THE
BIOLOGY OF
SENESCENCE

ALEX COMFORT

THIRD EDITION

 ELSEVIER · NEW YORK

First published in 1956 as THE BIOLOGY OF SENESCENCE
Revised and reset edition published in 1964 as AGEING: THE BIOLOGY OF
SENESCENCE by
Routledge & Kegan Paul Ltd
Broadway House, 68-74 Carter Lane
London, E.C.4

Published in the U.S.A., Canada, and Japan by Elsevier North Holland, Inc.
Published elsewhere by Churchill Livingstone, 23 Ravelston Terrace, Edinburgh EH4 3TL,
Scotland.

Library of Congress Cataloging in Publication Data

Comfort, Alexander, 1920–
    The biology of senescence.

    Rev. and reset ed. published in 1964 under title: Ageing, the biology of senescence.
    Bibliography: p.
    Includes index.
    1. Aging. I. Title. [DNLM: 1. Aging. WT104 C732b]
QP86.C57   1978   591.3′72   78-17546
ISBN 0-444-00266-9 (Elsevier North Holland, Inc.)
ISBN 0 443 01928 2 (Churchill Livingstone)

Printed in the United States of America

Ah quanta spes est, Lapidem sperare Sapientium! *What a hope that is, to have the Philosopher's Stone! Yet what shall it profit him if meanwhile he that has it sickens? if he groans in the torments of pain? if he rots in a merciless corruption? if wasting and the regiment of fevers contrive his death? To him that has riches and desires to have more, this is a most bitter fate . . . Yet none of these need the Chymist fear. His hope is fixed in the sufficiency of that secret in which he rejoices . . . For not only has this noble Medicine the virtue of combatting all the embattled forces of disease—it sustains the very vitals, nourishes the breath, and so conserves the natural heat that perfusing the whole body and entering all the limbs it ingenders and maintains there a constant motion and vigour . . . O Alchymist's hope, how you charm our minds, and with what promise you comfort us! To hold to an unfailing bodily health, a constant vigour and tranquillity of mind, to preserve these into a green and rugged old age, until, without a struggle or any sickness, soul and body dissever . . . The old granddam regains a merry suppleness, the long dry juice of her youth returns, as source and witness of her renewed fruitfulness. Grey hairs fall, and young curls appear; her teeth are renewed—new fingernails grow and the old are shed. The wrinkles of her brow fill and level, she straightens and she shines . . . Even old moulted fowls feather and lay eggs again. . . .*

Yet alas for that fortunate hope: the nearer they win to it, so much more does the possession threaten present dangers to them that all but have it. And how these may be avoided I do not know. . . .

Abram Kaau von Boerhaave, Declamatio academica
de Gaudiis Alchemistarum, 1737

—Sons of bitches! D'you want to live forever?
Frederick the Great to his Troops.

For
Leonard Hayflick
IN· CVIVS· CALVMNIATORES· MINGIMVS

Contents

Contents

Introduction

0.1 Introductory and Historical

If we kept throughout life the same resistance to stress, injury, and disease that we had at the age of ten, about one-half of us here today might expect to survive in 700 years' time. The reason we cannot is that in man, and in many, but probably not all, other animals, the power of self-adjustment and self-maintenance declines with the passage of time, and the probability of disease and death increases. The increase in man becomes eventually so steep that while exceptional individuals may outlast a century, there is an effective limit, depending upon our present age, upon the number of years for which any of us can reasonably expect to go on living. The uniformity of this process is one of the earliest unpleasant discoveries that every individual has to make, and although we have many psychological expedients to blunt its impact, the fact of this effective fixity of life-span, and of the decline in activity and health that often determine it, is always in the background of the human mind.

This process of change is senescence, and senescence enters human experience through the fact that man exhibits it himself. This close involvement with human fears and aspirations may account for the very extensive metaphysical literature on ageing. It certainly accounts for the profound concern with which humanity has tended to regard the subject. To a great extent human history and psychology must always have been determined and molded by the awareness that the life-span of any individual is determinate, and that the expectation of life tends to decrease with increasing age. The Oriental could say "O King, live for ever!" in the knowledge that every personal tyranny has its term. Every child since the emergence of language has probably asked "Why did that man die?" and has been told "He died because he was old."

Interesting psychological and historical speculation could be made on the part this awareness has played in human affairs. From the biologist's standpoint, its main importance has been the bias it has injected into the study of senescence. The child who asks the question, and receives the answer, is familiar with "old" clothes and "old" toys. He has always known that he, his pets, his cattle, and his neighbors will become increasingly prone to breakdown and ultimate death the older they get. He has observed from the nursery that inanimate and mechanical systems also deteriorate with the passage of time. He appears at a later age to derive some degree of comfort from the contemplation of the supposed generality, universality, and fundamental inherence of ageing—or alternatively from drawing a contrast between divine or cosmic permanence and his own transience. However inspiring this type of thinking may have been—and it features largely in the past artistic and philosophical productions of all cultures—its influence and its incorporation as second nature into the thought of biologists throughout history has seriously handicapped the attempt to understand what exactly takes place in senescence, which organisms exhibit it, and to what extent it is really analogous to processes of mechanical wear.

Our object in studying the biology of ageing is to find out why it occurs, and whether and how it can be controlled. This is not a new ambition. The fact that in past generations there was a much higher death rate at all ages did not make our ancestors any less inclined to rebel against the knowledge that they must decline with age; the protest took the form of legends in which fortunate mortals became actually or effectively immortal—sometimes with effects that punished their presumption. Aurora obtained the gift of immortality for Tithonus, but neglected to obtain perpetual youth. Cadmus and his wife, given the same opportunity, chose the rather wiser course of becoming animals of reputedly indeterminate, or at least very long, life-span, and were metamorphosed to

> two bright and aged snakes
> that once were Cadmus and Harmonia.

Legends of enormous longevity from natural causes, because they are cheering reservations on the normal life-span, have always been popular, and still exist to mislead research workers. Those for whom legends were not enough adopted another common expedient by making the unpleasant uplifting; and senescence is the subject of a vast body of edifying matter—literary, philosophical, and religious. One product of this attitude—the belief that it is impious, and must lead to some form of retributive disaster, to tamper with fate or the process of ageing—is with us today.

There have, however, always been ingenious men who were not prepared to accept these biological limitations in a contemplative spirit. Magic was first of all applied to ward off both disease and old age. With the rise of medicine, physicians came to distinguish between the two. Disease very often did respond to treatment, and it generally tended, in the young, to self-repair; age changes did not. The physicians tended more and more to devote their attention to acute processes of illness and injury, and to share the pious and fatalistic assessment of ageing. Attempts to alter the life-span fell again into the semi-magical province of sages, alchemists, and quacks. The Chinese sages had claimed substantial success in prolonging their own life-span—and that of their disciples—sometimes by a studied detachment from the world and its dangers, but also, with greater physiological likelihood, by systems of general and sexual gymnastics of a rather involved kind (Needham, 1957). One of the most successful was reputedly the sage Wei Po-Yang (second century A.D.), who may also have been the originator of the concept of the philosophers' stone, a substance capable both of producing gold from lead and of averting the changes of age. This idea played a significant part in scientific history, for the European alchemists of a later period divided their time between the transmutation of the elements and the elixir of life, which was to give them time to enjoy the gold they intended to make. By the end of the last century both these projects had come, with the growth of natural sciences, to be regarded as fundamental impossibilities that were suitable fields for charlatans and paranoiacs, and should be left alone by responsible scientists.

Of the two "fundamental impossibilities," the transmutation of the elements has beaten the control of ageing by a very long way. Travel to the moon, another uproariously unlikely project entertained by early alchemists, has done the same. Serious research into the control of ageing processes stands today at about the point where physical chemistry stood when Bécquerel first observed the spontaneous transmutation of a radioactive element. It has moved out of the field of eccentricity and is becoming the subject of more and more coordinated research by the standard methods of experimental biology. It now seems evident that while any large measure of control over human ageing might eventually prove impracticable, it is certainly not a fundamental impossibility or a verbal misconception of the circle-squaring variety, and we have the assignment of finding out by planned experiment how much can be done in this direction.

Technological research has, of course, the immense advantage over biological research that, in most cases, the problem is one of fulfilling known requirements—the mechanical requirements of space travel have been

known, in outline at least, for a century or more. In attempting to alter the
rate at which vitality declines with age, the requirements are not known, and
the initial problem is to ascertain them.

One result of the involvement of senescence with philosophy and the
"things that matter" has been the prevalence of attempts to demonstrate
general theories of senile change, including all metazoa and even inanimate
objects, which has had an edifying and a metaphysical cast. Prominent among
these have been attempts to equate ageing with development, with the
"price" of multicellular existence, with hypothetical mechanochemical
changes in colloid systems, with the exhaustion induced by reproductive
processes, and with various concepts tending to the philosophical contemplation of decline and death.

It is not unreasonable to point out that these theories have for the most
part deeper psychological and anthropological than experimental and observational roots. Some of them have a few facts on their side. "Reproductive
exhaustion" does appear to induce senescence in fish and in mollusca, and
flowering is a proximate cause of death in monocarpic plants, but the general
concept, especially when it is made a universal, owes a large debt to the
widespread belief in human cultures that sexuality "has its price." Extensions
of mechanical analogies from the wearing out of tools to the wearing out of
animal bodies are justifiable in a limited number of cases where structures
such as teeth undergo demonstrable wear with use and where this process
limits the life of the organism, but they have also shown a tendency to
become generalized in the hands of biologists who are devoted for philosophical, political, or religious reasons, to mechanism in the interpretation of
human behavior. Statements that "senescence is no more than the later stage
of embryology" resemble Benjamin Rush's great discovery that all disease is
disordered function. They belong to the category of word-rearrangement
games, which have long been played in those fields of study where there is as
yet no "hard news."

Although the religious, poetic, metaphysical, and philosophical literatures
of senescence will not be examined here, the detection and examination of
analogies based upon them, which have had a great, and generally adverse,
influence on the growth of our knowledge of age processes, must clearly play
a large part in any critical examination of the subject. The comments of
Francis Bacon, who was a philosophical originator of the scientific method as
well as the first systematic English gerontologist,[1] provide one of the best

---

[1] I dislike this word, but it is probably too well grown to be eradicated. It should
mean "a student of old men" (γέρων) and gerontology the study of old men. For the
study of age itself, the subject of this book, we require geratology (γῆραζ), upon
which it would be fruitless to insist. The correctly formed word, geriatrics, we owe to
the American Nascher.

critiques of the influence of such analogies and thought patterns, and they will be quoted without scruple here.

The practical importance of work upon the biology of senescence, beyond the fundamental information such work might give about the mechanisms of cell differentiation and renewal, can best be seen from the diagrams in Figures 0.2, 0.3, and 1.3. The advance of public health has produced a conspicuous shift in the shape of the survival curve in man so far as the privileged countries are concerned, from the oblique to the rectangular form. This has been due almost entirely to a reduction in the mortality of the younger age groups—the human "specific age" and the maximum life-span have not been appreciably altered. The medical importance of work on the nature of ageing lies at present less in the immediate prospect of spectacular interference with the process of senescence than in the fact that unless we understand old age we cannot treat its diseases or palliate its unpleasantness. At present aged-linked diseases are coming to account for well over half the major clinical material in any Western medical practice. We are producing Tithonuses. The physician is constantly referring to the biologist for a scientific basis of geriatrics, and finding that it is not there. The amount of material on which such a foundation could be built has increased, though not very rapidly, during the present century. Its quantity is still inversely proportional to the humane importance of the subject.

Science may affect human longevity favorably in two ways: by suppressing causes of premature death, or by postponing the ageing process that causes our liability to disease and death to increase logarithmically with the passage of time. The first of these two influences has already meant that in privileged countries more and more people reach the so-called "specific age" (75–80 years), but does not alter that age appreciably. The second, which is now in the stage of active research, aims at postponement or slowing of the ageing process itself.

It is highly important to recognize the difference between this approach, based on the search for a systems breakthrough, and the sum of all the other sociomedical advances. Figure 0.1 illustrates what has happened to date. The large changes in the survival curve of man over the last century represent, quite simply, the removal of causes of premature death, but the age at which a man becomes old, judged by the criteria of increasing infirmity and liability of death, is exactly what it was in Biblical times. Ageing itself, in the sense employed by gerontologists, is a progression that results in an increasing instability with time. This "loss of information" is multiform, but its rate, measured by the force of mortality, is highly stable, and the increase is roughly logarithmic. This stability is the basis of the well-justified assurance of actuaries that, with the exception of all premature causes of death, an annuitant will die between the ages of 70 and 100 years, regardless of any advance in the cure or prevention of specific diseases. There is in fact a

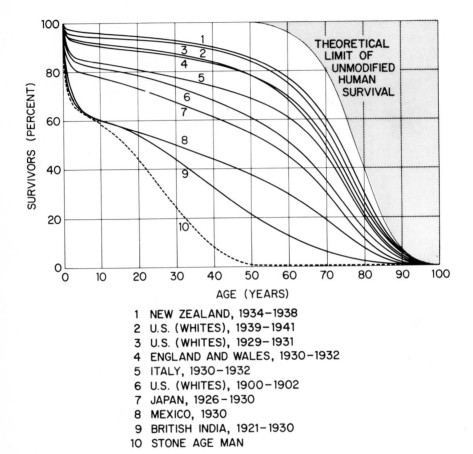

FIGURE 0.1   Historical changes in the human survival curve.

biological limit on human longevity that cannot be much transcended by conventional improvements in medicine or living conditions.

The last edition of this book appeared in 1964. Such has been the rate of advance of gerontology that we might well have canceled altogether the discussions of theory-in-the-abstract that constituted the subject at the time we reviewed it, and devoted the whole textbook to gerontology-in-practice, for although theory making continues unabated, it is now experimental in its outcome.

The illusion that science proceeds by classical induction is nowhere more evident than in our study of ageing. In fact, it proceeds by inspirational guesswork, experiment, serendipity, and finally confirmation and the emergence of a viable theory. Examples of such a progression are to be seen in Domagk's accidental discovery of sulfonamides while attempting to apply the theories of Ehrlich on bactericidal dyes and in the Wasserman reaction, which was developed on a wholly erroneous premise but worked. It is not cynicism to say that we shall discover the leading mechanisms of ageing by finding out what alters its rate and character, rather than the other way round: the function of pre-theory is simply to send us into the laboratory.

For this reason, separating immediately relevant theory, I have left intact the sections in this book dealing with the natural history of ageing and the past intellectual history of ageing research, and combined it with experimental work which was in hand at the time of this review, to constitute a review of "live" gerontological research. I have retained the descriptive matter and the historical debate because, first, nearly all possible models of relevant age processes must occur somewhere among the undergrowth of speculation, and second, human attitudes toward ageing expressed in theory have an anthropology of their own, from which even modern empiricism is not wholly immune.

The status of classical age studies in 1964 was one of pretheory, or pattern making: contemporary reviews include those of Lansing (1951, 1952), Birren (1959), Strehler (1962), and Korenchevsky (1961). Some of the more celebrated "general theories" had received unusually spirited treatment in a review by Medawar (1945). The literature of animal population statistics had been reviewed by Deevey (1947) and that of invertebrate senescence by Szabó (1935a,b) and by Harms (1949). The literature was reviewed in the bibliographies of Shock (1951) and of Nikitin (1958: Russian pre- and post-Revolutionary age studies). A great deal of clinicopathological material upon the age incidence of various human diseases and the weights of organs throughout life had been collected by Bürger (1954). Other reviews of specific topics will be cited in their place. The senescence of plants is not discussed here: it was well reviewed elsewhere (Crocker, 1939; Heath, 1957; Leopold, 1961).

Senescence is a general title for the group of effects that, in various phyla, lead to a decreasing expectation of life with increasing age. It is not, in this sense, a "fundamental," "inherent," or otherwise generalizable process, and attempts to find one underlying cellular property that explains all instances of such a change are probably misplaced. It is important and desirable to recognize the origins of many such general theories, which owe much to folklore on one hand, and to the emotional makeup of their authors on the other. The demoralizing effect that the subject of senescence exerted even on biologists of the highest competence and critical intelligence is well illustrated by the following passage from Pearl (1928), the father of animal actuarial studies:

> (Somatic death in metazoa) is simply the price they pay for the privilege of enjoying those higher specializations of structure and

function which have been added on as a sideline to the main business of living things, which is to pass on in unbroken continuity the never-dimmed fire of life itself.

Warthin (1929), whose insistence upon the fundamental impossibility of modifying the tempor of human ageing, now or at any time in the future, has an orgiastic tone quite out of keeping with the rashness of such a prediction, writes:

> We live but to create a new machine of a little later model than our own, a new life-machine that in some ineffable way can help along the great process of evolution of the species somehow more efficiently than we could do were we immortal. The Universe, by its very nature, demands mortality for the individual if the life of the species is to attain immortality through the ability to cope with the changing environment of successive ages. . . . It is evident that *involution* is a biologic entity equally important with *evolution* in the broad scheme of the immortal process of life. Its processes are as *physiologic* as those of growth. It is therefore inherent in the cell itself, an intrinsic, inherited quality of the germ plasm and no slur or stigma of *pathologic* should be cast upon this process. What its exact chemicophysical mechanism is will be known only when we know the nature of the *energy-charge* and the *energy-release* of the cell. We may say, therefore, that age, the major involution, is due primarily to the gradually weakening *energy-charge* set in action by the moment of fertilization, and is dependent upon the potential fulfilment of function by the organism. The immortality of the germ plasm rests upon the renewal of this energy charge from generation to generation.

This passage is highly typical of the subfossil and recent literature of old age. There can be few branches of biology in which uplifting generalization of this kind has so long been treated as a respectable currency for scientific thought.

In general, the more elaborate the attempts to depict senescence in overall mathematical terms, the more intellectually disastrous they proved. One of the most celebrated incursions of metaphysics into biology, that which postulates a separate "biological time," is best expounded in the words of its sponsor, Lecomte du Noüy (1936):

> When we refer to sidereal time as being the canvas on which the pattern of our existence is spread, we notice that the time needed

to effectuate a certain unit of physiological work of repair is about four times greater at fifty than at ten years of age. Everything, therefore, occurs as if sidereal time flowed four times faster for a man of fifty than for a child of ten. It is evident, on the other hand, that from a psychological point of view many more things happen to a child in a year than to an old man. The year therefore seems much longer to the child. . . . Thus we find that when we take physiological time as a unit of comparison, physical time no longer flows uniformly. This affirmation revolts one if the words are taken in a literal sense. But . . . the expression "flow of time" . . . is entirely false and does not correspond to a reality. When . . . we say that physical time measured by means of a unit borrowed from our physiological time no longer flows uniformly, it simply means that it does not *seem* to flow uniformly. . . . Must one consider this fact as the indication of a difference of magnitude between our short individual period and the immense periods of the universe? Must we see a proof of the existence of such periods? Who knows? All that we can say at present is that our crude language, lacking appropriate words, translates this knowledge into improper, inadequate expressions such as "There are two species of time" or "Physiological time does not flow uniformly like physical time." . . . We must not let ourselves be duped by these words, etc. . . .

It is startling how many distinguished biologists have subsequently quoted the notion of a distinct "biological" time with apparent sanction. Nonsense of almost Teilhardian proportions has even more recently been written on the same matter by Reichenbach and Mathers (1959). The alcoholic who draws on his bottle irregularly will find that its progress towards emptiness follows an irregular scale, "alcoholic time," so that judged by the rate of emptying of the bottle, "sidereal" time appears to progress unevenly. But variation in rate is hardly an occult, or even an unfamiliar, phenomenon. Like others before him, du Noüy has gone down clutching a platitude and come up embracing a metaphysical system.

In almost any other important biological field than that of senescence, it is possible to present the main theories historically and to show a steady progression from a large number of speculative ideas to one or two highly probable, main hypotheses. In the case of senescence this cannot profitably be done. The general theories of its nature and cause which have been put forward from the time of Aristotle to the present day have fallen into a number of overall groups that have been divided almost equally between fundamentalist theories which explain all senescence or treat it as an inherent property of living matter or of metazoan cells, and epiphenomenalist theories which relate it to particular physiological systems or conditions. They are also fairly evenly divided between the various categories of Baconian idola. It is a striking feature of these theories that they show little or no historical development; they can much more readily be summarized as a catalogue than as a process of developing scientific awareness. To the fundamentalist group belong, in the first place, all theories that assume the existence of cellular "wear and tear" (*Abnutzungstheorie*) without further particularization (Weismann, 1882; Pearl, 1928; Warthin, 1929); the mechanochemical deterioration of cell colloids (Bauer, 1924; Bergauer, 1924; Růžícká, 1924, 1929; Dhar, 1932; Lepeschkin, 1931; Szabó, 1931a,b; Marinesco, 1934; Kopaczewski, 1938; Georgiana, 1949); and pathological or histological elaborations of these, which attribute senescence to inherent changes in specified tissues—nervous (Muhlmann, 1900, 1910, 1914, 1927; Ribbert, 1908; Vogt and Vogt, 1946; Bab, 1948), endocrine (Lorand, 1904; Gley, 1922; Dunn, 1946; Findley, 1949; Parhon, 1955; to cite only a few from an enormous literature in which the endocrine nature of mammalian senescence is discussed, stated, or assumed), vascular (Demange, 1886), or even connective (Bogomolets, 1947). To the epiphenomenalist group belong toxic theories based on products of intestinal bacteria (Metchnikoff, 1904, 1907; Lorand, 1929; Metalnikov, 1937), accumulation of "metaplasm" or of metabolites (Kassowitz, 1899; Jickeli, 1902; Montgomery, 1906; Muhlmann, 1910; Molisch, 1938; Heilbrunn, 1943; Lansing, 1942, etc.), the action of gravity (Darányi, 1930), the accumulation of heavy water (Hakh and Westling, 1934; Griffiths, 1973), and the deleterious effect of cosmic rays (Kunze, 1933) or of oxidation (Molnár, 1972). There are also general developmental theories that stress the continuity of senescence with morphogenesis (Baer, 1864; Cholodkowsky, 1882; Roux, 1881; Delage, 1903; Warthin, 1929) or the operation of an Aristotelean entelechy (Driesch, 1941; Bürger, 1954), metabolic theories introducing the concept of a fixed-quantity reaction or of a rate/quantity relationship in determining longevity (Rubner, 1908; Loeb, 1908; Pearl, 1928; Robertson, 1923), attainment of a critical volume-surface relationship (Muhlmann, 1910, etc.), depletive theories relating senescence to reproduction (Orton, 1929), and finally an important group of theories that relate senescence to the cessation of somatic growth (Minot, 1908; Carrel and Ebeling, 1921; Brody, 1924; Bidder, 1932; Lansing, 1947, 1951). Most of the older theories have been reviewed, against a background of Drieschian neovitalism in the textbook of Bürger (1954), and historically by Grmek (1958). An extremely sensible undated book by Ernest (n.d.) seems to have been little noticed when it first appeared.

The distribution of dates in this catalog sufficiently indicates the state of the subject until about ten years ago. When Francis Bacon examined the relationship between animal-specific longevity, growth rate, size, and gestation period, he concluded that the available facts were unfortunately insufficient to support a general theory. That conclusion remains valid in practically all the instances quoted, but Bacon's self-denial failed to set a precedent for his successors. Almost all these theories, judging from the literature, continue at some point to influence biological thinking: some can be partially, or even largely, justified by the suitable selection of instances. Others did not bear critical inspection at the time they were first formulated, bearing in mind the known behavior of cells and the known discrepancies in longevity and in rate of ageing between animals of similar size, histological complexity, and physiological organization. Relatively few are supported by any body of fundamental experiment. The devising of general theories of senescence has employed able men, chiefly in their spare time from laboratory research, for many years. It seems reasonable to assume that almost all the mechanisms that might theoretically be involved have been considered, and if we are to understand what does in fact occur in a given ageing organism, we now need a combination of general observation and planned causal analysis in experimental animals.

The main early pretheories of ageing will be discussed in the text. They were admirably reviewed by Lipschutz in 1915, and have changed remarkably little since. There are, however, a few that should be outlined in greater detail here—either because they are still of importance, or because, though untenable, they have a considerable surviving influence.

The most influential nineteenth century contribution to this second category was probably that of Weismann, whose theory sprang directly from his distinction between germ plasm and soma. Weismann regarded senescence as an inherent property of metazoa, though not of living matter, since he failed to find it in protozoans and other unicellular organisms. Its evolution had gone hand-in-hand with the evolution of the soma as a distinct entity, and it was the product of natural selection, arising like other mutants by chance, but perpetuated as a positively beneficial adaptation, because "unlimited duration of life of the individual would be senseless luxury." "Death," according to this view, "takes place because a worn-out tissue cannot forever renew itself. . . . Worn-out individuals are not only valueless to the species, but they are even harmful, for they take the place of those which are sound" (1882). This argument both assumes what it sets out to explain, that the survival of an individual decreases with increasing age, and denies its own premise, by suggesting that worn-out individuals threaten the existence of the young. It had the advantage, however, of being an evolutionary theory, and we shall see later that this is the only type of theory that today seems likely to offer a general approach to the emergence of senescence in all the groups that exhibit it. The idea that all somatic cells must necessarily undergo irreversible senescence was challenged early in the century by the studies of Child (1915) upon planarians, and of Carrel (1912) upon tissue culture. The assumption that all higher metazoa must *ex hypothesi* exhibit senescence, however, dies hard, and the fallacious argument based on selection was constantly repeated (Metalnikov, 1936, 1937).

A considerable number of *metabolic* theories were based on the fact that an inverse relationship exists between length of life and "rate of living." On the basis of calorimetric experiments, Rubner (1908, 1909) calculated that the amount of energy required for the doubling of weight by body growth was approximately equal in a number of mammals. The energy requirement for the maintenance of metabolism, per unit adult body weight, was also approximately equal between species. Rubner inferred that senescence might, from these energy relationships, represent the completion of one particular system of chemical reactions, depending on a fixed total energy expenditure. He was obliged to erect a special category for man, whose energy requirement was found to be far higher than that in laboratory or domestic animals. Loeb (1902, 1908) attempted to find out whether the temperature coefficient of this hypothetical reaction was identical with that of general rate of development. Working with echinoderm eggs at various temperatures, and using a hatchability criterion to determine "senescence," if the word can be used in such a highly specialized instance, he concluded that the two coefficients were distinct. The importance of this work has been that its presuppositions have recurred in later studies, where some authors have based very similar inferences about the relationship of growth and senescence to a "monomolecular, autocatalytic reaction" on the shape and supposed mathematical proportions of the growth curve. As D'Arcy Thompson pointed out, this might equally prove the "autocatalytic" character of growth in a human population. In fact, with suitable adjustment, curves based on biological material can be made to provide support for almost any hypothesis of this kind.

Little need be said of the various *toxic* or *pathological* theories of mammalian senescence. There has been endless unfruitful discussion as to how far *senectus ipsa morbus* and how far pathological and physiological ageing can be separated: the most sensible exponent of a sharp distinction was Korenchevsky (1961) whose constant propaganda for more research on age processes makes him the obstetrician if not the father of modern gerontology. In his theory the distinction is chiefly a practical matter, since he believed that pathology was likely to yield to treatment, while "essential" ageing was not; his study makes little contribution to the understanding of the underlying vigor loss, and concentrates rather on endocrinal supplements. We are really left with five historically important theories, or groups of observations: the suggestion of Weismann that senescence is evolved, not intrinsic in all cellular matter; the work of Pearl (1928), which leads to the conception of a "rate of living," such that factors that retard development or reduce metabolism tend in many organisms to prevent or postpone senescence; the work of Minot (1908, 1913), of which the most important surviving parts are his relation of senescence to the decline of growth and his insistence upon its continuous and gradual character and its continuity with morphogenesis; the experimental studies of Child (1915), which showed that cellular differentiation and "senescence" in planarians is reversible, and of Carrel (1912), who demonstrated (wrongly, it now appears) that tissue cells derived from adult animals could be propagated indefinitely in vitro; and finally the theories of Bidder (1932).

Minot considered that senescence was the direct outcome of cell differentiation, that differentiated cells, by reason of the changes undergone (chiefly by their cytoplasm) in the course of morphogenesis, had become largely incapable of growth or repair. He believed that the negative acceleration of specific growth, found in a very wide variety of organisms, and ultimate senescence were products of this process, and that the first was a measure of the second. It followed from this that the rate of senescence, so defined, must actually be highest in embryonic life and in infancy, when the rate of differentiation is highest. Many of Minot's concepts, such as the rigid irreversibility of cell differentiation (echoed later by Warthin—1929), the incapacity of differentiated cells for growth, and the necessarily increasing liability to senescence of successive cell generations, are now disproved or at least impugned. His work, however, leaves with us the two important concepts of a gradual process of senescence linked to morphogenesis, and of a relation between it and the decline of growth potential. By using negative growth acceleration and rate of differentiation as a direct measure of senescence, Minot arrived at the conclusion that the rate of senescence is highest in fetal life, least in adult life. This concept has been widely adopted. Its validity depends upon the acceptance of Minot's definition; if senescence be regarded, as we shall regard it, in terms of deteriorative change in the organism's power of resistance, the idea requires qualification.

A far more important question, which had been latent in the literature since Ray Lankester (1870) pointed to the apparent non-senescence of fish, was raised by Bidder (1932). With the exception of Metchnikoff (1904, 1907), who was attempting to relate longevity to the form of the digestive tract, very nearly all biological theorists had assumed that senescence occurs in all vertebrates. This is probably so, but if it is not, then manifestly the general theories of senescence based on degree of tissue differentiation, irreplaceability of neurons, and other such systems fall to the ground. Bidder pointed out that there were several lower vertebrates in which there was no ground for suspecting that the mortality ever increased with increasing age, beyond the inevitable increment from accumulation of evident injuries. He suggested that vertebrate *senescence is a correlate of the evolution of determinate growth and of a final absolute size.* Bidder regarded determinate size as a property that had evolved as a result of the migration of vertebrates to dry land. He pointed to a number of instances in fish where constant expectation of life, capacity for growth, and general vigor appeared to persist indefinitely (Bidder, 1925). Bidder's argument is of importance, and is worth quoting in full.

> Giant trees, cultures of chick cells and of *Paramecium,* measurements of plaice and of sponges, all indicate that indefinite growth is natural. Galileo proved it fatal to swiftly moving land animals, therefore swiftly moving mammals and birds were impossible until their ancestors had evolved a mechanism for maintaining specific size within an error not impairing adequate efficiency. Even without evidence of evergrowing organisms, we could not suppose that the close correspondence to specific size, which we see in all swiftly moving creatures of earth or air, results from mere "senescent" fading out of the zygotic impulse to cell division and cell increase. Specific size is probably most important to birds, with their airplane mechanics strictly enjoining conformity of scale to plan; but to men it is most noticeable in man. Only familiarity prevents marvel at the rarity of meeting a man more than 20 percent taller or shorter than 5½ feet, or of discovering his remains in any place, or any race, or any epoch. Probably our erect posture enforces accurate propositions of length to weight, for running.
>
> Adequate efficiency could only be obtained by the evolution of some mechanism to stop natural growth so soon as specific size is reached. This mechanism may be called the regulator, avoiding the word "inhibitor" so as not to connote a physiological assumption. However ignorant we are of its nature, its action is traced in anthropometric statistics; a steady diminution in growth rate from a maximum at puberty to a vanishing point in the twenties. That the regulator works through change in the constitution of the blood is shown by the perpetual division of Carrell's chick cells in embryonic plasma, whereas cell division is ended in the heart of a hen.
>
> I have suggested that senescence is the result of the continued action of the regulator after growth is stopped. The regulator does efficiently all that concerns the welfare of the species. Man is within 2 cm of the same height between 18 and 60, he gently rises 2 cm between 20 and 27, and still more gently loses 1 cm by 40 or

thereabouts. If primitive man at 18 begat a son, the species had no more need of him by 37, when his son could hunt for food for the grandchildren. Therefore the dwindling of cartilage, muscle, and nerve cell, which we call senescence, did not affect the survival of the species, the checking of growth had secured that by ensuring a perfect physique between 20 and 40. Effects of continued negative growth after 37 were of indifference to the race; probably no man ever reached 60 years old until language attained such importance in the equipment of the species that long experience became valuable in man who could neither fight nor hunt. This negative growth is not the manifestation of a weakness inherent in protoplasm or characteristic of nucleated cells; it is the unimportant by-product of a regulating mechanism necessary to the survival of swiftly moving land animals, a mechanism evolved by selection and survival as have been evolved the jointing of mammalian limbs, and with similar perfection (Bidder, 1932).

Bidder's theory, besides raising the question of senescence as effect lying outside the "program" imposed by natural selection, posed the highly important suggestion that there might be two categories of vertebrates—those whose life-span is fixed, as in mammals, and those whose life-span is not fixed. From the theoretical point of view the establishment of the truth or falsity of this might have been the key problem in the elucidation of mammalian ageing, since the disproof of almost all the major existing theories of senescence would follow from the demonstration that it is not universally present in vertebrates. This might appear a simple issue of fact, but for reasons which will appear later a clear demonstration one way or the other was remarkably difficult to achieve.

Bidder's theory marks the last major attempt to produce a hypothesis of vertebrate senescence before the current eruption of physicists into the field of ageing studies, which followed the discovery of the apparent age-accelerating effects of radiation. These stochastic theories will be dealt with later: apart from them, no new picture of the general biology of ageing has been suggested since Bidder's, although its evolutionary basis has been discussed (Haldane, 1941; Medawar, 1952; Strehler, 1962). The decline in abstract speculation about old age is probably in itself a very good augury for research. Much of the previous published matter abundantly justified the view of Bacon that "the method of discovery and proof whereby the most general principles are first established, and then intermediate axioms are tried and proved by them, is the parent of error and the curse of all science.'

Despite the warnings of Bacon, general theories of ageing have continued to multiply. To the speculations of Minot, Bidder, and Warthin, based upon the supposed natural history of ageing, succeeded the stochastic models of Szilard (1959) and Failla (1960), the immunologic theories of Burnet (1959) and of Burch (1963a, b), the cross-linking theories of Bjorksten (1961), the error theory of Orgel (1936, 1970, 1973), a large range of theories based on hypothetical change in DNA (Ch. 9.1) or on the action of oxidative free radicals (Ch. 9.3), all of which will be dealt with in their place. Many of these pretheories have already generated important studies in confirmation or rebuttal, and the possibility remains that one or more of them may yet prove valid in explaining "primary" ageing. The primary assignment of gerontology—that of finding an accessible mechanism that times the human life-span as we observe it—remains undischarged. But it is nonetheless far closer to that objective today than when we last reviewed the subject—partly because, through the growth of experimental evidence which the pretheories of the past have generated, the possibility of a hierarchy of ageing processes integrated by a life-span "clock" has come to be recognized, and the nature of that clock is becoming clearer.

0.2   The Problem Today

The concern of scientists—as against mystics, quacks, and therapeutic optimists—with the control of human age processes, if we date it to Metchnikoff and Claude Bernard, is less than a hundred years old; the engagement of science in studying it as an immediately realizable project is less than thirty. Gerontology in its modern sense dates from about 1950.

In the first ten or twenty of these years its advocates generated a large body of printed matter, set up many institutes, and held many conferences, from which, so far as the fundamental understanding and control of age processes are concerned, virtually nothing hard emerged that could be put honestly to a lay committee as evidence of "definite progress." The view of some sources of research money that gerontology had now deservedly talked itself out of work was therefore comprehensible: but this ignores the time that must be spent, in any pioneer project, in cutting brushwood and reclaiming ground before a crop of fundamental experiments can be sown, let alone harvested. Though some of the time and effort spent so far had been wasted, a certain amount had been achieved in defining the problem, clearing old errors, raising a generation that knew the possibilities of age research, and discharging various ill-judged or superficial ideas that would have had to be voided at some point. Accordingly, although it bore no fruit in medicine, the work done may later prove more important than it now appears to be.

The root questions that determine the form of the age problem remain much as they were in 1950. In man and other warm-blooded vertebrates, vigor declines and disease susceptibility multiplies with increasing age. The rate of this increase under the best conditions has a characteristic value in each species, and is exponential, so that there is a maximum practicable lifespan that does not lengthen with further betterment.

Mammals are made up of three biological components: cells multiplying clonally throughout life (white corpuscles, epithelial cells), cells incapable of division and renewal (neurons), and non-cellular material which may have much or little turnover (collagen, intercellular substance). All of these are subject to an integrative physiological control. There are, accordingly, four grand classical hypotheses of the mechanism of senescence (not necessarily mutually exclusive), which must at some stage be dealt with: that vigor declines through change (epigenetic, mutational, infective, immunological) in the properties of multiplying cells; that it declines through loss of, or injury to, non-multiplying cells; and that it declines through primary changes in the "inert" materials of the body. All these are old hypotheses dating from Francis Bacon; none has yet been isolated by convincing experiment. At one time, interest in mutation and in matters such as somatic aneuploidy focused attention on the first hypothesis: that new cells in old animals are not so good as new cells in young animals. Szilard's speculations (1959a, b) fit better to the second hypothesis: that irreplaceable cells are lost with time. The third hypothesis has generated extensive and important work on collagen and related substances. The fourth hypothesis locates the timing mechanism of ageing not in the hardware of the body but in the software—in the overall program of regulation by which other aspects of the life cycle are governed, and which either determines ageing by a positive action, possibly related to earlier adaptive programming, or itself runs out of program when it passes beyond the reach of evolutionary selection.

One preliminary of any choice between these possibilities has been the need to observe the ageing and age-mortality relationship of animals other than men and rodents (which until recently were the only mammals for which we had life tables), and the study of factors that appear to hasten or delay the decline of vigor. This has been begun, though slowly. Another requirement is the detailed study of cell populations and numbers at different points in the life cycle; a third is the comparison of the new cells of old animals with those of young animals. The decline of brain-cell population at various ages in man, guinea pig, rat, and even the honey bee and termite has been very variously estimated, whereas histochemical studies of old and young animals still frequently fail to distinguish between young cells in an old organism and cells which are themselves old—or between animals such as rotifers, nematodes, and insect imagos, in which there is no cell division, or little, and mammals in which fixed and endlessly dividing cells exist together.

Throughout its history the study of ageing, as we have seen, has been ruinously obscured by theory, and particularly theory of a type which begets

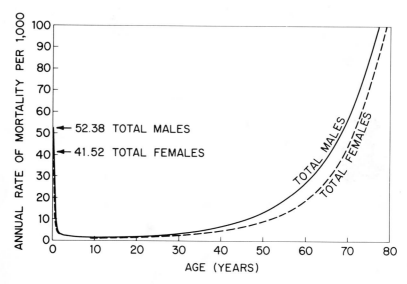

FIGURE 0.2   Annual rate of mortality per 1,000 by sex: United States, 1939–1941.

no experimental work. The discussion of methods that has taken place, and has been quantitatively the main activity of gerontology so far, has been worthwhile in laying to rest some of these philosophical ghosts, and though it is depressing to see them being raised again from time to time by the darkeners of scientific counsel, the most important recent contributions to theory all carry direct experimental consequences. It is noticeable that most of these theories have come from experimenters of international stature who are themselves working in other fields; serious progress in experimentation on age processes is really now waiting for some experimenter of equal caliber to devote all his time to it.

It will be necessary here to discuss a number of theories, most of which have been contributed in this way—leaving aside, on one hand, mere speculation, and on the other the contribution of information theory, which at present records only established actuarial concepts, though in a form that may prove instructive, or even decisive, in the end. We cannot as yet say which particular information store ageing makes its inroads, the answer depending upon the choice between our four overriding hypotheses: cell loss (predominantly of neurons, in this case), faulty copying, mechanochemical failure, and loss of physiological program. Thus, though the difference in life-span between species can be treated as a difference in initial information content, we are no nearer translating this into material terms. Even though none of the most recent suggestions seems likely in itself to "explain" ageing, they merit

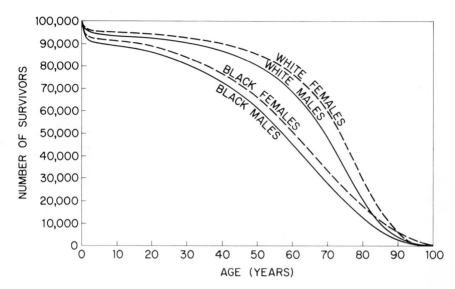

FIGURE 0.3   Number of survivors out of 100,000 born alive, for each race by sex: United States, 1939–1941.

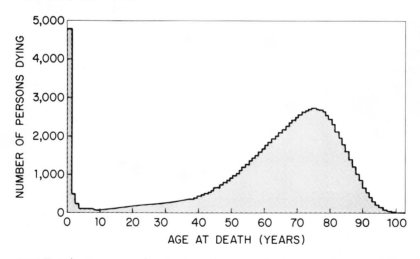

FIGURE 0.4   Frequency distribution of ages at death in a cohort starting with 100,000 live births, based on the mortality of white males: United States, 1939–1941.

close attention as evidence of the way in which ageing research and control have come to present themselves in practical terms to scientists of high ability, and it is this fact, rather than the theories themselves, that makes it possible that fundamental progress in the understanding of the loss of vigor with ageing may be closer than the standard of experimental papers might lead us to think. Understanding and control are of course very different things. The medical relevance of understanding the age process will depend upon what we understand it to be, and where its potential control resides.

1

The Nature and Criteria of Senescence: Historical

1.1   The Measurement of Senescence

Senescence is a deteriorative process. What is being measured, when we measure it, is a decrease in viability and an increase in vulnerability. Other definitions are possible, but they tend to ignore the raison d'être of human and scientific concern with age processes. Senescence shows itself as an increasing probability of death with increasing chronological age: the study of senescence is the study of the group of processes, different in different organisms, which lead to this increase in vulnerability.

The probability that an individual organism, which has survived to time x, will die before time $x + 1$ depends on the *rate of mortality* (q) per 1,000, meaning the number, out of 1,000 individuals living at time x, who have died by time $x + 1$. The *force of mortality* (μ) is given at any age x by

$$\mu_x = -n^{-1}\frac{dn}{dx} = \frac{-d}{dx}\,\mathrm{n} - n$$

where n is the number of individuals who have survived to age x.

In most organisms, the likelihood of dying within a given period undergoes fluctuations, often large, throughout the life-cycle. Senescence appears as a progressive increase throughout life, or after a given stadium, in the likelihood that a given individual will die, during the next succeeding unit of time, from randomly distributed causes; the pressure of the environment, which it has successfully withstood in the past, it now ceases to be able to withstand, even though that pressure is not increased. It is rare that we can determine the vulnerability of an individual. Our estimate of it is determined statistically, upon a population. The demonstration of such an increase in vulnerability is a necessary condition for demonstrating senescence: it is, obviously, only a sufficient condition if selective mortality from age-distributed external causes is ruled out. Real populations are subject to mortality both from random and from age-distributed causes. The variation of exposure rate throughout life is familiar in man; grown men are subject to risks that do not affect children, and so on. Differences in "risk" throughout life have been studied in some other animals, such as the locusts, whose causes of death were analyzed by Bodenheimer (1938) or the gall-fly Urophora (Varley, 1947). Pearson (1895), in his mathematical analysis of the curve of human survivorship into five components, attempted to limit the meaning of "senile mortality" to one such component, reaching its maximum incidence between 70 and 75 years of age. This would be an ideal solution if it were practicable, but Pearson's analysis is artificial in the extreme, and his "five separate Deaths" directing their fire at different age groups are not biologically identifiable. In general, however, a progressively increasing *force of mortality* and decreasing expectation of life in a population, if significant variation in exposure rate can be excluded, is evidence of the senescence of its individual members. The preliminary test for senescence in an animal species depends, therefore, on the life-table of an adequate population sample, studied with suitable precautions against selective causes of death.

The expected differences in behavior and form of life-table, between populations that age and those that do not age are shown in Figures 1.1a and

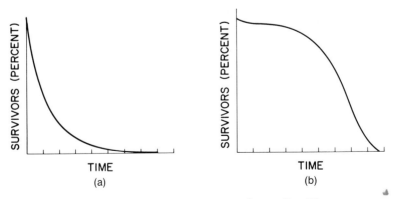

FIGURE 1.1a Survival curve at a constant rate of mortality (50 percent per unit time). 1.1b Survival curve of a population that exhibits senescence.

1.1b. In a population not subject to senescence and exposed only to random overall mortality, the decline of numbers is logarithmic, and animals die, *ex hypothesi,* from causes that would have killed them at any age. In a population exposed only to death from reduced resistance, due to senescence, the curve approaches a rectangular form: after a certain age, animals die from causes that would not have killed them in youth. In one case the force of mortality is constant; in the second it rises steadily with age. Thus in rats the force of mortality rises after the ninth month of life in a geometrical progression (Wiesner and Sheard, 1934). Real survival graphs are commonly intermediate in form between the two ideal contours. Pearl and Miner (1935) distinguished three main types of observed death curve, varying in skewness from the nearly rectangular in organisms with a low standing death rate throughout life, but showing a tendency to die almost simultaneously in old age, to the logarithmic decline characteristic of populations which show no senescence, or which die out before it can become evident (Figure 1.2). A fourth theoretical type, in which the curve is rectangular but inverse to that found in the ideal senescent population, was recognized by Pearl (1940) as a theoretical possibility; it seems to be realized in nature among organisms which have a high infant mortality, but whose expectation of life increases over a long period with increasing age. This pattern of survival is characteristic of some trees (Szabó, 1931a,b) but probably also occurs in animals. "There may be animals in which the expectation of life increases continuously with age. This may be so for many fish under natural conditions. It certainly goes on increasing for a considerable time. Thus in a species where the expectation of life was equal to the age, or better, to the age plus one week, no members would live for ever, but a small fraction would live for a very long time. A centenarian aware of the facts would pity a child, with an expectation of life of only a few years, but would envy a bicentenarian" (Haldane, 1953).

The simplest and oldest attempt to depict the age decline in terms of actuarial mathematics is that of Gompertz (1825), expressed in the function

$$R_m = -\frac{1}{n} \times \frac{dn}{dt} = R_0 e^{\alpha t}$$

where n = number of survivors at time $t,$ and α (the slope constant) and R_0 (the hypothetical mortality at time = 0) are constants.

Makeham's approximation simply adds to this a standing element of mortality independent of age, represented by the constant A

$$R_m = R_0 e^{\alpha t} + A$$

while Teissier's approximation describes those survival curves, common in laboratory practice where, owing to small samples, mortality is zero for the first few intervals, giving a "plateau of adult vigor" (Teissier, 1934)

$$\mu_x = e^{\alpha(x-b)}, \qquad x > b.$$

μ_x being the force of mortality at an age x, beginning to rise after the plateau of duration b has elapsed.

A number of more subtle theoretical models have been devised both by actuaries, who use them predictively, and by biometricians attempting to

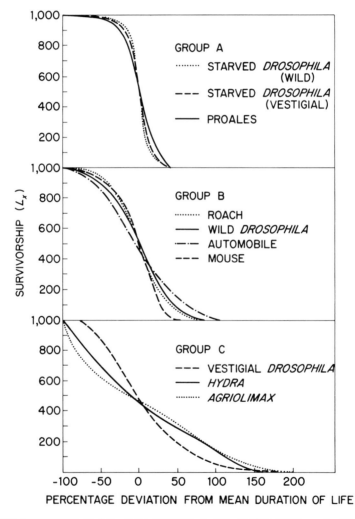

FIGURE 1.2   Types of survival curve. (From Pearl, after Allee, et al., 1949.)

formulate a hypothesis of ageing. Most of these depend on a combination of declining vigor, random environmental attack, and random oscillation of one or more physiological quantities about a fixed or a moving point of homeostasis. They were well reviewed by Strehler (Mildvan and Strehler, 1960; Strehler, 1962).

The accumulation of vulnerability with age is an all around and non-specific process. We can translate this into more concrete terms. The age distribution of pedestrian deaths in road accidents is similar in contour, excluding early infancy, to the general distribution of human deaths from all causes (Figure 1.3). This index is highly correlated with vigor, in its biological sense, for it represents a combination of sensory acuity, speed of avoidance, and power of recovery when hit.

No single parameter is sufficient to describe an observed survival curve. If the life-span of a species is to be given as a single figure, e.g., in comparing man and horse, the last decile is probably the most useful measurement, as the approximate proportions of the "physiological" curve can sometimes be guessed from it. The true index of the rate of ageing is presumably the differential of the force of mortality, and it would seem logical at first to

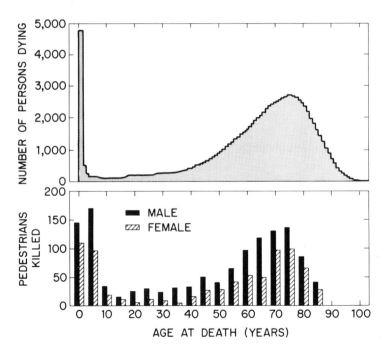

FIGURE 1.3   Distribution by age of all deaths in a privileged community (above) and of pedestrians in road accidents. (De Silva, 1938; Lauer, 1952.)

express all curves where ageing is in question in terms of mortality or its derivatives. But in real survival experiments all measures derived from q_x, the observed mortality, have a very large scatter, unless vast numbers are used, and standard smoothing techniques all introduce assumptions of regularity. Both the curve of survival (L_x/t) and the mean duration of life are largely affected by a few early deaths. Comparison of crude mean longevities, in particular, is quite meaningless in terms of the pattern of ageing, unless the causes and distribution of deaths are also compared.

Under good conditions the survival curves of mammals, and of many other organisms, tend to the form originally described by Gompertz (1825). This "physiological" curve represents the distribution of a vitality parameter. The smooth curve of survivorship drawn by actuaries is intended for prediction of average behavior. Unsmoothed curves for smallish populations, though consistent, are often better represented by straight-line approximations, or conform roughly to Teissier's equation (1934):

$$\mu_x = e^{\alpha(x-b)}$$

where μ_x is the force of mortality at age x, and $b < x$: in this case there is a well-marked period of adult vigor, and the curve begins with a plateau of zero mortality. If we assume that vitality declines continually according to some law (not necessarily linear), factors that uniformly raise the level of environmental attack or lower resistance to it will reduce b, whereas factors that alter the spacing of the lives in the vitality distribution will affect the slope of the subsequent decline.

Neary (1960) christened the period before the decline in vigor has brought any individual to the point at which the environmental attack is too much for it "induction"—it represents the plateau constant in Teissier's equation (1934).

When multiple life-shortening factors modify an arithmetic survival curve they commonly flatten it, first into a straight line, and, when still more severe, towards a logarithmic decay, the mortality being then independent of age. There is a tendency for the ends of the curve to remain pegged, however, the last half-decile succumbing only to very severe conditions.

The resulting family of hysteresis-like curves makes up the "parallelogram of survival," typical of animals having a definite life-span, and from which that life-span can be inferred. The pronounced "tail" is probably the result of heterogeneity; it might well not be found in experiments on F_1 hybrids between inbred lines. Curves of this kind are usually taken to represent an increment in general mortality rather than a change in the rate of ageing— there is no way of estimating from them how far age changes in survivors at a given time have been accelerated by previous hardship.

Some real animal populations decline in an approximately logarithmic manner. The "potential immortality" of individuals in a population following such a path of decline—an entirely meaningless phrase which has caused much philosophical agitation in the past—is not more significant as a practical issue than the "potential" meeting of any pair of railway metals at infinity. No population of organisms that is subject to a constant overall death rate contains "potentially" immortal individuals. The only advantage a non-senescent organism possesses over senescent forms is that the odds in favor of its death within a fixed period remain constant instead of shortening with the passage of time.

The survival curve of some 3,000 thoroughbred mares, from figures in the General Stud Book, is closely similar in form to that of civilized man (Comfort, 1958a, b; Figures 1.4, 1.5, and 1.6).

This human survival curve, in societies possessing developed medical services and a high standard of living, is intermediate between the rectangular and log-linear contours, but approaches the rectangular, with an initial decline due to infant mortality. Figures 0.2, 0.3, and 1.7 show, first, the comparative curves of mortality for populations in the present century living under different conditions of economic and climatic advantage, and second, the change in form of the life-table for North German populations between 1787 and 1800. Many life-tables for populations before the advent of scientific

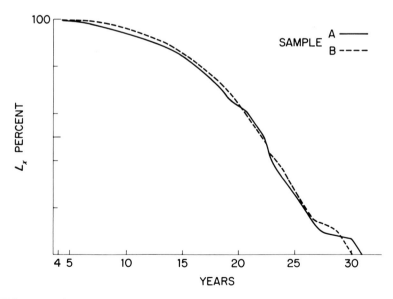

FIGURE 1.4   Survival curves of thoroughbred mares foaled in 1875–1880 (Sample A) and 1860–1864 (Sample B).

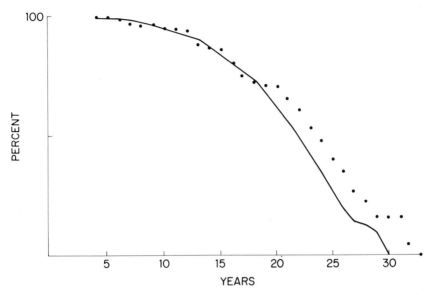

FIGURE 1.5   Survival curve of Arabian mares (dots) compared with the curve for English thoroughbreds (solid line).

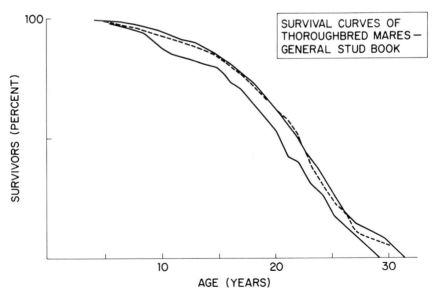

FIGURE 1.6   Survival curves of thoroughbred mares by coat color. (From Comfort, 1958a, b; 1961a.)

medicine are given by Dublin et al. (1949). The significance of technical and economic privilege is nowhere more evident than in the study of life-tables. The effects of public health upon the life-table are expressed rather in making it approach more closely to the rectangular shape than in prolonging the preinflectional part of the rectangle. In very many organisms, and in man under bad social and medical conditions, the infant mortality is so large as to obscure all subsequent trends, the curve coming to imitate Pearl's fourth, inverse rectangular, type (Figure 1.2). The terminal increase in liability to die may also be masked by cyclical variations in mortality associated with breeding or wintering, but the presence of such an increase remains an essential requisite for the demonstration of senescence in an organism. In many senescent populations, such as the sheep and cavies in Figures 1.12 and 1.13, the survival curve in adult life is not so much rectangular as arith-linear, a

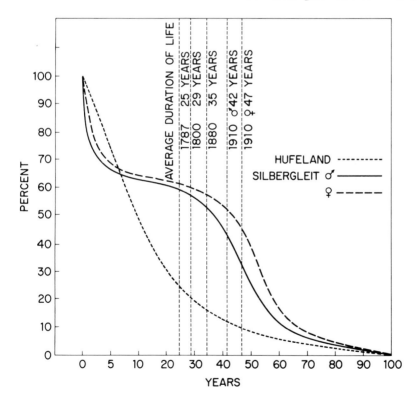

FIGURE 1.7 Survival curves of a German population. Hufeland's table (1798) is based on "experience" and estimates. Silbergleit's data are based on official statistics as given in the *Deutschen statistischen Jahrbuch* for 1915. Both sets of data relate to N. Germany. (From Vischer, 1947.)

constant *number* of individuals dying during each unit of time, the mortality necessarily decreasing as the supply of animals decreases, like the companions of Odysseus of whom Polyphemus ate a fixed number daily.

The breakage rate of crockery or glassware has sometimes been used to illustrate the decline of a non-senescent population (e.g., Medawar, 1952). A life-table for tumblers was actually constructed by Brown and Flood (1947)—that for annealed tumblers approaches the curve of constant mortality, though only roughly, while the decline of a smaller group of toughened glass tumblers was nearly arith-linear (Figure 1.8). Senescence, however, does apparently occur in tumblers, since abrasions of the lip make subsequent cracking more likely (Brown and Flood, 1947).

It is convenient to treat survival curves such as those of man or *Drosophila* as combinations of the log-linear "environmental" curve, found where the standing death rate is high, with a terminal rectangular decline due to

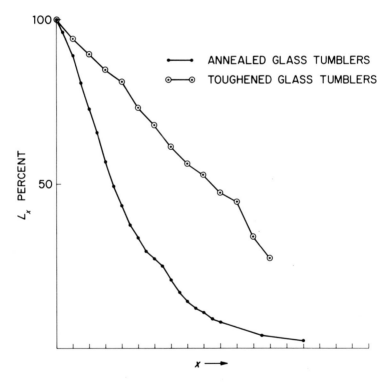

FIGURE 1.8   Survival curves for cafeteria tumblers. A: 549 annealed glass tumblers. B: 241 toughened glass tumblers. Time: 1 scale division = 2 weeks for Curve A, 5 weeks for Curve B. (Drawn from the data of Brown and Flood, 1947.)

senescence, since it is evident that not all those individuals who die in middle life owe any part of their misfortune to the senile increase in vulnerability, however early in life this is taken to begin.

Bodenheimer (1938) draws a useful distinction between the "physiological" longevity of a species—that attained under optimal conditions in a genetically homogeneous population and approaching the longest recorded life-span within the species—and the "ecological" longevity, which is the mean longevity observed empirically under given conditions. The ideal rectangular "physiological" curve postulated by Bodenheimer is a convenient abstraction at most, since the genetic and environmental conditions laid down for it cannot in practice be obtained in any real population. But in some forms the observed life-table in laboratory culture or domestication approximates the ideal rectangular form, and this approximation is closest of all in some human societies. It is, however, pointless in terms of the actuarial definition of senescence to pursue a "physiological" as opposed to a "pathological" senescence in most laboratory animals. In man, the typical pathological change of ageing is an increase in the number of pathological changes (Horak, 1968). If senescence is measured as increased *general* vulnerability, Bodenheimer's "physiological" longevity represents only the approximate region in which the rise in the curve of vulnerability to all assaults of the environment becomes so steep that even major protection against such assaults is insufficient to prolong life very greatly. The pattern can be modified and the apparent physiological longevity increased by removing specific causes of death—e.g., enteritis and ear disease in old rats (Korenchevsky, 1949), but the postponement of death obtainable in this way is itself limited, and argument about "natural" death, apart from pathological processes, in mammals is quite otiose.

It is manifestly impossible to demonstrate senescence from life-tables unless the mortality in early and adult life is sufficiently low, and the number of animals reaching old age is therefore sufficiently high, for an endogenous increase in susceptibility to death-producing factors of random incidence to be evident. Thus wild mice die at a rate that precludes their reaching old age, but mice kept under laboratory conditions have a life-table similar to that of Western European human populations in the year 1900 (Leslie and Ranson, 1940, Figure 2.42; Haldane, 1953): not even the most cherished laboratory population can receive the same social reinforcements of longevity as civilized man, but if such were possible, the life-table of mice might then approach that for Western European man today—always assuming that medicine has been the major agent in affecting longevity in man—the proposition has been strongly questioned (McKeown, 1971; Lalonde, 1974).

Organisms that undergo senescence, as judged by the life-table, also exhibit specific age, meaning an age at death that is characteristic of the species when living under conditions approaching Bodenheimer's "physiological" conditions.

Some of the limitations of the statistical definition of senescence were restated by Medawar (1952). It is obvious that any survival curve can be simulated by judicious, or injudicious, choice of material. Tables based only on age at death, a single arbitrary event, are open to serious criticism if they are used as indexes of a *continuous* process of declining vitality. The shape of such a curve is a measure of many things, including the genetic homogeneity of the sample. The incidence of various risks itself varies between age groups: the statistical appearance of senescence would, for example, be found in the life-table of any population of fish that was subject to frequent fishing with a net of fixed mesh size. Selective predation certainly produces effects of this nature. The increased force of mortality among men of military age during a war is not a manifestation of senescence. On the other hand, some causes of mortality, such as cancer (Rutgers, 1953; Freedman, 1976), have a curve of incidence that parallels the total curve of mortality. In employing the force of mortality as an index of senescence it is essential, as we have seen, to exclude so far as possible external factors which are not of random incidence in relation to age, yet this cannot be done with strict logical consistency. In the case of human life-tables, large secular changes in cause and incidence of death may occur within an individual life-span, while constitutional differences in rate of senescence between individuals ensure that the genetical composition of the survivors at, say, age sixty, is not representative of the whole cohort under study. These sources of error are, in fact, capable of avoidance or correction for most practical purposes, but they must always be recognized in inferring senescence from any life-table.

Since there is no direct way of measuring the liability of an individual to die without actually killing it, the statistical definition of senescence, although it reflects a real process in individuals, can only be tested upon a *population*. For this purpose the biologist uses tools originally made and sharpened by the actuary.

The differences between actuarial and biological approaches to mortality-measurements are in the main the differences between the prospective and retrospective use of statistics. The most practically important of these differences, for the kind of problems we have in hand, is the value we attach to smoothness. For almost all prospective purposes it is convenient in the first instance to assume some degree of uniformity, to recognize as few and as gross modalities as possible, and to deal with minor modalities by smoothing. For most retrospective purposes, the main consideration is to extract as much reliable, or even suggestive, information from scanty data as the limits of significance will allow. This will require the use of methods that will exaggerate fine structure where it is present. The biologist's main requirement in using standard actuarial techniques of research on age is that he shall be able to distinguish clearly between regularities that probably exist in the material, and any regularities that may result from the methods themselves. Most animal populations are heterogeneous for life-table purposes. Curves based on such material are averages, which are serviceable for prediction of limits, but often misleading as indications of the pattern of a biological process. Figure 1.9 illustrates such an effect in human growth curves, from the study by Tanner (1955); it compares the longitudinal plots of growth velocity against age in five individual children, the smoothed average that would be obtained by combining the measurements, as they would be combined in a cross-sectional study, and the same measurements as percentage deviates. The true age-velocity curves are typically peaked. Many instances quoted to demonstrate that "Nature does not progress by leaps" are a direct result of this type of treatment. Where, as in this case, longitudinal as well as cross-sectional studies are made, the error is evident: in the case of age-wise vigor loss we have still no means of doing this.

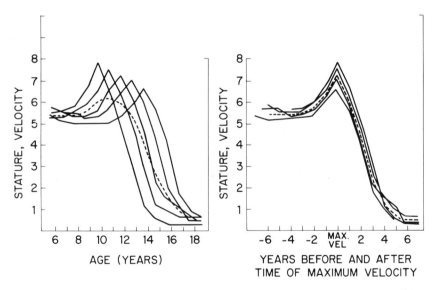

FIGURE 1.9 Relation between individual and mean velocities during the adolescent sport. Left: the height curves are plotted against chronological age. Right: they are plotted according to their time of maximum velocity. —, Individual curves; ----, mean curve. (From Tanner, 1955.)

It is evident that in applied biology, and especially in medicine, it is desirable to be able to infer not only the existence of senescence in a species but the degree of senile change in a given individual. This estimate must be based on secondary criteria, and can be made with accuracy only in forms whose life-cycle, like that of man or of *Drosophila,* has been subject to intensive study. The importance of the statistical definition of senescence is that it means we have to resort to adequate population studies. An over-common practice has been to keep a single specimen, a bird or a bullfrog, for ten or twenty years, and, when it is found dead, having been so for hours or possibly days, to describe histological appearances in its tissues in a note entitled "Senile change in the nervous system of *Passer* (or *Bufo*)." While senescence cannot be inferred from every life-table in which the force of mortality rises, neither can descriptions of "senile" changes be properly based on single observations upon supposedly ageing organisms belonging to groups whose life-cycle, in relation to senescence, is not fully known. In the same way many descriptions of supposedly "senile" changes in animals are based on comparison of infants with young adults. Really old animals are rare in laboratory populations.

In practice, other criteria than the life-table can be applied to organisms whose life-cycle is familiar, as secondary indexes of senescence; these are distinct from mere measures of chronological age, based upon the morphology of scales, teeth, or otoliths. Certain factors that are, in effect, direct measures of vigor or of vulnerability, such as the mortality from burns (Ball and Square, 1949), or even the annual absenteeism from sickness (Schlomka and Kersten, 1952), follow the general force of mortality in man. The supposed decline in the rate of wound healing proposed as a measure of senescence by du Noüy (1932) was based on grossly inadequate clinical material and is not supported by later work (Bourlière, 1950; Gillman, 1962), though the rate of contracture in full-thickness wounds is related to age (Billingham and Russell, 1956). The main age changes are in the character and composition of granulation tissue and in wound strength (Heikkinen, et al., 1971; Struck and Engelhardt, 1971; Engelhardt and Struck, 1972; Schilling, 1975). Less general criteria such as skin elasticity in man (Evans, et al., 1943; Kirk and Kvorning, 1949; Hollingsworth, et al., 1965), organ weight and relative organ hypoplasia in rats (Korenchevsky, 1942, 1949), heart rate in Cladocerans (Ingle, et al., 1937; Fritsch and Meijering, 1958; Fritsch, 1959; Meijering, 1958, 1960), milk yields in cattle (Brody, et al., 1923), egg production in fowls (Clark, 1940; Figure 2.6, p. 87), histological appearances of many kinds, and estimations of general or special metabolism are of value within sharply defined limits, but all are subject to considerable variation apart from the general senile process. In retarded Cladocera, for example, where mean life-span is artificially prolonged by postponing growth, the heart rate fails to decline before death to the low levels normally found in old age (Ingle, et al., 1937). Minot (1908), Hertwig, and others considered that a steady decrease in the nucleocytoplasmic ratio was a general feature of ageing in organisms, a suggestion that has not been upheld by later work, and that would today require translation into more precise biochemical terms. Dehydration was also formerly regarded as a general senile phenomenon. From a recalculation of older data, however, and from fresh material, Lowry and Hastings (1952) found that increased hydration, due perhaps to extracellular edema, loss of cells, and even gross pathological causes such as heart failure, is the most consistent finding in senile mammalian tissue. There is at present no biochemical sign characteristic of "oldness" in tissues or in cells, and the search for one may well reflect a fundamental misconception. It is in assessing the relevance of all such criteria to the main phenomenon of senescence, the decline in resistance to random stresses, that the statistical approach is essential. All assertions about senescence based upon pathological anatomy, or upon general theories that treat it as a single process, are open to question.

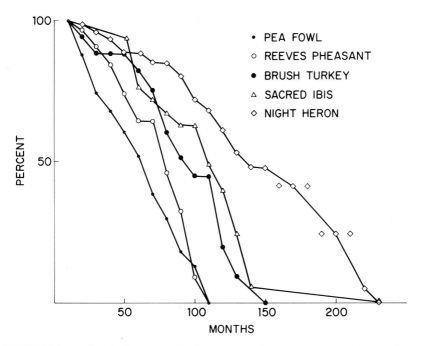

FIGURE 1.10 Survival curves of birds in the London Zoo, corrected for accidental deaths and losses. (From Comfort, 1962.)

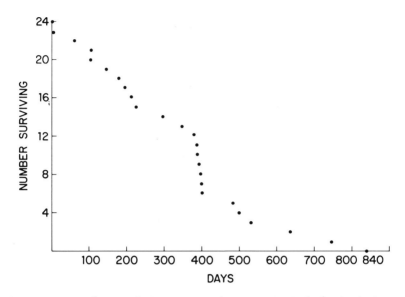

FIGURE 1.11   Orkney Vole *(Microtus orcadensis)*. Survival of 24 individuals, sexes combined (London Zoo).

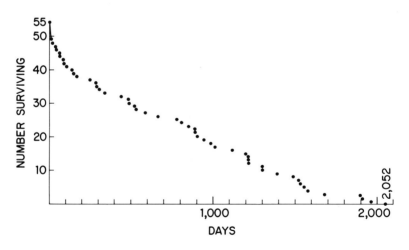

FIGURE 1.12   Patagonian Cavy *(Dolichotis patagona)*. Survival of 55 individuals, sexes combined (London Zoo).

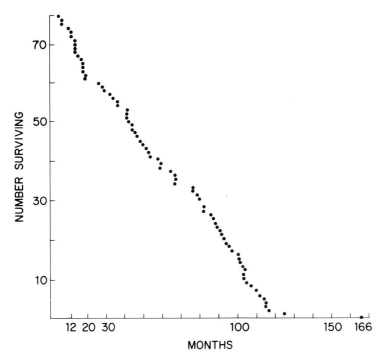

FIGURE 1.13 Mouflon Sheep *(Ovis musimon)*. Survival of 77 individuals, beginning at 12 months, sexes combined (London Zoo).

The *decline of growth rate* throughout life in some or all tissues appears to be a near-universal feature of metazoa.

> The specific growth rate always falls: living tissue progressively loses the power to reproduce itself at the rate at which it was formed. Minot arrived at this generalization, which should rightly be known as "Minot's Law," from the collation of his percentage growth-rate curves; and it was he who first recognized that the point of inflection of the integral curve of growth, and the division it makes between a period of positive and negative acceleration, is not of critical importance. The progressive dissipation of "growth energy," which this first law affirms, was thought by Minot to be an expression of the phenomenon of senescence—"ageing" with its everyday implications. Senescence is not, in this view, a process that sets in after a preliminary period of maturation has run

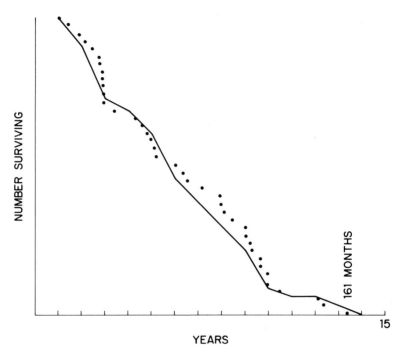

FIGURE 1.14   Irish Wolfhounds. Survival 67 individuals from 12 months of age, sexes combined. Line: whole sample, annual totals. Points: 38 individuals whose exact dates of death were known, to scale. (Data from D. Gardner.)

its course: senescence *is* development, looked at from the other end of life (Medawar, 1945b).

The use of this criterion, which is a readily measurable one, and can be applied to smallish groups of animals with suitable precautions, as well as to single tissues or organs, implies the acceptance of Minot's definition of senescence. The definition is defensible. On the other hand, the decline in specific growth rate is not a measure of senescence in its actuarial sense, since it does not run parallel with the force of mortality, and it would not be even an obligatory precursor of senescence if mortality only increased with age in those animals whose capacity for renewal or growth in some or all tissues has fallen to zero. It is with actuarial, deteriorative senescence that we are here concerned—if senility implied *only* the decline of growth rate in man, it would cause little public concern.

It is possible that future work will produce a workable and justifiable "direct measure" of senescence in individuals, based, for example, on the time-lag in cell division of tissue explants derived from old animals (Cohn and Murray, 1925; Suzuki, 1926; Medawar, 1940). The possibility of a multifactorial test is discussed in Chapter 10. A far more characteristic age change in mammals is the lag or delay in complex enzyme induction processes involving a hypothalamic stage (Adelman, 1971)—the location of this lag appears not to be cellular, and may prove to be central, an interesting possibility in the light of other work. Meanwhile the critical observations on the distribution of senescence in vertebrates have almost all had to be made upon organisms (large fish, crocodiles, tortoises) where life-table studies are out of the question. In these forms it is relatively easy to observe histologically or by a mating test, the degree of reproductive power persisting in individuals of known age. Inferences based on "reproductive" senescence are therefore easy to draw, compared with the insuperable difficulties involved in measuring the force of mortality in such cases.

Reproductive decline is a very general feature of those vertebrates that undergo senescence as judged by the increasing force of mortality: its evidences in various forms include gonadal changes, loss of secondary sexual characteristics, cessation of ovarian cycles, and a fall in sperm production, fertilizing power, hatchability, litter size, and viability. These changes follow a time scale that is different from that of the increase in force of mortality, however, and bears no constant relation to that increase in different species. The gonad often appears to behave as an "organism" having its own determinate life-span, but this is equally true of other structures, such as the thymus. The limited life of the gonad is in a special category only because, in terms of evolutionary teleology, the gonad is the significant part of the organism. Ageing of the whole organism after a prolonged postreproductive period is a process that is realized only by human interference, at least so far as most species are concerned, and not "envisaged" by evolutionary teleology. It could be argued that once gonadal senescence has become established in a species, eventual somatic senescence is as a rule inevitable from the withdrawal in postreproductive life of the selection-pressure towards homeostasis. A clear physiological link between the activity of the gonad and the growth and survival of the animal has been demonstrated in a few forms (e.g., Edlén, 1937, 1938), although even in *Daphnia,* oogenesis continues until death (Schulze-Röbbecke, 1951). In many vertebrates, however, even total castration has little or no adverse effect on longevity, and may increase it. Although senescence of the gonad is, in an evolutionary sense, the most important form of ageing, it is not self-evident that in the artificially protected animal it must always be followed by generalized somatic senescence, unless the two processes are causally related. Such an identification reflects, once more, a human preoccupation. Reproductive function, because of its ease of measurement, remains at most a justifiable test of continuing vitality in old animals—fertility indicating the absence of irreversible organ changes in one important system.

Metabolic decline, either measured directly by calorimetry and manometry or inferred from reduction in spontaneous activity, has also been regarded as an index of senescence—often on theoretical grounds, as representing the accumulation of inactive "metaplasm" at the expense of active protoplasm (Kassowitz, 1899, etc.) or the completion of a "monomolecular autocatalytic reaction" such as that postulated by Robertson (1923) or Bertalanffy (1941). The decline of heart rate in Cladocerans (Ingle, et al., 1937) has already been mentioned. The mean resting heart rate in man also tends to decline throughout fetal and postnatal life. Child measured the age of hydromedusae by the decline in their rate of pulsation (Child, 1918). In some invertebrates (planarians—Child, 1915; hydromedusae—Child, 1918; molluscan adductor muscle—Hopkins, 1924, 1930) and in some isolated vertebrate tissues (articular cartilages—Rosenthal, et al., 1940, 1941, 1942; rat blood vessels—Lazovskaya, 1942, 1943; avian muscle—Glezina, 1939; rabbit muscle—Cheymol and Pelou, 1944; rat brain homogenate—Reiner, 1947; liver, kidney, and heart homogenates—Pearce, 1936; mouse lymphoid tissue—Victor and Potter, 1935) O_2 uptake has been reported to decline with age.

In house-fly muscle Rockstein and Gutfreund (1961) found a decline in adenosine monophosphate and a piling up of triphosphate, which appears to be due to a loss of phosphatase activity. Calorimetric experiments on the whole mammal indicate a general decline in heat production with increasing age (Sondén and Tigerstedt, 1895; Benedict and Root, 1934; Magnus-Levy and Falk, 1899; Shock, 1942, 1948; Benedict, 1935; Boothby, et al., 1936; Kise and Ochi, 1934). This decline, however, like that of growth energy, is greatest in early life, and relatively slight in man after the age of 50 (Shock, 1953). It does not parallel the senescent increase in mortality. There is also gross individual variation. Kunde and Norlund found (1927) no significant decrease in the basal metabolism of dogs up to 12 years of age. In rats, Benedict and Sherman (1937) found a slight decrease in heat production with increasing age, measured in the same individuals, but with the onset of senescence the body weight itself declined, so that the metabolism per unit body weight appeared to increase. In man O_2 uptake per liter of intracellular fluid shows no decrease with age (Shock, et al., 1954). A fuller bibliography is given by Shock (1951, 1953). It is not so far possible, in most organisms, to base intelligible estimates of individual senescence upon changes in metabolic rate.

1.2 Forms of Senescence

Increase in death rate and decrease in resistance after a certain age might be expected in a number of model systems. The curve of failure rate for mechanical devices such as lamp bulbs, telephone switchboards (Kurtz and Winfrey, 1931), or radar units bears a superficial resemblance to the mortality curve of a senescent population, both in cases where all-or-none failure results from wear or from the passage of time (lamp filament failure, crystallization of metals, changes in condenser dielectrics) or where wear is cumulative and inefficiency increases to the point of failure (frictional wear, decline of cathode emission). The resemblance to biological senescence is closest in cases where several coincident processes ultimately become self-reinforcing. The "death-rate" of motor-cars, plotted by Griffin (1928) and Pearl and Miner (1935) is closely similar to that of wild-type *Drosophila* (Figure 1.2).

1.2.1 Mechanical Senescence

A few precise analogies to the failure of a non-replaceable part in a mechanical system are known to occur in organisms. Deterioration of the waxy epicuticle in insect imagines and of the teeth in the African elephant (Perry, 1953), the mongoose (Pearson and Baldwin, 1953), the shrew (Pearson, 1945; Pruitt, 1954), and some large carnivores are examples of strictly mechanical senescence. Such changes would ultimately kill the animal. Similar, though less obvious, mechanical changes may contribute to senescence in other forms. It is probable that the gradual loss of nephrons in the mammalian kidney is an example of the incidental loss of essential structures, but one that rarely reaches the point of causing death per se. On the other hand, the differences between an old cart and an old horse are sufficiently striking to make the extensive acceptance of "wear" as an explanation of senescence, and the resort to mechanical analogies based on the "spontaneous slow decomposition" of explosives (Lepeschkin, 1931) or the behavior of inanimate colloids (Růžícká, 1924; Dhar, 1932) difficult to accept. "The old organism does not contain old colloids, it contains newly formed colloids of an old character" (Lansing): this is not, however, universally true, and important molecules may in fact not be undergoing renewal (Gross, 1962). The mean half-life of human protein is 80 days; of liver and serum proteins, 10 days; and that of the carcase proteins, 158 days (Bender, 1953). High protein turnover in adult life has been found in some isotope studies (Shemin and Rittenberg, 1944); the turnover of other materials, such as collagen, decreases almost to zero with increasing age (Perrone and Slack, 1952; Neuberger and Slack, 1953). This possible distinction had been pointed out even before the discovery of colloids: "Quoniam vero duplex est duratio corporum: altera in identitate simplici, altera per reparationem: quarum prima in inanimatis tantum obtinet, secunda in vegetabilibus et animalibus; et perficitur per alimentationem" (*Hist. Vitae et Mortis*).[1]

But as Gross (1962) pointed out in a review article, it now looks as if the turnover of many body constituents, and not only of scleroproteins, has been considerably overrated in criticizing the theory of colloid ageing (Comfort, 1956)—"the point of view of the colloid ageing school might be summarized by asking the question: is it possible that at least one phase of the ageing process is a steady increase in crystalline order on the level of macromolecular aggregation, which requires little energy transfer, does not involve 'dynamic' processes, but does cause steady attrition by removing important molecular elements from the cellular machinery?" (Gross, 1962). It is certainly not *im*possible, in the light of the evidence that Gross summarizes. Electronic delocalization—"tautomeric shift and erroneous coupling"—has also been invoked as a subtler type of molecule spoilage leading to ageing (Pullman and Pullman, 1962); see also Bjorksten (1962).

A chemical extension of the idea of "mechanical" senescence could be based more plausibly on the existence of expendable enzyme systems renewable only by cell division, to explain the ultimate death of some fixed postmitotic cells (Cowdry, 1952); this concept will be discussed later on. In all organisms except those that are capable of total regeneration, mechanical injury of a more general kind must accumulate with time, but this process will vary greatly in rate under different environmental conditions. The constancy of the specific age in forms which senesce is a strong argument against the primacy of "mechanical" ageing: whether it negates chemomechanical ageing is more doubtful. The stability of the rate of age change in collagen suggests it does not.

1.2.2 *"Accumulation" and "Depletion"*

In addition to a limited number of cases in which mechanical wear normally, or potentially, terminates an animal life-cycle, most of the other postulated "causes" of senescence, such as the accumulation of metabolites (Metchnikoff, 1915; Jickeli, 1902) and the exhaustion of stored irreplenishable reserves, do very probably contribute to senescence in specific instances. The very large literature of calcium and pigment accumulation in the cells of

---

[1]Since there are in fact two ways in which bodies maintain their identity, the first, which applies only to inanimate objects, is simply by remaining the same. The second, which applies to plants and animals, is by renewing themselves; and they do this by means of nourishment.

higher animals (reviewed by Lansing, 1951) deals with changes that are probably reversible consequences, rather than primary causes, of an underlying senile process. Lansing (1942) and Sincock (1974) found, however, that reduction in the calcium content of the medium greatly increased the lifespan of rotifers. A similar increase was produced by a single immersion in weak citrate solution. Accumulation of calcium with age was demonstrated in the same organisms by microincineration. Similar processes are described in plants (Molisch, 1938; Ahrens, 1938; Lansing, 1942). The "life" of spermatozoa, though by no means analogous, has been shown to be prolonged by chelating agents that bind Cu^{++} and Zn^{++} (Tyler, 1953). In the case of the rotifer, at least, the evidence for an accumulative element in senescence is fairly strong.

Depletion certainly terminates the life-cycle of some non-feeding insect imagines, especially among Lepidoptera (Norris, 1934; Waloff, et al., 1947), and possibly other types of imago (Krumbiegel, 1929a, b). Many animals die or become more vulnerable, as a result of the depletion or physiological derangement caused by spawning (Orton, 1929). The life of female ticks, which normally die 4–5 days after oviposition, can be increased to 30 days by injecting sucrose into the body cavity (Achan, 1961). The incidence of parental mortality in molluscs is reviewed by Pelseneer (1935). Attempts to explain the human menopause in terms of exhaustion of the supply of ova will be discussed later. There is no evidence of a "depletive" senescence in mammals, unless the decline of growth rate is taken as evidence of the exhaustion of some hypothetical substance.

1.2.3 Morphogenetic Senescence

The accumulation of injuries presents no biological problem; it can easily be seen in structures such as skin, and the only serious difficulty lies in assessing how much it adds to ageing in particular structures or animal species.

But beside the processes of mechanical or metabolic senescence, and sometimes affecting the same organisms if they are protected from these, we also need a further, morphogenetic senescence to explain the sequence of events we see in many organisms. This senescence has been considered to arise directly from effects of the processes of cell development that give the species its typical shape, size, and organ structure, either through changes in cell behavior or through the effects of differential growth. It expresses itself as a decline in the capacity to regenerate or to maintain structures or conditions which, during growth and for a variable period after growth stops, are normally regenerated and maintained. Morphogenetic senescence is a cumulative failure of homeostasis, affecting the body as a whole, to which coincident or dependent mechanical failure or accumulative processes may contribute, but which appears to be part of the processes that control cell differentiation and regulation. More accurately, it appears to represent the withdrawal of coordination between these processes, so that physiological homeostasis "falls apart." The characteristic pathological change of ageing is an increase in the number of pathological changes. It is this form of senescence that characterizes higher vertebrates and is particularly well seen in man (Howell, 1968). The chief evidence that this morphogenetic senescence is more than the "sum of environmental insult," which was formerly invoked to explain it, is the existence in many organisms of specific age, analogous to specific size and possibly related to it, which displays little environmental, but marked interrace and interspecific variation.

Much information about the behavior of self-restoring and self-regulating systems, and a number of important general concepts, can be had from the study of mechanical models. These analogies can, strictly, only make clearer single components in the process of maintaining physilogical stability; the most important feature of "cybernetics" and homeostasis in the organism has no precise mechanical analogy. This is the fact that the homeostatic process, the state of quantitative invariance, or self-restoration, in various physiological systems, goes with qualitative and quantitative change in the nature of the systems themselves, their specificity, relative proportions, and function—in other words, it changes with developmental change. It looks very much as if senescence occurs when these long-term changes, which are probably controlled or initiated largely by the same humoral mediators which function in day-to-day homeostasis, pass out of control, or reach a point beyond which homeostasis is no longer possible.

This argument ultimately stands or falls by the result of our study of the phylogeny of senescence. Mammalian senescence seems to result from morphogenetic processes that ultimately escape from the homeostatic mechanisms that operate during adult vigor. If, on the other hand, some other vertebrates were able to reach a state of growing, or self-replacing, equilibrium, even over limited periods, such an equilibrium would be most likely to be found in those forms where differential growth is least evident. The evidence on this point will be examined later.

1.3   Senescence in Evolution

Senescence has often been regarded as an evolved adaptation, rather than as an inherent result of having a body. This view, which is reasonably well in accord with the existing, and very incomplete, evidence of its distribution in phylogeny, was held by Weismann in spite of his insistence on the constrast between germinal immortality and somatic mortality. Weismann, however, regarded senile change, and the limitation of the individual life-span, as a positively beneficial adaptation, and his argument is, as we have seen, at least potentially circular.

It is hard but not impossible to devise a system in which *short* life is selected as a character of fitness. Ribbands (1953) found an apparent example in worker bees, where the summer brood could increase its working life by consuming pollen, but uses it instead to rear additional larvae. The "clonal substance" of some protozoa may have adaptive uses of this kind (Nanney, 1974). Evidence of a hypothalamic "turning off" of reproduction in mammals might similarly be programmed, and Medvedev (1966) has postulated an evolved "destabilization" of cellular information with the same function of limiting individual life. In any circumstances where a high number of generations in unit time has an adaptive value, the Weismannian argument against individual longevity might hold. Leopold (1961) has argued a case for the adaptive value of parental death and of transience of organs in plants, and much of what he says could apply equally to seasonal animals. The most obvious modifications of life-span in phylogeny seem, however, to be chiefly in the other direction. The development of social insects probably depended upon the evolution of long-lived sexual forms, and it is very likely that something of the kind occurred in human phylogeny, in connection with the development of social behavior and the family unit. Neurons having a long potential life had to be evolved as a condition for the development of elaborate learned behavior and long parental dependence; with the development of rational power and social organization, the advantages of possessing the experience of even a few long-lived members was probably very high in any early hominid community. The social animals, especially man, provide one of the best examples where longevity depending on factors outside the reproductive period can theoretically be subject to positive selection in terms of fitness. Blest (1960) found a marked difference in the length of postreproductive life between species of butterflies with protective and with warning coloration—it is clearly advantageous to a species with warning colors that postfertile adults should be about for predators to experiment with, so as to educate them at the least cost to the fertile. Most of this argument is a full-blooded resort to Pangloss' Theorem.

The chief objection to Weismann's idea of senescence as an adaptive effect is the rarity of its demonstrable occurrence in nature. In all but a few forms among the larger animals senescence is a *potentiality*, not a benefit or a handicap; it is realized only when we interfere artificially with the animal or its environment, and it is arguable whether evolution can select for such potentialities. Bidder, it will be recalled, considered that senescence in mammals was an evolutionarily unimportant "by-product" of an important positive adaptation, the limitation of size. It would indeed be possible to attribute senile change to the effects of such by-products "coming home to roost" after the end of the reproductive period. More recently it has been suggested that senescence is to be regarded not as the positively beneficial character which Weismann believed it to be, but as a potentiality lying outside the part of the life-cycle which is relevant to evolution. It has certainly been "evolved," in that the living system that senesces has evolved, but it has not evolved as a physiological mechanism. The line of argument that appears most plausible is that suggested by Medawar (1945, 1952). It seems probable, for a number of reasons, that, except in certain social animals, there can be little effective selection pressure against senescence as such. In any wild communities of animals, even if they did not age, there will always be more young reproducing than old reproducing individuals; the difference is enough to offset the advantage in number of progeny that arises from a longer reproductive life. Death from senescence is itself in many species so rare in the wild state that failure to senesce early, or at all, has little value from the point of view of survival. In many forms the cessation or reduction of breeding capacity happens well before senescence proper—with certain exceptions in social animals. What happens later, in the postreproductive period, is theoretically outside the reach of selection, and irrelevant to it. Indeed, Medawar's view is really an evolutionary correction of one of Samuel Butler's bright ideas—that cells age for lack of a "racial memory" to instruct them how to go on living to ages of which their immediate ancestors had no experience, and that they die because they become puzzled how to continue. A consequence even more important than the mere failure of evolutionary processes to operate in favor of the postponement of senescence follows from the same facts. In view of the constant reproductive preponderance of young individuals, the postponement of the action of a harmful genetic effect until late in the reproductive life is almost as good, in selective value, as its complete elimination: the longer the postponement, the closer the equivalence. The evolutionary "demon" is concerned only to clear the part of the life-span in which he works, not the parts that might be reached if the environment were artificially made more favorable. This mechanism, by acting to move all adverse genetic effects that are capable of postponement and all the consequences of divergent but temporarily beneficial systems into the late reproductive or postreproductive life, may itself provide a partial explanation of the evolution of senescence, as Haldane (1941) has already suggested. In this case we would expect the balance in man to be such that the force of mortality is lowest when reproductive activity is potentially highest, though the observed lowest level falls rather earlier than this (10–12 years in males—Greville, 1946).

Mathematical models for the regulation of ageing by natural selection have been proposed by several workers (Hamilton, 1966; Edney and Gill, 1968; Klopfer, 1969; Ricklefs, 1969).

The selectionist argument, which regards senescence as the decline of evolved survival power through successive age groups, is most convincing when we apply it to mammals and birds: among invertebrates, reservations have to be made. In those that are predominantly seasonal, with a total life-span of less than one year, and that winter as fertilized adults, it is by no means true that at all times of the year young individuals must outnumber old in a free-running population. The autumn contingent of overwintering animals will consist of "old" individuals. In such forms, the selective advantage of different genotypes will vary from season to season, and there will be an ultimate requirement that the adult be capable of living long enough to overwinter. Forms producing two broods annually will tend to select fertility in the spring brood and longevity in the autumn, but with a time-lag of one generation between selection and potential expression. The mechanism of selection in such a system must be very complicated.

In mammals some selective advantage would also presumably attach to longevity where older males are polygamous and younger males compete for the remaining females (deer, baboons). The solipsist model of selection operating on "the individual" can obviously be upset by any selection pressures introduced into the system by interaction between individuals and by community patterns of ecological behavior in the species; the idea of an "individual" animal unsupported by the rest of the ecological community in which it lives is in fact unbiological, and large unpredictable selection pressures affecting the life-span may well arise from such hidden social relationships.

In spite of this criticism, the theory of senescence as a measure of declining selection pressure is important. The declining evolutionary importance of the individual with age may be expressed in another way in the "morphogenetic" senescence seen in mammals. At the point where a system of differential growth ceased to be regulated by forces that arose from natural selection, it would cease to be under effectively directional morphogenetic control, and would resemble an automatic control device which has "run out of program." In any such system the equilibrium must be increasingly unstable. These two views of senescence, as accumulation of delayed lethal or sublethal genetic effects, and as a withdrawal of the evolutionary pressure towards homeostasis with increasing age, are complementary, though probably only partial, pictures of its evolutionary significance. The concept of senescence as exhaustion of program also restores a far greater unity to our definition of ageing, which includes a great many effects having little in common beyond their destructive effect on homeostasis. All such effects fall within the idea of deterioration lying outside the "terms of reference" of each species, as laid down by natural selection. The "flying bomb" that failed to dive on its objective would ultimately "die" either of fuel exhaustion or through wear in its expendable engine. If its design had been produced by evolution, and its evolutionary relevance ceased at the moment of passing its objective or decreased as a function of the distance flown, both these events would be outside the program laid down by the selective equilibrium, as they were outside the calculation of the designing engineers. Death in such an expendable system may result from one of many factors, and even, as Bidder recognized, from the consequence of processes that contribute to fitness during earlier life, such as systems of differential growth. We shall find that a good deal of gerontology *is* primarily the study of a living system's behavior after its biological program is exhausted. The various evolutionary explanations of ageing already combine to offer us some idea of the reasons why this may be so, and lead to the model of a "hierarchy of clocks." See Section 6.2.

2
The Distribution of Senescence

2.1 Character of the Evidence

To find out which animals exhibit an increasing mortality with increasing age, we should ideally keep large numbers of each species, or of representative species, from birth to death, under optimal conditions of captivity. In point of fact, apart from the impracticability of keeping any significant number of species in this way, the results would be both artificial and potentially misleading. It is possible to invent about animal senescence a paradox rather analogous to the principle of physical uncertainty: it is "virtually unknowable" or, in other words, meaningless to ask, whether certain organisms are "susceptible to senescence," because the organism is biologically dependent on its environment. In the wild state these forms never normally live long enough to reach senescence, while domestication or protective interference with the environment brings about changes in physiology and behavior, which produce effectively a different organism. The object of the paradox is to point out the fruitlessness of argument over "potential" behavior that is practically unrealizable. Almost all our detailed knowledge of senescence comes either from the observation of man, or of domestication-artifacts such as the laboratory mouse or the laboratory strains of *Drosophila*. In the wild state it is most unlikely that any species of *Mus* or of *Drosophila* reaches old age with sufficient regularity to be subject to study.

In most cases we are creating for study a state that has no part in the life-cycle as it has been shaped by evolution, but is at most a potentiality. This must be taken into account on every occasion when theories of the evolution of senescence are being based on the appearance of senescence in domestic animals.

Life-tables for mammals other than man and the mouse are still few, though some data have been collected for horses (Comfort, 1958a, 1959), dogs (Comfort, 1956, 1960a), and various zoo animals (see Figures 1.4, 1.10–1.14).

2.1.1   Animal Life-Tables

If we had a comprehensive account of the relation between growth, development, mortality, and chronological age in a sufficient range of representative species, the truth of most of the general theories that have been put forward to explain senescence could probably be tested by inspection. The actuarial studies that we already have, combined with maximum age records, suggest that in invertebrates there is an inverse relationship between degree of cell replacement and liability to senile change. It is now of great importance to obtain accurate data for the relation of age to mortality in the main types of vertebrates, and in as many different species as possible. Ageing and general metabolic activity in rats are dissociable, at least prior to maturity, as growth and development are dissociable in the tadpole; it is therefore one of the most important problems of age studies to find out, if possible, which components of the developmental "program" in mammals determine the timing of senescence. Given a sufficient range of comparative information, we might expect to answer this question either directly, from observed correlations, or by a relatively small number of fundamental experiments.

There are no wholly consistent correlates of life-span beyond those suggested by Sacher (1959, index of cephalization). "Neither do those things which may seem concomitants give any furtherance to this Information (the greatness of their Bodies, the time of their bearing in the Womb, the number of their young ones, the time of their growth, and the rest) in regard that these things are intermixed—sometimes they concur, sometimes they sever" (Bacon). The metabolism of small birds measured by their oxygen consumption is higher than that of rodents, and apparently it does not decline with age like that of many mammals (Benedict and Talbot, 1921). This suggests that in phylogeny other causes than the increase in metabolic rates have operated to shorten the maximum life-span. The growth of birds, as Bacon (1645) pointed out, ceases relatively earlier than that of mammals, and much more definitively; the epiphyses of rats never join, and they may continue in growth, or be made to grow in response to somatotrophin, at any age, while no further growth occurs in birds after the attainment of adult size.

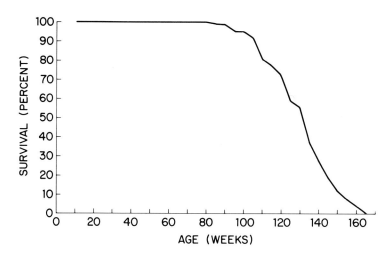

FIGURE 2.1   Survival curve of C67BL/6J male mice, based on 60 animals. (Mice were 10 weeks old at start of experiment; hence neonatal mortality is not considered.) (From Walford, 1976.)

There are also important discrepancies between the maximum ages reported in closely related mammals. The most extensive figures are for rodents: thus *Mus bactrianus* has been reported to live and remain fertile longer than any strain of *Mus musculus* (Green, 1932), while species of *Peromyscus* and *Perognathus* live almost twice as long: *Peromyscus maniculatus gambelli* 5 years 8 months (Summer, 1922); *Peromyscus maniculatus gracilis* 5 years 10 months (Dice, 1933; Rabb, 1960); *Perognathus longimembris* > 7½ years (Orr, 1939). These differences are not closely related to size: *Micromys minutus* reaches nearly 4 years in similar circumstances (Pitt, 1955). Leslie and Ranson (1940) and Leslie et al. (1955) found a difference in specific longevity between colonies of *Microtus arvensis* and *Microtus orcadensis,* though this might reflect the results of domestication and better culture. Such differences are clearly of great importance to our understanding of age processes, but so far none of the attempts to correlate them with quantities such as the duration of pregnancy or the relative length of preadult development is satisfactory, chiefly because the figures assumed for the specific ages of the different species are arbitrarily drawn from the maximum age records, some of them quite inaccurate. Most of the valid correlations which can be made out are those reviewed by Bourlière (1946).

The closest correlate of life-span in mammals is the "index of cephalization" or relative excess of brain weight over the predicted value derived from a universal brain–body weight equation (Friedenthal, 1910). Friedenthal's conclusion was that "der Klügste an längsten lebt."

The relation between brain weight and longevity, first pointed out by Friedenthal, has been carefully documented by Sacher (1959, 1965, 1966, 1975, 1976) in relation to gestation period (Sacher and Staffeldt, 1974) and to metabolic rate. For sixty-three mammals the life-span, L, was related to brain weight, E, and body weight, S, by the equation

$$\log L = 0.64 \log E - 0.23 \log S + 1.04$$

For Anthropoidea the equation is

$$\log L = 0.65 \log E - 0.20 \log S + 0.87$$

and for 85 wholly homeothermic species, resting metabolic rate, M, being expressed in cm^3 O_2/g per hour and deep body temperature T in °C

$$\log L = 0.62 \log E - 0.41 \log S - 0.52 \log M + 0.026\, T + 0.89$$

Hayflick (1975) has suggested that clonal longevity may be geared to overall life-span. In Sacher's view the determinant here may be the longevity imposed by larger brain size and the lower reproductive rate that accompanies it. These theories accord with the increasing evidence of a cerebral "clock" as the overriding determinant of ageing. Mallouk (1975) locates life-span in the exhaustion of a brain-sited Lebenssubstanz; a more likely explanation is in the existence of a timing mechanism, longer life-spans being made possible by secondary adaptations such as increased capacity for excision–repair of thymidine dimers (Hart and Setlow, 1974), or a slower rate of protein turnover (Spector, 1974).

In view of questions like these, one of the most important requisites for the understanding of mammalian age processes and the factors that time them is a full range of vertebrate vital statistics, based on animals living under conditions of captivity sufficiently good for a fair proportion of them to reach old age. These figures are almost wholly lacking. So far as can be ascertained, up to 1960 no life-table had been published for a captive population of any fish, reptile, or amphibian. There was one incomplete and ancient life table for domestic poultry, and it is based on an assumed equation to cover losses from culling (Gardner and Hurst, 1933); bird life tables are few to this day (Eisner and Etoh, 1967). Apart from these, we have had satisfactory actuarial data only for man, laboratory rats and mice, and a few other small rodents, with partial figures for culled populations of agriculturally important animals, e.g., Merino ewes (Kelley, 1939). There are thus no data for any vertebrates other than mammals; the figures that might throw light on the evolution of mammalian senescence, those for poikilotherms, birds, and marsupials, have never been sought.

One consequence of this lack of information is that we have no experimental mammal intermediate in size between man and the small rodents whose rate of ageing is actuarially known. There are no published actuarial data for rabbits: their modal specific age for all strains is probably about 8 years, but large hybrids may reach ages as great as 15 years (Comfort, 1956). Ten years has been reported in cottontails (Lord, 1961). Data for guinea pigs have been collected and briefly reported (Rogers, 1950) but we have no comparison of strains. Accordingly, many physiological and other differences described in the literature between young and "old" animals are in fact differences between infant and young adult animals, and even where this is not so it is impossible to establish correlations between such changes and the rate of ageing from maximum age records alone.

2.1.2 Methods of Obtaining Vertebrate Data

It is difficult, but not impossible, to obtain actuarial statistics for vertebrates, and as they are virtually essential to any biologically directed attack on age problems, we should devote our attention to getting them, as a matter of urgency. They represent an expendable problem, moreover, since time once spent will not need to be respent later.

Age-mortality data can be obtained in three ways: (1) from populations of animals specially kept under close observation throughout life, (2) from analysis of existing records; (3) by cross-sectional studies that indicate the simultaneous mortality in each age group over one period of time, instead of the successive mortalities of the survivors of a cohort followed throughout life. The results of (3) will differ numerically from those obtained from the

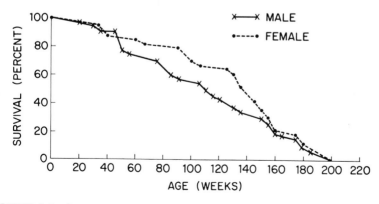

FIGURE 2.2 Survival curves of 35 male and 33 female Mongolian gerbils. Mean survival for males is 110 weeks; for females, 139 weeks. (From Troup, et al., 1969.)

same animals by the first two methods if there is a secular change in mortality during the lives of the longest-lived individuals. With this method we should include cross-sectional studies of animals that can be aged by inspection, particularly the analyses of fish populations by means of catch curves (Ricker, 1948). The number of instances in which wild populations can be used for ageing studies is, however, small as yet; although even in small birds whose mortality is substantially constant, ringing studies show that more individuals reach old age than the early death rates would lead us to expect (Haldane, 1953).

It is evident that we can expect to obtain figures for most of the long-lived animals only from existing records. These include kennel and stud books, notes kept by laboratories or by amateurs, and the record files of zoological gardens. The material varies greatly in quality, and the statistical treatment it requires is different from that which serves for laboratory or human actuarial work, since the data consist of multiple small samples, and in most cases there are substantial losses from the record by sale, culling, or deliberate killing in the course of experiments.

Within a single species, the difference in observed longevity of the various breeds of dog follow the direction predicted by Sacher (1959) from the distribution of life-span with brain and body weight in different groups of mammalian species. Table 2.1 gives some of Stephan's data (1954), together with the expected values of log x from Sacher's equation:

$$\log x = 0.636 \log z - 0.222 \log y + 1.035$$

where x = life-span in years, y = body weight, and z = brain weight, both in grams. Comparing these with observed or assumed values of $x(x^\circ)$, on the assumption that most of Sacher's figures for mammalian life-spans are derived

TABLE 2.1
Brain Weight, Body Weight, and Assumed Life-Span in Dogs

BREED	BODY WEIGHT (KG) y	BRAIN WEIGHT (G) z	LOG x_1	LOG x_2	LOG x^0	x^0 (YEARS)
Pekinese	5.6	58.7	1.40	1.28	1.30	20
Dachshund	8.2	70.9	1.33	1.20	1.28	19
Fox terrier	7.8	67.9	1.31	1.18	1.20	≮16
Mastiff	42.2	116.5	1.30	1.17	1.15	14
Leonberger	47.6	113.0	1.29	1.28	1.15	14
St. Bernard	47.0	113.7	1.34	1:20	1.15	14

log x_1 = 0.636 log z − 0.225 log y + 1.035 (Sacher's equation).
log x_2 = 0.6 log z − 0.23 log y + 0.99.
x^0 = Observed or assumed life-span.
Body and brain weights from Stephan (1954). Life-spans from Comfort (1960a).

from maximum records and that the longevity of other big breeds, which are known to be short-lived (such as the St. Bernard), resembles that of mastiffs, we find that most, although not all, of Stephan's data yield values for x that fit reasonably well to a similar equation with changed constants:

$$\log x = 0.6 \log z - 0.23 \log y + 0.99$$

The rest could no doubt be fitted by further manipulation, but more complex comparisons are pointless until the real life-span of more breeds is known. The figures so far are at least consistent, however, with the idea that the rule regarding index of cephalization applies empirically to interbreed as well as interspecific differences.

Domestic goats, 15 and probably up to 20 years (20 years 9 months, female wild goat, London Zoo).

Carnivora: *cats* are the longest lived of the small domestic mammals. Mellen (1940) from questionnaires sent out in Canada and the U.S.A. obtained these records: gelt males, 21, 21, 22, 23, 24, 24, 25, 28, 31 years; entire males, 23, 24, 26; females, 21, 21, 22, 31. These were owners' estimates, but at least one 31-year record was well supported. Thirty-three years has been claimed (Mellen, 1940). Figures for cats in England in recent years included at least ten apparently authentic cases over 20, and one gelt male alive at 28 (Comfort, 1956c).

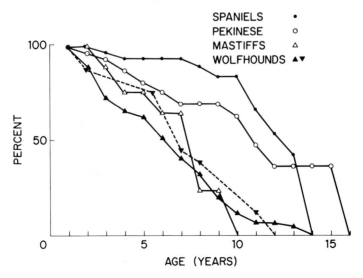

FIGURE 2.3 Survival curves of 4 breeds of dogs from 1 year of age. (From Comfort, 1960a.)

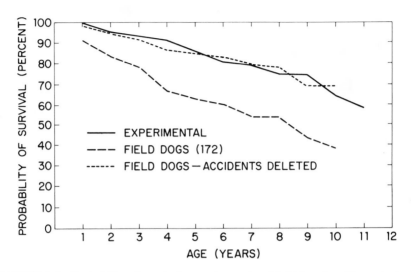

FIGURE 2.4   Probability of survival, experimental and field beagles. (From Andersen and Rosenblatt, 1965.)

TABLE 2.2
Longevity and Survival by Coat Color of Thoroughbred Mares
(from Comfort, 1958)

GROUP	n	$e_{x=4}$	V_e	MEDIAN
All colors:				
Foaled 1875	285	17.26	0.34	22.43
1876	245	17.65	0.21	22.43
1877	233	17.44	0.21	22.49
1878	248	17.49	0.30	22.15
1879	261	16.13	0.16	20.81
1880	221	16.01	0.18	21.81
1875–1880	1,492	17.04	0.046	22.18
1860–1864	1,250	17.31	0.044	22.07
Bays (1875–1879)	568	16.68	0.08	22.03
Blacks (1854–1900)	358	16.53	0.15	21.95
Chestnuts (1875–1879)	262	17.23	0.20	22.50
Greys (1845–1920)	200	15.57	0.28	20.43

Dogs very seldom exceed 18 years, and only exceptionally reach 20. There are remarkably few claims of greater longevity in the literature (34 years, Lankester, 1870). In many breeds the limit is far lower, large breeds being shorter-lived than small (see Table 2.3; Comfort, 1956b, 1960a). Size differences in dogs are predominantly differences in parenchymatous cell number,

TABLE 2.3
Survival of Four Breeds of Dogs from Kennel Records (from Comfort, 1960a)

Age (years)	Pekinese, Kennels D, K, Y ♂♀	Cocker Spaniels, Kennel M ♀	English Mastiffs, ♂♀	Irish Wolfhounds C	Irish Wolfhounds Kennel R ♂♀
N*	91	38†	23	9	91
1	1.0000	1.0000	1.0000	1.0000	1.0000
2	0.9663	1.0000	1.0000	0.88	0.8876
3	0.9301	0.9701	0.8857		0.7019
4	0.8741	0.9383	0.7440	0.88	0.6419
5	0.8062		0.7440	0.77	0.6049
6	0.7482		0.6377	0.77	0.4814
7	0.6880	0.9383	0.6377	0.44	0.3827
8		0.8935	0.2125	0.33	0.2716
9	0.6880	0.8394	0.2125		0.1728
10	0.6281	0.8394	0.0		0.0864
11	0.4711	0.6595			0.0370
12	0.3664	0.5396			0.0370
13		0.4197		0.0	0.0246
14		0.0			0.0
15	0.3664				
16	0.0				

*N = number from total sample alive at 1 year.

†Males omitted from computations because there was reason to suspect selection. Mean for 7 males 114 months, range 96–168.

(From Comfort, 1960a.)

not cell size (Rensch, 1954)—the same applies to neurons, judging from posterior root fiber counts in Terriers and Great Danes (Häggqvist, 1948). Crude comparisons of man-dog ages are of doubtful value in any breed (Cairey, 1954; LeBeau, 1953).

In a lifetime study of beagles (Andersen, 1961) about one-third had died by 10 years of age, but signs of "true senility" were said to be present from 5 years on, as judged by pathological findings (Figure 2.4; Andersen and Rosenblatt, 1965).

2.1.3   Age Determination in Animals

This usually depends on the presence of some structure that grows annually in a consistent pattern, making it possible, once the pattern is known and has been shown to be consistent, to age the animal as one ages a tree by the rings in its stump. Examples of such ring-producing structures include pelecypod (but not gastropod) shells, discussed later: otoliths, bones, teeth, horns, and fish scales. In mammals, the chief structures that can be used like this are the teeth of seals (by counting the incremental cementum layers: Laws, 1953; Schaffer, 1950; Hewer, 1960), the horns of sheep and goats (Murie, 1944; Ferrara, 1951), the wax earplugs of whales (Laws and Purves, 1956), and the antler-pedicles of caribou (Banfield, 1960)—the last not strictly ring-forming structures, though they undergo annual increment. Apart from progressive plumage changes like that in the lyrebird, there seem to be no incremental ageing methods for birds. Many reptiles can now be aged by growth zones in the bones—in particular, the ectopterygoids and squamosals of snakes (Bryuzgin, 1939; Petter-Rousseaux, 1953); Peabody (1958) found evidence of a drought some years previously in the zones laid down by a bullsnake *(Pituophis),* and readable zonation in the bones of lizards, crocodiles, and fossil Australian lizards (Peabody, 1961): these papers review the literature. There is a large literature of scale-reading in fish (see, for example, Frost and Kipling, 1949; pike, scales and opercular bones— Jhingran, 1957; Indian carp—Hartley, 1958; salmon, etc.). Other annulus-forming structures are the otoliths (Irie, 1957; *Gasterosteus*—Jones and Hynes, 1950; etc.), vertebrae (tuna—Galtsoff, 1952; *Raia*—Ishiyama, 1951; Daiber, 1960; shark—Haskell, 1948–1949), opercular bone (e.g., carp— Bardach, 1955), dermal spines and fin rays *(Squalus*—Holden and Meadows, 1962, Boyko, 1946; Channel catfish—Marzolf, 1955, etc.). Section of sturgeon fin rays has revealed ages up to 82 years (Chugunov, 1925; Milne and Milne, 1958). These references represent only a minute part of a vast literature of direct age determination by ring counting in fish. Of amphibians, only *Necturus* appears so far to have been aged by similar means (Senning, 1940).

Other methods of ageing animals, particularly mammals, are chiefly of use for population studies, and are not suitable for maximum age determination, since they distinguish only "old" from "young" without specific reference to years. They can sometimes give more precise information, however, if combined with year-group analysis of a population—here again, only representative papers can be quoted in this list. Such methods include the examination of teeth in horses; of the baculum; of tail pelage in squirrels (Sharp, 1958); moult pattern in *Microtus* (Ecke and Kinney, 1956); epiphyseal fusion in rabbits (Taylor, 1959)—a criterion that is much used in man, but is highly unreliable, owing to the large scatter in rates of development (Tanner, 1955)—ovum counts in primates (Laws, 1952); and tooth impressions in deer (Flyger, 1958). Age determination in game and furbearers is reviewed by Habermehl (1961).

Maximum longevity records of animal species have a definite, but limited, use in giving a comparative picture of the possible longevity in different forms. They can give no direct evidence of the distribution of senescence, but they can provide an important test of a number of general theories—those based, for example, on the exhaustion of neurons (Vogt and Vogt, 1946; Bab, 1948) are difficult to reconcile with the variation in specific age and potential longevity between closely related forms. A large scatter of maximum recorded ages is in itself suggestive, but not of course demonstrative, evidence of an indeterminate life-span, except in cases where it is evidence only of improving cultural methods and better understanding of the requirements of the animal under laboratory or domestic conditions. For a very large range of species we can readily infer a "potential" age that is never attained, either in the wild, because of accident and predation, or in captivity, because the animals cannot be kept alive in captivity—the "potential" longevity of snakes, chameleons (Flower, 1925, 1937), or mammals of little-known habits (pangolins—Flower, 1931) are cases in point. "Concerning the length and brevity of life in beasts, the knowledge which may be had is slender, the observation negligent, and tradition fabulous; in household beasts the idle life corrupts; in wild, the violence of the climate cuts them off" *(Historia Vitae et Mortis)*. With most birds, fully domestic mammals, hardy reptiles such as tortoises, and man, however, maximum records can be taken to represent in some real degree the extreme length of time for which the species, or its hardier genotypes, can remain self-maintaining if protected from gross disease or accident. Theories of senescence must fit these data, or at least not contradict them, to be available as working hypotheses.

2.2 Maximum Longevities in Animals

Apart from the observations collected by Bacon, which were remarkably critical and accurate compared with the wildness of later estimates, the accurate study of animal life-spans virtually begins with the enormously painstaking studies of Chalmers Mitchell (1911) and Flower (1925, 1931, 1935, 1936, 1937, 1938[1]) in purging a vast body of legendary and anecdotal material that encumbered the subject. Much of this legendary material unfortunately persists in other books and papers *(Tabulae Biologicae*—Heilbrunn, 1943; Nagornyi, 1948; Hammond and Marshall, 1952; Schmidt,

---

[1]Those references marked "Flower MS." refer to the card index of data and letters from biological workers which Flower was preparing against a revision of his first mammalian list, and which was uncompleted at his death. This index is in the library of the Zoological Society of London, and includes also bird and reptilian records and the skeleton of a list of invertebrate longevities.

1952; Wurmbach, 1951; Birren, 1959) deriving their data from Korschelt (1922). The skepticism of Flower's papers was very valuable, in view of the exorbitant claims made for parrots, elephants, and so on, but it seems probable that birds in particular are in fact capable of living considerably longer than Flower's maximum figures suggest. Better data may, in time, become available, though the value of such records is still not sufficiently widely appreciated and many opportunities must have been lost through failure to keep track of individual specimens. No recent writer has dealt equally painstakingly with the longevity of invertebrates.

The data on vertebrate senescence which follow are those of Flower, except where otherwise stated. Some more recent records have been added, including a number derived from the series of longevity studies published by the Penrose Laboratory of the Philadelphia Zoo in the years prior to 1942 (Duetz, 1938, 1939, 1940, 1942).

2.2.1   Mammals

The longest-lived species is man. *Elephas indicus* is known to reach 60 years: a few individuals may reach or exceed 70 in captivity (77?—Mohr, 1951). The only other mammals which are known to approach or exceed 50 years are the horse, hippopotamus (49 years 6 months: 1953—*Ann. Rep. N.Y. Zool. Soc., 53, 12*), *Rhinoceros unicornis* (49 years—Flower, 1931) and probably the ass (47 years?—Flower MS.). Many larger mammals, including baboons and other large primates, cats, bears, African elephant, equines, tapirs, can approach or exceed 30 years (chimpanzee, 39—Tomilin, 1936; baboon, *Papio papio,* 27—Duetz, 1938; *P. anubis,* 30+—Krohn, personal communication; gibbon, *Hylobates lar;* 32+—Duetz, 1938; (Tarsius? about 20—Ulmer 1960); domestic cat, 31—Mellen, 1939, 1940; 27, Comfort, 1955; Chapman's zebra, 40—Weber, 1942). A large group, including almost all ruminants, many medium-sized herbivores and carnivores, large bats, and the larger rodents (Beaver, capybara, the domestic rabbit) have recorded maximum ages between 12 and 20 years (golden agouti, 15—Duetz, 1938). The maximum ages of very many rodents and small carnivores are not accurately established, since few specimens have been kept, but it is likely that a very large group among these forms has a potential life-span approaching 10 years. (*Lutra canadensis,* ♂ 14½—Schaffer, 1958; fox, 15—Sheldon, 1949; ♂ fox, 14—Wheelwright, 1951; ♂ bobcat, 25—Carter, 1955; *Platypus,* 14—Manville, 1958.) The small Chiroptera certainly have a much longer life than most mammals of comparable size—ringed horseshoe bats have been recovered after at least 7 years (Bourlière, 1947), and have lived at least 16 years (Cockrum, 1956; Dorst, 1954; Van Heerdt and Sluiter, 1955). This agrees with their slow rate of reproduction.

The shortest-lived mammalian group (<5 years) includes rats, mice, voles and other small rodents, and the small insectivores. (Rat: 4 years 8 months in a white rat probably already 1 year old—Donaldson, 1924; Simms, 1958; laboratory mouse: 3 years 3 months—Kobozieff, 1931; *Apodemus sylvaticus,* 6 years—Neuhaus, 1957; *Micromys minutus,* nearly 4 years—Pitt, 1945; golden hamster *(Cricetus auratus),* usually 2–3 years maximum—Bruce and Hindle, 1934; Deansley, 1938; one specimen in London Zoo, 3 years 11 months—Flower MS.; guinea pig, 7 years 7 months—Rogers, 1950; *Blarina,* 18 months—Pearson, 1945; *Sorex fumeus,* 13–14 months—Hamilton, 1940; *Crocidina leucodon,* about 4 years—Frank, 1956). The real life-span of whales has never been established, but it is almost certainly not more than 30–50 years at the most (Ohsumi, et al., 1958), and probably less. The age of maturity of whales has been placed as low as 2 years (John, 1937). Ruud, et al. (1950) found that blue whales reach sexual maturity in about 5 years—no individual in their very large sample was apparently older than 12 years, judged by the baleen pattern. The life-span of dolphins in the wild appears to be of the same order (15 years—Sleptzov, 1940; 30+, one specimen— Parker, 1933). A female humpback whale is recorded with 95 striations in its wax earplug: reckoning 2 striations per year of life, this animal should have been about 47 years old. Few exceed 30 (Chittleborough, 1959) by this reckoning. There is uncertainty, however, as to the number of earplug zones laid down in each year. The subject is reviewed by Frigorio and Sachu (1968). Unfortunately, zonation in baleen is rarely readable (Yablokov and Andreyevna, 1965).

Little is known about longevity in marsupials or monotremes—or if known it has not been put on record *(Echidna* nearly 40 years—Duetz, 1942; *Platypus* certainly 10 and probably 14 years in captivity—Manville, 1958).

Detailed records of many other mammalian species are given by Flower.

Recent data on the longevity of seals were reviewed by Laws (1953), upon the basis of tooth sections. Captive records include *Otaria byronia,* 23 years; *Eumetopias stelleri,* 19 (Flower, 1931); one female, 22 (Fiscus, 1961); *Zalophus californianus,* 23; *Arctocephalus pusillus,* 20 (Bourlière, 1951); *Phoca vitulina,* 19 (Sivertsen, 1941); *Halichoerus grypus,* 41–42 (Matheson, 1950). In the wild, *Callorhinus ursinus* has reached 21+ years (Schaffer, 1950); *Mirounga leonina* ♂ 20, ♀ 18 (Laws, 1953).

The *maximum age records of horses and domestic pets* are of importance because these animals are the only mammals kept throughout life in sufficient numbers to give any estimate of the extreme age for the species. In spite of the likelihood of exaggeration and mistake, records of domestic pets kept singly, throughout life, by intelligent witnesses, provide evidence as good as that from laboratory stocks and sometimes better than that from zoos, since reliable mnemonic evidence is better than unreliable documents.

Horses very probably exceed 40; most higher claims refer to ponies. It is claimed, without published details, that in Lipizza horses ages of 30 are common. A Hafling mare foaled at 32 (Schotterer, 1939). Smyth (1937) reported a 46-year-old brood mare that foaled for the 34th time at 42—this case appears authentic. (Horse, 62—Flower, 1931: this is the celebrated but quite unauthenticated "Old Jack"; jennet, reputed 60—Wright, 1936; pony, 54—Rothschild *fide* Flower, 1931; Shetland pony, 58—The *Times,* May 3, 1944; roan pony, 52—The *Times,* April 12, 1944; all probably legendary. Iceland pony, 47—The *Times,* August 7, 1934; many records between 40 and 45.) A zebra has reached 40 in captivity (Weber, 1942). *Asses*—probably exceed 40 (47—Flower MS. from a press report; but an 86-year-old ass in *The Times,* November 29, 1937, can hardly be taken seriously). A 48-year-old mule is reported (Galea, 1936).

In an investigation of age records in the General Stud Book, the highest were reached by Arabians, three mares reaching 31 years, and one dying in its 33rd year (born 1911, died 1943; last covered, but barren, 1942). The two oldest thoroughbred mares in the sample were alive at 30 years. The Stud Book has not been searched in detail for higher records; the oldest mare so far encountered (Blue Bell, by Heron out of Jessie) was foaled in 1851 and died in 1885 at the age of 34. The stallion Matchem (1749–1781) reached a reputed age of 33: in the obituary lists of the Stud Book one other stallion reached 32, and four reached 31. For all mares reaching 4 years of age, the mean age of death was 21.2 years (Comfort, 1958).

Domestic goat: 15–20 years (20 years 9 months, female wild goat, London Zoo).

Carnivores: cats are the longest lived of the small domestic mammals. Mellen (1940) obtained records, from questionnaires sent out in the U.S. and Canada, of up to 31 years in gelt and entire males. Thirty-three years has been claimed. Figures for England in recent years include ten colorable cases over 20, and one gelt male alive at 28 (Comfort, 1955). *Dogs* only exceptionally reach 20 years, chiefly the smaller breeds; see pp. 59–62.

Rodents: the *rabbit* can almost certainly reach 15 years (10 years 3 months in the laboratory—Tegge [1936]; buck 13 years—Barrett-Hamilton [1911]; buck, chinchilla × Belgian hare, 11 years two cases; English buck, 14 years, both authenticated—Comfort, [1955]). American cottontail, 10 years in captivity—Lord (1961). Flower MS. contains a plausible correspondence with the owner of a rabbit (doe) that was said to have exceeded 18 years and was still alive.

Bats: The longevity of bats is of interest because their long survival contrasts with the short life of similar-sized rodents; this is often attributed to their status as partial poikilotherms. However, Herreid (1964) (see Table

2.4) found no difference in longevity between temperate zone bats, which hibernate, and tropical bats, which do not; the metabolism of both, however, is labile and falls to low levels when at rest.

2.2.2 Birds

Flower's longest "incontestable" record in captivity (Flower, 1925, 1938); (see Table 2.5) was 68 years in *Bubo bubo*. This is probably too low. Records

TABLE 2.4
Longevity Records of Bats (from Herreid 1964)

SPECIES	AGE (MAXIMUM, YEARS)
Megachiroptera	
Roussettus leachi	19.5
Pteropus giganteus	17.0
Microchiroptera	
Rhinolophidae	
Rhinolophus ferrumequinum	23.5
Rhinolophus hipposideros	14.5
Desmodontidae	
Desmodus rotundus	12.5
Vespertilionidae	
Myotis myotis	14.0
Myotis lucifugus	20.5
Myotis keenii	18.5
Myotis daubentoni	14.0
Myotis dasycneme	15.5
Myotis mystacinus	13.5
Myotis emarginatus	14.5
Myotis nattereri	14.0
Myotis sodalis	10.0, 11.0
Myotis subulatus	9.0, 12.0
Myotis thysanodes	6.0
Pizonyx vivesi	3.0, 10.0
Pipistrellus subflavus	10.0, 13.0
Eptesicus fuscus	19.0
Barbestella barbastellus	17.0
Plecotus auritus	12.5
Plecotus townsendii	10.0
Miniopterus schreibersi	14.5
Antrozous pallidus	8.0
Molossidae	
Tadarida brasiliensis	5.0

TABLE 2.5
Maximum Recorded Longevities in Forty-Five Species of Bird (from Flower, 1938)

	YEARS	
	PROVEN	REPORTED
Eagle Owl *(Bubo bubo)*	68	
Greater sulphur-crested Cockatoo *(Cacatua galerita)*	56	69, 80, 120
Bateleur Eagle *(Terathopsius ecaudatus)*	55	
Vasa Parrot *(Coracopsis vasa)*	54	
Condor *(Vultur gryphus)*	52	
White Pelican *(Pelicanus onocrotalus)*	51	
Grey Parrot *(Psittacus erythacus)*	49	73
Golden-naped Parrot *(Amazona auropalliata)*	49	
Australian Crane *(Megalornis rubicunda)*	47	
Golden Eagle *(Aquila chrysaëtos)*	46	80
Adalbert's Eagle *(Aquila adalberti)*	44	
Blue-and-yellow Macaw *(Ara ararauna)*	43	
Grey Crane *(Megalornis grus)*	43	
Leadbeater's Cockatoo *(Cacatua leadbeateri)*	42	60
Caracara *(Polyborus tharus)*	42	
Chilean Eagle *(Geranoaëtus melanoleucus)*	42	
White-tailed Eagle *(Haliaetus albicillus)*	42	
Sarus Crane *(Magelornis antigone)*	42	
Rough-billed Pelican *(Pelicanus erythrorhynchos)*	41	
Manchurian Crane *(Megalornis japonensis)*	41	
Asiatic White Crane *(M. leucogeranus)*	41	
Herring Gull *(Larus argentatus)*	41	44, 49
Banksian Cockatoo *(Calyptorrhynchus banksii)*	40	
Bare-eyed Cockatoo *(Cacatua gymnopis)*	40	
Western slender-billed Cockatoo *(Licmetis pastinator)*	40	
Tawny Eagle *(Aquila rapax)*	40	
King Vulture *(Sarcorhamphus papa)*	40	
Ceylon Fish Owl *(Ketupa zeylonensis)*	39	
Cinereous Vulture *(Aegypius monachus)*	39	
Red-and-blue Macaw *(Ara macao)*	38	64
Griffon Vulture *(Gyps fulvus)*	38	117
American Crane *(Megalornis americana)*	38	
Californian Condor *(Pseudogryphus californianus)*	37	
Shoebill *(Balaeniceps rex)*	36	
Domestic Goose *(Anser anser domesticus)*	35	80
Slender-billed Cockatoo *(Licmetis tenuirostris)*	34	85
Canadian Goose *(Branta canadensis)*	33	47
Orange-winged Parrot *(Amazona amazonica)*	30	71
Roseate Cockatoo *(Cacatua roseicapilla)*	30	47

TABLE 2.5
Maximum Recorded Longevities in Forty-Five Species of Bird (from Flower, 1938) (*Continued*)

	YEARS	
	PROVEN	REPORTED
Domestic Pigeon (*Columba livia domestica*)	30	35
Domestic Dove (*Streptopelia risoria*)	30	42
Emu (*Dromiceius novae-hollandiae*)	28	40
Ostrich (*Struthio camelus*)	27	40
Egyptian Vulture (*Neophron percnopterus*)	23	101
Crowned Pigeon (*Goura cristata*)	16	49, 53

exceeding 70 years in parrots, swans, and several large predators given by Gurney (1899), though less fully proven, are probably substantially correct (condor, 65—Sosnovski, 1957; goose, 46—Rankin, 1957; 33—Porter, 1958).

The maximum life-span in birds is not proportional to size (hummingbirds—two species 8 years in captivity, Conway, 1961). It is materially longer than in mammals of comparable size and activity. Many species can live 30–40 years (Herring gull, 36—Pettingill, 1967; Azure jay, >36—Conway, 1961), including small and active birds such as pigeons (Flower, 1938, Fitzinger, 1853; *Streptopelia risoria*, 40 years, *Columba livia,* 30 years, *Goura cristata,* ♂ 49, ♀ 53 years), while even the smaller passerines have a potential life of 10–15 or more years in captivity (29 years in a chaffinch—Moltoni, 1947) and ages of this order are occasionally reached even in the wild state (Perry, R., 1953). It has been properly remarked that

> *A robin redbreast in a cage*
> *Lives to a tremendous age.*

Extensive aviary records are given by Chalmers Mitchell (1911).

2.2.3 Reptiles

The longevity of tortoises is one of the few popular beliefs about animal life-span that is correct, though it has been exaggerated. There is no clear evidence that the larger species are potentially very much longer-lived than some small forms. The maximum authenticated records include *Testudo sumeirii,* 152+ (years); *T. elephantopus,* 100+; *T. graeca,* 102, 105; *T. daudini,* 100+; *T. hermanni,* 90+; *Emys orbicularis,* 70–120 (Flower, 1925, 1937; Rollinat, 1934; Korschelt, 1931); *Terrapene carolina,* 118+ (Ditmars, 1934), 88+ (Deck, 1926), 64 (Edney and Allen, 1951), the last two in the wild. The age of the royal tortoise of Tonga, said to have belonged to Captain

TABLE 2.6
Maximum Recorded Longevities of Chelonians (from Flower, 1937, except where otherwise stated)

SPECIES		YEARS	SOURCE
Testudo sumeiri	Marion's Tortoise	152+	
elephantopus	Galapagos Tortoise	100+	
graeca	Greek Tortoise	102, 105,	
	♀♀ alive	58	Moysey, (1963)
daudini	Daudin's Tortoise	100+	
hermanni	Hermann's Tortoise	90+	
radiata	Radiated Tortoise	85+	
gigantea	Giant Tortoise	68–180	
sulcata	Spurred Tortoise	42	
marginata	Margined Tortoise	28	
Terrapene carolina	Carolina Box-tortoise	123+	
		118+	Dittmars (1934)
		129	Oliver (1953)
		88+	Deck (1927)
		65	Edney and Allen (1951)
Emys orbicularis	European Pond-tortoise	70–120	Rollinat (1934)
Macroclemmys temminckii	Snapping Turtle	58+, 47	Conant and Hudson (1949)
Clemmys guttata	Speckled Terrapin	42+	
Pelusios derbianus	Derby's Terrapin	41+	
subniger		29+	Conant and Hudson (1949)
Sternotherus odoratus	Stinkpot Terrapin	52+	Conant and Hudson (1949)
Kinosternon subrubrum	Pennsylvania Terrapin	38+	
Chelodina longicollis	Longnecked Terrapin	37+	
		31+	Conant and Hudson (1949)
Caretta caretta	Loggerhead Turtle	33	
Malaclemmys centrata	Diamond-backed Terrapin	?40	Hildebrand (1932)
Cuora trifasciata	Three-banded Terrapin	26+	
Geoclemmys reevesi		24+	Conant and Hudson (1949)
Geochelone radiata		30+	Eglis (1960)

Cook (died May 1966), is unsupported by documents, but may well be authentic.

The longevity of turtles and luths (Parker, 1926, 1929) and of crocodiles has been assumed, upon a basis of recorded sizes, to be very great, though the longest captive record of a crocodile is 56+ years (Flower, 1937). *Alligator sinensis* has been kept 52 years (Lederer, 1941), and *A. mississippiensis* 41 years in the London Zoo (1912–1953). The records of snakes are limited by their poor survival in zoos (*Eunectes murinus,* 29 years—Flower, 1937; 28— Perkins, 1948; *Epicrates cenchris,* 27—Perkins, 1948). Lizards: *Anguis fragilis,* 33 years (Hvass, 1938), 32 (Flower, 1937), 27 (Thummel, 1938); *Sphenodon punctatus,* 28+ (Flower, 1937); *Heloderma suspectum,* 20 (Conant and Hudson, 1949); *Ophisaurus apodus,* 11 years 7 months (Conant and Hudson, 1949), 24 years (Perkins, 1948). The maximum life-span appears to be relatively brief in chameleons, but this may simply be due to failure to thrive in captivity.

2.2.4 Amphibians

"Amphibia, those cold and doubtful beings, can prolong their existence to an extraordinary length" (Hufeland, 1798).

Here again the figures in relation to size and growth give no very clear evidence that the life-span is sharply determined. The maximum records are in *Megalobatrachus* (52+ years—Flower, 1936; 65+ years—Schneider, 1932) but many small species are capable of very long life (*Triton* spp., 35 years—Smith, 1951; *Triturus pyrrhogaster,* 25—Walterstorff, 1928; *Amphiuma punctatum,* 25—Koch, 1952; *Triton marmoratus,* 24, 21—Wendt, 1934; *Pleurodeles waltl,* 20—Noble, 1931). *Siren,* 25 years, *Amphiuma,* 26— Noble, 1931; *Salamandra salamandra,* 24, *Bufo bufo,* 36, *Hyla coerulea,* 16, *Rana catesbiana,* 15, *Xenopus laevis,* 15 (Flower, 1925, 1936), *Rana temporaria,* 12+ years (Wilson, 1950), *R. esculenta,* 14+, 16+, *R. temporaria,* 9+ (Sebesta, 1935), *R. catesbiana* 8–10 years in wild and up to 16 in captivity (Durham and Bennett, 1963), *Gastrophryne olivacea,* 7–8 years in the wild (Fitch, 1956). *Leptodactylus pentadactylus,* 15 years 9 months (Conant and Hudson, 1949).

2.2.5 Fish

Seriously acceptable records of longevity in the larger fish are very few. The longest accepted by Flower are *Silurus glanis,* 60+ years, *Anguilla anguilla,* 55, *A. chrisypa,* 50 (Flower, 1935). Some of the more celebrated legends of fish longevity (up to 170, 200, 300, or 400 years in carp, and 250 years in pike) are revived by Backmann (1938) and by Wurmbach (1951). "Wenn auch diese Angaben hier und de übertreiben sein sollten," remarks Wurmbach, "so kann doch gar kein Zweifel daran herrschen, dass der

Karpfen wirklich ausserordentlich alt wird, und das Alter des Menschen weitaus übertrifft"—this is quite possibly true, but a 34-pound pike taken in 1961 proved on scale examination to be 13 or 14 years old. Many exaggerated estimates have been based upon size, as extrapolations of the normal mean growth rate for the species. Upon this basis, a 720-kg sturgeon should be about 200 years old, and occasional examples weighing 1,200–1,600 kg would be of fantastic antiquity. In no case, however, are any of these estimates supported by fin ray section studies, and the extrapolation is almost certainly unjustified. A beluga of 424 cm and just over 1 metric ton in weight was actually found to be about 75 years old.[2] It is a matter of considerable biological importance to get proper age determination upon exceptionally large specimens of this kind. Seventy-five-year-old sturgeons have been taken in Russia (Chugunov, 1949) and one 82-year-old in America (Milne and Milne, 1958). A halibut brought to Grimsby in 1957 was 10 feet long, weighed 36 stone, and was aged at 60+ years by scale examination. It was a female and apparently both fertile and growing.

The life-span of small fish is certainly limited in captivity (*Aphya pellucida*, 1 year; *Lebistes*, 1–2; *Xiphophorus*, 2–3; *Molliensia latipinna*, 3–4; *Betta pugnax*, 1½–2—Wurmbach, 1951). A few species of *Gobius* and *Latrunculus* must be regarded as annuals, even in captivity (Bourlière, 1946; Meyers, 1952) and the same applies to some species of Killifish (*Aphyosemon, Nothobranchius, Cynolebias*—Walford and Liu, 1965; Markovsky and Perlmutter, 1973). These are the shortest-lived available vertebrates for lifelong experiment. Apart from this important discovery, since the fish make excellent laboratory animals, in the general field of wild fish longevity there is little new information since the seventeenth century.

> The life of fishes is more doubtful than that of land beasts, since, living below the waters, they are less observed. Dolphins are said to live about 30 years; this is obtained by experiment upon some of them, the tail being marked by cutting; they grow for 10 years. In Caesar's fishponds certain *Muraenae* were found to have lived to the sixtieth year. Indeed, they were grown with long use so familiar, that Crassus the orator mourned for the death of one. The pike, of freshwater fish, is found to live the longest, sometimes to the fortieth year. But the carp, bream, tench, eel, and the like are not held to live above 10 years. Salmon grow quickly and live not long, as do also trout; but the perch grows slowly and lives longer. How long the breath governs the vast bulk of whales and

---

[2]I am very much indebted to Professor S. S. Turov of Moscow University Museum for a long series of sturgeon records.

orcae, we have no certain knowledge; neither for seals, nor for innumerable other fish[3] *(Hist. Vitae et Mortis).*

Most of these figures are reasonably congruent with Flower's list. Full lists of aquarium records were given by Hinton (1962).

2.2.6 Invertebrates

Previous lists of invertebrate longevities (*Tabulae Biologicae;* Heilbrunn, 1943; Nagornyi, 1948, etc.), apart from the excellent data collected by Weismann (1891), almost all spring directly from the opinions of Korschelt (1922). These are based on data from the older literature, largely unsupported by exact references, some accurate, but others highly speculative. The type of evidence that has got into such lists is well exemplified by the 15- to 20-year life-span of the crayfish. This, though probably correct, appears to owe its origin to an aside by T. H. Huxley (1880) to the effect that "it seems probable that the life of these animals may be prolonged to as much as fifteen or twenty years" (*The Crayfish,* p. 32). The large *Tridacna* may in fact be the longest-lived invertebrate, in view of high records of age in much smaller pelecypods, but the literature contains no information of any description about its life-span, and the relationship between great size and great age is perpetually being disproved in other animals. Of a supposedly 18-year-old *Helix pomatia* Korschelt writes elsewhere: "Gewiss hat diese Angabe von vornherein wenig Wahrscheinlichkeit für sich, aber als unmöglich wird man dieser Langlebigkeit nach dem, was man von anderen Tieren weiss, nicht bezeichnen dürfen"[4] (1922).

A proper survey of the longevity of invertebrates can hardly yet be undertaken—the information is mostly lacking. It seemed wisest in compiling Table 2.7, which includes a few of the longest and most interesting

---

[3]"Piscium vita magis incerta est, quam terrestrium, quum sub aquis degentes minus observantur. . . . Delphini traduntur vivere annos circa triginta; capta experimento in aliquibus a cauda precisa; grandescunt autem ad annos decem. Deprehensae sunt aliquando in piscinis Caesarianis muraenae vixisse ad annum sexagesimum. Certe redditae sunt longo usu tam familiares, ut Crassus orator unam ex illis defleverit. Lucius, ex piscibus aquae dulcis, longissime vivere reperitur; ad annum quandoque quadragesimum . . . at carpio, abramis, tinca, anguilla et huiusmodi non putantur vivere ultra annos decem. Salmones cito grandescunt, brevi vivunt, quod etiam faciunt trutae; at perca tarde crescit, et vivit diutius. Vastá illa moles balaenarum et orcarum, quamdiu spiritu regatur, nil certi habemus; neque etiam de phocis . . . et aliis piscibus innumeris."

[4]"No doubt these findings have little probability in themselves, but one cannot dismiss such longevity records as impossible, in view of what is known of other animals."

invertebrate records, to give not only the record and source, but the type of evidence upon which the record is based. In invertebrates that metamorphose, length of larval life often depends entirely upon environment and food, while in other forms adult life can be punctuated by very long spells of diapause. Figures for these forms should therefore when possible indicate the circumstances of life. Larval life-spans have in general been omitted from Table 2.7. The most reliable records are in all cases those of animals kept, like Labitte's (1916) beetles or the Edinburgh sea anemones (Ashworth and Annandale, 1904) under close observation in captivity. Evidence from growth rings requires very careful scrutiny. Some purely inferential evidence, as of the age of termite primaries, is probably reliable. There are also some surprisingly high records in the wild, especially for pelecypods, where the method of ageing by rings of growth has been well upheld by other evidence. The life-span of common invertebrates certainly remains a wide-open field for those with facilities and an unlimited capacity for taking pains, and one where any reliably attested information is worth putting on record.

The life-spans and senescence of molluscs may be taken as typical. The subject was first reviewed, and the literature cited with customary thoroughness, by Pelseneer (1935). The existing figures are here summarized in Table 2.7, which also shows the circumstances of the record (wild population, captive specimen, or specimens) and the nature of the evidence from which age has been estimated. I have drawn most of the records prior to 1935 from Pelseneer's bibliography (1935), adding symbols to classify the nature of the evidence, and subsequent records from the literature.

As in so many instances where age and longevity are discussed, many repeatedly quoted figures for molluscan life-spans (Korschelt, 1922; Heilbrunn, 1943; Spector, 1956; *Tabulae Biologicae*) are based on unsupported guesswork and require revision. Flower, to whom we chiefly owe the critical assessment of animal age records, unfortunately published only one unimportant paper on molluscs (1922) and did not live to complete a study of invertebrate life-spans. His notes for this study are in the Library of the Zoological Society, where the director has kindly allowed me to make use of them. Longevity is an aspect of animal life that is surprisingly often ignored, or treated by inference, in the discussion of life-cycles. Most of the accurate information that we have comes from the work of a few individuals (Hazay, 1881; Lang, 1896, etc.; Künkel, 1908, 1916, 1928; Weymouth, 1923, etc.; Oldham, 1930, 1942, 1942a; van Cleave, 1934, etc.) who have reared or observed molluscs and kept critical records.

We so far have laboratory life-tables only for a few small pulmonates (*Limnaea columella*—Baily, 1931; Winsor and Winsor—1935; *L. stagnalis appressa*—Crabb, 1929; Noland and Carriker, 1946; *Physa gyrina*— De Witt, 1954; *Bulinus truncatus, Planorbis boissyi*—Barlow and Muench, 1951).

TABLE 2.7
Maximum Recorded Longevities of Various Invertebrates

Porifera			
Suberites carnosus	15	c	Arndt (1941)
Adocia alba	9	c	Arndt (1941)
Coelenterata			
Actinia mesembryanthemum	65–70		Dalyell (1848)
		c	Korschelt (1922)
Cereus pedunculatus	85–90	c	Ashworth and Annandale (1904)
			Stephenson (1935)
			Warwick (1954) (personal communication)
Platyhelminths			
Schistosoma haematobium	25	h	Kirkland (1928)
	28	h	Christopherson (1924)
Clonorchis sinensis	25	h	Moore (1924)
Gastrodiscus aegyptiacus	9	h	Christopherson (1924)
Taeniorrhynchus saginatus	>35	h	Penfold, et al. (1936)
Diphyllobothrium latum	29	h	Riley (1919)
"Echinococcus cysts"	56	h	Lawson (1939)[*]
Dugesia tigrina			
(= *Planaria maculata*)	6–7	c	Goldsmith (1942)
Dendrocoelum lacteum	5	?	Bresslau (1928–1933)
Nematoda			
Loa loa	15	h	Coutelen (1935)
Wuchereria bancrofti	17	h	Knabe (1932)
Necator americanus	12	h	Sandground (1936)
Rolifera—see Table 2.8			
Annelida			
Eisenia foetida	3–4½	c	} Rabes (1901)
Lumbricus terrestris	5–6	c	}
Allolobophora longa	5–10	c	} Korschelt (1914)
Sabella pavonina	>10	c	Wilson D. P. (1949)
Arthropoda			
(Arachnida)			
"Tarantula" (aviculariid) ♀	11–20	c	Baerg (1945)
Avicularia avicularia ♀	>7	c	Didlake (1937)
Tegenaria derhami ♀	7	c	Savory (1927)
Filistata insidiatrix ♀	10, 11	c	Bonnet (1935)
Physocyclus simoni	4	c	Bonnet (1935)

TABLE 2.7
Maximum Recorded Longevities of Various Invertebrates (*Continued*)

Arthropoda

Teutana grossa ♀	6	c	Bacelar and Frade (1933)
Psalmopoeus cambridgii	5½	c	London Zoo (Flower MS)
Lasiodera curtior	4½	c	London Zoo (Flower MS)
(Crustacea)			
Astacus	15–25		inference Friedel (1880)
Homarus	50		inference Herrick (1898, 1911)
Leander serratus ♀	5–6		inference Solland (1916)
Oniscus asellus	4½	c	⎫
Philoscia muscorum	4	c	⎪
Porcellio scaber	3¾	c	⎬ Collinge (1944)
dilatatus	3½	c	⎪
Platyarthrus hoffmanseggi	5+	c	⎪
Armadillium vulgare	4+	c	⎭
Balanus balanoides	>5	w	Moore (1934)
(Insecta)			
Thysanura			
Ctenolepisma longicaudata	Total 7	w	Lindsay (1940)
Ephemeroptera			
Cloëon dipterum	Imago 4 wks	c	Vane (1946)
Isoptera			
Neotermes castaneus ♀ ♂	Imago >25 yrs	w	Snyder *fide* Howard (1939)
Nasutitermes-physogastric ♀	20–40	w	v. Hagen (1938)
"Termite primaries"	60–?	w	Richards (1953)
Lepidoptera			
Nymphalis antiopa	Imago 12 wks	c	⎫
Calliophrys rubi	Imago 6 weeks	c	⎬ Frohawk (1935)
Maniola jurtina	Imago 44 days	c	⎭
Coleoptera†			
Blaps gigas	Imago > 10 yrs	c	⎫
Timarcha sp.	Imago >5	c	⎬ Labitte (1916)
Carabus auratus	Imago 3–1	c	⎭
Dytiscus marginalis	Imago <3	c	Blunck (1924)
Prionotheca coronata	Imago 6, 7+	c	⎫ London Zoo (Flower MS)
Akis bacarozzo	Imago >4	c	⎭
Cybister laterimarginalis	Imago 5½	c	Sharp (1883)
Hymenoptera			
Apis mellifica ♀	Imago >5	c	Pflugfelder (1948)
Lasius niger ♀	Imago >19	c	Goetsch (1940)
Stenamma westwoodi ♀	Imago 16–18	c	Donisthorpe (1936)
Formica fusca ♀	Imago 10+	c	Janet (1904)
♀	Imago 15+	c	Lubbock *fide* Weismann (1882)

TABLE 2.7
Maximum Recorded Longevities of Various Invertebrates (*Continued*)

Hymenoptera

sanguinea	Imago 5+	c	Lubbock *fide* Weismann (1882)
Lasius niger ♀	Imago ⎤	c	Lubbock *fide* Weismann (1882)
Formica fusca ♀	Imago ⎦		

Echinodermata

Echinus esculentus	>8	w	Moore (1935)
Psammechinus miliaris	>6	c	Bull (1938)
Asterias rubens (reaches sexual maturity)	5–6	c	Bull (1934)
Marthasterias glacialis	>7	c	Wilson (1954) (personal comm.)
Ophiothrix fragilis	>5	c	*Zool. Gart.* (1930)

Gastropoda
Amphineura

Katharina tunicata	3	w	Heath (1905)
Ischnochiton magdalenensis	3–4	w	Heath (1905)
Chiton tuberculatus	12	w	Crozier (1918)
Cryptochiton stelleri	?4	w	Heath (1905)
Chaetopleura apiculata	4	w	Grave (1933)

Prosobranchia

Haliotis rufescens	>13	w g	Bonnot (1940)
Trochus niloticus	>12	w	Rao (1937); Pannikar (1938)
Gibbula umbilicalis	5	w	Pelseneer (1934)
Nerita japonica	2–3	w	Suzuki (1935)
Neritina fluviatilis	5	w	Geyer (1909)
Patella vulgata	15	w g	Fischer-Piette (1939)
Patina pellucida	1–2	w	Graham and Fretter (1944)
Acmaea dorsuosa	15	w g	Abe (1932)
Patelloida grata	>15	w g	Hamai (1937)
Valvata piscinalis	Annual	w g	Cleland (1954)
Calyptraea chinensis	5	w g	Wyatt (1961)
Littorina littorea	2–3?	w	Moore (1937)
	10	c	*fide* Marshall (1898)
	20	c	*fide* Pelseneer (1894)
scabra	♂ 4 ♀ 5	w	Sewell (1924)
obesa	3–4	w	Sewell (1924)
Rissoella diaphana *opalina* ⎤			
Skeneopsis planorbis ⎬	Annuals	w	Fretter (1947)
Omalogyra atomus ⎦			

TABLE 2.7
Maximum Recorded Longevities of Various Invertebrates (*Continued*)

Prosobranchia			
Hydrobia ulvae	5	c	Quick (1924)
	>3	w	Rothschild and Rothschild (1939)
Lioplax sp.	♂ 1 ♀ 2	w	van Cleave and Chambers (1935)
Paludina contectoides	<3	w	van Cleave and Lederer (1932)
	9	c	Geyer (1909)
contecta	♂ 4¹¹/₁₂ ♀ 5		
	♂ 3½ ♀ 4½	c	Oldham (1931)
bengalensis	♂ 1 ♀ 3	w c	Annandale and Sewell (1921)
malleata	♂ 4 ♀ 7	w	Niwa (1950
Campeloma rufum	>2	w	van Cleave and Altringer (1937)
	>4	w	Medcoff (1940)
Bithynia tentaculata	>2	w	Schäfer (1953)
Pila sp.	5	c	Flower (1922)
Prosobranchia			
Melanoides lineatus	2–3	c g	Sewell (1924)
Acrostoma variabile	2	c w	Sewell (1924)
Nassa obsoleta	3	w	Dimon (1905)
Nucella lapillus	>5	w	Moore (1938)
Trichotropis cancellatum	<3	w	Yonge (1962)
Opisthobranchia			
Haminea hydatis	4	w	Berrill (1931)
Philine aperta	3–4	w	Brown (1934)
Aplysia punctata	Annual	w	Eales (1921); Miller (1960)
Limapontia capitata	Annual	w	} McMillan (1947); Miller
	2	c	} (1962)
Limapontia depressa var. *pellucida*	Annual	w c	Kevan (1934, 1939, 1941)
Chromodoris zebra	Annual	w	} Garstang (1890)
nodosus	Annual	w	}
Melibe leonina	Annual	w	Guberlet (1928)
Eolis amoena	Subannual: 2 mos.	w	Risbec (1928)
Elysia viridis	Some >1	c w	}
Actaeonia senestra	Subannual	c w	}
Archidoris pseudoargus	>2	w	} Miller (1962)
Polycera quadrilineata	>1	w	}
Acanthodoris pilosa	2	w	}

TABLE 2.7
Maximum Recorded Longevities of Various Invertebrates (*Continued*)

Polycera quadrilineata			
Onchidoris fusca	2	w	⎫
muricata	Annual	w	⎪
pusila	Annual; some 2	w	⎪ Miller (1962)
Goniodoris nodosa	Annual; some 2	w	⎬
Doto coronata	1	w	⎪
Hero formosa	>2?	w	⎭
Pteropoda			
Limacina retroversa	>1	w	Redfield (1939)
Pulmonata			
Carychium tridentatum	Biennial	w c	Morton (1954)
Limnaea luteola	3	w	Seshiya (1927)
columella	Max. 139 days	c L	Bailey (1931)
	Max. 225 ⎱	c L	Winsor and Winsor (1935)
	Mean 128.8 ⎰		
palustris	Max. 8–10 mos.	c L	Forbes and Crampton (1942)
bulimoides	6 mos.	w ⎫	Olsen (1944)
	25 mos.	c ⎭	
stagnalis appressa	Max. 14 mos.	c	Noland and Carriker (1946)
Myxas glutinosa	Annual	w	Cooper (1931)
Bulinus truncatus3	Max. 13 mos.	c L	Forbes and Crampton (1942)
Planorbis corneus	2–3	w	Boycott (1936)
	6	c	Oldham (1930)
boissyi	1½	c L	Barlow and Muench (1951)
magnificus	2	w	Dale (1907)
Indoplanorbis exustus	2	c	Sewell (1924)
Ancylus fluviatilis	Annual	w g	Hunter (1935)
	>3	w g	Berg (1948)
Physa gyrina	Annual	w ⎫	De Witt (1954)
	3	c ⎭	
Abida secale	3	c	*fide* Flower MS.
Archachatina	10	w c	Plummer (1975)
Achatina zebra	6½	2	Longstaff (1921)
Rumina decollata	12	c	Vignal (1919)
Testacella spp.	5–6	?	*fide* Taylor (1907)
scutulum	>580 days	w, marked	Barnes and Stokes (1951); Stokes (1958)
haliotidea	>570 days		
Vitrina brevis	17 mos.	c	Künkel (1920)
pellucida	12–15 mos.	w	Taylor (1907)
Polita villae	5½	c	van der Horst (1929)

TABLE 2.7
Maximum Recorded Longevities of Various Invertebrates (*Continued*)

Pulmonata

Arion empiricorum	16–18 mos.	c	
simrothi	16–18 mos.	c	
subfuscus	12–13 mos.	c	Künkel (1916)
hortensis	11–12 mos.	c	
bourguignati	12–13 mos.	c	
Limax flavus	3	c	Szabó and Szabó (1929, 1936)
cineroniger	5	c	Oldham (1942a)
arborum	2½–3	c	Künkel (1916)
	17 mos.	c	Szabó and Szabó (1929, 1936)
	—	L	Pearl (1935)
Geomalacus maculosus	6½	c	Oldham (1942b)
Eulota fruticum	5–6½	w c	Künkel (1928)
Theba cantiana	2	w	Taylor (1917)
Helix pomatia	6–7	c	Künkel (1916)
	3	w	Lang (1896)
aspersa	5–6	c	Welch (1901)
	5½	c	Gain (1889)
	8–10	c	Welch *fide* Taylor (1907)
	10	c	Stelfox (1968)
(Cepaea) nemoralis	5–6	?	Lamotte (1951)
	7	c	Brockmeier (1888, 1896)
hortensis	9	c	Lang (1904)
Helix (Levantina)spiriplana	15	c	Vignal (1923)
(Arianta) arbustorum	5	c	Künkel (1916)
(Campyloea) cingulata	4–5	c	Künkel (1916)
Euparypha pisana	>3	w	Taylor (1907)
Cochlicella acuta	>1	w	De Leersnyder and Hoestlandt (1958)

Bivalvia

Nucula turgida	Max. 10–11	w g	Allen (1952–1953)
nucleus	>12	w g	Allen (1960)
sulcata	>17	w g	
Mytilus edulis	8–10	w g	Williamson (1908)
californiensis	>3	w g	Coe and Fox (1942)
variabilis	5	g	Sewell (1924)
Ostrea edulis	>12	w g	Orton and Amirthalingam (1930)
	12	L	Walne (1961)
virginiaca	4–6	w	Grave (1933)
Meleagrina vulgaris	7		Herdman (1904)

TABLE 2.7
Maximum Recorded Longevities of Various Invertebrates (*Continued*)

Bivalvia			
Pecten jessoensis	>8	w g	Bazykalova (1934)
irradians	2 (fished)	w	Gutsell (1930)
maximus	22	w g	Tang (1941)
Notovola meridionalis	>16	w g	Fairbridge (1953)
Dreisseria polymorpha	10	w g‡	Stanczykowa (1964)
Megalonaias gigantea	54, 36	w g	Chamberlain (1933)
	53	w g	Haas (1941)
Lampsilis anodontoides	>8	w g	Chamberlain (1931)
siliquoidea	>12	w g	Chamberlain (1931)
	>19		
recta	>18		
ovata	>19		
Fusconaia flava	12	w g	Grier (1922)
Amblema plicata	16		
Pleurobema coccincum	12		
Elliptio dilatatus	12		
Elliptio complanatus	12	w g	Matteson (1948)
Anodontoides subcylindraceus	9	w g	Grier (1922)
Tritogonia verrucosa	>11	w g	Chamberlain (1931)
Quadrula sp.	20–50	w g	Lefèvre and Curtis (1912)
	>30	marked	Isely (1931)
Margaritana margaritifera	70–80	w g	Rubbel (1913)
	>60	inference	Geyer (1909)
	100	inference	Israel (1913)
Unio crassus	15	w g	Brander (1956)
	16	w g	Tudorancea and Graia (1968)
tumidus	15	w g	Brander (1956)
	16	w g	Tudorancea (1969)
	>8	w g	Saldau (1939)
pictorum	13–15	w g	Brander (1956)
	>8	w g	Saldau (1939)
Pseudanodonta complanata	>14–15	w g	Brander (1956)
Anodonta piscinalis	10–15	w g	Brander (1956)
Sphaerium solidulum	<2	w	Foster (1932)
occidentale	>1	w	Herrington (1948)
Cumingia tellinoides	4	w	Grave (1933)
Tellina tenuis	5	w g	Stephen (1931)
Cardium corbis	>16	w g	Weymouth and Thompson (1930)
	7	w g	Fraser (1931)
edule	5	w g	Stephen (1931)

TABLE 2.7
Maximum Recorded Longevities of Various Invertebrates (*Continued*)

Cardium corbis	14	w g	Cole (1956)
Tivela stultorum	20	w g	Weymouth (1923)
	>12	w g	Coe (1947)
	53	wg	Fitch, (1965)
Dosinia exoleta	>7	w g	Kristensen (1957)
Venus mercenaria	25–40	w g	Hopkins (1930)
	17	w g	Belden (1912)
striatula	>10	w g	Ansell (1961)
Donax cuneatus	>3	w	Nayar (1955)
Venerupis pullastra	>8	w g	Quayle (1952)
Scrobicularia plana	18	w g	Green (1957)
Cochlodesma praetenue	4–5	w	Allen (1958)
Amphidesma ventricosum	>9	w g L	Rapson (1952)
Siliqua patula	19–25	w g	Weymouth and McMillin (1931)
Ensis siliqua	11–12	w g	Kristensen (1957)
Mya arenaria	>8	w g	Newcombe, (1935, 1936)
Teredo navalis	2	w	Grave (1928)
Cephalopoda			
Loligo pealii	3–4	w	Williams (1909)
subulata	1½	c	Flower (1922)
Spirula spirula	Annual	w g	Bruun (1943)
Octopus vulgaris ♂	3–4	w	Nixon (1969)
♀	Annual	w	Nixon (1969)

Ages are in years unless otherwise stated. The figures given represent the greatest age observed or inferred in the reference quoted, and include both extreme records and partial records, e.g., the statement that a species "is not sexually mature before 5 years of age" is scored as >5, and the statement "rarely survives into a fourth year"as <5. Symbols in the third column indicate the nature of the evidence cited, and are as follows: w = under wild conditions; c = individual(s) in captivity; g = estimate of age based on growth (annuli, yearly grouping, etc); L = full or partial actuarial data, life-table, survival curve.

*See also Coutelen, et al. (1950); Davaine (1877); Wardle and McLeod (1952, pp. 116–17).

†For a discussion of the longevity of beetle larvae, see Howard (1939); also Latter (1935—Cossus); Linsley (1938—Stromatium).

‡Assuming one ring per year.

Age-mortality studies in wild populations, depending on methods of year-group counting or ageing by growth rings, deal mainly with economically important bivalves, though van Cleave and co-workers (1932, 1934, 1935, 1937) and later authors (Hunter, 1953; Cleland, 1954) studied some fresh-water gastropods. Weymouth (1923) wrote of age determination in molluscs:

Of 14 papers by 13 different authors, 1 flatly denies that age can
be told from the shell, 2 are unwilling to commit themselves, 5
feel that there is some sort of connection between age and the
lines, but that they are of no material use even if their annual
recurrence could be established, and 6 go on record as believing
that the rings are annual. . . . In only 2 can the case be considered
as firmly established on adequate data.

It now seems agreed that growth rings can be used as a measure of age in
pelecypods, and that they give reliable results if estimates are confined to
species, and to localities, where annual deposition of a single ring, or a fixed
and consistent pattern of rings, can be confirmed experimentally (Fairbridge,
1953; Haskins, 1955). In some forms the sculpture bears no consistent
relation to seasonal growth. Other species that can be shown experimentally
to lay down well-defined yearly rings at one station may fail to do so at
another (Newcombe, 1936; Mead and Barnes, 1904—*Mya*). Rings are
produced by any check to growth that causes recession of the mantle edge
(Coker, et al., 1919) whether seasonal, climatic, or due to handling and other
experimental interference (Coe and Fox, 1942—*Mytilus*). Their relation to
the seasons differs from species to species, and where they are annual they
may represent the effects of temperature, of storm disturbance, or of growth-
suspension during spawning.

Sculptural rings in short-lived species are occasionally, but not consistently,
useful for the separation of broods. *Sphaerium solidulum* forms no annual ring
(Foster, 1932), but adults of the normally annual or biennial *Ancylus fluviatilis* show a sufficiently definite growth check to enable overwintered animals
to be identified (Hunter, 1953); a few may show as many as four rings (Berg,
1948). Ageing by annuli works best in pelecypods with a long life and growth
period and a large final size, and much work upon the life-spans of freshwater mussels depends upon ring determination. In *Quadrula* Isely (1931)
confirmed the one-for-one correspondence between annuli and years of life
by recovering marked specimens alive after a 15-year interval. By ring
measurements these mussels must have been at least 20 years old when
marked. Crozier (1918a,b) successfully aged *Chiton tuberculatus* by counting
the annual striae on the valves; opercular markings have also been used
(Hubendick, 1948; Kubo and Kondo, 1953), but there is no generally
available method of ageing gastropod shells or their opercula by inspection of
sculpture. There is also an obvious objection to the use of ages based on
annuli if conclusions are then to be drawn about the relation of senescence to
continued growth, since arrests of growth lasting for years would leave no
record in this system of notation, and the narrowness of the rings at high ages
may make them uncountable. Ring counting is clearly inapplicable to forms in

which growth at right angles to the mantle edge is determinate, ending with the formation of a definite lip, after which the only gain is in shell thickness (Foster, 1936—*Polygyra*). The alternative method of ageing from statolith sections, suggested by Pelseneer (1932), may be feasible, though the wild ages he quotes appear too high—but it has not been used in practice. For the study of large field samples it might conceivably be possible to recover the statoliths by some means other than individual dissection.

It may perhaps also be possible, over the next decades, to identify the growth rings in shells that have been deposited since large-scale radioactive pollution of sea and air began, at least in areas near the test sites, if not generally. If present estimates of ^{90}Sr and ^{45}Ca fallout are correct, the rise at each new atmospheric pollution may be detectable in the shells of European molluscs, especially those, like *Margaritana,* that concentrate calcium from acid and upland surface drainage water.

TABLE 2.8
Maximum Recorded Longevities of Rotifers (Bibliography from Hyman, 1951)

Asplanchna sieboldii	2–3 wks.	c*	Tannreuther (1919)
Proales decipiens	12 days	c	Leibers (1937)
sordida	22 days	c	Jennings and Lynch (1928)
			Lynch and Smith (1931)
Cupelopagis vorax	40 days	c	Cori (1925)
Euchlanis triquetra	21 days	c	Lehmensick (1926)
Epiphanes senta	8 days	c	Ferris (1932)
Brachionus pala	12–19 days	c	Chu (1934)
Euchlanis dilatata	23 days	c	Leibers (1937)
Keratella aculeata	29 days	c	Kolisko (1938)
Epiphanes brachionus	17 days	c	Kolisko (1938)
Floscularia conifera	18 days	c	Edmondson (1945a, b)
Lecane inermis	14 days	c	Miller (1931)
Philodina roseola	10 days		
citrina	21 days		
megalotrocha	17 days	c	Spemann (1924)
Rotaria macrura	58 days		
rotatoria	20–50 days		
Callidina sp.	5 mos.	c	Zelinka (1891)
Adineta vaga	15–22 days		
barbata	21 days		
Habrotrocha constricta	34 days		
Macrotrachela quadricornifera	2 mos.	c	Dobers (1915)
Mniobia russeola	30 days		

*c = individual(s) in captivity.

Diapause presents a special problem in estimating molluscan life-spans. Its duration cannot be determined by examining the shell, and periods spent in it almost certainly count little, if at all, towards the physiological age of the animal. Diapause in land forms and in the drought-resisting fresh-water species can certainly last for a substantial fraction of the "life-span" as ordinarily reckoned, and may well exceed it. According to Fischer (1931) normal hibernation in land molluscs may last annually for 5–6 months. *Cepaea nemoralis* in the Paris region hibernates intermittently from October to April (Lamotte, 1951). It has been claimed that *Oxystyla capax* has survived 23 years in aestivation (Baker, 1934). The evidence in support of this is equivocal, but there is no reason to doubt circumstantial accounts of prolonged diapause in some of the older literature (*Helix aperta,* 3 years— Darbishire, 1889; *Buliminus pallidior,* 6 years—Stearns, 1877). Even *Planorbis corneus* and *Limnaea peregra* are said to have remained alive for 3 years 7 months under dry conditions (Wilkins, 1948), and a freshwater bivalve (*Aspatharia*) survived a year in somebody's pocket (Dance, 1958). Some small species have an active life-cycle of considerably less than a year, which they expand by overwintering in the immature state at a much-reduced growth rate (*Omalogyra*—Fretter, 1947). In pluriennial forms, diapause represents a large and incalculable extension of the potential life, which needs to be considered in assessing marking records, and in making genetical or parasitological assumptions based on the usual length of generations.

In species with a wide climatic range, individuals from colder stations are longer lived and slower growing than those from warm stations (Weymouth and McMillin, 1931), but, in general, closely related species from temperate and tropical countries seem to have similar life-spans at the temperatures to which they are adapted. The life-spans of pluriennials with a wide altitude-range (e.g., *Arianta arbustorum*) may not differ very greatly at high and low altitudes if, as is possible, much the same fraction of the year in each case is spent in diapause.

In the laboratory, littermate *Planorbis* of an unidentified species (probably derived from *P. corneus*) placed individually in jars at 100 days of age, had median further life-spans of 125 days at a constant temperature of 23°C, and of 280 days at the room temperature of an unheated laboratory (range 7–20°C) (Comfort, 1957a).

2.3 Maximum Life-Span in Man

Human longevity records are even more notorious than those of animals. They depend largely on unsupported memory and tradition in a field where the emotional premiums of exaggeration are high.

Furthermore, even though this satisfaction and vanity, of which
we have spoken, were absent, yet such is the peculiar and perpetual wandering of the human Intellect, that it is more moved and
roused by affirmatives than by negatives, whereas properly it
ought to be just to both, nay even, in the forming of any axiom,
the force of the negative instance is the greater *(Novum Organum).*

King (1911) found in the 1911 census a discrepancy between the size of
the 85- to 90-year-old age group and that of the next higher group, which was
almost certainly due to exaggeration. William Thoms (1873), founder of
Notes and Queries, and Young (1899) devoted much time to exposing the
pretensions of past supercentenarians. In some of the "documented" cases,
the life-span of father, son, and grandson of the same names were apparently
conjoined in one record. Young's greatest authenticated record was a few
weeks short of 111 years.

The actuarial probability of an individual's exceeding the age of 150 years,
on the life-data of 1939, has been estimated at $(\frac{1}{2}^{50})$ (Greenwood and Irwin,
1939). Pütter (1921) calculated on a basis of German vital statistics for the
years 1871–1891 that ages over 105 were effectively impossible, and that for
every million persons reaching 20 years, the number reaching 109 would be
4.8×10^{-10}: "danach wäre es nunmehr wohl an der Zeit, die Berichte über
120, 130, 140, 150 usw.-jährige dahin zu verweisen, wohin sie gehören: ins
Reich der Fabel." This skepticism has proved excessive, especially as regards
the population-frequency of centenarians (see Freudenberg, 1951). The
existence of supercentenarians cannot be disproved by statistical means
unless the distribution of ages is really continuous, since ordinary life-tables
have no defense against, say, a rare genotype with double the normal
potential life-span. The number of persons reaching 100 years is in any event
too small for statistically significant estimates of the rate of increase in the
force of mortality after about 90 years of age. Pütter's estimate was based on
the assumption that this increase continued at the same rate as in earlier life.
The relation between observation and calculation in this part of the life-table
is fully discussed by Greenwood and Irwin (1939).

In a good many mammalian curves the "limit" is about twice the modal age
of adult death; this would give a "limit" in man of 150, if the analogy were
sound. In all probability it is not.

Subsequent writers have been content to rely on direct observation,
provided that only records supported by proper documentary evidence are
taken seriously (Forster, 1945; Tomilin, 1938). The minimum requirements
are these laid down by Thoms (1873): documentary evidence of *birth* (or
baptism), of *death or present age,* and of *identity.* The third of these, as Pearl

(1928) points out, is commonly the key to false records of extreme age. The best of such evidence, from compulsory birth certification, has been available in England since 1837, and would now be available for records up to 118 years (1955). By critical standards of comparable severity the greatest human age to be authenticated with reasonable certainty has been said to be 120 years (Fisher, 1923). A considerable number of cases between 110 and 115 years have also stood up to examination (e.g., Bowerman, 1939; Backman, 1945; Korenchevsky, 1947; Ernest [n.d.]). The greatest age to be authenticated in England and Wales by actual birth certificate, however, is now that of Mrs. Ada Roe, who died in 1970 at the age of 111 years and 339 days. When Mr. John Turner died in 1968, he was aged 111 years and 281 days.

Ernest (n.d.) accepts four records over 110 years, all colorably supported; these were Mrs. Ann Pouder of Baltimore, born 1807 in London, died 1917; Mrs. Ann Neve of Guernsey, born 1792, died 1903, 44 days before her 111th birthday; The Hon. Katherine Plunket, of Kilsaran, Ireland, born 1820, died 1932, aged 111 years 327 days (this lady's birth is recorded in a church register for 1820, but at one time she gave her own date of birth as 1834); and Pierre Joubert, of Quebec, born 1701, died 1814—his records

TABLE 2.9
**Number and Maximum Ages of
Centenarians Dying in England and Wales
(Registrar-General's statistics)**

| YEAR | NUMBER AND PROBABLE MAXIMUM AGE | |
	MEN	WOMEN
1940	20 (105)	102 (108)
1941	18 (112)	91 (108)
1942	12 (107)	79 (108)
1943	21 (108)	92 (106)*
1944	21 (109)	85 (105)*
1945	19 (105)*	71 (106)*
1946	22 (105)*	94 (108)*
1947	19 (106)*	97 (108)*
1948	19 (103)*	107 (115)
1949	27 (104)*	133 (106)*
1950	22 (102)*	131 (107)*
1951	33 (104)*	142 (109)*
1952	24 (105)	147 (107)*

*Verifiable by birth certificate.

were investigated in 1870 by the official statistician of Canada. This, if correct, makes him the present world titleholder for fully authenticated longevity, at 113 years 100 days. In America, Nascher's investigation of John Shell, reputed to be 131, showed him to be in fact about 100 years old (Nascher, 1920). In England and Wales, the oldest persons dying between 1930 and 1945 appear to have reached ages of 112 and 109 years (Korenchevsky, 1947). A woman who died at St. Asaph, Flintshire, in 1948 may have reached 115 years, and had certainly reached 111.

Claims of extreme longevity in particular districts abound. Metchnikoff investigated statements of this kind in Bulgaria and the Caucasus. Bazilievitch (1938a,b) led an expedition to investigate the celebrated longevity of Abkhasians, and examined several claimants in detail. Two of these were reputed to be over 130 years old. The evidence (identity papers and memory of events in the Caucasus during the early nineteenth century) is given by Bazilievitch in careful detail; much of it is extremely entertaining, but far from conclusive, although the subjects were certainly very old men (Bazilievitch, 1938b).[5] In recent years very large numbers of claims to extreme longevity have been made in Russia (e.g., Rokhlina, 1951; Nagornyi, 1948; Lukyanov, 1952; Nikitin, 1954). Dealing with the figures in the 1926 census of the U.S.S.R., which showed proportions of 3.5 and 3.8 centenarians *per thousand* gross population in Daghestan and Abkhasia respectively, as to 1.8 per million among Volga Germans, Tomilin (1938) says "We must doubt the factual truth of these figures, since no documentary evidence of the age of persons who had passed the century mark was produced." The analyzed distribution of age groups in the Abkhasian census shows exactly the same deficiency in the 85–89 and 95- to 99-year groups, compared with the 90–94 and 100+ groups, which was observed by King (1911) in England. "Without special documentary evidence of the accuracy of these age data, we cannot conclude definitely that the relative number of persons reaching the age of 100 and over in the general mass of the population of Abkhasia is really higher than in the population of Russia" (Tomilin, 1938). More recent figures for the Siberian provinces give proportions of centenarians ranging from 32 per 100,000 inhabitants in Yakutsk, 20 in Altai and 12–13 in a number of regions, to 1–0.5 in Sakhalin and Kamchatka. Among these centenarians villagers greatly outnumber townspeople (Berdishev and Starikov, 1960). The figure for the whole U.S.S.R. has been given as 21,708, or 10 per 100,000 (*Daily Telegraph,* April 5, 1961). The number of old people per unit

---

[5]Professor G. Z. Pitshelaouri, of Tbilisi University, who very kindly showed me his unpublished data on the longevity of Abkhasians, has found several subjects whose reputed age exceeds 130 years and is colorably supported by baptismal registers—one man still living took part in, and accurately describes, the Crimean war of 1854–1856. I have failed to obtain a paper by Mishaikov (1929) giving statistics for centenarians in Bulgaria.

of population is, of course, a very bad measure of longevity, for it can be sharply reduced by an increase in babies or a decrease in migration of young people to other areas, but it gives some idea of absolute numbers. It can also be lowered by more accurate census returns. The fall in the estimated number of centenarians in Yugoslavia per 100,000 inhabitants from 30 in 1921 to 10 in 1948 is probably due to this cause (Grmek, 1958).

Another unusually long-lived population at Vilcabamba in Ecuador has been studied by Leaf (1975) and by Davies (1975). In this case ages are not exorbitant, though 140 is claimed, and documentation is better than in the case of Abkhasia. In this population conditions are extremely arduous and caloric intake low; isolation from urban viruses may also be a factor. A more detailed study has been made of the demography of Vilcabamba by Salvator (1972). Unfortunately, careful scrutiny of the records indicates that most of the high ages in this population were exaggerated by between 10 and 30 years (Mazess* 1978).

---

*Mazess, R. B. (1978) Health and longevity in Vilcabamba. J. Amer. med. Ass. *240* 178

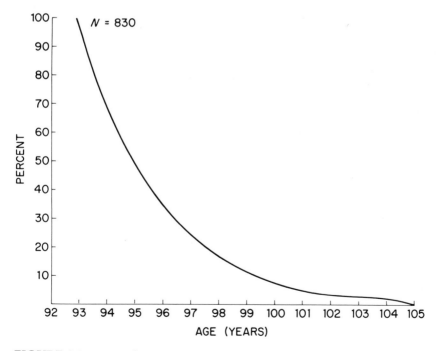

FIGURE 2.5 Form of the tail of the human survival curve above 92 years. (From the data of Greenwood and Irwin, 1939.)

Sporadic records of supercentenarians such as Old Parr, whose tomb in Westminster Abbey credits him with an age of 152 years, whose body was examined by Harvey, and whose complete lack of documentation was exposed by Thoms (1873), occur in almost all cultures: a long series of similar anecdotes is given by Gould and Pyle (1898). The best summary of these often-paraded examples is that of R. T. Gould (1945). Parr was beyond reasonable doubt an impostor (Ernest, n.d.). Walter Williams, the "Old Rebel," who died in 1959 in Texas, claimed to be 117 years old and the last survivor of the Confederate Army. He could not be traced in any army list, but received a military funeral, and was doubtless an old soldier in one sense or other (see *Illustrated London News,* January 2, 1960). Charles Smith, of Barton, Florida, claims to have been brought to the United States as a slave in 1854, at the approximate age of 12, and was still alive, with documentation acceptable to the American Medical Association and the Social Security Administration, in 1972, at the alleged age of 130 years (*Newsweek,* October 2, 1972). Though in most cases the stories conform closely to the childhood fantasy of "going on living for almost always," they may also indicate that authenticated records do not yet represent the extreme of human longevity under all conditions. There is some ground, apart from the absence of critical record in backward countries, to associate extreme *individual* longevity with a low rather than a very high standard of living throughout life (Gumbel, 1938), an argument which fortunately has not so far been advanced to justify starvation as a social policy. Extreme records in man, occurring in excess of statistical probability, are chiefly of interest in suggesting that after a certain age the rate of increase in the force of mortality is not maintained, either by reason of selection or from other causes.

2.4   Distribution of Senescence in Vertebrates

Actuarial senescence is known, or reasonably assumed, to occur in all mammals, provided they live long enough. It is less easily recognized, but apparently equally universal, in birds. There are so far no satisfactory life-table studies of birds under domestic conditions apart from a single paper on fowls already cited (Gardner and Hurst, 1933) and another on finches (Eisner and Etoh, 1967). But individuals kept as pets certainly become increasingly enfeebled after an age that is fairly constant for the species, and the reproductive senescence of poultry, marked by a steep decline in egg production, is well known to farmers (Clark, 1940; Brody, 1945; Figure 2.6). This decline can be reduced by mild hypothyroidism (Turner and Kempster, 1948). The pair of crowned pigeons that lived, according to Fitzinger (1853), for over 40 years, mated and laid throughout life, but hatched no offspring after the age

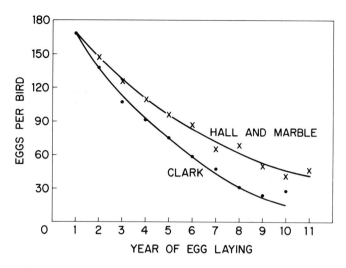

FIGURE 2.6 The decline in egg production in successive years of laying in domestic fowls. (Drawn from the data of Clark and of Hall and Marble.)

of 18 or 20 years (Flower, 1938). Spermatogenesis likewise appears to decline (Payne, 1952). The life-span of birds is longer in proportion to size and metabolic rate than that of mammals, and the scatter of age in senescence as shown by aviary records appears, superficially at least, to be rather greater within a species.

We are familiar with the ageing of warm-blooded animals because we keep them. It is among the "cold-blooded" vertebrates that uncertainty existed. We keep fish, but only the smaller forms; we do not, apart from zoological gardens and occasional pet tortoises, keep reptiles. As for amphibia, Hilaire Belloc wrote incontrovertibly concerning lonely people who keep frogs that

by the way
They are extremely rare.

The general assumption long remained that all vertebrates must necessarily undergo a senescence at least superficially similar to that of mammals, with the result that very little real information unbiased by this assumption has been published. The assumption is probably correct, but it cannot be lightly made. It is evident that some senile change, in the form of an accumulation of injuries, must occur in all vertebrates with the passage of time, and be reflected in the force of mortality. But this effect is certainly small and inconstant compared with the "morphogenetic" senescence that determines the life-span of mammals. It is this morphogenetic component that it was necessary to detect and estimate in lower vertebrates. Unfortunately for such a study, the life of many of these creatures, whether it ends in senescence or not, is, as we have seen, long enough to make ordinary short-term laboratory observation useless.

Bidder's opinions on the relation between perpetual youth and continuing growth have already been quoted. Three types of growth pattern are theoretically possible in vertebrates: growth to a maximum size, ceasing when this is reached; growth *toward* a limiting size which is approached asymptotically; and growth *without* a limiting size. In the third of these cases, the specific growth acceleration can be negative—i.e., the growth rate continually declines—but it could theoretically do so in such a way that, given a sufficiently long life, *any* final size could be reached. These last two modes of growth correspond to convergent and divergent series. Thus in the series

$$(1)\ 1 + \tfrac{1}{2} + \tfrac{1}{4} + \tfrac{1}{8} \cdots \lim 2,$$

and the series

$$(2)\ 1 + \tfrac{1}{2} + \tfrac{1}{3} + \tfrac{1}{4} + \tfrac{1}{5} \cdots,$$

the increment at each term decreases (the specific growth rate falls), but whereas in (1) the series tends to a limiting size (specific size), in (2) it does not, and can be indefinitely continued so that any sum is ultimately attained. The terms "indeterminate growth" and "indeterminate size" have been differently used by different writers. D'Arcy Thompson wrote, "It is the rule in fishes and other cold-blooded vertebrates that growth is asymptotic and size indeterminate" (1942). If the growth of an animal is in fact asymptotic, its size is limited by the sum of the asymptotic series. "Indeterminate" growth without limit, but with a decline in the specific growth rate, strictly follows the pattern of the divergent series. For this reason it would be desirable, but it is not empirically possible, given real biological material, to distinguish between "asymptotic" and "indeterminate" growth. In both cases the rate of growth delcines with advancing age; but in the second case the potential size is unlimited.

Distinctions of this kind, however, are based upon the fitting of equations to points derived by averaging observations upon populations of animals, and in spite of the real value of such biometric applications, in the study of growth curves they very often tended to lose contact with the real behavior of real animals. It is possible in practice to distinguish only between species, or particular populations of a given species, which continue throughout life to get tangibly bigger, given suitable conditions, and forms where the maximum size is reached relatively early in life, is fixed for the species, and does not increase further with increasing age even under the most favorable conditions. The chief obstacle to wide generalization about the determinacy or indeterminacy of growth in lower vertebrates, and in other forms such as pelecypods, lies in the fact that arrest of growth at an *apparent* specific size can be brought about by environmental conditions. In some cases growth can be resumed after stopping like this—in others, apparently, it cannot. There are also large differences within each of the main groups of poikilothermic vertebrates. In many reptiles and small fish, continued growth after a relatively early age is no more evident than in the male rat. In amphibia, "many species, particularly some tropical forms, seem to have an absolute size, which the males soon attain, but this does not hold for many salamanders, nor for some Northern frogs" (Noble, 1931). In many cases the male has an absolute size and the female has not. If enough data were available, the variety of growth-patterns would be more than sufficient to test Bidder's hypothesis—unfortunately, corresponding data upon age/mortality relations are almost entirely lacking.

The idea of a "self-maintaining" vertebrate is not impossible ex hypothesi. It is in fact what we should expect if growth cessation is an equilibrium process, if there is no important process of differential growth at work, and if there is no qualitative change in the regenerative power of cells throughout adult life. It is not self-evident, though it might be true, that an animal should be obliged to increase in size in order to retain the power of carrying out running replacements. It seems reasonable for our purposes to regard an animal of "indeterminate" growth as one in which the probability of nursing an individual to the point at which increase in somatic size has ceased is infinitely small, and an animal of "indeterminate" life-span as one in which the survival rate under favorable conditions is substantially independent of age, however long a population of that animal is observed from birth.

In all the groups that Bidder considered to be proof against senescence, there is wide variation in life-cycle and growth pattern, which is very probably reflected in differences of their capacity for age changes. Some aquarium species of fish certainly "age" as judged by their declining reproductive powers; in the larger sea fish this has not been clearly demonstrated. Contradictory views of fish senescence were given to Flower (1935) by two acknowledged authorities, one on aquarium and the other on marine ichthyology, and based on small and large teleosts respectively, but more recent work suggests that the distinction is artificial. In other forms there is an obvious sex difference in growth maintenance, in longevity, or in both. The specific age might also be indefinite in mammals which nevertheless became more liable to die, as individuals, with increasing age. It was implied by Ricker (1945) that fish might senesce individually, i.e., undergo a waning of vitality and resistance with age, but that there is no sharp *specific* age—the life-span of each individual would be limited by senescence, but the senile process would

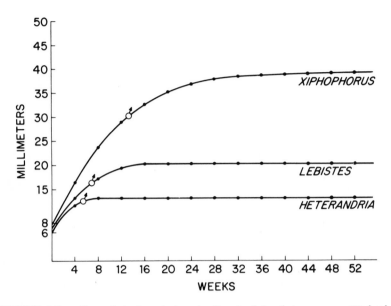

FIGURE 2.7a Growth in length (mm.) of male fish of the genera *Xiphophorus, Lebistes,* and *Heterandria* during the first year of life. Sexual maturity is indicated by ♂ . (From Wellensieck, 1953.)

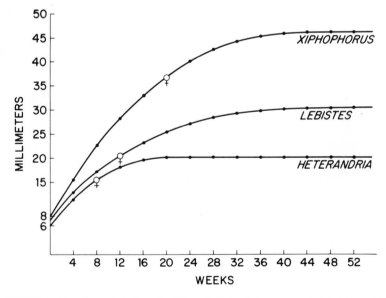

FIGURE 2.7b Growth in length of female fish of the genera *Xiphophorus, Lebistes,* and *Heterandria* during the first year of life. Sexual maturity is indicated by ♀. (From Wellensieck, 1953.)

reach its critical point at a much more variable age than in mammals: as if the menopause in human beings were to occur with approximately equal probability in any year after the menarche. Such senescence would be real, but could not readily be detected actuarially.

These speculative models retained their vitality so long as no data existed on the form of fish survival curves: they could conceivably be revived for speculation about very long-lived reptiles, where life-table studies are impossible, but the concept of the non-ageing vertebrate has ceased to be of real gerontological importance. Present evidence suggests that all vertebrates senesce, but some do so very slowly—probably so slowly that they are overtaken, like high-mortality birds and small mammals, by random mortality, but demonstrably nonetheless, as in the fibroblast culture experiment of Goldstein (1974) on the Galapagos tortoise.

2.4.1 Fish

The "indeterminate" growth of fish, on which Bidder based his hypothesis, was formerly much discussed (Hecht, 1916; Keys, 1928; Huxley, 1932; Vaznetzov, 1934; Thompson, 1942; Wellensieck, 1953). Many large species of teleosts can continue to grow throughout life, and the rate of decline of their growth rate is considerably slower than, for example, in most reptiles. The *locus classicus* of continued growth without evidence of senescence, actuarial or reproductive, is the female plaice. Here the evidence supports Bidder in that growth in the male plaice ceases relatively early, and there is evidence that it has a shorter life-span than the female (Wimpenny, 1953). On the other hand, in many small teleosts reproductive senescence is known to occur, and both the sexes appear to exhibit specific age, in spite of the fact that growth in the female may continue throughout life. The reproductive failure of many teleosts with increasing age is familiar to aquarists. So is the tendency of particular species to have a limiting age, although there have until lately been no published life-tables for any teleost in captivity by which this impression could be confirmed. The growth of some small teleosts has been studied (Felin, 1951; Wellensieck, 1953).

There is a good deal of evidence from wild populations that small teleosts, and perhaps teleost species generally, undergo both reproductive and actuarial senescence comparable to that of mammals (Gerking, 1957, 1959). The most dogmatic assertions on this score are those of pathological anatomists. On the basis of concretions occurring in the testis of a single teleost species (*Astyanax americanus*), Rasquin and Hafter (1951) held that the "appearance of senility changes shows that the teleosts conform to the common vertebrate pattern of ageing despite a widespread misconception to the contrary." The decline of fertility in some aquarium species provides more solid evidence in support of this view. Many species of fish are in any case exposed to a specialized series of fluctuations in mortality associated with reproduction.

The difficulties of treating these fluctuations as a form of senescence in those species which always die after breeding, such as the male of *Callionymus* (Chang, 1951) and the lamprey, are indicated by observations upon other fish in which there are a limited number of survivors from each breeding season, and these thereafter acquire a new lease on life. It is doubtful if any cyclical or potentially cyclical change in mortality can properly be called senile. In *Callionymus lyra* in the wild, the male appears to live 5 and the female up to 7 years. The males disappear after breeding once, probably through death, but possibly by migration to deeper water. Females may first breed in their third, fourth, or fifth year of life, depending on their rate of growth, and probably breed more than once (Chang, 1951). In such a case, the late-developing females would very probably have a longer total life-cycle.

Studies of wild populations are almost always conducted under conditions where the standing force of mortality throughout life is very high, and they therefore give little information about mortality trends in the latter part of the life-cycle of the longer-lived forms. Excluding the very high larval mortality, populations of many species of fish, studied in the wild, show an age structure and a pattern of death similar to that found in birds, i.e. a high constant mortality unrelated to age and a virtually constant expectation of life (Frost and Smyly, 1952—Figure 2.8 in this volume; Deevey, 1947). Substantial differences in life-span may be dictated by availability of food organisms of a size suited to adult feeding, and by competition between the fry of the observed species and adults of other species. Some populations of minnows show apparent specific age, which is exceeded in other populations of a closely-related species by a very large factor (Frost, 1943; Tack, 1940). In *Pimephales promelas,* Markus (1934) observed apparent specific size and specific age in all but a few exceptionally large individuals. This was apparently due to the fact that there was an overall mortality of 80 percent following spawning; the survivors, and individuals which took no part in breeding during their first year of maturity, continued growth until the next breeding season. If reproduction is avoided, life may be prolonged—Bidder (1932) points out that eels, which, it is believed, normally die after spawning, live many years in captivity (Flower, 1925). Frost and Smyly (1952) found considerable differences in growth rates and in the form of the growth curve between brown trout inhabiting tarns and those inhabiting Windermere (Figure 2.8). The age structure of the tarn population agreed well with a steady annual survival rate of 35 percent between the second and eighth year of life. In these fish growth had become very slow, whereas in the Windermere population individual fish were still growing at 7 years upon an approximately linear scale. The ability to continue growth may depend on attaining a size which makes it possible to prey on smaller fish. Long-lived fish such as pike certainly continue to grow measurably for very long periods (Schloemer,

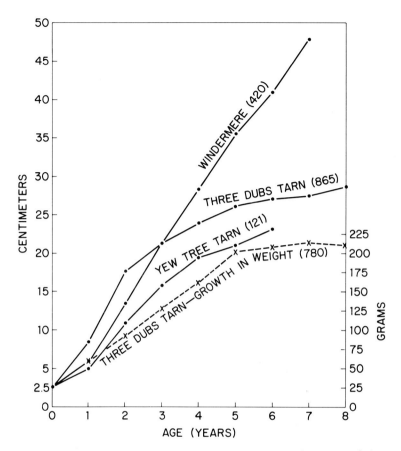

FIGURE 2.8 Growth in length and weight of trout in Windermere and the small tarns. (From Frost and Smyly, 1952.)

1936), but the increase in size is associated with an increase in the size of the prey taken (Frost, 1954). Ricker (1945) comments that "senile death is an everyday occurrence" in population studies of the Indiana sunfish. This conclusion is, however, based upon the failure of known sources of death (disease and predation) to account for the disappearance of fish. The overall mortality rates actually found in marking experiments were 56 percent for small and 58 percent for older specimens. But in many unfished populations of other species there is a steady increase in mortality with increasing age and size (Ricker, 1948). Gerking (1957) has collected strong evidence of ageing in a number of wild fish populations, and has reviewed the literature. An interesting special case is the parental death of Salmonids, which die after spawning from the endocrine changes that accompany migration; these changes are reversible, and non-migratory populations survive, and individuals breed many times. This question has been studied and reviewed by Robertson (Robertson and Wexler, 1959, 1962; Wexler, 1976; Robertson, et al., 1961); the cause of parental death is hypercorticoadrenalism, but the changes are very like those that occur with old age in fish protected from parental-migratory death by early castration.

A great deal of important information upon fish growth was collected by Schmalhausen (1928) from the data of a number of Russian workers (e.g., Tereschenko, 1917). In the sturgeon, growth continues actively throughout at least 30 years of life, with little decline in rate at sexual maturity (about 15 years) (see Royer, et al., 1968). In the bream, on the other hand, the growth constant shows a more regular and progressive decline. These fish were found to mature at about 3 years, and degenerative changes in the gonad were usually evident from the sixth year on—two definite stadia could be observed in the growth curve, one following puberty, and the other following this gonadal senescence, the growth coefficient settling down to a steady value thereafter without further decline up to 13 years of age (Figures 2.9, 2.10, and 2.11). This rather closely resembles the pattern reported in the goldfish.

In *Xiphophorus* and *Lebistes* the male exhibits sharp specific size, but the female may continue to grow measurably throughout life, the pattern of growth differing little from that of the plaice (Wellensieck, 1953). Yet in these forms previous experience suggests that there is no striking difference between the survivals of the two sexes in captivity (Bellamy, 1934). In *Heterandria* both sexes reach a virtual limiting size (Wellensieck, 1953) (see Figures 2.7a, b). In the goldfish, according to exhibition breeders, fertility

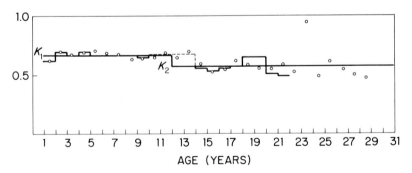

FIGURE 2.9   Growth constant for growth in length of the sturgeon, *Acipenser stellatus,* at various ages. Broken line, females; single points, males; thick line, mean value for males; dashes, mean value for females. $K_1=0.67$, $K_2=0.58$. (From Schmalhausen, 1928.)

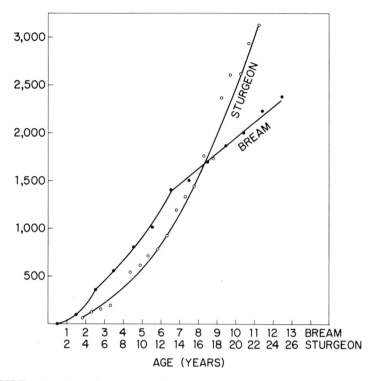

FIGURE 2.10 Growth in weight of the sturgeon *(Acipenser stellatus)* and the bream *(Abramis brama)*. Scale for *A. stellatus:* 1 Russian lb = 100. Scale for *A. brama:* 1 gram = 1. (After Schmalhausen, 1928.)

reaches a maximum under aquarium conditions in the third year of life, declining thereafter, and almost all fish are sterile by the seventh year. Breeding at 10 years is recorded (Hervey and Hems, 1948). When the reproductive life is over, however, the fish may improve greatly in condition, and appear much less sensitive to environmental damage than before. In exhibition fish the life-span appears to be about 17 years, though much older examples are known. The extreme record of longevity appears to be between 30 and 40 years. Rate of growth is extremely variable. One specimen, kept in a six-gallon tank, reached a length of only 4 inches in 25 years (Hervey and Hems, 1948).

In none of these cases is it clear how large a part of the potential life-cycle is actually covered by the observed growth curve. In most fish the rate of growth does in fact decline with age, though in many the effective reproductive life appears to have ceased long before this decline has produced an almost stationary body size. The reproductive decline, moreover, does not appear to involve any decrease in vigor, and may actually imply the reverse, in view of the hazards that reproduction involves for many fish.

In the small teleosts, most of these questions were finally answered by direct experiment. For this purpose the guppy *(Lebistes)* is a particularly suitable experimental animal, both because of the ease with which it can be reared and handled for purposes of measurement, and because of the neatness with which its growth can be controlled by varying the food intake and living space.

By combining restricted space with restricted diet, female *Lebistes* can be kept at a length of about 2 cm for as long as 600 days. In this state they are reproductively mature (unlike the rats subjected to retardation by McCay) and capable of resuming growth. There are "specific sizes" characteristic of each size of container and each level of nutrition—or, alternatively, of each population density in a tank, when a fish is promoted from one such container to a larger, or when fish are removed from a tank population, a new plateau is rapidly reached. The curve given by Wellensieck represents only one such equilibrium. The growth capacity also appears to decline somewhat throughout life, and there is a practical limit, as might be expected, to the size of guppy that can be produced at maximum food intake and maximum living space. The combination of variables in *Lebistes,* and the fact that the life-span of the nongrowing males is not, upon present data, grossly different from that of the growing females, suggest that a great deal about growth and senescence in fish can be learned by the collection of actuarial data for guppies subjected to different programs of growth.

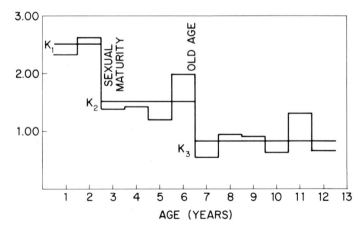

FIGURE 2.11   Growth in weight of the bream *(Abramis brama),* annual increments. The mean growth coefficients at various stadia (youth, maturity, postreproductive life) are indicated by transverse lines $K_{1\ 2\ 3}$. (From Schmalhausen, 1928.)

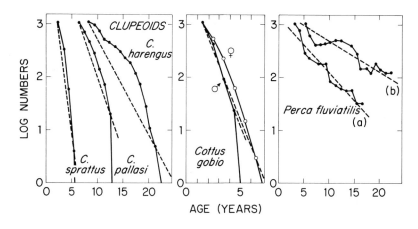

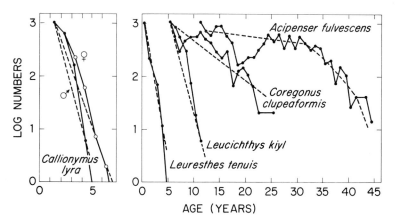

FIGURE 2.12 Some examples of survival curves in relatively unexploited fish populations. (From Beverton and Holt, 1959.)

A population study of guppies (*Lebistes reticulatus,* Peters) was begun in 1950 to find out whether their mortality under various conditions of culture increased with increasing age, and how this increase was related to growth (Comfort, 1960b, 1961; Comfort and Doljanski, 1959).

The main actuarial result appears clear-cut: the observed survival curves of *Lebistes* are not very different, either in form or in response to environment, from those of a small mammal under laboratory conditions. In all the series, under all the experimental conditions, the force of mortality rose steadily with age; there is a progressive squaring-up of the L_x curve and a decrease in variance with bettering conditions, but the curves are "pegged" at the ends, forming the typical "parallelogram of survival" seen in animals of fixed life-span.

The pathological findings in all of these guppies have been described by Woodhead and Ellett (1966, 1967a, b; 1969a, b). They indicate an endocrine senescence differing in detail but not in overall pattern from the changes seen in mammals.

Ageing in guppies appears to take place in the presence of the ability to grow. This negates Bidder's (1932) hypothesis: in the absence of evidence that all cells are equally renewable, it does not negate theories based on cell loss; renal degenerative changes, for example, do not appear histologically to be undergoing reversal, whether somatic growth is continuing or not. Whether what holds good for the growth of the guppy in relation to ageing is equally true of long-lived fish such as the sturgeon cannot be directly shown. In Beverton and Holt's (1957) terminology, the female guppy under favorable growth conditions has reached 75 percent of its eventual limiting size $L \infty$ by about 700 days of age, and its limiting age λ appears to be about 2,000 days, our oldest fish so far having reached 2,200 days. The corresponding value of $L \infty$ for plaice is reached by about 14 years (Beverton and Holt, 1957), giving an extreme longevity of 40 years if the same relationship holds.

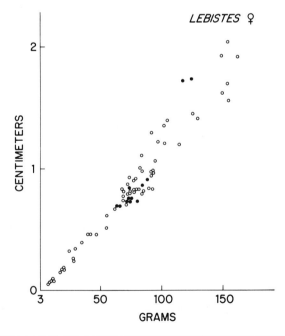

FIGURE 2.13a Weight-length relationship in female *Lebistes;* uninterrupted growth (open symbols) and checked and restarted growth (solid symbols). Scatter at higher ages is due to the presence in some fish of retained eggs.

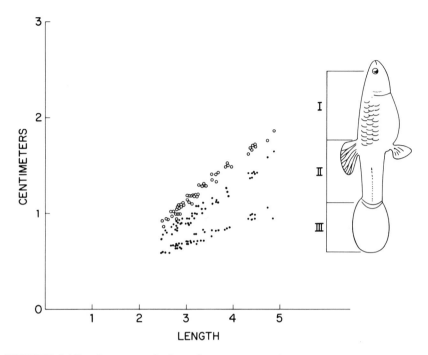

FIGURE 2.13b Isometry of rebound growth in checked female *Lebistes*. Abscissa, total length (cm); ordinate, mid-eye to anterior border of dorsal fin (circles), anterior border of fin to tail root (small circles), and tail root to tail tip (dots).

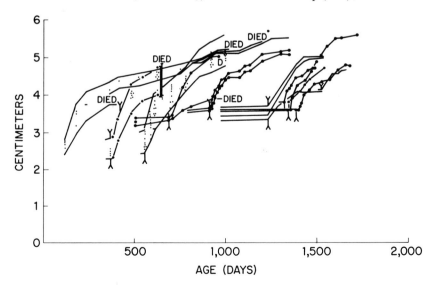

FIGURE 2.14 Growth in length of checked *Lebistes* females fully fed at the points marked ⅄Y.

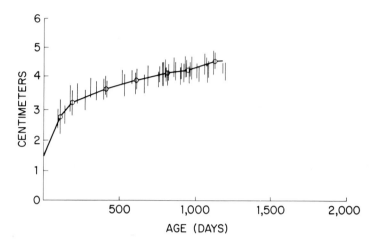

FIGURE 2.15   Growth in length of *Lebistes* females under "normal" aquarium regime permitting slow continuous growth. Columns indicate range in individual tanks, curve indicates mean of whole sample (48 individuals).

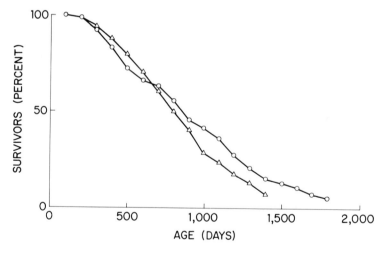

FIGURE 2.16   Combined survival curves of all tank-bred females (circles, N = 351) and all tank-bred males (triangles, N = 312).

The growth curve of the sturgeon shows no sign of flattening by the age of 30 years (Schmalhausen, 1926). Assuming that it reached 75 percent of the length asymptote by 45 years, we might on this basis expect a value of $\lambda\infty$ approaching 128 years. A record of at least 82 years has been claimed for sturgeon on the basis of fin sections (Milne and Milne, 1958).

   Taking the data of *Lebistes* it is possible to construct curves for other

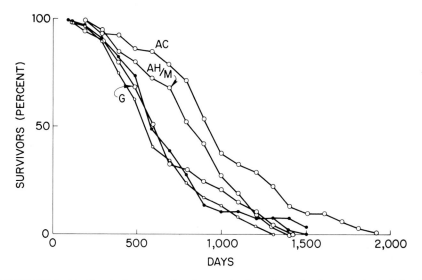

FIGURE 2.17   Survival curves of male guppies kept in tanks (large circles), 600-ml jars (small circles), and 250-ml milk bottles (small solid symbols).

species, showing what would happen to ability to survive if their growth and survival were in the same proportion. Figure 2.21 gives the growth curves of 87 tank-bred female *Lebistes* by batches with the observed survival curve for the whole sample to 1,100 days.

In Figure 2.22 the growth curves of four species in the wild (*Gasterosteus;* cod, plaice; hake) are plotted on time scales that bring their growth in length within the limits of the curve for *Lebistes.* The conversion factors for time are as follows:

$$500 \text{ days } (Lebistes) = 1.37 \text{ years}$$

Gasterosteus	1.25 years ×	0.91
Cod	5.0	3.65
Hake	10.0	7.3
Plaice	15.0	10.95

If these relationships hold good, populations with these growth curves would be expected to have declined by a quarter, from senescence alone, by 2.5, 10, 20, and 30 years respectively, and the four species would have limiting ages of 5, 20, 40, and 60 years respectively. *Gasterosteus* in the wild does in fact live 2–3 years, with a few individuals surviving longer. In the other species, if senescence were related to growth as in the guppy, senile mortality would not be significant within the normal expectation of life in fished populations—the modal age of plaice at catching being about 5 years.

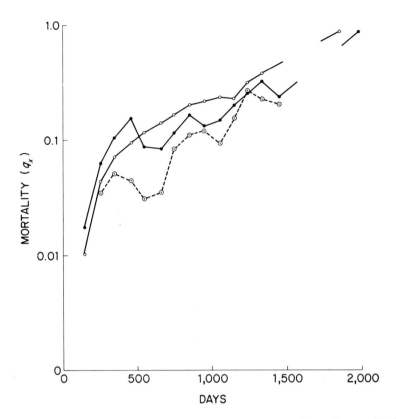

FIGURE 2.18   Mortality of guppies (q_x) against age: tank conditions. Circles, males; solid symbols, females; dotted line, epidemic "incidents" treated as individual lives.

The limiting ages seem likewise reasonable, except that on a basis of size one might expect the extreme life of cod to be more than 20 years.

Survival curves are now available for annual fish (*Nothobranchius*—Markovsky and Perlmutter, 1973; *Cynolebias*, Walford and Liu, 1965) and for the rice fish, *Oryzias* (Egami and Etoh, 1969): in each case the curve is indistinguishable from a mammalian survival curve.

There seems accordingly to be no reason from existing data to postulate a different pattern of mortality for small as against large fish.

It seems probable that there is as much variation in "senescence" as in growth patterns among teleosts. Some forms apparently resemble monocarpic plants, mortality being linked to reproduction. Some, in captivity, have a life-span determined by senescence, their mortality increasing with age on a

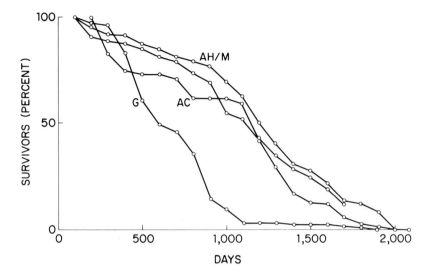

FIGURE 2.19 Survival curve of guppies kept in tanks (circles) and of breeding females transferred at various ages from tanks to 2-liter jars (hexagons).

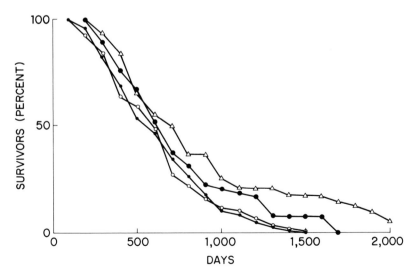

FIGURE 2.20 Survival curves of female guppies kept in 2-liter jars (triangles), 600-ml jars with full feeding (large solid symbols), 600-ml jars with restricted feeding (circles), and 250-ml milk bottles (small, solid symbols).

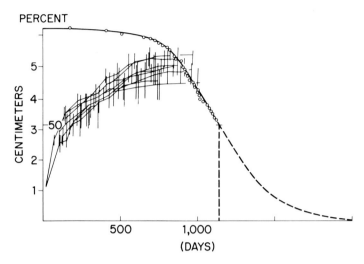

FIGURE 2.21 *Lebistes* females. Growth in length and survival. Compare with Figure 2.22.

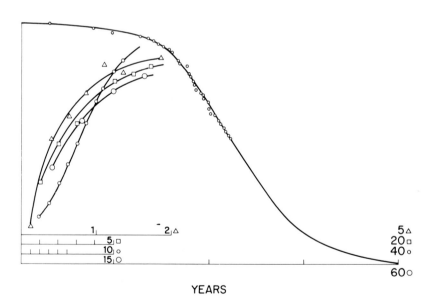

FIGURE 2.22   Growth and survival (extrapolated). Δ , sticleback; □, cod; ○, hake; ◇ plaice.

curve closely similar to that of mammals. Some forms, however, may conceivably have an effectively indeterminate life-span, though this may well mean only that their "determinate" maximum, as in wild birds, comes so late in relation to mortality as never to be reached in practice.

2.4.2 Reptiles and Amphibians

There are no published reptilian life-tables, but a number of careful studies of reptilian growth have been made (Sergeev, 1937; Townsend, 1931, 1937; Cagle, 1946). By collating these with maximum age records, a good deal of significant information can be obtained. Sergeev found that while, in all reptiles, early growth depends on environmental conditions, being sometimes very rapid, and growth-rate declines with increasing age, there are a number of forms where both sexes have an effective specific size which is reached early in life, and after the attainment of which no further growth occurs. The cessation of growth in these forms is apparently as definitive as that in mammals, and its timing does not appear to depend on the arrival of sexual maturity. There appears to be no close correlation between either of these two patterns of growth and the length of the life-span.

Among chelonians, both patterns of growth are known to occur. Continuous growth at a decreasing rate appears to be general in tortoises, the large species having inherently higher growth rates throughout. Townsend (1931,

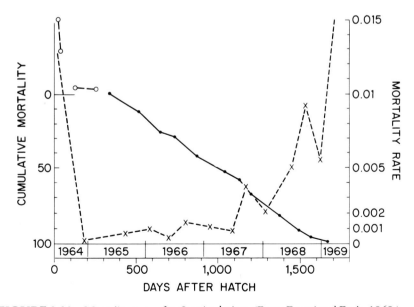

FIGURE 2.23 Mortality curve for *Oryzias latipes*. (From Egami and Etoh, 1969.)

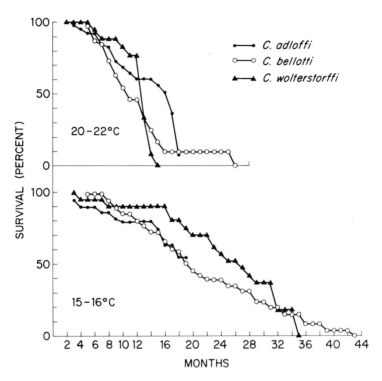

FIGURE 2.24   Representative survival curves of populations of three species of *Cynolebias* maintained at two temperature ranges. Data for males and females are combined. (From Liuand and Walford, 1970.)

1937) found that early growth in 100 specimens of the large *T. vicina,* kept in captivity, was potentially very rapid, and continued after the age of sexual maturity (about 20 years of age). Flower (1945) observed continuing growth in a 39-year-old specimen of *T. graeca.* The age of sexual maturity in the male *Terrapene carolina* appears to lie between 12 and 15 years (Nichols, 1939). All these are known to be long-lived forms. On the other hand, the majority of terrapins exhibit specific size. In *Emys* Sergeev (1937) found that growth cessation by the fifteenth year of life was as complete as in the adult mammal (Figure 2.26) although *E. orbicularis,* like *T. graeca,* is apparently capable of living 70–120 years and probably of breeding throughout life (Flower, 1937). Rollinat, however, on whose observations Flower's records were based, considered that growth in this form might continue for 30–40 years (Rollinat, 1934). Hildebrand (1932) studied the longevity and growth of over 1,000 specimens of *Malaclemmys centrata* in captivity—an investigation that is the nearest published approach to a chelonian life-table, but which was unfortunately continued in detail for only 10 years. He found the age of maturity

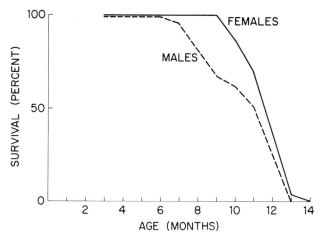

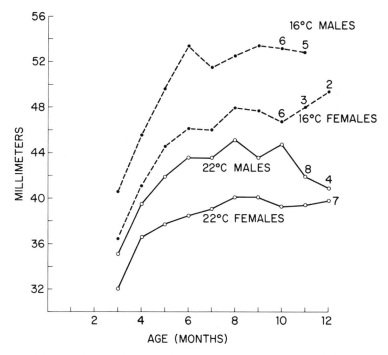

FIGURE 2.25a Percent survival of *Cynolebias adloffi* maintained since hatching at 22°C.

FIGURE 2.25b Average lengths of male and female *Cynolebias adloffi* maintained at 22 and 16°C. Each point is the average measurement of ten fish except where a lower number is indicated above some of the later points. (From Walford and Liu, 1965.)

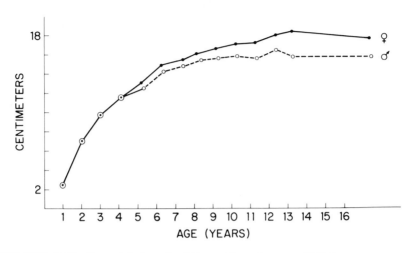

FIGURE 2.26   Growth in length of *Emys*. (From Sergeev, 1937.)

much more variable than in mammals, some individuals being full-grown in 8–9 years, others requiring 12–15. The oldest specimens in captivity were 21 years old, and "showed every appearance of being young animals," but other wild specimens taken when full-grown had been kept for 20 years without decline of vitality or reproductive power. Hildebrand placed the maximum life-span for this species at 40 years or more, but evidence from other small terrapins suggests that this may be a considerable underestimate. Although the only aquatic species which is known to have reached an age comparable with that of the land tortoises is *Emys orbicularis,* it would be very difficult to argue upon the existing evidence that specific size and determinate age are correlated in chelonians. Contrary to Bidder's hypothesis, specific size here seems to be an adaptation to carnivorous life in small pools, while continuing growth is found in land tortoises and marine turtles (Parker, 1926, 1929).

Crocodiles have also been credited with indeterminate growth:

> Crocodili perhibentur esse admodum vivaces, atque grandescendi periodem itidem habere insignem; adeo ut hos solos ex animalibus perpetuo, dum vivunt, grandescere opinio fit. . . . At de aliquo testaceo genere, nihil certi, quod ad vitam ipsorum attinet, reperimus.[6] *(Hist. Vitae et Mortis)*

---

[6]"Crocodiles are held to be very lively, and to have a notable span of growth—so that they alone of beasts, so opinion runs, grow so long as they live. . . . But of any hard-skinned beast, as pertaining to their length of life, we find nothing certain."

Claims of longevity are based on the exceptional size of some specimens. Large alligators have been observed in captivity to remain for 25 years in a non-growing state, e.g., *Alligator sinensis* (Dathe, 1935), though the difficulties of accurate length measurement are evident. Forty years has been reported (*Sunday Telegraph,* Jan. 12, 1964).

There is only one long-term study of ageing in amphibia, but the result is theoretically important: in *Xenopus,* Brocas and Verzar (1961b) found that collagen contractility changes steadily with age as in mammals, both in females, whose growth continues, and in males, which have a fixed size. There was no difference in the rate of collagen ageing between the sexes up to 13 years of age. Similar results have been achieved in snakes (Bourlière and Brocas, 1964). The high probability is that all reptiles and amphibians "age" if they live long enough; small forms (lizards, chameleons) appear to have limited lives, and the only question about published work on their pathology is whether the changes observed are in fact senile changes: in the larger forms the life-cycle is so easily modified by diapause, diet, temperature, and the like that individuals probably age at rates so different as to be beyond the access of actuarial statistics except in an experiment of intolerable length.

2.5 Distribution of Senescence in Invertebrates

Among invertebrates not only is there a demonstrable variety, greater than in vertebrates, in the nature of the preponderant senile process, but we have also the full range, from indeterminacy to very sharply defined determinacy of life-span. The gaps in our knowledge of life-cycles are so large that we cannot yet picture the distribution of senescence in invertebrate phylogeny: papers entitled "The life-history of . . ." only very exceptionally include reference to the senescence of the species under study—an extraordinary deficiency, which is a measure of the equally extraordinary lack of interest in age processes. It is fairly evident, however, that the distribution both of senescence in general and of any one process of senescence, such as depletion or mechanical deterioration, is quite discontinuous in phylogeny. This evolutionary discontinuity is what we should expect if "exhaustion of program" is the common basis of adverse age changes.

Senescence in some shape or form probably occurs in every group where the power of regeneration or fissile reproduction is less than total, or where body cells are not continuously and "indeterminately" replaced. Some forms that "degrow" under adverse conditions appear to be capable, in all probability, of unlimited alternate growth and degrowth, at least in the laboratory, while in a few, such as actinians, the adult can remain indefinitely in statu quo, though with a changing population of cells. Senescence is most striking in forms such as rotifers where determinacy of cell number is very highly developed and the power of regeneration is negligible. There do not appear to be any invertebrate cells (except possibly pelecypod neurons, of whose longevity and renewability we know little) that are called upon to remain for 100 or more years in active function, like a human neuron, or for still longer, like the neurons of the tortoise. The distribution of senescence in invertebrates suggests that in spite of the general argument against the selection of long-lived forms, relatively great longevity is sometimes an evolved adaptation, and that if some cold-blooded vertebrates age extraordinarily slowly, that, too, is likewise a specialized mechanism and not a primitive or an "inherent" mechanism which has been lost with increasing somatic complexity.

2.5.1 Porifera

Bidder infelicitously cited "the sea anemone, the bath sponge and the water-vole" as three organisms insusceptible to senescence. The only serious study of senescence in Porifera appears to be that of Arndt (1928) who concludes that it does not occur, although some sponges are fatally disrupted by their own larvae. Aquarium specimens have an effectively limited life, as in so many other groups, but sponges seem ideally able to conform to Bidder's expectation of them.

2.5.2 Coelenterates

In hydromedusae, Child (1918) observed a progressive decrease in metabolism and pulsation rate with increasing size, which he regarded as evidence of senescence. His work on the processes of ageing and rejuvenation in hydroids (1915) depends on the criterion of resistance to cyanide as evidence of "physiological age"—one that is hardly acceptable in this context. Child's results with Pennaria, using this test of age, were in any case less consistent than those he obtained with planarians, where cyanide resistance rose steadily throughout life (Child, 1915).

Evidence that the life-span of sea anemones is "indeterminate" is probably stronger than for any other metazoan group. Dalyell's (1848) celebrated specimens of *Actinia* lived for 70 years in captivity without any sign of deterioration. An even more famous batch of sea anemones were collected "some years prior to 1862," and were first identified as *Sagartia troglodytes* by Ashworth and Annandale (1904), later by Stephenson as *Cereus pedunculatus* (1935). They remained in the aquarium of Edinburgh University Department of Zoology until 1940 or 1942, when they were all simultaneously found dead. Budding continued freely throughout life, and the animals underwent no obvious change during 80 to 90 years of continuous observation (Warwick, 1954, personal communication). Whether gametogenesis likewise continued throughout life is not known.

Hydra. The long-standing controversy over the senescence of *Hydra* illustrates some of the difficulties of placing a gerontological interpretation on life-tables and histological appearances. *Hydra* was a favorite organism, earlier in the century, in the argument over the "potentielle Unsterblichkeit" of metazoa. Differences in culture conditions almost certainly account for the very irregular results obtained.

Early workers (Hertwig, 1906; Boecker, 1914; Berninger, 1910) on this question found it impossible to keep *Hydra* for long periods without the onset of "depression," evidenced by cloudy swelling and cytolysis. With better cultural methods Goetsch (1922, 1925) kept individuals of *Pelmatohydra oligactis, Hydra attenuata,* and *Chlorohydra viridissima* alive for 27 months. Goetsch considered that, like the actinians, *Hydra* was capable of remaining indefinitely in statu quo. Gross (1925), working with *P. oligactis,* failed to keep any individual alive for more than 349 days, "senescence" being evidenced by irregular and hypertrophic budding or by the animal becoming smaller and smaller in the presence of abundant food. "Senile" changes in Gross's material began after the fourth month of life. A life-table, drawn from Hase's (1909) data by Pearl and Miner (1935), extending over only 148 days, indicates some increase in mortality with age, but is closer to the log-linear than to the rectangular contour (see Figure 1.2, p. 24). Hartlaub (1916) had already described experiments on Syncorinae in which he concluded that the power of producing gametes was lost relatively early in life, while that of budding persisted.

David (1925) kept isolation records in cultures of *P. oligactis* and satisfied himself that in this form the individual animals tended to die between 20 and 28 months in approximate order of individual age—an important observation that has not been repeated. According to Schlottke, however (Schlottke, 1930), the material in David's histological sections was heavily parasitized. Schlottke's own observations suggested that all the tissues of *Hydra* are continuously replaced throughout life, from a subjacent reserve of interstitial cells. This view is supported by the work of Brien (1953), who showed by marking experiments that there is continuous growth in *Hydra* from front to back, the marked zone travelling down the animal and being ultimately rejected at the base: a case, in other words, of "indeterminate growth" coexisting with a final specific size. For the most recent discussion of this matter, see Strehler (1961, 1962).

In colonial hydroids, however, it seems to have been shown beyond reasonable doubt that the life-span of each hydranth is physiologically determinate. The resorption and involution of hydranths was described in full by Huxley and de Beer (1923); the hydranth shrinks, the gut becomes filled with cellular debris, and the degenerating material is returned to the colony by the contraction of the hydranth itself. In *Obelia* and *Campanularia* Crowell (1953) has shown that regression takes place strictly in order of age, each hydranth having a life of 4 days at 21°C and 7 at 17°C. When regression is accelerated by starvation or adverse culture conditions, the age order is still preserved. *Campanularia* has been used as a model "short-lived metazoan" for ageing studies (Strehler, 1966; Brock, 1970, 1971).

2.5.3 Other Invertebrates

Existing observations are scattered rather thinly over a number of groups. Child (1911, 1913, 1914, 1915, 1918) carried out exhaustive studies upon the regeneration of planarians, and upon their capacity for de-differentiation, to which subsequent research has been able to add little or nothing. Here again, as in *Pennaria,* he employed the increase in resistance to dilute cyanide solutions as a criterion of senescence, on the assumption that this change reflected a decrease in metabolic rate. While susceptibility decreased as a function of age in the growing animal, planarians kept for several months at a constant size showed no such increase, and planarians undergoing shrinkage under adverse food conditions showed a decrease in susceptibility. Child also demonstrated the "rejuvenation," partial or entire, of regenerating fragments of planarians. This further observation, using the same criterion of resistance to toxicity (1915), that a gradient of "rejuvenation" exists in *Stenostomum* (Rhabdocoela) during the production of new zooids has been confirmed by Sonneborn (1930) using direct life-table studies. Sonneborn's experiments showed that the regenerative effects of fission were markedly unequal in the two halves, since the head portions, which required only to regenerate tails, underwent typical senescence, and died after a limited number of divisions, while tails, which required to regenerate most of the body and nervous system, could be propagated indefinitely. Much of this work has been repeated by Haranghy and Balász (1964). Some authors have detected signs of senescence (chiefly somatic distortion) even in planarians (Balász and Burg, 1962), but, as in *Hydra,* it is hard to distinguish age changes from the pathologies inherent in prolonged culture.

In *Aeolosoma* (Oligochaeta), Haemmerling (1924) found that the anterior end of the body appeared to undergo eventual senescence, new worms being produced from the posterior end. Stolč (1902) had already given a circumstantial histopathological account of "senile" death in *Aeolosoma* as a whole, but the appearances observed might have resulted from almost any environmental cause. In *Nais* (Annelida), Stolte (1924, 1927) found extensive histological changes with age, with disappearance of the normal zones, degeneration of the visceral ganglia, and the cessation of reserve-cell production from the embryonic tissue persisting in the posterior end. The significance of these changes is again obscure, and no attempt was made to determine actuarially the mortality rates at different ages. Annelid regeneration and ageing appear to be controlled by the characteristic yellow-pigmented coelomic cells (Moment, 1974). Rhabdocoelians have (Bresslau, 1928–33) been observed to be increasingly susceptible to protozoan parasites the longer they live.

How far the capacity for "degrowth," which is found in planarians, is evidence of a potentially indeterminate life-span is not evident, but it seems likely that forms such as *Lineus* (Nemertinea), which revert on starvation over a period of years to a mass of cells resembling an embryo (Dawidoff, 1924), might be maintained indefinitely in alternate growth and degrowth until the patience of the investigator was exhausted.

The evidence in fissile worms at present suggests that nonsenescence depends upon fairly active replacement of cells, and that any organ that fails to take part in the regenerative process is liable to undergo senile change. Harms (1949) considered that the senescence of Serpulids was due primarily to changes in the nervous system, and rejuvenated old specimens of *Protula* by grafting young heads. Some further work on this subject as careful as that of Child and Sonneborn would probably be well worth undertaking.

The senescence of nematodes is now a *locus classicus* by virtue of the relative ease with which individuals can be synchronized and their enzymology studied. Following the work of Gershon, they have been widely used as models of biochemical change in fixed postmitotics (see Section 9). Changes have been reported similar to those observed in the decline-phase of limited fibroblast clones—loss of enzyme activity without loss of immunoreactive enzyme, appearance of heat-labile isozymes (Reiss and Rothstein 1974, 1975; Bolla and Brot, 1975), a peculiar and so far unexplained parallel to the behavior of a senescent clone. The life-cycle is manipulable—for example, by sterilization with acriflavin (Dougherty and Nigon, 1956) but experiments to differentiate cytoplasmic and nuclear influences, critical for the dissection of ageing effects, are unpromising in an organism wholly without cell division. Full electron microscopy of the nematode ageing process remains to be undertaken. For a review of error-theory experiments in nematodes see Section 9.5.

Morphogenetic loss throughout life of the power of regeneration in a nematode of determinate cell number was actually demonstrated by Pai (1928) in *Anguillula aceti*. Amputation of the tail with nuclear removal kills the animal at any age. In young individuals, provided the nucleus is left intact, wound healing and cytoplasmic regeneration can take place. In mature animals there is wound closure but no cytoplasmic regeneration, while in senile animals amputation is fatal. In *Anguillula* senescence follows a pattern very similar to that of rotifers (see below) and occurs at about 44 days. The degenerative cellular changes in ovaries, gut and nerve cells have been described: these appear in the two or three days preceding death (Pai, 1928; Bürger, 1954). Thickening of interchordal hypodermis and pigment accumulation are also recorded (Kisiel, et al., 1975).

2.5.4 Rotifers

The ageing of rotifers is one of the most spectacular examples of endogenous senescence in animals. It is also one of the most thoroughly studied, at least from the descriptive point of view. The life-span varies in different species from a few days to several months, and each species tends to exhibit very sharp specific age. After a period of growth, which takes place by increase in cell size, the nuclear number being fixed, and adult vigor, rotifers enter a period of senescence, with conspicuous loss of activity, degeneration of cells, deposition of pigment, and ultimate death in extension. In some forms the senescent phase is genuinely postreproductive, but in the majority it occurs while egg laying is still occurring at a diminished rate, and may be accompanied by the production of malformed eggs, or eggs of varying size.

The external appearances of rotifer senescence have been vividly described in several forms (*Callidina*—Plate, 1886; *Pleurotrocha*—Metchnikoff, 1907; *Proales*—Noyes, 1922; Jennings and Lynch, 1928; *Hydatina*—Plate, 1886; *Lecane*—Szabó, 1935; Miller, 1931; *Rotifer vulgaris*—Spemann, 1924; *Philodina*—Fanestil and Banous, 1966; *Mytilina*—Sincock, 1974). The animal becomes sluggish in behavior and reaction to jarring, the tissues and cuticle shrink and become opaque or granular in appearance, swimming is replaced by creeping, pigment accumulates in the gut, digestive gland, and mastax. The movements of the pharyngeal cilia are the last signs of life to persist.

It seems clear that this is an endogenous process of degeneration. A number of attempts have been made to correlate it with other features of rotifer organization. Plate (1886) considered that senescence in *Hydatina* occurred typically when the activity of the ovary, and the supply of germ cells, failed. This is not the case in all rotifers, however. In *Lecane inermis* Miller (1931) found that the mictic females cease egg laying early in life and have a relatively prolonged postreproductive period, while amictic females show signs of age before the last egg is produced, and all are dead within two days thereafter; the life-span of males is even shorter (Figure 2.27). In this species, fertilization of the mictic females does not appear to influence longevity. Miller attributes the difference in life-span between mictic and amictic females directly to the difference in fertility, but this is not fully borne out by her life-tables, the chief difference being in the longer postreproductive period of the mictic females. In *Hydatina senta* it is the amictic females which are the longer lived (Ferris, 1932; see also King, 1970). In both these species, however, the form having the higher reproductive rate in early life dies younger, an observation which supports Miller's suggestion that death

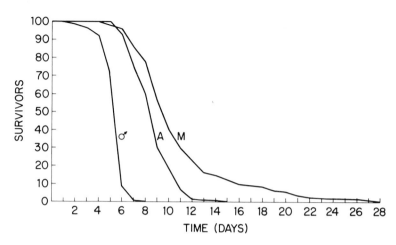

FIGURE 2.27   Survival curves for males, and mictic (M) and amictic (A) females of *Lecane inermis.* (From Miller, 1931.)

results from "exhaustion." Egg-laying in *Apsilus vorax* continues until death (Cori, 1925) and in *Proales,* appears itself to be adversely affected by somatic senescence, the egg substance failing to enter the eggshell, and eggs of bizarre size and shape and of low hatchability being produced (Jennings and Lynch, 1928). Old populations of *P. sordida* consist of two types of senile individuals, some thick and opaque, and others abnormally transparent, with pigmentation of the gastric glands. There is considerable individual variation in the length of survival once senescence is established.

Impairment of function in all the species that have been studied is so general during senescence that it is not possible to identify a pacemaker organ in the process, though in some cases it appears to be the digestive system that first deteriorates. The pattern is fully consistent with some or all of the somatic cells having a fixed survival time under normal metabolic conditions—a highly important precedent for the study of other types of metazoan senescence. The senescent change depends directly upon metabolism: encysted rotifers can survive for very long periods (59 years—Rahm, 1923) and display enhanced reproductive performance on emergence from diapause (Dobers, 1915).

It is particularly interesting that this dramatic senescence in rotifers accompanies a very strict determinacy of cell number, a lack of regenerative capacity, and in most species a very limited power of repair. Nuclear division after hatching has not been described in any rotifer. In many forms wound healing is confined to young animals; older animals die after amputation (Pai, 1934), but in young *Asplanchna brightwelli* (Pai, 1934) and *Stephanoceros*

(Jurszýk, 1926, 1927; Ubisch, 1926) the cytoplasm of the coronal lobes can be regenerated, as can parts of the coronal funnel in *Cupelopagis* (Huhner-hoff, 1931; references from Hyman, 1951). Ultrastructural changes have been seen in old rotifers (Herold and Meadow, 1970). The rate of rough reticulum formation declines with age, and free ribosomes become rarer (Lansing, 1964). In Herold and Meadow's study the chief age change was the accumulation of granular vesicles, which are probably primary lysosomes containing accumulations of waste material.

The somatic growth of rotifers has been studied by several workers. *Rotifer vulgaris* shows little or no change in size throughout life (Spemann, 1924). The growth curve of *Apsilus vorax* is a parabola, with shrinkage before death (Cori, 1925), while in *Philodina citrina* growth ceases by the sixth day (Lansing, 1948) (see Figure 2.28). Lansing also made the striking observation that if these rotifers are propagated in each generation from eggs laid at or after the fifth day of maternal life, the rate of development becomes progressively greater and greater from generation to generation, and the longevity of the individual less and less, so that clones propagated in each generation from old mothers invariably become extinct (Figures 2.29–2.31). Jennings and

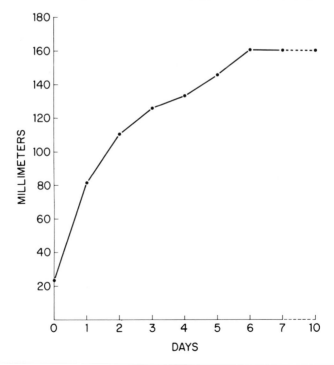

FIGURE 2.28   Growth in length of *Philodina citrina*. (From Lansing, 1948.)

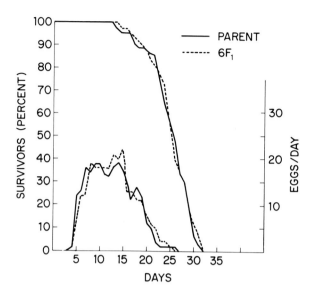

FIGURE 2.29 Life-span and egg-laying of *Philodina citrina* (Rotifera) over six generations in normal culture. (From Lansing, 1952.)

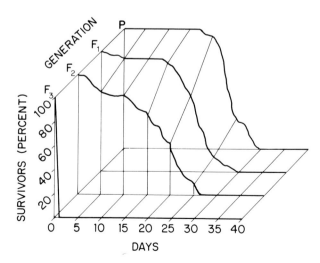

FIGURE 2.30 Progressive decline in life-span of a strain of *Philodina citrina* (Rotifera) raised in each generation from eggs laid by old mothers. (From Lansing, 1952.)

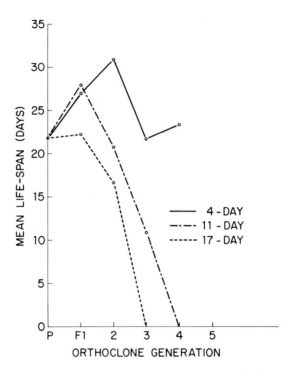

FIGURE 2.31   Life-span of successive generations of *Philodina* reared in each generation from the eggs of 4-, 11-, and 17-day-old mothers. (From Lansing, 1948.)

Lynch (1928) had already noted that the offspring of very old rotifers are less viable than those of vigorous adults. Lansing's results suggested that the effects of maternal age are cumulative from generation to generation: they were also reversible, the eggs laid by young members of such a clone being capable of giving rise to normally long-lived individuals. Lansing also found that clones propagated in each generation from the eggs of very young mothers showed an increase in longevity over the control stock. In *Euchlanis triquetra,* the "young" orthoclone could not be maintained, however, because within a few generations it gave rise largely to male-producing eggs. Lansing regards his ageing factor as a product of growth cessation, since it appears in the individual animal at the point where the negative specific acceleration of growth is greatest. Meadow and Barrows (1971a, b) found no orthoclone effect in a bdelloid rotifer: Lansing's findings were confirmed in other species by King (1967).

   The susceptibility of rotifer eggs to external influences affecting the life-cycle of the progeny has been much studied in forms that give rise periodically to mictic generations. The literature on sex determination in rotifers is reviewed by Hyman (1951). The longevity of the two types of female differs considerably:

> . . . somewhere in the ontogeny of the females, it must be deter-
> mined which kind of egg they are destined to lay. The determina-
> tion occurs during the maturation of the egg from which the
> female comes, that is, during the last few hours before the egg is
> laid. (Hyman, 1951)

Both internal and environmental factors of great complexity appear to operate in different forms. "The conclusion from numerous researches seems to be that, in addition to an inherent rhythm as regards male production, monotony of conditions suppresses mictic females, whereas any sudden change, especially of diet and of physiochemical composition of the water, induces the appearance of mictic females" (Hyman, 1951). The reason for the difference in longevity between Lansing's old and young orthoclones is not, it should be noted, entirely comparable to that between mictic and amictic females. It does not seem to represent a difference in specific age due to a shortening of that part of the survival curves that, owing to the low early mortality in rotifers, is usually horizontal, but rather a "breaking away" of this plateau by the introduction of a higher and higher early mortality, the curve becoming less and less rectangular and more and more oblique. If conclusions are to be drawn upon the effect of maternal age upon senescence, this difference is important.

It is unlikely that the uniform specific age of rotifer populations is due to *depletion*. Reproductive exhaustion has already been discussed. It is also known that the limited regeneration observed in *Stephanoceros* takes place at the expense of reproduction and of somatic growth. Little is known of the metabolic capacity of rotifers—they apparently store glycogen, but may be incapable of assimilating carbohydrate (Hyman, 1951). Sudden senescence might well represent the exhaustion of a metabolic substrate, or of a non-renewable system. *Accumulation* has also been suggested: pigment certainly does accumulate, probably secondarily to the ageing process, and old rotifers are full of lysosomal vesicles (Herold and Meadow 1970). Lansing (1942) demonstrated the accumulation of calcium in old rotifers, and succeeded in prolonging their life by immersion in dilute citrate solution; it is not clear how often this process can be repeated. A more curious factor influencing the life-span was observed by Edmondson (1945a, b) in *Floscularia conifera,* where individuals growing in aggregation reach twice the length, twice the age, and a higher level of fertility as against solitary specimens.

The peculiarities of rotifer organization are so numerous that some, if not all, of the mechanisms controlling their longevity are likely to be peculiar to the group. On the other hand, their short life-span makes them a suitable object for study, and they provide an unequivocal example of senescence coupled with cellular nonrenewal that calls for further investigation.

Systematic electron microscopy might prove very instructive. Massive increase in granular vesicles and detachment of ribosomes have been reported (Herold and Meadow 1969, 1970). Lansing (1964) found a decline in the rate of rough reticulum formation and a scarcity of free ribosomes. Although recent disillusion with invertebrate models is justified, the peculiarities of fixed-cell invertebrates (rotifers and nematodes) to some extent exempt them from the stricture; they remain models of fixed postmitotic behavior which should be worked out in detail.

2.5.5 Arthropods

Senescence in arthropods is widespread and probably universal. Those forms that have wings, jaws, bristles, and other chitinous tegumentary structures not renewed by moulting are particularly liable to genuinely "mechanical" senescence. In the forms that moult as adults, the time of ecdysis is a particularly arduous one, judged by the mortality, and many of these, such as *Daphnia* and large spiders, appear very often to die in the attempt to carry out a final moult.

"Physiological" senescence, in the sense in which nineteenth-century biology used the term, also appears in a convincing form for the first time in arthropods, since, as Metchnikoff first pointed out (1907, 1915), a non-feeding imago *must* be regarded as expendable from the evolutionary point of view. The evolution of short sexual life as a modification in some groups is balanced by the evolution of a very long sexual life in specialized individuals of other, social, species, as part of the adaptive development of a group existence—the longest life-span being reached in one or both sexual forms among true ants and termites.

There is no known case of arthropod indeterminacy comparable with that of actinians. Growth in most insect imagines is more or less rigidly limited, although the capacity for continued cell division persists in varying degrees. According to Harms (1959), somatic mitosis in many arthropod imagines is virtually confined to the midgut. Mitotic capacity has not been shown to bear any relationship to longevity, except perhaps in forms producing queens, where the relation of continued reproduction to long life might be either a direct example of cause and effect, or the result of two parallel adaptations. Some solitary arthropods are capable of very long life (20 years in tarantulas—Baerg 1945; possibly 50 years in lobsters—Herrick, 1896).

Crustacea. The small crustacea (Cladocerans, Copepods, Isopods) generally show very sharp specific age. There are good examples of senescence in *Ligia* (Inagaki, 1971; Berreurbon and Inagaki, 1970; Inagaki and Berreurbon

1970) and *Sphaeroma* (Charmant, 1971). In *Daphnia*[7] specific age appears to be definable in terms of instars, *D. longispina* living for 19–22 instars, the duration of which depend upon the conditions of culture (Ingle, et al., 1937) and *D. magna* for 17 instars (Anderson and Jenkins, 1942). Detailed studies upon factors that retard or accelerate the rate of development and life-span in *Daphnia* have been carried out (McArthur and Baillie, 1926 *seq.;* Ingle, et al., 1937; Anderson and Jenkins, 1942; Fritsch, 1953, 1959; Fritsch and Meijering, 1958; Meijering, 1958, 1960; von Reden, 1960, etc., *seq.*). In view of the availability of life-tables for *Daphnia,* the pattern of its normal growth is of particular interest. Edlén (1938) showed that the growth of normal daphnids takes place in two cycles, the first leveling off after three or four instars, and the second coinciding with the development of the gonad. He found three types of pattern in the growth of individual *D. magna*. In the majority of specimens (Figure 2.32) the two cycles of growth followed one another, the growth potential in the second cycle falling almost to zero with increasing age; this fall is accompanied by a decrease in egg size and number, and the animal finally dies after a short period in which growth has almost ceased. In individuals of the second type (Figure 2.33) the two growth cycles were superimposed—in these growth was very rapid, there was no prepubertal "shelf" in the curve of body size, and fertility was lost early, although the life-span appeared to be normal. The third type (Figure 2.34) showed only the first cycle of growth, but no gonadal function developed, and adult size was not attained. These forms died early. Edlén considered that the developing ovary exerts a hormonal control over growth, and possibly over the maintenance of life processes generally.

The chief senile changes in *Daphnia* appear to be in the fat body, intestinal epithelium, and musculature (Schulze-Röbbecke, 1951). This author found no evidence of the "cerebral death" that was once widely accepted as the general cause of invertebrate senescence (Harms, 1926; Muhlmann, 1900, 1911), and which was described by Walter (1922) in *Cyclops*. Withdrawal of ovarian activity does not seem to be the direct cause of senescence in *Daphnia*. Schulze-Röbbecke's oldest specimens still showed considerable

---

[7]There is a striking lack of unanimity in the literature over the "normal" life-span of various species of *Daphnia,* even when grown in apparently similar media. Fritsch (1953) has shown that this variation depends to some extent upon the amount of available pantothenic acid. Where Daphnids are fed upon living cultures of protozoans or algae, the food organism itself may metabolize and remove pantothenic acid. It is highly questionable in view of Fritsch's findings how far the life-tables obtained by workers using different culture techniques, or even by one worker at different times, are comparable. This is unfortunate, as Cladocerans are most useful organisms to gerontologists. Further standardization of culture techniques seems essential if they are to be used in this way, however.

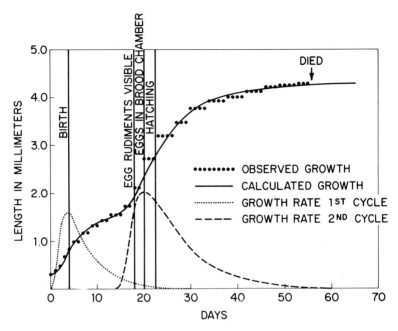

FIGURE 2.32   Growth in length of *Daphnia magna,* first type. (From Edlén, 1938.)

ovarian activity, and continued to lay eggs, though in reduced numbers, up to the time of death. Oocytes at all stages of maturation remained in the ovary to the last. Schulze-Röbbecke attributed the death of *Daphnia* in old age to failure of nutrition following degenerative changes in the gut.

Walter's work on *Cyclops* (1922) dealt with *C. viridis,* which has a life-span of about 9 months, "senile" change in gut epithelium and in the cerebral ganglia being evident from the fifth month. Somatic mitosis in adult life occurs only in the mid-gut of *Cyclops,* and in this region "senile" changes were not found (Harms, 1949). The most striking degenerative changes in *Cyclops* were found in the chromatin of the ganglion cells, with the appearance of large inclusion bodies suspiciously reminiscent of virus inclusions or fixation artifacts, and in the antennules. Gut degeneration occurred later in life, about the eighth month, and was confined to the anterior gut, mitosis continuing in other parts of the gut epithelium until the end. It is difficult to know what connection, if any, these changes have with the process of senescence.

Needham (A. E. Needham, 1950) has studied the growth rate of limb regeneration in *Asellus aquaticus;* growth in crustacea, according to Needham's figures for *Asellus* and *Carcinus,* is determinate and the curve sigmoid, the arithmetic rate of growth rising to a maximum and declining asymptoti-

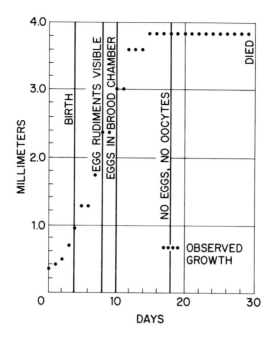

FIGURE 2.33   Growth in length of *D. magna,* second type: growth phases superimposed. (From Edlén, 1938.)

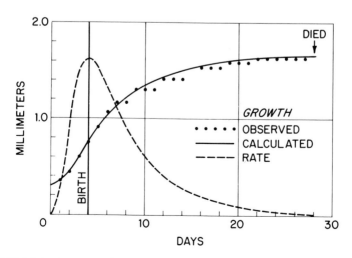

FIGURE 2.34   Growth in length of *D. magna,* third type. One growth cycle only. (From Edlén, 1938.)

cally thereafter to zero. The geometric rate of growth declines monotonically with age from the outset, and the rate of decline itself declines with increasing age. The specific regeneration rate decreases progressively with age, owing to the progressive increase in the duration of each instar; the rate of decline is much less than that of the normal growth rate, and itself declines with age. "In some crustacea the limiting size is attained at an age beyond the mean expected life-span. Growth is indeterminate in Crustacea only in this sense. They are not potentially immortal." This investigation illustrates once again the difficulty of characterizing the growth behavior of real organisms mathematically: the decline of arithmetic growth may be asymptotic, or tangible size increase may continue; in crustacea there is the additional difficulty that growth is discontinuous, being interrupted by stadia, which superimpose a "quantal" effect on the smooth ideal curve. The conclusion of Needham's studies is that the growth of crustacea follows a convergent series, and must cease, presumably, for practical purposes in any form that lives long enough.

Insects. It has long been recognized that several separate types of senile change may occur in insects. Mechanical damage to the cuticle (Blunck, 1924; Wigglesworth, 1945), depletion of reserves both in feeding and non-feeding imagines, accelerated in some cases by reproduction (Krumbiegel, 1929a, b; Bilewicz, 1953), accumulation of urates (Metchnikoff, 1915), deterioration of the nervous system (Hodge, 1894–1895; Pixell-Goodrich, 1920; Schmidt, 1923; Weyer, 1931, etc.) and "general senile decay" have all been demonstrated by more or less satisfactory evidence. The vast majority of holometabolous imagines give every evidence of having a sharp specific age, and this is a group in which we are unusually well equipped with life-tables. The nature of the processes which limit imaginal life seems, however, to vary widely, but they have the common property of being processes operating in a cellular system where little or no renewal, and no further morphogenetic development, are occurring.

One of the best general descriptions of insect senescence is given by Blunck (1924) for *Dytiscus marginalis:* he describes the main signs of advancing age as diminution in activity and deterioration of the epicuticle, with the growth of colonial protozoa on the dorsal shield, legs, and mouth parts, which the animal cannot any longer clean effectively. The cleaning secretions seem to be reduced, and the chitin appears brittle, whole legs or attennae occasionally snapping off in swimming. If pygidial gland secretion fails, air enters the subalar air chamber and the beetle drowns. In the beetles dissected by Blunck, the gonads had almost disappeared during the third year of life, the fat body was increased in size, almost filling the body cavity, but chalky and full of concretions. In some individuals there was almost complete atrophy of the wing muscles. The extreme life-span is under 3 years, females living longer than males: sexual activity usually ceases in the second year but may persist in individuals into the third. A number of senile processes, which may not be mutually dependent, can be detected in this description. The balance between mechanical, depletive, and "morphogenetic" senescence must vary considerably from species to species, and even from individual to individual. Blunck's description is of interest in providing not only an account of such a mixed senescence, but one of the very few instances where the "change in inert structures," so popular with colloid chemists investigating senescence, really seems to occur—in the progressive hardening and weakening of the chitin of *Dytiscus* elytra, which Blunck found to be a reliable rough measure of the age of specimens taken in the wild. On the other hand, a considerable part of this change, as Blunck himself suspected, may represent failure to secrete the normal lubricant coat—a cellular rather than a mechanical deterioration.

In many insects, especially lepidoptera, there is evidence that the fat body contains a definite reserve of materials, which are not replaceable during imaginal life. In females of the moth *Ephestia elutella,* longevity and fecundity are both functions of body weight at eclosion (Waloff, et al., 1947). Longevity is also greater in virgin females, possibly owing to the sparing of reserves through egg-rudiment resorption (Norris, 1933, 1934). Exhaustion of the fat body is characteristically found in *Ephestia* that appear to have died of old age. Norris (1934) found evidence that the fat body contains two types of store, one needed for the maintenance of the ovaries and the other for the maintenance of life. The second appears to be supplemented by feeding the imago, but not the first (Norris, 1933). Similar deterioration of the fat body has been described as a sign of senescence in *Carabus* and *Drosophila* (Krumbiegel, 1929b) and *Sitodrepa panicea* (Janisch, 1924), in which the period of depletion is apparently hastened by exposure to CO_2. This type of "depletion senescence" is, in fact, in one sense an extension of morphogenetic senescence, if in the transition from larva to imago the organism loses the power of synthesis or assimilation of some material which it is able to store during larval and pupal life. How far depletion of larval reserves is a general feature of insect senescence it is difficult to say. The nonfeeding or the starved imago is necessarily dependent upon what stores it has, although Metchnikoff (1915) from a careful study of *Bombyx,* favored an "accumulative" rather than a "depletive" mechanism to account for imaginal death. Other imagines probably vary a great deal in their biochemical accomplishments. Some lepidopteran imagines feed on nectar and are known to absorb water and sugars. Frohawk (1935) kept *Nymphalis antiopa* alive for three months from eclosion by feeding sugar solution. On the other hand, robust Coleoptera, such as *Blaps,* are fully capable of living on their intake and stores for ten years, while the mole cricket has been thought able to live much longer. Activity reduces the life-span: Camboué (1926) greatly pro-

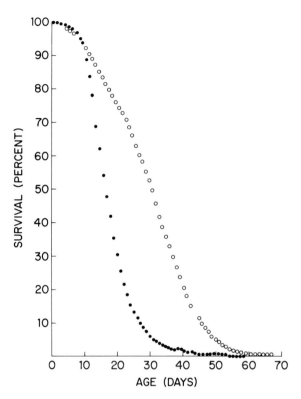

FIGURE 2.35   Survival curves of male and female houseflies. Males ●; females ○. (From Rockstein and Lieberman, 1958.)

longed the life of butterflies by decapitating them. The correlations between pre-imaginal and imaginal life-spans have been discussed by Balász (1960).

The influence of reproduction on life-span is equally variable, but it often seems to involve inroads upon stored and irreplaceable reserves. Unmated females of *Periplaneta* lay fewer eggs than mated females and live longer (Griffiths and Tauber, 1942). The life-span in both male and female *Drosophila* is substantially decreased by mating (Bilewicz, 1953). Krumbiegel found that the reserves in the fat body of Carabids decrease after first copulation, but increase again with feeding (1929). In the moth *Fumea crassiorella* Matthes (1951) found that the longevity of the female was halved by copulation if egg laying was allowed, and slightly reduced by it if egg laying was prevented (Figure 2.36).

Ageing in all diptera appears to be associated with a declining flight capacity, chiefly in duration of sustained flight. This correlates with biochemical and mitochondrial changes, and with changes in the structure of flight muscle. These last are not in themselves as a rule sufficient to explain the marked decline in function, and neurochemical changes must be involved. The decline has an orderly and programmed appearance. The extensive literature of microscopic, biochemical, and enzymic changes is reviewed by Baker (1976), by Sohal (1976), and by Webb and Tribe (1974).

The theory of "cerebral death" (Gehirntod) in insects arises chiefly from some long-standing work on bees. Hodge (1894, 1895), Pixell-Goodrich (1920), and Schmidt (1923) all described cerebral degeneration, reduction of cerebral cell number, and disorganization of the nervous system as characteristic and probably causal mechanisms in the senescence of worker bees. According to Hodge, the cell number in the brain of old workers was reduced by three-quarters. Pixell-Goodrich found that in diseased, and therefore inactive, workers, the cerebral architecture was more normal than in healthy workers. Schmidt attributed the reduction in cell size and cell number to direct "wear by use," the amount of work done by the insect being a fixed quantity. Holmgren (1909) found a similar deterioration in the supraesophageal ganglia of old termite primaries: the brain of old physogastric queens of *Eutermes* was reduced to two-thirds of the volume usually found in virgin queens. Other instances of "Gehirntod" in insects were described by Hansemann (1914) in *Bacillus rossi* (Phasmidae) and *Musca* (Sohal, 1972).

Quite apart from the fact that they have been indiscriminately transferred to mammals, these findings themselves have been open to intermittent criticism. Smallwood and Phillips (1916) were by no means satisfied that the

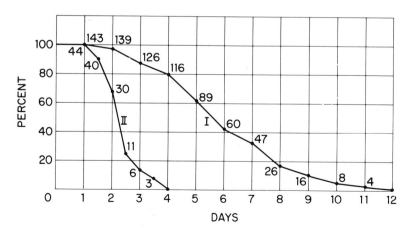

FIGURE 2.36 Survival curves of 145 isolated virgin females (I) and 44 isolated fertilized females (II) of the moth *Fumea crassiorella*. (From Matthes, 1951.)

changes in relative nuclear size described by Hodge in worker bees resulted from ageing or were in any way pathological. Weyer (1930) regarded the cerebral ganglion changes as secondary, since the supposedly senile degeneration appears remarkably suddenly, and only after evident deterioration in other organs. In a 5-year-old queen, Pflugfelder (1948) found some disturbances of cerebral histology especially in the corpora pedunculata, but no significant cerebral change in old drones and workers. Rockstein (1950), however, found a decline in cell number in the brain of worker bees from a mean 522 at eclosion to 369 at 6 weeks. The complex behavior of worker bees deteriorates suddenly just before death.

In some lepidoptera this change in behavior before death is very marked— so much so that it may have an adaptive function (Blest, 1960), there being aposematic species which, when no longer fertile, become behaviorally conspicuous to predators through overactivity.

Schulze-Röbbecke (1951) made a careful search for evidence of "cerebral death" in *Dixippus* and *Melolontha* and found no signs of it whatsoever, the primary senile deterioration being most evident in gut and musculature. "Vielleicht hat v. Hansemann bereits töte Tiere untersucht, was sehr leicht vorkommen kann, da bei den Stabheuschrecken infolge ihrer Reaktionsträgheit der Übergang von den letzten Lebensaüsserungen zum Tode nicht ohne weiteres festzustellen ist." The amount of senile change described either as a result of fixation artifacts or the sectioning of "that which dies of itself" has yet to be assessed in the literature.

A considerable amount of work has been done upon the physiological factors that influence longevity in worker bees. Winter bees are known to be considerably longer lived than the summer brood, even when they are kept under similar conditions of temperature and activity. Maurizio (1946) found that caged winter bees had a mean survival of 36 days from eclosion compared with 24 days in caged summer bees. The life-span of summer bees can be prolonged in two ways: by feeding pollen to caged bees (Maurizio, 1946), or by removing all the sealed brood regularly from the colony, so that the same bees continue with brood rearing throughout life. Under these conditions bees may live as long as 72 days (Moskovljević, 1939; Maurizio, 1950).

Two factors appear to influence the longevity of workers. One of these is certainly activity. Ribbands (1950) found that anesthesia with CO_2 had the effect of causing young bees to begin foraging earlier than usual: in bees that forage early, expectation of imaginal life is less (30.1 ± 1.2 days), but expectation of foraging life is greater (15.0 ± 1.2 days) than in late starters (37.1 ± 0.6 and 10.8 ± 0.8 days). The second appears to be dietary. Winter bees differ from summer bees in the greater development of their pharyngeal glands and their fat-bodies. This development results from autumn consumption of pollen, in excess of the requirements for immediate brood rearing. In queen-right colonies in summer, prevention of brood rearing can produce similar consequences, and in pre-swarming colonies temporary interruption of brood-rearing produces conditions different only in degree. In all these cases the increased expectation of life is associated both with enhanced development of the pharyngeal glands and fatbody, and with decreased activity (Ribbands, 1953). It appears that worker bees have a life-span that is partially expressible in "flying hours," and that this life-span, and the total output of work per life, can be increased by increasing pollen consumption (Maurizio, 1950), but summer bees only increase their life-span in this way if they are deprived of brood. There is also ground for believing that the activity of worker bees is reduced by the possession of internal food reserves. In winter bees, then, absence of brood leads to repletion, which in turn induces both quiescence and inherently greater longevity at a time when both are beneficial to survival. (See the review of bee nutrition and longevity by Maurizio, 1959.) The expectation of foraging life decreases in proportion to the age of the bee when it begins to forage; endogenous senescence therefore appears to play a part in limiting the life of workers, and they do not all die from accident alone (Ribbands, 1952). Queenless "indoor" bees, which are

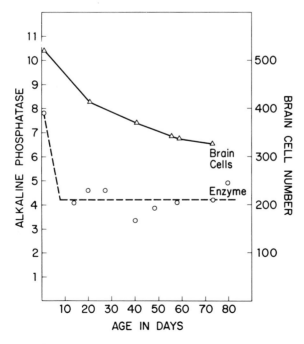

FIGURE 2.37 Alkaline phosphatase in whole body homogenates and brain cell number in the adult worker honey bee. (From Rockstein, 1953.)

not carrying out normal hive activities, live about 10 weeks (Rockstein, 1959). Whatever the facts concerning Gehirntod, this process of senescence appears to contain a major depletive element, combined, in all probability, with an element of mechanical damage. In this respect the senescence of worker bees conforms to a pattern that seems to be widespread in insects. Bees are, of course, a special case in that the far greater longevity of queens depends upon the developmental consequences of having been fed on "royal jelly." This substance has lately proved very effective in prolonging the life of pharmaceutical firms: there is no reason to think that it is otherwise effective in man.

Of all laboratory insects, the most popular is *Drosophila*. An immense volume of research on the longevity, pathology, and ultrastructural changes with age in this genus is reviewed in the critical bibliography of Lints (Soliman and Lints, 1976: 451 refs.) For a review of insect ageing generally see Clark and Rockstein (1964).

The formative papers in "geroentomology" are now mostly over 20 years old. With the advent of enzyme chromatography and electron microscopy, much new and chiefly negative information has accumulated.

In sum, the most gerontologically relevant changes in old insects concern pigment (as a possible measure of decline in defence against auto-oxidation) and mitochondrial morphology, with the appearance of "whorls," which may indicate decline in cytochrome oxidase (Webb and Tribe, 1974). Uncoupling of mitochondrial oxidative reactions (Sanadi, 1973; Chen, Warshaw and Sanadi 1972) has been found elsewhere during tissue ageing, but changes in mitochondrial morphology do not necessarily imply enzymatic or respiratory change (Wilson, et al., 1975).

In the area of pigment deposition, the work of Miquel (Miquel, et al., 1974a,b) has shown a steady pigment increase in *Drosophila* tissues, associated with lysosomal acid phosphatase activity, and accelerated by increased O_2 tension. Apart from these two useful model systems, however, the electron microscope has produced virtually nothing from the field of insect ageing which can be applied to the study of mammalian ageing processes—a disappointing conclusion in view of the immense amount of gerontological energy which has gone into the group, largely because of the ease of experiment which accompanies short life. A new geroentomology may soon emerge, however, aimed not so much at single-process models as at the identification of life-span control systems, neural and cytogenetic. These will not resemble the analogous systems in mammals, but the analogy will be instructive.

2.5.6   Molluscs

Pelseneer (1934) divides molluscs in the wild into annual species, pluriennial species with a short reproductive life, and pluriennial species with a long reproductive life. In some members of this last group, indeterminacy of life-span cannot be excluded. Most of the evidence is obtained from wild material. The combination of patterns appears analogous to that found in fish. Like fish, molluscs include short-lived forms, forms with a longer but apparently determinate life, and forms, especially among the larger pelecypods, which appear to have no maximum size.

The annual forms include many nudibranchs (Pelseneer, 1934, 1935) and probably most of the smaller freshwater species (*Paludestrina jenkinsi*—Boycott, 1936; *Ancylus*—Hunter, 1953). According to Boycott (1936), *Planorbis corneus* is the only British freshwater pulmonate which is not normally an annual. Many of these annual forms die immediately after reproduction. In *Viviparus contectoides* (van Cleave and Lederer, 1932) and *V. bengalensis* (Annandale and Sewell, 1921) the wild males live 1, and the females up to 3 years. In captivity (ldham kept male *V. contectus* for $4\frac{1}{2}$ and female for 5 years (Oldham, 1931), and living embryos were present at the time of death. Growth, judged by length, ceased in the second or third year of life. A number of other forms live for a maximum of 2 or 3 years in the wild, breeding during one or two seasons (*Lioplax*—van Cleave and Chambers, 1935; *Carychium,* 18 months—Morton, 1954; *Bithynia*—Boycott, 1936; Lilly, 1953; *Fossaria*—van Cleave, 1935; *Sphaerium*—Foster, 1932; *Teredo navalis*—Grave, 1928). Specimens of *Limnaea columella* kept in captivity under good conditions give a life-table showing a typical senile increase in force of mortality similar to that in *Drosophila* (Winsor and Winsor, 1935; Baily, 1931). The growth of *Limnaea* has been studied by Baily (1931) and Crabb (1929). Among rather longer-lived forms, Pelseneer (1934) found a complete cessation of shell growth and a decline in fertility with age in *Gibbula umbilicalis,* complete infertility being general at about 54 months, and the extreme life-span $4\frac{1}{2}$–5 years. In *Eulota fruticum* the relation of egg laying to age has been determined. According to Künkel, death takes place in captivity "when the germinal glands are exhuasted" (Künkel, 1928) (Figure 2.38). In *Physa gyrina* De Witt (1954) found a distinct postreproductive period, amounting to as much as 49 percent of the total life-span in mass culture, or 36 percent in isolation culture, the overall mean life-spans being 211 and 143 days respectively, while an individual *Limapontia,* normally an annual, lived a year in captivity after breeding (McMillan, 1947). Szabó and Szabó (1929–1936 *passim*) published a number of studies upon the "senescent" changes observable in the digestive gland and nervous system of *Agriolimax*: these, however, were inconstant from species to species, and a life-table (Figure 1.2) constructed from their data by Pearl and Miner (1935) shows a steady high mortality: it is probably that none of these slugs reached their maximum potential age.

Incidence of parasitic infection increases with age and size (*Bithynia*—Schäfer, 1953; *Littorina*—Moore, 1937). Wasting of the body tissues and

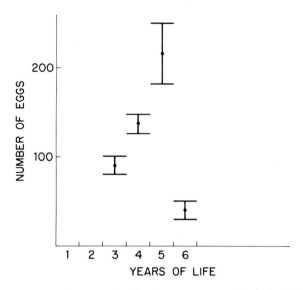

FIGURE 2.38   Egg production of *Eulota fruticum.* (From Künkel, 1928.)

fibrotic changes in the digestive glands are also described. Szabó and Szabó (Szabó, I., 1932a,b, 1935; Szabó, M., 1935a; Szabó and Szabó, 1929, 1930a, b, 1931a, b, 1934a) found degenerative changes and pigment deposition in ganglion cells of old specimens of *Helix* and *Agriolimax*. The most evident histological changes with age were in the digestive gland, which underwent fibrosis and loss of cells, but these changes were not consistent from species to species. Künkel (1928) wrote that *Eulota* dies "when the germinal glands are exhausted" and in old *Agriolimax* oocytes had almost wholly disappeared (Szabó and Szabó, 1935) perhaps as part of a progressive change to predominant maleness: in *Limnaea stagnalis appressa* under laboratory conditions "autopsy of senescent snails invariably discloses a badly atrophied liver, and the remaining organs, with the exception of the reproductive organs, are badly emaciated" (Noland and Carriker, 1946). There is evidently no basis here for any generalization.

Where there is a sex difference in the life-span of molluscs it appears to be in favor of the female, as in almost every other phylum (*Viviparus bengalensis*—Annandale and Sewell, 1921; *V. contectoides*—van Cleave and Lederer, 1932; *V. malleatus*—Niwa, 1950; *Lioplax*—van Cleave and Chambers, 1935; *Littorina scabra, L. obesa*—Sewell, 1924). But in *Chiton,* under wild conditions, Crozier (1918) found a progressive deficit of females in the higher age groups. The growth rate and final size of males are also more commonly the less, where a difference exists (*Hydrobia*—Rothschild and Rothschild, 1939); *Spirula* (Bruun, 1943) is an exception.

Very little evidence exists to relate the apparent senescence of short-lived molluscs in the wild to their growth pattern, or to their potential life-span in isolation. Van Cleave (1935) and Hoff (1937) considered that the snails *Fossaria* and *Viviparus* continue to grow throughout life; in these forms, according to van Cleave, the maximum size that is characteristic of the facies of any colony is secured by a combination of environmental effects on the growth rate and an endogenous process of senescence which kills the animal after the completion of its life-cycle, irrespective of its general somatic growth. In the large *Trochus niloticus*, Rao (1937) found no evidence of senile mortality, the upper limit of age being about 12 years in a wild population, and growth continuing at a decreasing rate throughout life. On the other hand, in spiral gastropods with an elaborate lip armature, growth must be *effectively* determinate so far as shell size is concerned. It has been suggested that in *Polygyra* growth in size ceases at lip formation, but body weight and shell thickness continue to increase (Foster, 1936). Przibram (1909) quoted observations by Taylor and de Villepoix that the gland cells of the mantle disappear in fully-grown specimens of *Helix aspersa, H. nemoralis,* and *Clausilia perversa.* The growth of molluscs is seasonal, and the development of the gonad appears in some forms to compete with, or inhibit, body growth—in oysters, the periods of shell growth occur in each year before and after spawning (Orton, 1928), while in *Hydrobia ulvae* parasitic castration leads to gigantism (Rothschild, 1935). The life-span of such giants was unfortunately not recorded. On a small series of *Limnaea columella* Baily (1931) found that shell growth ceased at or soon after sexual maturity, and that the shortest-lived individuals were those with the highest growth rates. A life-table was constructed for this species by Winsor and Winsor (1935) (Figure 2.40). Species whose life-cycle rarely exceeds 2 years may be capable of much longer life in captivity. Oldham (1930) kept *Planorbis corneus* in active reproduction up to 6 years of age. Many Helicidae, especially the smaller forms, have been regarded as annuals in the wild (Lamy, 1933; Pelseneer, 1935): the potential life of helicids and medium-sized land snails in captivity (excluding diapause, aestivation, and so on) may, however, reach or exceed 10 years (*Rumina decollata,* 12 years, *Helix spiriplana* 15 years—Vignal, 1919; *Helix pomatia,* 6–7 years—Künkel, 1916; 6–8 years—Cuénot, 1911; *H. hortensis,* 6 months). Deaths occurred chiefly in summer. The final intervals of this table do not seem to have been published, but Taylor (1907) states that specimens kept by Welch lived 8 or even 10 years; *Cepaea hortensis* was kept by Lang (1904) for over 9 years. Lamotte (1951), who carried out marking experiments, gives the mean wild longevity of *C. nemoralis* variously as 6–7 years and as 2–3 years (Lamotte, pp. 16, 100), but found that it was

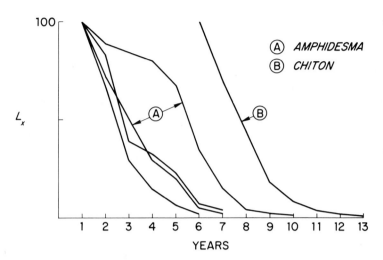

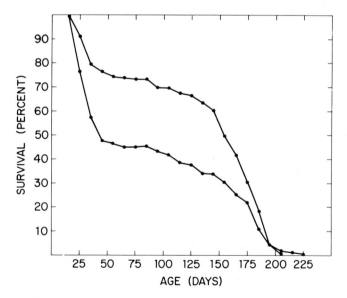

FIGURE 2.39 Survival curves of four wild populations of *Amphidesma ventricosum* drawn from the data of Rapson, 1952 (A); and of *Chiton tuberculatus* from the age of 6 years, from the data of Crozier, 1918 (B). (From Comfort, 1957a.)

FIGURE 2.40 Life-span of the pulmonate *Limnaea columella* at two different population densities. (From Winsor and Winsor, 1935.)

necessary to mark at least 1,000 specimens to be certain of recovering 10 after the lapse of two years.

In monocarpic forms, especially short-lived nudibranchs, there is some evidence that adult death is a normal sequel of spawning. "Parental death" due to the effects of reproduction occurs widely in insects and fish, though its physiology is not always plain. As in annual plants, death can in some cases be postponed indefinitely if reproduction is prevented. In female eels the life-span is determinate if the mating migration takes place, but not otherwise (Bertin, 1956), while non-spawners among minnows, which normally die after breeding, may live for a further year as unusually large specimens (Markus, 1934). Szabó (1932) found that mating shortened the life-span of *Agriolimax*: the effect of self-fertilization was less severe since fewer eggs were laid. There are no other experimental instances where the longer life of aquarium-bred snails can be shown to result from failure to breed. The amount of diversion of body activities into reproduction varies from species to species. Shell growth may be slowed or permanently stopped at maturity: Baily (1931) found that in the laboratory growth ceased with the onset of egg laying in *Limnaea columella* in other species the annual growth check coincides with spawning (*Pecten maximus*—Tang, 1941). It is more interesting from this point of view that parasitic castration produced by trematode infection of the gonad regularly induces gigantism in some species (*Hydrobia*—Rothschild, 1935; *Littorina neritoides*—Rothschild, 1941; *Zebrina detrita*—Boettger, 1953, 1953a). It has not been shown whether this is a hormonal effect, a sign of competition between somatic and gonadal requirements, or a specific growth stimulation by a product of the parasite. The life-span of such giants has not been described, and would be well worth noting. In general, heavily parasitized animals have their lives shortened, but any exception would have important epidemiological consequences. The power of inducing longer life might have evolutionary advantages to the parasite, equal to those of inducing large size and a consequently improved chance of being picked out by the secondary host.

The growth of the long-lived pluriennial lamellibranchs is in most cases indeterminate, in that it does not cease at a fixed adult size. There is, however, evidence that where mortality increases with age it may in some cases be size dependent, both in these forms and in some gastropods. In wild populations of annual and biennial molluscs there is no "plateau" at the end of the growth curve, and no relative accumulation of individuals in the large-size groups. Death occurs consistently in adults at an age when growth is apparently still in progress. Van Cleave (1935) first suggested that in *Fossaria modicella* attainment of a critical size might in itself lead to death from environmental causes. Hunter (1953) considered that relatively simple factors such as rate of stream flow and the growth of attached algae might determine the size at which adult *Ancylus* die. There is also a size effect in *Physa* and *Lymnaea* (Hunter, 1961).

Something similar occurs in several long-lived species, and in both cases it is open to a different interpretation. Fischer-Piette (1939) collected figures for the age and size of *Patella vulgata* from different sites, and found a definite inverse relation between growth rate and final age, judged by ring counting, in the different samples. Hopkins (1930) found that the oldest individuals of *Venus mercenaria* were usually not the largest. Some small specimens had as many as 40 growth-rings, and appeared to have grown abnormally slowly, while large shells rarely had more than 20 or 25. Colonies of *Siliqua patula* in California show twice the growth rate, but only half the final life-span, of the same species in Alaska (Weymouth and McMillin, 1931); Rapson (1952) found an abnormally high natural mortality in his fastest-growing colony of *Amphidesma* (Figure 2.39). This behavior closely resembles the results of experiment on animals that display "endogenous" senescence. It suggests that the life-span is fixed in terms of developmental program, rather than size alone, and that the rate of ageing is being modified by changes in nutrition and temperature. Although losses from selective predation often depend on size, the demonstration of any other environmental form of senescence due to pure size would be of great interest, for there is already a classical example of such a process in those fossil *Gryphaea* that finally became incapable of opening the shell (Westoll, 1950). A purely size-

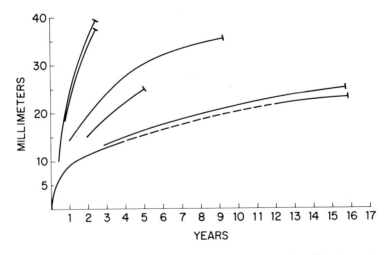

FIGURE 2.41   Growth in shell diameter and longevity of *Patella vulgata* in various stations, showing the short life of rapidly growing populations. (From Fischer-Piette, 1939.)

dependent effect does not seem the most probable general explanation of molluscan senescence, and the facts constitute strong evidence against regarding the life-span of any pluriennial molluscs as "indeterminate" in the same sense as that of actinians.

Growth continuing actively to the maximum recorded age has been found in many forms (*Cardium,* 16 years—Weymouth and Thompson, 1930; *Venus mercenaria,* 40 years—Hopkins, 1930; *Siliqua,* 14–16 years—Weymouth and McMillin, 1931; *Pecten jessoensis,* 8 years—Bazykalova, 1934; *Mya,* 7–8 years—Newcombe, 1935, 1936). The larger freshwater pelecypods, which have fewer enemies and are not subject to tidal disturbances, reach even greater ages.

The life-span of these freshwater mussels calls for special discussion. It has been widely studied because of their economic importance and depletion by fishing, but with inconclusive results, most of the argument turning on the interpretation of years (hybrid *H. hortensis* × *nemoralis,* 10 years—Cuénot, 1911), while *Oxystyla capax* has been revived from diapause after 23 years (Baker, 1934).

Even less is known about the longevity and liability to senescence of most marine gastropods. In *Acmaea dorsuosa* Abe (1932) found that growth continued in 15-year-old specimens from some localities, while in other localities an apparent specific size was reached at 5 years. Apparent specific size in certain colonies was also found by Hamai (1937) in *Patelloida grata.* The most suggestive evidence of a determinate life-span in limpets comes from Fischer-Piette's (1939) observations, which showed a definite inverse relationship between longevity, judged by growth rings, and rate of growth in different stations (Figure 2.41). This strongly suggests that a process of morphogenetic ageing is occurring at different rates depending on the rate of growth.

No increase in mortality with age has been demonstrated in many of the longest-lived pluriennials, the decline in their numbers being gradual, without any evidence of a sharp specific age. Crozier (1918a, b; Figure 2.39) obtained a survival curve for *Chiton tuberculatus* between 5 and 13 years, which is approximately logarithmic, and showed no sign of an age increase in mortality (younger ages could not be sampled on account of their habits). Rao (1937) found no increase in the mortality of *Trochus niloticus* up to 12 years. But in other species the specific age is well defined, and lies within the wild survival period. Some of these have a strikingly low adult mortality compared with small vertebrates. *Nucula turgida* shows only a very gradual decline in numbers until the 7th year, dying off thereafter to a limiting maximum age at about 11 years (Allen, 1952–1953): *Amphidesma ventricosum* begins its senile decline under favorable conditions at 4½ years and reaches a maximum age of about 10, 80 percent of yearlings surviving to 4 years (Rapson, 1952, Figure 2.39). The large Helices probably have survival curves both in the wild and in captivity of this type, which is that characterized by Teissier (1934), with a long initial plateau. *Eulota fruticum* has a specific age of about 6 years in captivity (Künkel, 1928). Welch (1901) collected forty specimens of *H. aspersa,* some of which were already adult; in captivity all survived at 15 months, 36 at 38 months, and 20, including two collected as adults, at 72 growth rings. There are apparently large differences in growth rate and wild longevity between species and in different stations. Some mussel populations show a combination of extremely slow and prolonged growth, long life-span, and low adult mortality which is perhaps unique in biology, but much of the evidence is inferential, especially for the European forms, and more experiment seems to be needed.

In several North American species annulus counts have been shown, on evidence already quoted, to be reasonably acceptable measures of age (Coker, et al., 1919–20; Isely, 1931). Washboard mussels (*Megalonaias gigantea*) with 53 and 54 such rings have been described, and even larger specimens exist, measuring as much as 280 mm in length. In the smaller species the growth rate has often declined so much by the 12th or 15th year that subsequent annuli cannot be counted satisfactorily (Matteson, 1948; Saldau, 1939).

It has long been suspected that *Margaritana margaritifera* has by far the longest life-span of any European species; ages of 60 or even 100 years in the wild have been inferred from its growth rate (von Hessling, 1859; Geyer, 1909; Israel, 1913; Korschelt, 1932). It forms rather ill-defined growth rings. Israel's estimate of 100 years is based in part on the extreme slowness of adult growth, but it also leans heavily on the finding of a shell marked "1851," which was still alive in 1911. This evidence gains a little credit from the habit among German pearlers of marking shells after partially opening them with a "key." Rubbel (1913) made a careful study of the growth of marked specimens over a 2-year period. He failed to detect consistent rings: the growth rate in length fell regularly with increasing size, from 1 mm/year in shells 60 mm long to 0.4 mm/year in shells 100 mm long. Assuming a 60-mm specimen to be at least 10 years old, Rubbel concluded that it should take another 20 years to reach 80 mm and a further 40 years to reach 100 mm. On this basis the natural life-span could not be less than 70–80 years.

The growth rate and size of *Margaritana* have been shown, however, to vary from place to place. Altnöder (1926) found that specimens from one locality bearing 20 annuli measured 11.6 mm in length, while from another they measured 12.4 mm with 60 annuli, and size relative to annulus number increased in a downstream direction. Altnöder accepts growth rings as a serviceable measure of age, having found that annuli produced during one year's observation in previously measured mussels agreed in breadth with the recently deposited "annual" rings.

Saldau (1939) from data obtained in the European part of Russia found that while growth in *Unio* continued in some waters after the 8th year, *M. margaritifera* was growing steadily without any evident falling-off in rate at the 13th year. Her age estimations also were based on rings, determined by transillumination. If the ages so obtained are correct, mussels in some rivers had reached 60 mm in length by 10 years of age and 70 mm by 13 years, while 13-year-olds in other rivers measured less than 50 mm. Ages over 13 years were not estimated, since "after this age the rings become too close." Brander (1956), while making no attempt to judge their ages, records a specimen of *M. margaritifera* 154 × 63 mm, and several others not much smaller.

The upper limit of life-span in other European Naiades cannot be determined with certainty from shell sculpture, because of the falling-off of growth at high ages. In some stations a virtual plateau of size is probably reached. In general, large shells represent a high growth rate rather than extreme age: from the counting of rings, the normal maximum (in *Unio* and *Anodonta*) is probably not much more than 20–30 years. Haranghy (Haranghy, et al., 1962) has described senile involutional changes in the gonad of *Anodonta*.

If the 100-year estimate of longevity in *M. margaritifera* is correct, it is the longest-lived invertebrate known, exceeding under wild conditions the 80- to 85-year record for the actinian *Cereus* in captivity (Ashworth and Annandale, 1904; Stephenson, 1935; Comfort, 1956). A life-span of this order in the wild would imply an exceedingly low adult mortality. Freshwater mussels are known to be attacked by rodents and birds, and *M. margaritifera* has also been fished for many centuries by man, often in a destructive manner. The same, however, could be said of the Pismo clam, for which an age of 53 years is recorded (Fitch, 1965)—this is a fishery species in which careful studies have been made. These ages are quite probably equalled by other large pelecypods.

The supposed longevity of *Tridacna* has already been mentioned, together with the fact that nothing whatever is known about its real life-span.

The pelecypods also illustrate the risks of purely ideal and mathematical representations of growth pattern. Pseudo-specific size from environmental causes is common. In *Siliqua* (Weymouth, 1931), some populations reach an apparent limiting size, cease altogether to grow thereafter, and die early: this, like Fischer-Piette's observation on limpets (1939), might suggest that a senile process is at work. Wild limpets apparently die while in active growth, but those that grow fastest die earliest (Figure 2.41). Other molluscan populations have growth records that, though fitted for practical purposes to an asymptotic curve, actually give observed readings in the highest age groups that lie well above such a curve, and indicate that in these groups growth is continuing (Weymouth, 1931). There is an obvious objection to the use of growth rings to measure age, however, if conclusions are then to be drawn about continuing growth. Arrest of growth lasting for years would leave no record of itself in this system of notation. The results obtained by the use of the ring method in pelecypods have so far been reasonably consistent (see Newcombe, 1936). The validity of growth rings as annual markers requires careful confirmation in each population examined, however (Haskings, 1954). Hopkins (1930) found that in *Venus mercenaria* growth was continuing actively at 20 years. The oldest specimens aged by growth rings were in general not the largest shells. Some small examples had reached an estimated age of 40 years, and appeared to have grown abnormally slowly.

2.6   Senescence in Wild Populations

Senescence as a potential part of the individual life-cycle is, as we have seen, widespread: in discussing the evolution of senile processes, however, it is important to know how far it really occurs in wild animals. The weight of evidence suggests that senescence in the wild is rare but not unknown. Its commonest form is undoubtedly the pseudo-senescence that follows reproduction, but genuine senescence analogous to that of man is occasionally reached, at least by individuals, while there are probably some forms in which it is normally reached. If our observation of animal life-cycles were confined to small birds and mammals in the wild, however, we should probably not recognize senescence as an entity except in ourselves.

2.6.1   Vertebrates

Although data from bird and small mammal populations have perhaps led to an overstatement of the case against "natural" senescence, old age is undoubtedly a relatively rare or very rare termination to the life-cycle of vertebrates studied in the field—as it is for man in societies where medical and economic conditions are bad. For large numbers of animal species, the typical curve is one in which a high or very high infant mortality rate is succeeded by a high adult mortality rate which does not increase with age. These species, even when they are capable of senescence, never reach it. This type of curve has been repeatedly demonstrated in population studies (see Lack, 1954); whereas in voles kept in the laboratory the survival curve approximates that of man (Leslie and Ranson, 1940, Figure 2.42), in wild voles (Hinton, 1925, 1926; Elton, 1942), and in *Peromyscus* (Burt, 1940) senescence is never observed, judging from the state of the teeth and bones of recent and fossil animals. In some populations the vole must be regarded as an annual (Elton, 1942). Tooth wear is a reliable index of age in short-tailed shrews, those over 2 years of age being edentulous, but age limitation by this mechanical form of senescence is more potential than actual since few survive

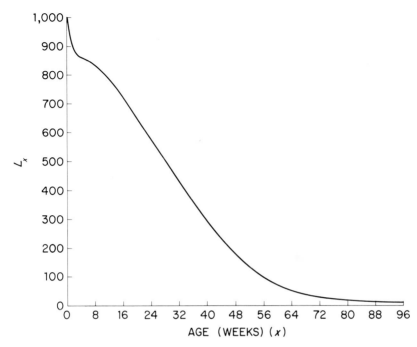

FIGURE 2.42   Smoothed survival curve for the vole *Microtus agrestis* in captivity. (From Leslie and Ranson, 1940.)

to exhibit it. They may survive in captivity up to 33 months (Pearson, 1945).

The log-linear pattern of decline in survivorship is highly characteristic of birds. It has been demonstrated in the blackbird, song thrush, robin, starling, and lapwing (Lack, 1943a, b, c); redstart (Buxton, 1950); American robin (Farner, 1945); and herring gull (Marshall, 1947). In a series of robins ringed by Lack (1943a), 111 out of 144 leaving the nest (77 percent) died in the first year. This compares with a maximum recorded age of 11 years, which is occasionally reached in the wild state. The succeeding annual mortality was at a steady rate approaching 50 percent. A survivorship curve for lapwings *(Vanellus vanellus)* calculated from 1,333 birds is closely fitted by a line corresponding to a constant mortality of 40 percent per annum (Kraak, et al., 1940; Lack, 1950). The rates of mortality for most birds that have been studied appear to fall between 30 and 60 percent per annum. Very much lower figures have been recorded for large sea birds such as cormorants (Kortlandt, 1942), in which the mortality was found to decline from 17 percent before fledging to an annual rate of 4 percent between the third and twelfth years. The annual mortality in one species of albatross (*Diomedea epomophora*) is only 3 percent. Such birds may well live to reach senescence, if their life-span is 50 years. But considerable evidence has accumulated, chiefly from ringing studies, to show that the expectation of life of some wild birds actually increases with age. Although the total of ringed birds recovered in Europe does not exceed 10,000 per year, a few individuals are known to have survived for longer than could be expected if the early mortality were maintained. R. Perry (1953) gives records of this kind (redwing— *Turdus musicus,* 17 + years; goldfinch, *Carduelis carduelis,* 16 + years; meadow pipit, *Anthus pratensis,* 13 years) all of them in species have mean annual survivals of the order of 50 percent (Lack, 1950). A ringed starling *(Sturnus vulgaris)* has been retaken after 18 years, and a herring gull after 36 (Pettingill, 1967). The probability of such records being obtained as a result of chance, bearing in mind how few birds are ringed, is very low indeed. An almost exactly similar situation has been observed in the human population of the Punjab, where, in spite of a very heavy early and adult mortality, very old individuals are not uncommon, and those who survive beyond middle life have an expectation of life comparable to that in Western Europe (Yacob and Swaroop, 1945). Bird survival curves in captivity closely resemble those of mammals (Comfort, 1962; Eisner and Etoh, 1967).

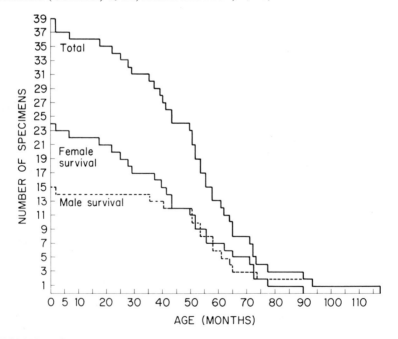

FIGURE 2.43   Survival curves for the Bengalese finch in captivity. (From Eisner and Etoh, 1967.)

In lizards, the wild mortality rate declines with increasing age (Sergeev, 1939): this result agrees with the ecological studies of Stebbings (Stebbings and Robinson, 1946; Stebbings, 1948) on *Sceleporus graciosus* in the wild. A very high proportion of the population was found to consist of lizards 6 to 9 years old (30 percent), and there were signs of a decreasing force of mortality with age. In some cases the decrease may be even steeper. In some vertebrates the enormous infant mortality would completely overshadow subsequent trends in any life-table based upon a cohort at birth: in the mackerel, for instance (Sette, 1943), survival to the 50-mm stage is less than 0.0004 percent.

There are a certain number of apparent instances where senescence occurs as a regular phenomenon in wild populations of animals, both vertebrate and invertebrate, quite apart from occasional records of "old" individuals (Bourlière, 1959). Murie (1944), from the examination of the skulls of 608 mountain sheep *(Ovis dalli)*, constructed a life-table in which the death rate was minimal between 1½ and 5 years of age, and climbed thereafter. The main deaths in old and young sheep appear to have been due to predation by wolves. The Arctic fin whales studied by Wheeler (1934) appeared to undergo an increase in mortality after the 15th year of age (in females); the apparent increase may, however, have been the result of the failure of the older specimens to return from their winter quarters to the regions where they can be caught and recorded. A good many larger carnivores and herding animals probably survive occasionally into old age in the wild state, though death must as a rule occur very early in the process of declining resistance. It is evidently impossible, in population studies, to assume either a constant mortality with age or a mortality increasing with increasing age, without some prior evidence of the behavior of similar forms.

The "normal" or "wild" pattern of mortality in man is, of course, an abstraction, since even man in modern urban society is, biologically speaking, living "in the wild," albeit after much social and behavioral adaptation. Early and primitive human societies almost certainly resembled in their ageing behavior those populations of animals that occasionally reach old age, and in which the force of mortality shows some decrease during middle adult life. This is the pattern one would expect in social animals, where the survival of certain experienced individuals has probably a positive survival value for the group, although in man the adaptation has been expressed in increasing capacity for abstract thought and social organization, rather than in increasing longevity per se. Although one may guess that early man occasionally reached the point at which his powers of homeostasis began to fail through age, he must have died through environmental pressure, like Murie's sheep, very early in the process. Out of 173 palaeolithic and mesolithic individuals whose age could be determined, only three (all males) appeared to have been older than 50 years, and none much older (Vallois, 1937). Palaeolithic man in the Chinese deposits normally died from violence at a presenile age (Wiedenreich, 1939). In rather more civilized societies, the fall in mortality with increasing age becomes more evident: according to Lack (1943a, 1954), the curve of mortality based on the ages given in Roman funerary inscriptions (MacDonnell, 1913) is much like that for birds. Hufeland's (1798) and Silbergleit's (Vischer, 1947) figures (Figure 1.7) illustrate further stages in the transition to the rectangular survival curve of modern societies in privileged countries: many other examples have been collected by Dublin and his fellow actuaries (1949).

2.6.2 Invertebrates

Senescence also occurs in the wild in some invertebrates, though it is often probably of the type of the "parental" deaths of shotten eels. Senescence in one form or another has been invoked to account for the fixity of size and

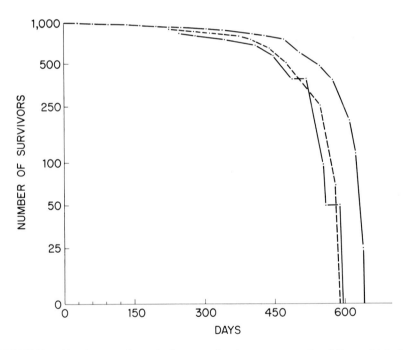

FIGURE 2.44   Corrected survival curves for three groups of ascidians which first appeared in August, September, and October 1957. · ——— ·: Group A, appearing in August; ·-----·: Group B, appearing in September; ·-------·: Group C, appearing in October. For the sake of clarity, curves *B* and *C* have not been carried back to the origin. (From Goodbody, 1962.)

life-span in some freshwater gastropods (Sewell, 1924; van Cleave, 1934, 1935). The figures of Fischer-Piette (1939), relating longevity inversely to growth rate in *Patella,* also suggest the operation of senescence. It very probably occurs in the long-lived sexual forms of social insects, such as termite primaries, and has been found to contribute to the mortality of worker bees (Ribbands, 1952). Among other insects, Jackson (1940) observed a factor of senescence in tsetse flies *(Glossina)* occurring only during the rainy season, when the life-span of the flies is longer. Dowdeswell, et al. (1940), infer the possibility of a decline in the viability of butterflies *(Polyommatus icarus)* throughout imaginal life. The position in insects is considerably complicated by the existence of specialized overwintering forms. Overwintering Gerrids show changes in the muscles that appear to precede natural death—mechanical wear of the rostrum, which occurs in old insects, is never far enough advanced to explain their decease (Guthrie, 1953, *personal communication*). Cladocera and Amphipoda, together with other small crustaceans, tend to exhibit constant specific age in the laboratory, and may also do so in the wild state. In a natural population of *Corophium volutator* (Watkin, 1941) the mortality in females rose sharply after maturity.

Several genera of rotifers also exhibit well-defined specific age in culture (Pearl and Doering, 1923; Pearl and Miner, 1935; Lansing, 1942, 1947a, b, 1948) and almost certainly undergo senescence with significant frequency in the wild state. A population of the tube-building *Floscularia* marked in the wild with carmine underwent a linear decline, followed by a steep increase in mortality in the final survivors (Edmonson, 1945a, b): the curve obtained in this marking experiment was not far different from those obtained in laboratory populations of rotifers.

3

Senescence in Protozoa

3.1 Senescence in Protozoan Individuals and Clones

Much theoretical study was devoted during the last century to the "immortality" of protozoans, and their insusceptibility to senescence, following the concepts put forward by Weismann. It was considered that in unicellular organisms generally, and in populations of metazoan cells undergoing division without differentiation, the product of a cell's division is always a pair of daughter cells having the same age status, and destined each to lose its identity in another division. This theory makes very important assumptions about the nature of the copying processes that underlie cell division. In the majority of cases to which it was applied, the assumptions are probably correct, although there seem to have been no direct experiments designed to show whether, in a given protozoan population, the diagram of lineages shows any tendency to segregate the deaths of individual cells towards its edges, as in a metazoan genealogy. The "immortality" of protozoa has been superseded by the study of stability in clones generally (see Ch. 9.4) but it remains of theoretical interest.

Weismann had been impressed (1882) that in protozoa there is no death because there is no corpse. "Natural death" of individuals (often apparently from strictly endogenous causes) does occur in protozoa, as Jennings (1945) has shown (see below); and the assumption that there is no unrenewable matter at cell division is not universally true; in many forms, especially those producing swarm spores, there may be a substantial corpse, at least as tangible as the rejected parental shell of the dividing radiolarian. This is less often demonstrably the case in somatic cells, and the analogy between strictly acellular organisms and tissue cells cannot now be wholeheartedly maintained: it is still generally held, however, that the outcome of a protozoan cell division is a pair of rejuvenated and infant cells rather than a mother and a daughter of different seniority.

The indeterminacy of cell lineages has on occasion been attacked with some ferocity, though on grounds of political philosophy rather than experimental evidence (Lyepeschinskaya, 1950). The question legitimately arises, however, particularly but not only in ciliates, how far the renewal of structures at mitosis is evenly distributed between the resulting cells (Taylor, 1958; Mortimer and Johnston, 1959; Eaves, 1973). Child (1915) noticed that in *Stentor* one of the progeny retains the old, while the other forms a new, peristome. From experiments he concluded that this made no difference to the age status of the inheritors, both being equally "young." The criterion of "youth," however, was high susceptibility to cyanide poisoning. The critical experiment of making a genealogical table to determine the order of death of the fission products over several generations on the pattern of Sonneborn's (1930) *Stenostomum* experiments does not appear to have been carried out.

True senescence, and a marked difference in age status between mother and progeny, certainly appears to occur in suctorians. Korschelt (1922) noticed this in several forms (*Acanthocystis, Spirochona, Podophrya,* etc.), while in *Tokophrya* the parent organism's life-span can be measured, and is increased by underfeeding (Rudzinska, 1952). In a far greater number of cases there are signs that the copying process at division only produces a new structure additional to one that already exists, not two new, or one new and one manifestly renovated, structure. The theoretical interest of this process (in *Euglypha*) and its bearing on protozoan "age" has been noticed before (Severtsov, 1934). In such cases, either the structure does not deteriorate with time, or it is maintained continuously during life, or its possession must ultimately confer a disadvantage on one or other of the division products.

Whereas in some protozoa organelles, axostyles, flagella, and cilia are visibly resorbed or shed at fission, and new ones produced for each fission product, in others, especially in ciliates, maternal organelles, flagella and other structures are shared between the progeny, being taken over by one daughter cell while copies are developed in the other. Of two closely related species of *Spirotrichonympha* infesting termites, for example, one divides longitudinally in the normal flagellate manner, while in the other division is transverse, the anterior daughter receiving all the extranuclear organelles of the parent cell except the axostyle, while new organs are formed for the posterior daughter. The axostyle is resorbed (Cleveland, 1938). The possibility that the "inheritance" of organelles may modify the age status of the inheritor certainly merits re-investigation.

A large part of the literature included in the bibliographies of senescence deals with the presence or absence of "ageing" in protozoan clones. Maupas (1886) appears to have been the first to draw an analogy between somatic ageing in metazoa and the behavior of protozoan populations. He predicted that such populations would display a life-cycle including a phase analogous to metazoan senescence, and ending in the death of the population, unless nuclear reorganization by conjugation, or some similar mechanism, brought about the "rejuvenation" of the stock. For many years a vigorous competition was conducted between protozoologists in seeing how many asexual generations of *Paramecium, Eudorina,* and similar creatures they could rear. In the course of this process much nonsense was written about "potential immortality," but a great deal was learnt about protozoan reproduction and culture methods. It became evident that some clones deteriorate and others, including somatic cells such as fibroblasts in tissue-culture, do not. Calkins (1919) in a classical study showed that strains of *Uroleptus mobilis* kept in isolation culture without conjugation underwent senescence characterized by a falling-off of growth potential, degeneration of nuclei, and ultimate loss of micronucleus. These strains ultimately became extinct. Conjugation at any stage of the process, and probably also endomixis, produced an immediate reversion to normal, regardless of whether the conjugates came from old or young isolation strains. Sonneborn (1938) succeeded, by selection of strains of *Paramecium* in which endomixis was long delayed, in breeding a race which no longer exhibited any kind of nuclear reorganization. These strains invariably died after 4 or 5 months. Rizet (1953) has recently reported similar results with an Ascomycete kept in continuous vegetative reproduction, and Muggleton and Danielli produced spanned stains of Amoeba by inhibiting growth (1968). On the other hand, Bélár (1924) maintained *Actinophrys sol* in isolation culture, without the occurrence of paedogamy, for 1,244 generations over 32 months, and observed no decline in the rate of cell division. Beers (1929) kept *Didinium nasutum* for 1,384 generations without conjugation or endomixis. Hartman (1921) kept *Eudorina elegans* in active asexual reproduction for 8 years. Woodruff's oldest culture of *Paramecium aurelia* persisted for over 15,000 generations but was undergoing autogamy. The conclusion must be that some clones are stable while others are not.

More light is thrown on this problem by the work of Jennings (1945) upon clones of *Paramecium bursaria.* He found that in this species the life-cycle fell into well-defined phases of growth, sexual reproduction by conjugation with other clones, and decline. The length and character of these phases differed substantially from clone to clone. In the decline phase the death of individual cells, and especially of the progeny of conjugation between old clones, becomes very common. The vitality and viability of the progeny of conjugation, even when the conjugant clones are young, varies greatly, and a very high proportion of ex-conjugants normally die. This mortality is highest among the progeny of conjugation between related clones. Of 20,478 exconjugants, 10,800 (52.7 percent) died before undergoing their fifth successive cell division, while 29.7 percent died without dividing at all. Most conjugations produced some nonviable clones, some weakly clones capable of limited survival, and a few exceptionally strong clones, some of which appeared capable of unlimited asexual reproduction. It is from these strong races that the population of laboratory cultures is normally obtained.

Jennings concluded as follows:

> Death did not take origin in consequence of organisms becoming multicellular . . . it occurs on a vast scale in the Protozoa, and it results from causes which are intrinsic to the organism. Most if not all clones ultimately die if they do not undergo some form of sexual reproduction. . . . Rejuvenation through sexual reproduction is a fact . . . yet conjugation produces, in addition to rejuvenated clones, vast numbers of weak, pathological or abnormal clones whose predestined fate is early death. The rejuvenating function of conjugation is distinct from, and in addition to, its function as a producer of variation by redistribution of genes. Among the clones produced (by conjugation) there are seemingly, in some species, some clones of such vigor that they may continue vegetatively for an indefinite period, without decline or death (Jennings, 1945).

Some authors have regarded the increased proportion of weak and nonviable conjugants of old clones as the outcome of an accumulation of unfavorable mutations. Comparable effects (Banta, 1914; Banta and Wood, 1937) have been described in clones of *Daphnia*. This was long since suggested by Raffel (1932) on the basis of *Paramecium* experiments. The type of lineal "senescence" that occurs in *Paramecium* is in some respects analogous to the processes that are familiar in inbred stocks reproducing sexually, for *Drosophila* to domestic cattle (Regan, et al., 1947), and described under the general title of inbreeding depression, but differs from it in that in clones the accumulation of mutations, rather than the segregation of existing genes and the loss of the advantages of heterozygy, have been held to be involved. The mortality among the progeny of autogamy in *Paramecium* is directly related to the length of time during which autogamy has been previously suppressed (Pierson, 1938). The time scale of the group "life-cycle" is modified by a great many physical and chemical agents; on the other hand, methylcholanthrene, normally a mutagenic agent, delays the decline of *Paramecium* clones (Spencer and Melroy, 1949). Sonneborn has found (Sonneborn and Schneller, 1960a, b) that clonal senescence in *Paramecium* depends, as other workers have foreseen (Fauré-Frémiet, 1953), on the peculiar mechanism in ciliates whereby the germinal and vegetative functions of the nucleus are divided between two separate structures. When *Paramecium* divides after a sexual process, the new nucleus of each daughter cell again divides into two. One of these products, the micronucleus, which reaches the anterior end of the cell, has the normal diploid number of chromosomes, and is apparently concerned solely with conveying the genotype: it is, in other words, the "germ plasm." The other portion, the macronucleus, controls the metabolism of the cell. It becomes highly polyploid, and at subsequent cell divisions, while the micronucleus divides evenly in the normal manner of nuclei, the macronucleus distributes its chromosomes at random to the daughter macronucleus arising from it. Because of the enormous number of sets which it contains, every cell in the earlier divisions has a fair chance of getting its quota, but with the passage of time more and more daughters receive an unbalanced set and a reduced physiological repertoire, and a chromosome once lost cannot be restored from the micronucleus except by sexual division—conjugation or autogamy. In the later stages of clonal senescence even sexual division is affected and abnormal or non-viable products increase. Sonneborn suggests that this is not due to the accumulation of mutations, since it can be prevented by periodic autogamy, even though this does not alter the genotype: it appears to be due to injury inflicted upon the micronucleus itself through the abnormal intracellular conditions produced by the defective macronucleus. In ciliates the germ plasm has to live in the cell where the processes of somatic maintenance are carried out, and it is therefore unusually exposed (Sonneborn, 1974). This is probably a unique situation—it does not even apply in other ciliates—and the division of function between vegetative and germinal nuclei is confined to this group. The existence of presumed cytoplasmic mutations, although there is no evidence to relate them to metazoan senescence as such, might be far more relevant to it than studies of protozoan clones. A kindred subject, that of somatic aneuploidy, is discussed in Ch. 6.4.3. It is in any case probably misleading to identify the decline of protozoan cultures with the metazoan senescence which it superficially resembles; it is doubtful if analogies can properly be drawn between acellular organisms and metazoan cells, and the only relevance of the whole question of "ageing" in protozoan clones to ageing in the metazoan body lies in the light it might possibly throw upon the effects of cell division in renewing expendable enzyme systems and organelles. There is no special reason, upon the present evidence, why the "senescence" of *Paramecium* should continue to figure as extensively as it has done in treatises devoted to gerontology. Nanney (1974), in reviewing much recent work on clonal changes in longevity, structural fidelity, and macronuclear composition in ciliates, draws attention to the capacity of these organisms for "temporal regulation" over intervals of a few dozen to several hundred cell divisions and their possible use of random events to measure biological time. There may here be analogies to the behavior of somatic cells in situ, but it is not clear what they are.

The "senescence" of some lines of plants in vegetative propagation apparently depends on the accumulation of exogenous viruses that hamper vigor (Crocker, 1939)—other agriculturally important varieties have been propagated vegetatively for years or centuries without deterioration. The accumulation of exogenous viruses itself raises interesting questions with regard to the possible accumulation of other, endogenous, intra- or extranuclear self-propagating materials.

Not all senescence or degeneration in clones, however, can be put down to the peculiarities of protozoa or to the action of viruses. A striking example of such a degeneration was studied at Oxford by K. G. McWhirter, to whom I am much indebted for his unpublished observations on it. This is the condition called "June Yellows," which affects strawberry plants propagated by runners, and impairs the formation of chloroplasts. It appears simultaneously in all plantations of a clone, even when they are geographically separated, and progresses in jumps, all the plants of the same clonal (but not individual) age passing synchronously from stage to stage. Usually in the end the clone dies out. The condition cannot be transmitted to adult plants by grafting. Transmission to seedlings is ambilinear through both egg cell and pollen. In the progeny of crosses between clones at different stages of degeneration it is matroclinous: seedlings of very degenerate "mothers" deteriorate most rapidly. As a clone degenerates, the tendency to transmit "yellows" to its offspring increases. The factor or factors remain latent in some clones, but "yellows" may appear after varying intervals in some of the selfed or crossed seedlings obtained from these clones, thus showing a latency reminiscent of that of the presumed oncogenic plasmagenes. This similarity has been pointed out before (Darlington, 1948; Darlington and Mather, 1949).

The behavior of this degeneration is like that of a mutation which is in part cytoplasmically controlled. Such conditions are characterized by a lag phase, by simultaneous appearance in all the members of a clone, noninfectivity, passage through a series of stable phenotypic stages, and interaction with growth and reproductive hormones. In some of McWhirter's material, "yellows" appeared to be aggravated during the flowering period, although it may occur in seedlings long before flowering.

4

The Influence of Genetic Constitution on Senescence and Longevity

4.1   Inheritance of Life-Span

4.1.1   General

It is evident in any comparison of laboratory stocks that differences of specific age are to some degree "inherited" (Pearl and Parker, 1922; Gonzales, 1923; Gruneberg, 1951), but detailed genetic knowledge of the manner of their inheritance is not plentiful. Much variation in life-span occurs between inbred lines. This variation is often related to a single heritable predisposition to die of cancer, renal disease, or some other single cause: in these cases it is often short life, not long life, which is capable of genetic selection in the homozygote. Bittner (1937) showed that in some cases it is possible to transpose the longevities of strains of mice by cross-suckling. In other cases, secondary causes, such as restricted capacity for activity in deformed stocks, affect the life-span. In a stock of mice bred by Strong (Strong, 1936; Strong and Smith, 1936) longevity increased the apparent incidence of disease by allowing animals to reach the cancer age. Two factors appear at first sight to be involved in inherited longevity: absence of genetic predisposition to specific causes of death, and a less definite quantity ("vigor") which contributes to Darwinian fitness because it is usually expressed both in fertility and in longevity. It is by no means certain that these factors are distinct. "Vigor" itself may in fact represent either the covering up of deleterious recessives by heterozygosis, or a state of overdominance, in which the heterozygote is inherently more vigorous than either homozygote.

Hereditary factors in human longevity have often been sought. Pearl and Pearl (1934a, b) found, for instance, that the summed ages at death of the six immediate ancestors of centenarians and nonagenarians were significantly greater than in a control series of the relatives of individuals not selected for longevity. 86.6 percent of long-lived (over 70) subjects had at least one long-lived parent, while 48.5 percent of nonagenarians and 53.4 percent of centenarians had two such parents, all these figures being significantly higher than in the control series. Kallman and Sander (1948, 1949) found that in 1,062 pairs of twins the mean difference in longevity between dizygotic twin individuals was twice as great as in monozygotics. These and other studies indicate that longevity is "hereditary," but unfortunately give little light on its genetics. When mares were grouped by parental longevity, the calculated means show differences of less than twice the standard error in favor of the groups with one long-lived parent; 113 mares with two long-lived parents had a mean expectation of life at 4 years of 18.07 ± 0.58 years, which is significantly more than the global mean, or the mean for any other group (Comfort, 1958a). Beeton and Pearson (1901) studied the longevity records

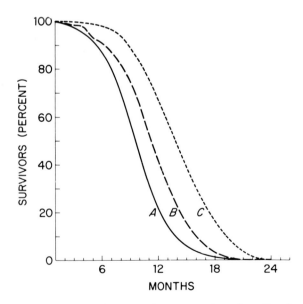

FIGURE 4.1   Survival curves of mice in laboratory culture, breeding females. Curve *A* based on 241 *dba* females, curve *B* on 730 Bittner albinos, curve *C* on 1,350 Marsh albinos. (From Gruneberg, 1951.)

of Quaker families, and found that the sib-sib correlation of longevity was nearly twice the parent-offspring correlation, in those individuals who died at 21 years of age or later, but that there was a far lower sib-sib correlation between those dying as minors. Haldane (1949) has pointed out that this is the type of correlation that would be expected where the heterozygote is fitter in the Darwinian sense than either homozygote: insofar as natural selection operates to eliminate homozygosis, not to promote it, such fitness must imply a higher correlation between sibs in an equilibrium population than between parent and child. In any case, the degree of parent-child correlation observed by Beeton and Pearson is only a quarter of that between parental and filial statures in comparable studies. The non-inheritance of "shortevity" from causes such as cardiovascular disease is a major factor in man (Hammond, et al., 1971).

> It will readily be seen that a vast number of those who attained a very old age passed through life remarkably free from disease; many never were ill, never took medicine, retained the powers of body and mind until the latest period, and seemed to sink suddenly into the arms of death without passing through any period of decay and decrepitude. (van Oven, 1853).

Dublin and his colleagues (1949) have summarized most of the historic studies on the inheritance of longevity in man. They conclude that the popular idea of inheritance as a factor in longevity is probably correct, that the evidence from actuarial studies is heavily vitiated by all kinds of environmental influences, and that the order of advantage to the sons of long-lived fathers is small compared with the secular increase in life-span during recent generations. The difference in life expectation at 25 years between those with better and poorer parental longevity records is between 2 and 4 years—this compares with a gain of 6.7 years in the general expectation of life at 25 years in the United States between 1900 and 1946. "It may be well, as has been suggested, to seek advantages in longevity by being careful in the choice of one's grandparents, but the method is not very practicable. It is simpler and more effective to adapt the environment more closely to man" (Dublin, et al., 1949).

It does not follow from these considerations that longer life cannot be obtained in a given population by selective breeding, and in mice this has, in fact, been done (Strong and Smith, 1936). There may well be single-gene characters where the homozygote is significantly longer lived. "Vigor," on the other hand, which is a correlate of both longevity and fertility, and hence of Darwinian fitness, is likely in most cases to be an expression of heterozygosis, and one would not expect to be able necessarily to produce abnormally long-lived animals by inbreeding long-lived parents.

Agricultural genetics, like natural selection, has for the most part attempted to increase lifetime production averages by increasing early output of eggs or offspring. Greenwood (1932) found that the fertility and hatchability of hens' eggs decline with age of the parent to such an extent that attempts to improve the stock by breeding from long-lived birds were economically impracticable. Apart from the obvious difficulty of breeding for long life in any animal with a substantial postreproductive period, which involves rearing all the progeny of large numbers of animals throughout life, the consequence of inbreeding per se, and the tendency of inbred laboratory stocks to reach a very stable equilibrium life-span (Pearl and Parker, 1922) militate against any such experiment. In Pearl's own experiments (Pearl, 1928) the long- and short-lived *Drosophila* segregates were identified in the F₁ by subsidiary, anatomical characters known to be associated with the desired lines. In *Drosophila subobscura* of the structurally homozygous Küssnacht strain, which had been in culture for about 3 years, and had reached an equilibrium life-span considerably shorter than that of wild-caught flies, breeding for eight generations over 1 year exclusively from eggs laid after the 30th day of parental life produced no significant alteration in mean imaginal longevity (Comfort, 1953) (Figure 4.2).

The inheritance of long life in man is presumably bound up with the inheritance of "general health" (Pearson and Elderton, 1913; Pearl, 1927), an element that is not more susceptible to analysis than "vigor," though it has been partially described in terms of response to stress (Selye, 1946). Robertson and Ray (1920) found that in a population of mice the relatively long-lived individuals formed a stable subgroup, displaying the least variation and the highest resistance to disturbing factors. In such a group the growth rate tends to be a measure of "general health," and rapid rather than retarded growth correlates with longevity. In other studies on groups of animals living under standardized conditions, rate of growth and length of life have been found to vary independently (Sherman and Campbell, 1935). The relation between growth rate and vigor in a mixed population has to be distinguished from the effect of growth retardation by dietary means in a homogeneous population; here the retarded growers live longer. As McCay (1952) points out, much early work on the relation between growth rate and longevity was vitiated by this confusion in experimental planning. The field was reviewed by Maynard Smith (1965).

4.1.2   Parental Age

The *age of the mother* is known in certain cases to modify the longevity of her offspring. This influence apparently includes a wide range of dissimilar effects, some strictly "genetic," and others operating at various stages in the process of embryogenesis, or, in mammals, on into lactation. Certain of these

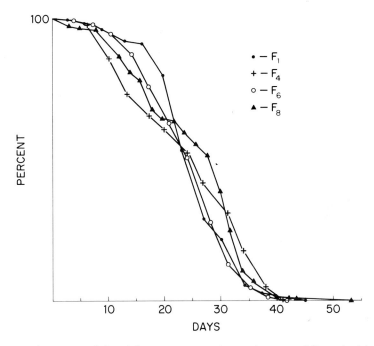

FIGURE 4.2 *Drosophila subobscura,* strain K. Survival curves of flies raised in each generation from eggs laid by adults which had passed the 30th day of imaginal life. (From Comfort, 1953.) Compare with Figure 4.3.

effects appear only in the F_1, while others, like the factor described by Lansing in rotifers, which leads to a decreasing life-span in successive generations of clones propagated exclusively from old individuals, appear to be cumulative and reversible.

The general question of maternal age effects in genetics is beyond the scope of this book. It has been reviewed (Miner, 1954; Parsons, 1964). In mammals the age of the mother exerts an influence on the vigor of the progeny that appears to vary greatly in direction and extent, even within a species. Sawin (in Miner, 1954) found that in one strain of rabbits, the early (under 6 months) mortality was lowest in the progeny of young mothers, and increased throughout maternal life, while in another larger strain it reached a minimum in the progeny of mothers 18 months old. These changes were not correlated with any differences in lactation or maternal weight. Suntzeff, et al. (1962) found that in mice there was no decline in longevity on repeated breeding from old mothers, but there was a significant increase in the age at which daughters became pregnant. Jalavisto (1950, 1959) found evidence that in man the expectation of life decreases with increasing maternal, but not paternal, age. The percentage of abnormal offspring is greatest in litters born to young guinea pigs (Wright, 1926) and elderly women (Murphy in Miner, 1954). It is possible that the association of mongolism with high parental age is a reflecton not of increasing fetal abnormality, but a decrease to the point of viability in an abnormality which, at younger maternal ages, is lethal (Penrose in Miner, 1954). Other workers have attributed it to accelerated maternal ageing (Emanuel, et al., 1972)—not judged, however, by actuarial criteria— where a defective child is born to a young mother. In some celebrated experiments upon mouse leukemia, McDowell and his co-workers showed that when susceptible males are crossed with resistant females, the age of onset of leukemia in the hybrid F_1 is significantly retarded in mice born to, or suckled by, old as compared with young mothers. At the same time, the mean longevity of mice that die of causes other than leukemia is also greatest in the progeny and nurslings of old mothers (McDowell, et al., 1951). Strong (in Miner, 1954) has described a factor influencing the latent period of sarcoma production after injection of methylcholanthrene into mice, which appears, like Lansing's rotifer longevity factor, to be cumulative—a line derived from seventh to ninth litters in each generation had a significantly increased and increasing latent period compared with a line derived from first and second litters. Unlike Lansing's effect, this increase has not been shown to be reversible in the progeny of young members of the "old" line. There is at present no evidence in mammals of any cumulative disadvantage in longevity accruing to "youngest sons of youngest daughters." In this connection Strong has, however, stressed on a number of occasions the need for further information on the relation between longevity and cumulative parental age in human genealogies. Such information is unfortunately hard to come by, and no large-scale study has yet been published. Comfort (1953) failed to find a comparable effect in *Drosophila,* but it was found by O'Brian (1961) and by Lints and Hoste (1974). In houseflies the 30-day mortality of female rises from 50 percent among offspring of 4- to 5-day-old parents to 90–95 percent in offspring from eggs laid at 27 days of age (Rockstein, 1958). The longevity of males was not affected. In *Drosophila,* Parsons (1962) found that variability in egg length and bristle characters increases with high maternal age. Lansing's effect has also been sought in the parthenogenetic Cladocera. In *Moina* it can occur, but is prevented by inositol or by giving liver extract (Murphy and Davidoff, 1972). The age of the mother affects the rate of development, and probably the longevity, of young *Daphnia.* Green (1954) found that the size of *Daphnia* at birth determines the instar in which maturity occurs, the largest becoming mature earliest. The birth size itself depends upon maternal age, being highest (in *D. magna*) in the third brood. Since the pre-mature phase is the part of the life-cycle in which most variation occurs, the mature phase being usually of fixed length, early developers might be expected to be significantly shorter-lived than late. Fritsch (1956) compared the longevity under carefully standardized conditions of successive generations of *Daphnia* raised wholly from first, third, and sixth hatchings, and found no significant trend in any of the orthoclones, the mean life-span in all remaining at about 30 days.

The critical issue with regard to parental-germinal theories of ageing is the presence or absence of a *paternal* age effect. The Stud Book could be expected to yield useful material for such studies. The search for parental age effects on the life-span of man is complicated by the high correlation between ages of spouses (Sonneborn, 1960; Jalavisto, 1959); there is no such correlation between ages of sire and dam in horse breeding, and both mares and stallions commonly remain at stud to advanced ages.

Vitt (1949) claimed that the longevity and racing performance of thoroughbred horses are substantially influenced by the age of both dam and sire, and that impairment of vigor by the use of old breeding stock is cumulative. He found that in a sample of 100 mares from vol. 1 of the General Stud Book, the progeny of dams 12 years old or less developed more slowly, judged by the age at first foaling, and lived longer ($e_{x=4} = 19.5$ years) than the progeny of dams aged 13 or more ($e_{x=4} = 16.4$ years). Absolute figures and standard errors are not cited, and it is not clear whether the estimates are corrected for losses or based on the distribution of recorded deaths alone. Vitt also compared the fertility and racing form of foals by old and young stallions, and concluded that there was an equally marked paternal age effect, the optimal performance being reached by the foals of stallions 8–16 years old out of mares 6–13 years old. Rather similar views have been expressed by other Russian mammal breeders (Eidrigevits and Polyakov, 1953; Isupov, 1949; Ponomareva and Spitskaya, 1953; Pospelov, 1952; Zamyatin, et al., 1946).

In a large series of Stud Book figures, the lives of mares were distributed (a) by age of dam at foaling, (b) by age of sire at covering, one year earlier, (c) by age of dam at foaling and sire at covering, where these fell in the same grouping interval. Of 1,492 lives, 1,342 were scored and grouped by age of dam, 1,355 by age of sire, and 719 by both. (Comfort 1958a, b; 1959b, c). There was no significant difference in expectation of life between foals of mares under and over 13 years of age (under 12, $e_{x=4} = 16.89$; over 13, $e_{x=4} = 16.86$ years). With further subdivision the progeny of the oldest mares had the shortest life-spans, but the largest difference was less than twice its standard error. Still smaller differences were obtained for the same lives grouped by paternal age alone. Of the 719 lives grouped by age of both parents, those whose dam and sire were under 13 years old lived slightly longer (17.39 ± 0.36) than those whose parents were over 13 (16.45 ± 0.48;

$t \neq 2.3$, $0.02 > P > 0.01$), and the difference was greater in the extreme segments of these groups (dam and sire < 9, 17.91 ± 0.47; > 16, 15.71 ± 0.83; $t \neq 2.3$, $0.02 > P > 0.01$). This difference is much smaller than that described by Vitt (1949) from maternal age alone, and is of the order of the difference between cohorts.

In a second series, the longest-lived group were the progeny of parents of 16 years and over, but the standard error was very large (17.26 ± 1.09): the 220 animals that were the progeny of two young parents had numerically the shortest life-spans (16.51 ± 0.52); none of the differences was significant, and all were in the reverse direction to those in the 1875–1880 sample.

One hundred twenty-one mares gotten during or after their sire's 20th year by 3 long-lived stallions had a slightly, but not a significantly, higher expectation than the global mean (16.65 ± 0.57). Only 41 mares were got by the 3 selected stallions in or after their 16th year upon dams 16 years old or more; these had a mean expectation of life of 16.29 ± 0.94 years. By combining these mares with all the progeny in other samples of parents 16 years old or over, we obtained 154 lives, with $e_{x=4} = 16.45 \pm 0.62$ years, which is less than any of the three global means, but not significantly so. These results, taken as a whole, seem to afford no evidence of any consistent effect of parental age on the longevity of mares.

4.2   Heterosis or Hybrid Vigor

Abnormally long-lived animals can regularly be produced by crossing certain pure lines, not themselves unusually long-lived, the effect being greatest in the hybrid F_1 and their offspring and declining rapidly on subsequent inbreeding. This is, in fact, the simplest method of increasing the specific age in many already inbred laboratory and domestic animals. Striking examples of this effect (heterosis) in increasing longevity have been recorded in mice. Gates (1926) by crossing Japanese waltzing with "dilute brown" strains produced a generation which was still actively breeding at 2 years of age. Chai (1959) gives details of the longevity of such crosses. "Supermice" produced by heterosis develop precociously, reach a large size, and remain in active reproduction much longer than their parents, thereby exhibiting a combination of rapid growth with increased longevity analogous to that of the rapid growers described by Robertson and Ray (1920). An example of the same effect in *Drosophila* is shown in Figure 4.3. The greater longevity of goldfinch-canary mules compared with the parent species is apparently well known to aviarists, and such techniques of crossing are of widespread agricultural and economic importance when applied to sheep or to plants. Vetukhiv (1957) (Figures 4.4, 4.5) has shown that in *Drosophila* there is considerable heterosis in crosses between natural populations from different places.

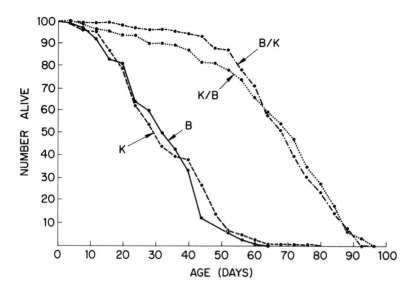

FIGURE 4.3   *Drosophila subobscura,* hybrid vigor and longevity. Survival curves for the inbred lines B and K, and for the reciprocal hybrids between them (sexes combined). (From Clarke and Maynard Smith, 1955.)

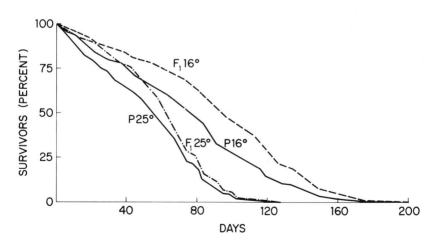

FIGURE 4.4   Survival curves of geographic populations of *Drosophila pseudoobscura* and their hybrids. Summarized data for all parental populations and for all F_1 hybrids at 16 and 25°C. Solid lines indicate parental populations; dashed lines, F_2 hybrids. (From Vetukhiv, 1957.)

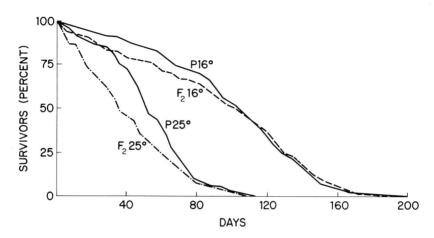

FIGURE 4.5   Survival curves of geographic populations of *Drosophila pseudoobscura* and their hybrids. Summarized data for all parental populations and F₂ hybrids at 16 and 25°C. Solid lines indicate parental populations; dashed lines, F₂ hybrids. (From Vetukhiv, 1957.)

The existence and magnitude of this effect should always be borne in mind in the planning of experiments on the life-span of animals drawn from closed laboratory stocks—such work can produce very seriously misleading results if unrecognized heterosis takes place. If an experiment in which the longevity of generations is compared begins with hybrid progeny, marked inbreeding depression can shorten the life-span of the succeeding generations if genetical precautions are not taken.

A fuller study of longevity in hybrids might provide useful information on the nature of "constitutional vigor" in relation to growth rate. The effect is variously explained. Some of the possible complications of heterosis in relation to the criteria of vigor are indicated by the findings of Rutman (1950, 1951), who compared the rates of methionine uptake in liver slices from a fast- and a slow-growing strain of rats. The methionine replacement rate in slices derived from the fast-growing strain was almost double that in the slow, but the growth rate of the slow strain could be made to approach that of the fast by transposing the litters during suckling, and appeared to be controlled by a milk-borne factor. Interstrain hybrids at first showed a growth pattern like that of the mother, but later followed that of the faster-growing strain.

Although by a very elegant experiment J. and S. Maynard Smith (1954) showed that in certain cases at least heterosis appears to result from orthodox heterozygy, in a number of instances cytoplasmic and environmental factors also appear able to evoke vigor. This is largely a reflection of the very heterogeneous character of "vigor." Borisenko (1939, 1941) reported an increase in vigor in the progeny of *Drosophila* matings where the inbred parents were reared under different environmental conditions. This observation does not appear to have been repeated. The question of the induction of vigor by non-genic means was at one time a favored field of ideological anti-Mendelians (Kurbatov, 1951; Hašek, 1953, etc.), but by no means all the positive results come from this school. As far back as 1928, Parkes observed that mice suckled by rats exhibited an extraordinary overgrowth, which results simply from excessive nutrition. Marshak (1936) found evidence of a maternal cytoplasmic factor influencing the increase of growth rate due to heterosis in mice. The increased "vigor" in progeny of pure-line ova transplanted to hybrid mothers (Kurbatov, 1951) is also found in transplanted fetuses (Venge, 1953). Hašek claimed (1953) that when parabiosis is carried out between Rhode Island and Leghorn embryos in the egg, by an ingenious technique, the pullets occasionally show even greater vigor than the progeny of R.I.R. × Leghorn crosses. The lamentable story of Michurinism should not obscure the fact, stressed in his lifetime by J. B. S. Haldane, that the last word has yet to be said on the nature of induced vigor, and that this can be of more than one kind. The whole problem is one which might be of considerable interest to gerontology, since in some cases "vigor" appears capable of induction postconceptually, or even postnatally. It is important to notice, however, that there is no clear evidence at present to show that the vigor and longevity obtainable by true heterosis are greater than those existing in *wild* strains. Heterosis should be regarded, in all probability, as the restoration of "wild" vigor, whether by restoring heterozygy or by other processes, in lines that have lost that vigor through inbreeding. How far the results of heterosis can be superior to those of wildness, in longevity or otherwise, remains to be demonstrated.

4.3   Sex Effects

4.3.1   *Feminine Advantage*

In most animals that have been studied, the male sex is the shorter lived. This is true in organisms as dissimilar as fish (Bidder, 1932; Wimpenny, 1953), spiders (Deevey and Deevey, 1945, Figures 4.6, 4.7), *Drosophila* (Alpatov and Pearl, 1929; Bilewicz, 1953), *Habrobracon* (Georgiana, 1949), *Tribolium* (Park, 1945, Figure 4.8), water beetles (Blunck, 1924), houseflies (Rockstein and Lieberman, 1948), and man (Daw, 1961). In exceptional cases the preponderance of male mortality can be reversed. Thus Woolley (1946) found that in crosses between dba female and c57 male mice, the virgin females of the F_1 had a mean life of 27 and the males 29 months: in the reciprocal cross, the females lived 30 and the males 33 months. Males of

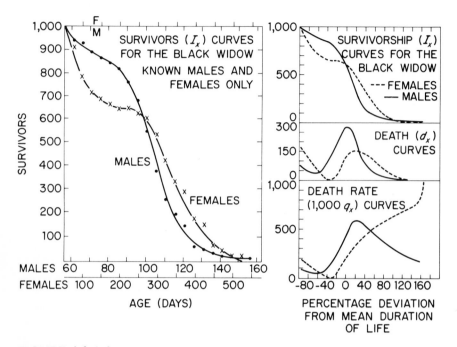

FIGURE 4.6 (left)   Survivorship curves for 82 males and 45 females of the black widow spider *Latrodectes mactans* (Fabr). Note that the male curve is shown to five times the time scale of the female curve. (From Deevey and Deevey, 1945.)

FIGURE 4.7 (right)   Survivorship, death, and death rate curve for the black widow. Note that the death curves are shown to twice the ordinate scale of the others. (From Deevey and Deevey, 1945.)

Rattus natalensis outlive the females (Oliff, 1953). Darwin (1874) regarded the shorter life of the male as "a natural and constitutional peculiarity due to sex alone." Attempts have also been made to explain it in genetic terms (Geiser, 1924–1925; Gowen, 1931, 1934). Gowen constructed life-tables for *Drosophila* intersexes and triploids, and concluded from his results that chromosome imbalance in itself exerted an adverse effect on life-span. In inbred *Drosophila* lines any pattern of sex advantage may appear, depending on the genes present (Maynard Smith, 1959b,c). In most of the forms where full life-tables have been made, the bias of mortality against the male follows the rule of greater vigor in the homogametic sex. McArthur and Baillie (1932) pointed out that if the lowered vitality of the male was due to greater homozygosis for adverse genes, the effect should be reversed in those forms where the female is heterogametic—notably lepidoptera and birds. Landauer and Landauer studied fowls (1931), Rau and Rau (1914) saturnid moths; they could find no evidence of such a reversal. Adequate life-table studies are still very scarce in these groups. In crosses, the difference in vigor between homogametic and heterogametic sexes may certainly be so great that only the homogametic reaches maturity; thus Federley (1929) found that in certain interspecific crosses in hawk moths, only the males survived pupation, though in reciprocal crosses both sexes survived. Beside these studies, that of Pearl and Miner (1936) upon *Acrobasis caryae,* which is one of the few actuarially-constructed lepidopteran life-tables that have been published, and an extensive study by Woodruffe (1951) on the survival of the moth *Hofmanophila pseudospretella* under different environmental conditions, both show a significantly higher female life-span. Alpatov and Gordeenko (1932), working on *Bombyx mori,* found no difference in longevity between unmated males and females, but a significantly longer male life in mated moths. Re-examining the results of Rau and Rau (1914), they concluded that in both *Samia cecropia* and *Calosamia promethea* the mated female had a shorter life-span than the male. This difference, however, might be due at least in part to the exhaustion of reserves by more frequent egg laying in mated females. The life-span of the female *Aglia tau* is said to be the shorter (Metchnikoff, 1907).

Rey (1936), working on the non-feeding imago of the moth *Galleria mellonella,* found that the males lived up to twice as long as the females, the difference being unaffected by humidity but exaggerated at low temperatures. He assumes this to be "the rule for lepidoptera."

In poultry, it seems to be established that the female is the more viable and

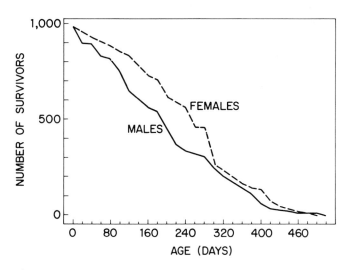

FIGURE 4.8 Survivorship curves for male and female *Tribolium madens* (radix of 1,000 imagines). (From Park, 1945.)

has the longer reproductive life (Pease, 1947), and observations such as those of McIlhenny on wild ducks (1940), which indicate an increase in the proportion of males with increasing age, are probably the result of differential risks. Male pigeons are reputedly the longer-lived sex (Levy, 1957) and the same applies to Bengal finches, in one of the few bird life-tables available (Eisner and Etoh, 1967). Longer life-span in males is also found in some other birds in the wild (Lack, 1954). In cyprinodont fishes, some of which have an atypical mechanism of sex determination, evidence is inadequate, but Bellamy (1934) found no conspicuous sex difference in longevity in a small series. An example of longer life in the male teleost occurs in minnows (van Cleave and Markus, 1929) but this refers to a wild population. It seems altogether likely that where a sex difference in longevity is observed it arises from the sum of differences in metabolic rate and behavioral pattern—in other words, from physiological sexual dimorphism. A number of invertebrate metabolic studies support such a view (*Daphnia*—McArthur and Baillie, 1929a, b; *Drosophila*—Alpatov and Pearl, 1929), by indicating that the "rate of living" in the male is in fact higher. The degree to which the inferior vitality of the male mammal results directly from the action of androgens was first discussed, and the whole question of male mortality reviewed at length, by Hamilton (1948). In man, the higher male mortality is present both in utero and in infancy. At later ages the question is, of course, complicated by social and occupational factors (Herdan, 1952). There are as yet no fully satisfactory human data on the relative longevity of castrates, though their life-span is certainly not grossly inferior to that of normals. Many of the highest recorded ages in cats have occurred in gelt males. The finding of Slonaker (1930) that castration produces a slight decrease in rat longevity was based on too few animals to be significant. Virgin and ovaryless *Drosophila* females live longer than normals, and sterilization increases the female life-span (Maynard Smith, 1958a, b).

Muhlbock (1959) found that virgin mice live longer than spayed females, while castrated and entire males have closely similar curves. The oldest survivors of all are castrates, however. In rats, Arvay, et al., (1963) found little difference between castrate and entire male longevity.

There is a strong possibility that the true explanation is immunological. Females may be more prone to, but less hurt by, autoimmune effects by reason of being "programmed" to live with a half-foreign fetus: the X chromosome controls immunoglobulin synthesis and thymic function, as well as the G6PD involved in phagocytosis (Schlegel and Bellanti, 1969). For this and possibly other (hormonal) reasons, the resistance of males to infection appears to be lower; the feminine advantage disappears in germ free mice (Gordon, et al., 1966). Add to this the fact that sex-rated data in offspring of human first-cousin marriages are consistent with considerable X heterosis (Hook and Schull, 1973) and much of the effect appears to be accounted for. See also p. 217.

4.3.2 Sexual Activity: Shunamitism

In some instances (*Drosophila*—Bilewicz, 1953) the life of the male is still further shortened by copulation or by egg laying. In others (*Latrodectes*— Shulov, 1939–1940) the male dies after a determinate short life-span, whether mated or not. While the mortality of Anglican clergy in England during the 1930s was only 69 percent of the general male mortality, and that of other Protestant clergy 74 percent, the mortality of Roman Catholic clergy was 105 percent (Registrar-General's statistics, 1938). This observation is complicated by a variety of factors; in rats, however, regular mating improves the condition and longevity of the male (Agduhr, 1939; Agduhr and Barron, 1938; Drori and Folman, 1969). Though there may be other reasons for the fact that married persons live statistically longer than unmarried persons (Sheps, 1961), this might tend to support the view that the virtues of "continence" in man, *vis-à-vis* longevity, have been overpraised by interested parties. In rats the greater longevity appears to result from greater activity due to higher testosterone levels (Drori and Folman, 1969).

One particularly odd finding is the vast excess of deaths from most causes, including tubercle, accident, and cardiovascular disease in the young widowed group of both sexes (Kraus and Lilienfeld, 1959). It has been variously suggested that the healthy widowed soon marry and leave the group, that assortation leads to a "mutual choice of poor-risk mates," that the survivor and deceased shared an unfavorable environment, and that early death— possibly psychogenic—is a direct effect of surviving a spouse. Between these choices a complete absence of facts leaves us freedom of choice at present.

One must here distinguish between the effects of sexual intercourse and *shunamitism,* the beneficial effect on old males of the proximity of a young female. Though it is an old notion of magical origin, Muhlbock (1959) has shown that this actually occurs in rats—old males live materially longer if one young female is introduced to groom them. After citing the opinion given by the Dutch physician Boerhave (1668–1738), who "recommended an old Burgomaster of Amsterdam to lie between two young girls, assuring him that he would thus recover strength and spirits," Hufeland (1798) remarks "We cannot refuse our approval to the method." It would seem by tradition to be applicable only to the male.

Apart from King David and the Burgomaster aforesaid, the *locus classicus* of magical shunamitism is the treatise *Hermippus Redivivus* of Cohausen (1742), which contains much engaging nonsense. The influence technically responsi-

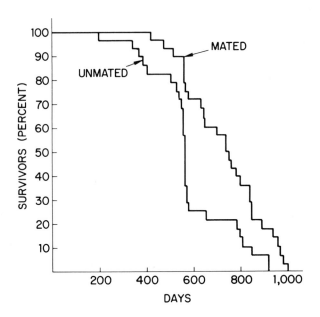

FIGURE 4.9   Survival of mated and unmated male rats. (From Drori and Folman, 1949.)

ble was the physical proximity or the "heat" or "breath" of a young virgin, coition being specifically excluded as dangerous to the failing constitution ("the King knew her not"), but the process was semiparasitic and took from the young what it gave to the old. In the Indian tradition, where the revivifying contact is specifically sexual, it was held particularly dangerous to lie with an old woman (see the *Ratimañjarī* of Jāyadeva).[1]

The magical idea of shunamitism might now be transferred *mutatis mutandis* to mere social contact, but there may well have been greater scientific value in the techniques adopted by the medieval Indian kings of Chandella, builders of the Khajurāho temples, who successfully pursued both longevity and proximity through industrious ritual coition with specially-instructed maidens (see Zannas and Auboyer, 1960), and in the popular notion of

---

[1]Bālā tu prāṇadā prottrā taruṇi prāṇahāriṇī/Praudhā karoti vṛddhatvaṁ vṛddhā maraṇamādiśet

"the young girl gives the breath of life,
the young woman takes the breath of life,
the grown woman hastens age,
the old woman brings death"   (*Ratimañjarī*, v. 24)

"grinding young": "while the miller grinds the old man's corn, the miller's daughter grinds the old man young again." Failing this, according to Marsilio Ficino (1498) "he should find a young, healthy, gay, and beautiful girl, attach his mouth to her breast, and drink her milk while the moon is waxing: and thereafter take *pulv. foeniculi* with sugar." This advice has perhaps some psychoanalytical virtue in acting out the regression seen commonly in old age. It has even been seriously revived under color of using milk as a "biocatalyst" (Gondos, 1965).

The mean age of ceasing regular coitus has been placed at 68 in married and 58 in unmarried men (Holland; Braadbart, 1961): Newman (1959) found that 70 percent of married American couples in his sample were sexually active at 60, many continuing into the late 80s. Regular coitus with mutual orgasm is recorded between a man of 103 and his wife aged 90 (Kinsey, et al., 1949) and fatherhood at 94 (Seymour, et al., 1935). Contrary to popular belief, there is little or no decline either in male potency or in woman's libido solely with age—in fact, it more often increases, up to at least the age of 60 (Kinsey, et al., 1953).

As far back as 1930 Raymond Pearl recorded nearly 4 percent of males between 70 and 79 having intercourse every third day and nearly 9 percent more were having it weekly. Kinsey's figures pointed to a decline in coital frequency in both sexes with age, but these figures were cross-sectional. In 1959 Finkle and co-workers questioned 101 men aged 56–86, ambulatory patients with no complaint likely to affect potency, and found 65 percent under age 69 and 34 percent over 70 still potent, with 2 out of 5 over 80 years old averaging ten copulations a year. When they went further into this, they found that some in the sample had never had intercourse. Others, though potent, had no partner. In the over-70 group the main reason given for sexual inactivity was "no desire"—in fact, of all the men over 65, only three gave as reason "no erection." Newman and Nichols (1960) questioned men and women from 60 to 93 years of age and found 54 percent active overall. No significant decline was found under 75. Over 75, 25 percent were still active, and the decrease was accounted for chiefly by illness of self or spouse. "Those who rated sexual urges as strongest in youth rated them as moderate in old age: most who described sexual feelings as weak to moderate in youth described themselves as without sexual feelings in old age," confirming Pearl's 1930 finding that early starters are late finishers. Pfeiffer, et al. (1968) at Duke studied 254 people of both sexes.

The median age for stopping "sexual activity" (presumably coitus, not masturbation) was 68 in men, range 49–90, and 60 in women with a high record of 81, the difference being due to the age differential (average 4 years) between spouses. The figures for regular and frequent intercourse were 47 percent between 60 and 71 and 15 percent age 78 and over. The most interesting part of this study is that unlike previous examinations it was longitudinal, not cross-sectional. Over a 5-year period, 16 percent of propositi reported a falling off of activity, but 14 percent reported an increase. What we are seeing in cross-sectional studies, therefore, is a mixture of high and low sexually active individuals, in which those whose sexual "set" is low for physical or attitudinal reasons drop out early—often using age as a justification for laying down what has for them been an anxious business. So much for the obsession with loss of sexual function which has so heavily influenced gerontology—senile asexuality is a sociogenic disorder.

Hypogonadal and so-called "climacteric" impotency respond to testosterone better than impotency, which appears to be mainly a learned behavior (Cooper, 1970). The role of androgen in the cycle of male excitation is not known—it is at least as likely that high levels result from, rather than cause, sexual arousal (Kraemer, et al., 1976). The overall but irregular decline in cross-sectional androgen levels reported by various authors with increasing age represents not only endogenous reduction, but quite probably the reduction in sexual activity imposed by a social "script" (Gagnon and Simon, 1973).

It seems probable that while female arousal can be reliably mediated by androgen, the control of male arousal depends on an earlier, probably oligopeptidic, neurohormone. Increased libido is consistently seen in males after administration of human chorionic gonadotrophin (HCG) (Amelar and Dubin, 1977) when it is given for infertility: this action probably depends upon follicular-stimulating hormone (FSH) or luteinizing hormone (LH), or both, or on a specific oligopeptide as yet unidentified, paralleling the arousal seen in animals of both sexes after intraventricular LHRH injection. This group of responses is insufficiently investigated to yield present clinical application, but the irregular response to androgen in cases of reduced male libido clearly indicates that other mechanisms are involved; to the extent that libidinal decline is not wholly sociogenic it may be integrated with some hypothalamic ageing "clock," similar to that which inaugurates the menopause.

Continued sexual activity is an evident correlate of continued vigor: as Hufeland dutifully puts it,

> The power of procreating others seems to be in the most intimate proportion to that of regenerating and restoring one's self: but a certain regularity and moderation are necessary in the employment of it, and marriage is the only means by which these can be preserved . . .

(1798). For life-tables of monks and nuns, see Madigan (1959) and Josephina (1955).

4.4 Progeria

Although the rate of senile deterioration varies between individuals, the specific age of genetically homogeneous animal lines is very stable; even in human populations the range of apparent variation is not very great, and the few descriptions of racially-distributed "premature senility," as in Eskimos (Brown, et al., 1948), are not actuarially supported, though such variation, genetic or environmental, may occur.

Sporadic cases of syndromes having some of the general characters of premature old age occasionally occur in man. It is not clear how far any of these syndromes can be regarded as genuine accelerations of the timing mechanisms that determine senescence. They are apparently pleiotropic genetic defects, occurring commonly in sibs, and are most conveniently mentioned here. They have been regarded as pluriglandular endocrine disturbances, but they affect many ectodermal structures and look in most respects much more like an inborn error of metabolism—possibly the deficiency of an enzyme system, or a chromosomal abnormality.

Infantile progeria (Hutchinson-Gilford syndrome) (Thomson and Forfar, 1950; Manschot, 1940, 1950) occurs in childhood. After an apparently normal infancy, the child begins to show retarded growth, with dwarfism and progressively increasing physical abnormality. The appearance becomes senile, the skin atrophic, and there is hypertension with extensive atheroma and calcification. Death usually occurs from coronary disease before the 30th year. The mental development of these children may be retarded, but is more typically precocious. Cataract may occur. The endocrine appearances at necropsy are inconstant, but pituitary eosinophils are reported to be reduced (Manschot, 1940).

Adult progeria (Werner's syndrome) was first described by Werner (1904) in four sibs. It bears some resemblance to a delayed infantile progeria, occurring after growth has been wholly or partially completed. The subjects are short and of unusual appearance. The symptoms begin in the third or fourth decade, with the development of baldness, greying, skin changes, cataract, calcification of vessels and occasionally of tissues, osteoporosis, hypogonadism, and a tendency to diabetes (Thannhauser, 1945). This seems in general a more promising source of analogy with normal senescence than does the infantile progeric syndrome. Extensive bibliographies of progeria are given by Thannhauser (1945), by Thomson and Forfar (1950), and by Epstein, et al. (1966). Electron microscopic studies do not support the

TABLE 4.1
Comparison of Features of Werner's Syndrome with Those of Ageing

	WERNER'S SYNDROME	AGEING
A. Similar findings		
1. Atherosclerosis, arteriosclerosis, and medical calcinosis		
2. Graying of the hair		
3. Hypermelanosis		
4. Cerebral cortical atrophy		
5. Lymphoid depletion and thymic atrophy		
B. Similar findings, but differences in degree		
1. Calcification of valve rings and leaflets*	Very severe	Moderate
2. Hyalinization of seminiferous tubules*	Very severe	Severe only in very aged
3. Atrophy of skin appendages*	Severe	Moderate
4. Osteoporosis*	Generalized, but found particularly in distal extremities	Generalized, spine particularly vulnerable
5. Loss of hair*	Generalized	Principally scalp

C. Features characteristic of
Werner's syndrome

	"Dystrophic" type: subcapsular and cortical	"Senile" type: cortical or nuclear (probably different from those of Werner'f syndrome)
1. Cataracts*		
2. Ulcerations and atrophy of extremities*	Non-trophic, very frequent	Trophic, infrequent
3. Short stature*	Primary	Acquired
4. Laryngeal atrophy*	Common	Unusual
5. Proportion of sarcomas and connective tissue tumors among neoplasms*	High	Low
6. Soft-tissue calcification*	Common	Unusual
7. Prostate	Atrophic epithelium	Benign prostatic hypertrophy
8. Adrenal glomerulosa	Conspicuous	Poorly demarcated
9. Parathyroid	Chief cell predominant	Oxyphils predominant

Source: Epstein, et al., 1966.
*Differences considered to be of principal significance.

analogy to premature aging (Spence and Herman, 1973). There is reason to believe that adult progeria is a genetic disorder—Epstein, et al. (1966), give detailed pedigrees. Fibroblast survival in culture is curtailed (Goldstein, 1969; Danes, 1971) and heat-labile enzymes in skin fibroblasts resemble those in Phase-III cultures (Goldstein and Moerman, 1975).

Other less generalized conditions with rather similar symptomatology have been described. "Senile" change may be limited to the extremities (acrogeria). The main interest of these conditions is in providing examples of mechanisms that may mimic the deteriorative changes of human old age. The conditions are all rare, and no parallels have been described in laboratory animals. In infant progeria, pituitary growth-hormone deficiency appears to play some part, though the condition differs markedly from straightforward dwarfism. The deficiency of oxyphil cells in some reported cases bears a resemblance to that which follows castration (Wolfe, 1941, 1943). Walford (1962) draws the analogy with autoimmune diseases.

Pearce and Brown (1960) described a progeric familial syndrome in the rabbit—this appears to represent the incomplete manifestation of a character which, in its severest form, produces infant death, since it occurs in a strain liable to produce nonviable young with parchmentlike skin. The "senile" changes are loss of coat, loss of weight, ulceration, cachexia, and ophthalmia, and the range of acute and chronic types is reminiscent of the range of human progeric syndromes. It does not appear to be identical with these, however, and calcification is not prominent. A much more human-looking animal "progeria" has been produced in rats by a type of experimental calcium hypersensitivity (Selye, 1962), induced by dihydrotachysterol.

Sudden "senescence" in adults, a great standby of the nineteenth-century dramatist, is an uncommon endocrine, or possibly hypothalamic, reaction to severe emotional shock or accident which, although not genetic, can conveniently be considered here because of its superficial affinity with progeria. In the interest of literary effect, the preliminary phase of sudden baldness is usually not stressed. The hair may fall out within 24 hours, to be replaced when it grows again after an interval, by white or structurally defective hair; impotence, depression, and cachexia are described as concomitants. The condition is recoverable, and appears to have more connection with Simmonds' disease than with senescence. A case was reported by Greene and Paterson (1943) in a railwayman who fell from a locomotive and suffered head injury and severe shock and another following a crush injury to the hand (Thomson, 1938; see also Fraser, 1943). In another case, a policeman rang the doorbell of a gas-filled house and was severely shocked by the explosion that followed (*Evening Standard* December 8, 1961). A few cases are alleged to have followed intense fear, as in battle. The pituitary may well be the endocrine chiefly responsible, and the primary site of the disorder the hypothalamus.

4.5 Choice of Material for Experimental Study of Age Effects

Research on the senescence of man and most large mammals necessarily involves work on genetically diverse populations. Where closed laboratory stocks are used, or the subject is a "genetical" domestic animal such as the mouse or *Drosophila,* genetic precautions are essential in ageing experiments, especially if comparisons are to be made between the life-spans of different groups or different generations. The size of the effect that can be produced in such stocks by heterosis has already been mentioned. The presence or absence of uniformity in the experimental population is also particularly important in research involving life-tables, since in many inbred lines the form of the life-table depends entirely on one cause of death that is not typical of the species, or even the phylum.

In non-genetical experiments (nutrition, biochemistry, growth rate, and so on) the choice lies between *inbred, hybrid,* and *random-bred* material. *Inbred* lines commonly have a life-span that is rather low for the species, and this may be advantageous. Their vigor is often low, though inbreeding depression is more evident in some species than others. Inbred lines are often chosen by non-genetical workers for bioassay, in the belief that they have the advantage of uniformity. This, however, is not so. Grüneberg (1954) has stressed two important characters of such lines: They cannot be relied upon to remain constant in their heritable properties with the passage of time, and may diverge rapidly when split into separate colonies; and they do not constitute phenotypically uniform material, but may, on the contrary, be strikingly more variable than F_1 hybrids between strains, and even than random-bred material (McLaren and Michie, 1954).

Hybrid material, bred in each generation by crossing inbred lines, suitably chosen, has a number of important advantages for general work upon ageing. In such crosses the life-span approaches the maximum for the species under the experimental conditions. Vigor is high, so that "background" losses due to temperature change, infection, operative mortality, and accident are much reduced, and variation between individuals is minimal. This uniformity is itself probably a reflection of vigor, in the form of better homeostasis (Robertson and Reeve, 1952). Hybrids can, like inbreds, be employed for transplantation experiments. Like inbreds, too, they may all die of a single cause, and will do so as a rule with greater unanimity in regard to age.

Random-mated material, when mating is genuinely random, and not occurring within an already highly-inbred colony or between such colonies, produces animals, the strongest of which exhibit a vigor and life-span approaching that of hybrids, more variable than hybrids, unsuitable for transplantation experiments, showing a variety of causes of death more closely resembling that in human populations, and, in general, resembling such populations more closely than hybrid or inbred lines.

The choice of inbred, hybrid, or random-bred material, when it is not dictated by the fact that no pure lines are available, will depend upon which of these attributes are most useful. The type of material must, however, be correctly stated, since it greatly affects the interpretation of results. Probably the most valuable approach to the comparative study of ageing, though not always a practicable one, would be a scheme of research carried out in parallel upon all three types of strain, in an animal that is already genetically familiar.

5

Growth and Senescence

5.1 "Rate of Living"

The idea of the life-span as a fixed quantity is an old one. In a great many organisms it has long been recognized that the contrast, perhaps originally moralistic, between a long life and a high "rate of living" had valid biological applications. The phrase "rate of living" we owe to Pearl, and it conveys the concept very satisfactorily without making too many assumptions. In many organisms the life-span, like the rate of development, is a function of the temperature over a considerable range. In such forms it appears that a fixed quantity of *something* that, for want of a better term, we have called "program," must run out and be succeeded by senescence. The organism must pass through a fixed sequence of operations, metabolic or developmental, the rate of its passage determining the observed life-span.

The period in which the kinetics of metabolism were being discovered expressed this "program" in directly chemical terms. Life had an observable temperature coefficient. Growth, in the classical conception of Robertson (1923), followed the same course as a monomolecular autocatalytic reaction. Loeb (1908) attempted to answer by the determination of temperature coefficients a fundamental question about the "rate of living" in relation to ageing—what is the nature of the "program" that has to be fulfilled before senescence begins? Is it a program of differentiation or growth, or maintenance metabolism, or of all three? Loeb's experiments showed that the temperature coefficient of the rate of "ageing" in echinoderm ova differed greatly from that of their respiration. Later work has shown the relationship between development and temperature to be too complex for simple estimation of coefficients. Morphogenesis depends upon a large number of simultaneous and occasionally contrary processes. We should almost certainly now be inclined to interpret the program fulfilled by an animal during its life-cycle in terms drawn from experimental morphology and from the study of control systems, rather than directly from physical chemistry.

The postulation that senescence always accompanies, or follows, the cessation of growth—which we owe originally to Minot (1908)—is, in fact, no more than a postulation, since, as we have seen, there may be organisms in which senescence occurs hand-in-hand with growth. Senescence in man, judged by the life-table, commences while active growth is in progress: Minot himself considered that the rate of senescence was actually greatest when growth rate was at its maximum.

The dissociability of growth from development was first shown by Gudernatsch's researches upon the action of thyroid in the developing tadpole (1912). Metabolism, measured by respiration, is dissociable from both. "The fundamental mechanisms are not separable only in thought: on the contrary, they can be dissociated experimentally or thrown out of gear with one another" (Needham). The fundamental problem in relation to the "rate of living" lies, therefore, in determining which of these processes, and in what proportions, make up the essential sequence of operations through which the organism must pass before senescence makes its appearance. In its crudest form the question is: Given that these processes, though dissociable, are normally interdependent, does this organism undergo senescence (1) when it reaches a particular stage of cellular differentiation; (2) when it has exhausted a particular store of "growth energy," whatever the nature of such a store; or (3) when it has carried out a certain stint of metabolism—a life-span measurable in calories or in liters of oxygen consumed? It is immediately evident that the program in real organisms is complex, that since senescence is a diverse process the pacemaker differs in different forms. In some cases, when (1) above has been satisfied, the further life-span of the *differentiated* cells may depend upon their metabolism, as in (3). All concepts based on "wear and tear" in neurons or other cells postulate a similar sequence: loss of regenerative power followed by mechanical or chemical exhaustion. In the rotifer the normal sequence of differentiation produces an organism that is almost incapable of cellular repair, and quite incapable of nuclear regeneration. The life-span of the adult, once this point in the program has been reached, is inversely proportional to temperature and metabolic rate over a certain range. How this effect operates we do not know. The encysted adult, although unable to survive in the complete absence of oxygen (Rahm, 1923), may pass years in diapause. The life-span of many larvae can be enormously prolonged by underfeeding or shortened by heating: once metamorphosis has taken place the program is resumed but still responds to changes in temperature by a change in pace. The longest-lived imagines, termite queens, do in fact increase in size after eclosion (Harvey, 1934). In mammals it has been postulated that, since the metabolic rate is held steady by various homeostatic devices, the essential ingredients of the program leading to senescence are growth and differentiation; that growth ceases as a result of some process or processes of differentiation, and that the absence of growth is a proximate cause of senescence.

We have already suggested that this is not in accordance with the evidence. The observational test—that no vertebrate that continues to grow undergoes "morphogenetic" senescence, even though all vertebrates that cease to grow are subject to it—is not satisfied, while the experimental test—the demonstration that the life-span of an adult vertebrate can be prolonged by keeping it artificially in continued growth, beginning after normal size and development have been attained—gave a negative result in Everitt's (1959) rat experiment with growth hormone. We cannot yet identify any single process that by its failure, produces the senile decline of homeostasis in mammals. It is, however, possible to treat the developmental sequence leading to senescence, in its relation to growth and to differentiation, as an "integrating system," of the type employed in various calculating and timing devices.

The most familiar example of such a system, functioning as a calculating device, is the taxi meter. This machine records time when the taxi is stationary, and distance, or time and distance, when it is moving. The real taxi meter does so upon an "open-ended" scale, the amount of the fare that can be rung up on the dial being theoretically unlimited, since the dials after reaching $99.99 return to zero. For the purpose of our argument, the biological taxi meter has been adapted by an anarchist to produce an undesirable result when a particular fare is reached, say $5; or, more correctly, an *increasing probability* of this result as $5 is approached and passed. An increasing impairment of the brakes and steering would be a suitable device. The meter records 10¢ per minute, so long as the taxi is stationary and 20¢ per mile plus 10¢ per minute so long as it is moving. In this case, if the journey never begins, the impairment will take place eventually, though not for a very long time. For an extended biological analogy it is probably better to take the case in which the conditions of the impairment reaching a disastrous stage are, first, that the fare shall reach $5, and second that the taxi shall have traveled at least a short distance from its starting point.

The question we have to ask is this: Does mammalian senescence effectively resemble such an integrating system, in which differentiation is the higher-scoring and the essential component, but in which retardation leading to continuance of growth directly or indirectly delays the point at which senescence appears; or does cessation of growth *itself,* whether it arises from some active mechanism of size limitation or through the attainment of an equilibrium state, directly cause the senile deterioration? The crude application of the calculating machine or the time-fuse analogy has many objections, the chief of them being that the senile decline in resistance in mammals is not a sudden process, as it is in the rotifer, but a smooth rise in the force of mortality beginning at an early stage. Mechanical timing devices produce as a rule a single event after a fixed program, not an increasing probability throughout the program, though this objection does not hold good for analog computing systems: it is relatively simple to devise an electronic taximeter-bomb in which the *probability* of an explosion increases with the increase of time and distance, or a system in which the steering of the taxi becomes increasingly impaired as the "program" continues. A far more serious objection is that in ordinary taxi meters time and distance are not normally interlocked, as growth and differentiation, though experimentally separable, are interlocked in the developing animal. It has been suggested that the two processes are in some degree mutually exclusive (Bertalanffy, 1933, 1941)— a conception that goes back to Minot. It seems probable that in most organisms it is the component of differentiation, not that of mere growth, that is responsible for senescence.

Analogies, in any case, are mostly of use as teaching illustrations. In the final analysis, any senescence, even if it never reaches the ideal state of being expressed as a sequence of chemical reactions and equilibria, must presumably be reducible to a series of definite processes—such-and-such a mechanism leads to the loss of dividing power in such-and-such cells, which then have a life-span limited by the non-renewability of their enzymes to so many chemical operations, after which they deteriorate with the following consequences. We are nowhere near such a picture of any one senile or developmental process in any organism, let alone of mammalian senescence or morphogenesis in general. A certain amount of experimental evidence has, however, accumulated—enough to indicate the directions in which further research might profitably be directed.

One of its most important—and theoretically distressing—findings is that the decrease in longevity of *Drosophila* imagines at high temperatures may not be a matter of simple thermal acceleration. Clarke and Maynard Smith (1961b) have kept *D. subobscura* at high temperatures and then transferred them back to lower temperatures, with a view to measuring the expected loss in life-span which the taxi meter analogy would predict. Apart from the special case of females, which are rendered sterile by heat and consequently live longer than usual, a period spent at a high temperature, provided it is less than the "plateau" in the survival curve that precedes the onset of deaths, subtracts nothing whatever from subsequent survival at a low temperature (Maynard Smith, 1958, 1959c; Clarke and Maynard Smith, 1961a, b). According to these authors, the decline in *Drosophila* "vitality" during the plateau, Neary's (1960) "induction period," is not accelerated by heating: flies in hot conditions die early not because their vitality is more rapidly impaired by age, but because the vitality required for survival is higher than in cool conditions. Further studies by Lamb (1968), Hollingsworth (1969), Strehler (1962), and Shaw and Bercaw (1962) confuse the picture still further. As Lints points out (1971) it looks as if neither the thermal-dependence nor the induction-threshold model applies satisfactorily to *Drosophila* ageing, and a great many other variables (effect of pre-imaginal conditions and differences between *D. melanogaster* and *D. subobscura* for a start) may contribute to the temperature response. The real problem is in the use of a nonspecific event, namely death, as measure of an ongoing process of failing homeostasis or rising attack—a universal problem in gerontology of which this particular controversy is a shining example.

5.2 Experimental Alteration of the Growth Rate

5.2.1 *Invertebrates*

In many invertebrates, the specific age is easily altered, either in response to temperature changes, to which it bears a simple relation, or by retardation of growth through the restriction of food. The total longevity of insects can be increased either by underfeeding the larvae, or by keeping any or all of the stages, from egg to imago, at low temperatures. The same applies to ticks— starvation will increase the life-span of some species from a few weeks to 2 years (Bishopp and Smith, 1938). Northrop (Northrop, 1917; Loeb and Northrop, 1917) kept Drosophila larvae for varying periods on a yeastless medium to delay growth and induce stunting: by this means the total life-span from hatching to death was increased. There is disagreement whether delayed growth of larvae leads to an increase in the life-span from eclosion. Northrop found no such increase in imagines reared from retarded larvae. Intermittent starvation of the imago of Drosophila shortens its life; retardation of the larvae of Lymantria also fails to increase the life-span of the imago, which cannot feed (Kopeć, 1924, 1928). Alpatov and Pearl (Alpatov and Pearl, 1929; Alpatov, 1930) found a slight increase in imaginal life-span in Drosophila when the larvae were retarded by development at 18°C. This effect was less evident in males, and appeared to be reversed in some experiments: where the imagines were kept at 25–28°C, larvae reared at 28°C gave longer-lived flies than those reared at 18°C. The statistical significance of the differences was in any case small.

In insects in which metamorphosis is incomplete, the optimal intake of food, and particularly of protein, for rapid growth produces a shorter total life-span than a poorer diet; in *Blatta orientalis* and *Periplaneta americana* the optimal protein intake for longevity of all the stages is about half that which gives the fastest development (Haydak, 1953). In holometabolous insects, dietary slowing is confined to the larval stages, which can be extended by intermittent fasting (*Lymantria*—Kopeć, 1924), with beetle larvae to many years; the life of imagines, on the contrary, usually seems to be increased by food supplements (butterflies—Frohawk, 1935) especially in females (*Musca domestica*—Rockstein, 1959), and still more by the prevention of egg laying (*Musca domestica*—Rockstein, 1959; *Ephestia*—Norris, 1934; Köhler, 1940), since in both feeding and non-feeding adults the longevity is determined by stored reserves, particularly of protein. Bees present a special problem; here feeding controls development and the choice between two life-cycles—that of a queen, lasting up to 5 years (Pflugfelder, 1948) and that of a worker, which depends directly on how much pollen protein is kept back for individual use, rather than used for rearing brood. Broodless or "winter" workers have a life-span of 300–400 days compared with 30–70 days when brood is present (Maurizio, 1959). Attempts have been made to increase the imaginal life-span of insects with vitamin supplements on the model of royal jelly, but with small effect (Gardner, 1948).

The life-span and final size of Daphnia (McArthur and Baillie, 1926) and *Moina* (Ingle, 1933; Terao, 1932, etc.) vary inversely with the temperature over a considerable range. Like *Drosophila, Daphnia* can be markedly retarded either by cooling or by underfeeding. A detailed study on the effect of retardation upon specific age and growth in *Daphnia* was carried out by Ingle, et al. (1937). By diluting the medium, it was shown that starvation of Daphnia for varying numbers of instars resulted in an increase of life-span approximately equal to the period of starvation, but that individuals starved only until the 11th or 17th instar lived longer than individuals starved throughout life. This prolongation of life was achieved by lengthening the duration of each retarded instar, the total number of instars remaining constant. In this species *(D. longispina)* the specific age appeared to lie between the 19th and 22nd instars, without reference to the chronological age these may represent (Figures 5.1, 5.2). In *D. magna,* Anderson and Jenkins (1942) found a mean life-span of 960 hours or 17 instars; the number of pre-adult instars varied from 4 to 6 and the differences in longevity between individuals represented differences in the length of the pre-adult period. (See also Dunham, 1938). The finding of Fritsch (1953) that the pantothenic acid content of the medium is a major factor in determining the life-span of *Daphnia* complicates the interpretation of some of these studies of dietary retardation, however. For other studies of the longevity and heart

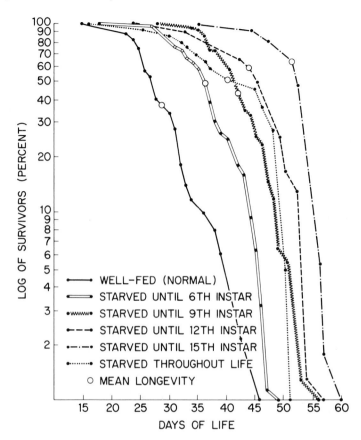

FIGURE 5.1 Effects of restricted food on the longevity of *Daphnia longispina*. (From Ingle, et al., 1937.)

rate of *Daphnia,* see Meijering (1958, 1960), V. Reden (1960), and Fritsch (1956, 1959).

5.2.2 *Insect Metamorphosis and Senescence*

A great many insects are capable of very long pre-imaginal life, the duration of which is largely determined by food supply. The "rate of living," as a simple quantity treated apart from morphogenetic processes, does not give an entirely satisfactory picture of insect development. We might possibly make an experimental approach to the study of insect senescence on the following lines. Senescence, of course, occurs in the ordinary course of events only in the imago. The larval or nymphal stages must be regarded as a system that is self-maintaining but tends towards ultimate metamorphosis.

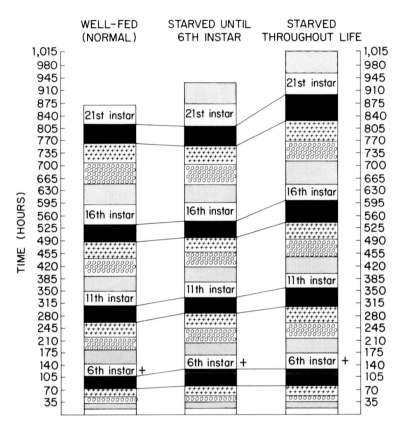

FIGURE 5.2 Effect of restricted food upon the duration of instars in *Daphnia longispina*. (From Ingle, et al., 1937.)

They are analogous to the young growing period of non-metabolous metazoa. The question arises how long, if metamorphosis could be indefinitely prevented, the metathetelic larva would remain self-maintaining as an equilibrium system. It might presumably do so indefinitely, or it might ultimately undergo a specialized type of senescence due to the suppression of development or to imbalance between continued, divergent growth processes; or it might nevertheless undergo senescence from the same cause, whatever that cause may be, that limits the life of the imago.

To ask whether a larva or a nymph would senesce if it did not metamorphose is not entirely idle speculation. The data that we have on the developmental physiology of *Rhodnius,* chiefly from the work of Wigglesworth, make it possible to contemplate interfering with the development of nymphs. The pre-imaginal phase of *Rhodnius,* during which growth takes place, is maintained by the so-called juvenile hormone.

During larval life, imaginal differentiation is suppressed because in the presence of the juvenile hormone secreted by the corpus allatum the intracellular system which leads to the production of larval structures takes precedence over the system which leads to the formation of adult structures (Wigglesworth, 1953b).

The influence of temperature on larval development appears to act through this system, high temperatures or low oxygen tensions depressing the juvenile hormone and producing prothetely, low temperatures enhancing its effect and producing metathetely. This system lends itself particularly well to analysis in terms of control mechanisms. The tendency of the cellular system in its "free-running" state appears to be towards the imaginal form. Moulting hormone from a fifth-stage larva will cause a first-stage larva *Rhodnius* to metamorphose (Wigglesworth, 1934). Second-instar moth larvae will metamorphose to minute pupae and adults if the corpora allata are removed (Bounhiol, 1938) and isolated fragments from the integument of newly-hatched moth larvae tend to pupate (Piepho, 1938). The function of the juvenile hormone appears to be to moderate or prevent this free-running tendency, though as a standing bias, not as a negative feedback. The point to which the free-running system tends, moreover, is an unstable one, ending in eventual senescence. In the fifth-stage *Rhodnius* nymph the thoracic gland undergoes very rapid disintegration as soon as metamorphosis takes place, and the possibility of moulting, and cuticular renewal is thereby lost, from lack of evocator, although the power of the dermal cells to respond to injected moulting hormone remains (Wigglesworth, 1953a). Long-term change in this system causes the bias to be overcome at the correct moment. The homeostasis achieved by the juvenile hormone is not absolute, otherwise metamorphosis would never take place; the metamorphosis-producing hormone ultimately carries the day. But occasional nymphs of *Rhodnius* devoid of the thoracic gland cannot metamorphose, and appear to live for long periods without senescence. This mechanism offers an opportunity for the dissection of just such a system of partial homeostasis, directed to act as a delay mechanism, as appears to underlie so many life-cycles that end in senescence. Work on insect senescence is in many respects unpromising as a source of principles that can be extended to the biology of vertebrate old age; such research is frequently confined to the very special circumstances that exist in the imago—in other words, to a system that is already in a time-limited equilibrium. For measures of interference with the growing organism, however, and attempts to stabilize the system in its earlier stages, insect material may prove the most manageable. Any example of indefinite stabilization at an immature stage, in any organism, would be of great biological interest. The degree of drift towards the unstable state probably varies throughout development in different insects; Bodenstein has shown (1943a, b) that in *Drosophila* early salivary glands implanted in late larvae are not immediately capable of metamorphosis: "Whether the organ discs respond with growth or differentiation depends on a definite relationship between hormone concentration and organ responsiveness" (Bodenstein, 1943b).

5.2.3 *Vertebrates*

The history of the growth–ageing hypothesis has already been told. It is no longer of more than historical interest, but it sired perhaps the most important practical observation to date for the control of ageing, that of caloric restriction effects in mammals.

The possibility of producing a long-lasting but recoverable delay in mammalian growth and development by underfeeding first arose from the studies of Osborne and Mendel (1915, 1916). The work of McCay on rats, which extended the results obtained by underfeeding upon arthropod growth directly to mammals, is well-known, but still very remarkable. It also still represents the only successful assault that has ever been made on the problem of mammalian specific age, which is itself the key problem of medical gerontology; and the rather exceptional growth pattern of rats in no way diminishes its interest. The experiments, first described in 1934 (McCay and Crowell, 1934; McCay, et al., 1939, 1956; Saxton, 1945), extended over years and are fully reviewed in retrospect by McCay (1952). Groups of rats were reared on a diet sufficient in all other constituents but deficient in calories, and their growth thereby retarded. After periods of retardation up to 1,000 days, the calorie intake was raised to permit growth. The animals then grew rapidly to adult size, even though the longest-retarded group had already exceeded the normal life-span for the strain, and continued to live to approximately twice the maximum age reached by unretarded controls (Figure 5.3). This long survival was accompanied by a decreased incidence of many chronic diseases, which appeared to represent a true diminution in senile liability to death from random causes. The chief specific diminution was in death rate from pulmonary diseases and from tumors. "In general, the retarded rat remains active and appears young whatever its chronological age. It is very alert. It tends to go blind in the second and third year of life. Its pulse rate of 340 beats per minute is about 100 below normal" (McCay, 1952). The basal metabolic rate of rats so retarded lay between that of normal young and normal old animals (Horst, et al., 1934). In rats retarded for 850 days, heat production per unit surface area was lower, but heat production

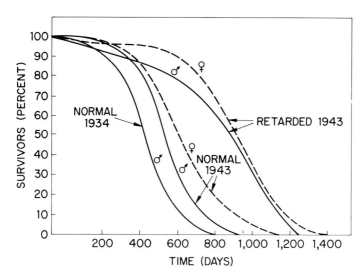

FIGURE 5.3   Survival curves of normal and retarded male and female rats, showing the effect of dietary restriction. (From McCay, et al., 1943.)

per unit weight higher, than in normal controls (Will and McCay, 1943). The aorta and kidneys of retarded rats showed in general a higher level of calcification than those of controls (Hummel and Barnes, 1938), perhaps on account of the relatively higher mineral concentrations in the restricted diet (Barnes, 1942). A further series of experiments in the dietary restriction of animals that had already reached maturity was unfortunately complicated by the introduction of many groups of variables (exercise, casein intake, liver supplements, etc.); in these experiments, underfeeding produced a significant increase in life-span compared with fully-fed controls, but the difference was far less conspicuous than in the retardation of young growing rats, and the most important factors in determining life-span were those that determined the degree of body fatness (McCay, et al., 1941; Silberberg and Silberberg, 1954). This difference was largely accounted for by the higher incidence of renal disease on a high protein diet and in obese animals (Saxton and Kimball, 1941); in contrast to the findings in animals retarded while young, the incidence of chronic pneumonitis and of tumors was not reduced by under-feeding in mature animals (McCay, et al., 1943; Saxon, 1945).

Basal metabolism in restricted rats is intermediate between that of normal young and normal adult rats (Will and McCay, 1943). Their size restriction is a restriction in cell number, retarded animals having the cellular population appropriate to size group, not age group (Fukuda and Sibatani, 1953). The operative effect seems to be mediated by the pituitary—it is a dietary

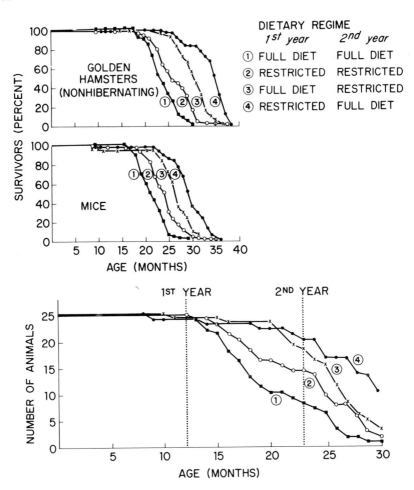

FIGURE 5.4   Survival curves for golden hamsters, mice, and rats kept on different dietary regimes as indicated. (From Stuchlíková, et al., 1975.)

hypophysectomy (Samuels, 1946) and is antagonized by extraneous growth hormone (Hrůza and Fábry, 1957). Tissues from retarded animals have a shorter latent period in tissue culture (Holečková, et al., 1959) and the tail collagen in such animals is "young" in its response to heat shrinkage (Chvapil and Hrůza, 1959). Evidence regarding food restriction in normally grown adult animals is less spectacular—gains in general seem to reflect the avoidance of overweight (McCay, et al., 1956).

Ross (1961, 1976) varied the components of the diet of rats separately—restriction of protein alone produced little gain in longevity; restriction of carbohydrate produced some gain, but less than when protein, calorie intake, and carbohydrate were all restricted. Rats on an unrestricted diet low in protein and high in carbohydrate restricted their own intake, and lived longer in consequence than other unrestricted groups (Figure 5.5).

Miller and Payne (1968) found that rats fed a high-protein diet for the first 120 days of life and a low-protein diet thereafter lived 28 percent longer than stock-diet controls. Stuchlíková, et al. (1975) found that the optimal régime for longevity in rats, mice, and hamsters was early restriction followed by full feeding—but the restriction in these experiments was moderately severe (50 percent of control diet) and the effect probably complex. See Fernandes, et al. (1976) for a review of mouse dietary effects.

In retarded rats the liver composition resembles that of much younger animals: the amount of RNA phosphorus in Edsall's reagent extractives is even higher at 12 months than in normal 1-month-old animals, and protein turnover appears to be enhanced compared with normals. On realimentation, these indexes rapidly "catch up" with the chronological age (Nikitin, 1962).

The results of these experiments indicate that at least some mammals are capable while immature of undergoing prolonged suspension of growth without any acceleration of senescence. The suspension is not complete, since deaths occur unless some increase in weight is allowed. The most important inference to be drawn from the work would appear to be that senescence itself is the direct consequence not so much of growth cessation as

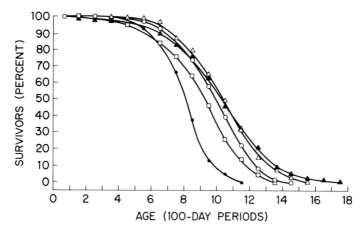

FIGURE 5.5 Percentage of survivors at successive 100-day periods of 4 groups of rats maintained on restricted intakes of semisynthetic diets and of one group of rats maintained *ad libitum* with a commercial diet. Key: ●, commercial laboratory chow; ○, high casein–high sucrose intake; Δ, high casein–low sucrose intake; □, low casein–high sucrose intake; ▲, low casein–low sucrose intake. (From Ross, 1961.)

that of the attainment of a developmental stage, the timing of which is partially, but not wholly, linked to the growth rate—there being no evidence that starved rats remain "young" indefinitely. By 1,150 days, moreover, only about half the retarded individuals were capable of resuming growth (McCay, et al., 1943). There is some evidence from later work that prolongation of the life-span, though in a smaller degree, can be produced by intermittent dietary restriction without any evident effect on the growth rate (Carlson and Hoelzel, 1946). Moreover, most of the changes that ultimately fix the specific age appear to have occurred at the time of maturity, since the increase in longevity obtained by underfeeding adult rats, is far less (McCay, et al., 1941; Ross, 1971).

In contrast to McCay's findings, retardation of rats *before* weaning leads to permanent undersize and tends to affect longevity adversely (Widdowson and Kennedy, 1962). Later work has shown a clear distinction between the effects of growth retardation, of dietary restriction without growth retardation but started early in life, and of dietary restriction in the mature rodent. Basically, moderate restriction started at weaning limits tumor incidence and perhaps life; restriction started early in life prolongs life without affecting tumor incidence; and late restriction limits chronic disease (Ross, 1961, 1969, 1976; Ross and Bras, 1965; Ross, et al., 1970). In all studies excessively rapid growth, dietetically induced, militates against longevity.

Less severe or intermittent restriction prolongs life, but chiefly by cutting early mortality, with less effect on the specific age. Riesen, et al. (1947) found that in Wistar rats the gain was roughly proportional to the severity of restriction: starvation for 1 day in 3 or 4 produces a significant increase in mean life. The benefit from retardation is greater in rats on an omnivorous than on a vegetarian diet (Carlson and Hoelzel, 1947, 1948). By fasting 1 day in 3, increases in mean expectation of 20 percent in males and of 15 percent in females are obtainable without arrest of growth (Carlson and Hoelzel, 1946). Thomasson (1955) found that the survival curve of rats receiving 27 percent fat in the diet in the form of butter was oblique, with little initial plateau. If rapeseed oil was substituted the plateau was prolonged by about 25 weeks, and the curve became more rectangular: Growth was slower— chiefly because appetite was decreased—and there was a marked reduction in renal disease. By reducing food intake only moderately, to a level that did not inhibit growth or retard sexual maturation, Berg and Simms (1962) have increased the life-span of rats by 25 percent (200 days) in females and 30 percent (300 days) in males, with corresponding delay in the onset of diseases and tumors.

Experiments of the same type have been made upon mice, with very similar results. Both total and reproductive life-span can be increased by calorie restriction. On a diet containing half the calories (as lard and dextrose) in the standard mouse diet, C_3H females which are normally sterile at 11–12 months were still rearing litters at 21 months, the longest records being in mice restricted for 11–15 months and then fully fed (Carr, et al., 1949); fasting on 2 days out of 7, with or without addition of nucleic acid to the diet, produced an increase of 50–60 percent in the life-span of albinos (Robertson, et al., 1934).

Mice have the advantage of being available as inbred lines, which vary in life-span and predominant cause of death. They are also free of the enzootic lung infections that complicate rat longevity studies. Several investigators have studied special effects of calorie restriction or of limiting intake of particular foodstuffs. Tannenbaum (1947) found that female DBA mice restricted to a weight of 19–20 g showed a striking absence of spontaneous tumors, which were the chief cause of death in 30-g controls. In YBR/Wi "yellow" mice, a high-fat diet reduced the incidence of amyloidosis but greatly shortened life (Silberberg and Silberberg, 1955, 1957b); but a high-carbohydrate diet, though it produced obesity, did not affect life-span. C57 mice responded to a high-fat diet by developing a high incidence of arthritis (Silberberg and Silberberg, 1957a). King, et al. (1955) found that in C_3H mice given a diet containing the normal trace-element additives, there was a high incidence of sudden heart failure after about a year, and of fetal resorption, which could be prevented either by added tocopherol or by omission of trace elements. "Obese" *(ob, ob)* mice whose weight was restricted by a diet low in calories have proved remarkably long-lived, reaching 1,027 days (Lane and Dickie, 1958): the gain from restriction was greater than in the nonobese hemizygotes *(ob, +)*. In a few instances vitamin supplements have been found to improve performance: vitamin A (Sherman and Trupp, 1940), pantothenic acid (Anonymous, 1949; Pelton and Williams, 1958), but the examples probably represent the remedying of deficiencies.

The mechanism of retardation by dietary restriction in growing mammals is partially known from other studies. It appears to be central and neuroendocrine. Inanition lowers the gonadotrophic activity of the pituitary; this was clearly shown by the transplantation studies of Mason and Wolfe (1930) on female rats, and again in male rats by Moore and Samuels (1931). In rats, reduction of the protein content of the diet below 7 percent produces anestrus from gonadotrophin deficiency (Guilbert and Goss, 1932).

Aside from any general action on the appetite-size control system, one crucial agent, acting by deficiency, appears to be tryptophan, and its lack probably operates to interfere with serotonin production (Segal and Timiras, 1976). The sensor is presumably hypothalamic, the limiting reaction in serotonin formation being the hydroxylation of tryptophan, and that in dopamine and norepinephrine synthesis the hydroxylation of L-tyrosine (Fernstrom, 1976). In the "pseudohypophysectomy" of malnutrition, pituitary growth hormone will reinitiate growth of the skeleton and decrease the rate of weight loss even without increase of food intake (Mulinos and Pomerantz, 1941; Samuels, 1946). The effects of restricted food intake on the neuroendocrine system probably play a major part in the alteration of apparent specific age. (See Section 9.7.)

In C$_3$H mice, Carr, et al. (1949) produced anestrus by reducing the standard calorie intake by half: at 14 months of age, single cycles were readily induced by administering dextrose, though the dose necessary to bring this about varied from 0.15 to 1.0 g. When the mice were permitted at the age of 21 months to feed at will, and mated, all became pregnant, and 10 out of an initial total of 17 were alive and sexually active at the age of 23 months.

We have no comparable observations in man. Malnutrition can produce gross retardation of puberty (as can disease or "indirect" malnutrition—the effects of bilharzia are particularly striking), but such malnutrition is always total and shortens life. In McCay's experiments the dietary restriction was confined to reduction of calories. The undernourished majority in the world at the present time derive no benefit in longevity from their circumstances. But it is not impossible, as Edmonds suggested in 1832, and as Sinclair (1955) and McCance and Widdowson (1955) repeated, that adult life might be shortened by the pursuit of excessively rapid growth during childhood. Human puberty can be accelerated by overfeeding (Bruch, 1941), and there is already evidence that while the maximum mean height of Englishmen has not increased during the last century, it is now reached no less than 5 years earlier (Morant, 1950), and the loss of height with increasing age shows a parallel advance. The main objections to such an argument are that the present acceleration of puberty is probably a return to normal rather than a fresh development, the age of menarche in the ancient world having been what it is now: and that the evolved "lag" in early human development, characteristic of the lengthened primate childhood, is likely to complicate any direct analogy with rodent growth and maturation (Tanner, 1955; Comfort, 1960c). Constitutional precocious puberty does not appear to shorten life (Jolly, 1955) (see Figure 6.3).

Much of this older literature is now of historical interest. In 1948, Evans, et al. confirmed with pure growth hormone Wiesner's (1932) original finding that rats could be kept in continuous growth throughout life by injections of pituitary growth hormone. Wiesner had reported some improvement in the condition of old male rats under the influence of growth hormone. The experiment of Evans, et al., was not designed to study the effect of growth on longevity, and they found that continued growth from hormone administration in rats itself leads to death from an increased incidence of tumors. The 12 animals in the original experiment of Evans, et al., were killed at 647 days for histological purposes. With small doses of the purified hormone, "drug-resistance" to the growth-promoting and nitrogen-retaining effects develops (Whitney, et al., 1948). In dogs and cats, continued administration of growth hormone after growth cessation produces not growth but diabetes, while in others (man) epiphyseal fusion prevents continued body growth after sexual maturity. Hopes were once entertained of using growth hormone to delay senescence. Moon, et al. (1952), found that massive administration of growth hormone (2 mg/day) to mice evoked tumors in only one of the tested strains. It appears, moreover, that growth hormone alone fails to induce tumors in hypophysectomized animals (Asling, et al., 1952a, b). The idea underlying this kind of investigation was already present in the work of Robertson (Robertson and Ray, 1919; Robertson, 1923) at a time when endocrinology was insufficiently advanced to enable it to be realized. The results they obtained in retarding growth with "tethelin" were almost certainly non-specific.

It is now clear that the emphasis on "growth" as a possible preventative of ageing, stemming as it does from Bidder and from an erroneous hypothesis, is a misdirection of energy—we should rather be looking for the site of the sensor by which calorie restriction is "read" and the rate of ageing consequently modified (Ch. 9.7). Everitt (1959) finds that growth hormone failed either to prolong life or to reverse indexes of senescence in ageing rats.

Attempts to *accelerate* mammalian senescence have been surprisingly unsuccessful. While laboratory animals can be prematurely killed by a number of drugs or deficiencies, these do not in general affect the process of senescence, radiation and the radiomimetic drugs excluded. Experimental efforts to accelerate ageing in rats with dinitrophenol (Tainter, 1936, 1938) and thyroid (Robertson, et al., 1933) or retard it with thiouracil (Hartzell, 1945) were uniformly unsuccessful in bringing about any change in the specific age. Petrova (1946) obtained evidence that induced neurosis at least shortens the life, if it does not affect the specific age, in dogs: it is significant that in man the most effective means of reducing the apparent rate of senile change, *ceteris paribus,* are psychological, social, and occupational.

5.3 Growth Cessation and Mammalian Senescence

Mammals in captivity under "optimal" conditions exhibit both specific size and specific age, and these vary widely between related species, and between genetic races of the same species. The mechanism that determines specific size has long been believed by some workers to intervene more actively in mammalian development and to be more selective in its action on tissues, than the mechanism that leads to the more gradual decline of growth in some reptiles and fish. In these forms, according to this view, the die-away curve of growth, which is generally exponential in relation to body weight, suggests a far more general process of size limitation affecting all the tissues approximately equally, and reaching the virtual limiting size without much alteration in the general physiology of the animal.

> It is the rule in fishes and other cold-blooded vertebrates that growth is asymptotic and size indeterminate, while in warm-blooded animals, growth comes, sooner or later, to an end. But the characteristic form is established earlier in the former case, and changes less, save for . . . minor fluctuations. In the higher animals, such as ourselves, the whole course of life is attended by constant alteration and modification of form" (D'Arcy Thompson, 1942).

The form of the mammalian, and especially the human, cycle both of growth and of senescence has frequently been interpreted as an active process of negative feedback, which operates unequally, and may contribute to the relatively sharp arrest of growth at the level represented by the specific size, but results in a "morphogenetic" senescence depending in turn upon a rather limited number of key physiological changes.

With the hypothetical relationship between growth cessation and senescence in mind, a number of attempts have been made in the past to interpret senile changes in terms of endogenous "growth inhibitors," whether these are regarded as substances or as physicochemical conditions (Baker and Carrel, 1926; Carrel and Ebeling, 1921; Simms and Stillman, 1936). The case for such an inhibiting system was stated by Bidder (1932) in the passage already quoted. The nature of influences determining mammalian organ size is virtually unknown. Some of these appear to be extracellular and inhibitory. In cultures, for example of diatoms, growth may be arrested by the accumulation of a metabolite (Denffer, 1948). The most primitive types of morphogenesis, such as that found in hydroids, depend on the acquisition by certain zooids of inhibitory powers over the development of others (Summers, 1938), although the inhibited cells retain the potentiality of growth. It is also known that some "old" tissue cells are capable of indefinite growth in cultivation.

The suggestions implicit in this type of reasoning are tempting, but there are evidential grounds for caution in postulating a simple "toxic" senescence due to the existence of a growth-inhibiting senile principle. Such a principle is not readily demonstrated. Bidder once rashly located it in the pineal gland; this is an example of scientific precognition, in that the pineal's association with biological "clock" processes has been reopened of late (Quay, 1972). Kotsovsky (1931) attempted successfully to retard the growth of tadpoles by feeding senile heart muscle—an improbable tissue for such a purpose—and

Grimm (1949) obtained similar results with senile plasma. Picado (1930) enhanced the growth of young rats by transfusions of adult plasma. More serious data, however, exist.

The best experimental evidence concerning growth limitation is probably that obtained from studies of mammalian liver. Although mitotic figures and binucleate cells decrease in mammalian liver throughout life, regeneration after hepatectomy occurs in senile rats, apparently at a rate not much lower, so far as replacement of cell number is concerned, than in young adults, though much less than in growing animals (Bucher and Glinos, 1950). As Minot pointed out (1908) the adult differs more from the infant than the old from the adult. The time lag between hepatectomy and maximum mitotic count increases with age (Marshak and Byron, 1945), thereby paralleling the difference between the behavior of tissues from young immature and young adult donors in tissue culture (Hoffman, et al., 1937), and confirming the universal finding of increased growth inertia, rather than decreased growth capacity, as the most conspicuous character of cellular explants with increasing donor age (Cohn and Murray, 1925; Suzuki, 1926; Medawar, 1940). In regenerating rat liver at all ages, however, the lag reverts to the value characteristic of young animals (Glinos and Bartlett, 1951). In young actively growing rats the restoration of liver mass after hepatectomy shows a considerable rebound phenomenon, reaching 145 percent of the original weight in 7 days (Norris, et al., 1942). All the general characteristics of tissue behavior during the attainment of specific size appear to be exemplified in liver. These include: (1) negative specific acceleration of growth; (2) retention of growth capacity after the limiting size has been attained, as demonstrated either by explants or, in this case, following partial removal of the organ; (3) increased growth inertia with increasing age; and (4) "postinhibition growth rebound." Medawar (1942) stresses the surprisingly wide distribution of this last effect, which is shown by tissue cultures (Spear, 1928) and *Amblystoma* larvae (Buchanan, 1938) retarded by cooling, and in rats or mice following brief restriction of diet (Osborne and Mendel, 1916; Clarke and Smith, 1938; Jackson, 1936).

Much is still on occasion made of the decline in rate of wound healing with age proposed by du Noüy (1916, 1932) as a criterion of senescence (Landahl, 1959). This entire theory was based on less than a dozen uncontrolled cases and should now be considered extinct. (Landahl, in citing it, appears to agree that it is probably wrong in fact—but what matter? It gives such a beautiful curve.) Experimental studies suggest that while actual cell replacement in wounded skin is highest in infancy, little difference in cell multiplication exists between adult and senile animals, though here again the time lag in reaching the peak mitotic rate becomes longer with age (Howes and Harvey, 1932; Bourlière, 1950) though the actual mitotic rate increases (Thuringer and Katzberg, 1959). Delayed healing of skin wounds is not clinically very evident in old people (Elman, 1953). In male mice the mitosis curve for skin in situ is bimodal, with peaks in infancy and again in middle age (Bullough, 1949). One easily-measured growth system that shows a steady decline throughout later life is that controlling fingernail growth (Knobloch, 1951; Bürger, 1954; Hamilton, et al., 1955).

Attempts have been made in the specific case of liver tissues to relate organ size to the existence of a mitotic inhibitor or inhibitors. Studies on plasmapheresis (Glinos and Gey, 1952) and parabiosis (Bucher, et al., 1950) after partial hepatectomy have yielded some evidence that a humoral inhibitor, of the kind envisaged by Carrel and Ebeling (1921), disappears from circulation after hepatectomy. These observations, though interesting, could provide a suspiciously simple picture of the dynamics of growth limitation, and of consequent senescence.

An opposing view to the humoral school was suggested by Medawar (1942). Both in whole animals and in specific organs and tissues the rate of growth declines throughout life. Medawar points out that it is not self-evident that this decline is the result of active growth inhibition.

> We are so deeply influenced by the spirit of Newton's First Law that we tend to think that whenever a *rate* falls off, something is actively suppressing it. This is true of rates of motion, but it is not true in quite the same sense of the rates of a type of change which we may call changes in *probability states*. The rate at which heat is lost from a cooling body is initially high, and falls off as its temperature approaches that of the environment. The rate at which the distribution of molecules in a closed-diffusion system tends towards uniformity is likewise rapid at first, and slower and slower thereafter. In these cases, and in other similar to them, we are dealing with rates that fall off 'of their own accord,' with systems that tend to a certain, most-probable state at a rate which depends upon how far they have yet to go to reach it. We may look in vain for inhibitors and controllers: they are not there. I do not know whether what I have called the 'kinetic picture' of growth will be found to fall within the domain of statistical mechanics. . . . It is simply a picture which we should keep in mind when thinking of growth processes, lest we should come to regard the doctrine of growth-controlling factors as self-evident; which it certainly is not.

This argument is graphical rather than explanatory, and the analogy it contains must be approached with caution. It is evident that organ size has certain properties of an equilibrium state, in approaching which the cell number and growth energy vary after the manner of potential energy in the process of redistribution. The equilibrating forces, however, manifestly arise, on the evidence of explantation, from the organ's and the cell's surroundings. Mathematically similar systems involving real energy loss, such as cooling, are in no real sense analogous, since they are examples of a process not subject to further analysis. The decline in human population growth is as fair a comparison. Although morphogenesis is no doubt ultimately expressible as a redistribution of energy, "inherent" decline of rate in approaching a most-probable state is only *explanatory*, in the sense of providing a satisfactory regression of causes to the limit of useful experiment, if "growth energy" is itself a form of energy in the physical sense, analogous to heat in a kettle or electrochemical energy in a battery; in the hypothetical case where a population of cells was restricted in growth by exhausting a particular energy source, employed only for growth and not for maintenance metabolism, such a system would apply, and would not only depict but "explain" the course of events.

The great value of the approach from probability, as Medawar points out, is in preventing a facile assumption that if a growth rate declines, this decline must result from the action of a specific toxin or inhibitor. This does not mean, however, that in a complex biological system we can avoid asking specifically *what* declines, since a decline in rate implies real quantitative and qualitative change in terms of chemical structure, and the investigation of these changes is practicable. It appears manifest that the reversion of explanted tissues to active growth is in fact caused by removal from their previous environment. It seems at least arguable whether the time lag in multiplication that characterizes aged explants is inherent in the cell at all. Simms found that the lag in cell division of aortic explants from old fowls can be reduced by a number of non-specific procedures such as papain digestion, or washing with an ultrafiltrate of serum (Simms, 1936; Simms and Stillman, 1937). Such effects might even be purely mechanical. For most purposes it is probably also desirable to regard growth energy less as a "store," since, to maintain the analogy, such a "store" must be almost immediately "replenished" after hepatectomy or explantation, than as a "space," with walls defined by the continuously varying properties of any individual cell in the growing tissue, and by the continuously varying properties of the "environment," in which are included all the adjacent cells of the same tissue. Such a concept, and, in fact, any concept of limiting size as an equilibrium process, would seem incidentally to imply the continuous replacement of any deciduous cells. The chief criticism of the humoral theories of growth limitation is their readiness to assume that the limiting factors derived from the "environment" can (a) be treated in isolation and (b) necessarily correspond to substances rather than to physicochemical states and gradients. That adjacent-cell effects need not depend upon molecular hormones is well shown by Whitaker's work on the mutual orientation of *Fucus* egg cells through a simple pH gradient (see J. Needham, 1942). The search for hormonal substances that can be isolated is abundantly justifiable, but the failure to find them should not be astonishing or discouraging. There is much evidence (reviewed by Stewart and Kirk, 1954) to suggest that the "inhibitors" detected in old serum by Carrel and his associates were non-specific mate rials, probably including the serum lipoproteins. This is not to say that such materials do not exert a growth-inhibiting effect in vivo, or that such an effect is without physiological significance, but most existing studies certainly support Medawar's conclusion (1942) that there is no simple extractable contact hormone in adult tissue that directly restrains the growth of cells. The "inflection" in the curve of absolute growth (weight/time) is still occasionally quoted as evidence of active growth inhibition, but this is a mathematical fallacy that has been repeatedly exposed (Minot, 1908; Schmalhäusen, 1929; Weymouth, 1931; Medawar, 1945).

The raising of this question, in relation to senescence rather than morphogenesis, turns once again on the supposed absence of age changes in some reptiles and fish, now exploded by observation. The possible association between size limitation and homeothermy is interesting in view of the different relationships between pituitary and thyroid hormones in the determination of growth which have been found in mammals and in amphibians (Evans et al., 1939; Scow and Marx, 1945; Steinmetz, 1954); at some point in vertebrate evolution, a balance mechanism between thyroid and growth hormone, which leads to gigantism in the thiouracil-treated tadpole, has become converted into a synergism such as normally operates in the rat or in man. Unfortunately for any phylogenetic theory, the pattern in fish appears to resemble that in mammals (Goldsmith, et al., 1944). This subject will be further considered in a subsequent chapter.

6

The Mechanisms of Senescence

6.1 Background

The early years of experimental gerontology were spent in cataloging every kind of change that might conceivably reduce the vigor of an organism with time. This was a necessary activity, but the mechanisms are numerous and—taken singly—misleading, since in any organism, whether mammal or insect, time-dependent adverse changes are integrated into a definite life-cycle. Occasionally a single change is obviously limiting, but such examples are rare; many time-dependent changes are uncoupled, or only loosely coupled, to the "clock" of life-cycle. They would become important in limiting life if the organism did not age as it now does. Such uncoupled processes are, however, attractive by reason of being easily isolated for study. In other cases in vitro study has masked the degree of coupling in vivo: clonal senescence, for example, is loosely coupled to endocrine controls and tightly coupled to the epigenetic controls for cell turnover; collagen cross-linking, though normally on its own "clock," is coupled to endocrine processes.

Approaching earlier work with hindsight, we can now identify the basic model as a hierarchy of "ageing" processes. The relevant assignment, curiosity aside, is to identify that or those that actually time the observed life-cycle in man and are accessible to interference. So far the trend has still been to identify individual age processes, such as clonal change or somatic mutation, and then attempt to erect a theory treating each as a prospective "cause," so-called unitary theories. This approach should now perhaps yield to a systems theory model, and the timing elements located in the body's main cybernetic areas (brain and chromatin)—where programmed interaction and drift may both be interactively located. In the set-point adjustments that pattern observed ageing in man, the brain overrides the chromatin-epigenetic system, though this system is a possible source of the secular change that powers the ageing "clock," and the points of likely first-instance intervention lie in the software, not in "inherent" or "unitary" processes.

The mathematics of systems theory, or of catastrophe theory as applied to the topological analysis of instability that ageing represents, will not be presented here, since they serve chiefly to rehearse the facts in an alternative language. In this chapter age change studies will be cataloged historically rather than grouped in a hierarchical model—chiefly because the hierarchy is no doubt different for every organism, or at least every phylum—while the changes that have occupied researchers are drawn from a vast array of organisms and must necessarily be treated in detail.

6.2   Concept of Hierarchy of Clocks

Lifespan determination can be accurately analogized on the model of a probe designed to fly past Mars. In such a device the components have individual "life spans" and are subject to ongoing deterioration with or without partial renewal, but their tolerances have been chosen to allow the mission to be completed with some reserve in hand. Moreover, homeostasis in the system is governed by an inflight computer which monitors subsystems, adjusts to failures, and can call on backup circuits when such failures occur. The actual lifespan of such a machine will now depend not on one component or system but on the homeostatic program. The mission completed, however, the computer control will either (1) continue as before but with decreasing accuracy as more and more systems run over tolerance, until a major failure, or a minor failure involving the control mechanism itself, takes place; (2) "lose interest" and discontinue maintenance operations such as battery recharging or attitude control; or (3) self-destruct if actively programmed to do so. A vehicle designed to self-destruct exhibits programmed ageing; a vehicle not so designed exhibits "running out of program." In the event that in the first situation the "clock" controlling self-destruct misses, or is artificially set slow, then the lowest component tolerances will in turn become the "clock" upon which the demise of the vehicle will depend.

It seems probable on present information that mammalian ageing is analogous to the behavior we describe here as programmed; whether biologically speaking it is truly programmed will depend on evidence of an active self-destruct process that has been selected as adaptive, rather than on elements of feed-forward in control systems that have escaped from natural selection for the reasons suggested by Medawar (1945, 1952). In either event the result has been the production of a highly-canalized life-span integrated with habits, size, reproductive rate, and population dynamics. At the same time there are open-ended processes—such as clonal exhaustion—that, while under partial control from the hypothetical "life-span clock," would eventually cause the death of the organism, and there are probably other processes—such as irreversible damage by background radiation, not under the control of the "life-span clock"—which would likewise eventually prove fatal. So long as the life-span remains limited by a more general interplay of homeostatic failures, however, these subsidiary ageing processes do not have the time to cause major life-limiting effects—as in the spacecraft that is summarily blown up at a set point in time metal fatigue or battery exhaustion appear only as pathologies, not as life-limiting mechanisms.

A more accurate model is perhaps that of a charge, representing eventual dyshomeostasis and death, connected to a large number of time-fuses set to different intervals (Figure 6.2). Some of these are autonomous, like the accumulation of mutational events. Others, such as clonal and immunological senescence, are probably subject to timing by an overall life-span-determining clock. In turn, this clock itself directly detonates the charge, and also activates dependent clocks with varying time intervals; we witness the activation of these clocks in the process of ageing, and they contribute to its features, but the terminal event is probably initiated by the master clock. Or possibly the master clock, rather than itself detonating the charge, arms the detonating circuit, but the charge is not exploded until one or more of the dependent clocks runs out its time interval and is also armed. The apparently "gradual" appearance of senile dyshomeostasis, expressed in the notion that "ageing begins at birth," may well be an illusion generated by the successive activation of these dependent processes, while actual deterioration and death are relatively late processes, reflecting the arming of a neuroendocrine destruct mechanism, which is the most likely candidate for the life-span–setting master. The main expository defect of this model, of course, is that what is set off is not a sudden explosion but a cessation of self-maintenance—as if, returning to the model of the spacecraft, self-destruct were achieved not by detonation but by the active cessation of battery recharging or some other maintenance function.

Various alterations of this model can accommodate most credible hypotheses of ageing: a neuroendocrine master clock might, for example, depend for its timing on late-acting genes, stochastic events, loss of cells, or clonal exhaustion, though straightforward overinhibition of peripheral function by feed-forward from rate of growth, body size, or similar developmental measures seems in this case more likely—an interesting reminiscence, in this context, of the "growth" theories of Bidder and others. For an integrative clock to override life-span, it stands to reason that other potential age processes such as clonal duration must have tolerances such that the set life-span can be attained without their running out. The real interest of the model is that if the concept of a life-span-integrative neuroendocrine mechanism were to prove correct, and that mechanism were to be artificially modifiable—rather as a conventional clock can be regulated fast or slow—the degree of possible regulation would determine not only life-span artificially attainable, but whether the form of natural ageing in the modified organism changed radically because some other unregulated mechanism of ageing now fired first. Caloric restriction can almost double rodent life-span, and the ageing seen in retarded rodents appears normal in pattern though it occurs later; this suggests that whatever is regulated by the maneuver carries with it such subprocesses as clonal exhaustion, or that any such processes that are not regulated have time-constants so long that they do not preempt the process. Thus in the study by Johnson and Erner (1972; Figure 6.1) neuron loss in mice appeared to have a reserve sufficient for that process never normally to proceed to deficit in the life-span of the strain, and since calorie-restricted mice do not become evidently demented we must assume the process to be lower in the hierarchy of clocks than the process that is delayed by calorie restriction. If the master clock were to be very much more slowed, however, either it, or one of these subprocesses, can be expected to reach the limit of effective regulation. The point of stressing this interaction is to counter the predictions, based on unitary models of ageing, that once the nature of "the" ageing process is identified, and that process modified, vast life-spans can be predicated on the mortality rates existing at the time of life when mortality is lowest; such a simplistic model is possible but evidentially unlikely. The clinical limits of age delay are probably those of the slowest possible set for the overriding clock. To go beyond that would almost certainly involve addressing and controlling successively further mechanisms that do not operate in the ageing process as we now observe it.

The utility of invertebrates and lower vertebrates as models for mammalian ageing does not depend on any simplistic view of a "universal" ageing process—still less on the assumption that

> the essential features of the ageing phenomenon are universal among metazoans; senescence and death being the results of an evolutionary development directly related to differentiation and stemming from a need to restrict population sizes (Gershon, 1970)

This being almost certainly not the case, ageing is far more likely, given the questionable evolutionary argument, to be a final common path. A more rational approach is to identify clearly what component of mammalian ageing a lower organism might conceivably model (e.g., fixed cell changes in the nematodes to which Gershon's generalization referred) and use them to elucidate that process, in the awareness that, while it may be "an ageing process" in mammals, it cannot be assumed to be the chief lifespan determinant, whether or not it is so in the lower organism under study.

6.3   Unitary Theories

The two "unitary" theories of mammalian ageing most fancied by gerontologists and their recent allies the radiobiologists, are that it represents either (1) progressive loss or functional deterioration of fixed postmitotics or (2) progressive accumulation of faulty copying in clonally dividing cells—attributed variously to somatic mutation aneuploidy, cross-linking effects in information-carrying molecules, or some other stochastic process that would enable natural ageing to be fitted with the findings concerning radiation-induced life-shortening. Either (1) or (2) could presumably act as a clock located, probably, in one or more key groups rather than in the generality of fixed or of non-fixed tissue cells and would initiate secondary types of mischief which would produce the exponential mortality rise we see in life-tables.

The formulation that would receive, perhaps, the widest assent, at least in the matter of human senescence, has been that morphogenetic processes lead to the differentiation of cells that have lost the capacity for division—such as neurons and skeletal muscle fibers—and to a suspension of division in others, and that processes of "wear and tear," chemical, mechanical, or of a degree of biophysical subtlety depending on the taste of the investigator, thereafter bring about the decline of some or all of the tissues thus deprived of the power of self-renewal. This is plausible and probably true. On the other hand, no satisfactory technique has been devised for the study of cell population in situ, apart from the search for mitotic figures in sections; we do not, therefore, know the life-span of most tissue cells in their natural situation; many of the descriptions of senile change in fixed postmitotics, especially neurons, are based upon the assumption that the life-span of cells specialized to this extent is limited by their incapacity for division, as appears to be the case in rotifer and *Anguillula* cells. The striking differences in specific age between related species do not disprove the contribution of cell ageing to general senescence, but they cast a great deal of doubt on any assumption that the effect of wear and tear upon neurons (Bab, 1948; Vogt and Vogt, 1946) or any similar process is the prime mover in determining the senile decline. The powers of self-renewal possessed by neurons apart from cell division have almost certainly been under- rather than overestimated. Neuron regeneration in

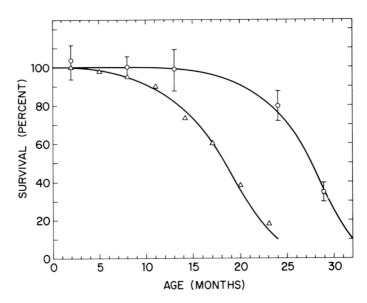

FIGURE 6.1   Percent survival of mice (Δ) and their neurons (○) versus age. Smooth curves are survival curves derived from the Gompertz relationship. (From Johnson and Erner, 1972.)

adult fish and amphibia can involve actual cell replacement from a reserve of neuroblasts:[1] in adult birds and mammals it is usually held to be limited to axon growth (see Clemente and Windle, 1955 for a review of the considerable literature). Radioactive thymidine incorporation in rat brain is usually limited to glia cells, which go on increasing throughout life (Smart and Leblond, 1961). The numbers of new glial cells appearing seem disproportionately high compared with the number of visible mitoses—some amitotic process may possibly be occurring to supplement them (Smart and Leblond, 1961). Cell division, however, may not be the only means of nuclear renewal (Pelc, 1965): the appearance of "binucleate" neurons in some old animals has been taken as evidence of a process of reconstitution (Andrew, 1955). Apart from this it is evident from observation that some neurons are capable of living and remaining in function for 100–115 years, unless we postulate a system of "reserve circuits" which has so far no evidence to support it. The distinction drawn by Weismann between immortal germ cells and mortal

---

[1] It has even been claimed that the Purkinje cells of the mammalian cerebellum, the least likely of all such cells to do so, undergo a cycle of periodic replacement from such a reserve (Baffoni, 1954). This is surely either a fundamental discovery or an egregious error, probably the second.

soma still persists in many of these assumptions, in spite of the growing number of instances where differentiated somatic cells in invertebrates are thought to give rise to germ cells, or to structures having the potentialities of germ cells (Brien, 1953).

The repeatedly cited "senile loss of brain tissue" now appears suspect (Tomasch, 1972). In mice, the main countable change with age seems to be in glia, which undergo a 40 percent reduction by 18 months, neurons and axons being unaffected (Sturrock, 1976). It is based largely on the findings of Andrew for the cerebellum (1955), which confirmed the work of Inukai in rats (1928). It is likely that selection of material, artifacts, viral and other diseases, and physiological processes of cell removal in the course of "programming" account for the wide discrepancies between investigators and tissues. Spinal cord and spinal root cell numbers have been said to decline

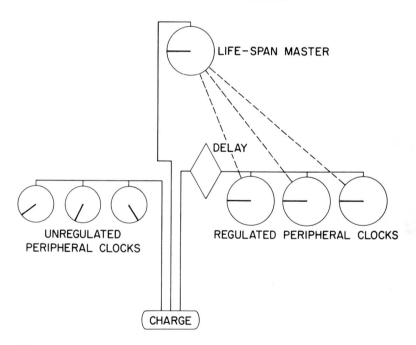

FIGURE 6.2   The determinant of life-span is normally the master, which fires first, either directly or via regulated secondary clocks with varying intervals after firing. Unregulated clocks are set "slow" and do not normally fire within the life-span. If the master were to be artificially slowed, one such unregulated clock might be able to "detonate" eventual ageing.

(mice—Wright and Spink, 1959; man—Arey and Bickel, 1935), remain constant (Duncan—1930), or increase slightly with age (cats—Moyer and Kalischewski, 1958). The cortical decline described in man by Brody (1970) was not confirmed in rats by Brizzee, et al. (1968), who found little change. Total longevity of the organism may of course make a difference, but it entails a rising incidence of specific pathologies and the determination of human cortical cell number, at best an arduous procedure, has never been correlated with cardiovascular or viral history. Mouse cortical cell number declines little, if at all, with age (Franks, et al., 1974). The decline it shows when estimated by a total-DNA method parallels the survival curve but lies to the right of it (Johnson and Erner, 1972), suggesting an ample reserve. An added complication is suggested by the finding of Balázs and Cotterrell (1972) that cortisol and thyroid reduce brain-cell number when administered during development.

6.4 Senescence in Cells

6.4.1 "Irreplaceable" Enzymes

There is no self-evident reason for the fact that the action of morphogenetic forces on cells, inhibiting their free division, should lead to their senescence. Mechanical and "colloidal" interpretations will not do; they fail to treat postmitotic cells as the dynamic systems which they certainly are. A theory of "mechanical ageing" in postmitotic cells could, however, be based on the exhaustion of specific cell constituents. It is reasonable to ask how much of the senescence of such cells, if they necessarily undergo senescence, is due to the existence of "expendable" enzymic or other intracellular structures, which can be replaced only at cell division.

The concept of an expendable "life-ferment" appears to have originated with Bütschli (1882), although he probably regarded it simply as a material undergoing distribution from the germ cells, where it is highly concentrated, to the somatic cells in which it is increasingly diluted by subdivision. We might now settle for a theory of enzyme exhaustion in postmitotics; we have to postulate (1) a fixed quantity of enzyme present in the cell and exhaustible by use, and (2) the existence of an essential enzyme replaceable only at cell division. The first proviso appears already to be largely met, since it is known that the effective life-span of enzyme molecules is finite in terms of molecule turnover (McIlwain, 1946, 1949; Theorell, et al., 1951).

The existence of enzyme systems renewed *only at cell division* has not, it seems, been demonstrated as such, but with the single general and large exception of "hereditary materials," nuclear and extranuclear, it has not been sought. Some direct evidence might be derived from the action of known selective blocking agents upon bacteria of protozoa. It will be evident, however, that the idea of an "enzyme replaced only by mitosis" falls very close to some biochemical models of the gene, which has been invested, either directly or at one remove, with direct catalytic properties. McIlwain (1946) has shown that in some catalytic systems the number of enzyme molecules per cell is of the order of unity. The inference from his figures is that if genes are not themselves molecules acting as catalysts, each gene during its "lifetime" (i.e., between one cell division and the next) produces one such molecule. McIlwain (1949) also calculated the life-span per molecule of the nicotinic acid co-enzyme component of *Lactobacillus arabinosus* as representing the production of 5.8×10^7 mol lactic acid. Theorell, et al., (1951) in tracer experiments demonstrated a very slow turnover of hemoprotein enzymes, the exception being liver catalase, which has a molecule life of only 4–5 days. The wastage of such systems is due, presumably, in part to side reactions and non-specific inactivation, and in part to competitive inhibition or blocking by metabolites partially resembling the correct substrate. If the determination of such a single-molecule system were a cause of cell senescence, and if the catalyst itself were to be identified with the gene, we would evidently need to postulate a copying mechanism at mitosis in which inactivation of the catalytic portion of the system (1) does not interfere with the production of a copy, and (2) is itself reversible: or, alternatively, one in which the products of division are two copies, not an original and a copy. It can, of course, be argued that when a differentiated cell in fact undergoes senescence, we cannot infer whether any system in it *would* be renewed by further division. Its failure to divide, even if that failure is a physiological one, leading to final differentiation, may be due to the loss of a copying mechanism. This type of problem has been encountered already, however, by workers attempting to explain some of the results of research on adaptive variation in Neurospora and yeasts. "Unless gene reproduction and gene action are totally independent of each other, we have to reconcile the uniformity in the reproduction of genes with the enormous variation in what we believe to be their primary products" (Pontecorvo, 1946). All of this speculation is now supplemented by work in nematodes which suggests faulty copying, or loss of the ability to translate RNA (Wallach and Gershon, 1974; see Ch. 9.1, 9.5).

Classical genetics, although it allocates an equal proportion of nuclear genic material to every cell, has so far given little direct information about the activity of this material in cells of different kinds at any time except during mitosis, and a new category of study ("epigenetics") has had to be coined to cover this activity. Of the large number of subsidiary copying processes which have been inferred from adaption experiments and work on anuclear portions of cells, some apparently continue undiminished throughout the intermitotic period. The power of adaptive enzyme production persists in yeasts rendered non-viable by x-rays (Spiegelman, et al., 1951). In a neuron, which may remain functioning in man for over a century, either the enzymic mechanism that maintains cell metabolism is continuously kept in repair, or it is of a kind that is almost invulnerable to incidental spoilage by use. The survival time of non-dividing cells varies greatly, even between closely related organisms: thus in rotifers, the life-span reaches 5 months in *Callidina* (Zelinka, 1891) and even, perhaps, several years in certain bdelloids (Murray, 1910). If "wear" is to be invoked in these cases where senescence occurs in the presence of cellular determinancy, then the susceptibility to it must vary enormously. Other cells—squamous epithelium, for example—have a function that depends on the progressive *change* in their structure and metabolism from formation to complete cornification. This implies a process of chemical heterauxesis within the cell, and all such "open-ended" systems, if they continue, must eventually destroy homeostasis. In Bullough's model (1967) cell longevity is fixed, though it remains subject to hormonal modification, at the point where a determined cell emerges from the mitotic cycle. Age control might depend in this case upon intervention to prolong the viability of postmitotics. The older idea of returning them to active mitosis (which is what appears in some instances to occur in malignancy) holds few attractions. It is, however, of interest to know how far they retain their original genetic potential intact. The development of histochemical methods of detecting enzymes in cells, and of selective blocking agents which irreversibly inactivate particular enzymes, already suggest experiments by which we might learn something of the limits of the postmitotic cell's power to regenerate its enzymic complement, and detect long-term changes in this power.

A special case of limited survival in the non-dividing cell is provided by the mammalian erythrocyte. This is one of the few cell types for which a life-table can be constructed. The form of the curves obtained by a variety of methods indicates that the decay of circulating erythrocytes is a true "senescence," i.e., that the probability of the destruction of a given cell increases markedly after it reaches a certain age. There is also, apparently, an "infant mortality" among newly-formed red cells to make the mimicry of a metazoan survival curve even closer.

The timing mechanism in this instance is the deleterious effect on other intracellular systems of the products of one particular oxidation-reduction system, in which methemoglobin is formed from hemoglobin (Lemberg and Legge, 1949). In this case we are dealing with a specialized, anuclear cell: in the nucleated avian erythrocyte, hemoglobin synthesis, and possibly other processes of renewal, continue in the circulation, but the life-span is, curiously enough, very much shorter (Hevesy and Ottesen, 1945; Hevesy, 1947) than that of the mammalian red cell. The relevance of red-cell turnover in general ageing is, however, small.

6.4.2   Cell Turnover

A popular notion among early medical writers on senescence was that cell turnover in the organs of the adult animal is virtually confined to such tissues as skin, and that the "cause" of senescence resides in the "exhaustion" of endocrine or other cells that have accompanied the individual throughout life. This might be true of some invertebrates, many of which have a wholly determinate cell number throughout, or in certain organs, such as the corpus allatum of bees (Pflugfelder, 1948); if the theory were to be applied to mammals the most probable candidates are nuerons. Definite loss of muscle cells, which are not normally replaced, was demonstrated by Yiengst, et al. (1959). Although the rate of turnover in liver cells decreases with age, and mitotic figures become few, the mean mitosis rate in adult rats is such as to double the volume of the organ in the animal's lifetime, if there were no incidental wastage.[2] This figure suggests that some liver cells may accompany the animals from cradle to grave, but that the majority do not. They do, however, undergo a peculiar process of nuclear multiplication with increasing polyploidy: in postoperative regeneration only the diploids divide to supply new cells (Doljanski 1960; review, Falzone, et al., 1959; Tanaka, 1951, 1953). Adrenal cortical cells are said to be continuously replaced in the adult cat (Lobban, 1952). Mitotic activity does, however, appear to decrease with advancing age (Blumenthal, 1945; Townsend, 1946; Korenchevsky, et al., 1950): in some other tissues, for example, skin, it increases (Thuringer and Katzberg, 1959). The generation cycle of mouse duodenal epithelium lengthens with age, and individual variation increases (Lesher, et al., 1961). The adrenals of old rats show various degenerative changes (Jayne, 1953). Mitosis varying in frequency with the sexual cycle occurs in the anterior pituitary (Hunt, 1942, 1943, 1947), though it may not affect all cell types equally, since the population changes in composition with advancing age (Parsons, 1936). There is no direct evidence that the power of cell replacement is lost in any endocrine gland with age, though there may be more general involutional changes at both cellular and tissue levels. The pattern of mammalian endocrine cell behavior is predominantly one of continual division and replacement, regulated in level by hormonal influences, and often occurring in cycles. It is impossible to say at present that there is not a single key exception to this pattern, but ageing is unlikely to be so simple a matter as the defection of one type of cell. It is significant that the syndrome of senescence cannot be produced experimentally by extirpating any one gland.

The morphological changes in endocrine cells with age have been widely studied, though here, as in all pathological studies of ageing, no line can be

---

[2]I am indebted to Professor M. Abercrombie, F.R.S., for this figure.

drawn between cause and effect. Such morphological changes in pituitary cells were reexamined by Weiss and Lansing (1953) and by Shanklin (1953), but without any new findings on the rate of cellular replacement. In some glandular organs, such as rat salivary glands, mitosis becomes both rare and abnormal in pattern after the end of active body growth, while in senile rats numerous imperfect mitoses occur (Andrew, 1953). For reviews of adult cell turnover, see Leblond and Walker (1956) and Abercrombie (1957).

6.4.3 Somatic Mutation

Somatic mutation as a cause of ageing owed its former popularity to three considerations: the fact that mutative change in cell lines would probably lead to eventual ageing if no other cause did so first; the prevalence of theories based upon it in cancer and radiation research; and the readiness with which it lends itself to speculative exercises in higher mathematics (Maynard Smith, 1962). An additional consideration was the intensely funded, if brief, excursion into radiobiology brought about by the nuclear weapons program.

The eruption of physicists into age studies—largely because of their involvement with radiation biology—produced a whole series of stochastic or "shooting" theories of ageing, which attempt to view it for purposes of description or explanation, in terms of a combination of random events, and these must now be examined if only for their historical interest.

The prototype of these theories is the idea that the predominant process in ageing is somatic mutation, leading to changes in the properties of clonally dividing cells and loss of capacity in fixed postmitotics. Its cause would be the sum of mutagenic influences on the body, and if radiation accelerated ageing, it would do so, in part at least, by increasing the mutation rate. The first suggestion of this in the literature seems to be that of Kunze (1933), who put it down to cosmic rays. In putting it forward again Failla (1960) points out that the large discrepancy between the observed and calculated "background equivalent" dose in irradiated mice can be removed if we allow for exposure to "background" in prenatal life, when radiation sensitivity is substantially higher. Failla is the originator of the term "hit" to describe a hypothetical lesion—point mutation, chromosome loss, or other—occurring in a cell and inactivating it. The term has been taken further in the elaborate stochastic model devised by Szilard (1959a, b).

Szilard assumes that the elementary step in ageing is a "hit" (not necessarily by a radiant particle) which renders inactive all the genes on one chromosome of a somatic cell. "Hits" are random events; the probability of any one chromosome being hit remains constant throughout life, and the overall rate of occurrence of hits is characteristic of the species. As a result of hits, the proportion of adequately functioning somatic cells declines with time until it reaches f^*, at which point the probability of death within unit time (in man, one year) is unity.

At the same time, each individual is assumed to carry a load of genetic "faults."

A "fault" is a mutation in one of the genes essential to the proper working of a somatic cell. Szilard assumes that the number of these genes in man is 3,000 out of a probable total of 15,000. A cell becomes inoperative when both of the pair of any such genes are put out of action. Accordingly, when a chromosome receives a hit, the cell will cease to function (a) if the homologous chromosome has already also received a hit, or (b) if the homologous chromosome carries a "fault" at any point. By assuming probable values for several quantities that no one accurately knows, Szilard proceeds from this model to draw plausible approximations to quantities that are known, such as the concordance between twin ages at death. He also proposes not an experimental proof, but at least one critical experiment—the reduction of life-span of the progeny of irradiated mice could support or negate the model.

The model itself has other interesting implications. One is that if m, the number of chromosome pairs, differs between species, the specific life shortening per rem will be greater for that in which m is the smaller, and vary inversely as $\sqrt{m}$. Szilard also works out, on the assumption of an average of $N = 2.5$ inherited faults per head for the human female, the modal longevity of a genetically perfect female with no such faults; it comes to 92 as against the present 80 years. If $N > 2.5$, it would be more.

Szilard's model is deeply ingenious, but for the biologist, as for the late Ernie Pyle, "the first word which comes to mind is But." Such simplified mathematical models can bring light to a subject—as did Morgan's assumption of the simple linearity of the genes—or merely darken it further. For the model to be relevant at all it seems essential that ageing should be timed by a fault in replication following the loss of one allele in the cell. This raises two grave objections, pointed out at once by Maynard Smith (1959b) and met by Szilard only at the expense of new variables (1959). The first is that, if the fault-hit hypothesis is right, the life of homozygous and inbred animals should be longer than that of heterozygous and hybrid animals, whereas the reverse is almost universally true. The second is that the only reason for Szilard's assumption that a hit inactivates a whole chromosome appears to be the need to find a hittable object yielding the right order of magnitude to account, for example, for the difference between male and female longevity, there being too many genes and too few cells to do so. It is also difficult to relate the whole model to the dynamics of cell division in a system that contains fixed and multiplying cells, where faults acquired by stem cells as the result of "hits" will be communicated to a varying cellular progeny. If the critical fraction f^* represents simply surviving cell number in general, it is difficult to credit either Failla's or Szilard's version of the cell-loss hypothesis, even if the effect of a "hit" is not necessarily the physical removal of the cell. Failla (1960), for example, assumes that "vitality" (the reciprocal of mortality) is ∞ f, the proportion of effective cells remaining, so that

$$\frac{f^t}{f^0} = e^{-\alpha t} = \text{spontaneous mutation rate, } \alpha \text{ being the slope}$$

factor of the Gompertz equation; and he points out that in this case the hitting process must damage rather than destroy the cell, as otherwise only 5.8 percent of the cells alive in man at the age of 35 would survive in him at the age of 65.[3] Szilard's theory seems to give an almost equally high rate of cell loss, whereas both completely ignore the question of replacement. If, on the other hand, f^* represents a fraction, not of cell number but only of an unspecified stuff "vitality," the further equations do no more than restate actuarial observation in new terms. To make them experimentally useful it would seem that ageing must be timed by the loss of key postmitotics (possibly in a single organ) or by a process with the same mathematical shape.

The third stochastic theory, by contrast with the Szilard-Failla model, places the emphasis specifically on the dividing cell, but on one particular clonal system. Antibodies are now thought to be produced by lymphocytes, and the acquired power of making a particular antibody appears to be transmitted by a lymphocyte to its progeny. A mechanism, not fully understood, determines that lymphocytes shall not normally respond to their proprietor's body constituents by forming antibodies against them.

Campbell and Work (1953) drew attention to the significance of the fact that animals cannot in general be immunized against their own proteins; and they suggest that the action of the genotype in determining specificity may be chiefly a negative one, in the prevention rather than the creation of a specific configuration. Burnet (1959) suggested that if mutation in lymphocytes followed by selection determines the various reactive capacities they show, and if one possible mutation is the loss of this negative specificity to homologous antigens, then the organism might be expected to face a steady increase in autoimmune reactions with the passage of time—reactions that might well be of precisely the polymorphic, diffuse, and variable type that characterizes the infirmities of ageing, whereas the statistical constancy of the mutation rate

---

[3]This is an arbitrary assumption, and Failla moreover undermines our confidence in this paper by devising a "constant," which is discovered by ceremoniously taking away the number he first thought of.

and/or the rate of occurrence of Szilardian "hits" would remain to provide the stability of the survival curve on which life assurance depends.

The revival of immunological age theories is an unexpected return to Metchnikoff (1899), who always predicted that the same cellular mechanism would prove to be morphogenetic in the embryo, defensive in the adult, and destructive in the end. Burnet's suggestion is open to experiment, and may possibly be confirmed or refuted reasonably quickly. Moreover, if true, it would mean that ageing was likely to be much more accessible to medical interference than it is now prudent to expect. It is not incompatible with some aspects of the Szilard-Failla model; the effect of a hit in this case is not that it removes a cell from useful activity, but that it puts a cell and its progeny into harmful activity. Burnet's general theory of "clonal selection" (1959) seems to imply that mutational instability in the lymphocyte system is used adaptively by the body, and moreover that the harmful mutation with loss of negative specificity also confers protection on the mutant against being "selected out" by normal body mechanisms, f^* being now no longer a cell balance below which we are bankrupt, but the fraction remaining after a lethal percentage of cells has become corrupted in this way. Burnet's theoretical argument persuasively urges that something of the sort ought to happen. What is now required is experimental evidence that it does so: Cole (1962) showed that the lymphocytes of old mice are less active in proliferating after isogenic transplantation, but not the reason for this behavior.

The gerontological interest of these suggestions lies in the fact that they come at a time when, in reviewing likely mechanisms of ageing, both somatic mutation and autoimmunity were avidly re-examined. The grounds for this re-examination were hypothetical, not experimental. In general the re-examiners argued on the following lines:

1. Somatic mutation causes divergence in tissue cells, albeit at an unmeasured rate. It would eventually impair tissue vigor if nothing else did.

2. Among its likely consequences is the production of new cells that are to some degree "not-self," as a result of the mutation of structural genes. If these cells are viable they will excite autoimmune reactions of varying degrees. The incidence of autoimmune disease increases with age in a Gompertzian manner (as do many other things—logarithms are great levelers).

3. The syndrome of chronic incompatibility ("runt disease") bears, to the eye of faith, certain resemblances both to senescence and to progeria (Tyler, 1960); more specifically, the splenic index and the incidence of hepatomegaly increase in ageing, progeria, and runt disease (Krumbhaar and Lippincott, 1939; Manschot, 1940; Simonsen, et al., 1958).

4. There is a suggestive three-cornered relationship between age processes, neoplastic processes, and autoimmune or supposedly autoimmune phenomena such as scleroderma.

5. Autoimmune phenomena are at present a "growth stock" and they should be re-examined in connection with every unsolved biological problem. This unspoken, but none the less defensible, argument applies equally to mutation, radiation-induced or otherwise.

All these arguments except the last have been intelligently amplified by Walford (1962). What has so far not appeared is the equally probable hypothesis that immune decline, like reproductive decline, is centrally mediated and coupled to a life-span "clock": immunologic ageing theories have for the most part been primary and cell-based, in spite of the finding of Price and Makinodan (1972a, b) that in cross-transplantation experiments both old cells and old environment are impaired.

Walford (1977) argues persuasively that much of observed ageing could represent increased auto- and decreased heteroimmunity. In long-lived strains of mice, dietary restriction delays maturation of immune-response capacity as well as prolonging life-span (Walford, et al., 1974; Gerbase-DeLima, et al., 1975; Walford, 1977). At a young age the cells of calorie-restricted mice show a diminished response to mitogens, but from 1 year of age onward their response is superior to that of controls: skin allograft survival is greatly prolonged, and does not reach normal values until over 1 year of age. Moreover, immunosuppression, either by low temperature or by immunosuppressants, may paradoxically correlate with increased life-span. Since it is now possible to reconstitute immune potential in old mice by irradiation and reimplantation of bone marrow and fetal thymus (Hirokawa and Makinodan, 1975), the extent to which failing immunity against pathogens and increasing autoimmunity against body constituents contributes to observed ageing should be measurable. Life-span experiments of this kind may also indicate whether immunological change is primary, and itself responsible for changes in response to protein hormones, or whether a hypothalamic "clock" is responsible for secondary immunological age effects. Both models are at present credible, especially as the role of immunity in controlling feed-forward end points in developmental response to protein hormones is at present unknown. There are experimental instances of immunological diversity in leukemias (Anderson, et al., 1961) and tumors generally (Tyler, 1960), but not very many in normal ageing—chiefly, perhaps, because they have not yet been extensively sought by the sophisticated methods now available for histocompatibility analysis. Mariani (Mariani, et al., 1960), grafting from male to female "A" strain mice of different ages, found signs of "a gradual immunologic maturation coupled with constantly changing skin properties": of the old–old grafts, none took. The present experimental study of immunology in relation to ageing is described in Ch. 9.8; mutation plays little part in it, however.

By locating the mutation in the antibody-producing cell rather than in the target tissue cell, Burnet's hypothesis steps over one prime difficulty of other somatic mutation hypotheses, that the likely mutation rate in tissue cells can hardly be high enough to account for ageing if cells are to be lost one by one, as they mutate—particularly if the mutant gene is recessive, or more than one mutation is involved. The gap we have to bridge to resolve this "bifurcation of Nature" is in finding some way in which somatic mutation of one cell could induce these mutationlike consequences in its unmutated neighbors of similar cell type. If it is the antibody-producing cell that is affected, this difficulty does not arise; it needs only one mutation, followed by rapid clonal multiplication, to do extensive damage to the correspondingly antigenic target tissue. The mutation need not, indeed, affect specificity; if, as Burnet suggests, "self"-reacting clones are inhibited by overstimulation, it need only affect sensitivity, and the setting of the stimulation-inhibition mechanism.

Burch's hypothesis of malignant change (1963a, b) involves the assumption that there are epigenetic regulators (of cell differentiation and, indirectly, of cell number) within the cell, which are accessible to immunological interference by antibody at the cell surface. Mutation in a structural gene leads to production of a sterically incorrect messenger substance, hence to an immunological incompatibility. This change, once it occurs, leads to disorganization of the endoplasmic reticulum and an irreversible loss of a control substance normally present in the cell, probably a lipoprotein. There is a schematic likeness between Burch's hypothesis of malignancy and Szilard's "hits" and "faults," in that it is assumed to depend on four events of mutation in each of two genes, probably in each member of two gene pairs, one structural and the other regulator, of which one or two are commonly prezygotic, and correspond to "faults." The balance between prezygotic and postzygotic mutations is further affected, however, because this is an autoimmune process, and the homozygote mutant will accordingly be tolerated.

For this mechanism to be fitted into general epigenetics we can consider the reaction at the cell surface, which precedes or initiates disturbance in hypothetical "differentiation-mitosis metabolites" of the cytoplasm, as an "echo" or negative feedback from the body's total immunological self-awareness evoked by a wrong identification signal. The mutated cell misidentifies itself to its cellular neighbors, thereby evoking immunological reprisals—which, in this case, instead of destroying the mutant cell, put it "out of control" by normal epigenetic mechanisms.

Burch has elaborated his whole model to account for one special case of what can happen when a cell, through mutation, misidentifies itself to a control mechanism: escape into malignancy. This is an easy consequence to detect, because a tumor is a visible object. If Burch is right, however, one might envisage a wide spectrum of other consequences of structural gene mutation depending on the kind of cell involved, the other genes or mutations present, the number and character of the structural mutations that had already appeared during the period of prenatal tolerance, and, most important, the nature of the feedback mechanisms normally present. One likely consequence would be cell deletion, but this, unlike tumor production, would not be detectable if it involved only the mutated cell. For an immunological mechanism to produce progressive cell loss, a "negative" malignancy, we should have to postulate either a loss of specificity in the immunological response of the body as a whole, or a response damaging to the mutated cell's neighbors. Burnet's suggestion gets over the difficulty by postulating a mutation in the antibody-producing, not the antigen-producing, side.

The answer to the impasse could also conceivably lie in the nature of the body's reply to a cell that misidentifies itself. In Burch's theory this is straightforwardly immunological. But there may be more than one reply. It is an old idea that a mutated cell might multiply anaplastically if through non-recognition it fails to evoke some hypothetical humoral feedback mechanism. The assumptions made about humoral influences in maintaining tisse structure and organ size have been criticized by Abercrombie (1957); Burch's hypothesis attributes malignancy to consequences of antibody reaction with the cell, not to its failure to evoke an extracellular negative feedback. We should mention this type of humoral hypothesis only because if it were true, and if mutation in a tissue cell were able to produce overcorrection, the difficulty over mutation rate and "negative" malignancy would be elegantly solved: mutation in one cell would then produce feedback effects not only on the mutated cell, but on all its normal neighbors of similar type.

It would now be tempting to bring Metchnikoff up to date on the lines along which Weiss (1950) and Burnet (1959a, b) were apparently thinking, by identifying the epigenetic "net" or mold that maintains somatic differentiation with two factors: cell surface effects and immunological factors that influence them, in response to the appearance not of "non-self" structural materials, but of cellular constituents that were absent, or occurred in subcritical amounts, at earlier stages of development. If this were so, it might mean that the "self" reacting lymphocyte clones postulated by Burnet are not abolished or held in a suppressed condition, so much as otherwise occupied as parts of a functioning epigenetic mechanism.

So far, so good—with a little ingenuity and in the absence of experimental fact we could very easily wrap up somatic mutation, Szilardian faults, autoimmunity, and senescence into a single package: loss of cells and loss of function are a polymorphic form of runt disease, due to growing diversity of body constituents and lymphocyte clones with age, and all reflecting the consequences of mutation. Unfortunately, the suggestions of Burch (1963c) also point to an important snag in Burnet's hypothesis, in so far as it is applied to explain ageing. Autoimmune phenomena increase regularly in incidence as a power of age, but are notoriously more prevalent in females: for inflammatory polyarthritis, the extrapolated age of 50 percent incidence is 230 years in males and 115 in females. On these and other grounds Burch has suggested that the site of autoimmunity should be a mutation on one or both X chromosomes. Following this line of argument, the mutation rate of lymphocytes should, in women, be double that in men: they should produce prohibited clones with a double frequency, but they should also have double the repertoire of competent antibody-producing clones in general, and, Burch argues, a correspondingly lower incidence of infectious disease—as, indeed, they have. On these assumptions they should, if Burnet's mechanism is responsible for ageing, age twice as fast as men, instead of somewhat more slowly, as they in fact do. Arguments about the X chromosome apart, the observed incidence of autoimmune disease between the sexes runs counter to the idea that autoimmunity, at least of the kind under discussion, is the chief timer of human ageing. As to the X chromosome, the findings of Jacobs and Court Brown (1963), concerning its disappearance in adult life suggest that there is a good deal still to be learned about the behavior of this structure in the two sexes with increasing age.

The activities of other mathematicians in speculating about the form of the mortality curve were reviewed by Mildvan and Strehler (1960). One fatal objection to any simple theory of ageing as a result of somatic mutation seems to have been removed by the finding that some, though not all, radiomimetic drugs can produce life-shortening (Alexander and Connell, 1960); but other, equally grave, objections remain. Maynard Smith (1962) has drawn attention to two of these. One is the huge somatic mutation rate that would be required to account for the observed rate of ageing: if we assume a rate in man of the same order as that assignable to germ cells, the likelihood that a given locus will have mutated in a man of 35 is 10^{-5}, and if the mutant is recessive the likelihood of its double occurrence is therefore 10^{-10}.[4] If there are 20,000 such cell-killing loci, the proportion of cells inactivated by mutation could not be much more than 2 per million at the age of 30, and perhaps 4 per million by the age of 60. This is not enough.

A second objection is that if ageing is due solely to point mutation the life of a haploid should be vastly inferior to that of a diploid. In haploid amphibia

---

[4]It is conceivable, of course, that there is a class of somatic mutations that are epigenetically dominant (due to "masking" of the other allele in certain body cells): such mutations would be tissue-selective in their expression.

it is, but they are poor things, while in *Habrobracon* haploid and diploid males have about equal life-spans, though the haploids are much more sensitive to radiation (Clarke, 1957; Clark and Rubin, 1961). Another, if weaker, objection is that dietary restriction slows ageing, but cannot slow mutation (Bjorksten, 1962)—it might presumably influence the expression of mutations that had already occurred, without preventing their occurrence, and certainly affects the number of cell generations in which mutations could be expressed.

It is necessary, however, to distinguish between somatic mutation of genes and other chromosomal damage, leading, for example, to aneuploidy. There may also be special effects whereby particular mutations produce peculiarly catastrophic results.

It is clear that if mammalian tissues exhibit either "distribution," as for example of the ability to translate particular codons (Strehler, 1969; Strehler, et al., 1971), or increasingly imperfect mitosis with increasing age, resulting in the accumulation of aneuploid or effectively aneuploid cells, this would lead to steady deterioration of equilibrium. Any difference in liability to senescence between mammals and lower vertebrates would be explicable, in terms of this theory, on the ground that mutation rate would be higher, in all probability, with higher temperatures and chromosome numbers.

This is another highly ingenious but unproven suggestion. Mammalian somatic cells are known to display some aneuploidy (Hsu and Pomerat, 1953; de Carli, 1961; a large and even more contentious body of data was reviewed by Sorokina, 1950).

If the copying mechanisms of somatic cells could be shown to deteriorate, like those of the *Paramecium* macronucleus, the further they travel from the germ line, senescence might result from the fact of cell turnover, not from its cessation. A possible mechanism for this was suggested to me by Dr. Helen Spurway. She suggests that as a result of somatic mutation the constituent cells of some mammalian tissues may lose their autarky and become a "community," in which both function and the capacity for replacement have undergone distribution. Such a community would contain both irreplaceable and indispensable members, and would therefore ultimately undergo senescence. Apart from actual aneuploidy, moreover, it appears from nuclear transplantation experiments that with differentiation there is a steady decline either in the completeness or in the availability of genetic information; in frogs, for example, the percentage of nuclei containing full genetic complements and able to generate a whole viable animal falls from 30 percent or more in the blastula to 3 percent in swimming tadpole gut epithelium (Gurdon, 1962). Whether parts of the complement are lost or only masked in not yet known.

Variation in chromosome number has been reported in human (Andres and Jiv, 1936; Timonen and Therman, 1950; Therman and Timonen, 1951) and pig embryos (Sorokina, 1950). In adult rat liver, Tanaka (1951, 1953) described wide variation in chromosome number. He found that cells with 42 chromosomes (diploids) contribute primarily to the growth of embryonic liver and to regeneration after hepatectomy in adults, and that growth and restoration were apparently confined to diploids and subdiploids. Walker and Boothroyd (1953) have shown that such "aneuploidy" is easily simulated by faulty technique. The polyploidy of mammalian liver is familiar. It is apparently under a general hormonal control (Swartz, et al., 1960; Geschwind, et al., 1959). As to aneuploidy, Y-chromosome loss is common in older men (Pierre and Hoagland, 1971, 1972; Inuma and Nakagome, 1972) and X-chromosome loss in older women (Fitzgerald, 1975; Fang, et al., 1975). Similar changes are reported in sheep (Bruere, 1967; see also de Galan, 1966; Neurath, et al., 1970; Fechheimer, 1972; Homa and Nielsen, 1976, Shoemaker, 1977). Jarvik (Jarvik and Kato, 1969) has detected correlation between organic brain syndrome in octogenarians and the occurrence of aneuploidy. As Finch (1976) points out, chromatin is itself a hormone-sensitive material, and changes in it are not necessarily primary. Court Brown found that aneuploidy in human leucocytes increases from about 4 percent at 10 years to 13–15 percent at 80 years (Jacobs, et al., 1961). Clearly chromosomal abnormality in the body or the liability to it in culture increase sharply with age in some cells at least. According to recent work, it looks as if only the sex chromosomes, not the autosomes, are affected by the presumed error of division.

The character of the proteins produced by the animal may also change in successive cellular generations. Apart from the theory of clonal selection in lymphocytes (Burnet, 1959; see p.) it was formerly suggested that senescence is a manifestation of an "immune" response to endogenous hormones (e.g., Picado and Rotter, 1936; Freud and Uyldert, 1947; Walford, 1962). A more subtle change in specificity of cell response, or of the properties of cellular products, whether it be interpreted immunologically, or, more probably, morphogenetically, cannot be ruled out. If cells in general or certain cells could be shown to acquire adaptive resistance to physiological regulators, as do bacteria to unfamiliar metabolites, from generation to generation, interesting possibilities would certainly be opened. Compensatory hypertrophy declines with age: Gregerman (1959), however, found no decline in the adaptive enzyme production of old rats, as judged by their ability to form tryptophan peroxidase and tyrosine transaminase (see also Bertolini, 1962.)

Gaillard (1942) carried out a long series of studies relating the degree of differentiation that can be produced and maintained in tissue explants to the age status of the press juice in which they are grown. According to these results, functional differentiation in endocrine and other explants can be obtained if they are grown successively in press juices from embryos of increasing age, while some degree of regression of structure occurs if the series is reversed, and explants are grown in juices of decreasing age order. These observations have never been repeated. No doubt if explants could be cultivated in media exactly simulating the chemical and physical environment and its changes through all the stages of development, they would pass through all the normal phases of in vivo histology. The point of interest to the gerontologist is to know how far it is possible to maintain a status quo at any point. Analysis of the power of tissues to mark time developmentally while retaining function requires more elaborate methods of organ and tissue culture than are so far available, but the explosion of Carrel's concept of clonal immortality suggests limits—as Daniel has found in explanted mammary duct (Daniel, et al., 1968). Gey (1952) indeed referred to the in vitro culture of "thyroid, parathyroid, adrenal cells, and the germinal epithelium of the ovary," even to the production of follicles, but these findings remain contentious.

6.4.4 "Cross-Linking" of Macromolecules

The thermal contractility of collagen in man, rat, mouse, chinchilla, and rabbit undergoes a progressive age change at a rate consistent for the species (Verzár, 1955, 1956, 1957, 1959a; Banfield, 1956; Banga, 1957; Brown and Consden, 1958; Kohn and Rollerson, 1960; Lupien and McCay, 1960; Chvapil and Hrůza, 1959; Hrůza, Chvapil and Kobrle, 1961). In scar tissue the collagen present has the age status, thus judged, of the scar, not of the animal (Verzár, 1964), while in dietarily retarded animals it remains apparently young (Chvapil and Hrůza, 1959). Pregnancy apparently hastens its ageing (Árvay, et al., 1963).

This process is a model for a revived form of the old hypothesis of colloidal ageing, which attributes age processes to slow physical change in body colloids of low turnover—based, now, not on progressive dehydration, as originally proposed by Růžícká (1924) and Marinesco (1934), but on the cross-linking of macromolecules, with consequent inactivation (Harman, 1955, 1956; Bjorksten, 1962, review; Miescher, 1955; Gross, 1962). According to this view, both radiation and chemical mutagens act on the age process by the liberation of free radicals and the promotion of cross linking in cell constituents generally—not necessarily nor only in the genetic information store—a seed that was to grow later into an extensive "free radical" theory, championed by Harman (1968) and Packer (1967), going far beyond cross-linking. The biological possibilities of simple cross-linking have been the subject of much work by Bjorksten (1968). The appearances in ageing collagen are consistent with cross-linking, but other changes occur, particularly in the associated polysulfates (Gross, 1962, review). The influence of dietary retardation and the fact that collagen is not significantly aged by x-ray exposure at levels that reduce the life-span (Sinex, 1957; Verzár, 1959) both have to be fitted into the theory. The thermal denaturation of bovine thymus DNA also changes signficantly with age (von Hahn and Verzár, 1963). That from old cows has a higher thermal stability to 0.0025 M NaNO$_3$ than DNA from calf thymus. According to Parhon, excision of the thyroid and gonad in rats appears to accelerate the age change in collagen (Parhon, 1962). In general, as has already been remarked, the idea of "colloidal" senescence looks no more plausible than it did a few years ago, and the turnover even of active body constituents seems to be more uneven than some of us expected. Free radical damage to membranes is, however, another matter (see Ch. 9.3).

6.5 Endocrine Senescence

6.5.1 General

The early discoverers of hormones were fully convinced that they had in their hands the key to the prevention of senescence in man. The fact that little of their enthusiasm bore fruit is due very largely to the manner in which the confluence of two deeply emotive subjects—ageing and the gonad—affected scientific judgment in the early years of the century. The hypotheses of the rejuvenators were in many respects reasonable, if their published claims were not. In any discussion of endocrine senescence it is probably worth restating (1) that organ and tissue grafting are appropriate and fully respectable techniques for the investigation of senile change, and that they have given misleading answers chiefly because the wrong questions were asked, (2) that the use of hormones in the palliation of senile changes in man, although it is largely ineffective, was a reasonable experiment which has not yet been exhausted, and (3) although gonadal "senescence" does not "cause" somatic senescence (this was self-evident in antiquity, from the life histories of eunuchs, long before testosterone was found to be unavailing in reversing general senile decay), it was a highly important model process, and a relatively accessible one for further study.

Gerontological endocrinology passed through two stages from which it is only now emerging: The first was covertly preoccupied with resexualization, while the second drew its focus from the conviction of most if not all gerontologists that ageing must be a process located either in cells or in the general chemical information store. There may indeed be such processes, but endocrine studies have tended, in spite of the warnings of Sacher (1968), to ignore the fact that not all ageing or age-dependent processes are necessarily "the" ageing process—that which is the leading timekeeper for the mammalian life-span, or for one of its aspects such as reproductive senescence. This timekeeper, or these timekeepers (since that for reproductive ageing may be distinct from the life-span clock, or only loosely coupled to it), are likely to be software processes, located in the control system—even if, as is possible, they are driven by a more fundamental change in DNA or cellular deterioration.

It is profitable to present historically the way in which gerontological endocrinology has developed, from preoccupation with growth as a preservative and with the search for remediable hormone deficiencies to the renewed and growing interest in hypothalamic timing mechanisms: this sequence admirably illustrates what we have said about the uses and dangers of pre-theory, for in fact both growth effects and the possibility of replacement therapy are implicit in the new model that is emerging, even though the lines of experimentation that produced it were if anything hindered by the hypotheses on which they were based.

Characteristic variations in hormone output occur throughout the mammalian life-cycle. They are of two types: cyclical and secular. These changes are the biochemical equivalent of the sudden movements of embryonic tissue which are seen in speeded-up films of developing organisms—they are part cause, part effect, and they represent only the outward and visible manifestation of changes in the quality and quantity of cell response. The hormones most likely to be linked directly with the senile process, such as the growth hormone of the pituitary could not at the time of much of this theorization be estimated in the intact animal. Of those that could be so estimated, the group of 17-ketosteroids showed a decline that continues with the rise of the force of mortality (McGavack, 1951; Kirk, 1949; Hamburger, 1948; Robinson, 1948; Hamilton and Hamilton, 1948; Hamilton, et al., 1954). The concept of an "adrenopause" analogous to the menopause seems now, however, to have little to support it. Apart from this, there was no single hormonal change that correlated with senescence; no single endocrine organ, of those which can be removed without fatal results, whose extirpation produced the syndrome of senility in mammals; and no hormone or combination of hormones that were known to produce more than a limited, and apparently secondary, reversal of senile changes. Ablation of a gland is not the same thing as its senescence in situ, and in surgical castration for prostatic and mammary cancer there is evidence that interconversion may take place between adrenal and gonadal steroids, but no simple hypothesis that senescence is a "withdrawal" effect was substantiated by the existing experimental evidence. It appeared that the sequence of developmental changes in endocrine activity that ends in senescence cannot be made to run backwards by hormone supplements, except in a very minor degree, if peripheral and trophic hormones used in clinical practice are considered alone. Whether neuroendocrine hormones of a more recent vintage can control ageing, and how far, is of course another matter.

In a long series of studies, Korenchevsky (e.g., Korenchevsky and Jones, 1947, 1948; Korenchevsky, et al., 1950, 1953; Korenchevsky, 1961) tried to show how far hormone supplements can reverse the senile process, judged by the restoration of the relative hypoplasia of organs. A great many of the senile structural changes described in endocrines were closely paralleled, though at a lesser level of severity, by the changes in structure that follow gonadectomy, and many of them are reversible by gonadal hormones. (Korenchevsky et al., 1950; McGavack, 1951). The peripheral effects of sex hormones in senility, such as the recornification of the vagina by estrogen (Loeb, 1944), are familiar enough. The decrease of mitotic rate and degree of vacuolation in the adrenal (Townsend, 1946; Blumenthal, 1945) and the increase of collagen and reticulum in the capsule and in the parenchyma (Dribben and Wolfe, 1947) that occur with advancing age were found to be partially reversible by estrogen, and more fully reversible by a combination of estrogen, androgen, and progesterone (Korenchevsky, et al., 1950). In the pituitary of the senile rat, Wolfe (1943) found a decrease in eosinophils, but no increase in basophils; vacuolation, like that which follows castration, occurred in the basophils with increasing age. These changes, particularly the decrease in eosinophils, were at least partially reversed by testosterone propionate (Wolfe, 1941). The senescent changes in fowl pituitary described by Payne (1949, 1952) were greatly hastened by gonadectomy. In other words, gonadal failure might contribute to senescence, but it probably does so only when it occurs at a certain point in the endocrine developmental program.

In some instances, direct estimations of the capacity of senile endocrines to respond to physiological stimuli began to be made. The thyroid of aged males shows no loss of capacity to respond to thyrotophic hormone (Baker, et al., 1959); it now appears that peripheral response to thyroxine is blocked by a pituitary hormone of long action (Denckla, 1974). Solomon and Shock (1950) tested the response of the adrenal cortex in 27 young and 26 old men to a dose of adrenocorticotrophic hormone (ACTH) and in 15 young and 13 old men to a dose of 0.4 mg adrenaline. No difference in eosinopenia was observed after ACTH, but adrenaline produced a significantly greater eosinophil depression in the young group. From this it was inferred that the senile cortex can still secrete 11, 17 oxysteroids without gross impairment, but that the response of the pituitary to acute adrenaline stimulation is lower in old than young subjects. Pincus (1950) likewise found no impairment of response to ACTH in old men compared with young controls. But with chromatographic techniques, Rubin, et al. (1955) examined the range of 17 α-ketosteroids produced at different ages. There is here little difference between men and women: in both, the greatest decline with age is in androsterone and aetiocholan-3α-ol-17-one, and the second greatest in the 5α, 11-oxygenated steroids. In men, production of steroids in the biosynthetic pathways to cortisol and to aldosterone decreases significantly with age

(Romanoff, 1975). Pregnanediol secretion falls off in the 50s, but does not decline further (Romanoff, et al., 1970)—effects that are not reversed by ACTH (Romanoff, et al., 1969). Ageing mammals maintain normal levels of adrenocorticoids despite a decline in secreting capacity (Riegele, 1976).

The hypophysis was clearly the site of election for "fundamental" and all-explaining endocrine changes leading to senescence—the part that it has played in the provision of such emotionally-satisfying theories follows naturally from the fact that it is known or credibly suspected to be involved in the regulation of almost all mammalian processes of homeostasis. Its proximity to the hypothalamus enables it to be linked with theories that locate senescence in the central nervous system. Hypophysial factors in senescence have also a special importance because of the relation of the hypophysis to the control of growth. In its simplest form, starting from cellular exhaustion, the idea of a primary pituitary senescence drew plausible anatomical arguments from the histological studies of Parsons (1936) and Simmonds (1914) on long series of glands from subjects of various ages, or from work such as that of Payne (1949, 1952) on the ageing fowl. The intuition, though a sound one, was never pushed to its logical conclusion.

If there was a tendency for the existence of the pituitary gland to serve as a pretext for vagueness of thought concerning the nature of senescence in mammals—the function formerly discharged by the pineal in the search for the seat of the soul—there were also solid arguments for its direct involvement, certainly as mediator, if not as originator, of senile processes. Because the pituitary is profoundly concerned with several processes of homeostasis, and is involved with morphogenetic timing mechanisms like that which initiates puberty, it would long have been possible to develop by hypotheses of pituitary senescence which did not depend upon an unbiological argument in terms of single hormones.

The function of trophic hormones appears to be the provision of one limb of a system of negative feedback, by which the level of effector-organ secretion is maintained and kept constant. If senescence be regarded as a continuously self-aggravating disequilibrium (a positive feedback process), then such a process can be induced in a model control system, normally dependent upon negative feedback, by several types of change.

Consider a system in which a device A produces a signal that increases the activity of a second device B, and in which, at the same time, the activity of B produces a signal that reduces the activity of device A. The properties of most self-regulating biological systems can be reproduced in this model by varying the characteristic of the stimulus A → B or the negative feedback B → A, and the number of stable states of A or B. If there is no time lag in either of these processes, the level of output B will tend to be constant and self-restoring. If there is an appreciable time constant in one limb of the circuit, the system will tend to function as a relaxation oscillator. In this case, A stimulates B, which does not immediately respond. Stimulus A → B continues to increase, reaching a level that corresponds to an ultimate response in B sufficient to inhibit A completely. The output of B then declines, permitting A to recover, and this represents one whole cycle. It is a requisite for the functioning of such a system that the unmodified output of A shall tend to increase in the absence of ouput B, i.e., that the state of A is inherently unstable. If output A be assumed to be the pituitary gonadotrophin and output B the gonadal hormone, then the immediate response of the pituitary to castration, or senile decline is gonadal response, is of the unstable type, though other mechanisms operate later to restore regulation. Where, as may be the case in the male, the pituitary-gonad balance oeprates as a level control, gradual failure of B's response would be expected to cause a gradual increase in output A. In a similar system containing a time constant, and therefore behaving cyclically, blocking would be expected to occur at one point in one particular cycle, with a proportionately greater rise in output A.

The importance of this homeostatic concept, even though in its simplistic form it contained no elements of secular feed-forward, is that in the simplified model self-regulating equilibrium can be turned to progressive disequilibrium by several types of change (see Dilman, 1971). Decline in the capacity of either A or B to respond to B → A or A → B will result in a permanently unstable state of A. If the response of A fails, B will also be driven into maximum output. Decline in the capacity of B to produce B → A will induce the unstable state of A. Decline in the capacity of A to produce A → B will lead to the relapse of B into its stable state of zero output. This, however, where B's output affects other systems, will cause disequilibrium in a complex physiology. In addition to these purely quantitative changes, biological cybernetic mechanisms are also capable of exhibiting, and in development, characteristically do exhibit, qualitative change in the specificity both of signal and response, which further complicates the picture.

Although analogies from circuits oversimplify the reality of mammalian homeostasis, they indicate the number of variables to be considered in studying the senescence of homeostatic systems; and they indicate some of the ways in which such senescence can be analyzed. Evidence suggests that in the case of the gonad it is the function of B that declines. With the pituitary trophic hormones, other than the gonadotrophins and ACTH, in vivo estimation of levels, corresponding to the measurement of output A, cannot as a rule be carried out. The action of these homeostatic systems, moreover, is not expressed through static components but through a developing organism in which long-term trends in cell specificity are themselves controlled by the signals involved in the homeostatic process—as if the system A ⇌ B were fitted in a vehicle whose movement it controlled, but which travelled into a hotter and hotter environment, thereby upsetting the characteristics of A and B.

These highly complex hormonal homeostatic systems are of the greatest importance in higher vertebrates, although the problem of "three-dimensional" homeostasis, or homeostasis superimposed on morphogenesis, is general in all developmental physiology. The views of Minot (1908) upon "cytomorphosis" (differentiation and maturation) as a cause of senescence carry the very important, and at first sight very probable, inference that no complex organism, and certainly no vertebrate, can remain in an indefinitely stable equilibrium. Where growth processes and differentiation are superimposed on homeostasis, they are analogous to "drift" in a control system; on this basis any system of differential growth must tend to increasing disequilibrium, unless the developmental "drift" itself modifies the homeostatic system to keep them appropriate to the altered situation. To this already complex model we must now add the possibility of "homeorrhesis" (Waddington, 1957) or moving homeostasis modulated by some ongoing hypothalamic program, which may include not only the reduction in central or peripheral responsiveness but also deliberate "shutting off" by means of blocking hormones. There is not only a "thermostat" responding to short-term changes: there may also be a "clock" that cuts off or switches on the feedback system at a predetermined time. For an analysis of one such model of progressive dyshomeostasis see Dilman (1971).

To the relatively simple, and now largely historical, concepts of endocrinological feedback, which by reason of long standing are those incorporated into clinical practice, it would now be necessary to add the whole neuroendocrine system, including the releaser and inhibitor oligopeptide hormones which represent both the link between enteroception and peripheral hormone secretion and, in all probability, the locus of longer-term cyclical and secular changes and the existence of a component not only of feedback but of feed-forward. The extent of this system within the nervous system is now being explored, but even while this exploration is in process the discovery of long-acting peripheral neurohomones (the endorphins, the thyroid-blocking hormone of Denckla) has introduced yet another level of complexity. The neuroendocrine hormones, moreover, differ from the peripheral and the releaser hormones of clinical application and from the neurotransmitters (catecholamines and other synaptic messengers) in their long time scale of effect. Changes in the activity of these substances, as well as straightforward morphogenetic change and maturation, may well represent the vector element in "homeorrhesis"—they are as likely a candidate as unexplained secular changes in target cells, and they may be the agent of such changes. It is only now becoming possible to see why the attempt to "explain," or even elucidate, ageing by looking at simple peripheral hormone and trophic hormone feedback loops met with no success.

6.5.2   *Gonad-Pituitary System*

Senescence of the *gonad* regularly precedes or accompanies senescence of the owner in a number of phyla—so much so that declining reproductive capacity has been taken as a token of senescence almost as valuable as the direct measurement of increased force of mortality. The relation of gonadal senescence to somatic senescence has clearly much evolutionary interest, since once the first is complete, in an organism, to the point at which that organism's contribution to posterity is no longer statistically significant, any further adverse change in viability is generally speaking inaccessible to the influence of natural selection, except in a very roundabout way.

In almost all litter-bearing mammals, a decline in litter size is characteristic of senescence. The long postreproductive period found in women is exceptional in mammals. It probably represents a genuine biological difference, quite apart from the far greater perfection of the techniques for keeping human beings alive (Bloch and Flury, 1959). Compared with the more gradual disappearance of fertility in other mammals, the human menopause is unusually complete and sudden. The range of this phenomenon among primates is not at present known. Few people have seen a postmenopausal monkey (Krohn, 1955). The age of menopause in *Macaca mulatta* has been given as 28–30 years, and in chimpanzees, greater than 44 years (Van Wagenen, 1970; Guilloud, 1968).

There is some cause for regarding gonadal senescence and the group of effects that follow senile gonadal withdrawal as a separate "senescence" from that of the animal as a whole, since gonadal supplements can reverse a whole series of subsidiary senile changes without materially reversing the progress of somatic senescence judged by survival. In the castrated male mammal, gonadal hormone supplements may perhaps actually shorten life. There is no demonstrable androgen deficiency in normal senile male rats (Korenchevsky, et al., 1953), nor, probably, in most old men (Stearns, et al., 1974).

Although sex hormones do not rejuvenate the organism in the manner envisaged by writers such as Voronoff, they produce a closer approach to "rejuvenation," covering more structures and body processes than do any other hormones that have been investigated except, perhaps, somatotrophin. In addition to their effects upon the secondary sexual characteristics, such as beard growth (Chieffi, 1949) or structure of vaginal epithelium (Loeb, 1944; Allen and Masters, 1948) and upon the genitalia themselves, androgens (Kenyon, 1942; Kochakian and Murlin, 1931; Kochakian, 1937) and probably also estrogens (Kenyon, 1942) exert an important "anabolic" effect with nitrogen retention and increased protein synthesis, and produce a number of unexpected peripheral changes, generally in the direction of a restoration of "young" structure (Korenchevsky, et al., 1953). Thus estrogens have been stated to produce a striking reversal of the atrophy of the senile nasal mucosa

(Kountz, 1950) and certainly produce extensive changes in senile skin, with dermal regeneration (Goldzieher and Goldzieher, 1950; Chieffi, 1950a) and restoration of elasticity (Chieffi, 1951). Their cosmetic use is now a medical commonplace. That the possibility of "rejuvenation by replacement" is limited, even where the reproductive organs are concerned, was shown by Kirk's failure (1948, 1949) to restore the phosphatase activity of senile prostatic secretion with androgens, although this activity is so restored in young hypogonadal males.

The relation of these changes and their reversal to the general picture of senescence in mammals was until lately extremely obscure. Of the more general processes in which gonadal hormone withdrawal plays a part, few had been identified with certainty. It has been suggested, for instance, that the osteoporosis of old age is a result of the withdrawal of gonadal anabolic hormones (Allbright, 1947).

The *initiation* of puberty is hypothalamic and closely linked to body weight (Fischer, 1973). Pituitary gonadotrophin is detectable in the hypophysis of the 17-cm pig fetus (Smith and Dortzbach, 1929) and the implantation of glands from 3-month-old rabbits is as effective in inducing puberty as implantation of adult glands (Saxton and Greene, 1939). The ovaries of immature rabbits do not respond to injected gonadotrophin (Hertz and Hisaw, 1943; Parkes, 1942–1944; Adams, 1953). On the other hand, it has long been known that when ovaries are transplanted reciprocally between young and old animals, it is the age of the recipient before or after puberty, not that of the ovary, which determines function or non-function (Foà, 1900, 1901; Long and Evans, 1922) and in some species gonadotrophin readily induces precocious ovarian and testicular development. Domm (1934) was able to induce crowing at 9 days of age and treading at 13 days in cockerel chicks by injections of pituitary gonadotrophins. The timing mechanism is stable within a species or a genetic strain. Human puberty very exceptionally occurs during childhood without any obvious pathological cause (constitutional precocious puberty"—Novak, 1944) and pregnancy has actually been reported in a child of five (Escomel, 1939). In albino rats, according to Mandl and Zuckerman (1952), genetic factors seem to play the major part in determining the age of puberty. Lorenz and Lerner (1946) likewise found clear evidence that age of sexual maturation in turkeys is heritable. "The reactivity of the gonads may be the most important factor in determining the time at which sexual maturity actually occurs, but the factors which affect this reactivity are largely unknown" (Robson, 1947). Change also takes place at puberty in the specificity of pituitary response: while estradiol induces pituitary and adrenal hypertrophy in rats castrated after puberty, it reduces pituitary and adrenal weight in animals castrated while still immature (Selye and Albert, 1942; Eldridge and McPherson, 1974).

The end of the reproductive period, as well as the beginning, is marked by changes in gonadal reactivity. These led some writers to regard the human menopause as a form of depletion-senescence (Swyer, 1954): Hertig (1944) describes the exhaustion of a "capital" of ova, which is not increased during postnatal life, but his findings suggested that the actual menopause precedes the end of all follicular activity. In man and many other mammals (the only admitted exceptions occur in Lemuroidea, the galago and the loris), the occurrence of any oogenesis during postpubertal life has been doubted. The case against it was persuasively put by Zuckerman (1951): this "perennial controversy" was continued by Parkes and Smith (1953), who found evidence of oocyte regeneration in rat ovaries grafted after freezing (see Davidson, 1968). There is certainly none in humans.

One of the most characteristic features of mammalian ageing is indeed the steady loss of oocytes from the ovary through follicular atresia. It apparently also occurs in birds (Dominic, 1962). Jones and Krohn (1961) investigated this process in mice—it is significantly retarded by hypophysectomy, but not arrested altogether. Explantation itself causes a massive loss of oocytes in the explanted ovary, but this appears to be due to anoxia when the blood supply is interrupted (Jones and Krohn, 1960b). There was never any good evidence that the menopause occurs in women because the supply of ova is exhausted: in mice, unilateral ovariectomy halves the total number of offspring and shortens reproductive life (Jones and Krohn, 1960a; Thung, 1962; Biggers, et al., 1962). Engle (1944) mentions the finding of apparently normal corpora lutea in women of 50: at the menopause most if not all ova and follicles have normally disappeared. Kurzrok and Smith (1938) found that in the human ovary, in contrast to the senile ovary of some other mammals, ova "cease to be found," and that this change occurs at or soon after the menopause. Subsequent work does not support this finding (Block, 1953; Novak, 1970).

Gardner (1952) transplanted ovaries between old and young rats, and apparently found a greater tendency to malignant change in old ovaries carried by young hosts. The ovary of the mouse, transplanted into an animal of a different age, was reported to behave likewise—passage in young mice did not prolong its life (Jones and Krohn, 1960b; Krohn, 1955); the ovary of the hypophysectomized mouse did not deteriorate with age, but remained able to function on explantation (Jones and Krohn, 1959).

From this confusion, the true picture of reproductive senescence is only now beginning to emerge. Aschheim (1964) demonstrated that transplants of ovaries from young to old rats did not lead to re-establishment of cycles. It is therefore clear that the senile loss of function in old rats did not originate in the ovary. He also showed that function in constant-estrus senile rats could be restored by injections of luteinizing hormone. The work of Clemens, et al. (1969) on electrical stimulation of the hypothalamus indicated that whatever incidental changes might occur with ageing elsewhere in the system of control, the end of reproductive life in female rats is predominantly a brain rather than a cytoendocrine phenomenon. The phenomena involved are complex and only now in the process of elucidation, and many hormones are involved in the senile picture.

Although the simple model of "running out of ova" does not account for the human menopause, the primary event in humans does appear to lie in the ovaries, which cease to respond to gonadotrophin. In the female rat, by comparison, the corresponding event—cessation of cycles—is triggered from the hypothalamic-pituitary system, probably by increased prolactin drive following a decline in both dopamine and serotonin (Meites, et al., 1978).

The steroidogenic cells of senile rat ovary are functional, and can respond to gonadotrophin—it is the stimulus that is deficient. The cells show no ultrastructural signs of ageing (Crumeyrolle-Arias, et al., 1976). The "senile" pattern of response appears to be due to failure of the prolactin-inhibiting factor to restrain prolactin secretion (Aschheim, 1972). Pituitaries of old rats are less responsive than those of young rats to luteinizing-hormone releasing hormone, and less readily sensitized to it by gonadal steroids (Watkins, et al., 1975). Stimulation of the pre-optic area produces release of luteinizing hormone and of prolactin in constant estrus but not in anestrus or pseudo-pregnant senile rats (Wuttke and Meites, 1973). A number of procedures restore ovulatory function in permanent-estrus rats, but the restoration is temporary (Aschheim, 1976).

The large body of studies upon altered behavior in gonads and endocrines appear, accordingly, to be relevant chiefly to peripheral or secondary effects of the ageing process—the fact that a mammal would eventually run out of ova is not the reason for the reproductive senescence we observe. It is now known that in constant-estrus rats (senile females where the capacity for response is not irreversibly compromised) both catecholamines and iproniazid, a monoamine oxidase (MAO) inhibitor, can reinitiate cycles (Quadri, et al., 1973). L-dopa can reinitiate menstruation in postmenopausal women (Kruse-Larsen and Garde, 1971; Hornykiewicz, 1966). These observations clearly locate the timing process of reproductive senescence in the same place as the initiation of puberty, namely the hypothalamus—where it is intimately related to the monitoring of such variables as caloric intake and body weight. Thus Aschheim (1966) found that brief caloric restriction in rats could itself initiate constant estrus. The "clock" mechanism itself is probably based on the sequence catecholamine $\rightarrow$ releaser hormone $\rightarrow$ gonadotrophin, and its firing tied to the shift in cerebral catecholamines with age (Sulman and Superstine, 1972; Finch, 1973), opening a field for experimental and clinical interference wider than could have been hoped in the early days of gerontological endocrinology, with the focus upon oligopeptide and intracerebral hormones rather than the peripheral variety.

The field of interrelation between effector hormones, trophic hormones, and releaser and inhibitor factors is constantly under review from current research. The main probable age changes in the hypothalamic-pituitary axis with age are reviewed with references by Everitt and Burgess (1976). Their comparison can be summarized as follows:

	Old human	Old rodent
GH production	Reduced during sleep	Reduced overall—; pituitary less responsive to GHRH
TSH	Reduced or no change—; response to TSHRH reduced	
Plasma ACTH	Unchanged; total secretion reduced?	
Blood LH, FSH	Increased in both sexes	LH reduced in old female
Serum prolactin	No change	Increased in female
ADH system	Vasopressin increased	ADH declines; response to dehydration slower
Pituitary tumor	Rare	Common
Pharyngeal pituitary	Activity increases	

The patterns of female reproductive senescence in rats and humans are entirely different (Aschheim in Everitt and Burgess, 1976), and different pituitary polypeptide species again have been detected in senescent mice (Wilkes, 1975). Other "clock" processes may also differ radically between species, a matter of some importance in transferring caloric-limitation results from mouse to man. Older studies on the mechanism of the menopause (Klebanow and Hegnauer, 1949) and of the striking rise of LH and FSH in men (Henderson and Rowlands, 1938) and postmenopausal women (Witschi, 1952) like that seen in young castrates (Hamilton, et al., 1944, 1945) require review in the light of better assay methods (Lazarus and Eastman in Everitt and Burgess, 1976). In the same treatise, Aschheim points out that this rise, reported in old female rats by earlier workers (Lauson, et al., 1939) is characteristic of the human, not the rodent, mode of reproductive cessation. The decline in ovarian reserve in terms of hormone production appears, however, to be genuine (Peng and Huang, 1972). The old observation that ovarectomy predisposes to adrenal carcinoma, preventable by estrogen, in

certain mouse strains (Wooley and Little, 1946) appears to have no direct
human relevance. There is no evidence that the high levels of LH and FSH in
elderly persons contribute to ageing, though they may produce the destruction of surviving ova and possibly mediate some of the late prostatic
pathologies.

Procaine which has been recommended on the basis of some papers that
appear humane and optimistic rather than critical (Aslan, 1956, 1957–1958;
Aslan and David, 1957) as a "remedy" for age changes, has been known for
years as a "mild activator of the pituitary-adrenal system" (Greene, 1959;
Anon., 1959). Ungar (1944) found that in the presence of an intact adrenal it
caused the release of a histamine antagonist. There is so far no satisfactory
evidence that it affects any basic ageing process, and it does not increase the
life-span of mice (Verzár, 1959b).

It is, however, a MAO inhibitor (Bucci and Saunders, 1960), which may
explain its apparent euphoriant action. The finding of Quadri, et al. (1973)
that isoproniazid is capable of reinitiating ovarian cycles indicates that the
physiological actions of procaine on ageing may be more extensive than can
be shown from life-table experiments. It is interesting that according to
Aslan, et al. (1965) procaine prolongs the life of male but not of female rats.
The possibility that it acts on a catecholamine-modulated clock might lead to
experiments with more toxic but more powerful MAO inhibitors such as
tranylcypromine. For a detailed review see Jarvik and Milne (1975).

6.5.3   *Hormonal Regulation of Growth in Vertebrates*

In mammals, where growth and differentiation are difficult to dissociate
experimentally, we have abundant evidence of senescence even in the longest-lived forms. In amphibians, where there is a clear-cut metamorphosis, and
where growth and differentiation can be manipulated with relative ease, we
have so far no direct evidence of senescence. We cannot readily find out
whether the life of intact amphibia, the neoteny of the axolotl, or the
gigantism of athyroid tadpoles, ends in senescence, for the practical reason
that axolotls may well be capable of living for 50, and normal frogs for 12, 15,
or 20 years. This conspiracy of circumstances perpetually recurs in the study
of ageing. The large literature of lower vertebrate endocrinology and morphogenesis cannot be brought to bear on the problem, for lack of actuarial
data.

Both homeotherms and poikilotherms, whether they metamorphose or
not, tend to pass through an earlier phase of active growth and a later phase of
active reproduction, each characterized by a separate type of endocrine
control, and the second by a relative loss of regenerative in favor of reproductive capacity. These phases are separated by the operation of a timing
mechanism which is linked to processes in the juvenile phase. In mammals,

.dy controlled by the pituitary growth and gonad-
successively. In lower vertebrates the differentiation
ation to adult function appears to depend on a pituitary-
ituitary growth hormone of mammalian origin is able to
wth of fish (Swift, 1954).

n between morphogenesis under the influence of gonadal hor-
loss of regenerative power has special interest in gerontology.
n (1947) found that when the gonopodium of poecilid fish differen-
tiates, under the influence of androgens, regenerative power is lost; he
stresses the analogy between this process and the loss of regenerative capacity
in the developing anuran limb. Such a change need not depend upon
irreversible loss of cellular capacity to grow—this does not appear to be the
case in amphibian limbs (Borssuk, 1935; Poležajev and Ginsburg, 1939), but
the physiological loss of repair power may be as complete, so far as the intact
animal is concerned, as is the loss of moulting power in Rhodnius once the
evocator is lost. There is clearly here, as Minot recognized, a possible
mechanism for the induction of senile change.

A certain amount of evidence is available concerning the hormonal influences that affect protein anabolism and regulate growth in mammals, especially in man. Where these factors have been studied, they give little support
to the idea of a simple relation between senescence and growth cessation, and
even less to the conception of a single, "master" endocrine inhibitor which
can be detached from the general pattern of progressing developmental
change. The pattern that exists in man has all the complication of a dynamic
system where homeostasis coexists with change. It is plain that in man, and
probably in some but not all other mammals, the "anabolic" stimulus to form
new protein is not the same throughout life. In adult life it is closely linked to
the gonadal cycle. The extent of the differences in endocrine control of
growth between determinate growers such as man and continual growers
such as the rat has not yet been mapped, and very little is known of the
hormonal control of growth in lower vertebrates. The existing evidence is
quite enough, however, to render any static conception of growth cessation in
terms of single-hormone deficiencies untenable. A more accurate picture
would perhaps be obtained by treating prepubertal and pubertal life as
separate instars separated by what amounts to a biochemical metamorphosis.

The growth of human beings, like that of Daphnia occurs in two overlapping cycles—one prepubertal, the other coinciding with puberty. (See
Figures 6.3, 6.4.) The prepubertal cycle has its most active phase during the
first 6 months of life. This cycle, according to Kinsell (1953), is almost wholly
controlled by the pituitary growth hormone. The pubertal cycle appears to be
evoked directly by anabolic steroid hormones derived from the gonad and
adrenal cortex. During both cycles a minimum output of thyroid hormone is
required to maintain growth and development. At puberty, in response to the

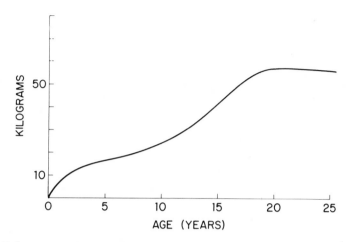

FIGURE 6.3   The postnatal growth in weight of male children (kg/years). (From the data of Quetelet.)

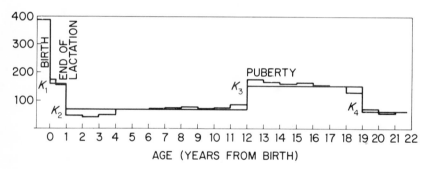

FIGURE 6.4   Annual growth increment in boys, from the data of Quetelet. K_1-K_4 = growth constants at each period. (From Schmalhäusen, 1928.)

pituitary gonadotrophins, the gonads produce steroid hormones which directly stimulate the growth of bone and of soft tissues. The process of bone growth in man is, however, self-limited, since the same hormones produce skeletal maturation and fusion of the epiphyses. There is reason to suspect that they also inhibit the production of pituitary growth hormone—probably through a negative-feedback system from the level of protein anabolism. It is particularly interesting to notice that acromegalic symptoms (McCullagh and Renshaw, 1934) or frank gigantism (Joedicke, 1919) are occasional sequels to castration in males; so, however, are polyuria and diabetes insipidus (Hamilton, 1948). Testosterone is a weak inhibitor of GHRH in the male—the intermediate in this process is probably an uncharacterized hormone released from the seminiferous tubule. The pubertal growth phase in girls appears to be largely of adrenal origin, since the growth-promoting effects of estrogens and of progesterone are less marked, except in the promotion of Ca and PO_4, retention, than those of androgens (Kinsell, 1953). It is generally held that thyroxine potentiates the action of pituitary growth hormone in mammals (Evans, et al., 1939; Scow and Marx, 1945) during the prepubertal phase, as well as hastening differentiation. This does not appear to be the case in anurans, where thiouracil produces pseudogigantism, and a balance between thyroid and pituitary has been postulated (Steinmetz, 1954), one evoking differentiation and the other growth and a "juvenile" condition.

This picture, which requires considerable amplification in terms of what is now known of somatotrophin and somatostatin interaction, accords reasonably well with the known effects of various endocrine deficiencies in producing dwarfism or gigantism in man. To some extent the appearance of the pubertal cycle curtails the prepubertal by inducing bone maturation. Epiphyseal union and the changeover to the pubertal phase of growth are delayed by administration of growth hormone (Freud, et al., 1939), as they are in natural gigantism. On the other hand, abolition of the whole gonadal influence by prepubertal castration has, at least, no gross effect on the life-span, and in cases of constitutional precocious puberty of genetic origin, where pubertal changes are complete by the age of six, and the lag phase of the growth curve is suppressed, the expectation of life is apparently normal (Jolly, 1955).

Various workers suggested that mammalian senescence "is" (or involves) the decline of growth hormone production, and that it "is" (or involves) the long-term effect of the pituitary gonadotrophin on non-gonadal tissues. There is no evidence of this decline in either males or females, though production of growth hormone during REM sleep and on waking may cease in women at menopause (for review see Finch, 1976). Moreover, the total absence of growth hormone does not induce premature ageing (Shire, 1973). In so far as senescence results from differentiation, the experimental question is rather this: to what extent can the administration of one or more "anabolic" hormones affect the power of continued homeostasis in adult animals? It was formerly argued that growth hormone itself may be the "juvenile hormone" of the mammalian pre-imaginal period. It is a primary stimulator of protein anabolism and somatic growth. (Oddly enough, the insect juvenile hormone also occurs in mammalian organs [Williams, et al., 1959]. What, if anything, it does there is quite unknown.) The change from a protein-building and nitrogen-retaining economy, and the negative specific acceleration of growth, are two of the most evident correlates of senescence (Mayer, 1949). The administration of growth hormone "confers strangely youthful proportions on the nitrogen, fat and water components of the body, even in old animals" (Asling, et al., 1952), but does not prolong life (Everitt, 1959). Change in specificity of tissue response to growth hormone certainly *appears* to occur in some mammals, and this change coincides with the attainment of maturity and the appearance of a fresh anabolism-maintaining mechanism. The experimental work of Young in England and Li in America suggested that before a critical time, injected growth hormone induces only protein anabolism; after that time, it also induces diabetes. This is the pattern in man, the kitten (Cotes, et al., 1949), and the dog (Campbell, et al., 1950), but not in the rat (Bennett, et al., 1948) or, apparently, the mouse (Moon, et al., 1952), which respond by continued growth. That the change in specificity involves endogenous as well as exogenous hormone is evident from the occurrence of diabetes in association with spontaneous acromegaly. Evidence for the existence of a separate diabetogenic principle is not very impressive (Raben and Westermeyer, 1952; Young, 1953). Todorov (1959) found chemical evidence of an "age change in response" to somatotrophin, even in the rat, in that the latent period of the response of rat liver RNA and DNA to its administration increases steadily with age, as in the enzyme-induction processes studied by Adelman (1970)—a general feature of induction with age, which may or may not in this case reside in DNA (Adelman, et al., 1972). Complete ablation of the anterior lobe in adults leads to failure of growth but not, in general, to other acceptable evidences of senility (in rats), though this cannot be shown from the life-table.

In experimental studies, even highly purified growth hormone administered to rats produces decreasing effects upon nitrogen retention and upon growth after repeated administration (Whitney, et al., 1948). These experiments, however, have often been carried out with heterologous (usually ox) hormones, and, as in the case of antigonadotrophic effects, no physiological importance can be attached to the apparent increase in tissue resistance.

Of the other hormones concerned in growth and differentiation, the pituitary thyrotrophic hormone appears in most mammals that have been studied (rats—Turner and Cupps, 1938; rabbits—Bergman and Turner, 1941; mice—Adams and Mothes, 1945; cattle—Reece and Turner, 1937) to reach a peak at or about puberty, with a subsequent decline that has never been followed by assay into old age. The decline of general metabolism with increasing age, which has been frequently linked with the decline of growth capacity as an index of "physiological ageing," appears to involve both a fall in thyroid activity and a decline in cell response, since thyroidectomized rats show no senile decline in heart-rate and O_2 uptake, and old normal rats are decreasingly responsive to thyroxine administration (Grad, 1953; Denckla, 1974). The declining heat production of ageing human subjects may well be a reflection as much of muscle atrophy as of thyroid involution: the power of the thyroid to respond to thyrotrophin is apparently unimpaired (Banks, et al., 1959).

The results obtained by McCay, using dietary restriction, could be regarded as the consequences of dietary hypophysectomy. Such a state of affairs interferes with the production of both growth hormone and gonado-trophin, and its effect is a general slowing of the "integrating system" of growth + development. Dietary retardation greatly postpones, but cannot be kept at such a level as to prevent, the onset of estrus (Asdell and Crowell, 1935). McCay, et al. (1943), found that the capacity of retarded rats to resume growth was ultimately lost if retardation was prolonged. Apparently if growth is delayed without differentiation, it may ultimately encounter a block at the cellular level.

There have been attempts at selective interference with mammalian differentiation by the school of Li and Evans (Walker, et al., 1952; Asling, et al., 1952a, b). Hypophysectomy in 6-day-old rats does not arrest the eruption of teeth or the opening of the eyes, but later sexual and presexual development is suppressed. Untreated animals ultimately die from paralysis due to cerebral compression, the brain outgrowing the cranium. Rats that survive the postoperative period have been maintained in good health by growth hormone supplements. In these supplemented rats, the rate of growth was only slightly less than that of unoperated controls. Skeletal development was normal, but adult organ differentiation and sexual maturation did not take place. Three such "metathetelic" individuals were kept for 200–300 days in an attempt to produce gigantism. It would be interesting to know how long such animals are capable of living, and what senile changes they ultimately exhibit.

Experiments with *Lithospermum* extracts first indicated that the chemical "dissection" of pituitary effects with chemical antagonists is not an unreasonable hope (Wiesner and Yudkin, 1952). Far more specific agents acting upon neuroendocrine transmitters are now available, and research interest will certainly shift to these. The effect upon life-span of inducing precocious puberty in mammals other than man, where it sometimes occurs spontaneously, does not appear to have been studied: mice, which mature very early, are not ideal subjects, and an experiment on longer-lived mammals encounters the familiar practical difficulties.

Rather than pursuing pituitary hormones analogous to some hypothetical "juvenile hormone," the deficit of which leads to senescence, most modern work tends rather to support Everitt (1973) in treating the adult pituitary as a source of "ageing hormones"—or, more accurately, as being controlled by hypothetical ageing signals derived from the hypothalamus, and probably distinct from the signals that induce adult differentiation; and the results obtained in caloric restriction experiments as being hypothalamic in site. The pituitary growth hormone is under noradrenergic control in the limbic system and hypothalamus (Martin, et al., 1973), and its actions are coupled to a variety of protein-synthetic reactions unsuspected when the theory of a "juvenile hormone" was being pursued. The adrenocorticotrophic hormone (ACTH) is similarly controlled (van Loon, 1973).

7

Ageing and the Effects of Ionizing Radiation

Ionizing radiation is harmful to living cells; the mischief it does depends on the kind and amount of radiation, the identity of the subject, and the dose-time relationship. One expression of the sum of this mischief is a reduction in the average life-span of animals acutely or chronically exposed. Part of this is due to specific and identifiable effects, such as radiation sickness and the induction of malignant tumors. Part is due to damage of a less easily identifiable kind.

Chiefly from a consideration of this second type of life-shortening, the view was early put forward that radiation increases the rate of ageing (Alexander, 1957). Since the cause and mechanism of natural ageing in man and animals are unknown, this assertion, if true, is of great interest to gerontologists. For the same reason, however, it cannot be tested in the most satisfactory manner by comparing natural ageing with the effects of radiation at a fundamental level. There is also a measure of ambiguity in the meaning that different workers attach to the statement. For most purposes, indeed, it is preferable to follow Mole (1957) in referring to the chronic toxicity of radiation.

If radiation increases the rate at which the force of mortality rises with age, and if, as is usually the case, increase in the force of mortality is an acceptable index of ageing, there is a sense in which the statement is true by definition. The same could be said of some but not all noxious influences that shorten life, particularly if, as has been maintained by Harden Jones (1955), physiological mischief is self-aggravating. The question is not whether radiation is a noxious influence of this kind, however, but whether its effect on general vigor is "something special"—whether in particular it acts by accelerating, augmenting, or simulating some of the processes that cause intact animals to age. The idea has been put forward (Kunze, 1933) that natural ageing itself is a toxic effect of background radiation; quantitative experiment does not seem to bear this out. The causes of natural ageing being unknown, however, radiation studies might possibly throw light on them. Evidence from the experiments that have so far been carried out, both by scientists on animals and by psychopaths on the human species, suggests that it is in any case important to understand the nature of the effect of radiation upon vigor.

Inspection of nonradiation effects suggests four main ways in which adverse factors can modify the survival curve.

Case 1. By producing an added standing mortality, as in zoo animals. The curve is intermediate between the "physiological" and the logarithmic—its exact form will depend on how much of the added component is itself age-dependent, and whether a resistant subgroup is selected. Age-dependence decreases as the total mortality increases. When the curve is a straight line there is no commonest age of adult death; when it is logarithmic, mortality is independent of age.

Case 2. By producing a general decrement of vigor that is roughly equal for all the affected animals. This appears to be the case in some but not all examples of inbreeding depression. Senile changes appear precociously but progress at the usual rate.

Case 3. By producing an acceleration of the whole process of mortality increase; i.e., the shape of the survival curve is virtually unaltered, but it is redrawn to a different time scale. The survival of *Daphnia* responds to moderate temperature increase in this way: McCay's rat curves are in much the same relationship, though the fit is considerably less good.

Case 4. By producing "all-or-none" damage. Certain animals die, at once or later; those that survive have undergone no loss of life-expectation.

Of these hypothetical "pure" instances, Cases 2 and 3 come nearest to representing a speed-up of age processes; in Case 2 ageing is precocious, in Case 3 it is precocious and itself accelerated. Specific increase in the rate of a hypothetical clock for natural ageing could presumably have either of these results, depending on the competence of the clock. But combinations of all four cases could produce curves of any shape, especially if some have latent periods and others show substantial recovery, and the most that can properly be said of a curve is that it is compatible or incompatible with a supposed process.

A factor could be said to cause "precocious ageing," beyond reasonable cavil over definitions, if: (1) it caused the force of mortality to rise more rapidly in affected than in control animals; (2) it brought forward the age of onset of diseases that affect the controls, but did not greatly alter the sequence or the incidence of causes of death; (3) it made any characteristic features of the ageing syndrome in that species—e.g., graying, loss of skin elasticity—appear at a proportionately lower age. In this case its effects could not be distinguished from those of an accelerated natural ageing, at least until more of the processes involved in natural ageing are known. It might act by accelerating the whole developmental program; in this case presenile landmarks in development, such as the age of puberty or bony union, would also be affected, but if its contribution were wholly to the deteriorative effects of development it need not do so.

We can translate this into more concrete terms. If radiation accelerates ageing, it should move the histogram of pedestrian road deaths (Figure 1.3) to the left—it need not alter its proportions. An irradiated population should retire earlier, though it might well leave school later, than an unirradiated.

7.1 Long-Term Effects of Irradiation on Survival Curves

7.1.1 *Chronic Exposure*

All the experimental studies that have appeared indicate that ionizing radiations, at least above a certain threshold of exposure, shorten life (Walburg and Hoel, 1972). The exceptions are in insects, where suppression of gonadal function can increase longevity (Benz, 1970) or with low doses, which appear to act as an evocator of stress response (Sacher and Trucco, 1962). The observations are difficult to compare because of their heterogeneity in type, relative efficiency, and dose of radiation, choice of animal and strain, method of analysis, and method of expressing result. They have been reviewed (Mole, 1957; Walburg and Hoel, 1972; van Dorp, 1970; Fry, et al., 1969; Lindop and Sacher, 1966); reference here will be confined to those giving enough of the survival curves of control and irradiated animals for their shapes to be compared. Much of the work on chronic irradiation has been concerned to establish a dose-response curve. The consistency of the published findings for mice, at least for doses of 10 rad/week or more (fast neutrons = 1 rad/week) is remarkable in view of the diversity of strain and experimental conditions (Blair, 1954).

Many of the results raise important questions of method. Survival is a most sensitive biological index, and the curves obtained in such experiments can be profoundly affected by minor environmental factors such as handling, temperature gradients, and population density in cages. Neary, et al. (1957) found that if, instead of four mice being kept in one cage, two were kept in a cage half the size, growth was almost completely arrested. The estrous cycle and tumor incidence of mice can be altered by the presence or absence of other individuals (Andervont, 1943–1944). Even in Neary's experiments, which were planned with great care to avoid such effects, there was a significant difference of 5 percent in the survival curves of randomly chosen control groups caged 20 ft apart. Mole (1957) has pointed out that a low-dose group of irradiated mice in the experiments of Lorenz, et al. (1954), which had an apparently increased life-span compared with controls, were kept in a different room, without air conditioning. Factors of this order are probably more serious hindrances to work on the effects of very low-level radiation than to assessments of the significance of larger life-span changes, but they cannot be ignored.

Some of the curves obtained by various investigators working on chronic irradiation are reproduced in Figures 7.1–7.3. Neary, et al. (1957) compared the effects of γ-irradiation and neutron irradiation of mice and analyzed the data to determine whether the shapes of the survival curves were in better accord with the hypothesis of excess mortality (Case 1), precocious ageing (Case 2), or accelerated ageing (Case 3). The fit to Case 1, by a probit transformation, was not convincing. Case 3 requires a general contraction of the time scale of the whole curve; the standard deviations of the mean survival times decreased with increasing dosage, but not greatly, and there was no evidence to suggest a more rapid advance of senile change once the decline had begun. Neary, et al. conclude that "the simple hypothesis of premature ageing represents our data reasonably well, particularly if early deaths are excluded."

In the earlier experiment of Lorenz, et al. (1954) the curves obtained by γ-irradiation of mice show some evidence of whole-scale contraction if control and maximally irradiated groups are compared, but mice at the lowest level of irradiation (0.11 γ/day) outlived the controls, as already mentioned: if this, and not the control curve, is taken as the base line, the decline in standard deviation at high doses is less evident, though still greater than in Neary's study (Figures 7.2, 7.3). According to Mole and Thomas (1961), when mice receive 3–200 rem daily, it is the initial dose-time that produces most of the observed life-shortening; i.e., the mechanism appears to saturate. The curve for guinea pigs is similarly intermediate between Case 2 and Case 3; their control curve is, incidentally, the first full survival curve to be published for these animals, apart from the brief account of their longevity given by Rogers and Rogers (1957). "Precocious" ageing would again seem the description of these results that begs fewest questions. In preparing most of the curves the sexes were combined, although there was separate analysis of the performance of each. Gowen (1961) recently found a signficant increase in life-

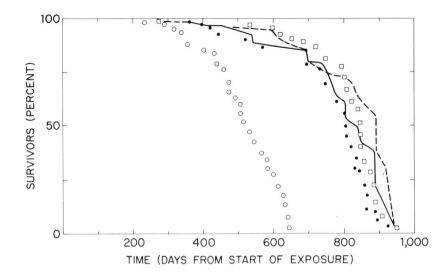

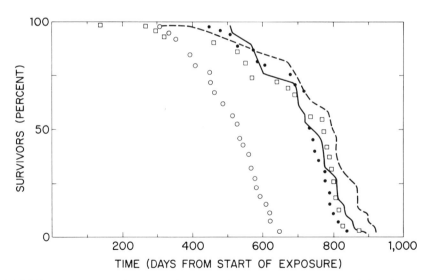

FIGURE 7.1 Survival curves of CBA male mice (lower graph) and female mice (upper graph) and duration of irradiation by fast neutrons (days): ○, fast neutrons, 6.4 rad/week; ●, fast neutrons, 0.54 rad/week; □, fast neutrons, 0.19 rad/week. Solid line: mice exposed to residual γ-ray component only. Dashed line: controls. (Adapted from Neary, et al., 1957.)

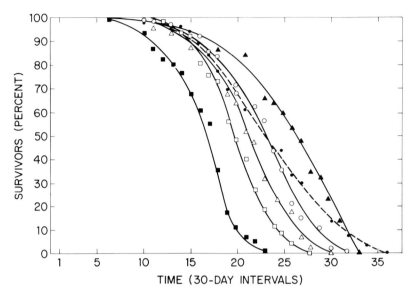

FIGURE 7.2   Survival curves of LAF₁ mice, showing percentage survivors at 30-day intervals: ○, controls; ▲, 0.11 rad/8-hr day; ◯, 1.1 rad/8-hr day; △, 2.2 rad/8-hr day; □, 4.4 rad/8-hr day; ■, 8.8 rad/8-hr day. (From Lorentz, et al., 1954.)

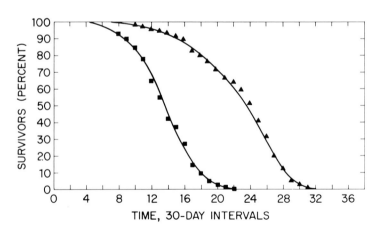

FIGURE 7.3   Survival curves of C₃Hb mice, showing percentage survivors at 30-day intervals; ▲, virgin control; ■, exposed to 8.8 rad/8-hr day. (From Lorentz, et al., 1954.)

expectancy of female mice after single x-ray doses, due wholly to the suppression of litter-bearing. Very low doses may also lenthen the life of animals whose health is suboptimal—possibly by doing more damage to the pathogens than to the mice, or through a "stress" effect (Sacher and Trucco, 1962).

Tumors apart, the long-term histological results of irradiation cannot usually be distinguished from those of natural ageing, though they can be induced locally (Casarett, 1956; Henshaw, 1944; Upton, 1957). The "characteristic pathological change" of mammalian ageing is probably an increase in the number of pathological changes. In animals short-lived as a result of irradiation the balance of these is in general preserved.

7.1.2 *Single Exposures*

Excluding acute and subacute mortality experiments, there is a shortage of completed survival curves for animals after one moderate or small dose of irradiation. In the original pile experiments of Henshaw, et al. (1947), the tails of the low-dosage curves were not completed: so far as they go, they suggest an increase in standing mortality as well as, or rather than, displacement of the adult mode. Furth, et al. (1954) studied the longevity and pathology of several thousand LAF_1 mice exposed to radiation from a nuclear bomb (chiefly gamma rays with an admixture of fast and slow neutrons). The tails of the curves are again not completed; for both males and females the scatter decreased slightly with increasing dose.

The decline in survivorship with age might be expected to begin unusually early after one dose and proceed unusually fast during continued exposure. This it apparently does (Sacher, 1959), but in chronic experiments most of the harm may well be done early (Neary, et al., 1957), though sensitivity has been reported to increase in animals already old (Sacher, 1957). The exact form of the survival curve depends on the strain of mouse used (Grahn and Hamilton, 1958). It is probable that the variance in control life-spans will fall steadily with better attention to biological conditions. In this context, however, *constant* conditions are not invariably optimal for longevity or for unanimity in dying.

To resolve some of these questions Lindop and Rotblat (1959a, b; 1961a, b, c) have carried out a very large-scale study of the effects of a single exposure to x-rays on the longevity of mice. Survival curves are being drawn for 3,500 SAS/4 mice exposed at 30 days of age to 15-MEV x-rays, in fourteen dose groups ranging from 50 to 850 rad, and for 1,200 sham-irradiated controls, with special attention to the age distribution and incidence of causes of death. A detailed postmortem was done on every animal, and physiological tests were carried out on random samples as subsidiary measurements of ageing. In a second experiment, on a further 5,000 mice, the sensitivity to radiation, judged both by LD_{50} and by life-shortening, were determined at a series of ages from 30 days onward. Breeding experiments were also undertaken, in which the longevity, leukemia incidence, and cause of death are compared in successive generations bred from irradiated and non-irradiated males. Special measures were taken in all this work to secure accurate dosimetry and to keep control and test series under biologically identical conditions.

The results indicate that the life-shortening produced by radiation is not due to a single disease, but to the bringing forward in time of all causes of death. The order and frequency of these causes is altered compared with controls—the result is not, therefore, identical with the effects of natural ageing, though it resembles them (Lindop and Rotblatt, 1960). A single genetic event has been postulated as the initiator of tumors and of early senescence (Curtis, 1967; Spalding, et al., 1971).

7.1.3   Effects in Man

Neither studies of occupational exposure nor military experiments, deliberate and accidental, on human populations have yet yielded satisfactory evidence about the long-term effects of radiation on human ageing. Warren (1956) compared the obituaries of radiologists with those of other physicians; he found not only a significant increase in leukemia but earlier death from each of a number of major diseases, the mean loss of life-expectation from all causes being 5.2 years. This is more than double Hursh's estimate (1957), since the average dose received would probably lie between 100 and 200 mrad/week (Osborn, 1955). Warren's computation has been cogently attacked (Seltser and Sartwell, 1958) because of his method of treating the age distributions involved. Court-Brown and Doll (1958) have analyzed the records of longevity in English radiologists from 1897 to 1958. They find no tendency to shorter life, even in the pioneer years when protection was minimal, apart from a small excess mortality from skin tumors. In their study, the performance of radiologists is if anything slightly better than that of comparable professional groups.

Data from atomic bomb and fallout casualties, though they have covered many types of illness and injury, have not so far proved more acceptable practically than ethically in assisting age studies. Some knowledge may in time be gained from them, but the two most heavily exposed populations are probably undergoing large social changes in age mortality. Accurate matching of human controls is not easy, and objective as well as subjective age changes can be modified in man by psychological as well as physical stress, even by the knowledge of having been exposed to radiation. "Early ageing" is occasionally mentioned in the victims of comparable maltreatment that did not include irradiation—in survivors of prison camps, for example. Effects on the human rate of ageing from exposure to atomic bombs appear to be minimal (Izumi, 1956; Hollingsworth, 1960; Anderson, 1971; Hollingsworth, et al., 1969; Anderson, et al., 1974; Belsky, et al., 1973).

7.2 Summary

It is difficult to draw a brief description of the effects of radiation on life-span from these data. One such description is that it seems to reduce vigor, in the same sense that heterosis increases it. The resemblance between the effects of irradiation and of inbreeding, like that between the effects of radiation and age changes, may be fortuitous, but is suggestive. The radiation resistance of hybrids is greater than of inbreds (Rugh and Wolff, 1958). Radiation, inbreeding, and ageing all diminish the resourcefulness of the organism in maintaining homeostasis against random environmental attack. In inbred animals, this instability is expressed as a high variability in characters such as drug resistance (McLaren and Michie, 1954); it would be interesting to compare the variability of irradiated animals by similar tests. Since inbreeding has acted throughout development, inbred animals are likely to be more variable in any case than those irradiated postnatally, but mice that had been reared under constant irradiation from conception (Neary, et al., 1957) were found to be very vulnerable.

Apart from the induction of tumors, radiation does not greatly alter the distribution of causes of death—the tendency is for irradiated animals to die earlier from all of them. Nor does it accelerate "development;" like inbreeding, it more commonly slows it.

Further experiment might show whether there is any real identity of process behind this resemblance. There are several hypotheses of ageing that are relevant to it, and to the possible mechanism of life-shortening by radiation (Strehler, 1959). Ageing has often been treated as the sum of inconstant changes due to external injury and to side effects of metabolism (Furth, et al., 1954; Jones, 1955; Sacher, 1955). Failure of repair with increasing age would then be due to differentiation, or to self-aggravation of changes when several happen to coincide (Hinshelwood, 1957; Sacher, 1956), the consistency of the survival curve being statistical rather than developmental. This dynamic version of the old theory of "wear" (*Abnutzungstheorie*) is more plausible when it is made more specific, and the changes are supposed to affect one or more groups of postmitotic cells that cannot be renewed by division. Ionizing radiation can increase the reactivity of structures normally stable and might hasten this type of deterioration as grit increases the rate of wear in bearings, by making the same changes occur for a smaller molecule tumor (Harman, 1957). There is here the possibility of a direct estimation, both of the molecule life of cells and of radiation effects on it, in animals of fixed cell number. The equally venerable theories of deterioration in the cellular or non-cellular microstructure (Marinesco, 1934; Rúzička, 1924) as manifestations of ageing, if not causes, have some support from recent work on collagen (Banga, 1947; Hall and Tunbridge, 1957; Verzár, 1957), but in this case the changes are not accelerated by local irradiation (Sinex, 1957). The identity of process between ageing and radiation damage may, indeed, be in the processes of repair rather than in the nature of the damage or changes induced (Stover, 1959).

For the kinetics of γ-irradiation damage in Drosophila imagoes see Dolkas, et al. (1975). Sacher (1965b) has proposed a mathematical test for the stochastic character of the damage done to longevity by radiation. The postulation of mechanisms has not always conformed to these strict criteria.

Most attention has naturally focused on the ability of radiation to disorganize chromatin. The similarity between mortality curves and entropy functions was noticed by Gompertz (1825). Perks (1932) remarked some time ago that loss of vigor, measured as "inability to withstand destruction," was of the same nature as "diminution of energy" in entropy theory, and the generation of a random element. It now seems likely that the information content of cell systems is the "biological energy" which was postulated in the last century, and thought to be dissipated with age. Inbreeding may reduce the fund of information by limiting the variety of genetic material present (Castle, 1926; Crow, 1948; Gowen, et al., 1946; Maynard Smith and Maynard Smith, 1954). Radiation might do so by its specific effects (point mutation, chromosome breakage) or merely by raising the noise level of the system; ageing might reflect a similar rise in noise level from metabolic "wear" of the molecules concerned, and from random injury. Mathematical consideration of such ideas (Sacher, 1955, 1956, 1961; Yockey, 1956) has so far outstripped experiment. They cannot yet be related, for example, to normal interspecific differences in life-span. Some, if not most, radiation damage to cells is extragenic, at least in ciliates (Power and Ehret, 1955); point mutation alone is probably not enough to account statistically for the observed rates of animal ageing (Failla, 1961). Russell (1957) has shown, however, that the shortening of life in male mice exposed to radiation from a nuclear bomb is transmitted to their progeny. Particularly interesting is Harman's finding (1957) that radiation-protective chemicals prolonged the life of unirradiated mice (see Ch. 9.3).

Hypothermia, like underfeeding, also gives some protection (Hornsey, 1959); underfed rats exposed to radiation fail, however, to resume growth when fed (Carroll and Brauer, 1961). All these results, however, depend chiefly on maintaining a rigid technique for survival experiments, and the difficulties of doing so are only now becoming evident. It is already clear, however, that polyploids are highly radioresistant (Sparrow and Shaiver, 1958) and that haploids (*Habrobracon*—Clark, 1960, 1961; Clark and Rubin, 1961) are more vulnerable than diploids to radiation-induced life-shortening. Curtis and Gebhard (1958) found that non-specific toxicity and nitrogen mustards did not accelerate ageing, but other chemical mutagens have been reported to produce life-shortening (Alexander, et al., 1959; Upton, et al., 1961; Conklin, et al., 1963) (see also Alexander and Connell, 1960).

Radiation biology can probably offer fundamental information about natural ageing processes. The most obvious field for this contribution, and one that need involve no assumptions about the identity of radiation damage with age changes, is in our understanding of the nature of vigor. Other possible applications may become evident as its cellular and physiological consequences are understood. Sufficient time has now been devoted to experiments in which radiations have been administered to animals and shown to do them no good. This point having been established, it should be possible to fix the requirements for more instructive comparisons.

> The most rational single explanation of the functional impairment of the ageing tissue is that it reflects an absolute loss in the cell population with replacement of these cells by extracellular fluid or connective tissue—the cell-deletion hypothesis (Handler, 1961).

But it is extremely difficult to relate this model to simple "genetic death" of fixed postmitotics resulting from mutation, for the reasons given—and still more difficult to relate it to a mutational theory of radiation life-shortening. Evidence suggests that at doses below 200 rad cell damage in mammals is chromosomal, with an average chromosome breakage dose of 19 rad, and the sensitivity of mammalian cells growing in tissue culture has been confirmed, to a large extent, in vivo, the mean lethal dose for the interphase human cell being put at about 86 rad. All the evidence contradicts equal sensitivity in fixed postmitotics, however (Hewitt and Wilson, 1959; Puck, 1961; Till and McCulloch, 1961): in animals without cell division, such as *Habrobracon*, radiation does indeed shorten life, and more in haploid than in diploid individuals, but only at doses one or two orders of magnitude greater than those that shorten the life of rodents (Clark, 1960, 1961; Clark and Rubin, 1961). Moreover, there are indications of change in the response of clonally-dividing mammalian cells, both to age and to low-dose irradiation; thus Pratt found that irradiated mice showed the same qualitative and quantitative lag in liver volume restoration after partial hepatectomy that is seen in old mice (Puck, 1961). Even if we substituted chromosomal damage for point mutation as the mechanism of age and radiation damage (assuming they are the same, which they may well not be) it looks as if survival of damaged but clonally viable cells may be more important than cell loss as a factor in reducing vigor and upsetting homeostasis (Puck, 1961). Loss of fixed postmitotics could be secondary—but if it is primary, we cannot say which of the two mechanisms is the overriding "clock" in fixing life-spans. Far more significant may be the extent and persistence of mechanisms for excision of error and for DNA repair.

8

Physiology, Homeostasis, and Ageing

Physiology is probably best regarded as the study of functioning homeostasis. The physiology described in the books is that of the young optimally functioning adult, human or animal.

Such a static and homeostatic physiology is the biological equivalent of the still photograph or of algebra prior to the invention of differential calculus. It has evident dynamic aspects within its own terms of reference, but it has also been superseded in biological thinking by a far wider concept of development process. While for initial study it is convenient and sensible to assume that there is one physiology of fat absorption or of neuromuscular conduction, once we obtain a picture of that physiology we are obliged at once to transfer it into a developmental context. The homeostasis that gives us our term of reference to "normal" function is in fact homeostasis about a developmentally changing point. There is one physiology for the newborn, another for the child, another for the adult, and another—or rather, several others—for the senescent man or animal.

If we look beyond "normal young adult" physiology, in so far as that can be normalized, we deal as developmental biologists with a sequence of physiologies beginning in the egg and ending in the grave which are related, when we treat them cross-sectionally, as are the frames of a motion picture, and in studying epigenetics or clinical medicine we are obliged to treat them as factors of process.

Developmental physiologists who deal with the end of this process, namely senescence, are in fact the only developmental physiologists for whom the transition from a static physiology to the process-centered kind presents any methodological problem. Embryonic and neonatal physiology may differ from the adult state, but because they are moving toward it, the fact that the point of homeostasis and the complexity of process are changing is not really troublesome. It is when we move on from optimal adult function into the consideration of senescence that we begin to have practical and intellectual difficulties.

Moving homeostasis, what Waddington (1957) has called homeorrhesis, is an easy enough idea. It involves us in more experiments, but whether we tackle it cross-sectionally or longitudinally it merely increases our comprehension of the resources of the organism. But ageing is at root an information loss: in the postadult phases we are studying, first, late developmental processes; then the consequences of deterioration in the system and the subsidiary compensations for these, the partial and often individually irregular failure of homeostasis; and finally, premortal deterioration. At no other stage of life is the complexity so great, nor the variation in individual patterns so marked—for the deterioration of homeostasis itself involves a steady increase in variance, and the variation among individuals as to which system leads the process of failure determines a still bigger variation in the surviving mechanisms of compensation.

We must accordingly ask how far there can be a physiology of ageing, or at least of its latter stages, except upon an individual basis. This is the point in the life-cycle at which genetic differences, including genetically determined idiosyncrasy in the rate of system failure, become manifest. These differences lead in turn to selection by death and further statistical divergence. If we tackle this phase of life cross-sectionally, by studying function and process in animals of a given senile chronological age, we are in fact transecting not a narrow distribution of characters but a wide and diverging distribution. The only comparable point in biology is in the immediately prepubertal phase in man, where individual genetic and environmental differences in the age of pubertal changes and in their order make cross-sectional study nearly meaningless (Tanner, 1955).

The diastolic blood pressure of women rises with age in approximately a straight line if we consider the mean, but the variance rises more steeply, and the range most steeply of all (Figure 8.1a) (Buerger, 1954). Physiological complexities underly this apparently simple curve; that of males is even more complex. If the curve were to be continued to still higher ages, the range might be expected to decline, through deaths of hypertensive old subjects, and the mean to decrease through the onset of cardiac failure in some of the survivors. A very large number of mensurables behave in this way with ageing

(Storer, 1965) (Figures 8.1–8.3). In most the variance and range increase, with the consequent requirement of larger samples at high ages, and if such samples are forthcoming the distribution may on inspection be found to be bimodal or plurimodal. Where in a straightforward deteriorative change the course of the curve is downward, but the variance does not increase, one cannot exclude the possibility—and on theoretical and rational grounds it is a probability—that a significant plurimodality is still concealed in the cross-sectional method.

All these difficulties are familiar in the statistical handling of human populations (Landowne, 1957). They can indeed be limited in animals by the use of inbred strains, but the limitation is deceptive, for if the degree of inbreeding is sufficient, it will give us the multiplied equivalent of studying a single genotype from a diverse population, while inbreeding itself can increase the range of homeostatic instability in a different way (McLaren and Michie, 1954).

There are indeed statistically identifiable changes, such as the decline in stroke index, or in 17-ketosteroid secretion (Hamilton and Hamilton, 1948; Landowne, 1957). Important research has been done both cross-sectionally and longitudinally in human populations by such workers as Shock and Verzár. Work of this type aims to characterize first, the general trends in physiological response with age, and second, the liability, viewed predic-

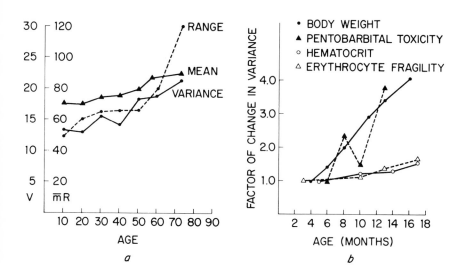

FIGURE 8.1 (a) Diastolic blood pressure, human female. (After Buerger, 1954.) (b) Factor of change in variance for a number of measurements as a function of age in C57BL/6J male mice. (After Storer, 1965.)

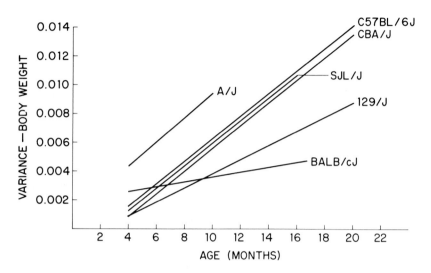

FIGURE 8.2   Regression of variance in body weight on age in six strains of female mice. (After Storer, 1951.)

tively, of particular individuals to particular changes. In spite of the utility of such studies, however, the processes that appear in the eventual distribution are subject to a peculiarity not found elsewhere in descriptive physiology: they contain the element of the unprogrammed, of progressive malfunction, not found elsewhere outside pathology. In this case, however, the malfunction and program loss are "normal," in the sense that they are inherent in the system, and this is what ageing implies.

This, then, is one uniqueness of senescent physiology viewed in gross. The homeostasis, or rather homeorrhesis, that has brought the system through epigenetic development to adult or "normal" function becomes increasingly unstable; the variations to which it must respond become larger, and its capacity to respond to them, less. Initial or incipient failures call into operation compensatory mechanisms at all levels which are programmed, as part of the "canalization" of function (in plain language, the existence of fallback mechanisms to cover failure in primary processes of adjustment). These are the adaptive age changes which have been studied by Frolkis and by Falzone, et al. (1967): they are not haphazard, but have presumably evolved pari passu with the long life of mammals such as man, where there is a long period of postreproductive life, at least in the female; they may well be the result of secondary and indirect natural selection—the result of the social advantage conferred by possessing elders and grandmothers. The adaptive changes can

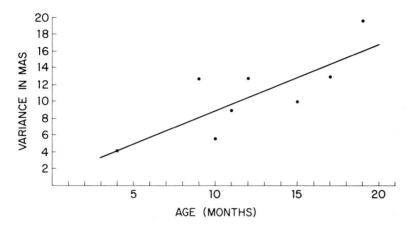

FIGURE 8.3   Change in variance in survival time under exposure to 100 rad/day (MAS) as a function of age in RF/J female mice. (After Storer, 1951.)

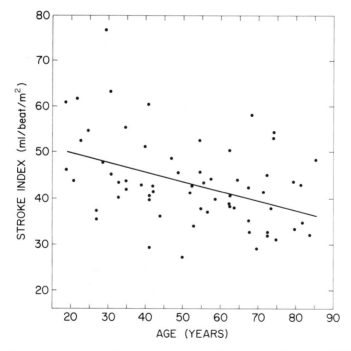

FIGURE 8.4   The relation between cardiac stroke index and age for 67 "normal" men. (After Landowne, 1957.)

be sufficient to mask an initial shift. Failure of peripheral cellular response may be met by increased output of a trophic hormone (the runaway production of gonadotrophin at the menopause is an extreme example of such a second-order control, one which is in this case ineffective in restarting ovulation. Such a second-order mechanism may remain virtually intact during the available life-span, or it may itself weaken in turn. Loss of nephrons may be met by hypertrophy of the surviving nephrons, but these in turn will eventually lose the capacity for further compensation, or renal function may deteriorate further after a plateau of compensation, through vascular, cellular, or extrarenal causes. It is this peculiarity of senescent deterioration, that it is in expression a multievent failure in a very well-buffered system, with several layers of precautionary response, which explains the rapid and diverse eventual collapse of homeostasis in many old subjects.

The other uniqueness of age physiology lies in the hierarchy of age changes already described—although ageing is an escape from homeostasis, it is also integrated by evolution into the profile of life-cycle in any animal that habitually, or even occasionally, reaches old age. The components of homeostatic breakdown and of turning-off are inextricable either by recourse to selectionist theory or—in most cases—by experiment; nor are they exclusive, since turning-off may be timed by failure of a previously homeostasized function. We are left accordingly with the description of a variety of observed changes—the "mechanisms" already cited—some evidence of their sequence or interrelation, and the need to elucidate in each organism the hierarchy of effects that lead to senescence as final common path.

It is essential to master this complexity before attempting to assess the practical relevance of modern experimental work on clonal ageing, genetic information loss, or other supposed primary processes. All are thinkably "primary," and provide attractive models for a simple overall senescence; all are, in fact, almost certainly loosely coupled to a more generally integrating life-cycle clock, of which any one of them might with further study eventually prove to be the mainspring. Thus if timed ageing is neurohormonally driven, cell loss or loss of genetic information might eventually be found to control the hormonal drift: a "primary" process might be only loosely coupled to ageing in some of its manifestations, or between organs.

Another consequence of this is that different physiological expedients for dealing with dyshomeostasis may be serially exposed at different points in the life-cycle, rather as an aircraft has a sequence of fallback systems to meet failures.

There have not been many physiological studies that concisely demonstrate the fact that the same homeostatic effect is being produced at different stages of the ageing process by different mechanisms. Arshavsky (1967) has demonstrated a whole successive repertoire of physiological devices by which dogs of increasing age respond to stress. Similar changes are seen throughout life in human response to acute infection, as expressed by the large clinical differences in the picture of lobar pneumonia in preantibiotic days as between children, young adults, middle-aged adults, and the old, in whom it could be virtually silent.

Sacher (1965) developed the mathematics of a homeostatic process with a specific point of failure. In real physiology, by reason of canalization, each such primary process is commonly overlapped by a secondary, fallback process, and this in turn has its point of failure. In the biology of any physiological mechanism there may be many, but rarely fewer than two, layers in such a stack. With the agewise deterioration of the homeostatic system as a whole, the magnitude of the swings to be corrected by a given primary process may increase, the failure threshold of the primary process may decrease, or both; but in the initial stages of the senile process, overlapping transfers the increased swing to the operation of secondary processes.

This system of overinsurance, of adaptive reaction by the body's residual potential to drift in each major system, is increasingly recognized today in the large number of recent studies on adaptive and compensatory mechanisms in ageing. The appearance of secondary, overinsurance mechanisms in part explains the failure of selection pressure to develop fundamentally non-ageing systems in higher animals, the need to increase life-span and consequently homeostatic reliability having been met by the development of late secondary adaptations rather than by making the primary process age-proof. Once committed to these, evolutionary correction of the original deficit becomes unlikely for lack of selection pressure: the same overinsurance principle probably applies at the cellular level as well as in gross physiology. Much past theory (Comfort, 1966; Curtis, 1967) has located the probable initial clock of age dyshomeostasis in damage to the nuclear information store or its transcribing mechanism, though whether fixed or clonally replicating cells are the chief determinant site of this loss, and whether it is general or timed by one or more cell groups, remains open. Its degree of coupling to the life-cycle is also unknown.

Attention is also focused on the repair mechanisms of DNA, as studiable through dose-time studies with ionizing radiation (Curtis, 1963, 1967; Sacher, 1965) and through the search for common or likely sources of nonreparable damage, such as the escape of lysosomal DNAase (Allison and Paton, 1965), which could represent an escape-point from programmed homeostasis. Besides random noise-type information loss of this kind, we have also to consider the possible role of programmed switching-off of intracellular physiological mechanisms in epigenesis, as suggested by Medvedev (1966). In this case too the principle of overinsurance as the evolutionary expedient for life prolongation is important. It may be that instead of evolving mechanisms to reactivate such masked genes, where the latent period of ensuing mischief is long, secondary but themselves limited methods of covering up the deficit have been the easier and preferred evolutionary option, and it is inherent in such overinsurance schemes that, like meeting one's debts by borrowing, the process is divergent to the point of failure.

There are already evidences of this kind in the findings of several studies on cellular senescence. In a number of these there is evidence of a terminal or subterminal metabolic "escape," characterized by rising O_2 uptake (Tribe, unpublished) and rising incorporation of label into DNA (Samis, et al., 1964), RNA (Wulff, et al., 1962), and protein (Clarke and Smith, 1966). It is tempting to interpret these as a terminal attempt at compensation for the increased production of nonsense materials, though such findings are susceptible to other interpretation, such as a failure of controlling feedback, or progressive damage to the cellular furniture by the escape of enzymes. The point in earlier ontogeny at which repair processes fail to the point of evoking secondary compensation is suggested, but has not yet been identified, through various dose-time studies of radiation damage. It seems highly probable that in so far as the noise component is concerned, nuclear information is subject to direct repair (of local defects, dimerization, etc.), secondary compensation through gene interaction to maintain the "canalized" condition, and selective deletion, both of nonsense or competitor molecules and of cells damaged by accumulation of errors. How far compensation will occur for any programmed switching-off of genes, on the lines postulated by Medvedev, is not known; the principle of evolutionary overinsurance rather than reform of process is on theoretical grounds very likely to apply equally to adaptive life prolongation in the presence of epigenetically determined loss of cell capacity. From the standpoint of controlling the rate of ageing, this would be a more difficult combination to control than that of noise increase plus compensation. If it were found to be the predominant cause of ageing, the finding would make the analogy between somatic and cellular age physiology extremely close, the "noise" accumulating in somatic physiology being already determined or programmed by events at a cellular level, whether these be random or themselves programmed, and depending in part on failure to distribute, rather than retain, information (Rose, 1967).

The mechanism of a failing but reinsured system of feedback is, accordingly, the field of study we designate as age physiology. The intracellular and intercellular mechanisms of ageing are likely to be schematically similar, for the reasons given. In the intracellular sphere we are concerned with chemical sources of program damage, repair processes of setting these, and compensatory mechanisms. In intercellular physiology we are concerned with normal or optimal feedback systems, sources of drift in these, secondary mechanisms of compensation, and the feedback between adjacent systems, such as muscular and vascular, vascular and renal, or muscular and protein-metabolic systems. It is these systems that integrate other age changes and set the life-span, and they represent the point at which gerontology must intervene. We are concerned with the changes in cellular response or capacity, in substrate susceptibility, and in hormone output. Thus in considering age changes in collagen metabolism, we need to reckon with decline in the capacity of tissue cells to produce collagenase, change in levels of cortisol output, and change in the colloidal and other properties of collagen (Houck et al., 1967). In considering the cardiovascular system we have to reckon with changes in the vascular wall, action of renal and cerebral homeostatic mechanisms and the drift in these, cardiac hypertrophy, and eventual myocardial degeneration, with multiple feedback loops between adaptive and pathological processes affecting all of these. The complexity of these interrelated mechanisms seems an ideal field for computer analysis with models, and one important aspect of age physiology applied to the understanding of senile function may well prove to be the construction of mechanical analog models in which drift, noise, and other properties of ageing systems can be simulated. There may be sizable contributions to be made here to cybernetic physiology in general, as well as to the identification of correctable key processes of drift, and to the particular genetic and individual circumstances that eventuate in stable senile equilibrium states—the situation we see in the healthy long-lived old.

This kind of optimized ageing is one possible target of gerontology. The broader, and actually—in view of the complexities outlined—the more credible target involves the identification of any life-cycle-controlling sequence that might be modified in rate. The experimentation described in the next chapter is primarily addressed to this wider objective, though some of its findings—if, for example, they led to the suppression of arterial disease in man—may actually contribute to the first objective.

9

The Position of Ageing Studies

If it were to prove feasible to tamper with the "clock" controlling information loss (whatever that may be), the possible outcome of such intervention would be to move the time of onset of the multiple vigor loss—and with it of almost all major deteriorations and malignancies that reflect it—to higher ages. Mammalian experiments involving relatively simple manipulations, such as calorie restriction (for review see Comfort, 1960; Ross, 1961) or the administration of hormones (Bellamy, 1968; Friedman and Friedman, 1964; Bodánzsky and Engel, 1966), indicate that this type of intervention is at least practicable in certain circumstances, and that the mammalian life-span is in principle modifiable. This is probably so in man, but if the leading process is, for example, one of exposure of uneliminated late-acting genes or otherwise an evolutionary or statistical entity only, it might prove inaccessible by reason of diversity (Medawar, 1945; Strehler, 1962; Hamilton, 1966; Wallace, 1967; Sacher, 1968), and research money would be better devoted to the piecemeal alleviation of senile disability through prosthetics and geriatrics. It now seems highly likely that the choice between these hypotheses could be made within a reasonably short time, given adequate research effort. At the moment the balance of evidence suggests that the first alternative—integral modifiability—is by far the more likely.

It seems rational to approach fundamental age research in the spirit of a stock-market analyst, starting with the main theoretical approaches, and thereafter selecting a portfolio. The projects that look most rewarding at the

TABLE 9.1
Ageing of Mammal—Intrinsic Models

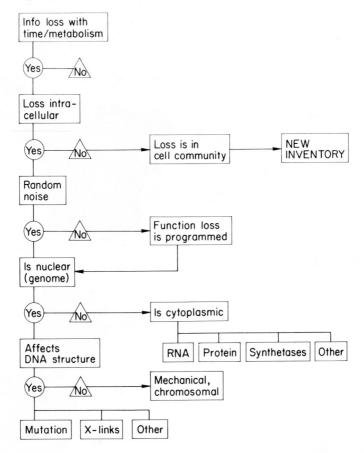

moment, from the viewpoint of understanding and modifying age processes, have in common the assumption that ageing represents an information loss; several involve a second assumption, that this loss occurs at a cellular level. If this second assumption is correct, it becomes necessary next to decide (a) whether the information loss is predominantly in fixed cells such as neurons, or in clonally dividing cells; and (b) whether the leading process in either case is one of noise accumulation in homeostatic and copying processes, or whether it is secondary to differentiation, depending on the irreversible switching-off of synthetic capacities with morphogenesis or an extrinsic process with similar consequences located in the software. Clearly, if we are dealing with a gramophone record that becomes scratched with repeated use to the point of unintelligibility, we might be able to lubricate the needle, or otherwise reduce the rate of noise injection. If we are dealing with a record that, once played, cannot be restarted, we need to devise a means of running it more slowly, though not so much more slowly as to spoil the music. Neither model is exclusive nor exhaustive; thus if switching-off is involved (as at some point in ontogeny it must be), we are still thereafter dealing with information loss depending on spoilage of irreplaceable structures (Bullough, 1971). The site of such spoilage offers further choices, and may include molecular, chromosomal, organelle, or membrane changes, or all of these. Any model of information loss, whether cellular, molecular, or intercellular, seems, moreover, mathematically and logically to require some kind of self-aggravating or feedback process if it is to explain the exponential character of ageing. Apart from verifying any model as a whole, one important experimental problem is accordingly to determine the size and site of the feedback loop. Another is to determine if there is one such loop or several. We need accordingly to look for evidence of misspecified or nonsense cells or materials accumulating with age, and, in particular, for sites at which misspecification would be self-propagating: for evidence of a nonsense material that either produces more of itself (an ageing pseudovirus, in other words) or one that produces increasing disorder of specification. The feedback loop could also lie in the community of cells, even if the original error is molecular.

9.1 "Primary Error" Hypotheses

The simplest "classical" hypothesis of intrinsic ageing was that information is being lost from DNA—either through mutation, through macromolecular damage, or through epigenetic masking, the last of these identifying ageing with differentiation. The mutational theories arise from the consideration of the supposed ageing effects of radiation, though the identity of these with natural ageing remains debatable and fails to agree with the data from radiosensitivity experiments in old mice (Yuhas, 1971): radiation administered in youth appreciably shortens life, but it appears to have therapeutic effects—possibly on neoplasia or the general stress reaction—when given in old age. Simple point mutation, until recently a popular hypothesis, is probably ruled out, both by the mathematics of the process (Maynard Smith, 1959a) and by the failure of chemical mutagens to induce radiation-type life-shortening unless they are capable of producing changes more extensive than point mutation—cross-linking, for example (Alexander, 1967; Alexander and Connell, 1960). Macromolecular genome damage by cross-links, irreparable strand breakage and the like are more acceptable, and would square with the postulated effects of radiation, mutagens, and free radicals. In the case of bacteria it has been computed that one mitomycin-induced cross-link per genome in DNA is lethal (Waring, 1968). Chromosomal abnormalities accumulate with age (Curtis, 1967) and appear, in the case of humans, to correlate with some mental changes (Jarvik and Kato, 1969; Nielsen, 1968). There is evidence that in brain cells of 10-year-old dogs genes coding for rRNA have actually been lost (Johnson and Strehler, 1972).

Many studies have been carried out upon differences between the DNAs and RNAs of "old" and young cells variously defined. Some of these are reviewed by Price and Makinodan (1973). Repair (Epstein, et al., 1973; Clarkson and Painter, 1974; Little 1976; Wheeler and Lett, 1974) of DNA strands has been found or hypothesized to differ between "old" and "young." The presence of single-stranded regions (Chetsanga, et al., 1975), RNA–DNA ratios in fixed cells (Chaconas and Finch, 1973), and template capacity (O'Meara and Herrmann, 1972) have been said to change during the course of ageing. Problems arise in all these studies over the definition of oldness in the material selected, which covers old fixed postmitotics, late generations of clonally dividing mitotics, or both. Until recently, moreover, gerontologists have not been sophisticated DNA chemists, or sophisticated DNA chemists gerontologists, with consequent artifactual and semantic problems. DNA repair capacity has been correlated with species life-span (Hart and Setlow, 1974), as has repetition of important sequences (Medvedev, 1972). There is some evidence that in mouse cells single-strand scission accumulates with age (Ono, et al., 1976).

Cross-linking in long-term molecules, favored by Bjorksten (1958), has drawn some popularity as a source of DNA damage from the large body of work on natural ageing of collagen, begun by Verzár and last reviewed in detail by Hall (1968) and by Deyl (1968). It may well affect the properties, for example, of organelles without involving the information store itself. Attempts to demonstrate it directly in "old" DNA have been made (Von Hahn and Verzár, 1963; Von Hahn and Fritz, 1966), but there are experimental difficulties in the direct comparison of function in "old" and "young" DNA (for review see Von Hahn, 1971). It is not demonstrable in Drosophila DNA (Massie, et al., 1975). More evidence may conceivably come from the attempts of Bjorksten to prepare and test bacterial enzymes directed against cross-linked materials in general (Bjorksten, et al., 1971; Schenk and Bjorksten, 1973). "Old" DNA has been said to differ from "young" in protein-binding power (Samis and Wulff, 1968) and possibly in unwinding capacity (Devi, et al., 1966). Its template activity has been variously reported (Devi, et al., 1966; Pyhtila and Sherman, 1968; Samis and Wulff, 1969), but seems to depend far more on RNA polymerase concentration than on donor age. Direct studies of nuclear DNA, conducted with gerontology in mind, have so far been made by less sophisticated techniques than those employed by the genetic chemists. In recent work on dogs, Shirey and Sobel (1972) found no transcriptional differences. There is difficulty in avoiding mixed nuclear populations of old fixed, younger fixed, and clonally competent cells even in a tissue such as myocardium.

There is a wide range of subsidiary theory about possible causes and manifestations of DNA error, involving, for example, immunity (Burch, 1968) or escape of lysosomal DNAases (Allison and Paton, 1965; Allison, 1966). At the same time, the direct demonstration that young DNA differs or does not differ from old seems likely to come from the further general advance of genetic chemistry rather than from ad hoc research, the role of gerontologists being to raise the possibility. There are a priori objections to a "primary" DNA lesion, moreover, including the need to explain why some clones, such as those of William pears, are stable, and why the rate of damage accumulation measured by mortality should be 50 times as great in the mouse as in man (Sacher, 1968). Masking by histones is another theoretical possibility (Von Hahn, 1971): epigenetic switching-on and switching-off must, it is held, occur at the nuclear level during differentiation. It could be timed by outside intercellular signals, and could even include an evolved life-span fixing, "destructor" mechanism (Medvedev, 1966) or changes in translational capacity from the turning-off of RNA species able to read particular codons (Strehler, 1969; Strehler, et al., 1971; Johnson and Strehler, 1972). Another possibility, raised by Medvedev (1972) and Cutler (1972) is that age sensitivity of codons depends on the number of available copies, rare or unrepeated information being perishable. Some processes, once switched off, might be irrecoverable within the differentiated state, and the life of cells in that state could accordingly be fixed by the life-span of irreplaceable secondary copies, enzymes and the like. Thus Bullough (1967, 1971) has drawn attention to the importance of substances that determine the postmitotic lifespan of cells passing out of the mitotic cycle into their determinate state: death in these cells may follow at a fixed interval after the closing of a developmental "gate," but with this interval and the position of the "gate" appear to be modifiable, e.g., by prednisolone.

A related line of thought is that pursued by Gelfant (Gelfant and Graham-Smith, 1972): that tissue maturation and subsequent ageing depend on epigenetic blocking of cells at either the G_1 or G_2 phase of the cycle, followed by non-renewal-type ageing. This block is releasable both by hydrocortisone and by other immunosuppressants (De Cosse and Gelfant, 1968) and may be immunodetermined. In Gelfant's view the well-known longer latent period of older tissues in culture represents only the higher proportion of cells in these tissues that are G_1 blocked (McCreight and Sulkin, 1959).

9.2 Non-DNA Error Theories

At the present moment it seems clear (a) that error accumulation in primary DNA has been neither demonstrated nor excluded as a "cause" of ageing, and (b) that all the arguments and mechanisms adduced for it could apply with equal force to error accumulation at a post-DNA level. This could be chromosomal (involving nuclear structures rather than molecular DNA) or it could involve later transcription steps (RNA, synthetases, and proteins), or the selective loss of ability to transcribe particular codons (Strehler, et al., 1971). Quantitative and qualitative changes with age in mouse spleen tRNAs have been described by Wust and Rosen (1972). Loss of sex chromatin with age occurs in normal women (Jacobs, et al., 1963) and chromosomal loss in other groups has been reported in connection with organic brain syndrome (Jarvik and Kato, 1969). Some argument has been based on the rate of visible nuclear error accumulation in long- and short-lived mouse strains (Curtis, 1967). By far the most coherent location of the likely primary error site, however, puts it at the RNA-synthetase step. This theory was developed by Orgel (1963, 1970, 1973), and is now having a profound influence on the study of limitation in clones. According to Orgel, stochastic error, either in RNA specification or in the production of synthetases from RNA templates, both cytoplasmic in site, would lead to precisely the required accumulation of further error through the machine-tool role of the synthetases (RNA polymerases and the like) in specifying both secondary templates and themselves. This would produce an eventual error crisis, bad copies driving out good—by which time misspecification would be present in all but the primary copies, and might finally affect these. The likelihood of such a crisis, which is not inevitable, is determined by the relative kinetics of misspecified molecules and protein copying generally (Orgel, 1970), so that the difference between limited and unlimited clones is explicable, as dependent upon relative rates of protein synthesis. If incorrect synthetases produce both further errors and more of themselves, they could exert a viruslike action both within the cell and, if transferred, in other cells. A model of this kind is in agreement with the work that has been done to locate error sites through the search for runaway synthesis of RNA, DNA, and protein, as possible compensation for nonsense material production (Samis, et al., 1964; Wulff, et al., 1962; Clarke and Maynard Smith, 1966). It also agrees extremely well with the results obtained in the studies of spanned clones (described below), and would gain still further in plausibility if it could be linked experimentally with one of the forms of chemical-stochastic attack incriminated by the free-radical and cross-linking schools. Attempts to demonstrate "runaway" synthesis at the mitochondrial level in old cells have so far consistently failed, however (Menzies and Gold, 1971). The Orgel model could not be substantiated in *Drosophila* by induced protein misspecification (Bozcuk, 1976), nor could altered enzyme be detected in mouse liver (Yagil, 1976) for glucose-6-phosphate dehydrogenase (G6PDH), though it was detected by Gershon and Gershon (1973) for aldolase.

The main investigable consequences of an Orgel-type error model would be (1) increasing clonal divergences with age, (2) aggravation by error agents

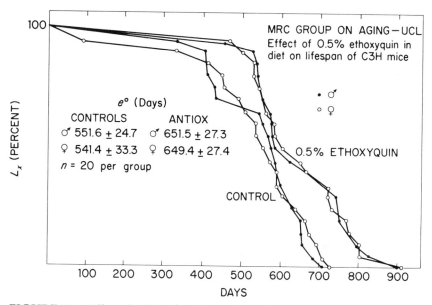

FIGURE 9.1   Effect of 0.5% w/w ethoxyquin on the survival curves of C3H mice. (From Comfort, 1971.)

such as unconventional amino acids that act directly on protein specification, and (3) cytoplasmic transmissibility.

It becomes profitable at this point to switch from the consideration of hypotheses to that of empirical research projects. In view of the large diversity of possible error sites inside and outside the cell, it now seems at least marginally more likely that the exact site, the size of the feedback loop, and the choice between primary DNA and later transcription faults will be settled from observing empirical agents acting on the life-span than the other way round. It is now possible to outline a scientifically accountable research "portfolio" that, while neither sufficient nor exhaustive, covers the market on reasonable investment principles. This is based (1) on maximum number of options, with regard to the theories laid down, and (2) the preferential use of life prolongation as the critical experiment: non-specific life-shortening is easy to produce, but prolongation of the active life of outbred animals much less so.

9.3   Protectant Substances

If information loss from cells is stochastic, and is comparable to that produced by γ-rays, then it ought to be possible to affect its rate chemically without further particularization of site. The earliest test of the chemical-stochastic hypothesis, other than by looking for life-shortening, was suggested by Harman (1961, 1962). If radiation accelerates ageing, then radio-protectants, and especially antioxidants, might reasonably be expected to delay it in the intact animal. The critical experiment, however, would be to define an antiradiation drug that delays ageing in the unirradiated animal.

Food antioxidants of the type used as preservatives in manufactured products have now been administered to rats or mice with varying degrees of life-span prolongation compared with controls (Harman, 1957, 1961, 1968a, b; Buu-Hoi and Ratsimamanga, 1959; Comfort, et al., 1971), but without clear evidence that the prolongations obtained depend on molecular protection. A substantial body of speculation has also grown up about the exact site of possible free-radical damage, and the chemistry of the reactions that might be involved (Tappel, 1968; Burlakova, et al., 1966; Dormandy, 1969; Kawashima, 1970; Barber and Bernheim, 1967; Pryor, 1970). The range of possible side reactions and attack sites is evidently wide, ranging from the genetic information store to mitochondrial and other lipids of fixed cells, with or without the formation of lipofuscin (Bjorkerud, 1964; Barber and Bernheim, 1967; Chio, et al., 1969).

Evidence of the validity of a free-radical theory of ageing would not only open an immediate prospect of clinical experiment, but also make available for the purpose of gerontology a large and important body of experience drawn from food and materials chemistry. All that remains is the exertion necessary to demonstrate whether the theory is correct or not. If indeed long-term molecules and sensitive copying mechanisms do not undergo changes analogous to those seen in stored foods and materials, it is reasonable to ask what protects them (Cain and Cunneen, 1962).

The probable candidates among chemical mechanisms have been considered by Harman (1957–1968), Tappel (1968), Dormandy (1969), and others. Lipoperoxidation is favored (Dormandy, 1969, review) because it is known to occur with ageing, e.g., in rat brain (Yoshikawa and Hirai, 1967), where α-tocopherol concentration fails to increase with age (Weglicki, et al., 1968). It can also be linked with lipofuscin chemistry, and has analogies with vitamin E deficiency and the widely studied toxic processes (encephalomalacia, exudative diathesis), which are controllable by adding antioxidant to animal feeds (Bunyan, et al., 1962; Machlin, 1963; Andrews, et al., 1960). These last are short-term processes due to an increased rate of lipoperoxidation, either from ingestion of preformed peroxides in food, or from high rates of free-radical initiator consumption in the absence of sufficient α-tocopherol. No experiments at lower levels of attack have been pursued into old age, using agricultural animals, and α-tocopherol itself appears relatively ineffective as a life-prolonging agent in mice on standard laboratory diets (Harmon, 1968b). The subject of tocopherol effects has been reviewed by

Dam (1967). It is no means certain that vitamin E acts, wholly or mainly, as an antioxidant (Green, 1972). Toxicity of unsaturated fats as free-radical sources in the absence of a high tocopherol intake is a possibility worthy of consideration in the planning of human atherosclerosis diets. Packer and Smith (1974) have claimed that vitamin E can suppress clonal senescence of fibroblasts, a finding not so far confirmed.

Mitochondrial damage has also been studied (Marco, et al., 1961; Tappel and Zalkin, 1959; Horton and Packer, 1970, review). Mitochondria, however, are replaceable structures. In order to "explain" ageing on the analogy of radiation-induced molecular attack we seem to require damage either to irreplaceable molecules, for example, in fixed cells or the genome, or to the copying mechanism of clonally dividing cells—possibly, on the basis of Orgel's hypothesis (1963), at the synthetase level.

In testing any supposed mechanism of natural ageing, we have to design experiments in such a sense that the positive result is the prolongation of the life—preferably of a mammal—beyond, and preferably greatly beyond, the normal species and strain performance; this is an unusual event, one not easy to produce non-specifically compared with premature death. So far, the only experiments in gerontology to meet this rubric have been the classical studies of dietary restriction (McCay and Crowell, 1934; Tannenbaum, 1947; Ross, 1961).

A number of antioxidants differing widely in chemical structure and given in heroic doses (up to 1% w/w diet) appear to prolong the life of rats or mice compared with the control groups on standard diets, the usual prolongation, judged as mean expectation or median, being around 15 to 20 percent. Colorable effects of this type are reported for 2-mercaptoethylamine (2-MEA), cysteine, 2,2'-diaminodiethylsulfide (Harman, 1957) di-*ter*butylhydroxytoluene (BHT) (Harman, 1968a, b), ethoxyquin (Harman, 1968b; Comfort, et al., 1970), ammonium diethyldithiocarbamate, sodium hypophosphite and sodium bisulfite (Harman, 1968a, b), and *nor*-dihydroguaiaretic acid (Buu-Hoi and Ratsimamanga, 1959). Selenium has been proposed for test (Tappel, 1968). Life-span increase has been reported in Wistar rats on a vitamin-replete diet when excess vitamins C and E were given in the form of fruit juice (Kayser, et al., 1966; Lavollay, 1968). 2-MEA and BHT also appear to diminish the life-shortening induced by chronic irradiation (Harman, 1968c), though it appears arguable whether the radioprotectant action of 2-MEA is due wholly to its antioxidant properties (Brown, 1967). In recent experiments by Kohn (1971) the life of C57BL mice was prolonged by BHT and 2-MEA only where colony survival was suboptimal, and the "prolonged" curves did not differ significantly from those of optimally fed and housed controls.

Harman's experiments are somewhat complicated by the short lives of

TABLE 9.2
Longevity of C3H Mice on Standard Diet and Diet Plus
0.5% w/w Ethoxyquin
    (mean, SE, and limit (days). N = 20 per group)

CONTROL	ETHOXYQUIN
551.6 ± 24.7 (711)	651.5 ± 27.3 (887)
541.4 ± 33.3 (722)	649.4 ± 27.4 (907)

controls fed on one of his standard laboratory diets. In our experiments (Comfort, et al., 1970) 40 male and 40 female 3-month-old C3H mice were randomly assigned in equal numbers to a standard pellet diet ("Oxoid" 41 B) and to the same diet with 0.5% w/w added ethoxyquin, both ad libitum.

No sex difference in survival was seen in either group, but survival curves for both sexes differed significantly in favor of the treated groups, with a curve displacement of about 100 days (Figure 9.2) (Tables 9.2, 9.3). Tumor incidence in both treated and untreated groups was low for the strain, which had an untreated survival curve similar to C3Hf (Muhlbock, 1959), but shorter. The antioxidant-fed mice were at all ages significantly lighter than the controls, and showed earlier weight loss. Activity and condition were strikingly better retained in the treated group. The form of the curves—and response to a mortality incident affecting all four groups between 500 and 600 days—which was probably infective or environmental, would be consistent with a postponement of some predominant age-dependent process by about 15 percent, rather than with the suppression of one incidental cause of senile mortality.

The converse experiment has been attempted, but incurs the reservations proper to all life-shortening experiments. Experiments with increased atmospheric O_2 tension have given equivocal results. Gerschman (1959) found a decrease in mouse longevity at O_2 tensions greater than 1 atmosphere, the effects being reversible by dithiocarbamates or Co^{2+} (Gerschman, et al., 1958). In acute experiments, mice deficient in α-tocopherol showed increased sensitivity (D. W. Taylor, 1958; Gerschman, et al., 1955) to O_2 excess, but Sobel (1970) failed to shorten life-span by intermittent exposure of mice to 1.08 atmosphere O_2 in youth and young adulthood.

In life-prolongation experiments the analysis of the curve is critical, since it is difficult to devise a statistical test to discriminate the removal of one late-acting cause of death from a general slowing of age processes. Change in the last decile is one such test, but requires huge samples; lifelong cross-kill pathological examination is another (Lindop and Rotblat, 1960), but with the same drawback for high age groups.

In the experiments so far published, "the results are significant, but God

TABLE 9.3

Weights of C3H Mice on Control (C) and Antioxidant-containing (A) Diets (gm.)
(mean, SD, and range)

				Age (days)			
	97	125	197	248	310	409	533
♂							
C	25.4 ± 1.86	27.7 ± 2.62	31.9 ± 2.84	32.6 ± 2.64	30.5 ± 1.73	30.5 ± 2.12	29.2 ± 3.04
	(22—30)	(23—31)	(29—36)	(29—34)	(26—33)	(26—32)	(26—31)
	N = 20	20	20	20	20	19	13
A	26.0 ± 1.79	28.3 ± 2.11	28.9 ± 2.29	27.9 ± 2.44	25.2 ± 2.72	26.3 ± 2.87	26.0 ± 3.04
	(23—29)	(25—34)	(25—36)	(24—34)	(22—29)	(22—30)	(22—36)
	N = 20	20	20	20	20	20	19
♀							
C	20.2 ± 1.30	22.1 ± 1.70	26.8 ± 2.59	28.7 ± 3.15	27.3 ± 3.03	26.6 ± 3.45	25.9 ± 2.99
	(18—23)	(20—25)	(22—31)	(24—33)	(23—33)	(21—31)	(25—32)
	N = 20	20	19	19	19	18	13
A	20.9 ± 2.27	22.3 ± 1.78	24.4 ± 2.37	24.1 ± 2.05	20.6 ± 2.04	21.0 ± 2.51	20.3 ± 1.78
	(16—28)	(20—28)	(21—29)	(22—28)	(18—25)	(17—25)	(17—24)
	N = 20	20	20	20	20	20	18

271

knows what they signify." While an effect is clearly present, and is compatible with the theory, attribution to molecular protection is still premature. A number of reservations attach to all of the published series. None of the data (unlike those from radiation studies) were obtained in a special-purpose life-table colony—an important reservation in the light of past experience. The maximum life-spans obtained with antioxidants are so far in all cases within the credible or recorded natural performance of the strains (Muhlbock, 1959) and the increments over controls smaller than those regularly obtainable by, for example, caloric restriction. In Harman's curves, the effect appears to be rather an improved survival into the last quartile than a bodily curve displacement, at least at the lower dose levels. In the C3H mice given an ethoxyquin 0.5% w/w diet by Comfort, et al. (1970), curve displacement is definite, and the limit increased by about 200 days. Most significantly, however, the weights of treated mice in all reported series tended to be grossly reduced by antioxidant treatment.

Beside the theory of molecular protection, there therefore appear at present to be several alternative explanations at least equally plausible for the effects observed.

1. Large amounts of chemicals may hinder assimilation or spoil the appetite of mice (Day, et al., 1969; Kormendy and Bender, 1971, for BHT), even in strict pair-feeding experiments, which have not so far been conducted. The effect could, therefore, easily represent covert calorie restriction. Some of Ross's experiments (1971) indicate that the major effect of lifelong calorie restriction, at least on tumor incidence, is exercised in the postweaning period; however, antioxidants were not being given during this period in the experiment of Comfort, et al. (1970). Lipolysis is enhanced by 0.5% BHT (Pascal, 1971).

2. For mice, as for broiler fowls (Machlin and Gordon, 1960; Machlin, 1963), excess antioxidant may merely limit the toxicity of a standard laboratory diet, adequate for all except life-span studies. Kohn's (1971) experiments suggest that it is environmental attack rather than ageing rate that is modified by BHT or 2-MEA.[1]

3. Many of the active materials, especially BHT (Gilbert and Goldberg, 1965, 1969; Nievel, 1969), are powerful enzyme inducers: ethoxyquin, at the doses given, produces marked liver enlargement (Wilson and de Eds, 1959). In Ross's dietary experiments (1969) hepatic enzyme levels were found to correlate strongly with further life expectancy in rats on a number of food régimes; the time lag of indirect enzyme induction is an excellent measure of age (Adelman, 1970), but little work has yet been done by way of an attempt

---

[1]For inhibition of tumorigenesis by BHT, see Ulland, et al. (1972).

to alter longevity through excess enzyme induction. Russian workers now report life-prolongation with phenobarbital (Emanuel, et al., 1977). That this effect is not simple is shown by the fact that cytochrome P450 induction is enhanced by excess peroxidated fatty acids and reduced by BHA (McLean and Marshall, 1971). Microsomal enzyme activity certainly appears to decline in mice with age (Baird, et al., 1971). It is known from the example of DDT that powerful enzyme inducers may derange steroid metabolism (Peakall, 1967; Fahim, et al., 1970). Longevity in rats is also increased slightly by added cyclamate (Dalderup and Visser, 1971), and by dieldrin (Walker, et al., 1969) and DDT (Laws, 1971); the second through tumor inhibition. Lifelong administration of DDT at levels that induce microsomal enzymes significantly prolongs the reproductive life of rats (Ottoboni, 1972) either by altering hormone turnover, or by a direct effect of the induction process. The whole extensive field of enzyme levels with age is exhaustively reviewed by Finch (1972). Antioxidants also reduce carcinogen-induced chromosome breakage (Shamberger, 1973).

4. A hypothesis of straightforward "chemical stress," germane to (3) above, with or without suppression of a predominant tumor, is a feasible model for longer gross survival in understressed laboratory animals living in constant conditions (Bullough, 1971). Adrenal enlargement is reported with BHT (Gaunt, et al., 1965).

None of these possibilities has as yet been excluded. The hypothesis that tocopherols act on the body mainly as simple antioxidants appears to be highly questionable; it is even more questionable in the case of selenium and of synthetics such as ethoxyquin, which protect against toxic liver necrosis. The literature of these interactions is reviewed by Green (1972).

The model of free-radical attack, however, remains interesting. If it were to prove correct, it would be necessary either to assume that it affects the contents of fixed cells and irreplaceable or low-turnover molecules, or to find a mechanism by which it might affect clonally-dividing cells. The antioxidant α-tocopherylquinone prolongs the adult life of nematodes (Epstein and Gershon, 1972): it must accordingly be acting upon fixed postmitotic cells rather than clonally-dividing cells, since nematodes have no cell division. Oxidative damage to genetic information appears to be of importance in radiation-induced mutation, and is a theoretical possibility in ageing. Mutation occurs in seeds with storage, depending upon physical conditions (Blakeslee, 1954). Conger and Randolph, studying ESR measurements (1968), failed to find any evidence of free-radical effects in seeds; the prevention of such processes might be one function of the high tocopherol content of wheat germ. Antioxidant administration, moreover, failed to influence the rate of accumulation of chromosomal abnormalities in mouse liver (Harman, et al., 1970). In theory, however, direct attack on the DNA–

TABLE 9.4
Agents that Might Modify the Rate of Ageing

NATURE	THEORETICAL BASIS	FINDINGS
Antioxidants	Scavenge free radicals, prevent attack on DNA *or* Some other system	"Prolong life" (mouse) but may not alter specific age (Harman, 1961, 1968).
Radioprotectants	Assume ageing similar in nature to radiation damage	Antagonize radiation life-shortening (Harman, 1968)
Protein synthesis inhibitors	Break "vicious circle" if synthetase faults involved	Untested experimentally
Lysosome stabilizers	Prevent escape of enzymes (including lysosomal DNAase)	See prednisolone
Immunosuppressants	Limit ageing effects due to autoimmune divergence	Azathioprine slightly prolongs mouse life (Walford, 1964)—splenectomy in old mice greatly prolongs it (Albright, et al., 1969). Predict antilymphocyte serum may limit some age changes but increase clonal divergence
Anti–cross-linking agents	Ageing reflects cross-linking in long-term molecules	BAPN may affect longevity (LaBella, 1968) and tumor incidence (Kohn and Leash, 1967). Penicillamine not yet tested.
Hormonal agents	Modify chemical allometry, retard senescent program	
Anabolics	Prevent decline in protein storage and muscle power, conserve Ca	Limited clinical effect in man
Somatotrophin	Maintains "young" pattern of tissue chemistry	Fails to prolong rat life (Everitt, 1959)
Prednisolone	Program-slowing, antiautoimmune. Lysosome stabilizer? Modifies life-span of postmitotics (Bullough, 1971).	Doubles life-span in short-lived mice (Bellamy, 1968). Increases amnion-cell survival (Yuan and Chang, 1969).
Postpituitary	Doubtful	Whole postpituitary prolongs rat life (Friedman and Friedman, 1964). Active substance may be oxytocin (Bodánszky and Engel, 1966)
Antimetabolic drugs	Simulate calorie restriction	Untested
Enzyme inducers	Life-span (Ross, 1961) and error expression may be affected by turnover.	Antioxidant inducers increase longevity. Try DDT, phenobarbital?

RNA step is not necessary to introduce error into a clonal system, provided that free-radical action can reduce the accuracy of the synthetase step, either at or after translation (Lewis and Holliday, 1970). Some radiation damage, expressed as accelerated ageing, may be of this kind (Ambe and Tappel, 1961), and radiation (albeit at high doses) has been shown to affect the specificity of poly-U RNA synthetase (Goddard, et al., 1969). The free-radical theory would gain greatly in plausibility if it could be shown that antioxidants influence the further clonal propagation either of limited fungal clones or of human untransformed diploid cells. This appears to be the case in *Neurospora* (Munkres and Minssen, 1976; Munkres, 1976). Other experiments must cover the pathological analysis of antioxidant-treated and control animals at a range of ages, comparing lipofuscin concentrations, liver mitochondrial function, enzyme levels, and age-dependent parameters generally.

The practical importance of any technique by which life prolongation can be obtained with low-toxicity agents, working on a model that does not require initial knowledge of the site of action for a serviceable clinical effect (if the theory is right, the sites are probably multiple) is potentially such that it would appear to call for a sizable short-term effort, either to demonstrate the hypothesis of "free-radical" ageing or to dispose of the error. The results so far are interesting, and might still provide evidence for the role of free-radical damage as a contributor to the ageing process, which has been persuasively argued by Tappel (1968). Any such demonstration would lead not only to a reexamination of natural molecular protection by such agents as tocopherols and -SH groups, but to a fresh look at the stability of "living" molecules against the kind of attack already familiar in food and materials chemistry and in the deterioration of synthetics. Within the same project range we may also include the extensive work done on lipofuscin pigment (as a probable product of intracellular lipid oxidation) and upon the lysosomes themselves, which appear to be concerned with it. (Bjorkerud, 1964; Strehler, 1964; Barber and Bernheim, 1967). Lipofuscin accumulation may be prevented (Nandy and Bourne, 1966) and the pigment granules themselves removed (Meier and Glees, 1971) by the drug meclofenoxate. The significance of this is unknown.

Other work has concentrated on agents that might affect the life-span by modifying cross-linking (LaBella, 1966, 1968; Kohn and Leash, 1967), lysosome stability (Allison, 1966), or protein synthesis. A repertoire of substances undoubtedly exists by means of which a high proportion of the subsidiary theories of noise accumulation with age could be tested (Comfort, 1966), and the search for protectants is clearly a valid approach to the fundamental questions that require answers. (Table 9.4). If, in toxicity testing of new substances—particularly preservatives and anticancer, immunosuppressant, antimetabolic, and radioprotectant drugs—investigators can be persuaded to run the experiment until natural death in both control and treated groups, we might get a great deal of valuable information. The large effects of single hormones in some mouse strains (Bellamy, 1968) open another field of investigation. The agent used by Bellamy (prednisolone) has been shown to prolong the postmitotic life-span of human cultured amnion cells (Yuan and Chang, 1969). Some or all of the phenomena of lipofuscinosis, antioxidant activity, and their relation to ageing may be connected fundamentally with the structure and deterioration of membranes, with which they seem to be involved (Allison, 1966; Hochschild, 1971; Sullivan and De Busk, 1973), and the stability of lysosomes, on which accuracy of protein synthesis may depend (Sullivan and De Busk, 1973). Concentration on the details of error theory, which may itself prove erroneous, should not exclude the possibility that ageing can be delayed and life-span modified at the somatic level: the nature of the delay in calorie-restricted rodents, long known (McCay and Crowell, 1934), has still not been elucidated, but it appears to involve a dietary hypophysectomy; the critical element may be reduced protein turnover. More sophisticated metabolic interference by lowering the overall metabolic rate is possible. If such measures fail to delay ageing that result in itself would be theoretically important for our understanding of the "clock."

9.4   Limitation in Clones

Carrel thought that somatic fibroblast cultures were immortal—that they were, in other words, stable clones. The facts now appear to be that stable clones exist—particularly for plant cells—but that somatic diploid cells in tissue culture under conventional nutritional regimes are not, or are not always, truly stable; that some if not all of such cultures appear intrinsically limited to approximately the number of doubling divisions they would undergo in the host animal; and that, judging from Kohn's transplantation experiments (1962), this number differs from cell to cell. The chief authority for the instability of somatic diploid clones is Hayflick (1965). It does not appear to apply to hemopoietic clones in vivo (Lajtha and Schofield, 1971). Evidence of the in vitro clonal senescence of antibody-forming cells has been obtained by Williamson and Askonas (1972). Argument continues over the nature of the instability observed by him, and over its inherence in somatic diploids. Hay and Strehler (1967) were unable to detect any reduction in the life-span of clones from old as opposed to young postembryonic donors, but this too has since been reported (Martin, et al., 1970). Clonal survival is also reduced in progeria (Goldstein, 1969). The latent period of growth initiation, an old index of ageing, might prove equally due for reinvestigation in resolving the nature of clonal age changes (Soukoupová, et al., 1965).

Of various in vivo models based on chimera formation, Krohn (1962, 1966) found that epidermis may be indefinitely propagable: mammary duct epithelium transplanted to its normal site in the fat pad shows a progressive age-dependent change, not in dividing capacity but in growth rate (Daniel, et al., 1968; Hoshino, 1970). There is no fall with passage in the percentage of takes, but the time taken to fill the available space increases linearly with clonal age. The clone can in this case outlive the donor, but there is a "counting" mechanism running, which is reflected in slower growth. This appears similar to the decline in colony-forming ability of transplanted marrow stem cells, which are otherwise clonally stable (Siminovitch, et al., 1964).

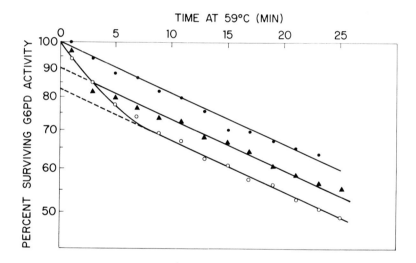

FIGURE 9.2   Inactivation at 59°C of glucose-6-phosphate dehydrogenase obtained from young, middle-aged, and senescent cells. Confluent cultures were rinsed with phosphate buffer saline (Dulbecco A) and harvested with trypsin. The cells were washed twice with 0.005 M Tris/HCl in 0.15 M NaCl (pH 7.4). The pellet was resuspended in 0.05 M Tris/HCl (pH 8.0) containing 10^{-3} M mercaptoethanol, 10^{-3} M EDTA, 4×10^{-3} M ϵ-amino-η-caproic acid and 10^{-3} M NADP, and the cells disrupted by sonication. Cell debris were removed by centrifuging at 18,000 rpm at 4°C for 30 min. The supernatant (approximately 0.6 ml per 20-oz culture bottle) was assayed for G6PD activity. The assay consisted of 0.02 ml enzyme and 0.78 ml 0.25 M Tris/HCl buffer (pH 8.6) containing 9.5×10^{-3} M glucose-6-phosphate (Na salt), 3.2×10^{-4} M NADP, and 1.9×10^{-2} M MgCl₂. The rate of increase in absorbance at 340 nm was measured with a Pye Unicam SP 1800 spectrophotometer, each assay being run for 1 min. The extraction and assay procedures are based on those of Steele. ●, passage 22; Δ, passage 48; ○, passage 61. (From Holliday and Tarrant, 1972.)

It seems empirically clear that mammals do not die through running out of further mitosis, at least in high-turnover tissues. At the same time, clonal finitude is a highly important concept for ageing studies even if only some somatic cells are limited in this way, as has been suggested in the genesis of human baldness (Barman, et al., 1969). It is still more significant as evidence in support of the various error theories. In this context the most interesting work is that on cytoplasmic agents controlling clone death. These studies date from the work of Rizet (1957) and Marcou (1957) on fungal clones, and have been continued at Buffalo by Muggleton and Danielli and at the Mill Hill National Institute of Medical Research by Holliday and Lewis.

Muggleton and Danielli (1968) took stable clones of *Ameba* and placed them under conditions that inhibited protein synthesis for long periods. Changes were induced in the treated clones which rendered them unstable in one of two ways: either they displayed stem-cell behavior, one product of each division dying without further doubling, or the entire clone died synchronously after a fixed number of divisions. By some elegant microtransplantation experiments, they showed that stem-cell behavior results from the implantation of a "spanned" nucleus in normal cytoplasm, but Hayflick-type limitation was transmissible to stable clones cytoplasmically, by very small inocula. This conforms closely to Rizet's (1953, 1956) observation, now confirmed by Holliday (1969), that in *Podospora,* hyphal senescence is preceded by the appearance in the cytoplasm of a material that can transmit premature senescence to young hyphae.

Holliday (Harrison and Holliday, 1967) originally attempted to confirm Orgel's hypothesis of synthetase error by the administration of unconventional amino acids to *Drosophila* larvae, with resultant life-shortening in the adult. He also (Holliday, 1969) investigated the clonal ageing of *Podospora* and *Neurospora* from this viewpoint. He found both an apparent increase in protein variation for "spanned" clones, judged by the appearance of variants in auxotrophes, and the presence of a cytoplasmically transmissible ageing factor. It becomes highly important to identify this material, in view of Orgel's suggestion that the stochastic error in ageing is cytoplasmic. By comparison of enzyme levels measured immunologically and in terms of activity, Lewis and Holliday have shown that in several fungal strains the proportion of misspecified enzyme increases sharply in the senescent phase of the clone. By genetic experiments it can also be shown that this change to misspecification is itself eventually mutagenic (Lewis and Holliday, 1970). An exactly similar misspecification of enzyme with ageing has been found by Gershon and Gershon in nematodes (1970) and in ageing mouse liver (Gershon and Gershon, 1973). By contrast Adelman (1970) found no evidence of enzyme misspecification in old mice, but marked delay in indirect enzyme induction.

All studies based on cross-reacting material are open to the objection that if the substrate is unpurified it is hard to know what is measured, while purification may lead to loss of any "error" material present—especially since what is being sought is the sum of random misspecified molecules. In preparative procedures these are unlikely to form a distinct zone. The urgent need to apply fungal conclusions to mammalian diploid cells while meeting these objections has been fulfilled by Holliday and Tarrant (1972), who have found evidence of the accumulation of molecular error in two rigorously characterized enzymes of limited fibroblast clones, glucose-6-phosphate dehydrogenase (G6PDH) and 6-phosphogluconate dehydrogenase (6PGD), during phase III. They used as an index the downward displacement of the normally loglinear thermal inactivation curve, which can be used to quantify the proportion of misspecified enzyme. This proportion rises from 5 percent for G6PDH at passage 20, to 25 percent at passage 61, the increase occurring precipitously during the last third of clonal life-span. Both this rise and an early senescence of the clone, morphologically similar to the natural phase III changes, can be accelerated by the error agent 5-fluorouracil, and is also accelerated in progeria (Holliday, in press). These findings support Orgel's hypothesis so far as the ageing of clones is concerned. Heat-denaturable fractions could also theoretically arise by somatic mutation or postsynthetically. In the first case, a proportion of senescent clone cells would be producing exclusively heat-labile enzyme; the findings require that by passage 61 the proportion of cells mutant for genes coding faulty G6PDH and 6PGD

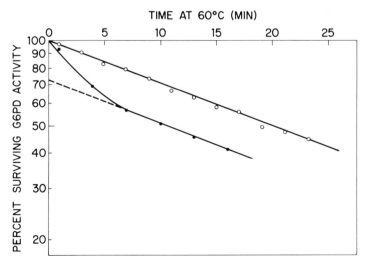

FIGURE 9.3   Inactivation at 60°C of G6PD obtained from young and senescent cultures. ○, passage 23; ●, passage 61. (From Holliday and Tarrant, 1972.)

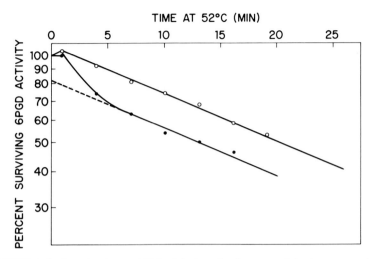

FIGURE 9.4   Inactivation at 52°C of 6-phosphogluconate dehydrogenase obtained from young and senescent cultures. The substrate was 7×10^{-4} M 6-phosphogluconic acid (Ba salt), otherwise the cell-free extract and enzyme assay was the same as with G6PD. O, passage 25; ●, passage 64. (From Holliday and Tarrant, 1972.)

would have to approach 25 percent. Mutation has been shown to increase non-linearly in ageing fungal clones, but the required rate to explain the effect seems improbably high: nearly 100 percent of glutamic acid dehydrogenase in senescent *Neurospora* is heat labile (Lewis and Holliday, 1970). This "ageing" is, however, postponed by antioxidants (Munkres and Minssen, 1976). Postsynthetic denaturation remains possible, assisted by the possibility of slowing turnover, but the percent heat-labile fractions is not increased in fibroblasts by omission of serum, by cyclohexamide, or by holding at 5°C. Gershon and Gershon (1973) have reported inactive aldolase molecules in the livers of ageing mice.

Whether the process in fibroblasts can be generalized to ageing in vivo remains to be tested: in this case mouse life should be shortened, and ageing accelerated, by 5-fluorouracil. Holliday *(personal communication)* also suggests that stable clones are those so intolerant of minimal error that an exponential error crisis is prevented by early selection against substandard cells precluding division. In any apparently normally vigorous clone of fibroblasts, the presence of an error level in G6PDH or 6PGD greater than 10 percent foreshadows the onset of phase III within a few passages. The theoretical and kinetic implications of error accumulation have been widely debated (Kirkwood and Holliday, 1975a, b; Lewis, 1972; Maceira Coelho, 1973).

It is possible and, indeed, likely that other processes contribute to clonal ageing besides the misspecification of proteins at translation (Waldenstrom, 1970): if all such proteins accumulate error, this will extend to RNA and DNA synthetases and support the faulty machine-tool hypothesis (Holliday and Pugh, 1975). Death could result not only from late mutation, but also primarily from DNA error or masking, even though lower stages of the cycle of misspecification are self-maintaining and cytoplasmically transmissible. Good and Watson (1973) found that failure to synthesize DNA often occurs pairwise in daughter cells of a limited fibroblast clone in media containing tritiated thymidine. Eaves (1973) suggests that the clonal stability of heteroploids may be due to total cellular RNA replacement at meiosis. In cultured liver cells, Kahn, et al. (1977) found no enzymatic deterioration in phase II or phase III: the thermal instability of G6PDH increased with age but decreased with further purification. The authors found no evidence of altered protein, either from missynthesis or from posttranslational change, and the altered enzyme stability appeared to result from the cell medium rather than the enzyme molecule. Gofman, et al. (1968) have claimed that Hayflick-type clones show a loss of E16 and increase in E17 chromatin. Transformation has also been said to involve balance between group 9 and group 5 chromosomes (Hitotsumachi, et al., 1971). From label incorporation studies Wulff, et al. (1962) had already suggested that faulty synthetase production might originate at the RNA-protein link, through "wear" affecting the sites of mRNA synthesis. This process they put down to mutation, but it seems equally likely that error in the specification of polymerases could itself eventually be mutagenic, as in fungi. Such mutagenic polymerases have been described (Speyer, 1965) and nucleotide incorporation in the nucleus by their action has been found even in fixed postmitotics (Von Borstel, et al., 1966). Changes in levels of N-methyltransferase are reported in ageing rodent tissue (Mays, et al., 1973). In plant clones Oota (1964) found a separation of ribosomal RNA from protein prior to cell ageing. For a validation of Orgel's hypothesis, any stochastic error either in RNA or in synthetase specification will serve, however. Other types of self-propagating error not primarily involving transcription but affecting it later could produce like effects: the self-propagating foci of polysaccharide cross-linking suggested by Field (1967, for the scrapie agent), for example. Other "slow virus" effects may be of this type: the boundary between a virus and a misspecified self-propagating cell constituent is semantic only, as evidenced by the potato spindle-tuber agent (Diener, 1972).

Clonal ageing studies accordingly become critical in working out possible feedback loops in cellular error theory. A character of Orgel's model is that it is in theory at least reversible, the fault being initially confined to high-turnover protein, leaving the DNA master copies intact until a later stage. Attempts to reverse the "spanning" of *Ameba* have so far failed (Muggleton and Danielli, 1968) and Marcou's (1957) reversal of aging in fungi appears to depend on selection of non-senescent revertants, but the idea is interesting.

Ageing may prove to be mediated at some stage through lysosomal or membrane damage (Allison, 1966; Hochschild, 1971). Inositol deprivation in inositol-requiring strains of *Neurospora* results apparently in membrane damage accompanied by enzymic mis-synthesis very like that seen in clonal ageing (Sullivan and De Busk, 1973)—some form of membrane damage could accordingly be responsible for error accumulation, arising from release of proteases and the consequent production of ribosomes damaged by partial hydrolysis which nonetheless continue to synthesize protein. Inositol itself modifies another "clonal deterioration"-type process, the orthoclonic Lansing effect in *Moina macropa* (Murphy and Davidoff, 1972).

Cells appear to become "committed" to senescence (Kirkland and Holliday, 1975) possibly through the appearance of a defective cytoplasmic particle. On this model, diploid mammalian fibroblasts would be "immortal" if a means were found of separating uncommitted cells in culture. The model expresses the differences between stable and unstable clones in terms of the probability of committal, the incubation period of senescence, and the population size. A paradoxical conclusion is that error agents that reduced the incubation period might prolong as well as reduce clonal longevity. Stable clones may possess a mechanism for the selective removal of misspecified proteins, as in *E. coli* (Goldschmidt, 1970). It becomes urgent both to determine which somatic cells accord with Hayflick's finding, having due regard to nutritional and other factors in culture (Hay, 1964; Hay, et al., 1968), and to pursue transmissible cytoplasmic factors in clones generally. The microsome-inhibiting protein described by Hrachovec (1969) might be one such (Gordon, 1971). The occurrence or non-occurrence of "error crisis" appears to be kinetically determined (Orgel, 1970; Lewis and Holliday, 1970; Kirkwood and Holliday, 1975), the risk being highest at high rates of protein turnover (Gordon, 1971; Lewis, 1972). This perhaps could explain, among other things, some effects of dietary restriction. It is also possible that the character imparted by transforming viruses which prevents clonal senescence is a byproduct of kinetic rearrangement, rather than a possible associate of malignancy such as the possession of a reverse replicase—whence, for example, the reduced serum requirement of transformed clones (Dulbecco, 1970; Clarke, et al., 1970). The senescence of cultured fibroblasts is hastened by a chromatographically separable fraction, probably a glycoprotein, released from old cells when they are disrupted (Milo, 1973)—a possible analog of the cytoplasmic factor reported in fungi by Rizet (1957). As against the model of an overriding error, it has been reported that Phase III clones can be rescued by hybridization (Goldstein and Lin, 1971). Price, et al. (1971), comparing neuron changes in ageing and in irradiation, suggest that in fixed cells of this type, DNA single-strand breakages may accumulate, either through loss of function in repair enzymes, or through escape of lysosomal hydrolases. In fibroblast lines derived from cases of xeroderma pigmentosum, where repair enzymes are known to be defective, ultraviolet sensitivity is increased, but clonal duration is not affected: this would seem to exclude repair-enzyme defect as a cause of Hayflick's effect in dividing cells (Goldstein, 1971).

9.5 Fixed Cell Phenomena

Gershon's studies (1970) suggest that if progressive misspecification of enzymes occurs in the clones studied by Holliday (1969; Lewis and Holliday, 1970) it also occurs in fixed cells. Presence of inactive enzyme has been confirmed in nematodes by Reiss and Rothstein (1974). On the other hand, Pelc (1965) observed label incorporation into DNA of non-dividing cells in adult animals without cell division or endopolyploidy; he infers that these cells have powers of chromosomal repair that mitigate genetic damage with age. A similar process occurs in old *Drosophila* imagoes (Bozcuk, 1972). As to organelles, one of the main observed changes in ageing nematode cells is redistribution of ribosomes with an accumulation of 60S particles, which may be associated with incorrect mRNA translation (Wallach and Gershon, 1974). Deficits in striped muscle which occur with human ageing may be cellular or a consequence of general changes in the internal environment: more direct attempts have been made to relate cellular dysfunction to intracellular mechanisms in the course of attempts to modify functional brain loss during human ageing. On a basis of age changes in the conformation of polyribosomes, Gordon (1971) has reviewed the purported action of a number of substances—including pemoline and inosine—upon senile memory function, and has tried to relate ribosomal error accumulation to ageing and to the activation of latent viruses. The distinction between Orgel's hypothetical "misspecified synthetase" and an exogenous viral agent might be difficult to draw. The extent of viral responsibility for the changes commonly attributed to "normal ageing," as well as for supposedly genetic syndromes, is wholly unknown, but long-term fixed cells as well as clones undoubtedly accumulate inclusions. Some of these are pigmentary, others appear to be viruses or virus products (Fraser, et al., 1970; Field and Peat, 1971). Slow viruses are now known to be responsible for the Jakob-Creuzfeld type of presenile dementia (Gibbs, et al., 1968) where a kuru-type virus seems to be involved, and a similar etiology is thinkable for Alzheimer's disease. Field and Shenton (1973) have detected a steady increase in scrapie-like antigens of mouse and human tissue with age, especially in brain and spleen, using electrophoretic migration of sensitized guinea-pig macrophages.

Inosine itself is an antiviral agent (Gordon, 1971) and clinical trial of this and of amantadine in human senile dementias seems a possible development for future research.

In Gordon's experiments, inosine was complexed with alkylamino-alcohols. Many of these substances, including procaine and meclofenoxate, are membrane-active and possess neurological actions. Meclofenoxate has special interest as one of the three substances claimed to inhibit or remove lipofuscin pigment in neurons (Nandy and Bourne, 1966; Meyer and Glees, 1971), the others being kavain and orotic acid (Hochberg and Rosdahl, 1953; Földi, et al., 1970; Várkonyi, et al., 1970). It has been tested in man to alleviate senile memory loss (Geauz, et al., 1972). Lipofuscin is itself probably a product of lipoperoxidation (Barber and Bernheim, 1967)—though its presence reflects long-term free radical attack, no evidence exists so far to indicate whether it interferes with function simply by being there. Zeman (1971) has uncovered an important model for the process and consequences of lipofuscinosis in the constitutional lipofuscin accumulation disease known in man as Batten's disease, and described also in dogs (Koppang, 1974). Of other neuroactive dialkylamino compounds, procaine, which has acquired notoriety through the work of Aslan and her co-workers (Aslan, et al., 1965), appears to act chiefly as a euphoriant (Bucci and Saunders, 1960; Chebotarev, 1969). No action on lipofuscin has so far been reported for this substance. It appears to be a monoamine oxidase (MAO) inhibitor, however (Bucci and Saunders, 1960; Hrachovec, 1972), and its radioprotectant action is equal to that of 2-mercaptoethylamine (Cheymol, et al., 1960). Sulman and Superstine (1972) have related some age processes to adrenal exhaustion dependent on monoamine depletion and raised MAO levels, a suggestion that may explain some of the effects attributed to procaine in the old. Even more important is the possible action of catecholamines upon a brain clock (Ch. 9.7). The attempt to influence brain function in age involves a complex mixture of processes concerned with ribosomal synthesis, pigment accumulation, viruses, oxygen deficit, and general neurophysiology. It is accordingly a poor model for critical experiments on fixed cell behavior, despite its great clinical importance. The loss of brain cells with age which figures widely in the literature is still apparently not established for mammals, and studies on different animals and brain areas are hard to reconcile (Comfort, 1971; Johnson and Erner, 1972; Tomasch, 1972). A more significant change than loss of neurons may prove to be the loss of interneuronal spaces with age (Bondareff and Narotzky, 1972).

9.6 Caloric Restriction

Reduction of calorie intake remains the most effective known method of modifying the apparent rate of rodent senescence. In the early work of McCay (McCay, et al., 1934, 1939) this was effected by gross restriction from

TABLE 9.5
Experimental Substances Reputed to Affect the Senile Brain

SUBSTANCE	REFERENCES	$N\langle^R_R$ R =	CNS ACTIVITY	MEMBRANE ACTIVITY	AFFECTS LIPOFUSCIN
Procaine	Bucci and Saunders (1960)	C_2H_5	Euphoriant; MAO inhibitor	Local anesthetic	?
p-acetyl-ABA dimethylamine	Barsa and Saunders (1959)	CH_3	Euphoriant; MAO inhibitor	Local anesthetic	?
Di-ethylamine ethanol	Grothe (1950) Valasquez and de Jalon (1942)	C_2H_5	Euphoriant; Acetylcholine precursor	Membrane active	?
Na pangamate	Shevliagnina (1967)	CH_3	?	Protects against anoxia, toxins	?
Meclofenozate	Nandy and Bourne (1966)	CH_3	Stimulates glucose metabolism	Protects against anoxia	++
Kavain	Földi, et al. (1970) Hun, et al. (1967)		Sedative	Local anesthetic	+
Mg orotate	Földi, et al. (1970) Hun, et al. (1967)		?	?	+

TABLE 9.6

$$H_2N-\bigcirc-CONH\cdot CH_2CH_2N\Big\langle{}^{CH_2CH_3}_{CH_2CH_3}\cdot HCl \quad \text{procain}$$

$$Cl-\bigcirc-O\cdot CH_2COO\cdot CH_2CH_2N\Big\langle{}^{CH_3}_{CH_3} \quad \text{meclophenoxate}$$

$$Na\cdot COO(CHOH)_4 CH_2 COO\cdot CH_2 N\Big\langle{}^{CH_3}_{CH_3} \quad \begin{array}{l}\text{sodium}\\ \text{pangamate}\end{array}$$

kavain

(COO)$_2$Mg

Mg. orotate

Source: Bucci and Saunders (1960), Barsa and Saunders (1959), Grothe (1950), Valasquez and de Jalon (1942), Shevliagnina (1967), Nandy and Bourne (1966), Földi, et al. (1970), Hun, et al. (1967), Bouchard and Rigal (1970), Judge and Urquhart (1972), Bouvier, et al. (1974).

weaning to a level that inhibited growth. More recent work indicates that a restriction to 60 percent of the ad libitum calorie intake, which reduces final weight but has little effect on rate of development, is effective in prolonging life by between 15 and 40 percent in long-lived strains, whether it be achieved by continuous restriction or by intermittent feeding. Comparable life-span effects have been observed in other forms from suctorians up; the literature prior to 1960 has been reviewed elsewhere (Comfort, 1960). Restriction prolongs not only life but reproduction and adult vigor. Total tumor incidence is reduced. Collagen cross-linking is delayed (Chvapil and Hrůza, 1959; Giles and Everitt, 1967; Everitt, 1971) but not abolished; the latent period of cells in culture is also shortened compared with that in old full-fed controls (Holečková, et al., 1959). Immunologic ageing appears to be slowed (Walford, et al., 1974). Metabolic rate is not reduced, and bodily activity is slightly increased. Calorie-restricted animals have the appearance and behavior of younger individuals.

Dietary effects of specific constituents vary with strain of animal, and are complex. In the most recent and detailed studies of Ross on rats (Ross, 1961) the longest survivals, as between isocaloric diets, were attained on high-protein–high-sucrose and low-protein–low-sucrose intakes, the shortest on low-protein–high-sucrose diets. Increase of life-span similar to that induced by calorie restriction has been reported in Wistar rats following selective vitamin restriction, both with and without growth limitation (Kayser, et al., 1972).

In view of its importance as a tool in slowing actuarial ageing of mammals, dietary restriction has received inadequate study by critical experiment. The slowing, if real, might involve program retardation, including delay in clone turnover, "stress" enhancement of homeostasis, kinetic effects on the prevalence of miscopied synthetases or RNAs via changes in protein turnover, reduction in free-radical or other side reactions, sparing of irreplaceable cells or mechanisms, conservation of microsomal enzyme activity, immunologic and metabolic effects, or some or all of these. There is no evidence whether comparable effects could be obtained in man, aside from the prevention of specific disorders due to overconsumption of fats or sugar, but the probability is reasonably high. The major effects on tumor postponement in the rat depend on restriction during the postweaning period, but later restriction has still a measurable influence on life-span (Ross, 1971).

9.7 Cerebral "Clock" Mechanisms

By far the most important implication of the calorie restriction effect is the likelihood that "dietary hypophysectomy" is mediated through a control centre in the hypothalamus: the comparable effect on ageing rate of tryptophan restriction almost certainly depends upon modified serotonin metabolism (Segall and Timiras, 1976). While caloric restriction, even if it were shown to work in man, is unlikely to be a popular life-prolonging agent—unless it can be simulated pharmacologically by interfering with absorption—identification of a cerebral clock would open the way to intervention, either by "fooling" the clock as to the level of caloric intake, or by identifying and interfering with its controlling outputs. By placing one overriding process of "senescence" in the brain, it also opens the way to purely neuropsychological investigation into possible control by biofeedback. In this case the yogis and George Bernard Shaw might be proven embarrassingly prescient.

Brain catecholamines, the probable modulators of many cyclic or "clock" processes, are known to change in concentration with age (Finch, 1973). Their ability to reinitiate reproductive cycles in senile animals and in women suggest that they play a part in the reproductive "clock." Whether, or how closely, this "clock" is coupled to the general "clock" controlling senescence is unknown, but the effect of caloric, and more particularly of tryptophan, restriction is general, and affects the whole of the senile vigor loss. Moreover L-dopa has been shown to increase life-span in adapted mice (Cotzias, et al., 1974). All catecholamine levels are simply modulated by diet (Fernstrom, 1976).

The implications of this important model have been most fully expounded by Finch (1972, 1973, 1975, 1976), and by Samorajski (1977). In contrast to the large number of theories, reviewed elsewhere in this book, which start with the basic assumption of an overriding intrinsic "cause" of ageing located in the cell or in its genetic program, Finch draws attention to the large number of instances in which genomic activities are themselves sensitive to hormones (even to the point of chromosome loss; see Ch. 6.4.3). There may in fact be, and probably is, a hierarchy of coupled age processes, but observed reproductive, hormonal, and enzymatic changes, and the various peripheral ageing processes appear to be integrated into a characteristic lifespan by central, neuroendocrine controls. There is abundant evidence, reviewed by Finch (1976), that brain monoamines change systematically with age. The origin of these age-related changes, many of them highly localized, is unknown, but the decline of catecholamines is the basis for specific senile pathologies, notably parkinsonism, tremor, increased liability to depressive illness, modification of the sleep cycle, and increasing incidence of cardiac arrhythmias in man and in rats. It is also the probable basis for alteration of hypothalamic response to hormonal feedback. Dilman (1971) has pointed out in the case of the somatotrophin–insulin–glucose interaction how a vicious circle of metabolic disturbance can arise on a time scale that is slow with respect to the life-span.

A neuroamine–drift–modulated system would affect not only hormone levels and responses but also other hormone-sensitive molecules such as steroid-binding proteins, which are associated with chromatin or with tRNA. It seems likely (Finch, 1972, 1976; Samorajski, 1977) that the brain loci acting as pacemakers of ageing are in the parts of the hypothalamus and limbic system, associated with the detection of humoral signals, and that these are analogous, though not necessarily identical, with the pacemakers controlling growth and maturation. All of these "clocks" are, however, seen as being coupled in a hierarchy of control mechanisms.

There is in fact no good in vivo evidence for widespread failure of genomic control, nor are the various attempts to demonstrate irreversible "ageing" of DNA, of a kind significant for the life-cycle, convincing. There is, by contrast, abundant evidence of the control of transcription and translation in peripheral tissues by neurohumoral action. We cannot yet address the question whether the basic neuroamine shift that is the mainspring of the "clock" is the result of localized primary pathology, including actual cell loss, beyond pointing out once more that the legend of "brain cell loss" in age is in all probability precisely that (see p. 284). The shift would appear equally likely to be itself an evolved adaptation—the evolved adaptation, in fact, by which life-cycle, including reproductive rate, has been specified. Whether it has the "deliberate" destructor character attributed by Medvedev (1966) to noise-generating genes, or whether its ultimate adverse effects are secondary to earlier adaptive programming cannot be inferred. But the link between neuroamines and long-cycle "clock" processes is already familiar from the observation of recurrent affective illness.

It seems fairly obvious that this possibility, often foreshadowed in theories that located ageing in the brain and/or the pituitary gland, would have commanded attention far sooner if the research goals of gerontology had not been focused by "pre-theory" on intrinsic cellular and molecular–genetic changes. It was necessary for endocrinology to demonstrate continued competence in old tissues, and for enzymology (notably in the work of Adelman and his school) to demonstrate continued enzymatic induction modulated only in rate and by non-cellular, probably central, influences, for the model to achieve its present position at the head of the agenda of gerontological research. Had investigation proceeded from observation—in this case by analysis of the site of action of calorie restriction—we would not have had to wait so long.

Watkins, et al. (1975) have suggested that the reproductive decline seen characteristically in mammals with age, and manifest in the human menopause, is partly due to alterations in the hypothalamic-anterior pituitary regulation of gonadotrophin secretion. Partial restoration of reproductive function in rodents has been observed following electrical stimulation of the preoptic area of the hypothalamus (Clemens, et al. 1969) or injection of L-dopa, iproniazid, or epinephrine (Quadri, et al., 1973) and in postmenopausal women following L-dopa (Kruse-Larsen and Garde, 1971; Hornykiewicz, 1966). In the case of tissue response to thyroid hormones, Denckla (1974) has described a long-acting hormone originating in the anterior pituitary which blocks the peripheral action of thyroxine. The effect of this substance persists for 28 weeks after hypophysectomy, but after this interval the peripheral response of hypophysectomized rats returned to juvenile levels. The production of this blocking hormone is a hypothalamus-controlled age effect. Denckla guesses that the intervention of this mechanism explains the poorer life-prolongation obtained by underfeeding adult as against prepubertal rats. In the case of adrenocorticoids, a number of studies (e.g., Romanoff and Baxter, 1975) indicate that the observed postmature changes are due not to limitation of adrenal biosynthetic capacity but to alterations in the feedback mechanisms, probably under hypothalamic control, which regulate steroidogenesis.

The mechanism of the "clock," and the factors controlling it, are unknown; it appears, however, to be coupled to the shorter-term cycles (diurnal and lunar) evident in primates. The age of menarche is linked to vision, being strikingly earlier in blind girls (Magee, et al., 1970); evidence has been adduced of a pineal timing mechanism, originally photic, though it can hardly be so in man (Quay, 1972). It is also—and more significantly for the

TABLE 9.7
Hypothetical Model of a Central Ageing "Clock."

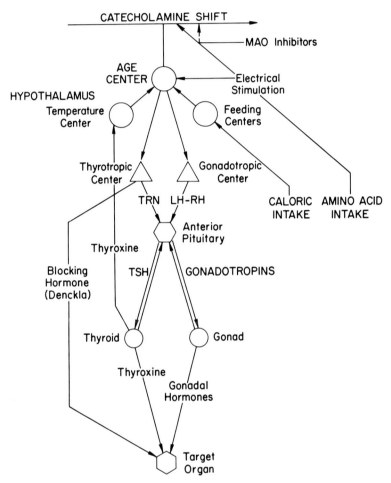

explanation of calorie restriction experiments—closely coupled to critical body weight (Frisch, 1973), and to amino acid intake (Fernstrom, 1976). In humans the pineal has optic connections which replace the direct pineal photo reception of, e.g., birds.

The most plausible model for a hypothalamic ageing clock localizes the time-keeping mechanisms in the neuroendocrine transducer cells, which both monitor circulating hormones and act as secretors. This region is the richest in significant catecholamines, and also the site of choice for any age-setting process dependent on selective cell death (Dilman, 1971). With ageing there is a significant decline in the dopamine content of the caudate nucleus and putamen (Bertler, 1961; Carlsson and Winblad, 1976) but little change in hindbrain 5-HT or 5-HIAA, and there is a steady increase in monoamine oxidase activity (Nies, et al., 1973; Robinson, et al., 1972; Robinson, 1975).

Ageing mediated by a hypothalamic clock might accordingly be a "hardware" process resting on cell loss or neural enzymic changes in vulnerable fixed postmitotics. It might equally be a programmed or "software" process dependent on a timed feedback system similar to the shorter-term catecholamine-modulated processes involved in circadian rhythms and in longer-term cyclic mood changes. Whether it results from changes actively programmed to set life-span or from changes reflecting an "escape" from selection pressure is chiefly of academic interest, and it is easier to hypothecate mechanisms for a programmed start phenomenon such as puberty than for a programmed stop phenomenon such as menopause. A life-span clock regulating general homeostasis is likely to be distinct from the reproductive clock but coupled to it. The high canalization of life-span indicates that all lower clocks in the hierarchy are either coupled to the overriding clock, or have tolerances high enough to ensure that they do not fire within the evolved life-span.

The structure of the hypothetical "clock" has not been plausibly presented, let alone investigated. Apart from actual loss or incapacitation of neuroendocrine transducer cells (which only moves the "fundamental" process a stage backward), possible models include secular change in catecholamine balance (Finch, 1976) analogous to those that appear to drive diurnal rhythms and the longer affective cycles seen in depressive cyclical illness; the model is possible, though it is academic to argue about cyclicity in a process exhibiting one cycle only. The involvement of serotonin, or of serotonin–dopamine balance, has been suspected from the large influence of tryptophan restriction on the longevity and apparent ageing rate of mice (Segall and Timiras, 1976)—there have so far been no published studies of any comparable influence on lifespan of parachlorophenylalanine, the specific inhibitor of tryptophan hydroxylase, which is the limiting step in serotonin production. Other high experimental priorities in elucidating, or rejecting, a hypothalamic ageing clock are the reexamination of age changes in diurnal hormone periodicity, both in human subjects and in rodent parabionts of unequal age; and the search for extracerebral influences which may mimic, interfere with, or unbalance neuroendocrine homeostasis. Such factors include autoimmune reactions which produce immunoglobulins capable of blocking endocrine control at the cell surface. The "long-acting thyroid stimulator" (LATS) of thyrotoxicosis may be of this kind; Denckla's "long-acting thyroid inhibitor" (Denckla, 1974) appears, however, to be of pituitary origin. There may however be physiological immune-mediated pathways involved in long-term and levelsetting homeostasis. The relation of brain clocks to cyclicity and puberty

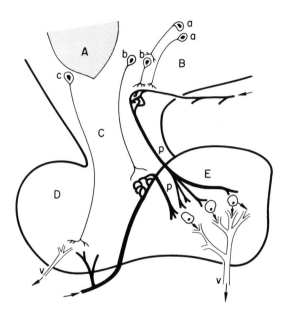

FIGURE 9.5   Structure of the neurohypophyseal pathways. (A) 3rd ventricle; (B) hypothalamus; (C) stalk; (D) neurohypophysis; (E) adenohypophysis; (a,a) monoaminergic neurons; (b,b) peptidergic (releaser) neurons; (c) supraopticohypophyseal neuron (vasopressin secretor); (p,p) portal systems; (v) vein. (From Samorajski, 1977.)

timing, and of puberty timing to blindness (Magee, et al., 1970) raise the possibility that the melatonin cycle is also at some point involved (Quay, 1972), although the instances of precocious puberty in pinealoma are most probably due to pressure effects on the hypothalamus rather than specific pineal hormones. One major difficulty of the hypothalamic clock is that if it exists it should on occasion be disordered, and there are no convincing examples of spontaneous neuroendocrine premature ageing: in progeria there are no consistent endocrine abnormalities, and the syndrome seems to be due to an inborn deficit in connective tissue. The cachexia in some cases of "sudden senescence" of hypopituitary origin is the nearest approach to a disorder of neuroendocrine age-timing which is clinically familiar.

The points of access to this "clock" appear to be (1) the dietary and metabolic rate in general, (2) as a modulator of this, the appetite control center; the set-point of this is modifiable and may be chemically accessible by reversible agents, as is shown by its derangement in anorexia nervosa and the apparent correction of this by alpha-blocking agents such as phenoxybenzamine (Redmond, et al., 1976)—the critical adjustment may be a dopamine–norepinephrine balance (Margules, 1970; Mawson, 1974; Samorajski, 1977);

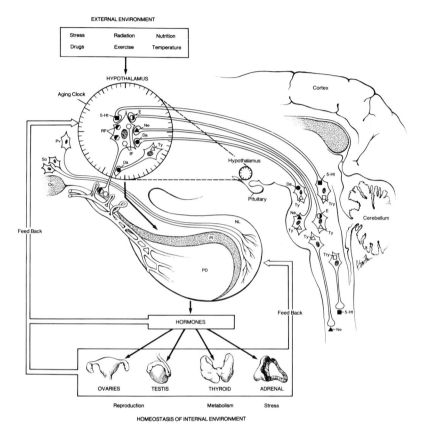

FIGURE 9.6 Neuroaminergic pathways in a hypothetical ageing "clock." NE, norepinephrine; DA, dopamine; 5-HT, serotonin; Ty, tyrosine; Try, tryptophan; RF, releaser factors; IF, inhibitor factors; So, supraoptic nucleus; Oc, optic chiasma. (From Samorajski, 1977.)

(3) the hypothetical ageing-development center or centers, the life-cycle effector clock (these must be systems of high stability, since changes in rate of overall ageing are extremely rare; their set-points are almost certainly genetic) (4) the brain–catecholamine shift, accessible to tryptophan supply, MAO inhibitors, and single catecholamines. How far a manipulation in fact affects the clock is experimentally hard to prove, since catecholamine-modulated processes are involved not only in the drive and set of such clocks but in the inputs to them and the outputs from them. Thus slowed ageing would be expected to depend on increased clock catecholamines, but might result from decreased dopamine in the appetite–caloric input system, as in tryptophan restriction (Segall and Timiras, 1976); (5) the humoral output of the hypo-

thalamus, which modulates peripheral set-points in somatic ageing; the substances involved are oligopeptides and probably prostaglandins, either of which may be excitatory, inhibitory, or both; (6) the peripheral responses themselves—the field of classical gerontological endocrinology.

Clearly the further back in the sequence, the more complete and physiological will be the effect of an intervention, and the more effective the regulation of coupled but potentially autonomous age processes such as clonal and immunological ageing and macromolecular damage.

The ageing hypothalamus shows changes in structure (Frolkis, 1976) which may be primary or secondary: its threshold of response to chemoception is apparently raised (Dilman, 1971, 1976), possibly by pineal "blocking" hormones—though these more probably act on the pituitary (Everitt, 1976).

The model of catecholamine-modulated hypothalamic age control opens a number of fields of research. It should be possible to identify the cerebral system responsible for monitoring calorie intake and body weight (a subject, oddly enough, of concern to space medicine, investigating the effects on longevity of increased and decreased levels of g (Oyama and Platt, 1965, 1967). It should also be possible to unravel some part of the mechanism by which altered hypothalamic response affects longevity, though this is complex enough at the endocrine level alone, and may well also involve central control over, for example, immunology (Magaeva, 1972; Stein, et al., 1976; Ader and Cohen, 1976; Freedman, 1976), thereby transferring immunogerontology from the intrinsic to the extrinsic field. It offers a number of possible sites for short-cut direct experimentation, with monoamines and with MAO inhibitors—the effect of L-dopa on life-span is an example of this class of experiment (Cotzias, et al., 1974). The cause of the age-dependent catecholamine drift also remains to be investigated, and might be found to reinstate the primacy of one of the many postulated intrinsic mechanisms, though it may depend on actual hypothalamic cell damage (Frolkis, 1976). An important practical link is that between this field of study and the badly underfunded field of psychobiochemistry. We have seen the effects of the injection of molecular biology and of radiobiology into gerontology in leading to an emphasis on intrinsic age processes: a serious attack on brain neurotransmitters, their function and control might lead by contrast to an advance of physiology in depth, from ageing and mental disorder to cancer control (Frantz, et al., 1972; Freedman, 1976). Such an emphasis appears more physiological and more rewarding because less limited in approach. Finally, the central location of an ageing clock opens the way to psychobiological research into the numerous effects of mental state on physiology and survival familiar to all physicians and so far attributed without further analysis to "suggestion," a name that explains nothing—the human capacity for voluntary illness and for the willed postponement of death is a case in point (Phillips and Feldman, 1973).

9.8 Autoimmune Phenomena

If ageing reflects cellular divergence, as in fungi—whatever its site—and affects endogenous mechanisms of quality control, it would be reasonable to look for immunological factors in its development arising from the presence of cells that are "not self." A parallel between ageing and autoimmunity has been suggested by a number of investigators (Burch, 1963, 1968; Walford, 1962 [review] 1969; Burnet, 1970; Makinodan, Perkins, and Chen, 1971). Autoimmunity is a pleiotropic process of exactly the kind that might give rise to the widely diverse appearances seen in ageing. Direct evidence of immunological diversity with ageing is so far not very strong—chiefly because it has not yet been sought by the sophisticated methods now available for histocompatibility analysis. Mariani (Mariani, et al., 1960), grafting from male to female Strong "A" strain mice of different ages, found signs of age-linked immunological changes in skin: of the old–old grafts, none took. Later transplantation work by Makinodan, et al., suggests that in old animals both "seed" and "soil" are impaired, i.e., both cell and environment (Hanna, et al., 1967; Makinodan, et al., 1971; Price and Makinodan, 1972a, b). Implantation of old T-cells in young irradiated hosts lowers the host level of immune response to that characteristic of old mice, while establishment of normal lymphocyte function abolishes a progerialike syndrome in hypopituitary dwarf mice (Fabris, et al., 1972). Reports of decreased immunocompetence with age in mice continue to accumulate (Hanna, et al., 1967; Price, 1971). Greater competence is said to be restored by some chemical agents (Renoux and Renoux, 1972). Pantelouris (1972) suggests that thymic involution with age leads to loss of IgG antibodies, and a reliance mainly on low-specificity IgM antibodies, with consequent increases in autoimmune phenomena (see also Sigel and Good, 1972).

Much of the original interest in autoimmune age changes derives from the idea of somatic mutation, leading to misspecified cells. This concept has been the basis of elaborate theories (Burch, 1963, 1968), but it can be extended to other forms of clonal divergence or molecular error. Burnet (1959, 1967) has suggested that mutation in lymphocyte clones might cause them to lose their inhibition against the production of antibodies for correctly specified body tissues—one of the few simple mutative models that satisfies the observed mathematical findings—or that clonal exhaustion may occur in the immunocyte line (Burnet, 1970; Denman and Denman, 1970; Williamson and Askonos, 1972; Fabris, et al., 1972; Hijmans and Radl, 1972). Another possibility is that the efficacy of the filter mechanism against misspecification itself declines with age. Teller and co-workers (Aoki and Teller, 1966; Teller, et al., 1964) found that the immunological response of old mice to tumors and heterografts is markedly impaired. Albright and Makinodan (1966) found that senile mouse spleen cells were themselves toxic to nonsenile, lightly irradiated recipients, and that in old animals there was a decay in the number of immunologically competent "progenitor" cells; this might reflect exhaustion of a stem-cell store or clonal limitation in the immunocyte line—an important instance, if valid, because impairment here could remove the somatic censorship on other misspecified cells. The homogeneity of immunoglobulins described by other workers in human old age may reflect the exhaustion of specific clones of precursor cells (Hijmans and Radl, 1972). Splenectomy itself produces in old mice one of the largest recorded increases in lifespan (Albright, Makinodan, and Deitchman, 1969). If this is an immunological rather than a viral effect, it appears highly important. Hotchkin (1972) has compared the effects on mice of ageing and of early infection with LCM virus, which appears to accelerate it. He suggests that autoimmune ageing effects may prove to be virus induced, and that if infected animals meet the criteria of accelerated ageing laid down in future rate-measurement studies, viral autoimmunity may prove to be a tool to assess the autoimmune component in natural ageing.

Walford (1964) has found that mouse life-span can be marginally prolonged by immunosuppressants (Imuran), though far less than, for example, by calorie restriction. Life-time studies on complete immunosuppression with antilymphocytic serum (ALS.) have not yet been published, though these may well resolve the problem. Burnet's original theory would lead us to expect an amelioration of ageing with ALS. It seems more likely, however, that the action of immunosuppressants will prove to be more like that of antiinflammatory agents, i.e., that they will limit some of the reactive pathology seen in ageing, but aggravate any consequences of clonal divergence by removing the filter mechanism. Increased tumor incidence is already reported (Allison, 1970), though there is reason to think that this is viral rather than a result of withdrawn surveillance. Aside from the prevalence of autoimmune phenomena, the immune mechanisms of old animals show marked impairment, of which one consequence appears to be failure to censor malignant cells (Makinodan, et al., 1971), though the mechanism responsible is unknown. What we shall need in this case is a way of enhancing rather than stopping the elimination of misspecified cells and molecules, and autoimmune diseases could be evidence only of the body's attempts to do this. Energetic application of new immunological knowledge is clearly an important field in age research both theoretically and practically.

Bliznakov (1978) has shown that in 22-month-old female CFI mice, hemolytic antibody response can be raised to levels approaching those in young mice by administration of Coenzyme Q_{10} (2,3-dimethoxy-5-methyl-6-deca-prenyl benzoquinone), possibly by restoration of mitochondrial energy-linked processes. Moreover the decline in immune response may have effects not confined to the immune system: Piantanelli, et al. (1978) have grafted young thymus into "nude" or thymectomized mice and into old normals with restoration of normal triiodothyronine and insulin levels, raising the possibility that some endocrinological age processes in the intact animal might be immunogenetic and thymus-mediated. The loss of function appears to be in the thymus itself, since old thymus fails to thrive in young recipients.

It is still perfectly credible that ageing is, at its manifest level, chiefly or wholly an immunological process, whether the immunological changes themselves are genetically programmed, hypothalamically controlled, error-dependent, or based on clonal exhaustion. Greenberg and Yunis (1972) have suggested that the evolutionary determination of the life-span of species may be immunologically mediated: either the thymus acts as a "clock" synchronized with processes of clonal exhaustion, or T-cell maturation decays through decline in trophic and maturation factors or an increase in suppressor cell activity. Even the life-shortening produced by single radiation doses may prove to be immunological—the experiment of immunocyte replacement in mice exposed to a single life-shortening dose does not appear to have been done as yet.

9.9   Metabolic Program Retardation

Metabolic retardation other than by calorie restriction is feasible in mammals without reducing activity, and has been suggested by Strehler (unpublished). In humans it might even be achieved by biofeedback methods if an operant were identified. Whether or not it would retard ageing is not a priori predictable, in view of the fact that temperature effects on ageing are not apparently invariably additive (Clarke and Maynard Smith, 1961), at least in insect imagoes, though full hibernation retards collagen cross-linking (Hrůza, et al., 1966). Hypothermia also appears to exert an effect on autoimmune mechanisms (Szilagyi, et al., 1971). In spite of the careful work of Ross (1961, 1969), the dietary restriction phenomenon remains unexplained at the fundamental level, though it might be related to copying errors, to enzyme turnover, or to action on a brain "clock." The revised theory of Orgel (1970) leaves room for large influences upon error rate due to differential changes in protein turnover—in general the higher the turnover, the greater the probability that an erroneous synthetase will replicate itself. The sensitivity of collagen cross-linking to dietary, hormonal, and other metabolic influences does not necessarily indicate a similar sensitivity for intracellular molecules, but in general, agents that delay collagen cross-linking appear to affect other age indices as well. The prolongation of life obtained in old rats by whole posterior pituitary (Friedman and Friedman, 1964) is also unexplained. The active principle appears to be oxytocin (Bodánszky and Engel, 1966). *General comparative studies* provide a repertoire of test cases by which theories can be initially screened. They also act as an insurance against overcommitment to molecular error theories. It could well still prove that whatever the eventual rate of cellular misspecification, human ageing as we see it is primarily timed by some mechanical and somatic process such as cellular membrane alteration, or the rundown of a specific cerebral clock. The wise investor will leave room in his portfolio for such eventualities, and the collection of a wide range of life-table and physiological data for the largest possible variety of living systems is clearly a sound investment. From his comparison of body weights, metabolic rates, and life-spans in mammals, Sacher (1959, 1968; Sacher and Trucco, 1962) points out that longevity correlates with two main characters— positively with the amount of homeostatic information in the system, including the brain; and negatively with gram/calorie metabolism—and theories, whether of error or of general homeostatic instability, must square with these findings to be acceptable. Another unexplained but strikingly close correlate of longevity in mammals is an inverse relation with the ability of their fibroblasts to activate mutagenicity of 7,12-dimethylbenzanthracene (Schwartz, 1975).

The picture of fundamental research in ageing has been greatly altered over the last decade. Though it is diverse, there is now a convergence in the diversities. Another decade of application might well see the diversities resolved—even if our present attempts to resolve them are incorrect—and its clinical possibilities revealed.

The most urgent need at the moment is for the development of methods to measure human ageing rates in the short term (Comfort, 1969). Given suitable multiparametric tests it would be possible, and is now urgent, to leapfrog long-lived mammal experiments and work directly on humans, who are the intended beneficiaries of the research; so long as this involves 50- to 60-year experiments, gerontological intervention is effectively confined to mice by reason of tedium. It is extremely likely that the known techniques of rodent life-span modification would produce some effects on human ageing rates if they could be quickly and ethically tested. The investigation of this possibility is likely to begin within the next few years.

10

Measuring the Human Ageing Rate

The concept of measuring ageing biologically rather than chrono-
logically is of enormous general interest, of importance in indus-
try, and indeed in all areas of human endeavour, but has received
relatively little attention from medical scientists. (Hollingsworth,
et al., 1965)

It was, in fact, an early and highly unfruitful concern of *savants calculs* such
as du Nouy. But for a proper account of ageing it has so far been necessary to
insist on the force of mortality as the sole generally applicable criterion, in the
absence of any definite information about the nature and identity of the
"clock."

A new attempt to work out battery tests of human physiological age is now
overdue. It is justified by experimental necessity. Agents are known which
seem to prolong the life-span of rats and mice: one (dietary restriction) has
been known for over 30 years. It is highly probable that some of these would
affect human life-span if they could be tested briefly and ethically. That we
can now think in terms of human experiment is due to the large recent
increase in information from longitudinal and cross-sectional sample studies
on time-dependent variables in man, the availability of computers and of
automated clinical chemistry, and the application (e.g., by Gitman, 1969) to
routine screening tests.

Experimental gerontology may well prove the medical growth stock of the next decade, and its philosophy requires brief restatement. Ageing is the process or group of processes that cause the eventual breakdown of mammalian homeostasis with the passage of time. The timing of these processes, although it shows some genetic scatter, is uncommonly stable. It is the universal experience of man that while we may die sooner from single causes, between 70 and 90 years of age homeostasis declines "across the board," causes of sickness accumulate, and causes of death become multiple. Between 65 and 70, the average number of unrelated lesions per individual at necropsy is 5.71; by 80–85 years it has risen to 8.42 (Howell, 1968).

We require a battery of tests by which rates of ageing could be examined in treated and untreated humans in a study of feasible size. For this purpose the variables chosen must meet the following criteria:

1. They must be sufficiently diverse and unrelated to any single assumed process for it to be highly likely that a maneuver which is found to stabilize all of them will also affect the rate of actuarial ageing.

2. They must correlate closely with chronological age, either directly or in a simple transformation.

3. They must change sufficiently, and sufficiently regularly, with age for us to expect significant differences over a 3- to 5-year run at the selected age of test.

4. They must be measurable in volunteers without unacceptable hazard, discomfort, labor, or expense.

Age-dependent variables in man show three main patterns of change. In one large group, change is greatest between infancy and adulthood and negligible thereafter. It was this group that prompted repeated statements by twentieth-century biophilosophers that "the rate of ageing is highest in infancy." This assertion indicates that age-dependent variables are limited in their usefulness as alternative indices to mortality. Others exhibit peaking (blood cholesterol) or are suspect by reason of covert selection (blood pressure). Of the serviceable variables, we select from those that are arithlinear with age, regardless of sign, and those that are Gompertzian or log-linear with age, paralleling the force of mortality. Mortality itself is lowest at around 12 years, but by reason of the large dispersion at low ages when the function is inverted to read off chronological age from the other variables, rather than vice versa, useful curves are best taken from an arbitrary origin of about 40 years (i.e., from the end of the plateau of adult vigor rather than from the low point of the Gompertz curve). Other indices that are more consistently linear (e.g., collagen contractility) are therefore best adapted to the same arbitrary origin, and the test period set between 40 and 70 years. The ideal battery accordingly measures what happens at the point of maximal change, and after the end of the period of adult vigor. The function(s) fit better with Teissier's (1934) convention than with the conventional Gompertz-Makeham function giving

$$\mu_x = e^{a(x-b)}; \ x > b$$

rather than

$$\mu_x = \mu_0 e^{at} + A$$

The duration of the "plateau" as seen in small population samples is represented by b. The samples will in any case be small by actuarial standards. In fact, however, the postulated origin at about 40 years corresponds roughly with the origin of the linear part of the Gompertz curve allowing for the irregularity seen in real human mortality curves at earlier ages. The study should in any case be set for choice at age 50–55 or age 60–65 where mortality will be significant and the rate of change in log mensurables large.

The battery is based on that described by Hollingsworth, et al. (1965), which was designed to measure rate of ageing in Hiroshima survivors, from studies of about 450 Japanese. Here nine functions selected from seventeen functions examined gave a correlation with age of nearly 0.90. Compared with other attempts (e.g., Ciuca and Jucovski, 1969), which lean heavily on clinical impressions, this study appears the best available starting point. It can, however, be expanded considerably in both number and variety of indices. (Davis and Hayen, 1970; Conrad, 1960; Baier, et al., 1971; Parot, et al., 1969; Bourlière, 1969; Ciuca and Jucovski, 1970; Bocher and Heemskerk, 1969). For our objective, viz., leapfrogging dog or primate studies and testing non-hazardous procedures directly on man, the most numerous and available primate—as well as the beneficiary in view—we require a test procedure of realistic size and duration, comparable, for example, to dietary studies or clinical trials on a single lesion. This means, in effect, a procedure giving reasonable expectation of significance for between 100 and 500 subjects including controls, with the probability of having to settle for the smaller number. The same battery could be used both for gerontological work and for environmental or radiation studies (which are now, in man, both contradictory and necessarily retrospective). Experience gained here, even if the tested agent proves inactive and both series are pooled as controls, will be invaluable in the next 10–20 years if reported influences on human longevity multiply.

10.1. Test Battery

For initial use, the test age should be 50 years and the sample should be confined to males to avoid further statistical breakdown and complications associated with differences in age of menopause, which affects some variables.

Available test procedures fall into three groups: straightforward (anthropometry, clinical and chemical examination, sensory tests, psychometric tests); those requiring, for example, biopsy; and those depending on the fact that deaths will occur in the test samples. The 'straightforward' groups might be modeled on the procedure used for clinical screening by Gitman (1969), based on a flow-type center using lay staff, and the psychometric tests should be automated, probably by means of the machine devised by Gedye and Wedgwood (1969).

The inclusion or exclusion of biopsy procedures would be a matter for a policy decision. The draft (see Table 10.1) includes four possible tests requiring live tissue: fibroblast clone duration, culture latency period, thigh-skin melanocyte count, and wound healing. Collagen testing is barely feasible in man except at necropsy, and is covered in part by other measurements (skin elasticity, vascular state, blood elastase). Lymphocyte RNA/DNA, ratio (Sakai, et al., 1965) and leucocyte chromosome count are in theory derivable from a blood sample, though there is evidence that for the second of these sternal puncture would be preferable (Chlebovsky, et al., 1966). On grounds of labor most of these more elaborate, though theoretically important, tests would probably have to be limited to one-fifth or one-tenth of the sample.

Mortality would be expected in a 50-year-old sample. For United States or United Kingdom white males we would expect thirty deaths between 50 and 55, and about fifty between 60 and 65 for a sample n of 500 lives (i.e., too few for significance if the sample were any smaller, but enough to give some necropsies). A full legal consent and pathological program should be written in, however, to secure these. Necropsy-based measurements would include cause of death, number of lesions present, lipofuscin, collagen, cell counts, presence of amyloid and atheroma, and organ weight.

In Hollingsworth's series of seventeen tests, the highest age correlations were for characters (hair graying, skin elasticity), which contribute most to the "clinical impression" of age, and eleven of seventeen overlap Gitman's test battery. Hair graying was excluded from the final Hiroshima series because of difficulty in quantification. Various ways of estimating it have been suggested (Hollingsworth, et al., 1961, percent gray hairs per axilla) and if skin biopsy were done, skin melanocyte concentration might prove an alternative (Snell and Bischitz, 1963; Fitzpatrick, et al., 1964; Walsh, 1964). Besides the Hollingsworth-Gitman series, a number of additional tests are

suggested in Table 10.1, either because they are easy, even if poorly correlated with age (anthropometry), or because they are evidence of things not
seen (nail calcium accumulation, which parallels aortic calcification in time—
Mattei, et al., 1955; Bürger, 1954) or because, though speculative, they are
theoretically important (blood copper content—Harman, 1965; blood elastase, autoantibodies—Hildemann and Walford, 1966; Makinodan and Peterson, 1966). These are chosen on the basis of the most accessible measure—
e.g., skin elasticity rather than skin collagen properties, nail calcium rather
than aortic calcium. Anthropometric age measures are worth confirming and
give little trouble. The most promising seem to be seated stature, trunk
height, and biacromial diameter (Parot, 1969), though the change is greatest
in females and is less than one standard deviation over the interval 50–85
years. Psychometric tests are highly important: several (vocabulary, digit
symbol, similarity, block designs, digits forward and backward, and tapping
tests) correlate with 5-year survival (Jarvik and Falek, 1963) as well as with
chromosome-error accumulation (Jarvik, et al., 1969). Others (e.g., serial
choice task performance) seem to correlate with cardiovascular status (Szafran, 1965; Spieth, 1965), though at a low level of significance. Psychometric
changes may reflect both normal ageing and subclinical disease (Davies,
1968). It would be valuable to extend our knowledge of these correlations.
Automation of the Wechsler adult intelligence scale (WAIS) test battery
should be feasible (Gedye and Wedgwood, 1969; Schonfield and Robertson,
1968). Sensory tests (audiometry, flicker-fusion frequency, optometry),
though time-consuming, are also potentially of use.

It should in theory be possible to measure homeostatic failure directly by
measuring variance (Storer, 1965), but this has pitfalls arising from the ageing
organism's capacity for improvisation, as well as from the selection exercised
at high ages by mortality itself (Comfort, 1969); however, it may shortly be
possible to measure, for example, the proportion of misspecified enzyme in
certain systems (Gershon and Gershon, 1970), and new measures of this kind
may well multiply over the next 5–10 years. The Gitman battery has a
statistical advantage in that it can show not only whether the observed values
are in the normal range, but also the trend of readings in the individual at
reexamination. It was designed as a clinical screen, not a measure of ageing,
but includes a great many indices which have been independently standardized against age, albeit in only a small sample ($N = 47$) (Libow, 1963). Serum
cholesterol is an unsuitable direct measure of ageing, since it commonly rises
until age 50 and falls thereafter (Keys, 1952) and the results in different
studies have been discrepant (Libow, 1963; Nowlin, et al., 1969). Of the
other age-related variables in Libow's paper (Libow, 1963, Nowlin, et al.,
1969), serum albumin ($r = -0.267$) decline and protein-bound iodine ($r = -0.33$), maximal breathing capacity ($r = -0.43$), and vital capacity ($r =$

−0.50) correlate with age at levels approaching those selected by Hollingsworth, et al. (1965).

We should ideally now search among endocrine and enzyme-induction responses for those most closely correlated with actuarial ageing. This approach comes close to the idea of a single index parameter; if such were to be found, it would in all probability be extremely close to the major life-cycle "clock" in man. At the moment we have no test of this kind, though some enzyme-induction processes studied by Adelman (1970) approach it. The clumsiness inherent in multiparametric tests would make them a poor substitute if a more fundamental test were available.

10.2. Procedure

The battery is essentially designed to test any non-hazardous agent or maneuver that might be offered as likely to affect the ageing clock.

The feasible size of an ageing study depends on the number of available volunteers, and on the procedure (diet, injections, or additives) required in the treated group. Recruitment of volunteers would normally be from a large employer, a closed group (monks, prisoners, pensioners), or from a profession (physicians, academics, government employees). Administration and supervision of treatments cannot be discussed in vacuo. The most likely agents for trial within the next 5–10 years would appear to be diets, antioxidants, psychological maneuvers, and possibly anticaloric or anti–cross-linking drugs. All these create problems of supervision and continuity, and English society provides few healthy closed communities from which volunteers could be recruited; some of the major difficulties of long-term diet experiments were well illustrated by a Veterans Administration trial on cholesterol and atheroma (Dayton, et al., 1969). This type of experiment does, however, provide a practical and ethical model. Had these investigators, moreover, had access to the kind of test battery I am suggesting, important information about potential free-radical effects in accelerating certain age indices might conceivably have been obtained as a by-product of the main study (Harman, 1971).

As an example of the type of experiment to which the method could be applied, consider the testing of antioxidant or enzyme-inducing agents in man — the counterpart of recent rodent experiments. Such a trial, if it seemed desirable, would probably be feasible, although the dose levels would be heroic by comparison with current permitted use in foodstuffs (a full and frequent review of hematology and side effects would in this case be needed, multiplying the number of attendances and involving a complete health-check battery in addition to the running measurements). Substances that we already ingest have their attractions for trial purposes, but the known safety

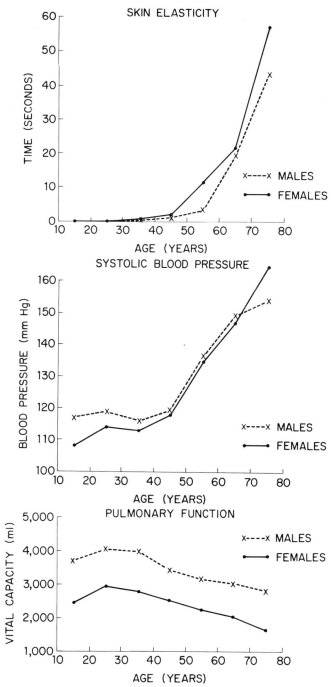

FIGURE 10.1 (From Hollingsworth et al., 1965.)

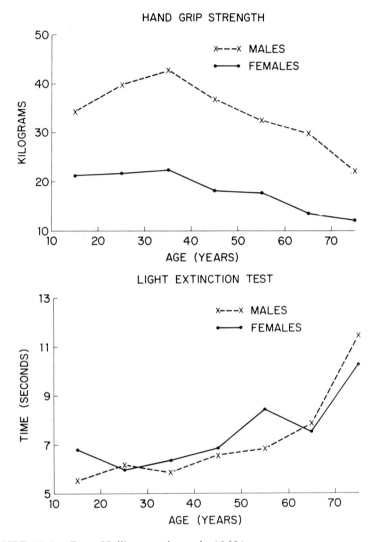

FIGURE 10.2   (From Hollingsworth, et al., 1965.)

of, for example, *ter*-butylhydroxytoluene as a food additive could be more than offset by the risk of sensitization to most process foods, for which the volunteer would not thank us. It might in this case be wiser to use a low-toxicity antioxidant not already widespread in groceries. Naturally occurring antioxidants might well be tested in this way (tocopherols, ubiquinones, -SH donors). Lifetime administration of known inducers (phenyltrin, phenolbar-

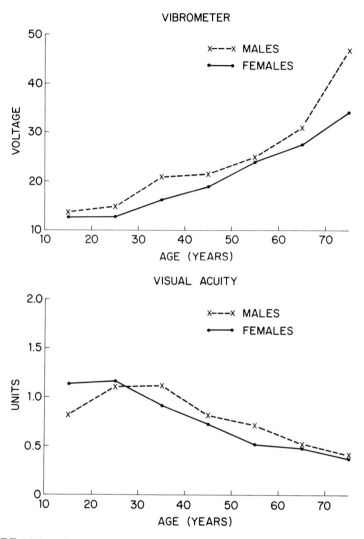

FIGURE 10.2 (Continued.)

bitol) already occurs in the control of epilepsy. Physicians are a potential source of volunteers: they might in theory be self-policing, and they would certainly be capable of giving themselves a parenteral agent, if one were available for trial. Choice of a 50- or 60-year baseline makes the problem of a controlled population of willing volunteers more complex by excluding students or soldiers, for example, but it must be part of the philosophy of

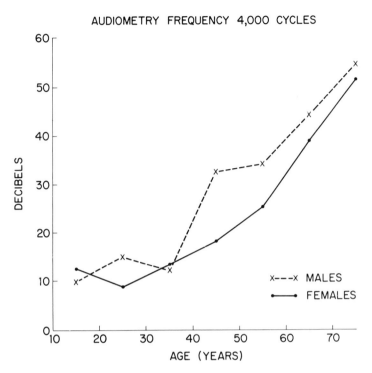

FIGURE 10.3   Correlation of the final "physiological age" determination with chronological age. (From Hollingsworth, et al., 1965.)

attempts at age control that we should aim, initially at least, at the possibility of a late-acting agent, so as to reduce the total span of treatment required.

This may, of course, prove impossible. Nor may it be possible (or desirable) to run even a superficially harmless procedure, such as the use of low-calorie foods, without a separate and frequent "toxicity" assessment; it might, indeed, have been wise and profitable to include one in the dietary cholesterol studies already cited (Dayton, et al., 1969). Viewed purely as an ageing test the model requires annual or twice-yearly attendance, depending on numbers, at a clinical center, which will also provide records storage, a secretariat, and a manned telephone to give appointments. A small sample (N = 100) could be dealt with surgery fashion, by hand. It seems preferable, however, to aim at a Gitman-type flow system set up, for example, in an empty ward, with patients admitted in batches of four, and with all tests requiring more than 5 minutes (e.g., audiometry and ECG) duplicated. While it may be necessary to limit the tests strictly to those required by the study, there is a case for giving the full Gitman screening battery so as to provide a

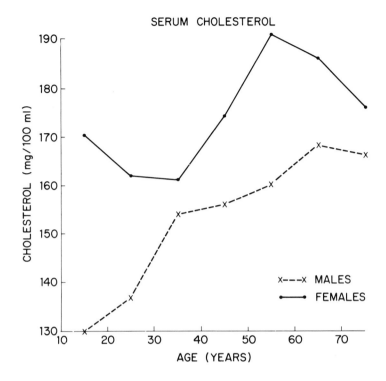

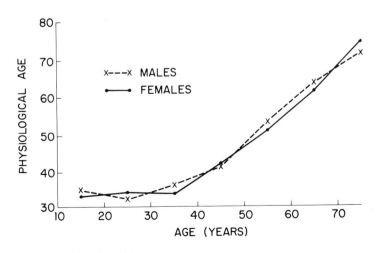

FIGURE 10.3   (Continued.)

TABLE 10.1
Draft Test Battery for Physiological Age in Man

TEST	REFERENCES	*r*
Hair-graying score	Hollingsworth, et al. (1965); Flugel (1971)	0.717
Skin elasticity[a]	Hollingsworth, et al. (1965); Robertson, et al. (1969); Anderson (1965); Grahame and Holt (1969)	0.604
Systolic blood pressure[a,b]	Hollingsworth, et al. (1965); Pflanz and Torok (1969)	0.519
Diastolic blood pressure[b]	Hollingsworth, et al. (1965)	0.409
Heart size[b]	Hollingsworth, et al. (1965)	0.294
Thorax size[b]	Hollingsworth, et al. (1965)	−0.124
Total vital capacity[a,b]	Hollingsworth, et al. (1965); Rosenzweig, et al. (1966)	−0.402
Tidal volume[b]	Hollingsworth, et al. (1965)	
One-second expiratory volume[b]	Hollingsworth, et al. (1965); Rosenzweig, et al. (1966)	−0.126
Hand-grip strength[a]	Hollingsworth, et al. (1965, 1969)	−0.323
Light-extinction test[a]	Hollingsworth, et al. (1965)	0.488
Vibrometer[a]	Hollingsworth, et al. (1965)	0.537
Visual acuity[a,b]	Hollingsworth, et al. (1965)	−0.432
Audiometry 200 cps[b]	Hollingsworth, et al. (1965); Jalavisto (1965)	0.445
Audiometry 4,000 cps[a,b]	Hollingsworth, et al. (1965); Jalavisto (1965)	0.596
Serum cholesterol[a,b]	Hollingsworth, et al. (1965); Libow (1963); Keys (1952)	0.234
Total serum albumin[b]	Hollingsworth, et al. (1965); Wagner (1971)	−0.267
Albumin/globulin ratio[b]	Bürger (1954); Wagner (1971)	
Plasma water	Hall (1968)	
Mean venous pressure[b]	Bürger (1964)	
Protein-bound iodine[b]	Libow (1963)	0.33
Enzyme-induction rate	Adelman (1970)	
Serum copper	Harman (1965)	
Serum elastase	Hall (1966)	
Serum RNAase	Sved, et al. (1967)	
Nail calcium content	Mattei, et al. (1955)	
Stature[b]	Parot (1959); Dequeker, et al. (1969)	−0.532
Seated stature[b]	Parot (1959)	−0.53

TABLE 10.1 (*Continued*)
Draft Test Battery for Physiological Age in Man

Test	References	r
Trunk height[b]	Parot (1959)	−0.34
Biacromial diameter	Parot (1959)	−0.40
Metacarpal osteoporotic index	Dequeker, et al. (1969)	−0.786
Lean body mass	Forbes and Reina (1970)	
Lymphocyte RNA/DNA ratio	Sakai, et al. (1968)	
Explant latency[c]	Medawar (1940); Soukoupová, et al. (1964); Walters and Walford (1970); Heine and Parchwitz (1957)	
Serum growth promotion	Carrel and Ebeling (1921); Baker and Carrel (1926)	
Biopsy healing and contraction[c]	Howes and Harvey (1932); Billingham and Russell (1956); Landahl (1959)	
Clonal further viability[c]	Hayflick (1965); Hay and Strehler (1967); Hay, et al. (1968); Martin, et al. (1970)	
Leucocyte aneuploidy	Jacobs, et al. (1963); Goodman, et al. (1969)	
Autoantibody titers	Hildemann and Walford (1966); Makinodan and Peterson (1966)	
Skin melanocyte count[c]	Snell and Bischitz (1963); Fitzpatrick, et al. (1964); Walsh (1964)	
WAIS tests (automated set)	Gedye and Wedgwood (1969); Jarvik and Falek (1963); Libow (1963); Jalavisto (1965)	
similarities		
digit span		
vocabulary		
digit symbol		
block design		
digit copying		
tapping test		−0.44
Reaction time, ruler test	Jalavisto (1965)	0.48
Reaction time, light	Jalavisto (1965)	0.35
Flicker-fusion frequency	Jalavisto (1965)	−0.48
Taste sensitivity	Hughes (1969)	
Total 5-year mortality[d]		

TABLE 10.1 (*Continued*)
Draft Test Battery for Physiological Age in Man

Test	References	r
Organ weights[d]	Tauchi (1961)	
Disease specific mortality[d]		
Tumor incidence, living[b]		
Tumor incidence, necropsy[d]		
Arterial pathology[d]		
Amyloidosis, stain[d]		
Cartilage H_2O content[c,d]	Bihari-Varga and Biró (1971)	
Lipofuscin amount[d]	Strehler, et al. (1959)	
Aortic calcium[d]	Lansing, et al. (1950); Bürger (1954)	
Collagen contractility[d]		
Collagen fluorescence[c,d]	LaBella and Paul (1965)	

[a]Selected for Hollingsworth battery. [b]Included in Bitman inventory. [c]Biopsy dependent. [d]Necropsy dependent.

periodic checkup as a direct incentive to volunteers, with a physician present to answer questions and deal with anxieties. The clinically relevant parts of the printout should be sent to the volunteer's physician.

10.3. Payoff

Testing of specific agents apart, the creation of an "ageing assessment unit" in this country, though not cheap, is likely to be a rewarding investment.

It is almost certain to be needed some time before 1985 if clinical trial of possible approaches to the slowing of the ageing clock are not to be confined to rats or to patients in other countries. Tests of this kind are already in preparation in the United States, but encounter increasing legal restrictions.

If the agent or procedure first chosen for test proves wholly inactive, the results will still be of prime importance as a test run of the parameters chosen, the administrative structure, and the cooperation of physicians and volunteers. We need to find out how to do this kind of experiment, and the "know-how" obtained could well be a prime tool in the experimental medicine of the 1980s, as well as in the assessment of diets, environmental hazards, and radiation effects. It is an interesting thought that acceleration (or delay) in the process of ageing, which would affect the age of onset of all diseases—not the frequency of one—is a perfectly possible side effect of drugs or environmental factors now current. It would also be, at present, undetectable unless gross enough to influence the life-table for the whole population, and then only inferentially and in retrospect. An ageing battery would bring this kind of effect within the scope of immediate detection.*

The Gitman-type clinical screening center is a possible tool for future group practice and health-service use. Whether clinical screening is economically effective as a means of early diagnosis is still questionable; but if it is, we need experience with it. This would be obtainable without additional cost as a by-product of the kind of ageing study here proposed, and might render the investment acceptable while the importance of rate modification in the preventive medicine of the future is being realized by the scientific community.

10.4   A Special Application: Aerospace Gerontology

One consequence of the U.S.N.A.S.A. shuttle program is that two additional disciplines—gerontology and geriatrics, the study of fundamental ageing mechanisms with a view to their control, and the medicine of later life—have become highly relevant to aerospace medicine.

The occasion for introducing geriatrics into aerospace medicine is practical. As long as crew selection for space flight was confined to fully trained professional astronauts and involved exceptionally arduous requirements, space physiology was limited to the responses of the young fit adult. The shuttle program, however, gives the facility to fly passengers, including specially qualified older persons—senior scientists and technicians. This change in selection criteria makes it essential to examine response to acceleration, weightlessness and re-entry over the whole adult lifespan, not only its second quartile. The practical and immediate aim is to avoid hazard to passengers and the need for emergency return to Earth. But, because medicine has never been able to undertake it on the scale or with the resources now needed to establish flight criteria, the fundamental study of unconventional stress response at higher ages has great potential value for geriatrics in the nonflight context.

One example of the probable spinoff is already evident: It has long been clinically known that bed-rest is increasingly deleterious to patients as they grow older, but only when bed-rest was studied operationally (Donaldson, et al., 1970, Miller, et al., 1965) as a model of weightlessness were systematic studies of its physiological effects made available on a large scale. The establishment of flight criteria, as they will be based on performance tests, not arbitrary age qualifications, also promises to contribute to a key practical

---

*A recent example of genetic longevity has been described in hypobetalipoproteinemia (Kahn, J. A., Glueck, C. J. (1978) *J.A.M.A.* 240 (1):47.

problem of both geriatrics and gerontology, the nonactuarial estimation of biologic age (Comfort, 1972). Another innovative area is the investigation of system trainability in the control of response at high ages, which has novel therapeutic possibilities. While geriatricians have expertise to contribute to the special problem of flying older persons, aerospace—with its excellent physiological resources—has the potential to contribute large medical benefits to the medicine of later life in the course of addressing its own agenda.

10.4.1   Geriatric Aspects

The classic pattern of change in physiologic response with age is that observed by Verzár in relation to cold adaptation (Verzár, 1963). Response becomes later and in some systems lower overall, though delay is more prominent than deficiency, as in the case of enzyme-inductive processes where one system component is located in the hypothalamic system (Adelman, 1975). Pathologies also accumulate with age, and variance in most parameters increases in both Man and rodents (Storer, 1965), so that individual assessment becomes mandatory—where variance appears to decline, this is usually because responsive reserve is decreased and the old organism is living close to maximal response. Thus, further loading may cause system failure rather than mobilization of reserve capacity.

Besides these more general characters of older organisms, a number of physiological areas in normal ageing can be pinpointed as likely to be exacerbated by weightlessness, particularly calcium loss from bones and muscular atrophy. On the other hand, the point at which trouble is most likely for the older fit passenger is not during the weightless state but in readapting to gravity on return to Earth, at which time effects such as joint pains, vestibular disorientation, and "labor" with voluntary movements (Gibson, 1977) as well as other phenomena which are minor in younger crew (gravitational purpura, for example [Hordinsky, 1977] may last longer, or be more severe, on both, in older subjects. During readaptation, old subjects may require, for example, protection by gravity suits which are unnecessary in young subjects. Side-effects may occur after brief exposure to weightlessness which are characteristic of far longer exposure in the young, which do not occur in the young at all, or which resolve far more rapidly in the young. If not guarded against, some such effects—for example, on joints—may trigger prolonged disability. Some of these problems can be forseen from the model of bed-rest and others from basic geriatric experience, but all need to be explored now.

10.4.2   Fundamental Gerontology

The fundamental elucidation of ageing mechanisms has an interest in space research which arises primarily from the possibilities of using weightlessness in one of its critical experiments.

The present model of ageing is that, although a number of ongoing age processes continue to be identified in cells, organs, and molecules at the subcellular level, "universal" and simplistic pictures of ageing attributing it to a single local change fail to explain the phenomenon of lifespan. Similar animals (sheep and goats, *Mus* and *Peromyscus*) may differ radically in lifespan; moreover, the rate of ageing has long been known to be easily modified by simple *general* interventions such as caloric restriction. We have already discussed the possibility that the actual, observed lifespan, which has every appearance of being an evolutionarily programmed rather than a purely statistical phenomenon, is timed by a "clock" or "clocks" in the hypothalamus coupled to metabolism, which may also be responsible for fixing the reproductive rate and the rate of development, quantities that must for population-dynamic reasons be integrated with species longevity.

One result of the model is that weightlessness, which cannot be produced on Earth, and hypergravity, which can, become attractive tools for the analysis of the weight–metabolism–longevity loop. The question is not whether the body has a direct mode of baroception—in the case of bone or of cardiac load it clearly has—but whether the integrative "clock" has one; and whether the hypothalamus, which is chiefly a chemical sensor, reads body weight as an index of instantaneous body mass, either directly or by a second-order derivate from proprioception. If it does, then changing g can be used to dissect the inputs to the "clock" or to identify some of its outputs in oligopeptide hormones. If it does not, altered g will create an unconventional discrepancy between the clock and general homeostasis, which is partly baroceptive and responds to mechanical loading, for example, of the heart and muscles, with potentially instructive results.

The analysis of the hypothetical "clock" is important to clinical gerontology because it cannot easily be attacked by direct calorie restriction in Man. Human application depends clearly on analysis of how dietary restriction operates, with large possibilities for much simpler intervention if this can be done. Critical to this analysis is an understanding of precisely how the "clock" compares caloric intake with growth and body mass. An example of this aspect of the clock can be seen in the coupling of menarche to body weight, and of the continuance of menstruation to projected weight-for-age (Frisch, 1973).

Such short-term analytic experiments designed to settle specific problems have attractions as part of the shuttle program. Study of appetite, caloric intake and balance, circadian rhythms, and neurohormonal levels in brain and organs—especially somatotrophin, somatostatin, and prolactin might used to investigate the transduction of "size" to the neurohormonal clock within the 7-day limit of early projected shuttle flights. Because most hormone levels in the brain are likely to be disturbed by re-entry, they could not be reliably done on recovered animals. Experiments might be performed at hypergravity in centrifuge studies such as those of Oyama (Oyama and Platt, 1965), but these, for the reason given above, really call for a ground-based centrifuge facility designed to allow material such as brain to be collected at steady state without stopping the centrifuge. Apart from difficulty of manipulation, this method might well prove more expensive than the use of the shuttle.

The development of Cosmos and Skylab indicate that lifetime mammal studies will eventually be able to be conducted under weightlessness, but there is no apriori reason to forecast either major changes in life-span in adapted rats, or the sign of any changes that occur. To be significant in gerontology, serendipity would have to give a prolongation of life-span in weightlessness. The life of rats can be shortened by nonspecific assaults of all kinds; only gross prolongation over Earth findings would be of interest, and there is no reason to expect this. The time has passed for shotgun experiments based on the idea that because weightless conditions are available they should be tried, on age-related as well as on other processes, to see what if anything happens. More important is the recognition of (a) key specific experiments, like the analysis of size-proprioception; and (b) extension of other nongerontological types of experiment, human and animal, to include high-age groups as well as young adults, so that a complete age spectrum of process becomes available.

The data derived from all experiments in aerospace physiology should also be scrutinized with gerontology in mind. As an example of the spinoff from such monitoring, most easily conducted when a gerontologist is included in the flight task forces, is the fact that much theory has been devoted to the crosslinking of collagen as a mechanism of ageing or as an index of physiologic age. In recent flight experiments, it has been found that weightlessness appears from urinary aminoacid levels to mobilize pre-formed collagen (Leach and Rambaut, 1977). Thus, contractility and fluorescence estimates of collagen age on weightless animals become well worth making, for an object unconnected with ordinary aerospace physiology but one very interesting to experimental gerontologists. Clearly, findings of similar interest can be expected, or could be secured if protocols were run by a gerontologist in the course of preparation for other kinds of experiment.

10.4.3 Futurology

It is also interesting to look to the long term. Argument about such matters as the Einstein effect as a "gerontological" factor apart, long weightless missions are clearly likely to occur. These still give rise to anxiety on the ground that humans, being adapted to Earth gravity, are bound to encounter eventual disadaptation with its withdrawal. Present emphasis on weightlessness as "stress" may overlook the fact that it may equally represent stress-reduction for a highly orthostatic animal such as Man. Bed-rest, which in many ways approximates to weightlessness in its initial effects, is the traditional medical expedient to reduce physiological demand. In designing a hypothetical future space colony that would derive gravity from rotation, we might normally opt for $g = 1$ on the basis that this is the adapted optimal. But it is equally possible that $g = 0.75-0.8$ or thereabouts would yield a better adaptation, less physiologic stress, and greater well-being, similar to the lightness and freedom experienced by the disabled when salt-water swimming.

The projected Cosmos program will include flying a disc-type centrifuge in which animals will be able to select values of g between 0 and 1—it will be interesting to see their preference. The use of weightlessness as a rescue therapy in certain conditions has already been mooted as a long-term possibility (Kerwin, 1977).

During the childhood of gerontology it was occasionally speculated that "gravity is the cause of ageing" (Vrbiescu and Domilescu, 1965; Dárányi, 1930), presumably by some effect at a subcellular level. In less naive terms there is a connection, though unfortunately not of a kind which leads to practical intervention. All known organisms depend on chemical transduction of energy. They both evolved and are adapted to living in a gravity well, because they depend on availability of large and heterogeneous amounts of matter—phenomena such as predation, parasitism, and numerous degenerative side-reactions, all of which contribute to the evolution of an equilibrium lifespan and to decrease selective pressure with increased age are features of this "life style." Overcoming gravity accounts for much of the energy requirement of organisms. A hypothetical organism that "ate" energy directly and only ingested matter in minimum amounts for structural and reproductive purposes would avoid high concentrations of matter and high-gravity areas like the plague, and might indeed be highly durable. How such an organism could evolve, in terms of present ideas of biogenesis, and whether it would incur the side-effect of ageing, are science fiction questions, useful only to illustrate what the relation between gravity and senescence actually is. But if it did exist, high-gravity areas such as the surface of planets would be the wrong place to look for it.

10.4.4 Planning

The main points in a program of aerospace gerontology and geriatrics can be listed as follows: its mission would be to apply geriatric knowledge to aerospace problems and aerospace capacity to specific, clearcut, gerontological problems in short-term experiments, and the presence of geriatric and gerontological investigators in the aerospace establishment should be used to ensure a two-way flow of information from and to the clinical and research areas of these subjects. Definite areas of study should include

1. determination of flight criteria for ages greater than 50 years

2. physiological research on effects of acceleration, weightlessness, and other relevant factors in humans and animals throughout life, not only in young adults

3. study of individual variation and the development of non-actuarial measures of homeostasis and "physiologic age "—in the first place for crew selection, but with a constant eye on general clinical, actuarial and other applications

4. investigation of specific changes such as bone Ca loss which mimic those of ageing and may be exacerbated by it: measures to limit loss in weightlessness might provide protection against senile osteoporosis, and so on

5. study of readaptation of older subjects to re-entry, with a precautionary emphasis, and of control of adverse reactions by training

6. specific flight and ground experiments aimed at defined questions, such as the analysis of the lifespan "clock"

7. gerontological and geriatric presence in aerospace programs to identify problems and unrecognized sources of information

These objects alone are more than sufficient to establish the reality of "aerospace gerontology" as a necessary area of interest and to ensure the harvesting of valuable data from missions in hand.

11

Prospect

In so far as biology is more than a branch of idle curiosity, its assignment in the study of old age is to devise, if possible, means of keeping human beings alive in active health for a longer time than would normally be the case; in other words, to prolong individual life. People now rightly look to "science" to provide the practical realization of perennial human wishes which our ancestors have failed to realize by magic—or at least to investigate the prospect of realizing them. Under the influence of the study that is necessary to fulfill such wishes, the character of the wish itself generally changes in the direction of realism, so that most people today would be inclined to prefer the prospect of longevity, which may be realizable, to a physical immortality which is not, and, pari passu, "potentielle Unsterblichkeit" is already disappearing from the biological literature. An analogous process can be seen in the psychology of individual growing-up.

The objective of prolonging human life is one that can bear aggressive restatement from gerontologists, particularly at a time when there are scientists who seek ethical reasons why human life ought not to be prolonged, at least in communities of which they are not themselves members. Although it has much fundamental interest, we have seen that senescence is not, biologically speaking, a very satisfactory entity. It appears in most animals only under artificial conditions, and it would probably seem to most of us pointless to devote great effort to so arbitrary a part of development if it were not involved with a primary human desire. As it is, medicine has always accepted the prolongation of active and healthy human life in time as one of its self-evident objects, and this object has only been seriously challenged in the past two decades by the growth of pathological forms of antiliberalism. Gerontology differs from other fields of medical biology only in the fact that while most medical research is directed to making the curve of human survival as nearly as possible rectangular, gerontology is directed to prolonging the rectangle, and shifting the point of decline further in time from the origin. Population is indeed now an overriding issue, but the anxieties of such writers as W. Vogt (1949) still merit the rebuke of James Parkinson (1755–1824), that "if the population exceeded the means of support, the fault lay not in Nature, but in the ability of Politicians to discover some latent defect in the laws respecting the division and appropriation of property."

Technological forecasters refer to the point at which a theoretically attainable goal is seen to be practically feasible as the Hahn-Strassmann point, from the analogy of the demonstration of nuclear fission. The curve of subsequent development from that point consists of a number of envelopes determined chiefly by the amount of financial investment in the subject (Prehoda, 1967, 1968), but even at the lowest level of investment, the goal—in this case, a 15–20 percent prolongation of the human presenile period—is likely to be attained eventually, short of a total collapse of technological society. Although gerontology is now a worldwide study, only the United States possesses the resources in volume and quality of biological research to implement this possibility at the highest attainable rate, combined with the anthropological, unconscious, and attitudinal drives in its public and leaders which make such a maximal effort likely; it is, in other words, the country where dissatisfaction with the existing life-span is combined with the pragmatism necessary to attack it practically. Confidence in science, though it has been shaken by such things as pollution and the abuse of technology for psychopathological projects, remains the American resource in the face of overriding human desires of this kind; a growth in humane concern is more likely to divert the direction of scientific effort into the realization of needs than to dry up the pragmatic intention.

In the long term a society based on increased life-span and low turnover would be stable. Since reduction in reproductive rate is now a worldwide necessity to which the only alternative is disaster, whether or not gerontology succeeds in prolonging adult vigor, this looks like the pattern of the future ("zero population growth demands long-term people") but the model has so far attracted little predictive attention. Contingency planning of this kind, as well as action by scientists to prevent the abuse or distortion of the outcome by commercially or politically motivated groups, is already overdue. Such abuse could range from paternalistic suppression to denial of medical advances to unpopular or exploited sections of mankind, or their hogging by powerholders—either deliberately or, as with public health generally, through the maintenance of a more general worldwide social injustice. If the potentiality of longer life exacerbates the demand for human equality, it will only add to a demand, already certain to become irresistible, based on the end of exploitation and the fair division of all resources.

The scenario used by Prehoda (1968) envisages two additive increments in vigorous longevity—each of 15 percent—one cheap and simple, the other complex and costly. Taking the models of penicillin use and kidney grafting, and their application worldwide by developed and underprivileged countries, it is possible on this model to forecast a gerontology-dependent increase of 7 percent overall in world population by 2020. Other scenarios would yield other results. The concentration of extra longevity would in most such forecasts be chiefly in privileged societies, and is insignificant compared with the natural population increase expected from decreasing child mortality and the slow application of medical research and social justice in the developing countries. The envelope curves for this process assume only two increment-yielding procedures: in practice, if we take as a model not single discoveries but speed of transportation or growth of communication media, a continuing series of further increments seems highly probable, and the rate of invest-ment in these will be hastened both by the first success in the field and by the intense economic pressure arising from the burden of degenerative disease upon urban cultures. Such processes tend to be exponential in their early stages.

Postponement of old age, like all the other advances in human control of environment, must involve corresponding social adjustments: in the preven-tion of presenile mortality, as the graphs in Figure 11.1 abundantly indicate, social, economic, and political factors clearly predominate already. But what-ever problems might be raised by future increases in the human specific age, in this and other fields medicine can afford to treat protests based upon an interested misreading of the biology of human societies with the contempt they deserve, as a compound of illiberal opinions and bad science. The emotional preoccupation of former workers with magical rejuvenation did no good to the progress of science, but it was at least a humane preoccupation.

The social correlates of longevity, which are probably its most important practical aspects, have been omitted altogether from consideration in this book. It is clear throughout phylogeny that there is a relation between survival into the senile period and the existence of a social mode of life. In some cases longevity has evolved as a prerequisite of social organization, in others social organization itself increases the possibility of survival into old age, while the social group very probably draws adaptive benefits from the existence of old individuals. Both these trends appear to be at work in social primates. The potential life-span in palolithic man probably resembled our own: its realization has been possible through the development of a complex social and rational behavior. While therefore it is legitimate to abstract the idea of an evolutionary program in morphogenetic or physiological terms when we discuss the development and senescence of an individual man or of a worker bee, in neither case is this "program" really detachable from the social program which coexists with it, and which plays an equally important part in the determination of selection or survival. The irrelevance of discussing the biology of *individual* animals, even of non-social species, divorced from their ecology, has long been evident. Prolongation of the social activity and significance of the individual human being almost certainly leads to a change in the shape of the life-table, other things being equal. Continuance of active work, retention of interests, of the respect of our fellows, and of a sense of significance in the common life of the species, apparently make us live longer—loss of these things makes us die young. This is a result we might have expected, but which we still largely ignore in practice. Much of senile "involution" is the effect of the compulsory psychological and social "winding-up" imposed on the human individual by our form of society and our norms for the behavior of old people, and the most important measures for the prolonging of useful individual life that come within the range of the immediately practicable are all concerned with social adjustment. In point of fact, any increase in the life-span produced by slowing down the process of ageing would be an increase in the working life-span of already productive persons—the training of a doctor or a farmer now occupies nearly one-third of his total life-span and a half his expected working life. The exact demographic effects of an increase cannot be known until the pattern of the increase is known (whether childhood, old age, or both are prolonged in step with adult vigor, or not; and the relative proportions of the new survival curve) but any gain in period of maximum vigor and in working life is a free gift to the productivity of the world, and a decrease in the relative proportion of life spent in apprenticeship or dependency of various kinds. The contrast between the place of the (relatively few) aged in primitive societies (Simmonds, 1945, 1946) and the relatively many in our own (Sheldon, 1949; Sanderson, 1949) is particularly striking. In primitive cultures, stated Simmonds (1946),

> important means of security for old people are their active association with others and assistance in their interests and enterprises. They are regarded as repositories of knowledge, imparters of valuable information, and mediators between their fellows and the fearful supernatural powers. . . . The proportion of the old who remain active, productive, and essential in primitive societies is much higher than in advanced civilization, for they succeed to

an amazing degree in providing cultural conditions which utilize the services of their few old people.

How little this applies to our own culture is evident from the studies of Sheldon (1949) and Butler (1975); other evidence suggests that although in certain groups (Lehman, 1943), such as amateur naturalists—or among those who retain, perhaps, some of the magicosocial functions of the primitive elder (politicians, judges, and clergy)—the element of social support based upon continued activity leads to an apparently superior retention of the capacity for public life, the society of compulsory retirement, individual privacy, and the small family has little to offer to old people. This is a topic that cannot be pursued here, but its importance in the social medicine of age is paramount at present. Ageism is similar to racism: it consists in the imposition of roles based on ignorant prejudice. Wisdom would suggest that the most foolish and least affordable of prejudice is that directed against a group which we must all join.

"Civilized races," said Metchnikoff, "do not act like the Fuegians or other savages: they neither kill nor eat the aged, but none the less life in old age often becomes very sad" (1907). It was once believed that with the removal of "pathological" causes of death the specific age would rise very rapidly in man and approach the recorded maximum, about 120 years. We know much less about the diseases of later life than about life-saving by means of surgery and epidemiology in early life, but it seems possible that even with increased control over malignant tumors and blood-vessel disease the age at death might only come to be more and more normally distributed about 75 or 80 years. The characteristic pathological change of age is an increase in the number of pathological changes, and most people who die *late in life* from one of these causes also exhibit several other pathological processes which would probably have killed them very soon, had they survived the actual cause of their deaths.

The most important single change in our world, where life-span is concerned, is that in privileged countries our children grow up and reach old age and our wives no longer die in childbirth. We now know more accurately than ever before when we are likely to die. The most important future change, if it proves possible to control human ageing, may be that we no longer "look to our end," certainly as that end will come. The likelihood of such a change depends on the progress of our understanding of fundamental age processes. If the present trend of medicine continues without such progress, all that will happen is that the commonest age of dying will shift from being nearer 75 to being nearer 85, and the commonest causes may change so that we die of conditions which are not now so common, today's most frequent killers having been removed to uncover the next layer of the onion. If this is all, not many more than the present 1 in 100 born will reach 90, and not many more than the present 1 in 1,000 will reach 100. Those who do will still be the progeny of long-lived stocks, and owe more to their parents' genes than to medical science.

If, on the other hand, fundamental interference does become possible, so that we can modify not the diseases of age but the rate of ageing itself, the picture will be different. In what way and to what extent it will differ from the life-table today we do not know. There are several possibilities. It might conceivably prove possible, first of all, to lengthen the period of adult vigor without increasing the final life-span. This would produce a nearly square survival curve with its limit short of the century, and a situation like that in Huxley's *Brave New World,* where people remained apparently young until high ages and then died suddenly at approximately the usual time. This seems biologically the least likely pattern for us to achieve. More probably we might find means of prolonging the period of adult vigor, either alone, or with proportional prolongation of the pre-adult and the senile stages—a scalar expansion of our present survival pattern. Finally, and perhaps least profitably, it might be possible to prolong the total duration of life only by prolonging the stages prior to maturity. Its utility in man would depend entirely how late in the process of development it could be made to operate. There would be little point in interpolating 5 or 10 years at a physical and mental age of 12, except perhaps to make a longer period of pre-adult training possible. If there is any way of stopping or slowing the clock at a later age, that would represent a more significant achievement—a marking-time for, say, 5 years at the apparent age of 20 or 30, after which bonus we should complete a normal life-cycle. Of all the possible modifications the system childhood–adulthood–senescence could undergo, this comes nearest to the aims of von Boerhaave's alchemist, leaving aside the reversal of established senility, and it seems the most socially desirable. It is also by far the most likely. Where there is a rate it can usually be altered, and it is easier to alter a rate than to rewrite a biological program.

The problem of medical gerontology at the biological level, then, is to prolong the human life-cycle in time, either by deformation and stretching or by addition, and in particular to prolong that part of it which contains the period of "adult vigor." Such a problem could theoretically be solved in any of three ways, bearing in mind the evidence regarding the existence of a developmental "program"—that program could be prolonged by the provision of new developmental operations; or its movement, throughout or in part, could be slowed down; or active life could be maintained after the expiry of the program by piecemeal adjustment of homeostatic mechanisms with supplements, medicaments, and prostheses of various kinds.

The first of these possibilities, though it is biologically the most interesting, does not merit discussion at present, at any rate in relation to man. We do not know enough about morphogenesis to interfere with it clinically, except in a few simple deficiency states, let alone devise and apply a sequence of self-regulating operations in growth or development subsequent to normal adulthood. The third possibility is already receiving the greater share of the energy devoted to clinical studies upon human ageing, as opposed to fundamental research into its biology. We might in theory expect that the removal of successive causes of death would increase the expectation of life of the old as well as the young. It is interesting to notice that there is so far very little evidence of such an effect from the general advance of medicine in the last century (Figure 11.1). It may be that the time scale of the adult period, after somatic growth has ceased, is not susceptible to any major interference without at the same time destroying normal function. To assess the possibilities of such interference we need to know how far "marking time" at each stage of the mammalian developmental program is possible, and, if possible, is compatible with functional health. It is also a matter of practical import whether the rate of child growth influences the length of the period of adult vigor in man (Sinclair, 1955). The degree of linkage between growth, development, and metabolism may vary considerably at different periods of the life-cycle, and the bulk of the work upon their separation has been carried out only in non-mammalian embryos and larvae. We have to reckon with the possibility that the postpubertal mammal behaves like an imago—that its life-span is closely linked to metabolism, which, in homeotherms, is virtually invariable by the methods that can affect it in invertebrates, and that the fundamental change that leads to eventual senescence has already taken place at puberty. In this case, interference with the length of the adult phase could only be prosthetic.

Some biologists would share the pessimism formerly expressed by Strehler (1962) about the practicality of a fundamental intervention in human age processes. This suggests that the only unity in age effects may be a "loss of program," due to the failure of natural selection to secure homeostasis at high ages. Strehler goes on: "The evolutionary dereliction is probably so manifold and so deeply ingrained in the physiology and biochemistry of existing forms, including man, that the abolition of the process is a practical impossibility." At the same time, such pessimism, while it might eventually prove correct, is less in evidence than it was 10, or even 5 years ago. The operational attempt to interfere in age processes is now, at least, being taken seriously by people other than quacks and the obsessed: the number of teams clocking in daily to work on the project, in the United States alone, was over 1,000 in 1976, and is going up in the same country by about 200 a year. In fact, no medical field carries greater promise than gerontology, nor can medicine progress until this field is properly addressed.

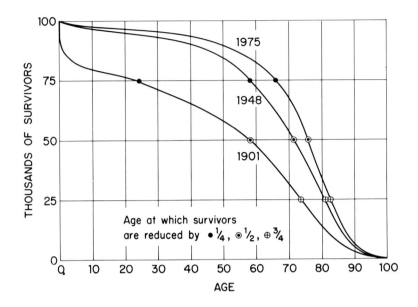

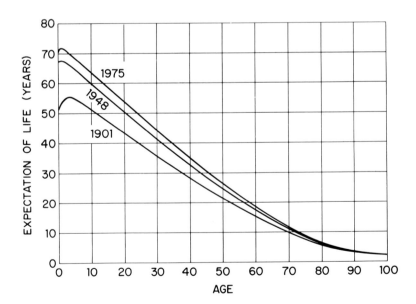

FIGURE 11.1   Comparison of survivorship and expectation of life: life-tables for the United States, 1901 to 1948, and forecast for 1975.

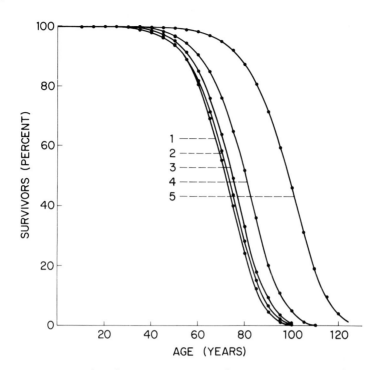

FIGURE 11.2 Predicted power law plots of survivorship curves for humans, assuming cures of the three major causes of death according to the assumptions described in the text. Curve 1 is for white males, U.S., 1967 data. The median survival time is 71.8 years. Curve 2 assumes a cure of vascular lesions, yielding a median survival time of 73.0 years. Curve 3 assumes a cure for cancer, yielding a median survival time of 74.8 years. Curve 4 assumes a cure for heart diseases, yielding a median survival time of 80.5 years. Curve 5 assumes all three diseases are cured, yielding a median survival time of 98.8 years. It is implicit in these calculations that a cured individual does not have an enhanced susceptibility to any other cause of death. (From Rosenberg, et al., 1973.)

There is probably a hierarchy of ageing mechanisms, some tightly and others loosely coupled. Accordingly the control or slowing of one leading mechanism may be expected to be limited in its effect by the exposure of others not coupled to it—by a form of discovered check. It is extremely likely that caloric restriction, even in adult life, could with proper dietary design be made to delay human senescence, and extremely unlikely, in the absence of a non-actuarial method of assay, that it will be applied. Since the gain from this cause alone could, on a rodent analogy, be 10–20 percent, making it take 70 years to reach physiological age 60, the effort would be worthwhile. Specific control of the hypothalamic "clock," though rather

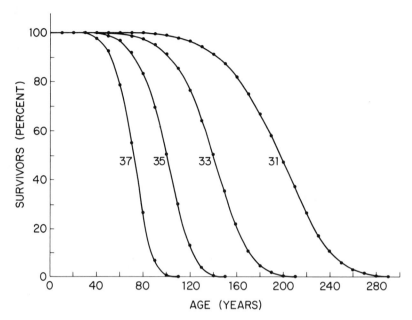

FIGURE 11.3   Predicted power law plots of survivorship for humans as a function of mean core body temperature using white males, U.S. 1967 data. For Curve 1, the standard plot, authors assumed a mean core body temperature of 37°C; for Curve 2, 35°C; for Curve 3, 33°C; and Curve 4, 31°C. The median survival times are; (1) 71.8 years; (2) 100 years; (3) 140 years; and (4) 198 years. (From Rosenberg, et al., 1973.)

further ahead, would carry so rich a harvest in reducing the non-actuarial burdens of ageing (mental disorder, reproductive decline, immunological insufficiency, and heart disease among them) that it would come near to meriting the panegyric of von Boerhaave quoted at the beginning of this volume.

It is clear that a cycle of medicine—that devoted to the control of infections, making way for the growth of surgery—is at an end. In the cycle that is beginning, there may be two main trends: a medicine of self-maintenance and self-knowledge ("preventive" or "positive" medicine), and a medicine of rate control, focused upon cyclical and secular processes in the body, of which ageing is one. Should the cerebral control of ageing be coupled to body-image in such a way that it is accessible to body-image manipulation, whether by traditional or by technological methods, the two trends will coalesce. Rather than speculate on the psychogenic character of illness, in the tradition of psychoanalysis, the newer medicine will be concerned with the mechanisms—brain mechanisms—by which psychic states are converted into symptomatology, as Freud himself believed would occur. Some of the brain-tissue signal paths uncovered in the analysis of ageing throw light on this group of phenomena. It is no longer soft-headed to cherish a "clinical impression" that the site, or even the occurrence, of a malignancy is a part of the patient's self-perception: mechanisms clearly exist through which this may be so.

In the meantime gerontology requires increased investment to elucidate the ageing clock or clocks, and a concerted search for non-actuarial means by which experimentation can be transferred to humans, who are the beneficiaries in mind: nobody needs long-lived mice.

The longevity of human tissues in storage is not, perhaps, likely to have a great influence on our longevity as individuals. There is the same fallacy in the conception of spare parts as a fundamental remedy for senescence, as in the idea that better medical services will push up the limit of the life-span; some of us certainly age more rapidly in one system than in another, but ageing is characteristically an increase in the number and variety of homeostatic faults. For this reason alone the interest of grafting and storage techniques for age studies is still much more for their contribution to theory than for the chance of using them as a prosthetic remedy for ageing. Krohn's work in making age chimeras by grafting mouse ovaries from old to young and from young to old is an elegant example of this kind (Jones and Krohn, 1960; Krohn, 1962), where the investigators used orthotopic grafting to discover whether the ageing of mouse ovary was a somatic or a tissue-sited process, and found that the transplanted ovary did not gain in longevity from being in a young environment.

Both organ culture and organ storage might throw some light on the role of somatic ageing in mutation, and on the related problem of the general stability of somatic cell-clones.

There remains the possibility that a substantial change in the specific age, and in the duration of healthy life, might result from *one particular* adjustment. This was the hope that led to the use of sex hormones for purposes of "rejuvenation," and which was largely disappointed.

The most likely sites for such an intervention are those suggested by caloric restriction—not perhaps *tout simple,* but through a readback of its influence on hypothalamic mechanisms. A close second is in the field of immunology.

To the question "Can the effective human life-span be prolonged artificially?" the most probable answer, based on all these possibilities, would appear to be "Yes." To the further question "By what factor?" no meaningful answer can be given until we know more of the nature of the predominant processes that determine human senescence. Supplementary questions dealing with the degree of reversibility in established senile change cannot at present be answered at all, beyond the conjecture that the morphogenetic program in man is hardly likely to be simply reversible in any fundamental sense, but that the irreversibility of local changes in ageing is at present probably over- rather than underestimated.

The only excuse for such speculation is, in any case, the possibility that it will drive us into the laboratory to ascertain the facts and to answer the questions it raises, thereby removing gerontology from the field of "entelechies" and "inherent principles" into that of intelligible evidence.

With the growth of international gerontology we no longer find ourselves waiting for the main problems of understanding age processes to be solved *incidentally,* in the course of general biological research upon other topics, but even so much of the information that is missing on other specific points is likely to be derived eventually from studies in endocrinology or morphogenetics which are not undertaken ad hoc; this type of background research cannot be hurried on, ahead of the general progress of knowledge, except by the cultivation of interest in ageing among biologists of all kinds.

Three main types of research have so far been involved in the investigation of ageing: study of the phylogeny of senescence in vertebrates; study of the correlations and the experimental modification of growth and development in populations where the life-span can be concurrently measured; and study of tissue-environment relationships through the creation of age chimeras. To these succeeded radiation biology, cell chemistry, and direct attempts to distinguish between age effects due to changes in cell number and in cell quality. Later still came molecular biology, but the clinical harvest was still delayed. It may well lie in an integrated neuroendocrine physiology of development.

The whole group of studies that need to be undertaken in determing the factors that predominate in mammalian ageing, or which can modify it, encounter a built-in different obstacle, since it is necessary either to work on forms whose life-span is short compared with that of the investigator, or to use elderly individuals whose early history has not been followed. The complication which this time factor introduces is of great importance for the planning of research. Man is by far the most numerous senile animal, and his life-cycle is extremely well known—even to the point at which we can estimate his physiological age by inspection; some research on senile men can be justified ethically, but the gerontological aspects of laboratory animal-breeding cannot much longer be neglected, since in many problems no further progress is possible until mammals of known life-cycle, heredity, and physiology are available in quantity. At present the choice lies between experiment on patients, the basing of general conclusions upon the behavior of invertebrates and small rodents, and postponing investigation for several years while a chosen population of larger mammals completes its life-cycle, though lifetime studies of dogs have been initiated for radiation research nevertheless (AEC Projects Nos. 4 and 6, University of California). Failure to deal with the logistics of this problem now will hinder research in 10 or 20 years' time, and that hindrance could be avoided by forethought.

Apart from specialized investigations, serious progress outside medicine now depends on the cultivation of general awareness among biologists of the importance of prolonging their study of every animal into the senile period, of collecting and publishing life-tables, especially for vertebrates under good laboratory conditions, and of seeking confirmatory evidence of the distribution of senescence in phylogeny. A few years of propaganda to biologists and administrators has already brought in a rich factual harvest. Much modern research into ageing tends still to be desultory, although the single subjects with which it deals are important in themselves. We ought to try to devise critical experiments, and if we destroy more hypotheses than we demonstrate, this is a subject that can well stand such treatment in contrast to the speculation that has gone before. The most desirable condition for progress in gerontology at the moment is still that the exact nature and scope of the problems raised by senescence should be understood, and the possibility of new experimental evidence borne in mind, during the planning and assessment of all biological and medical research, even when it is primarily directed to other objects. Senescence, like Mount Everest, challenges our ingenuity by the fact that it is there, and the focusing of our attention on it is unlikely to be fruitless.

References

Abdel-Malek, E. T. (1950). Susceptibility of the snail *Biomphalaria biossyi* to infection with certain strains of *Schistosoma mansoni*. *Am. J. Trop. Med. Hyg.* 30:887–888.

Abe, N. (1932). The age and growth of the limpet (*Acmaea dorsuosa* Gould). *Sci. Rep. Res. Inst. Tohoku Univ.* 7:347–363.

Abeloos, M. (1942). Sur la régénération de la tête des mollusques gasteropodes. *C. R. Acad. Sci.* 214:883–884.

Abercrombie, M. (1957). Localized formation of new tissue in an adult animal. *Symp. Soc. Exp. Biol.* XI:235–254.

Achan, D. N. (1961). On prolonging the longevity of the dog tick *Rhipicephalus sanguineus* after oviposition. *Curr. Sci.* 30:265–266.

Adams, A. E., and Mothes, A. M. (1945). The thyrotrophic potency of the pituitaries of albino mice with respect to age and sex. *Anat. Rec.* 91:21.

Adams, C. E. (1953) Mammalian germ cells. *Ciba Found. Symp.* London: Churchill, p. 198.

Adelman, R. C. (1970a). A biochemical parameter of aging. *Gerontologist* 10:24.

———— (1970b). Age-dependent effects in enzyme induction—a biochemical expression of aging. *Exp. Gerontol.* 6:75–88.

———— (1970c). Reappraisal of biological aging. *Nature* 228:1095.

———— (1970d). The independence of cell division and age-dependent modification of enzyme induction. *Biochem. Biophys. Res. Comm.* 38:1149–1153.

———— (1971). Age-dependent effects in enzyme induction—a biochemical expression of aging. *Exp. Gerontol.* 6:75–88.

———— (1975). Disruptions in enzyme regulation during aging. *Basic Life Sci.* 6:304–311.

Adelman, R. C., Stein, G., Roth, G. S., and Englander, D. (1972). Age-dependent regulation of mammalian DNA synthesis and cell proliferation in vivo. *Mech. Ageing Dev.* 1:49–59.

Ader, R., and Cohen, N. (1976). *Psychosom. Med.* 37:333–340.

Agduhr, E. (1939). Internal secretion and resistance to injurious factors. *Acta Med. Scand.* 99:387.

Agduhr, E., and Barron, D. H. (1938). Further observations on the increased resistance of mated animals to toxic agents: medinal. *Arch. Int. Pharmacodyn. Ther.* 58:351.

Ahrens, K. (1938). Lokaler Nachweis von Kalzium in den Membranen des Elodea-blattes mittels Natriumoleat. *Protoplasma* 31:508.

Albright, F. (1947). Osteoporosis. *Ann. Intern. Med.* 27:861.

Albright, J. F., and Makinodan, T. (1966). Growth and senescence of antibody-forming cells. *J. Cell. Physiol.* 67, Suppl. 1:185–206.

Albright, J. F., Makinodan, T., and Deitchman, J. W. (1969). Presence of life-shortening factors in spleens of aged mice. *Exp. Gerontol.* 4:267–276.

Alexander, P. (1957). Accelerated ageing—a long-term effect of exposure to ionizing radiations. *Gerontologia* 1:174–192.

—— (1967). The role of DNA lesions in processes leading to aging in mice. *Symp. Soc. Exp. Biol.* 21:29–50.

Alexander, P., and Connell, D. I. (1960). Shortening of the lifespan of mice by irradiation with x-rays and treatment with radiomimetic chemicals. *Radiat. Res.* 12:510–525.

Alexander, P., Connell, D. I., Brohult, A., and Brohult, S. (1959). Relation of radiation-induced shortening of the life-span by a diet augmented by alkoxyl glycerol esters and essential fatty acids. *Gerontology* 3:147–152.

Allee, W. G. , Emerson, A. E., Park, O., Park, T., and Schmidt, K. P. (1949). *Principles of Animal Ecology.* Philadelphia: W. B. Saunders Co.

Allen, J. A. (1952–1953). Observations on *Nucula turgida* Marshall and *N. moorei* Winckworth. *J. Mar. Biol. Ass. (U.K.)* 31:515–527.

Allen, W. M., and Masters, W. H. (1948). Investigation of sexual rejuvenation in elderly women. *10th Conf. Probl. Aging.* Josiah Macey, Jr. Foundation.

Allison, A. C. (1966). The role of lysosomes in pathology. *Proc. R. Soc. Med.* 59:867–868.

—— (1970). Tumor development following immunosuppression. *Proc. R. Soc. Med.* 63:1077–1080.

Allison, A. C., and Paton, G. M. (1965). Chromosome damage in human diploid cells following activation of lysosomal enzymes. *Nature* 207:1170–1171.

Alpatov, W. W. (1930). Experimental studies on the duration of life. XIII. The influence of different feeding during the larval and imaginal stages on the duration of life in the imago of *Drosophila melanogaster. Am. Nat.* 64:37.

Alpatov, W. W., and Gordeenko, N. A. (1932). Influence of mating on the longevity of silk-moths. *Zool. Zh.* 11 (2):60.

Alpatov, W. W., and Pearl, R. (1929). Experimental studies on the duration of life. XII. Influence of temperature during the larval period and adult life on the duration of life in the imago of *Drosophila melanogaster. Am. Nat.* 63:37.

Altnöder, K. (1926). Beobachtungen über die Biologie von *Margaritana margaritifera* und über die Ökologie ihres Wohnorts. *Arch. Hydrobiol.* 17:423–451.

Ambe, K. S., and Tappel, A. L. (1961). Oxidative damage to amino acids, peptides and proteins by radiation. *J. Food Sci.* 26:448–451.

Andersen, A. C., and Rosenblatt, L. S. (1965). Survival of beagles under natural and laboratory conditions. *Exp. Gerontol.* 1:193–200.

Anderson, B. G., and Jenkins, J. C. (1942). A time study of events in the life-span of *Daphnia magna. Biol. Bull. Wood's Hole* 83:260.

Anderson, R. E. (1965). Aging in Hiroshima atomic bomb survivors. *Arch. Pathol.* 79:1–6.

—— (1971). Delayed consequences of exposure to ionizing radiation: pathology studies at Atomic Bomb Casualty Commission. Hiroshima and Nagasaki, 1945–1970. *Hum. Pathol.* 2:567.

Anderson, R. E., Yamamoto, T., and Thorslund, T. (1974). Aging in Hiroshima and Nagasaki atomic bomb survivors: Soluble-insoluble collagen ratio. *J. Gerontol.* 29:153–156.

Anderson, R. L., and Doyle, P. C. (1961). Leucocyte antibodies in acute leukaemia of the monocytic and monocytoid forms. *Am. J. Clin. Pathol.* 36:25–30.

Andres, A., and Jiv, B. V. (1936). Somatic chromosome complex of human embryos. *Cytologia* 7:371.

Andrew, W. (1953). Phenomena of abnormal nuclear division in relation to the ageing process. *J. Gerontol.* 8:372.

Andrews, J. S., Griffith, W. H., Mead, J. F., and Stern, R. A. (1960). Toxicity of air-oxidised soybean oil. *J. Nutr.* 70:199–210.

Andusen, A. C. (1961). *10th Ann. Progr. Rep. of A.E.C. Proj. No. 4.* Univ. of Calif. Veterinary School, Davis, Calif.

Annandale, N., and Sewell, R. B. S. (1921). The banded pound-snail of India—*Viviparus bengalensis. Res. Indian Mus.* 22:215–248; 279–286.

Aoki, T., and Teller, M. N. (1966). Aging and cancerigenesis. III. Effect of age on isoantibody formation. *Cancer Res.* 26:1648–1652.

Arey, L. B., and Bickel, W. H. (1935). The number of nerve fibers in the human optic nerve. *Anat. Rec.* 61.

Arndt, W. (1928). Lebensdauer, Altern und Tod der Schwammer, S. B. *Ges. Naturf. Fr. (Berl.)* 23:44.

Arshavsky, I. A. (1966). Physiological mechanisms of the lifespan in mammals. *Trans. Moscow Soc. Nat.* 17:72–85.

——— (1966). The problems of physiological mechanisms determining Severtosov's apomorphosis and idioadaptation. *Zool. Zh.* 45:1308–1322.

Árvay, A., Takács, J., and Verzár, F. (1963). Der Einfluss von Graviditäten auf das Altern des Kollagens. *Gerontologia* 7:77–84.

Aschheim, P. (1976). In *Hypothalamus, pituitary and aging.* (eds. Everitt, A., and Burgess, J. A.). Springfield, Ill.: C. C. Thomas Co.

——— (1964). Resultats fournis par la greffe hétérochrone des ovaires sur l'étude de la regulation hypothalamo-hypophyso-ovarienne de la ratte senile. *Gerontologia.* 10:65–75.

——— (1972). Differentiation and neuroendocrine regulation in the hypothalamo-hypophysical-gonadal system, in Doerner, G. (ed) *Endocrinology of Sex.*

Asdell, S. A., and Crowell, M. F. (1935). The effect of retarded growth upon the sexual development of rats. *J. Nutr.* 10:13–24.

Ashworth, J. H., and Annandale, N. (1904). Observations on some aged specimens of *Sagartia troglodytes* and on the duration of life in Coelenterates. *Proc. R. Soc. Edinb.* 25:295.

Aslan, A. (1956). Eine neue Methode zur Prophylaxe und Behandlung des Alterns mit Novocain. *Therapiewoche* 7:14–22.

Aslan, A., and David, C. (1957). Ergebnisse der Novocain-Behandlung "Stoff H." bei dysmetabolischen Arthropathien. ibid., 8, 1–5.

Aslan, A., Vrabiescu, A., Domilescu, C., Campeanu, L., Costinu, M., and Stanescu, S. (1965). Longterm treatment with procaine in albino rats. *J. Gerontol.* 20:1–8.

Asling, C. W., Moon, H. D., Bennett, L. L., and Evans, H. M. (1952a). Relation of the anterior hypophysis to problems of ageing. *J. Gerontol.* 7:292.

Asling, C. W., Walker, D. G., Simpson, M. E., Li, C. H., and Evans, H. M. (1952b). Deaths in rats submitted to hypophysectomy at an extremely early age and the survival effected by growth hormone. *Anat. Rec.* 114:49.

Bab, H. (1948). The process of ageing. *Br. Med. J.* 1:1000.

Bacelar, A., and Frade, F. (1933). Sur la longevité chez les araignées. *C. R. Soc. Biol.* 113:523.

Backmann, G. (1938). Wachstumszyklen und phylogenetische Entwicklung. *Lunds Univ. Arskrift, N.F. Avd.* 2 (5):34.

——— (1945). Altern und Lebensdauer der Organismen. (Uppsala and Stockholm).

Bacon, F. (1645). *Historia Vitae et Mortis.* Dillingen.

Baer, K. (1864). *Reden.* St. Petersburg.

Baerg, W. J. (1945). The black widow and the tarantula. *Trans. Conn. Acad. Arts Sci.* 36:99.

Baffoni, G. M. (1954). La citomorfose degli elementi di Purkinje del cervelletto. *Ricere. Scient. (Rome)* 24:1641.

Baily, J. L. (1931). Some data on growth, longevity and fecundity in *Limnaea columella.* Say. *Biol. Generalis* 7:407–428.

Baird, M. B., Samis, H. V. , and Massie, H. R. (1971). Recovery from zoxazolamine paralysis and metabolism in vitro zoxazolamine in ageing mice. *Nature* 233:565–566.

Baker, F. (1934). A conchological Rip van Winkle. *Nautilus (Phil)* 48:5.

Baker, G. T. (1976). Insect flight muscle: maturation and senescence. *Gerontology* 22:334–362.

Baker, L. E., and Carrel, A. (1926). Au sujet du pouvoir inhibiteur du sérum pendant la vieillesse. *C. R. Soc. Biol.* 95:958.

Baker, S., Gaffney, G., Shock, N., and Lansdowne, M. (1959). Physiological responses of five middle-aged and elderly men to repeated administration of thyrotropin. *J. Gerontol.* 14:37–47.

Balász, A. (1960). Die Korrelation der praeimaginalen Lebensdauer und gerontologische Prozesse bei holometabolen Insekten, in *The Ontogeny of Insects.* Prague: Nakladelstvi Ceskoslovenske Akademie.

Balász, A., and Burg, M. (1962). Span of life and senescence of *Dugesia lugubris. Gerontologia* 6:227–236.

Balázs, R., and Cotterrell, M. (1972). Effect of hormonal state on functional as number and maturation of the brain. *Nature (New Biol.)* 236:348–350.

Ball, J. P., and Squire, J. R. (1949). A study of mortality in a burns unit. *Ann. Surg.* 130:160.

Ball, Z. B., Baines, R. H., and Visscher, M. B. (1947). The effects of dietary caloric restriction on maturity and senescence, with particular reference to fertility and longevity. *Am. J. Physiol.* 150:511–519.

Banfield, A. W. F. (1960). The use of caribou antler pedicles for age determination. *J. Wildl. Manag.* 24:99–102.

Banfield, W. G. (1952). The solubility and swelling of collagen in dilute acid with age variations in man. *Anat. Rec.* 114:157.

Banga, I. (1957). Der Effekt der schwachen organischen Säuren auf die Rattenschwanz-Kollagenfasern von jungen und altern Tieren. *Gerontologia* 1:325–346.

Banta, A. M. (1914). One hundred parthenogenetic generations of *Daphnia* without sexual forms. *Proc. Soc. Exp. Biol. Med.* 11:7.

Banta, A. M., and Wood, T. R. (1937). The accumulation of recessive physiological mutations during long-continued parthenogenesis. *Genetics* 22:183.

Barber, A. A., and Bernheim, F. (1967). Lipid peroxidation: its measurement, occurrence and significance in animal tissues. *Adv. Geront. Res.* 2:355–403.

Bardach, J. E. (1955). The opercular bone of the yellow perch, *Perca flavescens,* as a tool for age and growth studies. *Copeia* (1955), 107–109.

Barlow, C. H., and Muench, H. (1951). Life span and monthly mortality rate of *Bulinus truncatus* and *Planorbis boissyi,* the intermediate hosts of Schistosomiasis in Egypt. *J. Parasitol.* 37:165–173.

Barman, J. M., Pecoraro, V., and Astore, I. (1969). Biological basis of the inception and evolution of baldness. *J. Gerontol.* 24:163–168.

Barnes, D. W. H., Loutit, J. F., and Westgarth, D. R. (1959). Longevity of radiation chimeras. *Gerontologia* 3:137–146.

Barnes, H. F., and Stokes, B. M. (1951). Marking and breeding *Testacella* slugs. *Ann. Appl. Biol.* 38:540–545.

Barnes, L. L. (1942). The deposition of calcium in the hearts and kidneys of rats in relation to age, source of calcium, exercise and diet. *Am. J. Pathol.* 18:41.

Barrett-Hamilton, G. E. H. (1911). *History of British Mammals*. London.

Bauer, E. (1924). Beiträge zum Studium der Protoplasmahysteresis, usw. II. *Arch. Mikr. Anat.* 101:483; VIII:521.

Bazilievitch, I. V. (1938a). The syndrome of normal old age. *Proc. Conf. Probl. Old Age Kiev,* p. 255.

——— (1938b). Sur l'âge des viellards centenaires d'Abkhasya. *Medits. Zh.* 8:7.

Bazykalova, A. (1934). *Pecten jessoensis* Jay. (Age and growth-rate of *P.j.*) *Bull. Acad. Sci. (U.R.S.S.)* 2–3:389.

Beers, C. D. (1929). On the possibility of indefinite reproduction in the ciliate *Didinium* without conjugation or endomixis. *Amer. Nat.* 63:125.

Beeton, M., and Pearson, K. (1901). On the inheritance of the duration of life, and on the intensity of natural selection in man. *Biometrika* 1:50.

Beier, W., Brehmer, K. H., and Wiegel, D. (1971). Eine Möglichkeit zur Ermittelung des wahrscheinlichen biologischen Altern. *Z. Alternsforsch.* 24:77–78.

Bélár, K. (1924). Untersuchungen an *Actinophrys sol* Ehrenburg. II. Beiträge zur Physiologie des Formwechsels. *Arch. Protistenk.* 48:371.

Bellamy, A. W. (1934). Life span of *Platypoecilus, Xiphophorus* and their hybrids in the laboratory. *Science* 80:191.

Bellamy, D. (1968). Longterm action of prednisolone phosphate on a strain of shortlived mice. *Exp. Gerontol.* 4:327–334.

Belsky, J. L., Tachikawa, K., and Jablon, S. (1973). The health of atomic bomb survivors; a decade of examinations in a fixed population. *Yale J. Biol. Med.* 46:284–296.

Bender, A. E. (1953). Recent advances in protein synthesis. *Lancet* ii, 1142.

Benedict, F. G. (1935). Old age and basal metabolism. *N. Engl. J. Med.* 212:1111.

Benedict, F. G., and Root, H. F. (1934). The potentialities of extreme old age. *Proc. Natl. Acad. Sci. (USA)* 20:389.

Benedict, F. G., and Sherman, H. C. (1937). Basal metabolism of rats in relation to old age and exercise during old age. *J. Nutr.* 14:179.

Benz, G. (1970).Lebensverlängernde Wirkung von Gamma-strahlen auf Männchen des Larchen-wicklers (*Zeiraphera diviana*).

Berdishev, G. D., and Starikov, N. M. (1960). Longevity in Siberia and Far Eastern Russia. *2nd Conf. Gerontol Geriatr, Moscow Natural Society,* pp. 25–26.

Berg, B. N. (1960). Nutrition and longevity in the rat. I: Food intake relative to size, health and fertility. *J. Nutr.* 71:242–254.

Berg, B. N., and Simms, H. S. (1960). Nutrition and longevity in the rat. II. Longevity and onset of disease with different levels of food intake. *J. Nutr.* 71:255–263.

——— (1962). Relation of nutrition to longevity and onset of disease in rats. *Biol. Asp. Aging (N.Y. & Lond.),* pp. 35–37.

Berg, K. (1948). Biological studies on the River Susaa. *Folia Limnol. Scand.* 4:1–318.

Bergauer, V. (1924). Beiträge zum Studium der Protoplasmahysteresis, usw. III; VI; VII. *Arch. Mikr. Anat.* 101:489, 508, 512.

Bergman, A. J., and Turner, C. W. (1941). Thyrotropic hormone content of rabbit pituitary during growth. *Endocrinology* 29:313.

Berninger, J. (1910). Über Einwirkung des Hungers auf *Hydra. Zool. Anz.* 36:271.

Berreurbon, J., and Inagaki, H. (1970). Senescence of male woodlouse *Ligia oceanica* (L). *C. R. Soc. Biol.* (Paris) 164:516.

Berrill, N. J. (1931). The natural history of *Bulla hydatis* Linn. *J. Mar. Biol. Ass. (U.K.)* 17:567–571.

Bertalannfy, L. von. (1933). *Modern Theories of Development*. London: Humphrey Milford.

——— (1941). Stoffwechseltypen und Wachstumstypen. *Biol Zbl.* 61:510.

Bertin, L. (1956). *Eels, A Biological Study*. London: Cleaver-Hume Press.

Bertolini, A. M. (1962). Modification of cellular enzyme systems during ageing. *Gerontologia* 6:175–187.

Beverton, R. J. H., and Holt, S. J. (1959). A review of the life-spans and mortality rates of fish in nature. *Ciba Found. Colloquia on Ageing* 5:142–177.

Bidder, G. P. (1925). The mortality of plaice. *Nature* 115:495.

――― (1932). Senescence. *Br. Med. J.* 115:5831.

Biggers, J. D., Finn, C. A., and McLaren, A. (1962). Long term reproductive performance of female mice. I: Effects of removing one ovary. *J. Repr. Fertil.* 3:303–312.

Bihari-Varga, M., and Biró, T. (1971). Thermoanalytical investigations on the age-related changes in articular cartilage, meniscus and tendon. *Gerontologia* 17:2–15.

Bilewicz, S. (1953). Dóswiadczenia nad wplywem czynności rozrodczych na dlugóśc życia u muchy owocowej *Drosophila melanogaster*. (Influence of mating on the longevity of *D.m.* *Folia Biol. (Warsaw)* 1:175.

Billingham, R. E., Brent, L., and Medawar, P. B. (1953). Actively acquired tolerance of foreign cells. *Nature* (Lond.) 172:603.

Billingham, R. E., and Russell, P. S. (1956). Studies on wound healing with special reference to the phenomenon of contracture in experimental wounds in rabbits' skin. *Ann. Surg.* 144:961–981.

Birren, J. E., ed. (1961). *Handbook of Aging on the Individual*. Chicago: Univ. Press.

Bishopp, F. C., and Smith, C. N. (1938). The American dog tick, eastern carrier of Rocky Mountain spotted fever. *Circ. U.S. Dept. Agric.* No. 478:1.

Bittner, J. J. (1937). Mammary tumors in mice in relation to nursing. *Am. J. Cancer* 30:530.

Bjorkerud, S. (1964). Isolated lipofuscin granules, a survey of a new field. *Adv. Geront. Res.* 1:257–288.

Bjorksten, J. (1958). A common molecular basis for the aging syndrome. *J. Am. Geriatr. Soc.* 6:740–748.

Bjorksten, J. A. (1962). Aging: present status of our chemical knowledge. *J. Am. Geriatr. Soc.* 10:125–139.

Bjorksten, J., Weyer, E. R., and Ashman, S. M. (1971). Study of low molecular weight proteolytic enzymes. *Finska Kernist. Medd.* 80:70–87.

Blair, H. A. (1954). A formula of the relation between radiation dose and shortening of lifespan. *Peaceful Uses of Atomic Energy (Geneva)* XI.

Blakeslee, A. F. (1954). The aging of seeds and mutation rates. *Ann. N.Y. Acad. Sci.* 57:488–490.

Blest, A. D. (1960). A study of the biology of saturniid moths in the Canal Zone biological area. *Smithsonian Rep., 1959,* pp. 447–464.

Bliznakov, E. G. (1978). Immunological senescence in mice and its reversal by coenzyme Q_{10}. *Mech. Aging Devel.* 7:189–197.

Bloch, S., and Flury, E. (1959). Untersuchungen über Klimakterium und Menopause an Albino-Ratten, II. *Gynaecologia* 147:414–438.

Block, E. (1953). *Acta Anat.* 17:201.

Blumenthal, H. (1945). The ageing process in the endocrine glands of the guinea pig. I. The influence of age, sex and pregnancy on the mitotic activity and the histological structure of the thyroid, parathyroid and adrenal glands. *Arch. Pathol.* 40:284.

Blunck, H. (1924). Lebensdauer, Fortpflanzungsvermögen und Alterserscheinungen beim Gelbrand (*Dytiscus marginalis* L.) *Zool. Anz.* 58:163.

Bocher, W., and Hermskerk, J. J. (1969). Zur Problematik des funktionalen Alters. *Z. f. Gerontol.* 2:339–349.

Bodánszky, M., and Engel, S. L. (1966). Oxytocin and the lifespan of male rats. *Nature* (Lond) 210:751.

Bodenheimer, F. S. (1938). *Problems of Animal Ecology*. London:Oxford Univ. Press.

Bodenstein, D. (1943a). Factors influencing growth and metamorphosis of the salivary gland in *Drosophila*. *Biol. Bull. Wood's Hole* 84:13.

—— (9143b). Hormones and tissue competence in the development of *Drosophila. Biol. Bull. Wood's Hole* 84:35.

—— (1953). Endocrine control of metamorphosis. *Proc. IX Int. Congr. Entom. (Amsterdam)* 1951.

Boecker, E. (1914). Depression und Missbildungen bei *Hydra. Zool. Anz.* 44:75.

Boettger, C. R. (1953). Grossenwachstum und Geschlechtsreife bei Schnecken und pathologische Riesenwuchs folgen einer gestorben Wechselwirkung beider Faktoren. *Zool. Anz.* 17, Suppl-Bd.:468–487.

—— (1953). Riesenwuchs der Landschnecke *Zebrina (Z.) detrita* (Muller) als Folge parasitären Kastrations. *Arch. Molluskenk.* 82:151–152.

—— (1957–1958). Neue Erfuhrungen über der verjüngende Wirkung des Novocains. *Zool. Anz.* 8:3–12.

Bogomolets, A. A. (1947). *The Prolongation of Life.* New York:Duell Sloan and Pearce.

Bolla, R., and Brot, M. (1975). Age-dependent changes in enzymes involved in macronuclear synthesis in *Turbatrixaceti. Arch. Biochem. Biophys.* 169:227–236.

Bondareff, W., and Narotzky, R. (1972). Age changes in neuronal microenvironment. *Science* 176:1135–1436.

Bonnet, P. (1935). La longévité chez les araignées. *Bull. Soc. Int. Fr.* 40:272.

Bonnot, P. (1940). California abalones. *Calif. Fish. Game* 26:200–211.

Boothby, W. M., Berkson, J., and Dunn, H. L. (1936). Studies of the energy metabolism of normal individuals. *Am. J. Physiol.* 116:468.

Borisenko, E. Ya. (1939). Influence of conditions of development on the effects of inbreeding. *Yarovizatsiya* 5–6:162.

Borssuk, R. A. (1935). Untersuchung des Verlustes der Regenerations-fähigkeit der hinteren Extremität von *Rana temporaria. Arch. EntwMeck. Org.* 133:349.

—— (1941). On inbreeding in animal husbandry. *Trud. Sel. Khoz. Acad. Timiryazeva* 5:5.

Bounhiol, J. (1938). Recherches expérimentales sur la déterminisme de la métamorphose chez les Lepidoptères. *Biol. Bull. Suppl.* 24:I.

Bourlière, F. (1946). Longévité moyenne et longévité maximum chez les vertébrés. *Année Biol. (Paris)* 22:10.

—— (1947). Quelques remarques sur la longévité des petits mammifères sauvages. *Mammalia* 11:111.

—— (1950). Sénescence et vitesse de cicatrisation chez le rat. *Rev. Med. (Liege)* 5:669.

—— (1951). *Vie et moeurs des mammifères.* Payot:Paris.

—— (1959). Life-spans of mammalian and bird populations in nature. *Ciba Found. Symp. Ageing* 5:90–103.

—— (1969). Les méthodes de mesure de l'âge biologique de l'homme. *Cah. Santé Publ.* 37, Geneva, World Health Organization.

Bourlière, F., and Brocas, J. (1964). Le vieillissement du collagène et l'évolution avec l'âge du métabolisme basal chez un Ophidien, la couleuvre à collier. *Gerontologia* 9:98–106.

Bowerman, W. G. (1939). Centenarians. *Trans. Actuarial Soc. Amer.* 40:360.

Boycott, A. E. (1934). The habits of land mollusca in Great Britain. *J. Ecol.* 22:1–38.

—— (1936). The habits of freshwater mollusca in Britain. *J. Anim. Ecol.* 5:116–186.

Boyko, E. G. (1946). Age determination in fishes based on examination of fin ray sections. *C. R. Acad. Sci. U.R.S.S.* 53:483–484.

Bozcuk, A. N. (1967). Testing the protein error hypothesis of aging in *Drosophila. Exp. Gerontol.* 11:73–78.

—— (1972). DNA synthesis in the absence of somatic cell division association with ageing in *Drosophila subobscura. Exp. Gerontol.* 7:147–156.

Braadbart, S. (1961). (no title). *Lancet* II:764.

Brander, T. (1956). Über Dimensionen, Gewicht, Volumen und Alter grosswüchsiger europäischer Unionazeën. *Arch. Molluskenk* 85:65–68.

Bresslau, E. (1928–1933). *Turbellaria,* in *Handbuch der Zoologie,* II (eds. Kükenthal, W., and Krumbach, T.).

Brien, P. (1953). La pérennité somatique. *Biol. Rev.* 28:308.

Brizzee, K. R., Sherwood, N., and Timiras, P. S. (1968). A comparison of cell populations at various depth levels in cerebral cortex of young adult and aged Logan Evans rats. *J. Gerontol.* 23:289–297.

Brocas, J., and Verzár, F. (1961a). Measurement of isometric tension during thermic contraction as criterion of the biological age of collagen fibres. *Gerontologia* 5:223–227.

—— (1961b). The ageing of *Xenopus laevis,* a South African frog. *Gerontologia* 5:228–240.

Brock, M. A. (1970). Ultrastructural studies on life cycle of a short-lived metazoan, *Campanularia flexuosa. J. Ultrastruct. Res.* 32:118.

Brockmeier, H. (1888). Zur Fortpflanzung von *Helix nemoralis* und *H. hortensis* in der Gefangenschaft. *Nachrbl. Deutsch. Malak. Ges.* 20.

—— (1896). Beiträge zur Biologie unsere Süsswassermollusken. *Nachrbl. Deutsch. Malak. Ges.* 57.

Brody, H. (1970). Structural changes in the aging nervous system. *Intersc. Top. Gerontol.* 7:9–21. Basel: Karper.

Brody, S. (1924). The kinetics of senescence. *J. Gen. Physiol.* 6:245.

—— (1945). *Bioenergetics and Growth.* Baltimore: Williams and Wilkins.

Brody, S., Ragsdale, A. C., and Turner, C. W. (1923). The rate of growth of the dairy cow. IV. Growth and senescence as measured by the size and fall of milk secretion with age. *J. Gen. Physiol.* 6:31.

Brown, G. W., and Flood, M. M. (1947). Tumbler mortality. *J. Am. Statist. Ass.* 42:562.

Brown, H. H. (1934). A study of the Tectibranch Gastropod Mollusc, *Philine aperta* (L). *Trans. R. Soc. Edinb.* 58:179–210.

Brown, M., Sinclair, R. G., Cronk, L. B., and Clark, G. C. (1948). Some remarks on premature aging in the Eskimos. *Rev. Canad. Biol.* 7:178.

Brown, P. C., and Consden, R. (1958). Variation with age of shrinkage temperature of human collagen. *Nature* (Lond.) 181:349–350.

Brown, P. E. (1967). Mechanism of action of aminothiol radioprotectors. *Nature* 213:363–364.

Bruce, H. M., and Hindle, E. (1934). The golden hamster, *Cricetus (Mesocricetus) auratus* Waterhouse. Notes on its breeding and growth. *Proc. Zool. Soc. (Lond.),* p. 364.

Bruch, H. (1941). Obesity in relation to puberty. *J. Pediatr.* 19:365.

Bruere, A. N. (1967). Evidence of age aneuploidy in the chromosomes of sheep. *Nature* (Lond.) 215:658–659.

Bruun, A. F. (1943). The biology of *Spirula spirula* (L). *Dana Rep.* 4:1–44.

Bryuzgin, V. L. (1939). A procedure for investigating age and growth in reptilia. *C. R. Acad. Sci. (U.R.S.S.)* 3:403.

Bucci, L., and Saunders, J. C. (1960). A psychopharmacological evaluation of 2-diethylamino para-aminobenzoate (procain). *J. Neuropsychiatr.* 1:276–281.

Buchanan, J. W. (1938). Developmental acceleration following inhibition. *J. Exp. Zool.* 79:109.

Bucher, N. L. R., and Glinos, A. D. (1950). The effect of age on the regeneration of rat liver. *Cancer Res.* 10:324.

Bucher, N. L. R., Scott, J. F., and Aub, J. C. (1950). Regeneration of liver in parabiotic rats. *Cancer Res.* 10:207.

Buerger, M. (1954). *Altern und Krankheit.* Berlin:G. Thieme.

Bull, H. O. (1934). Aquarium observations on the rate of growth and enemies of the common starfish (*Asterias rubens* L.) *Rep. Dove Marine Lab.* Series 3, 2:60.

—— (1938). The growth of *Psammechinus miliaris* (Gml) under aquarium conditions. *Rep. Dove Marine Lab.* 6:39.

Bullough, W. S. (1949). Age and mitotic activity in the male mouse, *Mus musculus* L. *J. Exp. Biol.* 26:261.

—— (1967). *The Evolution of Differentiation.* London:Academic Press.

—— (1971). Ageing of mammals. *Nature* (Lond.) 229:608–610.

Bunyan, J., Diplock, A. T., Edwin, E. E., and Green, J. (1962). Exudative diathesis and lipid peroxidation in the chick. *Br. J. Nutr.* 16:519–530.

Burch, P. R. J. (1963a). Carcinogenesis and cancer prevention. *Nature* 197:1145–1151.

—— (1963b). Human cancer: Medelian inheritance or vertical transmission? *Nature* (Lond) 197:1042–1046.

—— (1963c). Autoimmunity: some aetiological aspects. *Lancet* I:1253–1257.

—— (1968). *An Inquiry Concerning Growth, Disease and Aging.* Edinburgh: Oliver and Boyd.

Bürger, M. (1954). *Altern und Krankheit,* 2. Aufl. Leipzig:G. Thieme.

Burlakova, E. B., Khrapova, N. G., Shtol 'ko, V. N., and Emanuel, N. M. (1966). The kinetic criterion of the applicability of inhibitors of free-radical processes in radiobiology and oncology. *C. R. Acad. Sci. (U.S.S.R.)* 169:688–691.

Burnet, F. M. (1959a). Clonal selection. *Croonian Lecture, R. Coll. Phys. (London).*

—— (1959b). *The Clonal Selection Theory of Acquired Immunity.* Cambridge: Univ. Press.

—— (1961). The new approach to immunology. *N. Engl. J. Med.* 264:24–34.

—— (1967). Concepts of autoimmune disease and their implications for therapy. *Perspect. Biol. Med.* 10:141–152.

—— (1970a). An immunological approach to ageing. *Lancet* II:358–360.

—— (1970b). *Immunological Surveillance.* Oxford: Pergamon Press.

Burt, W. H. (1940). Territorial behavior and populations of some small mammals in southern Michigan. *Misc. Publ. Mus. Zool. Univ. Mich.* 45:1–58.

Butler, R. N. (1975). *Why Survive? Being Old in America.* New York: Harper and Row.

Bütschli, O. (1882). Gedanke über Leben und Tod. *Zool. Anz.* 5:64.

Buu-Hoi, N. P., and Ratsimamanga, A. R. (1959). Retarding action of *nor*-dihydroguaiaretic acid on aging in the rat. *C. R. Soc. Biol. (Paris)* 153:1180–1182.

Buxton, J. (1950). *The Redstart.* London: Collins.

Cagle, F. R. (1946). Growth of the slider turtle, *Pseudemys scripta elegans. Amer. Midl. Nat.* 39:685.

Cain, M., and Cunneen, J. I. (1962). Fundamental approaches to aging problems. *Rev. Gen. Caoutchouc* 39:1940–1950.

Cairey, C. F. (1954). Simplified comparison of man-dog age. *J. Am. Vet. M.A.* 125:56.

Calkins, G. N. (1919). *Uroleptus mobilis* Eng. II. Renewal of vitality through conjugation. *J. Exp. Zool.* 29:121–156.

Camboué, P. (1926). Prolongation de la vie chez les papillons décapités. *C. R. Soc. Biol. (Paris)* 183:372.

Campbell, J., Davidson, I. W. F., Snair, W. D., and Lei, H. P. (1950). Diabetogenic effect of purified growth hormone. *Endocrinology* 46:273.

Campbell, P. N., and Work, T. S. (1953). Biosynthesis of proteins. *Nature* (Lond) 171:997.

Carlson, A. J., and Hoelzel, F. (1946). Apparent prolongation of the life-span of rats by intermittent fasting. *J. Nutr.* 31:363–375.

—— (1947). Growth and longevity of rats fed omnivorous and vegetarian diets. *J. Nutr.* 34:81–96.

—— (1948). Prolongation of the life-span of rats by bulk formers in the diet. *J. Nutr.* 36:27.

Carr, C. J., King, J. T., and Visscher, M. B. (1949). Delay of senescence infertility by dietary restriction. *Fed. Proc.* 8:22.

Carrel, A. (1912). On the permanent life of tissues, *J. Exp. Med.* 15:516.

Carrel, A., and Ebeling, A. H. (1921). Antagonistic growth principles of serum and their relation to old age. *J. Exp. Med.* 38:419–425.

Carroll, H. W., and Brauer, R. W. (1961). Residual radiation injury: impaired regrowth of realimented hypocalorically reared rats. *Am. J. Physiol.* 201:1078–1082.

Carter, T. O. (1955). Remarkable age attained by a bobcat. *J. Mammal.* 36:290.

Castle, W. E. (1926). A further study of size inheritance in rabbits with special reference to the existence of genes for size characters. *J. Exp. Zool.* 53:421.

Chaconas, G., and Finch, C. E. (1973). Effect of aging on RNA-DNA ratios in brain-regions of C57BL-6J male mouse. *J. Neurochem.* 21:1469–1473.

Chai, C. K. (1959). Life-span in inbred and hybrid mice. *J. Hered.* 50:203–208.

Chamberlain, T. K. (1931). Annual growth of freshwater mussels. *Bull. U.S. Bur. Fish* 46:713–739.

—— (1933). Ages and shell measurements of two large specimens of *Megalonaias gigantea* Barnes. *Nautilus* 47:29.

Chang, H. S. (1951). Age and growth of *Callionymus Iyra* L. *J. Mar. Biol. Ass. (U.K.)* 30:281.

Charmant, G. (1971). Physiological research in *Sphaeroma serratum* (Fabricius) (crustacea, isopoda)—influence of size on ion regulation—possible existence of senescent state in large males. *C. R. Acad. Sci.* 273:211.

Chebotarev, D. F. (1969). *Osnovyi Gerontologii.* Moscow:Medgiz.

Cheimer, R. S. (1972). Causal basis of chromosome abnormalities. *J. Reprod. Fertil.* 15, Suppl:79–98.

Chen, J. C., Warshaw, J. B., and Sanadi, D. R. (1972). Regulation of mitochondrial respiration in senescence. *J. Cell Physiol.* 80:141.

Chetsanga, C. J., Boyd, V., and Peterson, L. (1975). Single stranded regions in DNA of old mice. *Nature* 253:130–131.

Cheymol, J., Chabrier, P., Adolphe, M., and Selim, M. (1960). Procaine et dérivés dans la protection chimique contre les radiations du ^{60}Co. *C. R. Soc. Biol.* 154:1761–1762.

Cheymol, J., and Pelou, A. (1944). La réspiration du muscle du lapin suivant l'âge. *C. R. Soc. Biol. (Paris)* 138:91.

Chieffi, M. (1949). Effect of testosterone administration on the beard growth of elderly males. *J. Gerontol.* 4:200.

—— (1950). An investigation of the effects of parenteral and topical administration of steroids on the elastic properties of senile skin. *J. Gerontol.* 5:17.

—— (1951). The effect of topical oestrogen application on the elastic properties of the skin of elderly men. *J. Gerontol.* 5:387.

Child, C. M. (1911). A study of senescence and rejuvenation based on experiments with planarians. *Arch. EntwMech. Org.* 31:537.

—— (1913). The asexual cycle in *Planaria velata* in relation to senescence and rejuvenescence. *Biol. Bull. Wood's Hole* 25:181.

—— (1914). Asexual breeding and prevention of senescence in *Planaria velata*. *Biol. Bull. Wood's Hole* 26:286.

—— (1915). *Senescence and Rejuvenescence.* Chicago: Univ. Press.

—— (1918). Physiological senescence in hydromedusae. *Biol. Bull. Wood's Hole* 34:49.

Chio, K. S., Reiss, U., Fletcher, B., and Tappel, A. L. (1969). Peroxidation of subcellular organelles—formation of lipofuscin-like fluorescent pigments. *Science* 166:1535–1536.

Chittleborough, R. G. (1959). Determination of age in the humpbacked whale *Megaptera nodosa* (Bonaterre). *Aust. J. Mar. Freshw. Res.* 10:125–141.

Chlebovsky, O., Praslica, M. and Horak, J. (1966). Chromosome aberrations—increased incidence in bone marrow of continuously irradiated rats. *Science* 153:195–196.

Cholodkowsky, N. (1882). Tod und Unsterblichkeit in der Tierwelt. *Zool. Anz.* 5:264.

Christopherson, J. B. (1924). Longevity of parasitic worms: the term of living existence of *Schistosoma haematobium* in the human body. *Lancet,* p. 742.

Chu, J. (1934). Reproduction, life-span, growth and senescence of *Brachionus. Sci. Rep. Univ. Chekiang,* No. 1.

Chugunov, N. I. (1925). On the methods of age determination in sturgeons. *Bull. Fish. Econ. (U.R.S.S.)* 11:33.

―――― (1949). *Economic Fishes of the U.S.S.R.* Moscow.

Chvapil, M., and Hrůza, Z. (1959). The influence of aging and undernutrition on chemical contractility and relaxation of collagen fibres in rats. *Gerontologia* 3:241–252.

Ciuca, A. and Jucovski, V. (1969). Recherches concernant la détermination de "L'âge biologique moyen." *Riv. Espan. Gerontol.* 4:97–116.

―――― (1970). Studium über Alterswandel der somatophysiometrischen Indikatoren. *Z.f. Gerontol.* 3:133–230.

Clark, A. M. (1957). The relation of genome number to radio sensitivity in *Habrobracon. Am. Nat.* 91:111–119.

―――― (1960). Modification of life span by X-rays for haploids and diploids of the wasp *Habrobracon* sp. *Biol. Bull.* 119:292.

Clark, A. M., and Rockstein, M. (1964). Aging in insects. *Physiology of Insecta* 1.

Clark, A. M., and Rubin, M. A. (1961). The modification by X-irradiation of the life span of haploids and diploids of the wasp *Habrobracon* sp. *Radiat. Res.* 15:244–253.

Clark, T. B. (1940). The relation of production and egg weight to age in White Leghorn fowls. *Poultry Sci.* 14:54.

Clarke, G. D., Stoker, M. G. P., Ludlow, A., and Thornton, M. (1970). Requirement of serum for DNA synthesis in BHK 21 cells; effects of density, suspension and virus transformation. *Nature* 227:798–801.

Clarke, J. M., and Maynard Smith, J. (1955). The genetics and cytology of *Drosophila subobscura.* XI. Hybrid vigor and longevity. *J. Genet.* 53:172.

―――― (1961a). Two phases of ageing in the *Drosophila subobscura. J. Exp. Biol.* 38:679–684.

―――― (1961b). Independence of temperature of the rate of ageing in *Drosophila subobscura. Nature* (Lond.) 190:1027–1028.

―――― (1966). Increase in the rate of protein synthesis with age in *Drosophila subobscura. Nature* 209:627–629.

Clarke, M. F., and Smith, A. (1938). Recovery following suppression of growth in the rat. *J. Nutr.* 15:245.

Clarkson, J. M., and Painter, R. B. (1974). Repair of X-ray damage in aging WI-38 cells. *Mutat. Res.* 23:107–112.

Cleland, D. M. (1954). A study of the habits of *Valvata piscinalis* (Muller) and the structure and function of the alimentary canal and reproductive system. *Proc. Malac. Soc. (Lond.)* 30:167–202.

Clemens, J. A., Amenomori, Y., Jenkins, T., and Meites, J. (1969). Effects of hypothalamic stimulation, hormones and drugs on ovarian function in old female rats. *Proc. Soc. Exp. Biol. Med.* 132:561–563.

Clemente, C. D., and Windle, W. F. (1955). Regeneration of severed nerve fibres in the spinal cord of the adult cat. *J. Comp. Neurol.* 101:691.

Cleveland, L. R. (1938). Longitudinal and transverse division in two closely-related flagellates. *Biol. Bull. Wood's Hole* 74:1

Cockrum, E. L. (1956). Homing, movements and longevity in bats. *J. Mammal.* 37:48–57.

Coe, W. N. (1947). Nutrition, growth and sexuality of the Pismo clam (*Tivela stultorum.) J. Exp. Zool.* 104:1–24.

Coe, W. R. (1948). Nutrition, evironmental conditions, and growth of marine bivalve mollusks. *J. Mar. Res.* 7 (3):586–601.

Coe, W. R., and Fox, D. L. (1942). Biology of the California mussel (*Mytilus californiensis*). 1.

Influence of temperature, food supply, sex and age on the rate of growth. *J. Exp. Zool.* 90:1–30.

Cohausen, J. H. (1742). *Hermippus Redivivus,* sive exercitatio physico-medica curiosa de methodo raro ad CXV annos prorogandae senectutis per anhelitum puellarum, ex veteri monumento Romano deprompta, etc. Frankfurt.

Cohn, A. E., and Murray, H. A. (1925). The negative acceleration of growth with age, as demonstrated by tissue culture. *J. Exp. Med.* 42:275.

Coker, R. E., Shira, A. F., Clark, H. W., and Howard, A. D. (1919–1920). Natural history and propagation of the freshwater mussels. *Bull. U.S. Bur. Fish.* 37:75.

Cole, H. A. (1956). A preliminary study of growth rate in cockles (*Cardium edule* L.), in relation to commercial exploitation. *J. Cons. Int. Exp. Mer.* 22:77–90.

Cole, L. J. (1962). Ageing at the cellular level. Differential effect of transplanted isogenic lymphoid cells from old versus young mice. *Gerontologia* 6:36–40.

Collinge, W. E. (1944). Notes on the terrestrial Isopoda (Woodlice). *Northw. Natl.* 19:112.

Comfort, A. (1953). Absence of a Lansing effect in *Drosophila subobscura. Nature* 172:83.

—— (1954). Biological aspects of senescence. *Biol. Rev.* 29:284–329.

—— (1956a). Maximum ages reached by domestic cats. *J. Mammal.* 37:118–119.

—— (1956b). The longevity and mortality of Irish wolfhounds. *Proc. Zool. Soc. (Lond.)* 127:27–34.

—— (1957a). The biological approach in the comparative study of ageing. *Ciba Found. Colloquia on Ageing* 3:2–19.

—— (1957b). The duration of life in molluscs. *Proc. Malac. Soc. (Lond.)* 32:219–249.

—— (1957c). Survival curves of mammals in captivity. *Proc. Zool. Soc. (Lond.)* 128:349–364.

—— (1958a). Coat color and longevity in thoroughbred mares. *Nature* 182:1531–1532.

—— (1958b). Mortality and the nature of age processes, *Alfred Watson Memorial Lecture. J. Inst. Act.* 84:263–280.

—— (1958c). The longevity and mortality of thoroughbred mares. *J. Gerontol.* 13:342–350.

—— (1959a). Natural ageing and the effects of radiation. *Radiat. Res. (Suppl.),* 1, Suppl:226–234.

—— (1959b). Studies on the longevity and mortality of English thoroughbred horses. *Ciba Found. Colloquia on Ageing* 5:35–54.

—— (1959c). The longevity and mortality of thoroughbred stallions. *J. Gerontol.* 14:9–10.

—— (1960a). Darwin and Freud. *Lancet* II:107–111.

—— (1960b). Longevity and mortality in dogs of four breeds. *J. Gerontol.* 15:126–129.

—— (1960c). Nutrition and longevity in animals. *Proc. Nutr. Soc.* 19:125–129.

—— (1960d). The effect of age on growth-resumption in fish (*Lebistes*) checked by food restriction. *Gerontologia* 4:177–186.

—— (1961a). A life table for Arabian mares. *J. Gerontol.* 17:14.

—— (1961b). The expected rate of senescence and age-dependent mortality in fish. *Nature* 191:822–823.

—— (1961c). The longevity and mortality of a fish (*Lebistes reticulatus* Peters) in captivity. *Gerontologia* 5:209–222.

—— (1962). Survival curves of some birds in the London Zoo. *Ibis* 104:115–117.

—— (1966). The prevention of ageing in cells. *Lancet* II:1325–1329.

—— (1969). Test battery to measure aging rate in men. Lancet II:1411–1415.

—— (1971a). Neuromythology. *Nature (Lond.)* 229:282.

—— (1971b). Antioxidants and the control of ageing. *Nederl. Tijds. Gerontol.* 2:82–87.

—— (1972). Measuring the human aging rate. *Mech. Aging Devel.* 1:101–110.

Comfort, A., and Doljanski, F. (1959). The relation of size and age to rate of tail regeneration in *Lebistes reticulatus. Gerontologia* 2:266–283.

Comfort, A., Youhotsky-Gore, I., and Pathmanathan, K. (1971). The effects of ethoxyquin on the longevity of C3H strain mice. *Nature* (Lond.) 229:254–255.

Conant, R., and Hudson, R. G. (1949). Longevity records for reptiles and amphibia in the Philadelphia Zoological Garden. *Herpetologia (San Diego)* 5:1–8.

Conger, A. D., and Randolph, M. L. (1968). Is age-dependent genetic damage in seeds caused by free radicals? *Radiat. Bot.* 8:193–196.

Conklin, J. W., Upton, A. C., Christenberry, K. W., and McDonald, T. P. (1963). Comparative late effects of some radio-mimetic agents and of X-rays. *Radiat. Res.* 19:156–168.

Conrad, R. A. (1960). An attempt to quantify some clinical criteria of aging. *J. Gerontol.* 15:358–365.

Conway, W. G. (1961). Humming birds with wrinkles. *Animal Kingdom* (New York) 64:146–150.

Cooper, J. E. (1931). Life history of *Myxas glutinosa* (Muller). *J. Conchol.* 19:180.

Cori, C. I. (1925). Morphologie und Biologie von *Apsilus vorax*. *Z. Wiss. Zool.* 125:557.

Cotes, P. M., Reid, E., and Young, F. G. (1949). Diabetogenic action of pure anterior pituitary growth hormone. *Nature* (Lond.) 164:209.

Cotzias, G. C., Miller, S., Nicholosn, A. R., Matson, W. H., and Tang, L. C. (1974). Prolongation of lifespan in mice adapted to large amounts of L-dopa. *Proc. Natl. Acad. Sci.* (U.S.A.) 71:6.

Court Brown, W. M. (1962). Role of genetic change in neoplasia. *Br. Med. J.* 1:961–963.

Court Brown, W. M., and Doll, R. (1958). Expectation of life and mortality from cancer among British radiologists. *Br. Med. J.* 1958 2:181–189.

Coutelen, F. (1935). La longévité de la filaire *Loa loa* (Guyet 1778) et des embryons de filaires. *Bull. Soc. Path. Exot.* 28:126.

Coutelen, F., Razemon, P., and Biguet, J. (1950). La longévité des échinocoques—étude critique. *Ann. Parasitol.* 25:267.

Cowdry, E. V. (1952)., in Lansing, A. I.: *Problems of Ageing.* Baltimore: Williams and Wilkins Co.

Crabb, E. D. (1929). Growth of a pond-snail, *Limnaea stagnalis appressa,* as indicated by increase in shell size. *Biol. Bull.* 56:41–63.

Crocker, W. (1939). Ageing in plants, in Cowdry, E. V.: *Problems of Ageing,* 1st Ed. Baltimore: Williams & Wilkins.

Crowell, S. (1953). The regression-replacement cycle of hydranths of *Obelia* and *Campanularia*. *Physiol. Zool.* 26:319.

Crozier, W. J. (1914). The growth of the shell in the lamellibranch *Dosinia discus. Zool. Jb. (Anat.)* 38:577–583.

——— (1918a). Growth and duration of life in *Chiton tuberculatus. Proc. Natl. Acad. Sci. U.S.A.* 4:322–325.

——— (1918b). Growth of *Chiton tuberculatus* in different environments. *Proc. Nat. Acad. Sci.* 4:325–328.

Crumeyrolle-Arias, M., Scheib, D., and Aschheim, P. (1976). Light and electron microscopy of the ovarian interstitial tissue in the senile rat. *Gerontology* 22:185–204.

Cuénot, L. (1911). *La genèse des espèces animales.* Paris.

Cumming, R. B., Walton, M. F. and Winton, W. (1971). Modification of acute toxicity of mutagenic and carcinogenic chemicals in the mouse by antioxidant prefeeding. *Science* (in press).

Curtis, H. J. (1963). Biological mechanism underlying the ageing process. *Science* 141:686–694.

——— (1967a). Biological mechanisms of delayed radiation damage in mammals. *Curr. Top. Rad. Res.* 3; 140–173.

——— (1967b). Radiation and aging. *Symp. Soc. Exp. Biol.* 21:51–64.

Curtis, H. J., and Gebhard, L. (1958). Comparison of life shortening effects of toxic and radiation stresses. *Radiat. Res.* 9:104.

Cutler, R. G. (1972). Redundancy of critical genes in mammlian species of different maximum lifespans. *Proc. 25th Ann. Mtg. Geront. Soc. (U.S.A.),* Puerto Rico, p. 40.

Daiber, F. C. (1960). A technique for age determination in the skate, *Raja eglanteria. Copeia* (1962):258–260.

Dalderup, L. M., and Visser, W. (1971). Influence of extra sucrose, fats, protein, and of cyclamate in the daily food on the lifespan of rats. *Experientia* 27:519–521.

Dall, W. H. (1907). (no title). *Nautilus* 21:90.

Dalyell, J. G. (1848). *Rare and remarkable animals of Scotland,* II. London: Chapter 10.

Dam, H. (1967). *Carenze di vitamina E e rapporti con i lipidi alimentari Monogr. Centr. Stud. Lipid. Aliment.* 1.

Dance, S. P. (1958). Drought resistance in an African freshwater bivalve. *J. Conchol.* 24:281–283.

Daniel, C. W., De Ome, K. B., Young, J. T., Blair, P. B., and Faulkin, L. J. (1968). The in vivo lifespan of normal and preneoplastic mouse mammary glands. *Proc. Natl. Acad. Sci. (U.S.A.)* 6d:53.

Darányi, G. (1930). Fejlödés, fajfenntartás és öregedés természetben. *Term. Tud. Közl.* 62:305.

Darbishire, R. D. (1889). (no title). *J. Conchol.*6:101.

Darlington, C. D. (1948). The plasmagene theory of the origin of cancer. *Br. J. Cancer* 2:118.

Darlington, C. D., and Mather, K. (1949). *The Elements of Genetics.* London: Allen and Unwin.

Darwin, C. (1874). *The Descent of Man.* London: John Murray.

Dathe, H. (1935). *Zool. Garten (Leipzig)* 7:303.

Davaine, C. (1877). Traité des Entozooaires et des maladies vermineuses de l'homme et des animaux domestiques, 2nd Ed. Paris: Baillière.

David, K. (1925). Zur Frage der potentiellen Unsterblichkeit der Metazoen. *Zool. Anz.* 64:126.

Davidson, E. H. (1968). *Gene Activity in Early Development.* New York: Academic Press.

Davies, A. D. M. (1968). in *Interdisciplinary Topics in Gerontology* (eds. Chown, S. S., and Rieyel, K. F.). Basel.

Davies, D. (1975). *The Centenarians of the Andes.* London: Barry and Jenkins.

Davis, R. L., and Hayen, S. M. (1970). Biomedical studies of different aging populations. *Gerontologist* 10:3103.

Daw, R. H. (1961). The comparison of male and female mortality rates. *J. R. Statist. Soc.* 124(A):20–43.

Dawidoff, C. (1924). Sur le retour d'une Némerte, *Lineus lacteus,* en inanition, à un état embryonnaire. *C. R. Acad. Sci. (Paris)* 179:1222.

Day, A. J., Johnson, A. R., O'Halloran, M. W., and Schwartz, C. J. (1969). The effect of the antioxidant BHT on serum lipid and glycoprotein levels in the diet. *Aust. J. Exp. Biol. Med. Sci.* 37:295.

Dayton, S., Pearch, M. L., Hashimoto, S., Dixon, W. J., and Tomiyasu, U. (1969). *Am. Heart Assn. Monogr.* 25.

Deansley, R. (1938). The reproductive cycle of the golden hamster. *Proc. Zool. Soc. Lond.* 31.

De Carli, L. (1961). I cromosomi nella vecchiaia. *Georn. Geront.* 9:849–857.

Deck, R. S. (1936). Longevity of *Terrapene carolina* Linn. *Copeia* 160:179.

De Cosse, J. J., and Gelfant, S. (1968). Noncycling tumor cells: response to antilymphocytic serum. *Science* 162:698–699.

Deevey, E. S. (1947). Life tables for natural populations of animals. *Q. Rev. Biol.* 22:283.

Deevey, G. B., and Deevey, E. S., Jr. (1945). A life table for the black widow. *Trans. Conn. Acad. Arts Sci.* 36:115.

de Galan, E. H. K. (1966). Age and chromosomes. *Nature* (Lond.) 211:1324–1325.

Delage, Y. (1903). *L'Hérédité et Les Grandes Problèmes de la Biologie.* Paris.

De Leersnyder, M, and Hoestlandt, H. (1958). Extension du gastropode méditerranéen *Cochlicella acuta* (Mull), dans le sud-est de l'Angleterre. *J. Conchol.* 24:253–264.

Demange, E. (1886). Études cliniques et anatomopathologiques de la vieillesse. Paris: Baillière.

Denckla, W. D. (1974). Role of the pituitary and thyroid glands in the decline of minimal O_2 consumption with age. *J. Clin. Invest.* 53:572–581.

Denffer, D. V. (1948). Über einen Wachstumshemmstoff in älternden Diatomeenkulturen. *Biol. Zbl.* 67:7–13.

Denman, A. M., and Denman, E. J. (1970). Depletion of longlived lymphocytes in old New Zealand black mice. *Clin. Exp. Immunol.*

Dequeker, J. V., Baeyens, J. P., and Claessens, J. V. (1969). The significance of stature as a clinical measurement of aging. *J. Am. Geriatr. Soc.* 17:169–179.

De Silva, H. R. (1938). Age and highway accidents. *Sci. Mon.* 47:536–545.

Devi, A., Lindsay, P., Rainer, P. L., and Sarkar, N. K. (1966). Effects of age on some aspects of the synthesis of RNA. *Nature* (Lond.) 212:474–475.

De Witt, R. M. (1954). Reproductive capacity in a pulmonate snail, *Physagyrina* Say. *Am. Nat.* 88:159–164.

Deyl, Z. (1968). Macromolecular aspects of aging. *Exp. Gerontol.* 3:91–112.

Dhar, N. H. (1932). Senescence, an inherent property of animal cells. *Q. Rev. Biol.* 7:70.

Didlake, M. L. (1937). In *Culture Methods for Invertebrate Animals* (ed. Needham, J. G.). New York: Comstock, p. 244.

Diener, T. O. (1972). Is the scrapie agent a viroid? *Nature (New Biol.)* 235:218–219.

Dilman, V. M. (1971). Age-associated elevation of hypothalamic threshold of feedback control and its role in development, aging and disease. *Lancet* I:1211–1219.

—— (1976). In *Hypothalamus, Pituitary and Aging* (eds. Everitt, A., and Burgess, J. A.). Springfield, Ill.: C. C. Thomas Co.

Dimon, A. C. (1905). The mud snail *(Nassa obsoleta). Cold Spr. Harb. Monogr.* 2:1–48.

Dittmars, R. L. (1934). A review of the box turtles. *Zoologica (N.Y.)* 17:1.

Dobers, E. (1915). Biologie der Bdelloidea. *Int. Rev. Ges. Hydrobiol.,* Series 6, Suppl. 7.

Doljanski, F. (1960). The growth of the liver with special reference to mammals. *Int. Rev. Cytol.* 10:217–241.

Dolkas, C. B., Atlan, H., Dolkas, G., and Miquel, J. (1975). A mathematical analysis of the mortality kinetics of *Drosophila melanogaster* exposed to gamma radiation. *Mech. Ageing Dev.* 4:59–69.

Dominic, C. J. (1962). The ovary of the domestic pigeon, *Columbia livia,* with special reference to follicular atresia. *Proc. Ind. Sci. Congr.* 49:405.

Domm, L. V. (1934). The precocious development of sexual characters in the male chick by daily injections of thebin. *Anat. Rec.* 58:6.

Donaldson, C. L., Hulley, S. B., Vogel, J. M., Hattner, R. S., Bayers, J. H., and McMillan, D. (1970). Effect of prolonged bed-rest on bone mineral. *Metabolism* 19:1071–1084.

Donaldson, H. H. (1924). The rat. *Mem. Wistar Inst. Philadelphia,* No. 6.

Donisthorpe, H. (1936). The oldest insect on record. *Ent. Rec.* 48:1.

Dormandy, T. L. (1969). Biological rancidification. *Lancet* II:684–689.

Dorst, J. (1954). La longévité des Chiroptères. *Mammalia* 18:231–236.

Dougherty, E. C., and Nigon, V. (1956). The effect of acriflavin on the growth of the nematode *Caenorrhabditis elegans. Proc. XIV Intl. Cong. Zool. (Copenhagen, 1953).* p. 248-249.

Dowdeswell, W. H., Fisher, R. A., and Ford, E. B. (1940). The quantitative study of populations in the Lepidoptera. I. *Polyommatus icarus* Rott. *Ann. Eugen. (Camb.)* 10:123.

Draper, C. C., and Davidson, G. (1935). A new method of estimating the survival rate of anopheline mosquitoes in nature. *Nature* (Lond.) 172:503.

Dribben, I. S., and Wolfe, J. M. (1947). Structural changes in the connective tissue of the adrenal glands of female rats associated with advancing age. *Anat. Rec.* 98:557.

Driesch, H. (1941). Zur Problematik des Alterns. *Z. Altersforsch.* 3:26.

Drori, D., and Folman, Y. (1969). The effect of mating on the longevity of male. *Exp. Gerontol.* 4:263–266.

Dublin, L. I., Lotka, A. J., and Spiegelman, M. (1949). *Length of Life: A Study of the Life Table.* New York: Ronald Press.

Duetz, G. H. (1938). Comments on longevity and average exhibition ages during the year 1937. *Lab. Rep. Zool. Soc. (Philadelphia)* 66:31.

——— (1939). Revised tables of maximum exhibition periods for animals in the Philadelphia Collection. *Lab. Rep. Zool. Soc. (Philadelphia)* 67:22.

——— (1940). *Ibid.* 68:26.

——— (1942). *Ibid.* 70:23.

Dulbecco, R. (1970). Topoinhibition and serum requirement of transformed and untransformed cells. *Nature* 227:802–806.

Duncan, D. (1930). The incidence of secondary (Wallerian) degeneration in normal mammals compared in certain experimental and diseased individuals. *J. Comp. Neurol.* 104:1–16.

Dunham, H. H. (1938). Abundant feeding followed by restricted feeding and longevity in *Daphnia. Physiol. Zool.* 11:399.

Dunn, C. W. (1946). Endocrines in senescence. *Clinics (Phil.)* 5:847.

Du Noüy, P. L. (1916). Cicatrization of wounds. *J. Exp. Med.* 24:461.

——— (1932). Une mesure de l'activite physiologique. *C. R. Soc. Biol. (Paris)* 109:1227.

——— (1936). *Biological Time.* London: Methuen.

Duran-Reynals, F. (1940). Neutralization of tumor viruses by the blood of normal fowls of different ages. *Yale J. Biol. Med.* 13:61.

Durham, L., and Bennett, G. W. (1963). Age, growth and homing in the bullfrog. *J. Wildl. Manag.* 27:104–123.

Dykhuizen, D. (1974). Evolution of cell senescence, atherosclerosis and benign tumors. *Nature* (Lond.) 251:616–619.

Eaves, G. (1973). A consequence of normal diploid cell mortality. *Mech. Ageing Dev.* 2:19–21.

Ecke, D. H., and Kinney, A. R. (1956). Aging meadow mice *(Microtus californicus)* by observation of moult progression. *J. Mammal.* 37:249–254.

Edlén, A. (1937). Experimentelle Wachstumstudien an *Daphnia magna. Lunds Univ. Arsberatt,* Avd. 2, 34:1.

——— (1938). Geburt, Geschlechtsreife und Vermehrung in Beziehung zum Wachstumsverlauf bei *Daphnia magna. Arch. EntwMeck.* 137:804.

Edmonds, T. R. (1832). *Life Tables Founded upon the Discovery of a Numerical Law.* London: J. Duncan.

Edmondson, W. T. (1945a). Ecological studies of sessile Rotatoria. I. *Ecol. Monogr.* 14:15.

——— (1945b). Ecological studies of sessile Rotatoria. II. *Ecol. Monogr.* 15:141.

Edney, E. B., and Gill, R. W. (1968). Evolution of senescence and specific longevity. *Nature* (Lond.) 220:281–282.

Edney, J. M., and Allen, W. R. (1951). Age of the box turtle, *Terrapene carolina carolina. Copeia* 312:644.

Egami, N. (1971). Further notes on the life span of the teleost, *Oryzias latipes. Exp. Gerontol.* 6:379.

Egami, N., and Etoh, H. (1969). Lifespan data for the small fish *Oryzias latipes. Exp. Gerontol.* 4:127–130.

Eglis, A. (1960). Hardy rayed tortoise from Brooklyn. *Herpetologica* 16:28.

Eisner, N., and Etoh, H. (1967). Actuarial data for the Bengalese finch *(Lonchura striata)* in captivity. *Exp. Gerontol.* 2:187–189.

Ejiri, J. (1936). Studien über die Histologie der menschlichen Haut. II. Über die Alters und Geschlechtsverschiedenheiten der elastischen Fäsern. *Jpn. I. Derm. Urol.* 40:173.

Eldridge, J. C., and McPherson, J. C. (1974). Maturation of the negative feedback control of gonadotropin secretion in the female rat. *Endocrinology* 94:1536–1540.

Elman, R. (1953). Surgical problems in the aged, in *Problems of Ageing,* 2nd Ed. (ed. Cowdry, E. V.).

Elton, C. (1942). *Voles, Mice and Lemmings. Problems in Population Dynamics.* Oxford: Clarendon Press.

Emanuel, I., Sever, L. E., Milham, S., and Thuline, H. C. (1972). Accelerated aging in young mothers of children with Down's syndrome. *Lancet* II:361–362.

Emanuel, N. M., Obukhnova, L. K., Naidich, V. I., Murza, L. I., and Bunto, T. V. (1977) (no title) *Dokl. Acad. Nauk SSSR* 253:975–1060.

Engelhardt, G. H., and Struck, H. (1972). Effect of aging on wound healing. *Scand. J. Clin. Invest.* 29:10.

Engle, E. T. (1944). The menopause, an introduction. *J. Clin. Endocrinol.* 4:567.

Epstein, C. J., Martin, G. M., Schultz, A. L., and Motulsky, A. G. (1966). Werner's syndrome. *Medicine* 45: 177–221+.

Epstein, J., and Gershon, D. (1972). Studies on aging in nematodes (IV). The effect of antioxidants on cellular damage and lifespan. *Mech. Ageing Dev.* 1:257–264.

Epstein, J., Williams, J., and Little, J. B., (1973). Deficient DNA repair in progeria and senescent human cells (meeting abstr.). *Radiat. Res.* 55(3):527.

Ernest, M. (n.d.). *The Longer Life.* London: Adam and Co.

Escomel, E. (1939). La plus jeune mère du monde. *Presse Méd.* 47:875.

Everitt, A. (1976). In *Hypothalamus, Pituitary and Aging* (eds. Everitt, A., and Burgess, J. A.). Springfield, Ill.: C. C. Thomas Co.

Everitt, A. V. (1959). The effect of pituitary growth hormone on the aging male rat. *J. Gerontol.* 14:415–424.

——— (1971). Food intake, growth and the aging of collagen in rat tail tendon. *Gerontologia* 17:98–104.

——— (1973). The hypothalamic-pituitary control of ageing and age-related pathology. *Exp. Gerontol.* 8:265–278.

Everitt, A. V., and Burgess, J. A. (1976). *Hypothalamus, Pituitary and Aging.* Springfield, Ill: C. C. Thomas Co.

Evans, H. M., Simpson, M. E., and Li, C. H. (1948). The gigantism produced in normal rats by injection of the pituitary growth hormone. I. Body growth and organ changes. *Growth* 12:15.

Evans, H. M., Simpson, M. E., and Pencharz, R. I. (1939). Relation between the growth-producing effects of the pituitary and the thyroid hormone. *Endocrinology* 25:175.

Evans, R., Cowdry, E. V., and Nielson, P. E. (1943). Ageing of human skin. *Anat. Rec.* 86:545.

Fabris, N., Pierparli, W., and Sorkin, E. (1972). Lymphocytes, hormones and aging. *Nature* (Lond.) 240:557–559.

Fahim, M. S., Bennett, R., and Hall, D. G. (1970). Effect of DDT on the nursing neonate. *Nature* (Lond.) 228:1222–1223.

Failla, G. (1960). The aging process and somatic mutations. *The Biology of Aging, AIBS Symp., Publ.* No. 6, Washington, D.C., pp. 170–175.

Fairbridge, W. S. (1953). A population study of the Tasmanian "commercial" scallop, *Notovola meridionalis* (Tate). *Aust. J. Mar. Freshw. Res.* 4:1–40.

Falzone, J. A., Barrows, C. H., and Shock, N. W. (1959). Age and polyploidy of rat liver as measured by volume and D.N.A. content. *J. Gerontol.* 14:2–8.

Falzone, J. A., Samis, H. V., and Wulff, V. J. (1967). Cellular compensations and controls in the aging process. *J. Gerontol.* 22, Suppl:42–52.

Fanestil, D. D., and Banous, C. H. (1966). Aging in the rotifer. *J. Gerontol.* 20:462–469.

Fang, J. S., Jagiello, G., Ducayen, M., and Graffeo, J. (1975). Aging and X chromosome loss in the human ovary. *Obstet. Gynecol.* 45:455–458.

Farner, D. S. (1945). Age groups and longevity in the American robin. *Wilson Bull.* 57:56.

Fauré-Frémiet, E. (1953). L'hypothese de la senescence et les cycles de réorganisation nucleaire chez les Ciliés. *Rev. Suisse. Zool.* 60:426.

Federley, H. (1929). Über subletale und disharmonische Chromosomenkombinationen. *Hereditas* 12:271.

Feliksiak, S. (1947). Essai sur la régénération de la tête chez *Physa acuta* Dp. *Ann. Mus. Zool. Polon.* 14:7–11.

Felin, F. E. (1951). Growth characteristics of the poeciliid fish, *Platypoecilus maculatus. Copeia,* p. 15.

Fernandes, G., Yunis, E. J., and Good, R. A. (1976). Influence of diet on the survival of mice. *Proc. Natl. Acad. Sci. (U.S.A.)* 73:1279–1283.

Fernstrom, J. D. (1976). The effect of mutational factors on brain amino acid levels and monoamine synthesis. *Dev. Proc.* 35:1151–1156.

Ferrara, B. (1951). *La determinazione dell' età negli animali domestici.* Naples: Ed. Scientifiche Italiane.

Ferris, J. C. (1932). Comparison of the life histories of mictic and amictic females in the rotifer, *Hydatina senta. Biol. Bull. Wood's Hole* 63:442.

Ficino, M. (1498). *De triplici vita libri tres.* Venice.

Field, E. J. (1967). The significance of astroglial hypertrophy in scrapie, kuru, multiple sclerosis and old age. *Dtsch. Z. Nervenheulk.* 192:265–274.

Field, E. J., and Peat, A. (1971). Intranuclear inclusions in neurons and glia—study in aging mouse. *Gerontologist* 17:129.

Field, E. J., and Shenton, B. K. (1973). Emergence of scrapie-like antigenic properties in aging human tissues. *IRCS Int. Res. Comm.* (73-7) 5-10-4.

Finch, C. E. (1972). Enzyme activities, gene function and aging in mammals. *Exp. Gerontol.* 7:53.

———— (1973). Catecholamine metabolism in the brains of aging male mice. *Brain Res.* 52:261.

———— (1975). Aging and the regulation of hormones. *Adv. Med. Biol.* 61:229–238.

———— (1976). The regulation of physiological changes during mammalian aging. *Q. Rev. Biol.* 51:49–83.

Findley, T. (1949). Role of neurohypophysis in the pathogenesis of hypertension and some allied disorders associated with ageing. *Am. J. Med.* 7:70.

Fischer, P. H. (1931). Recherches sur la vie ralentie de l'Escargot (*H. pomatia* Linn). *J. Conchyl.* 75:5–100, 111–200.

Fischer-Piette, E. (1939). Sur la croissance et la longevité de *Patella vulgata* L. en fonction du milieu. *J. Conchyl.* 83:303.

Fiscus, C. H. (1961). Growth in the Steller sea lion. *J. Mammal.* 42:218–223.

Fisher, I. (1923). Report on National Vitality, Its Wastes and Conservation, Washington, D.C.

Fitch, H. S. (1956). Early sexual maturity and longevity under natural conditions in the Great Plains narrow-mouthed frog. *Herpetologica* 12:281–282.

Fitch, J. E. (1965). A relatively unexploited population of Pismo clams, *Fed. Proc. Tivela Stultorum* 36:309–312.

Fitzgerald, P. H. (1975). A mechanism of X chromosome aneuploidy in lymphocytes of aged women. *Humangenetik* 28:153–158.

Fitzinger, L. J. F. J. (1853). *Versuch einer Geschichte der Menagerien des Österreichisch-Kaiserlichen Hofes,* Vienna.

Fitzpatrick, T. B., Szabo, G., and Mitchell, R. E. (1964). Age changes in the human melanocyte system. *Adv. Biol. Skin* 6:35–50.

Flower, S. S. (1922). Longevity of molluscs. *Cairo Sci. J.* 10:115.

—— (1925). Contributions to our knowledge of the duration of life in vertebrate animals. I. Fishes. Ibid., 247. II. Batrachians. Ibid., 269. III. Reptiles. Ibid., 911. IV. Birds. Ibid., 1365.

—— (1931). V. Mammals. Ibid., 145.

—— (1935). Further notes on the duration of life in animals. I. Fishes. Ibid., 265.

—— (1936). II. Amphibians. Ibid., 369.

—— (1937). III. Reptiles. Ibid., 1.

—— (1938). IV. Birds. *Proc. Zool. Soc. (Lond.)* A:195.

—— (1945). Persistent growth in the tortoise, *Testudo graeca,* for 39 years, with other notes concerning the species, *Proc. Zool. Soc. (Lond.)* 114:451.

Flyger, V. F. (1958). Tooth impressions as an aid to the determination of age in deer. *J. Wildl. Manag.* 22:442–443.

Foà, C. (1900). La greffe des ovaires en rélation avec quelques questions de biologie générale. *Arch. Ital. Biol.* 34:43.

——(1901). Sur la greffe des ovaires. *Arch. Ital. Biol.* 35:364.

Földi, M., Zoltan, O. T., and Gyori, L. (1970). Über die Wirkung von Kavain und Mg. Orotat auf die funktionellen Störungen bei den experimentellen lymphogenen Enzephalopathie. *Z. Gerontol.* 3:97–108.

Forbes, G. B., and Reina, J. C. (1970). Adult lean body mass declines with age: some longitudinal observations. *Metabolism* 19:653–663.

Forbes, G. S., and Crampton, H. E. (1942). The effect of population density upon growth and size in *L. palustris. Biol. Bull.* 82:283–289.

Forster, A. (1945). Longevity. *Br. Med. J.* II:545.

Foster, T. D. (1932). Observations on the life history of a fingernail shell of the genus *Sphaerium. J. Morphol.* 53:473–497.

—— (1936). Size of shell in land snails of the genus *Polygyra* with particular reference to major and minor varieties. *Am. Midl. Nat.* 17:978–982.

Frank, F. (1956). Höhes Alter bei der europäischen Feldspitzmaus *Crocidina 1. leucodon* (Hermann, 1780). *Saugetierk, Mitt.* 4:31.

Franks, L. M., Wilson, P. D., and Whelan, R. D. (1974). The effects of age on total DNA and cell number in the mouse brain. *Gerontologia* 20:21–26.

Frantz, A. G., Habif, D. V., Hyman, G. A., and Suh, H. K. (1972). *Clin. Res.* 20:234.

Fraser, C. McL. (1931). Notes on the ecology of the cockle *Cardium corbis* Martyn. *Trans. R. Soc. Can.* 25:59.

Fraser, H., Smith, W., and Gray, E. W. (1970). Ultrastructural morphology of cytoplasmic inclusions within neurons of aging mice. *J. Neurol. Sci.* 11:123–127.

Fraser, R. (1943). Sudden senescence. *Lancet* II:275.

Freedman, A. (1976). In *Hypothalamus, Pituitary and Aging* (eds. Everitt, A., and Burgess, J. A.). Springfield, Ill.: C. C. Thomas Co.

Fremont-Smith, F. (1965). In *Aging and Levels of Biological Organization.* (eds. Brues, A. M., and Sacher, G. A.) Chicago: Univ. Press.

Fretter, V. (1947). The structure and life history of some minute prosobranchs of rock pools. *J. Mar. Biol. Ass. (U.K.)* 27:597–623.

Freud, J., Levie, L. H., and Kroon, D. B. (1939). Observations on growth (chorionotrophic) hormone and localization of its point of attack. *J. Endocrinol.* 1:56.

Freud, J., and Uyldert, E. (1947). A new idea about senility. *Acta Brev. Neerl. Physiol.* 14:18.

Freudenberg, K. (1951). Die natürliche Lebensdauer der Menschen. *Z. Altersforsch.* 5:241.

Friedel, E. (1880). Die lebenden Wassertiere auf der Internationalen Fischerei-Ausstellung zu Berlin im Jahr 1880. *Zool. Gart.* 21:323.

Friedenthal, H. (1910). Über die Gultigkeit der Massenwirkung für den Energieumsatz der lebendigen Substanz; II. *Zbl. f. Physiol.* 24:321–327.

Friedman, S. M., and Friedman, C. L. (1964). Prolonged treatment with pituitary powder in aged rats. *Exp. Gerontol.* 1:37–48.

Frigorio, N. A., and Sachur, G. A. (1968). The determination of whale lifespans. *U.S.A.E.C.* ANL-7535:116–118.

Frisch, R. (1973). Influences on age at menarche. *Lancet* I:1007.

Fritsch, R. H. (1953). Die Lebensdauer von *Daphnia* spec. bei verschiedener Ernährung, usw. *Z. Wiss. Zool.* 157:35.

——— (1956). Drei Orthokolone von *Daphnia magna* Straus ohne Lansing-Effekt. *Publ. Stat. Zool. Napoli* 28:214–224.

——— (1959). Herzfrequenz, Häutungsstudien und Lebensdauer bei Männchen von *D. magna* Straus. *Z. Wiss. Zool.* 161:266–276.

Fritsch, R. H., and Meijering, M. P. D. (1958). Die Herzfrequenz-Kurve von *Daphnia magna* Straus innerhalb einzelner Haütungsstudien. *Experientia* 14:346–347.

Frohawk, F. W. (1935). Feeding butterflies in captivity. *Entomologist* 68:184.

Frolkis, V. (1967). Adaptive mechanism of the aging organism. *Symp. Inst. Gerontol. (Kiev).*

——— (1976). *Hypothalamus, Pituitary and Aging* (eds. Everitt, A., and Burgess, J. A.). Springfield, Ill.: C. C. Thomas Co.

Frost, W. E. (1943). The natural history of the minnow, *Phoxinus phoxinus. J. Anim. Ecol.* 12:139.

——— (1954). The food of pike, *Esox lucius* L. in Windermere. *J. Anim. Ecol.* 23:339.

Frost, W. E., and Kipling, C. (1949). The determination of age and growth of the pike (*Esox lucius* L.) from scales and opercular bones. *J. Cons. Exp. Mer.* 24:314–341.

Frost, W. E., and Smyly, W. J. P. (1952). The brown trout of a moorland fishpond. *J. Anim. Ecol.* 21:71.

Fry, R. J. M., Grahn, D., Griem, M. L., and Rust, J. H. (1969). *Late effects of radiation.* London: Taylor & Francis.

Fukuda, M., and Sibatani, A. (1953). Biochemical studies on the numbers and composition of liver cells in post-natal growth of the rat. *Jpn. Biochem. J.* 40:95.

Furth, J., Upton, A. C., Christenberry, K. W., Benedict, W. H., and Moshman, J. (1954). Some late effects in mice of ionizing radiation from an experimental nuclear detonation. *Radiology* 63:562–570.

Gaillard, P. J. (1942). *Hormones Regulating Growth and Development in Embryonic Explants.* Paris: Hermann.

Gain, W. H. (1889). A few notes on the food and habits of slugs and snails. *Naturalist,* pp. 55–59.

Galea, P. H. (1936). Longevity of a mule. *Field,* p. 1556.

Galtsoff, P. S. (1952). Staining of growth rings in the vertebrae of Tuna (*Thynnus thynnus*). *Copeia,* p. 103.

Gardner, G., and Hurst, H. (1933). Life-tables for White Leghorn chickens in the State of Utah. *Proc. Utah Acad. Sci.* 10:149.

Gardner, T. S. (1948). The effect of yeast nucleic acid on the survival time of 600 day old albino mice. *J. Gerontol.* 1:445.

Gardner, T. S., and Forbes, F. B. (1946). The effect of sodium thiocyanate and yeast nucleic acid on the survival time of 700 day old albino mice. *J. Gerontol.* 1:453.

Gardner, W. K. (1952). Some endocrinological aspects of ageing. *J. Gerontol.* 7:293.

Gates, W. H. (1926). The Japanese waltzing mouse. *Publ. Carneg. Instit.* 337:83.

Gaunt, I. F., Fenner, G., Fairweather, F. A., and Gilbert, D. (1965). Liver response tests IV. Application to short-term feeding studies with RHT and BHA. *Food Cosmet. Toxicol.* 3:433–443.

Gedye, J. L., Exton Smith, A. N., and Wedgwood, J. (1972). A method of measuring mental performance in the elderly. *Age and Aging* 1:74–80.

Gedye, J. L., and Wedgwood, J. (1969). The use of an interactive computer terminal for assessing the mental state of geriatric patients. *Proc. 8th Intl. Gerontol. (Washington),* abst. 134.

Geiser, S. W. (1924–1925). The differential death-rate of the sexes among animals. *Wash. Univ. Stud.* 12:73.

Geldiay, R. (1957). Studies on local populations of the freshwater limpet Ancylus fluviatilis (Muller). *J. Anim. Ecol.* 25:389–402.

Gelfant, S., and Graham-Smith J. G. (1972). Aging: noncycling cells—an explanation. *Science* 178:357–361.

Georgiana, M. (1949). Longevity of the parasitic wasp, *Habrobracon uglandis* Ashmead. *Am. Nat.* 83:39.

Gerking, S. D. (1957). Evidence of aging in natural populations of fishes. *Gerontologia* 1:287–305.

—— (1959). Physiological changes accompanying ageing in fishes. *Ciba Found. Colloquia on Ageing* 5:181–207.

Gerschman, R. (1959). Oxygen effects in biological systems. *Proc. XXI Intl. Congr. Cienc. Physiol. (Buenos Aires)* 1:1.

Gerschman, R., Gilbert, D. L., and Caccamise, D. (1955). Effect of various substances on survival times of mice exposed to different high oxygen tensions. *Am. J. Physiol.* 192:563–571.

Gerschman, R., Gilbert, D. L., Nye, S. W., and Fenn, W. O. (1955). Role of antioxidants and glutathione in oxygen poisoning. *Fed. Proc.* 14:56.

Gershon, D. (1970). Studies on aging in nematodes. I. The nematode as a model organism for aging research. *Expl. Gerontol.* 5:7–12.

Gershon, H., and Gershon, D. (1970). Detection of inactive enzyme molecules in aging of the organism. *Nature* 227:1214–1217.

—— (1973). Inactive enzyme molecules in aging mice liver aldolase: *Proc. Natl. Acad. Sci.* 7:909–913.

Geschwind, I. I., Alferd, M., and Schooley, C. (1959). Liver regeneration and hepatic polyploidy in the hypophysectomised rat. *Exp. Cell. Res.* 15:232–235.

Gey, G. O. (1952). Cellular gerontologic research. *J. Gerontol.* 7:294.

Geyer, D. (1909). *Die Weichtiere Deutschlands.* Stuttgart: G. Thieme.

Gibbs, C. J., Gajdusek, D. C., Asher, D. M., Alpers, M., Beck, E., Daniel, P. M., and Matthews, W. B. (1968). Creuzfeld-Jakob Disease: transmission to the chimpanzee. *Science* 161:3839.

Gibson, E. G. (1977). Skylab 4 crew observations. In *Biomedical results from Skylab,* NASA SP 377.

Gilbert, D., and Goldberg, L. (1965). Liver response tests III. Liver enlargement and stimulation of microsomal processing activity. *Food Cosmet. Toxicol.* 3:417–432.

Giles, J. S., and Everitt, A. V. (1967). The role of thyroid and of food intake in the aging of collagen fibres. *Gerontologia* 13:65–74.

Gillman, T. (1962). in *Structural Aspects of Ageing.* (ed. Bourne, G.). London: Pitman Medical.

Gitman, L. (1969). *Multiphasic Health Screening Center Manual.* Brookdale Hospital Center, N.Y.

Gley, E. (1922). Senescence et endocrinologie. *Bull. Acad. Med. (Paris)* 87:285.

Glezina, O. M. (1939). Age changes in oxidation-reduction processes in the muscle tissue of birds. *Biokhim. Zh.* 13:105.

Glinos, A. D., and Bartlett, E. G. (1951). The effect of regeneration on the growth potential *in vitro* of rat liver at different ages. *Cancer Res.* 11:164.

Glinos, A. D., and Gey, G. O. (1952). Humoral factors involved in the induction of liver regeneration in the rat. *Proc. Soc. Exp. Biol. Med.* 80:421.

Glover, J. W. (1921). *U.S. Life Tables, 1890, 1901, 1910 and 1901–10.* Washington, D.C.: U.S. Bureau of Census, p. 301.

Goddard, J. P., Weiss, J. J., and Wheeler, C. M. (1969). Error frequency during *in vitro* transcription of poly-y with y-irradiated RNA polymerase. *Nature* 222:670–671.

Goetsch, W. (1922). Lebensdauer und geschlechtige Fortpflanzung bei Hydra. *Biol. Zbl.* 42:231.

———(1925). Beiträge zum Unsterblichkeitsproblem der Metazoen. V. *Biol. Zbl.* 45:192.

———(1940). *Vergleichende Biologie der Insektenstaaten.* Leipzig.

Gofman, J. W., Minkler, J. L., and Tandy, R. K. (1967). A specific common chromosomal pathway for the origin of human malignancy. *Resp. Univ. Calif. Radiat. Lab. (Livermore, Calif.),* UCRL 50356.

Goldschmidt, E. (1953). Multiple sex chromosome mechanisms and polyploidy in animals. *J. Genet.* 51:434–440.

Goldschmidt, J., Hoffman, R., and Doljansky, L. (1937). Étude comparative sur la duree de la période de latence pour la croissance des tissus embryonnaires et adultes explantés *in vitro. C. R. Soc. Biol. (Paris)* 126:380.

Goldschmidt, R. (1970). In vivo degradation of nonsense fragments in *E. coli. Nature* 228:1151–1154.

Goldsmith, E. D. (1942). Sexuality in *Dugesia trigrina* (syn. *Planaria maculata*). *Nature* 150:351.

Goldsmith, E. D., Nigrelli, R. F., Gordon, R. S., Charipper, H. A., and Gordon, M. (1944). Effect of thiourea upon fish development. *Endocrinology* 35:132.

Goldstein, S. (1969). Survival of cultured cells in progeria. *Lancet* I:424.

——— (1971). The role of DNA repair in aging of fibroblasts from xeroderma pigment and normals. *Proc. Soc. Exp. Biol. Med.* 137:730–734.

——— (1974). Aging in vitro: growth of cultured cells from Galapagos tortoise. *Exp. Cell. Res.* 83:297–362.

Goldstein, S., and Lin, C. C. (1971). Rescue of senescent human fibroblasts by hybridisation with cultured hamster cells. *J. Clin. Invest.* 50:A37.

Goldstein, S., and Moerman, E. (1975). Heat-labile enzymes in skin fibroblasts from subjects with progeria. *N. Engl. J. Med.* 292:1305–1309.

Goldzieher, J. W. (1949). The direct effect of steroids on the senile human skin. *J. Gerontol.* 4:104.

Goldzieher, J. W., and Goldzieher, M. A. (1950). Effect of steroids on the ageing skin. *J. Gerontol.* 5:385.

Gondös, M. (1965). *Proc. Intl. Congr. Gerontology (Budapest).* Budapest: Hungarian Academy of Sciences.

Gonzales, B. M. (1923). Experimental studies on the duration of life. VIII. The influence upon duration of life of certain mutant genes of *Drosophila melanogaster. Am. Nat.* 57:289.

Good, P., and Watson, D. (1973). Pairwise loss of mitotic ability by human diploid fibroblasts. *Exp. Gerontol.* 8:147–152.

Goodbody, I. (1962). The biology of *Ascida nigra* (Savigny); I. Survival and mortality in an adult population. *Biol. Bull.* 122:40–51.

Goodman, R. M., Fechheimer, N. S., Miller, F., et al. (1969). Chromosomal alterations in three age groups of human females. *Am. J. Med. Sci.* 258:26–34.

Gordon, H. A., Bruckmen-Kardoss, G., and Wastmann, B. S. (1966). Aging in germfree mice. Life-tables and lenius observed at natural death. *J. Gerontol.* 21:380.

Gordon, P. (1971). Molecular approaches to the drug enhancement of deteriorated functioning in the aged. *Adv. Geront. Res.* 3:199–248.

Gosden, R. G., and Walters, D. E. (1974). Effects of low-dose X-irradiation on chromosomal non-disjunction in aged mice. *Nature* 248:54–55.

Gould, G. M., and Pyle, W. T. (1898). *Anomalies and Curiosities of Medicine.* London: Rebman.

Gould, R. T. (1945). *Enigmas,* 2nd Ed. London: Bles.

Gowen, J. W. (1931). On chromosome balance as a factor in duration of life. *J. Gen. Physiol.* 14:447.

Gower, J., and Stadler, J. (1956). Life-spans of different strains of mice as affected by acute irradiation with 100 PKV X-rays. *J. Exp. Zool.* 132:133–156.

Grad, B. (1953). Changes in oxygen consumption and heart rate of rats during growth and ageing; role of the thyroid gland. *Am. J. Physiol.* 174:481.

Graham, A., and Fretter, V. (1946–1947). The life history of *Patina pellucida* Linn. *J. Mar. Biol. Ass. (U.K.)* 26:590–601.

Grahame, R., and Holt, P. J. L. (1969). The influence of aging on the in vivo elasticity of human skin. *Gerontologia* 15:121–139.

Grahn, D., and Hamilton, K. (1958). Survival of inbred mice under daily γ-irradiation as related to control survival and the genetic consitution. *Radiat. Res.* 9:122–123.

Grave, B. H. (1928). Natural history of the shipworm, *Teredo navalis,* at Wood's Hole, Mass. *Biol. Bull.* 55:260–282.

——— (1933). Rate of growth, age at sexual maturity and duration of life of certain sessile organisms at Wood's Hole, Mass. *Biol. Bull.* 65:375–386.

——— (1934). The gene in pathology. *Cold Spr. Harb. Symp. Quant. Biol.* 2:128.

Green, J. (1954). Size and reproduction in *Daphnia magna. Proc. Zool. Soc. (Lond.),* p. 535.

——— (1957). The growth of *Scrobicularia plana* (da Costa) in the Gwendraeth estuary. *J. Mar. Biol. Ass. (U.K.)* 36:41–47.

——— (1972). Vitamin E and the biological antioxidant theory. *Ann. N.Y. Acad. Sci.* 203:29–44.

Greenberg, L. J., and Yunis, E. J. (1973). Immunologic control of aging: a possible primary event. *Gerontologia* 18:247–266.

Greene, R. (1959). A remedy for ageing. *Lancet* I:786.

Greene, R., and Paterson, A. S. (1943). Sudden senescence. *Lancet* II:158.

Greenwood, A. W. (1932). The value of progeny in relation to age of dam. *Harper-Adams Util. Poult. J.* 17:478.

Greenwood, M., and Irwin, J. O. (1939). The biostatistics of senility. *Hum. Biol.* 11:1.

Gregerman, R. I. (1959). Adaptive enzyme responses in the senescent rat: tryptophan peroxidase and tyrosine transaminase. *Am. J. Physiol.* 197:63–64.

Greville, T. N. E. (1946). *United States Life Tables and Actuarial Tables, 1939–1941.* Washington, D.C.: U.S. Bureau of Census.

Grier, N. M. (1922). Observations on the rate of growth of the shell of the lake-dwelling freshwater mussels. *Amer. Midl. Nat.* 8:129–148.

Griffin, C. E. (1928). The life history of automobiles. *Michigan Business Studies* (Univ. Mich.), 1.

Griffiths, J. T., and Tauber, O. E. (1942). Fecundity, longevity and parthenogenesis of the American roach *(Periplaneta americana* L.) *Physiol. Zool.* 15:196.

Griffiths, T. R. (1973). A new unifying theory for the initiation of aging mechanisms and processes. *Mech. Ageing Dev.* 2:295–307.

Grimm, H. (1944). Der Lebenslauf der Organismen nebst kritischen Betrachtungen zu meiner Wachstumstheorie. *Z. Altersforsch.* 4:237.

——— (1949). Wachstumsfordernde und wachstumshemmende Stoffe im menschlichen Blut-serum. *Z. Altersforsch.* 5:197.

Grmek, M. D. (1958). On ageing and old age—basic problems and historic aspects of gerontology and geriatrics. *Monogr. Biol.* 5, No. 2.

Grobstein, C. (1947). The role of androgen in the declining regenerative capacity during morphogenesis of the *Platypoecilus maculatus* gonopodium. *J. Exp. Zool.* 106:313.

Gross, J. (1925). Versuche und Beobachtungen über die Biologie der Hydriden. *Biol. Zool.* 45:192.

—— (1962). In *Structural Aspects of Ageing* (ed. Bourne, G.). London: Pitman Medical.

Gross, J., and Schmitt, F. O. (1948). The structure of human skin collagen as studied with the electron microscope. *J. Exp. Med.* 88:555.

—— (1950). Connective tissue fine structure and some methods for its analysis. *J. Gerontol.* 5:343.

Grüneberg, H. (1951). *The genetics of the mouse.* The Hague.

—— (1954). Variation in inbred lines of mice. *Nature* 173:674.

Guberlet, J. E. (1928). Observations on the spawning habits of *Melibe leonina* (Gould). *Pub. Puget Sd. Mar. Biol. Sta.* 6:263–270.

Gudernatsch, J. F. (1912). Feeding experiments on tadpoles. I. The influence of certain organs given as food on differentiation. *Arch. EntwMeck. Org.* 35:57.

Guilbert, H. R., and Goss, H. (1932). Some effects of restricted protein intake on the oestrous cycle and gestation in rats. *J. Nutr.* 5:215.

Guilloud, N. B. (1978). In (eds., Finch, C. E., and Hayflick, L.) *Handbook of the biology of aging.* New York: Van Nostrand, p. 319.

Gumbel, E. J. (1938). La durée extrême de la vie humaine. *Actualités Sci. Indust.* 520:1.

Gurdon, J. B. (1962). Adult frogs derived from nuclei of single somatic cells. *Dev. Biol.* 4:256–273.

Gurney, J. H. (1899). On the comparative ages to which birds live. *Ibis,* pp. 19–42.

Guthrie, D. M. (1953). *Personal communication.*

Gutsell, J. S. (1930). Natural history of the bay scallop. *Bull. U.S. Bur. Fish.* 46:569–632.

Haas, F. (1941). Records of large freshwater mussels. *Zool. Sci. Rep. Field Mus. Nat. Hist.* 24:259–270.

Habermehl, K. H. (1961). *Die Altersbestimmung bei Haustieren, Pelztieren und beim jagdbaren Wild.* Berlin and Hamburg: Parey.

Haemmerling, J. (1924). Die ungeschlechtliche Fortpflanzung und Regeneration bei *Aeolosoma lemprichii. Zool. Jb.* (1 Abt.) 41:581.

Haggvist, G. (1948). Nervenfaserkaliber bei Tieren verschiedener Grosse. *Anat. Anz.* 96:398–412.

Hakh, I. W. D., and Westling, E. H. (1934). A possible cause of old age. *Science* 79:231.

Haldane, J. B. S. (1941). *New Paths in Genetics.* London.

—— (1949). Paternal and fraternal correlations of fitness. *Ann. Genet.* 14:288.

—— (1953). Some animal life tables. *J. Inst. Actu.* 79:351.

Hall, D. A. (1963). Age changes in the water content of human plasma. *Geront. Clin.* 10:193–200.

—— (1966). Elastase and the aging subject. *Proc. 7th Intl. Congr. Gerontol. (Vienna)* Abst. 40.

—— (1968). The aging of connective tissue. *Exp. Gerontol.* 3:77–90.

Hall, G. O., and Marble, D. R. (1931). The relationship between the first year egg production and the egg production of later years. *Poultry Sci.* 10:194.

Halpern, B., Emerit, I., Housset, E., and Feingold, J. (1972). Possible autoimmune processes related to chromosomal abnormalities (breakage) in NZB mice. *Nature (New Biol.)* 235:214–215.

Hamai, I. (1937). Some notes on relative growth, with specific reference to the growth of limpets. *Sci. Rep. Res. Inst. Tohoku Univ.* [*Biol.*] 12:71–95.

Hamburger, C. (1948). Normal urinary excretion of neutral 17-ketosteroids with special reference to age and sex variations. *Acta Endocrinol.* 1:19.

Hamilton, J. B. (1948). The role of testicular secretions as indicated by the effects of castration in man and by studies of pathological conditions and the short life span associated with maleness. *Recent Prog. Horm. Res.* 3:257.

Hamilton, J. B., Catchpole, H. R., and Hawke, C. C. (1944). Titres of urinary gonadotropins in old eunuchs. *Anat. Rec.* 88:435.

——— (1945). Titres of gonadotropins in urine of aged eunuchs. *J. Clin. Endocrinol.* 5:203.

Hamilton, J. B., and Hamilton, H. B. (1948). Aging in apparently normal men. I. Urinary titres of ketosteroids and of hydroxyketosteroids. *J. Clin. Endocrinol.* 8:433.

Hamilton, J. B., Hamilton, H. B., and Mestler, G. E. (1954). Ageing in apparently normal men. II. Androgenic activity of urinary ketosteroids and of their alpha and beta fractions. *J. Clin. Endocrinol. Metab.* 14:139.

Hamilton, J. B., Terada, H., and Mestler, G. E. (1955). Studies of growth throughout the life-span in Japanese: growth and size of nails and their relationship to age, sex, hereditary and other factors. *J. Gerontol.* 10:401–415.

Hamilton, W. D. (1966). The moulding of senescence by natural selection. *J. Biol.* 12:12–45.

Hamilton, W. J. (1940). The biology of the smoky shrew (*Sorex fumeus fumeus* Miller). *Zoologica (N.Y.)* 25:473.

Hammond, E. C., Garfinkel, L., and Seidman, H. (1971). Longevity of parents and grandparents in relation to coronary heart disease. *Circulation* 43:31–44.

Hammond, J., and Marshall, F. H. (1952). The life cycle. in *Physiology of Reproduction* (ed. Marshall, F. H.). London: Longmans.

Handler, P. (1961). Biochemical consideration of relationships between effects of time and of radiation on living systems. *Fed. Proc.* 20, Suppl. 8:8–13.

Hanna, M. G., Nettesheim, P., Ogden, L., and Makinodan, T. (1967). Reduced immune potential of aged mice. *Proc. Soc. Exp. Biol. Med. (N.Y.)* 125:882–886.

Hansard, S. L., Comar, C. L., and Davis, G. K. (1954). Effects of age upon the physiological behaviour of calcium in cattle. *Am. J. Physiol.* 177:383.

Haranghy, L., and Bal ́asz, A. (1964). Aging and rejuvenation in planarians. *Exp. Gerontol.* 1:77–84.

Haranghy, L., Balász, A., and Burg, M. (1962). Histological and histochemical analysis in mussels (*Anodonta*) of the involution of the genitals. *Proc. 1st Intern. Congr. Hungarian Gerontologists (Budapest)*.

Harman, D. (1955). Aging—a theory based on free radical and information theory. *U.C.R.L.* Publ. 3078, Univ. of Calif.

——— (1956). Aging—a theory based on free radical and radiation chemistry. *J. Gerontol.* 11:298–300.

——— (1957). Prolongation of the normal life span by radiation protection chemicals. *J. Gerontol.* 12:257–263.

——— (1961). Prolongation of the normal life span and inhibition of spontaneous cancer by antioxidants. *J. Gerontol.* 16:247–254.

——— (1962). in *Biological Aspects of Aging* (ed. Shock, et al.). New York: Columbia Univ. Press.

——— (1965). The free radical theory of aging: effects of age on serum copper levels. *J. Gerontol.* 20:151–154.

——— (1968a). Free radical theory of aging: effect of free radical reaction inhibitors on the mortality rate of male LAF$_1$ mice. *J. Gerontol.* 23:476–482.

——— (1968b). Free radical theory of aging: effect of free radical inhibitors on the lifespan of LAF$_1$ mice. *Gerontologist* 6:13.

——— (1968c). Relation between anti-aging and chronic-radiation protection agents. *Radiat. Res.* 35:547.

——— (1971). Free-radical theory of aging: effect of amount and degree of unsaturation of dietary fat on mortality rate. *J. Gerontol.* 26:451–456.

Harman, D., Curtis, H. J., and Tilley, J. (1970). Chromosomal aberrations in liver cells of mice fed free-radical reaction inhibitors. *J. Gerontol.* 25:17–19.

Harms, J. W. (1926). *Verjungung des Lebens.* Senckenberg-Bucher II. Berlin: Bermuhler.

——— (1949). Altern und Somatod der Zellverbandstiere. *Z. Alterforsch.* 5:73.

Harms, W. (1912). Beobachtungen über den natürlichen Tod der Tiere. I. Hydroides pectinata. *Zool. Anz.* 40:117.

Harris, J. A., and Benedict, F. G. (1921). A biometric study of basal metabolism in man. *Carnegie Inst. Wash. Publ.,* p. 303.

Harrison, B. J., and Holliday, R. (1967). Senescence and the fidelity of protein synthesis in Drosophila. *Nature* 213:990–991.

Hart, R. W., and Setlow, R. B. (1974). Correlation between deoxyribonucleic acid excision-repair and life-span in a number of mammalian species. *Proc. Natl. Acad. Sci.* 71.

Hartlaub, C. (1916). Über das Altern einer Kolonie von *Syncoryne. Wiss. Meersuntersuch.* 11.

Hartley, W. G. (1958). The microscopical study of salmon scales. *J. Queckett Micr. Club* 28:95–98.

Hartman, M. (1921). Untersuchungen über die Morphologie und Physiologie des Formwechsels der Phytomonadinen (Volvocales). III. Mitt. Die dauernd agame Zucht von *Eudorina elegans:* experimentelle Beiträge zum Befruchtungs—und Todproblem. *Arch. Protistenk.* 43:7.

Hartzell, A. (1945). Thiourea (thiocarbamide)—adult life span feeding experiments in rats. *Conts. Boyce Thompson Inst.* 13:501.

Harvey, P. A. (1934). In *Termites and Termite Control,* (ed. Kogoid, C. A.). Berkeley: Univ. Calif. Press, p. 227.

Hase, A. (1909). Über die deutschen Süsswasserpolypen *Hydra fusca. Arch. f. Rassen-u. Gesellschafts-Biologie* 6:721.

Hašek, M. (1953). Vegetative hybridization in animals through embryo parabiosis. *Česk. Biol.* 2:267.

Haskell (1948–1949). No title. *Ann. Rep. Mar. Lab. (Texas Game and Fish Commission),* pp. 212–217.

Haskins, H. H. (1955). Age determination in molluscs. *Trans. N.Y. Acad. Sci.* 16:300–304.

Hay, R. J. (1967). Cell and tissue culture in aging research. *Adv. Geront. Res.* 2:121–158.

Hay, R. J., Menzies, R. A., Morgan, H. P., and Strehler, B. L. (1968). The division potential of cells in continuous growth. *Exp. Gerontol.* 3:35–44.

Hay, R. J., and Strehler, B. L. (1967). The limited growth span of cell strains isolated from the chick embryo. *Exp. Gerontol.* 2:123–136.

Hayflick, L. (1965). The limited *in vitro* lifetime of human diploid cell strains. *Exp. Cell Res.* 37:614–636.

——— (1975). Cell biology of aging. *Bioscience* 25:629–637.

Hayflick, L., and Moorhead, P. S. (1961). The serial cultivation of human diploid cell strains. *Exp. Cell Res.* 25:585–621.

Hazay, J. (1881). Die Mollusken-Faune von Budapest. *Malak. Blätt* 3:1–69, 160–182; 4:3–224.

Heath, H. (1905). The breeding habits of chitons of the Californian coast. *Zool. Anz.* 29:390–393.

Heath, O. V. S. (1957). Ageing in higher plants. *Symp. Inst. Biol.* 6:9–20.

Hecht, S. (1916). Form and growth in fishes. *J. Morphol.* 27:379.

Heikkinen, E., Aalto, M., Vihersaari, T., and Kulonen, E. (1971). Age factor in the formation and metabolism of experimental granulation tissue. *J. Gerontol.* 26:294–298.

Heilbrunn, L. V. (1943). *An Outline of General Physiology,* 2nd ed. Philadelphia and London: W. B. Saunders.

Heine, U. I., and Parchwitz, E. (1957). Explantationsversuch am Herzen und an den Haut verschieden alter Mmusc. *Arch. Geschwulstforsch.* II: 111–114.

Henderson, W. R., and Rowlands, I. W. (1938). The gonadotrophic activity of the anterior pituitary gland in relation to increased intracranial pressure. *Br. Med. J.* I:1094.

Herdan, G. (1952). Causes of excess male mortality in man. *Acta Genet. (Basel)* 3:351.

Herold, R. C., and Meadow, N. D. (1970). Age related changes in ultrastructure and histochemistry of otoeferean argaus. *J. Ultrastruct. Res.* 33:203–218.

—— (1969). *Proc. 8th Inter. Congr. Gerontology. Abst.* 36.

Herreid, C. F. (1964). Bat longevity and metabolic rate. *Exp. Gerontol.* 1:193–200.

Herrick, F. H. (1896). The American lobster. *Bull. U.S. Fish Comm.* 15:1.

—— (1911). Natural history of the American lobster. *Bull. U.S. Bur. Fish.* 29:149.

Herrington, H. B. (1948). Further proof that *Sphaerium occidentale* does not attain full growth in one year. *Can. Field Nat.,* 62:74–75.

Hertig, A. T. (1944). The ageing ovary—a preliminary note. *J. Clin. Endocrinol.* 4:581.

Hertwig, R. (1906). Über Knospung und Geschlechtentwicklung von *Hydra fusca. Biol. Zbl.* 26:489.

Hervey, G. F., and Hems, J. (1948). *The Goldfish.* London: Batchworth Press.

Hertz, R., and Hisaw, F. L. (1943). Effects of follicle-stimulating and lutenizing pituitary extracts on the ovaries of the infantile and juvenile rabbit. *Am. J. Physiol.* 108:1.

Hevesy, G. (1947) Report of the eleventh International Congress of Pure and Applied Chemistry. *Nature* (Lond.) 156:534.

Hevesy, G., and Ottesen, J. (1945). Life cycle of the red corpuscles of the hen. *Nature* (Lond.) 156:534.

Hewer, H. R. (1960). Age determination in seals. *Nature* (Lond.) 187:959–960.

Hewitt, H. B., and Wilson, C. W. (1959). A survival curve for mammalian cells irradiated *in vivo. Nature* (Lond.) 183:1060–1061.

J. B. (1976). Relationship between DNA repair capacity and cellular aging. *Gerontology (Basel)* 22:3–8.

Hijmans, W., and Radl, J. (1972). Immunology of aging—experimental approach and application. *Tno Nieuws,* pp. 687–691.

Hildebrand, S. F. (1932). Growth of diamond-backed terrapins: size attained, sex ratio and longevity. *Zoologica (N.Y.)* 9:551.

Hildemann, W. H., and Walford, R. L. (1966). Autoimmunity in relation to aging as measured by the agar plaque technique. *Proc. Soc. Exp. Biol. Med.* 123:417–421.

Hinton, M. A. C. (1925). *Proc. Linn. Soc.* 138:18.

—— (1926). *Monograph of the Voles and Lemmings.* London: British Museum.

Hinton, S. (1962). Longevity of fishes in captivity as of September 1956. *Zoologica (N.Y.)* 47:105–116

Hitotsumachi, S., Rabinowitz, Z., and Sachs, L. (1971). Chromosomal control of reversion in transformed cells. *Nature* (Lond.) 231:511–514.

Hochberg, I., and Rosdahl, K. G. (1953). The influence of orotic acid on the lateral anterior horn cells of the rat. *Acta Pathol. Microb. Scand.* 33:36–43.

Hochschild, R. (1971). Lysosomes, membranes and aging *Exp. Gerontol.* 6:153–166.

Hodge, C. G. (1894–1895). Changes in human ganglion cells from birth to senile death. Observations on man and honey-bee. *J. Physiol.* 17:129.

Hoff, C. C. (1937). Studies on the Limnaeid snail *Fossaria parva* Lea. *Trans. Ill. Acad. Sci.* 30:303–306.

Hoffman, R. S., Goldschmidt, J., and Doljanski, L. (1937). Comparative studies on the growth capacities of tissues from embryonic and adult chickens. *Growth* 1:228.

Holden, M. J., and Meadows, P. S. (1962). The structure of the spine of the spur dogfish (*Squalus acanthias* I.) and its use for age determination. *J. Mar. Biol. Ass. (U.K.)* 42:179–198.

Holečková, E., Fabry, P., and Poupa, O. (1959). Studies in the adaptation of metabolism. VIII. The latent period of explanted tissues of rats adapted to intermittent starvation. *Physiol. Bohemoslov.* 8:15–21.

Holliday, R. (1969). Errors in protein synthesis and clonal senescence in fungi. *Nature* 221:1224–1228.

Holliday, R., and Pugh, J. E. (1975). DNA modification mechanisms and gene activity during development. *Science* 187:226–232.

Holliday, R., and Tarrant, G. M. (1972). Allied enzymes in aging human fibroblasts. *Nature* 23:26–28.

Hollingsworth, D. R., Hollingsworth, J. W., Bogitch, S., and Keelin, R. J. (1969). Neuromuscular tests of aging in Hiroshima survivors. *J. Gerontol.* 24:276–283.

Hollingsworth, J. W., Hashizume, A., and Hablon, S. (1965). Correlations between tests of aging in Hiroshima subjects: an attempt to define "physiologic age." *Yale J. Biol. Med.* 38:11–26.

Hollingsworth, J. W., Ishi, G., and Conrad, R. A. (1961). Skin aging and hair graying in Hiroshima. *Geriatrics* 16:27–36.

Hollingsworth, M. J. (1969). Fluctuating temperature and the length of life in *Drosophilia*. *Nature* 221:857–858.

Holmgren, N. (1909). Termitenstudien. *Kon. Svensk. Vetensk. Akad. Handl.,* 44.

Homma, A., and Nielsen, J. (1976). Chromosome aneuploidy associated with aging. *Neuropsychobiol* 2:104–111.

Hook, E. B., and Schull, W. J. (1973). Why is the XX filter? *Nature* 244:570–573.

Hopkins, H. S. (1924). Respiration in the tissues of mollusks in relation to age. *Anat. Rec.* 29:91.

——— (1930). Age difference and the respiration of muscle tissue of mollusks. *J. Exp. Zool.* 56:209.

Hordinsky, J. R. (1977). Skylab crew health—crew surgeons' reports. In *Biomedical results from Skylab,* NASA SP 377.

Hornsey, S. (1959). Fertility and life span of mice protected by hypothermia against total body irradiation. *Gerontologia* 3:128–136.

Hornykiewicz, O. (1966). *Proc. 2nd Symp. Parkinson's Disease Inf. Res. Cr.* New York: Raven Press.

Horst, K., Mendel, L. B., and Benedict, F. G. (1934). The influence of previous diet, growth, and age upon the basal metabolism of the rat. *J. Nutr.* 8:139.

Horton, A. A., and Packer, L. (1970). Interactions between malonyldialdehyde and rat liver mitochondria. *J. Gerontol.* 25:199–204.

Hoshino, K. (1970). Indefinite *in vitro* lifespan of serially isografted mouse mammary gland. *Experientia* 26:1393–1395.

Houck, J. C., De Hesse, C., and Jacob, R. (1967). The effect of aging on collagen catabolism. *Symp. Soc. Exp. Biol.* 21:403–426.

Howard, L. O. (1939). Ageing of insects, in *Problems of Ageing* (ed. Cowdry, E. V.). London: Bailliere, Tindall and Cox.

Howell, T. (1968). Multiple pathology in a septuagenarian. *J. Am. Geriat. Soc.* 16:760–762.

Howes, E. L., and Harvey, S. C. (1932). The age factor in the velocity of the growth of fibroblasts in the healing wound. *J. Exp. Med.* 55:577–590.

Hrachovec, J. P. (1969). Age changes in amino acid incorporation by rat liver microsomes. *Gerontologia* 15:52–63.

——— (1972). Inhibitory effect of gerovital H3 on rat liver monoamine oxidase. *Proc. 25th Ann. Mtg. Geront. Soc. (U.S.A.),* Puerto Rico p. 31.

Hrůza, A., and Fábry, P. (1957). Some metabolic and endocrine changes due to long-lasting caloric under-nutrition. *Gerontologia* 1:279–287.

Hrůza, Z., Chvapil, M., and Kobrle, V. (1961). The effect of ageing and castration on the tensile strength, elasticity and swelling of rat collagen fibres. *Physiol. Bohemoslov* 10:291–295.

Hrůza, Z., Vrzalová, Z., Hrabalová, Z., and Hlavačcová, V. (1966). The effect of cooling on the speed of aging in collagen *in vitro* and in hibernation of the fat dormouse *(Glis glis). Exp. Gerontol.* 2:29–36.

Hsu, T. C., and Pomerat, C. M. (1953). Mammalian chromosomes *in vitro.* III. On somatic aneuploidy. *J. Morphol.* 93:301.

Huang, H. H., and Meites, J. (1975). Reproductive capacity of aging female rats. *Neuroendocrinol.* 17:289–295.

Hubendick, B. (1948). Über den Bau und des konzentrischen Opercular-typus bei Gastropoden. *Arch. Zool.* 40 (A10):1–28.

Hufeland, C. W. (1798). *Makrobiotik, oder der Kunst das menschliche Leben zu verlängern.* Jena.

—— (1829). *The Art of Prolonging Human Life.* London: Simpkin Marshall (Eng. trans.).

Hughes, G. (1969). Changes in taste sensitivity with advancing age *Gerontol. Clin. (Basel)* 11:224–230.

Huhnerhoff, E. (1931). Über ein bisher unbekanntes Larvenorgan und die Regeneration bei *Apsilus vorax. Zool. Anz.* 92:327.

Hummel, K. P., and Barnes, L. L. (1938). Calcification of the aorta, heart and kidneys of the albino rat. *Am. J. Pathol.* 14:121.

Hunt, T. E. (1942). Mitotic activity in the anterior hypophysis of female rats. *Anat. Rec.* 82:263.

—— (1943). Mitotic activity in the anterior hypophysis of mature female rats of different age groups and at different periods of the day. *Endocrinology* 32:334.

—— (1947). Mitotic activity in the anterior hypophysis of ovariectomized rats after injection of oestrogens. *Anat. Rec.* 97:127.

Hunter, W. R. (1953). On the growth of the freshwater limpet, *Ancylus fluviatilis* Müll. *Proc. Zool. Soc. (Lond.)* 123:623–626.

—— (1961). Annual variations in growth and density in natural populations of freshwater snails in the West of Scotland. *Proc. Zool. Soc. (Lond.)* 136:219–253.

Hursh, J. B. (1957). The effect of ionising radiation on longevity. *A.E.C. Rep.* UR-506.

Hutt, F. B. (1949). *Genetics of the Fowl.* New York: McGraw-Hill.

Huxley, A. (1937). *After Many a Summer.* London: Chatto and Windus.

Huxley, J. S. (1932). *Problems of Relative Growth.* London: Methuen.

—— (1942). *Evolution: the Modern Synthesis.* London: Allen and Unwin.

Huxley, J. S., and de Beer, G. R. (1923). Studies in dedifferentiation—IV. Resorption and differential inhibition in *Obelia* and *Campanularia. Q. J. Micr. Sci.* 67:473.

Huxley, T. H. (1880). *The Crayfish.* London: Kegan Paul.

Hvass, H. (1938). *Zool. Garten, Lpz.* 10:229.

Hyman, L. H. (1951). *The Invertebrates,* Vol. III. London and New York: McGraw-Hill.

Inagaki, H. (1971). Weight and calcium concentration exuvium of woodlouse *Ligia oceanica* L. in bearing on its senescence. *C. R. Soc. Biol.* 165:571.

Inagaki, H., and Berreurbon, J. (1970). Growth and senescence in an isopod crustacea *Ligia oceanica. C. R. Acad. Sci.* [D.] *(Paris)* 271:207.

Ingle, L. (1933). Effects of environmental conditions on longevity. *Science* 78:511.

Ingle, L., Wood, T. R., and Banta, A. M. (1937). A study of the longevity, growth, reproduction and heart rate in *Daphnia longispina* as influenced by limitations in quantity of food. *J. Exp. Zool.* 76:325.

Inukai, T. (1928). On the loss of Purkinje cells with advancing age from the cerebellar urtea of the albino rat. *J. Comp. Neurol.* 45:1–31.

Inuma, K., and Nakagome, U. (1972). Y-Chromatin in aged males. *Jpn. J. Hum. Genet.* 17:57.

Irie, T. (1957). On the forming season of annual rings in the otoliths of several marine teleosts. *J. Fac. Fish and Anim. Husb. (Hiroshima University)* 1:311–317.

Isely, F. B. (1931). A 15-year growth record in freshwater mussels *(Quadrula). Ecology* 12:616–618.

Ishiyama, R. (1951). Studies on the rays and skates belonging to the family *Rajidae* found in Japan and adjacent regions. (in Japanese-English summary). *Bull. Jpn. Soc. Sci. Fish.* 16:112–118, 119–124.

Israel, W. (1913). *Biologie der Süsswassermuscheln.* Stuttgart:G. Thieme.

Izumi, N. (1956). Effect of the atomic bomb on school children in Urakami district, Nagasaki. *Rep. Jpn. Soc. Prom. Sci.* pp. 1701–1707.

Jackson, C. H. N. (1940). The analysis of a tsetse fly population. *Ann. Eugen. (Lond.)* 10:332.

Jackson, C. M. (1936). Recovery in rats upon re-feeding after prolonged suppression of growth by dietary deficiency in protein. *Am. J. Anat.* 58:179.

Jacobs, P. A., Brown, W. M. C., and Doll, R. (1961). Distribution of human chromosome counts in relation to ageing. *Nature (Lond.)* 191:1178–1180.

Jacobs, P. A., Brunton, M., Court Brown, W. M., Doll, R., and Goldstein, J. (1963). Change of human chromosome counts with age: evidence of a sex difference. *Nature (Lond.)* 197:1080–1081.

Jalavisto, E. (1950). The influence of parental age on the expectation of life. *Rev. Méd. Liège* 5:719.

———— (1965). In *Behavior, Aging and the Nervous System* (eds. Welford, A. T., and Birren, J. F.) Springfield, Ill.: C. C. Thomas, p. 353.

James, B. S. (1971). Progeria—cell-culture study on aging. *J. Clin. Invest.* 50:2000.

Janet, C. (1904). *Observations sur les fourmis.* Limoges.

Janisch, E. (1924). Über die experimentelle Beeinflussung der Lebensdauer und des Alterns schädlicher Insekten. *Arb. Biol. Reichsart. f. Land.-u. Fortwirtschaft.* 13:173.

Jarvik, L. F., and Falek, A. (1963). Intellectual stability and survival in the aged. *J. Gerontol.* 18:173–176.

Jarvik, L. F., and Kato, T. (1969). Chromosomes and mental changes in octogenarians. *Br. J. Psychiatry* 115:1193–1194.

Jarvik, L. F., and Milne, J. F. (1975). Genesis and Treatment of Psychological Disorders in the Elderly, in *Aging,* 2 (eds., Gershon, S., and Rasking, A.) New York: Raven Press.

Jarvik, L. J., Plum, J. E., and Kato, T. (1969). Chromosomal changes and psychometric scores. *Proc. 8th Intl. Congr. Gerontol.* (Washington) Abst. 43.

Jayne, E. P. (1953). Cytology of the adrenal gland of the rat at different ages. *Anat. Rec.* 115:459.

Jennings, H. S. (1945). *Paramecium bursaria:* life history. V. Some relations of external conditions, past or present, to ageing and to mortality of exconjugants, with summary of conclusions on age and death. *J. Exp. Zool.* 99:15.

Jennings, H. S., and Lynch, R. S. (1928). Age, mortality fertility and individual diversity in the Rotifer *Proales sordida* Gorse. I.I. *J. Exp. Zool.* 51:339.

Jhingran, V. G. (1957). Age determination of the Indian major carp (*Cirrhina mrigala* Ham) by means of scales. *Nature (Lond.)* 179:468–469.

Jickeli, C. F. (1902). *Die Unvollkommenheit des Stoffwechsels als Veranlassung für Vermehrung usw.* Friedländer: Berlin.

Joedicke, P. (1919). Ein Beitrag zum eunuchoiden Riesenwuchs. *Z. ges. Neurol. Psychiat.* 44:385.

John, D. D. (1937). Antarctic whales. *J. Soc. Pres. Fauna Emp.* 31:15.

Johnson, A. H., and Erner, S. (1972). Neuron survival in the aging mouse. *Exp. Gerontol.* 7:111–117.

Johnson, R., and Strehler, B. L. (1972). Loss of genes coding for ribosomal RNA in ageing brain cells. *Nature* 240:412–414.

Jones, D. B. (1951). Sex differences in the growth of young rats and the survival of adult rats fed protein-deficient diets. *J. Nutr.* 44:465–475.

Jones, E. C., and Krohn, P. (1959). Influence of the anterior pituitary on the aging process in the ovary. *Nature (Lond.)* 183:1155–1158.

―――― (1960a). The effect of unilateral ovariectomy in the reproductive life span of mice. *J. Endocrinol.* 20:129–134.

―――― (1960b). Orthotopic ovarian transformation in mice. *J. Endocrinol.* 20:135–146.

―――― (1961). The effect of hypophysectomy on age changes in the ovaries of mice. *J. Endocrinol.* 21:497–509.

Jones, H. B. (1955). A special consideration of the aging process, disease and life expectancy. *Adv. Biol. Med. Phys.* 4:281–337.

Jones, J. W., and Hynes, H. B. N. (1950). The age and growth of *Gastrosteus aculeatus, Pygosteus pungitius* and *Spinachia vulgaris* as shown by their otoliths. *J. Anim. Ecol.* 19:59–73.

Josephina (Sister), C. S. J. (1955). Longevity of religious women. *Rev. Religious* 14:29–30.

Jurczyk, C. (1926). Zur Regeneration bei *Stephanocerus. Zool. Anz.* 67:333.

―――― (1927). Beiträge zur Morphologie, Biologie und Regeneration von *Stephanocerus fimbriatus* Goldfuss. *Z. Wiss. Zool.* 129:103.

Kallman, F. J., and Sander, G. (1948). Twin studies on ageing and longevity. *J. Hered.* 39:349.

―――― (1949). Twin studies in senescence. *Am. J. Psychiatry* 106:29.

Kassowitz, M. (1899). *Allgemeine Biologie.* Vienna.

Kawashima, S. (1970). The possible role of lipoperoxidation in aging. *Nagoya J. Med. Sci.* 33:303–326.

Kayser, J., Neumann, J., and Lavollay, J. (1966). Effect du jus d'orange sur la longevité du rat Wistar nourri ad libitum. *C. R. Acad. Sci. (Paris)* 263:994–997.

―――― (1972). Effets favorables exercices sur la longevité du rat Wistar par divers types de restrictions vitaminiques. *C. R. Acad. Sci.* 274:3593–3596.

Kelley, R. B. (1939). Female aspects of relative fertility in sheep. *Aust. Vet. J.* 15:184.

Kenyon, A. T. (1942). The comparative metabolic influences of testicular and ovarian hormones in man. *Biol. Symp.* 9:11.

Kershaw, W. E., Lavoipierre, M. M. J., and Chalmers, T. A. (1953). Studies on the intake of microfilariae by their insect vectors, their survival, and their effect on the survival of their vectors. I. *Diroflaria immitis* and *Aedes aegypti. Ann. Trop. Med. Parasitol.* 47:207.

Kerwin, J. P. (1977). Skylab 2 crew observations and summary. In *Biomedical results from Skylab,* NASA SP 377:27–29.

Kevan, D. K. McE. (1934). *Limapontia depressa* (A. and H.) var. nov. in Scotland. *J. Conchol.* 20:16–24.

―――― (1939). Further notes on *Limapontia depressa* var. *pellucida* Kevan, *J. Conchol.* 21:160–162.

――――(1941). Notes on *Limapontia depressa* var. *pellucida* kept under artificial conditions. *J. Conchol.* 21:301–302.

Keys, A. B. (1928). The weight-length relation in fishes. *Proc. Natl. Acad. Sci.* 14:922.

Keys, A. (1952). The age trend of serum concentration of cholesterol and of Sf 10-20 ("G") substance in rats. *J. Gerontol.* 7:201–206.

King, C. E. (1967). Food, age and the dynamics of a laboratory population of rotifers. *Ecology* 48:111–128.

―――― (1970). Comparative survivorship of mictic and amictic rotifers. *Physiol. Zool.* 43:206–212.

King, H. D. (1915). Growth and variability in body weight of the albino rat. *Anat. Rec.* 9:751.

―――― (1939). Life processes in gray Norway rats during 14 years in captivity. *Am. Anat. Mem.* 17:1.

King, J. T., and Visscher, M. B. (1950). Longevity as a function of diet in the C_2H mouse. *Fed. Proc.* 9:70.

King, W. G. (1911). *Census of England and Wales,* Vol. 7, p. 46.

Kinsell, L. W. (1953). Hormonal regulation of human growth, in *Protein Metabolism, Hormones and Growth.* New Jersey:Rutgers Univ. Press.

Kinsey, A. C., Pomeroy, W. B., Martin, C. E., and Gebhard, P. H. (1953). *Sexual Behavior in the Human Female*. Philadelphia: W. B. Saunders.

Kirk, E., and Kvorning, S. A. (1949). Quantitative measurement of the elastic properties of the skin and subcutaneous tissue in young and old individuals. *J. Gerontol.* 4:273.

Kirk, J. E. (1948). The acid phosphatase concentration of the prostatic fluid in young, middle-aged and old individuals. *J. Gerontol.* 3:98.

———— (1949a). The effect of testosterone administration on the acid phosphatase concentration of the prostatic exprimate in old men. *Urol. Cut. Rev.* 53:683.

———— (1949b). The urinary excretion of neutral 17-ketosteriods in middle-aged and old men. *J. Gerontol.* 4:34.

———— (1951). Steroid hormones and ageing. A review. *J. Gerontol.* 6:253.

Kirkland, H. T. (1928). A case of schistosomas is presenting some unusual features. *J. Trop. Med. Hyg.* 31:78.

Kirkwood, T. B. L., and Holliday, R. (1975a). Commitment to senescence: a model for the finite and infinite growth of diploid and transformed human fibroblasts in culture. *J. Theor. Biol.* 53:481–496.

———— (1975b). The stability of the translation apparatus. *J. Mol. Biol.* 97:257–265.

Kise, Y., and Ochi, T. (1934). Basal metabolism of old people. *J. Lab. Clin. Med.* 19:1073.

Kisiel, M. J., Castillo, J. M., Zuckerman, L. S., Zuckerman, B. M., and Himmelback, S. (1975). Studies on aging in *Tubtatrix aceti*. *Mech. Ageing Dev.* 4:81–88.

Klebanow, D., and Hegnauer, H. (1949). Die germinative Insuffizienz der alternden Frau. *Z. Altersforsch.* 5:157.

Klopfer, P. H. (1969). Evolutionary origins of mortality. *Duke Univ. Coun. Aging Hum. Dev. Proc. of Seminares 1965–1969*, pp. 279–285.

Knabe, K. (1932). Beitrag zur Dauer von Filarieninfektion. *Arch. f. Sch. u. Tropenhyg.* 36:496.

Knobloch, M. (1951). Fingernagelwachstum und Alter. *Z. Altersforsch.* 5:357.

Kobozieff, N. (1931). Mortalité et âge limite chez la souris. *C. R. Soc. Biol. (Paris)* 106:704.

Koch, C. (1952). Von meinen ältesten Urodelen. *Aquar. Terrar. Z.* 5:9.

Kochakian, C. D. (1937). Testosterone and testosterone acetate and the protein and energy metabolism of castrate dogs. *Endocrinology* 21:750.

Kochakian, C. D., and Murlin, J. R. (1931). The effect of male hormone on the protein and energy metabolism of castrate dogs. *J. Nutr.* 10:439.

Kohn, R. R. (1971). Effects of antioxidants on lifespan of C57BL mice. *J. Gerontol.* 26:378–380.

Kohn, R. R., and Leash, A. M. (1967). Longterm lathyrogen administration to rats, with special reference to aging. *Exp. Mol. Pathol.* 1:354–361.

Kohn, R. R., and Rollerson, E. (1960). Aging of human collagen in relation to susceptibility to the action of collagenase. *J. Gerontol.* 15:10–15.

Kolisko, A. (1938). Lebensgeschichte der Rädertiere auf Grund von Individualzuchten. *Arch. Hydrobiol.* 33:165.

Kopackzewski, W. (1938). Probleme de vieillissement: recherches sur les colloides. *Protoplasma* 30:291.

Kopéc, S. (1924). Studies on the influence of inanition on the development and duration of life in insects. *Biol. Bull. Wood's Hole* 46:1.

———— (1928). On the influence of intermittent starvation on the longevity of the imaginal stage of *Drosophila melanogaster*. *Br. J. Exp. Biol.* 5:204.

Koppang, N. (1974). Canine ceroid-lipofuscinosis—a model for human neuronal ceroid-lipofuscinosis and aging. *Mech. Ageing Dev.* 2:421–445.

Korenchevsky, V. (1942). Natural relative hyperplasia and the process of aging. *J. Pathol. Bacteriol.* 54:13.

———— (1947). The longest span of life found in the records of centenarians in England and Wales. *Br. Med. J.* II:14.

—— (1948). Effect of sex and thyroid hormones on the process of ageing in female rats. *Br. Med. J.* I:728.

—— (1949). The problem of ageing. Basic difficulties of research. *Br. Med. J.* I:66.

—— (1961). *Physiological and Pathological Ageing.* Basel:Karger.

Korenchevsky, V., and Jones, V. E. (1947). The effects of androsterone, oestradiol, and thyroid hormone on the artificial premature "climacteric" of pure gonadal origin produced by ovariectomy in rats. III. Effects on histologic structure of vagina, uterus, adrenals and thyroid. *J. Gerontol.* 2:116.

—— (1948). The effects of androsterone, oestradiol, and thyroid hormone on the artificial premature "climacteric" of pure gonadal origin produced by ovariectomy in rats. *J. Gerontol.* 3:21.

Korenchevsky, V., Paris, S. K., and Benjamin, B. (1950). Treatment of senescence in female rats with sex and thryoid hormones. *J. Gerontol.* 5:120.

—— (1953). Treatment of senescence in male rats with sex and thryoid hormones and desoxycorticosterone acetate. *J. Gerontol.* 8:415.

Kormendy, C. G., and Bender, A. D. (1971). Chemical interference with aging. *Gerontologia (Basel)* 17:52–64.

Korschelt, E. (1908). Versuche an Lumbriciden und deren Lebensdauer im Vergleich mit andern wirbellosen Tieren. *Verh. Deutsch. Zool. Ges.,* p. 113.

—— (1914). Über Transplantationsversuche, Ruhezustände und Lebensdauer der Lumbriciden. *Zool. Anz.* 43:537.

—— (1922). *Lebensdauer, Altern und Tod.* Jena:Fischer.

—— (1925). *in Leben, Altern Tod.* Senckenberg-Bücher II. Berlin: Bermuhler-Verlag.

—— (1931). Über das vermütliche Alter der Riesenschildkroten. *Zool. Anz.* 96:113.

Kortlandt, A. (1942). Levensloop. samenstelling en structuur de Nederlandse aalscholver bevolking. *Ardea* 31:175.

Kotsovsky, D. (1929). The origin of senility. *Am. J. Physiol.* 90:419.

—— (1931). Allgemeine vergleichende Biologie des Alters. *Ergeb. Physiol.* 31:132.

Kountz, W. B. (1950). Restoration of body function in the aged. *J. Gerontol.* 5:385.

Kraak, W. K., Rinkel, G. L., and Hoogerheide, J. (1940). Oecologische beweging van de Europese ringgegevens van de kievit *(Vanellus vanellus L.). Ardea* 29:151.

Kraus, A. S., and Lilienfeld, A. M. (1959). Some epidemiological aspects of the high mortality rate in the young widowed group. *J. Chron. Dis.* 10:207–217.

Kristensen, I. (1957a). De artemisschelp *(Dosinia exoleta). Lev. Natuur* 59:82–84.

—— (1957b). De groeisnelheid van het Tafelmescheft *(Ensis siliqua). Lev. Natuur* 60:93.

—— (1957c). Differences in density and growth in a cockle population in the Dutch Wadden Sea. Doctoral Thesis, Univ. of Leiden.

Krohn, P. L. (1955). Tissue transplantation techniques applied to the problem of the ageing of the organs of reproduction. *Ciba Found. Colloquia on Ageing* 1:141.

—— (1962). Heterochronic transplantation in the study of ageing. *Proc. R. Soc. (Biol).* 157:128–147.

—— (1966). Transplantation and aging, in *Topics of the Biology of Aging,* (ed. Krohn, P. L.). New York:John Wiley & Sons.

Krull, W. H. (1931). Importance of laboratory raised snails in helminthology with life-history notes on *Gyraulus parvus. Occ. Pap. Mus. Zool. Univ. Mich.* 226:1–10.

Krumbhaar, E. B., and Lippincott, S. W. (1939). Postmortem weight of "normal" human spleens at different ages. *Am. J. Med. Sci.* 197:344–358.

Krumbiegel, I. (1929a). Lebensdauer, Altern und Tod in ihren Beziehungen zur Fortpflanzung. *S. B. Ges. Naturf. Fr. Berl.* 94:1928–1929.

—— (1929b). Untersuchungen über die Einwirkung auf Altern und Lebensdauer der Insekten ausgeführt an *Carabus* und *Drosophila. Zool. Jb.* (2 Abt.) 51:111.

Kruse-Larsen, C., and Garde, K. (1971). Postmenopausal bleeding: another side effect of L-dopa. *Lancet* I:707–708.

Kubo, I., and Kondo, K. (1953). Age determination of the *Babylonia japonica* (Reeve), an edible marine gastropod, basing on the operculum. *J. Tokyo Univ. Fish.* 39:199–207.

Kunde, M. M., and Norlund, M. (1927). Inactivity and age as factors influencing the basal metabolic rate of dogs. *Am. J. Physiol.* 80:681.

Künkel, K. (1908). Vermehrung und Lebensdauer der *Limnaea stagnalis* L. *Nachrbl. Deutsch. Malak, Ges.* 40:70–77.

—— (1908). Vermehrung und Lebensdauer der Nacktschnecken. *Verh. deutsch. zool. Ges.,* 18, 153–61.

—— (1916). *Zur Biologie der Lungenschnecken.* Heidelberg, pp. 316 ff.

—— (1928). Zur Biologie von *Eulota fruticum* Muller. *Zool. Jb. (Zool.),* 45, 317–342.

—— (1929). Experimentelle Studie über *Vitrina brevis* Fer. *Zool. Jb. (Zool.),* 46, 575–626.

Kunze, (1933). Cited by Bürger, M. (1954).

Kurtz, E. B., and Winfrey, R. (1931). Life-characteristics of physical property. *Bull. Iowa Eng. Exp. Station* No. 103.

Kurzrok, R., and Smith, P. E. (1938). The pituitary gland. *Proc. Assn. Nervous and Mental Diseases* No. 17, Chap. xvii.

LaBella, F. S. (1966). Pharmacological retardation of aging. *Gerontologist* 6:46–50.

—— (1968). The effect of chronic dietary lathyrogen on rat survival. *Gerontologist* 8:13.

LaBella, F. S., and Paul, G. (1965). Structure of collagen from human tendon as influenced by age and sex. *J. Gerontol.* 20:54–59.

Labitte, A. (1916). Longévité de quelques insectes en captivité. *Bull. Mus. Hist. Nat. (Paris)* 22:105.

Lack, D. (1943a). *The life of the Robin.* London:Witherby.

—— (1943b). The age of blackbirds. *Brit. Birds,* 36, 166.

—— (1943c). The age of some more British birds. *Brit. Birds* 36:193, 214.

—— (1946). Do juvenile birds survive less well than adults? *Brit. Birds* 39:258.

—— (1950). Population ecology in birds. A review. *Proc. Xth Intl. Ornith. Congr.*

—— (1954). *The Natural Regulation of animal numbers.* Oxford: Univ. Press.

Lajtha, L. G., and Schofield, R. (1971). Regulation of stem cell renewal and differentiation. *Adv. Geront. Res.* 3:131–146.

Lalonde, M. (1974), A new perspective on the health of Canadians. Ottowa: Govt. of Canada.

Lamb, M. J. (1968). Temperature and longevity in *Drosophilia. Nature* 220:808–809.

Lamotte, M. (1951). Recherches sur la structure génétique des populations naturelles de *Cepaea nemoralis* L. *Bull. Biol. France (Suppl.)* 35:1–238.

Lamy, E. (1933). Quelques mots sur la durée de la vie chez les Mollusques. *J. Conchol.* 77:483–502.

Landahl, H. D. (1959). In *Handbook of Aging and the Individual* (ed. Birren, J. E.) Chicago:Univ. Press.

Landauer, W., and Landauer, A. B. (1931). Chick mortality and sex ratios in the domestic fowl. *Amer. Nat.* 65:492.

Landowne, M. (1957). Methods and limitation in studies of human organ function. *Ciba Found. Colloquium on Ageing* 3:73–91.

Lane, P. W., and Dickie, M. M. (1958). The effect of restricted food intake on the life span of genetically obese mice. *J. Nutr.* 64:549–554.

Lang, A. (1896). Kleine biologische Beobachtungen über die Weinbergschnecke (*Helix pomatia* L.). *Vierteljahr. Ges. Zurich* 61:488.

—— (1904). Über Vorversuche zu Untersuchungen über die Varietätenbildung von *Helix hortensis* und *Helix nemoralis. Denkschr. d. Med. Naturwiss. Ges. Jena* II:437–505.

——— (1908). *Uber die Bastarde von Helix bortensis* und *Helix nemoralis, Eine Untersuchung zu experimentelle Vererbunslehre.* Jena:Fischer.

Lansing, A. I. (1942). Some effects of hydrogen ion concentration, total salt concentration, calcium and citrate on longevity and fecundity in the rotifer. *J. Exp. Zool.* 91:195.

——— (1947a). A transmissible, cumulative and reversible factor in ageing. *J. Gerontol.* 2:228.

——— (1947b). Evidence for ageing as a consequence of growth cessation. *Anat. Rec.* 99:579.

——— (1948). The influence of parental age on longevity in rotifers. *J. Gerontol.* 3:6.

——— (1951). Some physiological aspects of ageing. *Physiol. Rev.* 31:274.

——— (1952). In *Problems of Ageing* (ed. Cowdry, E. V.). Baltimore:Williams and Wilkins.

——— (1964). Age variations in the cortical membranes of rotifers. *J. Cell Biol.* 23:403–422.

Lansing, A. I., Roberts, E., Ramasarma, G. B., Rosenthal, T. B., and Alex, M. (1951). Changes with age in amino acid composition of arterial elastin. *Proc. Soc. Exp. Biol.* (N.Y.) 76:714.

Lansing, A. I., Rosenthal, T. B., and Alex, M. (1950). Significance of medial age changes in the human pulmonary artery. *J. Gerontol.* 5:211–215.

Lansing, A. I., Rosenthal, T. B., and Kamen, M. D. (1949). Effect of age on calcium binding in mouse liver. *Arch. Biochem.* 20:125.

Lansing, A. I., and Wolfe, J. M. (1942). Changes in the fibrillar tissue of the anterior pituitary of the rat associated with advancing age. *Anat. Rec.* 83:355.

Latter, O. H. (1935). Unusual length of life and curious site of larva of *Cossus ligniperda. Proc. R. Soc. (Lond.)* 10:41.

Lauer, A. R. (1952). Age and sex in relation to accidents in "road users" characteristics. *Natl. Acad. Sci. N. R. C. Highway Res. Bd. Bull.* 60.

Lauson, H. D., Golden, J. B., and Severinghaus, E. L. (1939). The gonadotrophic content of the hypophysis throughout the life cycle of the normal female rat. *Am. J. Physiol.* 125:396.

Lavollay, J. (1968). Effects exercices par les jus de fruits sur la durée de vie chez le rat. *Proc. 7th Congr. Intl. Jus de Fruits,* pp. 19–36.

Laws, E. R. (1971). Evidence of anti-tumorigenic effects of DDT. *Arch. Environ.* 23:181–184.

Laws, R. M. (1952). A new method of age determination for mammals. *Nature* (Lond.) 169:972.

——— (1953). The elephant seal (*Mirounga leonina* L.). I. Growth and age. *Falkland Ids. Dependencies Survey Sci. Rep.* No. 8.

Laws, R. M., and Purves, P. E. (1956). The earplug of the Mysticeti as an indication of age, with special reference to the North Atlantic Fin Whale (*Balacnoptera physalus* Linn). *Norsk Hvålfangstid* 45:413–425.

Lawson, T. C. (1939). Echinococcus cysts of the liver of 56 years' duration. *J.A.M.A.* 112:1331.

Lazovskaya, L. N. (1942). Age modifications of respiration of blood vessels. *Biul. Eksp. Biol. Med.* 14:46.

——— (1943). The change in respiration of blood vessels with age. *Biokhimia* 8:171.

Leach, C. S., and Rambaut, P. C. (1977). Biochemical responses in Skylab crewmen—an overview. In *Biomedical Results from Skylab,* NASA SP 377.

Leaf, A. (1975). *Youth in Old Age.* New York: McGraw-Hill.

Leathem, J. H. (1949). The antihormone problem in endocrine therapy. *Rec. Prog. Horm. Res.* IV:115.

LeBeau, A. (1953). L'âge du chien et celui de l'homme. *Bull. Acad. Vet. (France),* 26:229–232.

Leblond, C. P., and Walker, B. E. (1956). Renewal of cell populations. *Physiol. Rev.* 36:255–276.

Lederer, G. (1941). Zur Haltung des China-alligators (*Alligator sinensis* Fauvel). *Zool. Gärt. (Lpz.)* 13:255.

Lefèvre, G., and Curtis, W. C. (1912). Studies on the reproduction and artificial propagation of freshwater mussels. *Dept. Comm. Lab. Bull. Bur. Fish.* 30:105.

Lehman, H. C. (1943). The longevity of the eminent. *Science* 98:270.

Lehmensick, R. (1926). Zur Biologie, Anatomie und Eireifung der Rädertiere. *Z. Wiss. Zool.* 128:37.

Leibers, R. (1937). Beitrage zur Biologie der Rädertiere: Untersuchungen an *Euchlanis dilatata* und *Proales decipiens. Z. Wiss. Zool.* 150:206.

Lemberg, R., and Legge, J. W. (1949). *Hematin Compounds and Bile Pigments.* New York: Interscience Publ.

Leopold, A. C. (1961). Senescence in plant development. *Science* 134:1727–1732.

Lepeschkin, W. W. (1931). Death and its causes. *Q. Rev. Biol.* 6:167.

Lesher, S., Fry, R. J. M., and Kohn, H. I. (1961). Aging and the generation cycle of intestinal epithelial cells in the mouse. *Gerontologia* 5:176–181.

Leslie, P. H., and Ranson, R. M. (1940). The mortality, fertility and rate of natural increase of the vole (*Microtus agrestis*) as observed in the laboratory. *J. Anim. Ecol.* 9:27.

Levy, W. M. (1957). *The Pigeon.* Sumter, South Carolina.

Lewis, C. M. (1972). Protein turnover in relation to Orgel's error theory of aging. *Mech. Ageing Dev.* 1:43–47.

Lewis, C. M., and Holliday, R. (1970). Mistranslation and ageing in *Neurospora. Nature (Lond.)* 228:877–880.

Lewis, C. M., and Tarrant, G. M. (1972). Error theory and aging in human fibroblasts. *Nature (Lond.)* 239:316–318.

Libow, L. S. (1963). in *Human Aging, a Behavioral and Biological Study* (ed. Birren, J. E., Butler, R. N., Greenhouse, S. W., Sokoloff, L., and Yarrow, M. R.). Bethesda, Md.: USPHS 986, p. 37.

Lilly, M. M. (1953). The mode of life and the structure and functioning of the reproductive ducts of *Bythinia tentaculata* (L). *Proc. Malac, Soc. (Lond.)* 30:87–110.

Lindop, P. J., and Rotblat, J. (1959). Aging effects of ionizing radiation. *Prog. Nucl. Energy* 6(2):58–69.

——— (1959). Shortening of life-span of mice as a function of age at irradiation. *Gerontologia* 3:122–127.

——— (1960). Longterm effects of a single wholebody exposure of mice to ionising radiation. I. Life shortening. II. Cause of death. *Proc. R. Soc.* B 154:332–349.

——— (1961). Long term effects of a single whole body exposure of mice to ionizing radiations. *Proc. R. Soc.* (B), 154:332–349, 350–368.

——— (1961). Shortening of life and causes of death in mice exposed to a single whole body dose of radiation. *Nature (Lond.)* 189, 645–8.

Lindop, P. J., and Sacher, G. A. (1966). *Radiation and Aging.* London: Taylor & Francis.

Lindsay, E. (1940). The biology of the silverfish, *Ctenolepisma longicaudata* Esch. with particular reference to its feeding habits. *Proc. R. Soc. Victoria* 52:35.

Linsley, E. G. (1938). Longevity in the Cerambycidae. *Pan-Pacif. Ent.* 14:177.

Lints, F. A. (1971) Life span in *Drosophilia. Gerontologia* 17:33–51.

Lints, F. A., and Hoste, C. (1974). The Lansing effect revisited. I. Life-span. *Exp. Gerontol.* 9:51–70.

Lipschutz, A. (1915). *Allgemeine Physiologie des Todes.* Braunschweig: Fr. Vieweg.

Liu, R. K., and Walford, R. L. (1970). Observations on the lifespans of several species of annual fishes and of the world's smallest fishes. *Exp. Gerontol.* 5:241–246.

Lobban, M. C. (1952). Structural variations in the adrenal cortex of the cat. *J. Physiol.* 118:565.

Loeb, J. (1908). Über den Temperaturkoeffizienten für die Lebensdauer kaltblütiger Tiere usw. *Pflugers Arch.* 124:411.

Loeb, J., and Northrop, J. H. (1917). On the influence of food and temperature on the duration of life. *J. Biol. Chem.* 32:103.

Loeb, L. (1944). Hormones and the process of ageing. *Harvey Lecture* 36:228.

Long, J. A., and Evans, H. M. (1922). The estrous cycle in the rat and its associated phenomena. *Mem. Univ. Calif.* 6.

Longstaff, J. (1921). Observations on the habits of *Cochlitoma zebra* var. *fulgurata* Pfr. and *obesa* Pfr. in confinement. *Proc. Zool. Soc. (Lond.)* pp. 379–387.

Lorand, A. (1904). Quelques considérations sur les causes de sénilité. *C. R. Soc. Biol. (Paris)* 57:500.

—— (1929). La rôle de l'autointoxication intestinale dans la production de la vieillesse. *Clinique (Paris)* 24:205.

Lord, R. D. (1961). Potential life span of Cottontails. *J. Mammal.* 42:99.

Lorenz, T. W., and Lerner, I. (1946). Inheritance of sexual maturity in male chickens and turkeys. *Poult. Sci.* 25:188.

Lowry, O. H., and Hastings, A. B. (1952). Quantitative histochemical changes in ageing, in *Problems of Ageing* (ed. Cowdry, E. V.) New York: Williams and Wilkins.

Lupien, P. J., and McCay, C. M. (1960). Thermic contraction of and elasticity in the Chinchilla tendon fiber as influenced by age. *Gerontologia* 4:90–103.

Lynch, R. S., and Smith, H. B. (1931). A study of the effects of modification of the culture medium upon length of life and fecundity in a Rotifer (Proales sordida), etc. *Biol. Bull. Wood's Hole* 60:30.

MacDonnell, W. R. (1913). On the expectation of life in ancient Rome and in the provinces of Hispania and Lusitania, and Africa. *Biometrika* 9:366.

Maceira Coelho, A. (1973). Aging and cell division. *Front. Matrix Biol.* 1:46–77.

Machlin, L. J. (1963). The biological consequences of feeding polyunsaturated fatty acids to antioxidant-deficient animals. *J. Am. Oil Chem. Soc.* 40:368–371.

Machlin, L. J., and Gordon, R. S. (1960). Linoleic acid as causative agent of encephalomalacia in chickens fed oxidised fats. *Proc. Soc. Exp. Biol. Med.* 103:659–663.

Madigan, F. C. (1959). A life table for religious priests, 1953–1957. *Rev. Religious* 18:225–231.

Magaeva, S. V. (1972). Possible hippocampal-hypothalamic interaction in the regulation of immunogenesis, in *Questions of Neuroendocrine Pathology and Gerontology*, USSR:Gorkyi, pp. 35–37.

Magee, K., Basinska, J., Quarrington, B., and Stancer, H. C. (1970). *Life Sci.* 9:7.

Magnus-Levy, H., and Falk, E. (1899). Der Lungengaswechsel der Menschen in den verschiedenen Alterstugen. *Pflugers. Arch. Ges. Physiol.* Physiol. Suppl.: 314.

Makinodan, T., Chino, F., Lever, W. E., and Brewer, B. S. (1971). The immune systems of mice reared in clean and dirty conventional laboratory farms. *J. Gerontol.* 508–514.

Makinodan, T., Perkins, E. A., and Chen, M. G. (1971). Immunologic activity of the aged. *Adv. Geront. Res.* 3:171–198.

Makinodan, T., and Peterson, W. J. (1966). Secondary antibody forming potential of mice in relation to age. *Dev. Biol.* 14:96–111.

Mallouk, R. S. (1975). Longevity in vertebrates is proportional to relative brain weight. *Fed. Proc.* 34:2102–2103.

Malpas, A. H. (1933). Further observations of the age and growth rate of the Ceylon pearl oyster, *Margaritifera vulgaris. Bull. Ceylon Fisheries* 5:21–48.

Mandl, M., and Zuckerman, S. (1952). Factors influencing the onset of puberty in albino rats. *J. Endocrinol.* 8:357.

Manschot, W. A. (1940). Een geval van progero-nanie (Progeria von Gilford). *Nederl. Tijdschr. Geneesk* 84:3374.

—— (1940). *Over Progeronanie.* Amsterdam: Van Gorcum & Co.

—— (1950). *Acta Paediatr. Stockh.* 158.

Mansfield, A. W., and Fisher, H. D. (1960). Age determination in the harbour seal, *Phoca vitulina* L. *Nature* 186:92–93.

Manville, R. H. (1958). Concerning platypuses. *J. Mammal.* 130:582–583.

Marco, G. J., Machlin, L. J., Emery, E., and Gordon, R. S. (1961). Dietary effects of fats upon fatty acid composition of the mitochrondria. *Arch. Biochem. Biophys.* 94:115–120.

Marcou, D. (1957). Rajeunissement et arrêt de croissance chez *Podospora anserina. C. R. Acad. Sci.* 244:661–662.

Margules, D. L., (1970). *J. Comp. Physiol. Psychol.* 71:1.

Mariani, T., Martinez, C., Smith, J. M., and Good, R. A. (1960). Age factor and induction of tolerance to male skin grafts in female mice subsequent to the neonatal period. *Ann. N.Y. Acad. Sci.* 87:93–105.

Marinesco, G. (1934). Nouvelle contribution à l'étude du mécanisme de la viellesse. *Bull, Acad. Med. (Paris)* III:761.

———— (1934). Études sur le mécanisme de la vieillesse. *Rev. Soc. Argent. Biol.* 10:355.

Markofsky, J., and Perlmutter, A. (1973). Growth differences in subgroups of varying longevities in a laboratory population of the male annual cyprinodont fish *Nothobranchius guentheri* (Peters). *Exp. Gerontol.* 8:65–74.

Markus, H. C. (1934). Life history of the blackhead minnow. *(Pimephales promelas). Copeia* 116–122.

Marshak, A. (1936). Growth differences in reciprocal hybrids and cytoplasmic influence on growth in mice. *J. Exp. Zool.* 72:497.

Marshak, A., and Byron, R. L. (1945). The use of regenerating liver as a method of assay. *Proc. Soc. Exp. Biol. (N.Y.)* 59:200.

Marshall, H. (1947). Longevity of the American herring gull. *Auk* 64:188.

Marshall, J. T. (1898). Additions to British conchology. *J. Conchol.* 9:120–138.

Martin, G. M., Sprague, C. A., and Epstein, C. J. (1970). Replicative lifespan of cultured human cells. *Lab. Invest.* 22:86–91.

Martin, J. B., Kontor, J., Mead, P. (1973). *Endocrinology* 92:1354.

Marzolf, R. C. (1955). Use of pectoral spines and vertebrae for determining age and rate of growth of the Channel Catfish. *J. Wildl. Manag.* 19:243–249.

Mason, K. E., and Wolfe, J. M. (1930). The physiological activity of the hypophyses of rats under various experimental conditions. *Anat. Rec.* 45:232.

Massie, H. R., Baird, M. B., and Williams, T. R. (1975). Lack of increase in DNA crosslinking in *Drosophila* with age. *Gerontologia* 21:73–80.

Masters, W. H. (1952). The female reproductive system, in *Problems of Ageing* (ed. Cowdry, E. V.) New York: Williams and Wilkins.

Matheson, C. (1950). Longevity in the grey seal. *Nature* 166:73.

Mattei, C., Cognasso, P. A., and Torazzo-Gazzera, M. (1955). Sul contenuto in calcio delle unghie nelle varie et`a dell'uomo. *Giorn. Gerontol.* 3:511–517.

Matteson, M. R. (1948). Life history of *Elliptio complanatus* (Dillw.) *Am. Midl. Nat.* 40:690–723.

Matthes, E. (1951). Der Einfluss der Fortpflanzung auf die Lebensdauer eines Schmetterlings *(Fumea crassiorella). Z. Vergl. Physiol.* 33:1.

Maupas, E. (1883). Contribution à l'étude morphologique et anatomique des Infusoires ciliés. *Arch. Zool. Exp. Gen. S.* 2:1.

———— (1886). Recherches expérimentales sur la multiplication des Infusoires ciliés. *Arch. Zool. Exp. Gen. S.* 2:6.

Maurizio, A. (1946). Beobachtungen über die Lebensdauer und den Futterverbrauch gefangen gehaltener Bienen. *Beih. Schweiz. Beinenzig.* 2:1.

———— (1950). Untersuchungen über den Einfluss der Pollennährung und Brutpflege auf die Lebensdauer und den physiologische Zustand von Bienen. *Schweiz. Beinenztg.* 73:58.

———— (1959). Factors influencing the life span of bees. *Ciba Found. Colloquia on Ageing* 5:231–243.

Mawson, A. R. (1974). *Psychosom. Med.* 4:289.

Mayer, J. (1949). Definition and quantitative expression of ageing. *Growth* 13:97.

Maynard Smith, J. (1958a). The effects of temperature and of egg laying on the longevity of *Drosophila subobscura. J. Exp. Biol.* 35:832–842.

—————— (1958b). Prolongation of the life of *Drosophila subobscura* by a brief exposure of adults to a high temperature. *Nature (Lond.)* 181:496–497.

—————— (1959a). A theory of ageing. *Nature (Lond.)* 184:956–958.

—————— (1959b). Rate of ageing in *Drosophila subobscura. Ciba Found. Colloquia on Ageing* 5:269–281.

—————— (1959c). Sex limited inheritance of longevity in *Drosophila subobscura. J. Genet.* 56.

—————— (1962). The causes of ageing. *Proc. R. Soc. (B),* 157:115–127.

—————— (1965). Aging. *Heredity* 20:147.

Maynard Smith, J., and Maynard Smith, S (1954). Genetics and cytology of *Drosophila subobscura.* VIII. Heterozygosity, viability and rate of development. *J. Genet.* 52:152.

Mays, L. L., Borek, E., and Finch, C. E. (1973). Glycine N-methyl transferase is a regulatory enzyme which increases in aging animals. *Nature* 243:411–413.

McArthur, J. W., and Baillie, W. H. T. (1926). Sex differences in mortality and metabolic activity in *Daphnia magna. Science* 64:229.

—————— (1929a). Metabolic activity and duration of life. I. Influence of temperature on longevity in *Daphnia magna. J. Exp. Zool.* 53:221.

—————— (1929b). Metabolic activity and duration of life. II. Metabolic rates and their relation to longevity in *Daphnia magna. J. Exp. Zool.* 53:243.

—————— (1932). Sex differences of mortality in Abraxas-type species. *Q. Rev. Biol.* 7:313.

McCance, R. A., and Widdowson, A. M. (1955). A fantasy on ageing and the bearing of nutrition upon it. *Ciba Found. Colloquia on Ageing* 1:186.

McCay, C. M. (1952). in *Problems of Ageing* (ed. Lansing, A. I.) Baltimore: Williams and Wilkins.

McCay, C. M., and Crowell, M. F. (1934). Prolonging the lifespan. *Sci. Mon.* 39:405–414.

McCay, C. M., Maynard, L. A., Sperling, G., and Barnes, L. L. (1939). Retarded growth, lifespan, ultimate body size and age changes in the albino rat after feeding diets restricted in calories. *J. Nutr.* 18:1–13.

McCay, C. M., Maynard, L. A., Sperling, G., and Osgood, H. S. (1941). Nutritional requirements during the latter half of life. *J. Nutr.* 21:45.

McCay, C. M., Pope, F., and Lunsford, W. (1956). Experimental prolongation of the life span. *Bull. N.Y. Acad. Med.* 32:91–101.

McCay, C. M., Pope, F., Lunsford, W., Sperling, G., and Samvhavapol, P. (1957). Parabiosis between old and young rats. *Gerontologia* 1:7–17.

McCay, C. M., Sperling, L. S., and Barnes, L. L. (1943). Growth ageing and chronic diseases and life span in the rat. *Arch Biochem.* 2:469.

McCreight, C. E., and Sulkin, N. M. (1959). Cellular proliferation in the kidneys of young and senile rats following unilateral nephrectomy. *J. Gerontol.* 14:440–443.

McCullaugh, E. P., and Renshaw, J. F. (1934). The effects of castration in the adult male. *J. A. M. A.* 103:1140.

McDowell, E. C., Taylor, M. T., and Broadfort, T. (1951). *Carnegie Inst. Wash, Year Book* 50:200.

McGavack, T. H. (1951). Endocrine patterns during aging. *Am. J. Int. Med.* 35:961.

McIlhenny, E. A. (1940). Sex ratio in wild birds. *Auk* 57:85.

McIlwain, H. (1946). The magnitude of microbial reactions involving vitamin-like compounds. *Nature (Lond.)* 158:898.

—————— (1949). Metabolic changes which form the basis of a microbiological assay of nicotinic acid. *Proc. R. Soc. (B),* 136:12.

McKeown, T. (1971). A historical appraisal of the medical task, in *Medical History and Medical Care.* Oxford: Univ. Press.

McLaren, A., and Michie, D. (1954). Are inbred strains suitable for bioassay? *Nature (Lond.)* 173:686–687.

McLean, A. E. M., and Marshall, W. J. (1971). Effect of linoleic acid, peroxidation and antioxidants on induction of cytochrome-P-450 in rat liver. *Biochem. J.* 123:28P.

McMillan, N. F. (1947). The ecology of *Limapontia capitata* (Muller). *J. Conchol.* 22:277–285.

Mead, A. D., and Barnes, E. W. (1904). Observations on the soft-shelled clam. *34th Rep. Comm. Inland Fish. (Rhode Island).*

Meadow, N. D., and Barrows, C. H. (1971a). Studies on aging in a *bdelloid rotifer.* I. Effect of various culture systems on longevity and fecundity. *J. Exp. Zool.* 176:303.

—— (1971b). Studies on aging in the brachoid rotifers. II. The effects of various environmental conditions and maternal age on longevity. *J. Gerontol.* 26:302–309.

Medawar, P. B. (1940). The growth, growth-energy and ageing of the chicken's heart. *Proc. R. Soc. (B),* 129:332–340.

—— (1942). Discussion of growth and new growth. *Proc. R. Soc. Med.,* 35: 500.

—— (1945). Old age and natural death. *Mod. Quart.* 1:30.

—— (1952). *An Unsolved Problem of Biology.* London: H. K. Lewis.

Medcof, J. C. (1940). On the life cycle and other aspects of the snail *Campeloma* in the Speed River. *Can. J. Res.* 18D:165–172.

Medvedev, Zh. A. (1966). *Protein Biosynthesis.* London: Oliver and Boyd.

—— (1972). Possible role of repeated nucleotide sequences in DNA in evolution of lie spans of differentiated cells. *Nature* (Lond.) 237:453–472.

—— (1972). Repetition of molecular-genetic information as a possible factor in evolutionary changes of lifespan. *Exp. Gerontol.* 7:227–238.

Meier, C., and Glees, P. (1971). Effect of centrophenoxin on old age pigment in satellite cells and neurons of rat spinal ganglia. *Acta Neuropathol.* 17:310–321.

Meijering, M. P. D. (1958). Herzfrequenz und Lebensablauf von *Daphnia magna* Straus. *Z. f. Wiss. Zool.* 161:239–265.

—— (1960). Herzfrequenz und Herzschlagzählen zwischen Häutung and Eiablage bei Cladoceren. *Z. f. Wiss. Zool.* 164:127–142.

Meites, J., Huang, H. H., and Simpkins, J. W. (1978). The aging reproductive system, in *Aging,* 4 (ed., Schneider, E. L.). New York: Raven Press.

Mellen, I. (1939). *A Practical Cat Book for Amateurs and Professionals.* New York: Scribner.

—— (1940). *The Science and Mystery of the Cat.* New York: Scribner.

Menzies, R. A., and Gold, P. H. (1971). The hormones of mitochondria in a variety of tissues of young adults and aged rats. *J. Biol. Chem.* 246:2425–2429.

Metalnikov, S. (1936). L'évolution de la mort dans le règne animal. *Rev. Gen. Sci.* January 31, 1936.

—— (1937). *La lutte contre la mort.* Paris: Gallimard.

Metchnikoff, E. (1904). *The Nature of Man.* London: Heinemann.

—— (1907). *The Prolongation of Life—Optimistic Studies.* London: Heinemann.

—— (1915). La mort du papillon du murier—un chapitre de thanatologie. *Ann. Inst. Pasteur,* p. 477.

Meyers, G. S. (1952). Annual fishes. *Aquar. J.* 23:125.

Miescher, K. (1955). The problem of ageing. *Experientia* 11:417–440.

Mievel, J. G. (1969). Effect of Coumarin, BHT and phenobarbital on protein synthesis in the rat liver. *Food Cosmet. Toxicol.* 7:621–634.

Mildvan, A. S., and Strehler, B. L. (1960). A critique of theories of mortality, in *The Biology of Aging, AIBS Symp.,* Publ. No. 6:216–235.

Miller, D. S., and Payne, P. R. (1968). Longevity and protein intake. *Exp. Gerontol.* 3:231–234.

Miller, H. M. (1931). Alternation of generations in the rotifer *Lecane inermis* Bryce. I. Life histories of the sexual and non-sexual generations. *Biol. Bull. Wood's Hole* 60:345.

Miller, M. C. (1962). Annual cycles of some Manx nudibranchs. *J. Anim. Ecol.* 31:545-569.

Miller, P. B., Johnson, R. L., and Lamb, L. E. (1965). Effects of moderate physical exercise during four weeks' bed rest on circulatory functions in man. *Aerospace Med.* 36:1077-1082.

Milo, G. E. (1973). Enhancement of senescence in low passage human embryonic lung cells by an agent extracted from phase-III cells. *Exp. Cell Res.* 79:143-151.

Miner, R. W. (1954). Parental age and characteristics of the offspring. *Ann. N.Y. Acad. Sci.* 57:451.

Minot, C. S. (1908). The problem of age, growth, and death; a study of cytomorphosis, based on lectures at the Lowell Institute, March 1907, London. (1913). *Moderne Probleme der Biologie (Jena).*

Miquel, J., Lundgren, P. R., and Bensch K. G. (1974a). Effects of oxygen-nitrogen 1:1 at 760 Torr on the lifespan and fine structure of *Drosophila melanogaster. Mech. Aging Devel.* 4: 41-57.

Miquel, J., Tappel, A. L., Dillard, C. J., Herman, M. M., and Bensch K. G. (1974b). Fluorescent products and lysosomal components in aging *Drosophila melanogaster. J. Gerontol.* 29: 622-637.

Mishaikov, D. (1929). (title unknown). *Trimesechno Spisanie Glavnata Direkt. Statist.* 1:153, 174.

Mitchell, P. C. (1911). On longevity and relative viability in mammals and birds, with a note on the theory of longevity. *Proc. Zool. Soc.* 1:425.

Mohler, S. R. (1961). General biology of senescence. *Postgrad. Med.* 30:527-538.

Mohr, E. (1951). Lebensdauer einiger Tiere in zoologischen Garten. *Zool. Gart. (Lpz.)* 18:60.

Mole, R. H. (1957). Shortening of life by chronic irradiation—the experimental facts. *Nature* (Lond.) 180:456-468.

Mole, R. H., and Thomas, A. M. (1961). Life shortening in female CBA mice exposed to daily irradiation for limited periods of time. *Int. J. Radiat. Biol.* 3:493-508.

Molisch, H. (1938). *The Longevity of Plants.* New York: Botanical Garden.

Molnar, K. (1972-1973). Subbiological aspects of aging and the concept of cathode protection. *Mech. Ageing Devl.* 1:319-326.

Moltoni, E. (1947). Fringuello vissuto in schiavitù per ben 20 anni. *Riv. Ital. Orn.* 17:139.

Moment, G. B. (1974). The possible roles of coelomic cells and of their yellow pigment in annalid regeneration and aging. *Growth* 38:209-218.

Montgomery, T. H. (1906). On reproduction, animal life cycles and the biological unit. *Trans. Tex. Acad. Sci.* 9.

Moon, H. D., Simpson, M. E., Li, C. H., and Evans, H. M. (1952). Effects of pituitary growth hormone in mice. *Cancer Res.* 12:448.

Moore, C. R., and Samuels, L. T. (1931). Action of testis hormone in correcting changes induced in rat prostate and seminal vesicles by vitamin B deficiency or partial inanition. *Am. J. Physiol.* 96:278.

Moore, D. (1924). Note on the longevity of *Clonorchis sinensis. U.S. Publ. Hlth Rep.* 39:1802.

Moore, H. B. (1934). The biology of *Balanus balanoides.* I. Growth rate in relation to size, season and tidal level. *J. Mar. Biol. Ass. (U.K.)* 19:851.

——— (1935). A comparison of the biology of *Echinus esculentus* in different habitats. *J. Mar. Biol. Ass. (U.K.)* 20:109.

——— (1937). The biology of *Littorina littorea.* I. Growth of shell and tissues, spawning, length of life and mortality. *J. Mar. Biol. Ass. (U.K.)* 21:721-742.

——— (1938). The biology of *Purpura lapillus* (Part III): Life history and relation to environmental factors. *J. Mar. Biol. Ass. (U.K.)* 23:67-74.

Morant, G. M. (1950). Secular changes in the heights of British people. *Proc. R. Soc. (B)* 137:443.

Mortimer, R. K., and Johnston, J. R. (1959). Life span of individual yeast cells. *Nature* 183:1751-1752.

Morton, J. E. (1954). Notes on the ecology and annual cycle of *Carychium tridentatum* at Box Hill. *Proc. Malac. Soc. (Lond.)* 31:30-45.

Moskovljević, V. (1939). *Bce World* 20:83; 21:39–41.

Moyer, E. K., and Kalischewski, B. F. (1958). The number of nerve fibers in motor spinal nerve roots of young, mature and aged cats. *Anat. Rec.* 131:681–750.

Moysey, F. E. (1963). A tale of two tortoises. *Trans. Proc. Torquay Nat. Hist. Soc.* 13:7–12.

Muggleton, A., and Danielli, J. F. (1968). Inheritance of the "lifespanning" phenomenon in *Amoeba proteus. Exp. Cell. Res.* 49:116–120.

Muhlbock, O. (1959). Factors influencing the lifespan of inbred mice. *Gerontologia* 3:177–183.

Muhlmann, M. S. (1900). *Über die Ursache des Alters.* Wiesbaden: Bergman.

—— (1911). Das Altern und der physiologische Tod. *Samml. Anat. Physiol. Vortr.* 1:455.

—— (1924). Meine Theorie des Alterns und des Todes; zugleich zur Abwehr. *Virchows Arch.* 253:225.

—— (1927). Wachstum, Altern und Tod. Über die Ursache des Alterns und des Todes. *Ergcb. Anat. EntwGesch. (Anat. Abt.)* 27:1.

Mulinos, M. G., and Pomerantz, L. (1941). Hormonal influences on weight of adrenal in inanition. *Am. J. Physiol.* 132:368.

Munkres, K. D. (1976). Induction of cellular death and clonal senescence of an inositol-less mutant by inositol starvation and the protective effect of dietary antioxidants. *Mech. Ageing. Dev.,* 5:163–170.

Munkres, K. D., and Minssen, M. (1976). Aging of *Neurospora crassa.* 1. Evidence for the free-radical theory. of aging from studies of a natural-death mutant. *Mech. Ageing Dev.* 5:79–98.

Murie, A. (1944). *The Wolves of Mount McKinley.* Washington, D. C.: U.S. Dept. Int. Natl. Park Service.

Murphy, J. S., and Davidoff, M. (1972). The result of improved nutrition on the Lansing effect in *Moina macropa. Biol Bull.* 142:302–309.

Murray, J. (1910). Antarctic Rotifera. *British Antartic Expedition, 1907–1909* 1(3):41.

Murray, W. S. (1934). The breeding behaviour of the dilute brown M stock of mice (Little *dba*). *Am. J. Cancer* 20:573.

Murray, W. S., and Hoffmann, J. G. (1941). Physiological age as a basis for the comparison of strains of mice subject to spontaneous mammary carcinoma. *Cancer Res.* 1:298.

Nagornyi, A. V. (1948). *(Old Age and the Prolongation of Life.)* Moscow: Sovietskaya Nauka.

Nandy, K., and Bourne, G. H. (1966). Effect of centrophenoxin on the lipofuscin pigments in the neurones of senile guinea-pigs. *Nature (Lond.)* 210:213–314.

Nanney, D. L. (1974). Aging and longterm temporal regulation in ciliated protozoa: a critical review. *Mech. Ageing Dev.* 3:81–105.

Nascher, I. (1920). A noted case of longevity—John Shell, centenarian. *Am. Med.* 15:151.

Nayar, K. N. (1955). Studies on the growth of the wedge clam *Donax (Latona) cuneatus* Linn. *Ind. J. Fish.* 2:325–349.

Neary, G. J., Munson, R. J., and Mole, R. N. (1957). *Chronic Irradiation of Mice by Fast Neutrons.* Oxford: Pergamon Press.

—— (1960). Ageing and radiation. *Nature (Lond.)* 187:10–18.

Needham, A. E. (1950). Growth and regeneration rates in relation to age in Crustacea. *J. Gerontol.* 5:5.

Needham, J. (1942). *Biochemistry and Morphogenesis.* Cambridge: Univ. Press.

Neuberger, A., and Slack, H. G. B. (1953). The metabolism of collagen from liver, bone, skin and tendon in the normal rat. *Biochem. J.* 53:47.

Neuhaus, W. (1957). Höhes Alter ciner Waldmaus *(Apodemus sylvaticus* L., 1758). *Saugetierek. Mitt.* 5:171–172.

Neurath, P., DeFemer, K., and Bell, B. (1970). Chromosome loss compared with chromosome size, age and sex of subjects. *Nature (Lond.)* 225:281–282.

Newcombe, C. L. (1935). Growth of *Mya arenaria* in the Bay of Fundy region. *Canad. J. Res. (Ottawa)* 13:97–137.

——— (1936). Validity of concentric rings of *Mya arenaria* L. for determining age. *Nature (Lond.)* 137:191–192.

Newman, G. (1959). Communication to 12th Ann. Mtg. Gerontol. Soc. Amer. *J. Gerontol.* 14:491–515.

Newman, G., and Nichols, C. R. (1960). Sexual activities and attitudes in older persons. *J.A.M.A.* 173:33–35.

Nichols, J. T. (1939). Data on size, growth and age in the box turtle, *Terrapene carolina. Copeia,* 14.

Nielsen, J. (1968). Chromosomes in senile dementia. *Br. J. Psychiatry* 114:303–309.

Nikitin, V. N. (1954). (Longevity). *Sci. & Life (Moscow)* 8:27.

——— (1958). *(Russian Studies of Age, Physiology, Biochemistry and Morphology.)* Kharkov: Univ. Press.

——— (1960). (Influence of prolonged calorie-deficient feeding on longevity, metabolism and endocrine glands in rats.) In *(Questions of Gerontology and Geriatrics).* Leningrad: State Medical Publishing Ho.

Niwa, N. (1950). Life of *Viviparus malleatus. Bull. Jpn. Soc. Sci. Fish.* 16:108–110.

Nixon, M. (1969). The lifespan of *Octopus vulgaius.* 38:529–540.

Noble, G. K. (1931). *The Biology of the Amphibia.* New York: McGraw-Hill.

Noland, L. E., and Carriker, M. R. (1946). Observations on the biology of the snail *Limnaea stagnalis appressa* during 20 generations in laboratory culture. *Amer. Midl. Nat.* 36:467–493.

Norris, J. L., Blanchard, J., and Polovny, C. (1942). Regeneration of rat liver at different ages. *Arch. Pathol. (Lab. Med.)* 34:208.

Norris, M. J. (1933). Contributions toward the study of insect fertility. II. Experiments on the factors influencing fertility in *Ephestia kuhniella* Z. *Proc. Zool. Soc. (Lond.)* 903.

——— (1934). Contributions toward the study of insect fertility. III. Adult nutrition, fecundity and longevity in the genus *Ephestia. Proc. Zool. Soc. (Lond.)* 334.

Northrop, J. (1917). The effect of prolongation of the period of growth on the total duration of life. *J. Biol. Chem.* 32:123.

Novak, E. (1921). *Menstruation and Its Disorders.* New York: Appleton.

——— (1944). The constitutional type of precocious female puberty, with a report of nine cases. *Am. J. Obstet. Gynecol.* 47:20.

——— (1970). *Obstet. Gynecol.* 36:903.

Nowlin, J. B., Eisdorfer, C., and Bates, E. (1969). A longitudinal appraisal of serum cholesterol in a geriatric population. *Proc. 8th. Intl. Congr. Gerontol. (Washington)* Abst. 167.

Noyes, B. (1922). Experimental studies on the life history of a rotifer reproducing parthenogenetically *(Proales decipiens). J. Exp. Zool.* 35:222.

O'Brian, D. M. (1961). Effect of parental age on the life cycle of *Drosophila melanogaster. Ann. Entom. Soc. Am.* 54:412–416.

Ohsumi, S., Nishiwaki, M., and Hibiya, T. (1958). Growth of fin whales in the northern part of the N. Pacific. *Sci. Rep. Whales Res. Inst.* 13:97–133.

Oldham, C. (1930). Fecundity of *Planorbis Corneus. Naturalist,* p. 177.

——— (1931). Note on *V(iviparus) contectus. J. Conchol.* 19:179.

——— (1942a). Autofecundation and duration of life in *Limax cinereoniger. Proc. Malac. Soc. (Lond.)* 25:9.

——— (1942b). Notes on *Geomalacus maculosus. Proc. Malac. Soc. (Lond.)* 25:10.

Oliff, W. D. (1953). The mortality, fecundity and intrinsic rate of natural increase of the multimammate mouse *Rattus (Mastomys) natalensis* Smith in the laboratory. *J. Anim. Ecol.* 22:217.

Oliver, J. A. (1953). Young Billy Johnson's old box turtle. *Animal Kingdom* 56:154.

Olsen, W. W. (1944). Bionomics of the lymnaeid snail *Stagnicola bulimoides techella,* the intermediate host of the liver fluke in southern Texas. *J. Agric. Res.* 69:389–403.

O'Meara, A. R., and Herrmann, R. L. (1972). A modified mouse liver chromatin preparation displaying age-related differences in salt dissociation and template ability. *Biochim. Biophys. Acta* 269:419–427.

Ono, T., Okada, S., and Sugahara, T. (1976). Comparative studies of DNA size in various tissues of mice during the aging process. *Exp. Gerontol.* 11:127–132.

Oota, Y. (1964). RNA in developing plant cells. *Ann. Rev. Plant Physiol.* 15:17–36.

Orgel, L. E. (1963). The maintenance of the accuracy of protein synthesis and its relevance to aging. *Proc. Natl. Acad. Sci. (Wash.)* 49:517–521.

—— (1970). The maintenance of accuracy of protein synthesis and its relevance to aging: a correction. *Proc. Natl. Acad. Sci. (Wash.)* 67:1476.

—— (1973). Aging of clones of mammal. *Nature (Lond.)* 243:441–445.

Orton, J. H. (1928). On rhythmic periods of shell growth in *Ostrea edulis* with a note on fattening. *J. Mar. Biol. Ass. (U.K.)* 15:365.

—— (1929). Reproduction and death in invertebrates and fishes. *Nature (Lond.)* 123:14.

Orton, J. H., and Amirthalingam, C. (1930). Giant English Oysters. *Nature (Lond.)* 126:309.

Osborne, T. B., and Mendel, L. B. (1914). The suppression of growth and the capacity to grow. *J. Biol. Chem.* 18:95.

—— (1915). The resumption of growth after long-continued failure to grow. *J. Biol. Chem.* 23:439.

—— (1916). Acceleration of growth after retardation. *Am. J. Physiol.* 40:16.

Ottoboni, A. (1972) Effect of DDT on reproductive lifespan in the female rat. *Tox. Appl. Pharmacol.* 22:497–502.

Oyama, J., and Platt, W. T. (1965). Effects of prolonged centrifugation on growth and organ development of rats. *Am. J. Physiol.* 209:611–615.

Packer, L., Deamer, D. W., and Heath, R. L. (1967). (ed. Strehler, B. L.) *Adv. Geront. Res.* 2:77.

Packer, L., and Smith, J. R. (1974) Extension of the lifespan of cultured normal human diploid cells by Vit. E. *Proc. Natl. Acad. Sci.*

Pai, S. (1928). Die Phasen des Lebenzyklus der *Anguillula aceti* Ehr. und ihre experimentellmorphologische Beeinflussung. *Z. Wiss. Zool.* 131:293.

—— (1934). Regenerationsversuche an Rotatorien. *Sci. Rep. Univ. Chekiang,* 1.

Pannikar, N. K. (1938). Recent researches on Trochus. *Curr. Sci. (Bangalore)* 6:552–553.

Pantelouxis, E. M. (1972) Thymic involution and aging: a hypothesis. *Exp. Gerontol.* 7:73–82.

Parhon, C. I. (1955). *Biologia Vîrstelor—cercetari clinice şi experimentale.* Bucharest: Acad. R. P. R.

Parhon, C. I., Pitis, M., Stan, M., and Petresco, S. (1961). Étude physiologique de la fibre collagène du rat blanc thyreo-gonadectomisé. *Gerontologia* 6:118–125.

Park, T. (1945). Life tables for the black flour-beetle, *Tribolium madens* Charp. *Amer. Nat.* 79:436.

Parker, G. H. (1926). The growth of turtles. *Proc. Natl. Acad. Sci. (Wash.)* 12:422.

Parker, W. R. (1933). Pelorus Jack. *Proc. Linn. Soc.* p. 2.

Parkes, A. S. (1928). Note on the growth of young mice suckled by rats. *Ann. Appl. Biol.,* 16, 171.

—— (1942–1944). Induction of superovulation and superfecundation in rabbits. *J. Endocrinol.* 3:268.

Parkes, A. S., and Smith, A. U. (1953). Regeneration of rat ovarian tissue grafts after exposure to low temperatures. *Proc. R. Soc.* (B) 140:455.

Parot, S. (1959) Recherches sur la biométrie du vieillissement humain. *Bull. Soc. Anthropol.* 2:299–341.

Parot, S., Jacquemin, E., and Poitremaud, J. (1969). La capacité des sujets âgés et très-âgés. *J. Physiol. (Paris)* 61:265–276.

Parsons, P. A. (1962). Maternal age and developmental variability. *J. Exp. Biol.* 39:251–260.

—— (1964). Parental age and the offspring. *Rev. Biol.* 39:258–267.

Parsons, R. J. (1936). In *Medical papers dedicated to H. A. Christian.* Baltimore.

Pascal, G. (1971). Effets metaboliques d'un additif alimentaire à propriété antioxygène: le BHT. *J. Physiol. (Paris)* 63:260–261.

Payne, F. (1949). Changes in the endocrine glands of the fowl with age. *J. Gerontol.* 4:193.

—— (1952). Cytological changes in the cells of the pituitary, thyroids, adrenals and sex glands of the ageing fowl, in *Problems of Ageing* (ed. Lansing).

Peabody, F. E. (1958). A Kansas drouth recorded in growth zones of a bull snake. *Copeia* pp. 91–94.

—— (1961). Annual growth zones in living and in fossil vertebrates. *J. Morphol.* 108:11–62.

Peakall, D. B. (1967). Pesticide-induced enzyme breakdown of steroids in birds. *Nature* 216:505–506.

Pearce, J. M. (1936). Age and tissue respiration. *Am. J. Physiol.* 114:255.

Pearce, L., and Brown, W. H. (1960). Hereditary premature senescence in the rabbits. *J. Exp. Med.* 11:485–516.

Pearl, R. (1927). On the distribution of differences of vitality among individuals. *Am. Nat.* 61:113.

—— (1928). *The Rate of Living.* New York: Knopf.

—— (1930). *The Biology of Population Growth.* New York: Knopf.

—— (1940). *Introduction to Medical Biometry and Statistics,* 3rd Ed. Philadelphia: W. B. Saunders.

Pearl, R., and Doering, C. R. (1923). A comparison of the mortality of certain lower organisms with that of man. *Science* 57:209.

Pearl, R., and Miner, J. R. (1935). Experimental studies in the duration of life. XIV. The comparative mortality of certain lower organisms. *Q. Rev. Biol.* 10:60.

—— (1936). Life tables for the pecan-nut case bearer *(Acrobasis caryae,* Grote). *Mem. Mus. Hist. Nat. Belg.* 3:169.

Pearl, R., Park, T., and Miner, J. R. (1941). Experimental studies on the duration of life. XVI. Life-tables for the flour beetle *Tribolium confusum* Duval. *Am. Nat.* 75:5.

Pearl, R., and Parker, S. L. (1924). Experimental studies on the duration of life. IX. New life-tables for *Drosophila. Am. Nat.* 58–71.

—— (1922). Experimental studies in the duration of life. II. Hereditary differences in duration of life in line-bred strains of *Drosophila. Am. Nat.* 56:174.

Pearl, R., and Pearl, R. de W. (1934). *The Ancestry of the Long-Lived.* London: H. Milford.

——(1943). Studies on human longevity. VI. Distribution and correlation of variation in the total immediate ancestral longevity of nonagenarians and centenarians in relation to inheritance factor in the duration of life. *Hum. Biol.* 6:98.

Pearson, K. (1895). Mathematical contributions to the theory of evolution. II. Skew variations in homogeneous material. *Phil. Trans. R. Soc.* 186, Series A:343.

Pearson, K., and Elderton, E. M. (1913). On the hereditary character of general health. *Biometrika* 9:320.

Pearson, O. P. (1945). Longevity of the short-tailed shrew. *Am. Midl. Nat.* 34:531.

Pearson, O. P., and Baldwin, P. H. (1953). Reproduction and age structure of a mongoose population. *J. Mammal.* 34:436.

Pease, M. (1947). How long do poultry breeding stock live? *J. Ministr. Agric.* 54:263.

Pease, M. S. (1928). Experiments on the inheritance of weight in rabbits. *J. Genet.* 20:261.

Pelc, S. R. (1965). Renewal of DNA in nondividing cells and aging. *Exp. Gerontol.* 1:215–222.

Pelseneer, P. (1894). Introduction à l'étude des mollusques. *Mem. Soc. R. Malac. (Belg.)* 37 (1892):31–243 (p. 54).

—— (1932). Un moyen de déterminer la durée de la vie des mollusques. *C. R. Ass. Franc. Av. Sci.* 56:289.

────── (1934). La durée de la vie et l'âge de la maturité sexuelle chez certains mollusques. *Ann. Soc. Zool. (Belge)* 64:93.

────── (1935). *Essai d'Ethologie Zoologique.* Bruxelles.

Penfold, W. J., Penfold, H. B., and Phillips, M. (1936). A survey of the incidence of *Taenia saginata* infestation in the population of the State of Victoria, etc. *Med. J. Austr.* (23rd Yr.) I:283.

Peng, M. T., and Huang, H. H. (1972). Aging of hypothalamic ovarian function in the rat. *Fertil. Steril.* 23:535–542.

Perkins, C. B. (1948). Longevity of snakes in captivity in the U.S. *Copeia,* p. 217.

Perks, W. (1932). On some experiments in the graduation of mortality statistics. *J. Inst. Actu.* 63:12–57.

Perrone, J. C., and Slack, H. G. B. (1952). The metabolism of collagen from skin, bone and liver in the normal rat. *Biochem. J.* 49:lxxii.

Perry, J. S. (1953). The reproduction of the African elephant, *Loxodonta africana. Phil. Trans. R. Soc. (B)* 237:93.

Perry, R. (1953). Some results of bird ringing. *New Biol.* 15:58.

Petter-Rousseaux, A. (1953). Recherches sur la croissance et le cycle d'activité testiculaire de *Natrix natrix helvetica* (Lacépède). *Terre et Vie* 100:175–223.

Pettingill, O. S. (1967). A 36-year old herring gull. *Auk* 84:123.

Pfeiffer, E., Verwoerdt, A., and Wang, H. S. (1968). Sexual behavior in aged men and women. *Arch. Gen. Psychiatry* 19:753–758.

Pflanz, H., and Torok, M. (1969). Steigt der Blutdruck mit den Alter an? *Z. f. Gerontol.* 2:156–167.

Pflugfelder, O. (1948). Volumetrische Untersuchungen an den corpora allata der Honigbiene *(Apis mellifica). Biol. Zbl.* 67:223.

Phillips, D. P., and Feldman, K. A. (1973). A dip in deaths before ceremonial occasions. *Am. Soc. Rev.* 38:678–696.

Piantanelli, L., Basso, A., Muzzioli, M., and Fabris N. (1978). Thymus dependent reversibility of physiological and isoproterenol evoked age-related parameters in athymic (nude) and old normal mice. *Mech. Aging Devel.* 7:171–182.

Picado, T. C. (1930). Effets des injections de serum homologue sur la taille et croissance des animaux. *Ann. Inst. Pasteur* 44:584.

Picado, T. C., and Rotter, W. (1936). Précipitines anti-glandes endocrines et longevité chez quelques espèces de vertebres. *C. R. Soc. Biol. (Paris)* 123:869.

Piepho, H. (1938). Über die Auslosbarkeit überzähliger Häutungen und vorzeitiger Verpuppung an Hautstücken bei Kleinschmetterlingen. *Naturwiss.* 26:841.

Pierre, R. V., and Hoagland, H. C. (1971). X cell lines in adult men: loss of Y chromosome, a normal phenomenon? *Mayo Clin. Proc.* 46:52.

────── (1972). Age-associated aneuploidy—Loss of Y-chromosome from human bone-marrow cells with aging. *Cancer* 30:889.

Pierson, B. F. (1938). Relation of mortality after endomixis to the prior interendomitotic interval in *Paramecium aurelia. Biol. Bull. Wood's Hole* 74:235.

Pincus, G. (1950). Measures of stress responsivity in younger and older men. *Psychosom. Med.* 12:225.

Pitt, F. (1945). Breeding of the harvest mouse in captivity. *Nature (Lond.)* 155:700.

Pixell-Goodrich, H. (1920). Determination of age in honey bees. *Q. J. Micr. Sci.* 64:191.

Plate, L. (1886). Beiträge zur Naturgeschichte der Rotatorien. *Jena Z. f. Naturwiss.* 19:1.

Plummer, J. M. (1975). Observations on the reproduction, growth and longevity of a laboratory colony of *Archachatina marginata* Swain. *Proc. Malac. Soc. Lond.* 41:395–413.

Poležaiev, L. V., and Ginsburg, G. I. (1939). Studies by the method of transplantation on the loss and restoration of the regenerative power in the tailless amphibian limbs. *C. R. Acad. Sci. (U.R.S.S.)* 23:733.

Pontecorvo, G. (1946). Microbiology, biochemistry and the genetics of microorganisms. *Nature (Lond.)* 157:95.

Porter, A. (1958). A venerable gander. *Country Life,* October 30, 1958, p. 1010.

Posgay, J. A. (1954). In Haskins, H. H. (1955). Age determination in molluscs. *Trans. N.Y. Acad. Sci.* 16:300–304.

Prehoda, R. W. (1967). *Designing the Future—the Role of Technological Forecasting.* Philadelphia: Chilton.

—— (1968). *Extended Youth.* New York: Putnam.

Price, G. B., and Albright, J. F. (1971) Cellular defects in immune responses of aging mice. *Fed. Proc.* 30(A):526.

Price, G. B., and Makinodan, T. (1972a). Immunologic deficiencies in senescence. I. Characterization of intrinsic deficiencies. *J. Immunol.* 108:403–412.

—— (1972b). Immunologic deficiencies in senescence. II. Characterisation of extreme deficiencies. *J. Immunol.* 108:413–417.

—— (1973). Aging: Alteration of DNA-protein information. *Gerontologia* 19:58–72.

Price, G. B., Modak, S. P., and Makinodan, T. (1971). Age-associated changes in DNA of mouse tissue. *Science* 171:917–920.

Pruitt, W. O. (1954). Ageing in the masked shrew, *Sorex cinereus cinereus* Kerr. *J. Mammal.* 35: 35.

Pryor, W. A. (1970). Free radicals in biological systems. *Sci. Am.* 223:70–76.

Przibram, H. (1909). *Experimental-Zoologie* Vol. II. Vienna, p. 126.

Puck, T. T. (1961). Cellular aspects of irradiation and aging in animals. *Fed. Proc.* 20, Suppl. 8:31–34.

Pullman, B., and Pullman, A. (1962). Electronic delocalization and biochemical evolution. *Nature* 196:1137–1142.

Pütter, A. (1921). Die ältester Menschen. *Naturwiss* 9:875.

Pyhtila, M. J., and Sherman, F. G. (1968). Age-associated studies on thermal stability and template effectiveness of DNA and nucleoprotein from beef thymus. *Biochem. Biophys. Res. Comm.* 31:340–344.

Quadri, S. K., Kledzik, G. S., and Meites, J. (1973). Reinitiation of estrous cycles in old constant-estrous rats by central-acting drugs.

Quay, W. B. (1972). Pineal homeostatic regulation of shifts in circadian activity rhythm during maturation and aging. *Trans. N.Y. Acad. Sci.* 34:239.

Quayle, D. B. (1952). The rate of growth of *Venerupis pullastra* (Montagu) at Millport, Scotland. *Proc. R. Soc. Edinb.* 64:384–406.

Quick, H. E. (1924). Length of life of *Paludestrina ulvae. J. Conchol.* 17:169.

Rabb, G. B. (1960). Longevity record for mammals at the Chicago Zoological park. *J. Mammal.* 41:113–114.

Raben, M. S., and Westermeyer, V. W. (1952). Differentiation of growth hormone from the pituitary factor which produces diabetes. *Proc. Soc. Exp. Biol.* 80:83.

Rabes, O. (1901). Über Transplantations-Versuche an Lumbriciden. *Biol. Zbl.,* p. 633.

Raffel, D. (1932). The occurrence of gene mutations in *Paramecium durelia. J. Exp. Zool.* 63:371.

Rahm, P. G. (1923). Beiträge zur Kenntnis der Moosfauna. *Z. Allg. Physiol.* 20:1.

Rankin, N. (1957). A goose nearly 50 years old. *Country Life,* February 7, 1957.

Rao, H. S. (1937). On the habitat and habits of *Trochus niloticus* Linn. in the Andaman seas. *Rec. Ind. Mus. (Calcutta)* 39:47–82.

Rapson, A. M. (1952). The Toheroa, *Amphidesma ventricosum* Gray (Eulamellibranchiata): development and growth. *Am. J. Mar. Freshw. Res.* 3:170–198.

Rasquin, P., and Hafter, E. (1951). Age changes in the testis of the teleost, *Astyanax americanus*. *J. Morphol.* 89:397.

Rau, P. (1924). The biology of the roach, *Blatta orientalis* Linn. *Trans. Acad. Sci. (St. Louis)* 25:57.

Rau, P., and Rau, N. (1914). Longevity in saturnid moths and its relation to the function of reproduction. *Trans. Acad. Sci. (St. Louis)* 23:1.

Redfield, A. C. (1939). The history of and population of *Limacina retroversa* during its drift across the Gulf of Maine. *Biol. Bull.* 76:26–47.

Redmond, D. B., Swann, A., and Heninger, G. R. (1976). Phenoxybenzamine in anorexia nervosa. *Lancet* II:307.

Reece, R. P., and Turner, C. W. (1937). The lactogenic and thyrotropic hormone content of the anterior lobe of the pituitary gland. *Univ. Missouri Agr. Exp. Sta. Res. Bull.* 266:1.

Regan, W. M., Mead, S. W., and Gregory, P. W. (1947). The relation of inbreeding to calf mortality. *Growth* 11:101.

Reichenbach, H., and Mathers, R. A. (1959). In *A Handbook of Aging and the Individual*. (ed. Birren, J. E.). Chicago: Univ. Press.

Reiner, J. M. (1947). The effect of age on the carbohydrate metabolism of tissue homogenates. *J. Gerontol.* 2:315.

Reiss, U., and Rothstein, M. (1974). Heat-labile isozymes of isocitrate lyase from aging *Turbatrix aceti*. *Biochem. Biophys. Res. Comm.* 61:1012–1016.

———— (1975). Age-related changes in isocitrate lyase from the free-living nematode *Turbatrix aceti*. *J. Biol. Chem.* 250:826–830.

Renoux, G., and Renoux, M. (1972). Restauration par le phenyl-imidothiazole de la résponse immunologique des souris âgées. *C. R. Acad. Sci. (Paris)* 274:3034–3035.

Rensch, B. (1954). The relation between the evolution of the central nervous functions and the body-size of animals, in *Evolution as a Process*. (eds. Huxley, J., Hardy, A. C., and Ford, E. B.). London: Allen and Unwin.

Rey, P. (1936). La longévité des *Galleria* adultes, mâles et femelles. *C. R. Soc.Biol.* 121:1184.

Ribbands, C. R. (1950). Changes in the behaviour of honey-bees following their recovery from anaesthesia. *J. Exp. Biol.* 27:302.

———— (1952). Division of labour in the honey-bee community. *Proc. R. Soc.* 140(B):32.

———— (1953). *The Behaviour and Social Life of Honey Bees*. London: Bee Research Ass. Ltd.

Ribbert, H. (1908). *Der Tod aus Altersschwäche*. Bonn: Cohen.

Richards, O. W. (1953). *The Social Insects*. London: MacDonald, p. 188.

Ricker, W. E. (1945). Natural mortality among Indiana blue-gill sunfish. *Ecology* 26:111.

———— (1948). Methods of estimating vital statistics of fish populations. *Ind. Univ. Publ. Sci. Ser.* 15:1.

Ricklefs, R. E. (1969). Natural selection and the development of mortality rates in young. *Nature* 223:922–925.

Riegele, G. (1976). In *Hypothalamus, Pituitary and Aging* (eds. Everitt, A., and Burgess, J. A.).

Riesen, W. H., Herbst, E. J., Walliker, C., and Elvekjem, C. A. (1947). The effect of restrictive calorie intake on the longevity of rats. *Am. J. Physiol.* 148:614–617.

Riley, W. A. (1919). The longevity of the fish tapeworm of man, *Diphyllobothrium latum*. *J. Parasitol.* 5:193.

Risbec, J. (1928). De la durée d'évolution chez *Aeolidia amoena* Risb. *C. R. Acad. Sci. (Paris)* 191:278–280.

Rizet, G. (1953). Sur l'impossibilité d'obtenir la multiplication vegetative ininterrompue et illimitée de l'Ascomycète *Podospora anserina*. *C. R. Acad. Sci.* 237:828–830.

———— (1957). Les modifications qui conduisent à la sénescence chez *Podospora:* sont-elles de nature cytoplasmique? *C. R. Acad. Sci.* 244:663–666.

Robertson, E. G., Lewis, H. E., Billewicz, W. Z., and Foggett, I. N. (1969). Two devices for quantifying the rate of deformation of skin and subcutaneous tissue. *J. Lab. Clin. Med.* 73:594–602.

Robertson, F. W., and Reeve, E. C. R. (1952). Heterozygosity, environmental variation, and heterosis. *Nature* 170:286.

Robertson, O. H., Drupp, M. A., Thomas, S. F., Favom, C. B., Hane, S., and Wexler, B. C. (1961). Hyperadrenocorticism in spawning migratory and non-migratory Rainbow Trout *(Salmo gairdnerii);* comparison with Pacific Salmon *(Genus Oncorhynchus).* *Endocrinology* 1:473–484.

Robertson, O. H., and Wexler, B. C. (1959). Hyperplasia of the adrenal cortical tissue in Pacific salmon and Rainbow trout accompanying sexual maturation and spawning. *Endocrinology* 65:225–238.

—— (1962). Histological changes in the organs and tissues of senile castrated Kokanee Salmon. *Gen. Comp. Endocrinol.* 2:458–472.

Robertson, T. B. (1923). *The Chemical Basis of Growth and Senescence.* Philadelphia: Lippincott.

Robertson, T. B., Dawbarn, M. C., Walters, J. W., and Wilson, J. D. O. (1933). Experiments on the growth and longevity of the white mouse, II. *Aust. J. Exp. Biol. Med. Sci.* 11:219.

Robertson, T. B., Marston, H. K., and Walters, J. W. (1934). *Aust. J. Exp. Biol. Sc.* 12:33.

Robertson, T. B., and Ray, L. A. (1919). Experimental studies on growth, XI. The influence of pituitary gland tissue, tethelin, egg lecithin, and cholesterol upon the duration of life in the white mouse. *J. Biol. Chem.* 37:427.

—— (1920). Experimental studies on growth. XV. On the growth of relatively long-lived compared with that of relatively short-lived animals. *J. Biol. Chem.* 42:71.

Robson, J. M. (1947). *Recent Advances in Sex and Reproductive Physiology.* London: Churchill.

Rockstein, M. (1950). The relation of cholinesterase activity to change in cell number with age in the brain of the adult worker honey bee. *J. Cell. Comp. Physiol.* 35:11.

—— (1953). Some aspects of physiological aging in the adult worker honey bee. *Biol. Bull.* 105:154–159.

—— (1958). Heredity and longevity in the animal kingdom. *J. Gerontol.* 13, Suppl. 2:7–13.

—— (1959). The biology of aging in insects. *Ciba Found. Colloquia on Ageing* 5:247–263.

Rockstein, M., and Gutfreund, D. E. (1961). Age changes in adenine nucleotides in flight muscles of male house fly. *Science* 133:1476–1477.

Rockstein, M., and Lieberman, H. M. (1958). Survival curves for male and female house-flies *(Musca domestica* L.) *Nature* 181:787–788.

Rogers, J. B. (1950). The development of senility in the guinea pig. *Anat. Rec.* 106:286.

Rokhlina, M. L. (1951). (The road to longevity.) Moscow: Pravda.

Rollinat, R. (1934). *La vie des reptiles de la France centrale.* Paris.

Romanoff, L. P. (1975). The effect of age on production of adrenal corticosteroids by men. *Proc. 10th Intl. Congr. Gerontol.,* Jerusalem, Israel.

Romanoff, L. P., and Baxter, M. N. (1975). The secretion rates of deoxycorticosterone and corticosterone in young and elderly men. *J. Clin. Endocrinol. Metabol.* 41:630–633.

Romanoff, L. P., Baxter, M. N., Thomas, A. W., and Ferrechio, G. B. (1969). Effect of ACTH on the metabolism of pregnenolone-7a-^{3}H and cortisol-4-^{14}C in young and elderly men. *J. Clin. Endocrinol. Metabol.* 29:819–830.

Rose, S. M. (1967). The aging of the system for the transmission of information controlling differentiation. *J. Gerontol.* 22(Suppl.):28–41.

Rosenberg, B., Kemeny, G., Smith, L. G., Skurnick, I. D., and Bandwiski, M. J. (1973). The kinetics and thermodynamics of death in multicellular organisms. *Mech. Ageing Devel.* 2:275–294.

Rosenthal, O., Bowie, M. A., and Wagoner, G. (1940). Metabolism of cartilage (bovine) with particular reference to the effects of ageing. *J.A.M.A.* 115:2114.

——— (1941). Studies in the metabolism of articular cartilage. I. Respiration and glucolysis of cartilage in relation to age. *J. Cell. Comp. Physiol.* 17:22.

——— (1942). The dehydrogenetic ability of bovine articular cartilage in relation to its age. *J. Cell. Comp. Physiol.* 19:333.

Rosenzweig, D. Y., Arkins, J. A., and Schrock, L. G. (1966). Ventilation studies on a normal population after a 7-year interval. *Amer. Rev. Resp. Dis.* 94:74–78.

Ross, M. H. (1961). Length of life and nutrition in the rat. *J. Nutr.* 75:197–210.

——— (1969). Aging, nutrition and hepatic enzyme activity patterns in the rat. *J. Nutr.* 97, Suppl. 1:565–601.

——— (1971). The lasting influence of early calorie restriction on the prevalence of age-related diseases and longevity of rats. *VII Ann. Symp. AUA-ANL: 9-11.* Argonne Nat. Lab., Illinois.

——— (1976). Nutrition and longevity in experimental animals. *Curr. Concepts. Nutr.* 4:61–76.

Ross, M. H., and Bras, G. (1965). Tumor incidence patterns and nutrition in the rat. *J. Nutr.* 87:245–260.

Ross, M. H., Bras, G., and Ragbeer, M. S. (1970). Influence of protein and calorie intake upon spontaneous tumor incidence of the anterior pituitary gland of the rat. *J. Nutr.* 100:177–189.

Rothschild, A., and Rothschild, M. (1939). Some observations on the growth of *Peringia ulvae* (Penn) in the laboratory. *Novit. Zool.* 41:240–247.

Rothschild, M. (1935). Gigantism and variation in *Peringia ulvae* Penn, caused by infection with larval trematodes. *J. Mar. Biol. Ass. (U.K.)* 20:537.

——— (1941–1943). The effect of trematode parasites on the growth of *Littorina neritoides* (L). *J. Mar. Biol. Ass. (U.K.)* 25:69–78.

Roux, W. (1881). *Der Kampf der Teile im Organismus.* Leipzig. ·

Royer, L. M., Atton, F. M., and Cuerrier, J. P. (1968). Age and growth of lake sturgeon in the Saskatchewan River delta. *J. Fish. Res. Bd. Canada* 25:1511–1516.

Rubbel, von A. (1913). Boebachtungen über das Wachstum von *Margaritana margaritifera. Zool. Anz.* 41:156–162.

Rubin, B. L., Dorfman, R. I., and Pincus, G. (1955). 17-ketosteroid excretion in ageing subjects. *Ciba Found. Symp. Ageing* 1:126.

Rubner, M. (1908). Probleme des Wachstums und der Lebensdauer. *MittGes. Inn. Med. (Wien)* 7:58.

Rudzinska, M. (1951). The influence of amount of food on the reproduction rate and longevity of a Suctorian *(Tokophyra infusionum). Science* 113:10–11.

——— (1952). Overfeeding and life-span in *Tokophyra infusionum. J. Gerontol.* 7:544.

Rugh, R., and Wolff, J. (1958). Increased radioresistance through heterosis. *Science* 127:144–145.

Russell, W. L. (1957). Shortening of life in the offspring of mice exposed to neutron radiation from an atomic bomb. *Proc. Natl. Acad. Sci. (U.S.)* 43:324.

Rutgers, A. J. (1953). Mortality by cancer as a function of age. *Experientia* 12:470.

Rutman, R. J. (1950). A maternal influence on the incorporation of methionine into liver protein. *Science* 112:252.

——— (1951). The inheritance of rates of methionine uptake by rat liver protein and relations to growth. *Genetics* 36:59.

Ruud, J. T., Jonsgard, A., and Ottestad, P. (1950). Age studies in blue whales. *Hvalrad. Skr.* 33: 1.

Růžícká, V. (1924). Beiträge zum Studium der Protoplasmahysterethchen Vorgänge (Zur Kausalität des Alterns). *Arch. Mikr. Anat.* 101:459.

——— (1929). Beiträge zum Studium der Protoplasmahysteresis, usw. (Zur Kausalität des Alterns). *Arch. EntwMeck. Org.* 116:104.

Sacher, G. A. (1956). On the statistical nature of mortality, with expecial reference to chronic radiation mortality. *Radiology* 67:250–257.

—— (1957). Dependence of acute radiosensitivity on age in adult female mouse. *Science* 125:1039–1040.

—— (1958). Entropic contributions to mortality and aging, in *Symp. on Inform. Theory Biol.* Cambridge, England: Pergamon Press.

—— (1958). Reparable and irreparable injury, in *Radiation Biology and Medicine* (ed. Claus, W. D.). Reading, Mass.: Addison-Wesley.

—— (1959). Relation of lifespan to brain weight and body weight in mammals, in *Ciba Found. Colloquia on Ageing* (eds. Wolstenholme, G. E. W., and O'Connor, M.). London: Churchill, pp. 115–133.

—— (1965a). *Aging and Levels of Biological Organisation.* Chicago: Univ. Press.

—— (1965b). Lethal effects of whole-body irradiation in mice. *Radiol. Clin. North Am.* 3:227–241.

—— (1966). Abnutzungstheorie, in *Perspectives in Experimental Gerontology* (ed. Shock, N. W.). Springfield, Ill.: Thomas, pp. 326–335.

—— (1968). Molecular versus systemic theories on the genesis of aging. *Exp. Gerontol.* 3:265–272.

—— (1975). Maturation and longevity in relation to cranial capacity in hominid evolution, in *Primate Functional Morphology and Evolution* (ed. Tuttle, R.). The Hague: Mouton Pub., pp. 417–442.

—— (1976). Evaluation of the entropy and information terms governing mammalian longevity, in *Interdisciplinary Topics in Gerontology* (ed. Cutler, R. G.). Basel: Karger.

Sacher, G. A., Grahn, D., Hamilton, K., Gurian, J., and Lesher, S. (1958). Survival of LAF mice exposed to Co^{60} γ rays for the duration of life at dosages of 6–20,000 r/day. *Radiat. Res.* 9:175–176.

Sacher, G. A., and Staffeld, E. F. (1974). Relation of gestation time to brain weight for placental mammals: implications for the theory of vertebrate growth. *Am. Nat.* 108:583–615.

Sacher, G.A., and Trucco, E. (1962). A theory of the improved performance and survival produced by small doses of radiations and other poisons, in *Biological Aspects of Aging* London & New York: Columbia Univ. Press.

Sacher, G. A., and Trucco, E. (1962). The stochastic theory of mortality. *Ann. N.Y. Acad. Sci.* 96:985–1007.

Sakai, H., Kato, E., Matsuki, S., and Asano, S. (1968). Age and lymphocyte nucleic acids. *Lancet* I:818–819.

Saldau, M. P. (1939). (Growth rate of commercially valuable molluscs in some districts of the ' European part of the USSR.) *Bull. Inst. Freshw. Fish. (Leningr.)* 22:244–269.

Salmon, T. N. (1941). Effect of pituitary growth substance on the development of rats thyroidectomised at birth. *Endocrinology* 29:291.

Salvator, M. (1972). *Vilcabamba, Tierra de Longevos.* Quito, Ecuador: Casa de la cultura ecuadoreana.

Samis, H. V., and Wulff, V. J. (1969). The template activity of rat liver chromatin. *Exp. Gerontol.* 4 (in press).

Samis, H. V., Wulff, V. J. and Falzone, J. A. (1964). The incorporation of ^{3}H cytidine into RNA of liver nuclei in young and old rats. *Biochem. Biophys. Acta* 91:223–230.

Samorajski, T. (1977). Central neurotransmitter substances and aging—a review. *J. Amer. Geriat. Soc.* 25:337–348.

Samuels, L. T. (1946). The relation of the anterior pituitary hormones to nutrition. *Rec. Prog. Horm. Res.* 1:147.

Sanderson, W. A. (1949). Report of British Association Symposium on social and psychiatric aspects of ageing. *Nature* 163:221.

Sanadi, D. R. (1973). Decline of respiratory activity of myocardial mitochondria in senescence. *Rec. Adv. Stud. Cardiac Struct. Metab.* 3:91–96.

Sandground, J. H. (1936). On the potential longevity of various helminths, with a record from a species of *Trichostrongyhus* in man. *J. Parasitol.* 22:464.

Savory, T. H. (1927). *The Biology of Spiders*. London: Sidgwick and Jackson.

Sawin, P. B. (1954). In *Parental Age and Characteristics of the Offspring* (ed. Miner, R. W.). *Ann N.Y. Acad. Sci.* 57:451.

Saxon, J. A. (1945). Nutrition and growth and their influence on longevity in rats. *Biol. Symp* 11:177.

Saxton, J. A., and Kimball, G. C. (1941). Relation of nephrosis and other diseases of albino rats to modifications of diet. *Arch. Pathol.* 32:951.

Saxton, J. H., and Greene, H. S. N. (1939). Age and sex differences in hormone content of the rabbit hypophysis. *Endocrinology* 24:494.

Schäfer, H. (1953). Untersuchungen zu Okologie von *Bithynia tentaculata*. *Arch. Molluskenk.* 82:67–70.

Scheffer, V. B. (1950). Growth layers on the teeth of Pinnipedia as an indication of age. *Science* 112:309.

―――― (1958). Long life of a River Otter. *J. Mammal.* 39:591.

Schenk, R. U., and Bjorksten, J. (1973). The search for microenzymes. *Finska Kernist. Medd.* 82:24–46.

Schilling, J. A. (1975). Wound healing and the inflammatory response in the aged. *Maj. Probl. Clin. Surg.* 17:24–38.

Schlegel, R., and Bellanti, J. A. (1969). Increased susceptibility of males to infection. *Lancet* II:826–827.

Schloemer, C. L. (1936). The growth of the muskellunge, *Esox masquinongy immaculatus* (Garrard) in various lakes and drainage areas of Northern Wisconsin. *Copeia*, p. 185.

Schlomka, G., and Kersten, E. (1952). Über Möglichkeiten einer statistischen Altenscharakteristik auf Grund von Morbiditätszählen. *Z. Altersforsch.* 6:306.

Schlottke, E. (1930). Zellstudien an *Hydra*. I. Altern und Abbau von Zellen und Kernen. *Z. Mikr.-Anat. Forsch.* 22:493.

Schmalhäusen, I. (1928). Das Wachstumsgesetz und die Methode der Bestimmung der Wachstumskonstante. *Arch. Entw/Meck. Org.* 113:462.

―――― (1929). Zum Wachstumstheorie. *Arch. Entw/Meck. Org.* 116:5677.

Schmidt, H. (1923). Über den Alterstod der Biene. *Jena Z. f. Naturwiss.* 59:343.

Schmidt, W. J. (1952). Einiges über das Altern der Tiere. *Z. Altersforsch.* 6:344.

Schneider, K. M. (1932). Zum Tode des Leipzigen Riesensalamanders. *Zool. Gart. (Lpz.)* 5: 142.

Schonfield, D., and Robertson, E. A. (1968). The coding and sorting of digits by an elderly sample. *J. Gerontol.* 23:318–323.

Schotterer, A. (1939). Alters-und Fruchtbarkeitsrekorde der Häflingerstute "Venus" und "Leda". *Dtsch. Landw . Tierz.* 43:228–229.

Schulze-Röbbecke, G. (1951). Untersuchungen über Lebensdauer, Altern, und Tod bei Arthropoden. *Zool. Jb.* 62:366.

Schwartz, A. E. (1975). Correlation between species lifespan and capacity to activate 7,12 dimethylbenz-*d*-anthracene to a form mutagenic to a mammalian cell. *Exp. Cell Res.* 44:445–457.

Scow, R. O., and Marx, W. (1945). Response to pituitary growth hormone of rats thyroidectomized on the day of birth. *Anat. Rec.* 91:227.

Sebesta, F. (1935). Beobachtungen über das Alter der Raniden. *Blatt. Aq. Terrar.* 46:115.

Segall, P. E. and Timiras, P. S. (1976). Pathophysiologic findings after chemic tryptophan deficiency in rats. *Mech. Ageing Dev.* 5:109–124.

Sekera, E. (1926). Beiträge zur Kenntnis der Lebensdauer bei einigen Turbellarien und Süsswassernemertinen. *Zool. Anz.* 66:307.

Seltser, R., and Sartwell, P. E. (1958). Ionising radiation and the longevity of physicians. *J.A.M.A.* 166:585–587.

Selye, H. (1946). General adaptation syndrome and diseases of adaptation. *J. Clin. Endocrinol.* 6:117.

——— (1962). *Calciphylaxis.* Chicago: Univ. Press.

Selye, H., and Albert, S. (1942). Age factor in responsiveness of pituitary and adrenal folliculoids. *Proc. Soc. Exp. Biol. (N.Y.)* 50:159.

Senning, W. C. (1940). A study of age determination and growth of *Necturus maculosus* based on the parasphenoid bone. *Am. J. Anat.* 66:483.

Sergeev, A. (1937). Some materials to the problem of the reptile postembryonic growth. *Zool. Zh.* 16:723.

——— (1939). *Probl. Ecol. Biotsen. (Leningr.)* 4:276.

Seshiya, R. V. (1927). On the breeding habits and fecundity of the snail *Limnaea luteola* Lk. *J. Bombay Nat. Hist. Soc.* 32:154.

Sette, O. E. (1943). Biology of the Atlantic mackerel *(Scomber scombrus)* of North America. I. Early life history including the growth, drift and mortality of the egg and larval population. *Bull. U.S. Fish. Wildl. Serv. Fish.* 50:147.

Severtsov, A. N. (1939). (Morphological laws of the evolutionary process.) *Sorena* 3:23.

Sewell, R. B. S. (1924). Observations on growth in certain molluscs and on the changes correlated with growth in the radula of *Pyrazus palustris. Rec. Ind. Mus. (Calcutta)* 27:529–548.

Seymour, F. I., Duffy, C., and Koerner, A. (1935). A case of authenticated fertility in a man aged 94. *J.A.M.A.* 105:1423.

Shamberger, P. J. (1973). Disease cardiogen chromosome breakage. *Proc. Am. Ass. Cancer* 14:9.

Shanklin, W. M. (1953). Age changes in the histology of the human pituitary. *Acta Anat. (Basel)* 19:290.

Sharp, D. (1883). Longevity in a beetle. *Entom. Monthly Mag.* 19:260.

Sharp, W. M. (1958). Aging gray squirrels by the use of tail pelage characteristics. *J. Wildl. Manag.* 22:39–44.

Shaw, R. F., and Bercaw, B. L. (1962). Temperature and life span in poikilothermous animals. *Nature* 196:454–457.

Sheldon, J. H. (1949). *Social Medicine of Old Age.* London: Oxford Univ. Press.

Sheldon, W. G. (1949). Reproductive behaviour of foxes in New York State. *J. Mammal.* 30:236.

Shemin, D., and Rittenberg, D. (1944). Some interrelationships in general nitrogen metabolism. *J. Biol. Chem.* 153:401.

Sheps, M. C. (1961). Marriage and mortality. *Am. J. Public Health* 51:547–555.

Sherman, H. C., and Campbell, H. L. (1935). Rate of growth and length of life. *Proc. Natl. Acad. Sci. U.S.A.* 21:235.

Shire, J. G. M. (1973). Growth hormone and premature aging. *Nature* (Lond.) 245:215–216.

Shirey, T. L., and Sobel, H. (1972). Compositional and transcriptional properties of chromatins isolated from cardiac muscle of young-mature and old dogs. *Exp. Gerontol.* 7:15–30.

Shock, N. W. (1942). Standard values for basal oxygen consumption in adolescence. *Am. J. Dis. Child.* 64:19.

——— (1948). Metabolism in old age. *Geriatrics* 1:232.

——— (1951). *A Classified Bibliography of Gerontology and Geriatrics.* Palo Alto, Calif.: Stanford Univ. Press.

Shock, N. W., Watkin, D. M., and Yiengst, M. J. (1954). Age changes in renal function and basal oxygen consumption as related to total body water. *Fed. Proc.* 13:136.

Shoemaker, R. H. (1977). X chromatin and aging. *Acta Cytol.* 21:127–131.

Shulov, A. (1939–1940). On the biology of *Latrodectes* spiders in Palestine. *Proc. Linn. Soc. (Lond.)* 309.

Sigel, M. M., and Good, R.A. (1972). Tolerance, autoimmunity and aging. Springfield, Ill.: Thomas.

Silberberg, M., and Silberberg, R. (1951). Diet and life-span. *Physiol. Rev.* 35:347–362.

——— (1954). Factors modifying the life span of mice. *Am. J. Physiol.* 177:23.

Siminovitch, L., Till, J. G., and McCulloch, E. A. (1964). Decline in colony-forming ability of marrow cells subjected to serial transplantation in irradiated mice. *J. Cell. Comp. Physiol.* 64:23–27.

Simmonds, L. W. (1945). *The Role of the Aged in Primitive Society.* New Haven, Conn.: Yale Univ. Press.

——— (1946). Attitudes toward ageing and the aged: primitive societies. *J. Gerontol.* 1:72.

Simmonds, M. (1914a). Über embolische Prozesse in der Hypophysis. *Arch. f. Pathol. Anat.* 217:226.

——— (1914b). Zur Pathologie der Hypophysis. *Verh. Dtsch. Path. Ges.* 17:808.

Simms, H. S. (1936). The effect of physiological agents upon adult tissues *in vitro. Science* 83:418.

——— (1958) Aging and longevity of rats under favourable conditions. *Publ. Hlth. Rep. U.S. Publ. Health Svc.* 73:1115–1116.

Simms, H. S., and Stillman, N. P. (1936). Substances affecting adult tissue *in vitro.* II. A growth inhibitor in adult tissue. *J. Gen. Physiol.* 20:621.

——— (1937). Substances affecting adult tissue *in vitro.* III. A stimulant (the "A" factor) in serum ultrafiltrate involved in overcoming adult tissue dormancy. *J. Gen. Physiol.* 20:649.

Simonsen, M., Engelbreth-Holm, J., Jensen, E., and Poulsen, H. (1958). A study of the graft-versus-host reaction in transplantation to embryos, F_1 hybrids and irradiated animals. *Ann. N.Y. Acad. Sci.* 73:834–839.

Sinclair, H. M. (1955). Too rapid maturation in children as a cause of ageing. *Ciba Found. Colloquia on Ageing* 1:194.

Sincock, A. M. (1974). Calcium and aging in the rotifer *Mytilina brevispina* var. *redunca. J. Gerontol.* 29:514–517.

Sinex, F. M. (1957). Aging and the lability of irreplaceable molecules. *J. Gerontol.* 12:190–198.

Sivertsen, E. (1941). On the biology of the Harp Seal, *Phoca groenlandica* Ersel. *Hvalrad. Skr. (Oslo)* No. 26.

Sleptzov, M. M. (1940). Détermination de l'âge chez *Delphinus delphis* L. *Bull. Soc. Nat. (Moscow)* 49:43.

Slonaker, J. R. (1912). The normal activity of the albino rat from birth to natural death, its rate of growth and the duration of life. *J. Anim. Behav.* 2:20.

——— (1930). The effect of the excision of different sexual organs on the development, growth and longevity of the albino rat. *Am. J. Physiol.* 93:307.

Smallwood, W. M., and Phillips, R. L. (1916). The nuclear size in the nerve cells of bees during the life cycle. *J. Comp. Neurol.* 27:69.

Smart, I., and Leblond, C. P. (1961). Evidence for the division and transformations of neuroglia cells in the mouse brain as derived from radioautography after injection of thymidine-H^3. *J. Comp. Neurol.* 116:349–366.

Smith, M. (1951). *The British Amphibians and Reptiles.* London: Collins.

Smith, P. E., and Dortzbach, C. (1929). The first appearance in the anterior pituitary of the developing pig foetus of detectable amounts of the hormones stimulating ovarian maturity and general body growth. *Anat. Rec.* 43:277.

Smyth, N. (1937). Longevity in horses. *Cavalry J.* 27:101.

Snell, R. S., and Bischitz, P. G. (1963). The melanocytes and melanin in human abdominal wall skin. *J. Anat.* 97:361–376.

Sóbel, H. (1970). Follow-up on mice exposed to 1.08 ATS oxygen in nitrogen for a substantial portion of lifespan. *Aerospace Med.* 41:524–529.

Sohal, R. S. (1972). Senescent changes in brain of housefly. *Tex. Rep. Biol.* 30:192.

—— (1976). Age changes in insect flight muscle. *Gerontology* 22:317–333.

Soliman, M. H., and Lints, F. A. (1976). Bibliography on longevity, aging and parental age effects in *Drosophila*. *Gerontology* 22:380–410.

Solland, E. (1916). Recherches sur la biologie des "Palemonides" des côtes de la France. *Rec. Fonds Bonaparte* 1:69.

Solomon, D. R., and Shock, N. W. (1950). Studies of adrenal cortical and anterior pituitary function in elderly men. *J. Gerontol.* 5:302.

Sondén, K., and Tigerstedt, R. (1895). Die Respiration und der Gesammtstoffwechsel des Menschen. *Skand. Arch. Physiol.* 6:1.

Sonneborn, T. M. (1930). Genetic studies on *Stenostomum incaudatum* n. sp. I. The nature and origin of differences in individuals formed during vegetative reproduction. *J. Exp. Zool.* 57:57.

—— (1938). The delayed occurrence and total omission of endomixis in selected lines of *Paramecium aurelia*. *Biol. Bull. Wood's Hole* 74:76.

—— (1960). The human early foetal death rate in relation to the age of father, in *The Biology of Aging*, AIBS Symp., Washington, Publ. No. 6. p. 288.

—— (1974). In *Handbook of Genetics* (ed. King, R. C.). New York: Plenum.

—— (1960a). Physiological basis of aging in *Paramecium*. *Ibid.* 283–284.

Sonneborn, T. M., and Schneller, M. (1960b). Age-induced mutations in *Paramecium*. AIBS Symp. Washington Publ. No. 6, 286–287.

Sorokina, M. I. (1950). Variability of the chromosome complex in tissue cells of warm-blooded animals. *Bull. Acad. Sci. (U.R.S.S.)* 6:97.

Sosnovski, I. P. (1957). On the longevity of animals in the Moscow Zoo. *Priroda* 9:119–120.

Soukoupová, M., Holeckova, E., and Cinnerova, O. (1965). Behaviour of explanted kidney cells from young, adult and old rats. *Gerontologia* 11:141–152.

Soukoupová, M., and Holečková, E. (1964). The latent period of explanted organs of newborn, adult and senile rats. *Exp. Cell Res.* 33:361–367.

Spalding, J. F., Brooks, M. R., and Archulet, R. F. (1971). Possible single gene locus effect on life-span. Radiation-resistance and activity. *Radiat. Res.* 47:287.

Sparrow, A. H., and Shaiver, L. A. (1958). The radioresistance of high polyploids. *Radiat. Res.* 9:187.

Stebbings, R. C., and Robinson, H. B. (1946). Further analyses of a population of the lizard *Sceleporus graciosus gracilis*. *Univ. Calif. Publ. Zool.* 48:149.

Stein, M., Schiavi, R., and Camerino, M. (1976). *Science* 191:435–440.

Steinmetz, C. H. (1954). Some effects of thyroxine and antithyroid compounds on tadpoles and their relation to hormonal control of growth. *Physiol. Zool.* 27:28.

Stelfox, A. W. (1968). On the inheritance of scalariformity in *Hulix aspersa*. *J. Conchol.* 26:329–332.

Stephan, H. (1954). Die Anwendung der Snell'schen Formel $h = k^3 p$ auf die Hirn-Körpergewichtsbeziehungen bei verschiedenen Hunderassen. *Zool. Anx.* 153:15–27.

Stephen, A. C. (1931). Notes on the biology of certain lamellibranchs on the Scottish coast. *J. Mar. Biol. Ass. (U.K.)* 17:277–300.

Stephenson, R. A. (1935). *British Sea Anemones*. London: The Ray Society.

Sterns, E. L., MacDonnell, J. A., and Kaufman, B. J. (1974). Declining testicular function with age. *Am. J. Med.* 57:761–766.

Stevenson, J. A. (1932). Growth in the giant scallop squid *(Loligo pealii)* at St. Andrews N.B. *Ann. Rep. Biol. Bd. (Ottawa)*, pp. 37–38.

Spear, F. G. (1928). The effect of low temperature on mitosis *in vitro*. *Arch. Exp. Zelforsch.* 1:484.

Spector, I. M. (1974). Animal longevity and protein turnover rates. *Nature (New Biol.)* 249:66.

Spector, W. S. (1956). *Handbook of Biological Data.* Philadelphia: W. B. Saunders.

Spemann, F. W. (1924). Über Lebensdauer, Altern und andere Fragen der Rotatorien-Biologie. *Z. Wiss. Zool.* 123:1.

Spencer, R. R., and Melroy, M. B. (1949). Studies of survival of unicellular species. I. Variations in life expectancy of a *Paramecium* under laboratory conditions. *J. Nat. Cancer Inst.* 10:1.

Speyer, J. G. (1965). Mutagenic DNA polymerases. *Biochem. Biophys. Acta* 91:223–227.

Spiegelman, S., Baron, L. S., and Quastler, H. (1951). Enzymatic adaptation in non-viable cells. *Fed. Proc.* 10:130.

Spieth, W. E. (1965). In *Behaviour, Aging and the Nervous System* (ed. Welford, A. T., and Birren, J. F.). Springfield, Ill.: Thomas, p. 366.

Stanczykowa, A. (1964). On the relationship between abundance, aggregation and condition of *Dreissena polymorpha* pall in Masurian Lakes. *Ekol. Ph.* A12:653–690.

Stearns, R. E. C. (1877). On the vitality of certain land molluscs. *Amer. Nat.* 11:100–102.

Stebbings, R. C. (1948). Additional observations on home ranges and longevity in the lizard *Sceleporus graciosus. Copeia,* p. 20.

Stewart, D. C., and Kirk, P. L. (1954). The liquid medium in tissue culture. *Biol. Rev.* 29:119.

Stokes, B. (1958). The worm-eating slugs *Testacella scutulum* Sow. and *T. haliotidea* Drap. in captivity. *Proc. Malac. Soc. (Lond.)* 33:11–20.

Stolč, A. (1902). Über den Lebenszyklus der niedrigsten Süsswasserannulaten und über einiger sich anschliessende biologische Fragen. *Bull. Int. Acad. Sci. (Boheme)*

Stolte, H. A. (1924). Altersveränderung bei limicolen Oligochaeten. *Verhand. Deutsch. Zool. Ges.* 29:43.

———— (1927). Studien zur Histologie des Altersprozesses. *Z. Wiss. Zool.* 129:1.

———— (1937). Gestaltung, Zeichnung und Organabbau unter dem Einfluss normaler und "alternden" Gonaden bei *Polyophthalmus pictus* (Polychaeta). *Z. Wiss. Zool.* 150:107.

Storer, J. B. (1959). Rate of recovery from radiation damage and its possible relation to life-shortening in mice. *Radiat. Res.* 10:180–185.

———— (1965). In *Aging and Levels of Biological Organisation* (ed. Brues, A. M., and Sacher, G. A.). Chicago: Univ. Press, p. 192.

Strehler, B. L. (1959). Origins and comparisons of the effects of time and high energy radiations on living systems. *Q. Rev. Biol.* 34:117–142.

———— (1961). Aging in coelenterates, in *Biology of Hydra and other Coelenterates* (eds. Lenhoff, H. M., and Loomis, W. F.). Univ. Coral Gables, Fla.: Univ. Miami Press.

———— (1962). Further studies on the thermally-induced aging of *Drosophila melanogaster. J. Gerontol.* 17:347–352.

———— (1962). *Time, Cells and Aging.* New York: Academic Press.

———— (1964). On the histochemistry and ultrastructure of age pigment. *Adv. Geront. Res.* 1:343–348.

———— (1966). In *Perspectives in Experimental Gerontology* (ed. Shock, N.). Springfield, Ill: Thomas.

———— (1969). Molecular biology of aging. *Naturwiss.* 56:57–71.

Strehler, B. L., Hirsch, G., Gusseck, D., Johnson, R., and Bick, M. (1971). Codon-restriction theory of aging and development. *J. Theor. Biol.* 33:429–474.

Strehler, B. L., Mark, D. D., Mildvan, A. S., and Gee, V. (1959). Rate and magnitude of pigment accumulation in the human myocardium. *J. Gerontol.* 14:430–439.

Strong, L. C. (1936). Production of CBA strain inbred mice: long life associated with low tumour incidence. *Br. J. Exp. Pathol.* 17:60.

Strong, L. C., and Smith, G. M. (1936). Benign hepatomas in mice of the CBS strain. *Am. J. Cancer* 27:279.

Struck, H., and Engelhardt, G. H. (1971). Altersabhängigkeit der Wundheilung. *Z. f. Gerontol.* 4:356–362.

Stuchlíková, E., Juricobá-Horaková, M., and Deyl, Z., (1975). New aspect of the dietary effect of life prolongation in rodents. What is the role of obesity in aging? *Exp. Gerontol.* 10:141–144.

Sturrock, R. R. (1976). Changes in neuroglia and myelination in the white matter of aging mice. *J. Gerontol.* 31:513–522.

Sullivan, J. L., and De Busk, A. G. (1973). Inositol-less death of *Neurospora* and cellular aging. *Nature (New Biol.)* 243:72–74.

Sulman, F. G., and Superstine, E. (1972). Aging and adrenal-medulla exhaustion due to lack of monoamines and raised monoamine oxidase levels. *Lancet* II:663.

Summers, F. M. (1938). Form regulation in *Zoothamnion alternans. Biol. Bull. Wood's Hole* 74:130.

Suntzeff, V., Cowdry, E. V., and Hixon, B. B. (1962). Possible maternal influence on longevity of offspring in mice, in *Biological Aspects of Aging* New York & London: Columbia Univ. Press.

Suzuki, S. (1935). On the age and growth of *Nerita japonica* Dunken. *Sci. Rep. Res. Inst. Tohuku Univ.* [Med] 10:247–246.

Suzuki, Y. (1926). A study of the resistance of animals by the tissue culture method. *Mitt. Allg. Pathol. Sendai* 2:191.

Sved, S., Kral, V. A., Enesco, H. E., Solyon, L., Wigdor, B. T., and Mauer, S. M. (1967). Memory and serum ribonuclease activity in the aged. *J. Am. Geriatr. Soc.* 15:629–639.

Swartz, F., Sams, B. F., and Barton, A. G. (1960). Polyploidization of rat liver following castration of males and females. *Exp. Cell Res.* 20:438–446.

Swift, D. R. (1954). Influence of mammalian growth hormone on rate of growth of fish. *Nature (Lond.)* 173:1096.

Swyer, G. I. M. (1954). *Reproduction and Sex.* London: Routledge.

Szabó, I. (1931a). Absterben und Entwicklung. *Biol. Gen.* 7:163.

―――― (1931b). The three types of mortality curves. *Q. Rev. Biol.* 6:462.

―――― (1932a). Das Alterspigment bei einigen Schnecken, untersucht an überlebenden Ganglienzellen. *Arb. Ung. Biol. Forsch. Inst.* 5:38.

―――― (1932b). *Elettartam és öregedés.* Budapest.

―――― (1935). Senescence and death in invertebrate animals. *Riv. Biol.* 19:377.

Szabó, I., and Szabó, M. (1929). Lebensdauer, Wachstum und Altern, studiert bei der Nacktschneckenart *Agriolimax agrestis. Biol. Gen.* 5:95–118.

―――― (1930a). Todesursachen und pathologische Erscheinungen bei Pulmonaten. *Arch. f. Mollusk.* 62:123.

―――― (1930b). Vorläufige Mitteilung über die an der Nacktschnecke *Agriolimax agrestis* beobachten Altersveränderungen. *Arb. Ungar. Biol. Forsch. Inst.* 3:350–357.

―――― (1931a). Histologische Studien über den Zusammenhang der verschiedenen Alterserscheinungen bei Schnecken. I and II. *Z. vgl. Physiol.* 15:329, 345.

―――― (1931b). Lebenszyklen der Nacktschnecke *Limax flavus* L. *Zool. Anz.* 96:35–38.

―――― (1931c). Todesursachen und pathologische Erscheinungen bei Pulmonaten. H. Hautkrankheiten bei Nacktschnecken. *Arch. Molluskenk* 63:156–160.

―――― (1934a). Alterserscheinungen und Alterstod bei Nacktschnecken. *Biol. Zbl.* 54:471–477.

―――― (1934b). Lebensdauer und Körpergrösse einiger Nacktschnecken. *Zool. Anz.* 106:106–111.

―――― (1936). Histologische Untersuchungen über den Zusammenhang zwischen Langlebigkeit und Fortpflanzung. *Zool. Anz.* 113:143–153.

Szabó, M. (1935a). On a culture method for the rotifer *Lecane Inermis* Bv. together with some notes on the biology of this animal. *Arb. ung. Biol. Forsch. Inst.* 8.

―――― (1935b). Pathologische Erscheinungen bei Schnecken. *Allattani Kozl. T.* 32:132.

Szafran, J. (1965). Age differences in sequential decisions and cardiovascular status among pilots. *Aerospace Med.* 36:303–310.

Szilagyi, T., Csernyani, H., Csako, G., and Benko, K. (1971). Influence of hypothermia on the Arthus phenomenon and leukotaxis. *Experientia* 27:1469.

Szilard, L. (1959). On the nature of the aging process. *Proc. Natl. Acad. Sci.* (U.S.A.) 45:30–45.

――― (1960). Dependence of the sex ratio at birth on the age of the father. *Nature* (Lond.) 186:649–650.

Tack, E. (1940). Die Ellritze (*Phoxinus laevis* Bg.): eine monographische Bearbeitung. *Arch. Hydrobiol.* 37:321.

Tainter, M. L. (1936). Dinitrophenol in diet, on growth and duration of life of the white rat *(sic)*. *Proc. Soc. Exp. Biol.* 31:1161.

――― (1938). Growth, life-span and food intake of white rats fed dinitrophenol throughout life. *J. Pharmacol.* 63:51.

Tanaka, T. (1951). A study of the somatic chromosomes in various organs of the white rat (*Rattus norvegicus*) especially in regard to the number and its variation. *Res. Genet.* 2:39.

――― (1953). A study of the somatic chromosomes of rats. *Cytologia* 18:343.

Tang, S. F. (1941). The breeding of the escallop *Pecten maximus* (L) with a note on the growth rate. *Proc. Lpool. Biol. Soc.* 54:9–28.

Tannenbaum, A. (1947). Effects of varying caloric intake upon tumor incidence and tumor growth. *Ann. N.Y. Acad. Sci.* 49:6–17.

Tanner, J. M. (1955). *Growth at Adolescence.* Oxford: Blackwell.

Tannreuther, G. (1919). Studies on *Asplanchnia ebbesborni* with special reference to the male. *Biol. Bull. Wood's Hole* 37:194.

Tappel, A. L. (1968). Will antioxidant nutrients slow aging process? *Geriatrics* 23:97–105.

Tappel, A. L., and Zalkin, H. (1959). Inhibition of lipid peroxidation in mitochondria by Vit. E. *Arch. Biochem. Biophys.* 30:333–336.

Tauchi, H. (1961). On the fundamental morphology of the senile changes. *Nagoya J. Med. Sci.* 8:1–22.

Taylor, D. W. (1958). Effects of tocophenols, methylene blue and glutathione on the manifestations of oxygen poisoning in Vit. E. deficient rats. *J. Physiol.* 140:37–47.

Taylor, J. W. (1894–1924). *Monograph of the Land and Freshwater Mollusca of the British Isles.* Leeds:Taylor.

Taylor, M. (1958). Longevity of the Proteus group of amoebae. *Nature* 182:1245.

Taylor, R. H. (1959). Age determination in wild rabbits. *Nature (Lond.)* 184:1158–1159.

Tegge, M. S. (1936). Length of life of a rabbit. *Science* 84:575.

Teissier, G. (1934). Recherches sur le vieillissement et sur les lois de la mortalité. II. Essai d'interprétation générale des courbes de survie. *Ann. Physiol. Phys-Chim. Biol.* 10:260–284.

Teller, M. N., Stokes, G., Curlett, W., Kubisek, M. L., and Curtis, D. (1964). Aging and cancerigenesis. I. Immunity to tumor and skin grafts. *J. Natl. Cancer Inst.* 33:649–656.

Terao, A. (1931). Change of vitality with age as based on the living unit of the organism. I. Oxygen consumption in the daphnid *Simocephalus exspinosus. Proc. Imp. Acad. (Tokyo)* 7:23.

――― (1932). Duration of life in the water flea *Moina macropa Straus,* with special reference to rate of living. *J. Imp. Fish. Inst.* 27:63.

Terao, A., and Tanaka, T. (1930). Duration of life in the water flea *Moina macropa* Straus in relation to temperature. *J. Imp. Fish. Inst.* 25:67.

Tereschenko, K. K. (1917). La brême (*Abramis brama*) de la région du Volga et de la mer Caspienne. *Trav. Lab. Ichthyol. Astrakhan* 4:2.

Thannhauser, S. J. (1945). Werner's syndrome (progeria of the adult) and Rothmund's syndrome:

2 types of closely related hereditofamilial atrophic dermatoses with juvenile cataracts and endocrine features; a critical study with 5 new cases. *Ann. Intern. Med.* 23:559.

Theorell, H., Beznak, M., Bonnichsen, R., Paul, K. G., and Akeson, A. (1951). Distribution of injected radioactive iron in guinea pigs and its rate of appearance in some hemoproteins and feuritins. *Acta. Chem. Scand.* 5:445.

Therman, E., and Timonen, S. (1951). Inconstancy of the human somatic chromosome complement. *Hereditas* 37:266.

Thompson, D'Arcy W. (1942). *On Growth and Form,* new Ed., Cambridge: Univ. Press, p. 199.

Thoms, W. J. (1873). *The Longevity of Man: Its Facts and Fictions.* London.

Thomson, A. P. (1938). Sudden appearance of senility after an accident. *Lancet* II:135–136.

Thomson, J., and Forfar, J. O. (1950). Progeria (Hutchinson-Gilford syndrome). Report of a case and review of the literature. *Arch. Dis. Child.* 25:224.

Thummel, E. (1938). Lebensdauer einer Blindschleiche. *Zool. Garten. (Lpz.)* 10:153.

Thung, P. J. (1962). In: *Structural Aspects of Ageing.* (ed. Bourne, G.) London: Pitman Medical.

Thuringer, J. M., and Katzberg, A. A. (1959). The effect of age on mitosis in the human epidermis. *J. Invest. Dermatol.* 33:35–39.

Till, J. E., and McCulloch, E. A. (1961). In vivo radiosensitivity of bone marrow. *Radiat. Res.* 14:213.

Timonen, S., and Therman, E. (1950). Variation of the somatic chromosome number in man. *Nature (Lond.)* 166:995.

Tomasch, J. (1972). Gibt es einen altersbedingten kontinuerlichen Neuronenverlust? *Klin. Wochenschr. (Wien.)* 84:169–170.

Tomilin, M. I. (1936). Death of the oldest chimpanzee in captivity. *Science* 83:103.

Townsend, C. H. (1931). Growth and age in the giant tortoise of the Galapagos. *Zoologica (N.Y.)* 9:469.

—— (1937). Growth of the Galapagos tortoise, *Testudo vicina,* from 1928 to 1937. *Zoologica (N.Y.)* 22:289.

Townsend, F. (1946). Ageing processes in the endocrine glands. *J. Gerontol.* 1:278.

Tribe, M. A. (19   ). Age-related changes in the respiratory physiology of flight muscles from the blowfly, *Calliphora erythrocephala. Exp. Gerontol.* 2:113–122.

Troup, G. M., Smith, G. S., and Walford, R. L. (1969). Life span, chronologic disease patterns, and age-related changes in relative spleen weights for the Mongolian gerbil (Meriones unguiculatus). *Exp. Gerontol.* 4:139–144.

Tudorancea, C. (1969). Comparison of the populations of *Unio tumidus,* Phil. from the complex of Crapire-Jijila marshes. *Ekol. Polka.* 17:185–204.

Tudorancea, C., and Gruia, L. (1968). Observations in the *Unio crassus* Phil. population from the Nera River. *Trav. Mus. Hist. Nat. Grigore Antipa* 8:381–394.

Turner, C. W., and Cupps, P. T. (1938). The thyrotropic hormone of the pituitary in albino rats during growth, pregnancy and lactation. *Endocrinology* 24:650.

Turner, C. W., and Kempster, H. L. (1948). Mild hypothyroidism maintains egg production with advancing age. *Poult. Sci.* 27:453.

Tyler, A. (1953). Prolongation of the life span of sea urchin spermatozoa and improvement of the fertilization reaction, by treatment of sperm and eggs with metal chelating agents. *Biol. Bull. Wood's Hole* 104:224.

—— (1960). Clues to the etiology, pathology, and therapy of cancer provided by analogies with transplantation disease. *J. Nat. Cancer Inst.* 25:1197–1229.

Ubisch, L. (1926). Untersuchungen über Bau, Funktion, Entwicklung und Regeneration der Rense des Weibchens von *Stephanoceros eichorni. Z. Wiss. Zool.* 127:590.

Ulland, B. M., Weisburg, H. H., Yamamoto, R. S., and Weisburg, E. K. (1972). Antioxidants and carcinogenesis. *Tox. Appl. Pharmacol.* 22:281(a).

Ulmer, F. A. (1960). A longevity record for the Mindanao Tarsier. *J. Mammal.* 41:512.

Ungar, G. (1944). The inhibition of histamine release by a pituitary-adrenal syndrome. *J. Physiol.* 103:333–343.

Upton, A. C. (1957). Ionizing radition and the aging process. *J. Gerontol.* 12:306–313.

—— (1960). Ionizing radiation and aging. *Gerontologia* 4:162–176.

Upton, A. C., Kimball, A. W., Furth, J., Christenberry, K. W., and Benedict, W. H. (1960). Some delayed effects of atom-bomb radiations in mice. *Cancer Res.* 20:1–62.

Upton, A. C., McDonald, T. P., Christenberry, K. W., and Gude, W. D. (1961). Delayed somatic effects of radiometric agents and X-rays. *Biol. Div. Semiannual Progr. Rep.*, (Oak Ridge Natl. Lab. Publ. 3095), February 15, 1961, p. 84.

Vallois, H. V. (1937). La durée de vie chez l'homme fossile. *C. R. Acad. Sci.* 204:60.

van Cleave, H. J. (1934). Length of life-span as a factor in regulating populations. *Ecology* 15:17.

van Cleave, H. J., and Altringer, D. A. (1937). Studies in the life-cycle of *Campeloma rufum*, a freshwater snail. *Amer. Nat.* 71:167–184.

van Cleave, H. J., and Chambers, R. (1935). Studies in the life history of a snail of the genus Lioplax. *Am. Midl. Nat.* 16:913.

van Cleave, H. J., and Lederer, L. C. (1932). Studies on the life cycle of the snail *Viviparus contectoides*. *J. Morphol.* 53:499.

van Cleave, H. J., and Markus, H. C. (1929). Studies on the life cycle of the blunt-nosed minnow. *Amer. Nat.* 63:530.

van der Horst (1929). Lebensalter und Schalengrösse. *Arch. Mollusk.* 61:46.

Van Dorp, N. (1970). Ionising radiations and ageing. *Nucl. Energy* 11:115.

Vane, F. R. (1946). Longevity of mayflies. *Northw. Nat.* 21:252.

van Heerdt, P. F., and Sluiter, J. W. (1955). Longevity in bats. *Natuur-hist. Maandbl.* 44:35.

van Loon, G. R. (1973). In *Frontiers in Neuroendocrinology* (eds. Ganong, W. F., and Martini). New York: Oxford.

Van Wagenen, G. (1970). Menopause in a subhuman primate. *Anat. Rec.* 166: 392.

Varkonyi, T., Domokos, H., Maurer, M., Zoltan, O. T., Czillik, B., and Foldi, M. (1970). Die Wirkung von dl Kavain und Mg-Orotat auf die feinstrukturellen neuropathologischen Veränderungen der experimentellen Lymphogenen Enzephalopathie. *Z. Gerontol.* 3:354–360.

Varley, G. C. (1947). The natural control of population balance in the knapweed gall-fly (*Urophora jaceana*). *J. Anim. Ecol.* 16:139.

Vaznetzoff, V. V. (1934). Versuch einer vergleichenden Erforschung des Wachstums der Cypriniden. *Zoo. Zh.* 13:540.

Venge, O. (1953). Studies of the maternal influence on the growth in rabbits. *Acta Agric. Scand.* 3:243.

Verzár, F. (1955). Veränderung der thermoelastischen Eigenschaften von Sehnenfasern beim Altern. *Experientia* 11:230.

—— (1957). Aging of connective tissue. *Gerontologia* 1:363–378.

—— (1959a). Influence of ionizing radiation on the age reaction of collagen fibres. *Gerontologia* 3:163–170.

—— (1959b). Note on the influence of procain (Novocain) para-aminobenzoic acid or diethylethanolamine on the ageing of rats. *Gerontologia* 3:351–358.

—— (1963). *Lectures on Experimental Gerontology.* Springfield, Ill.: Thomas.

—— (1964). Factors which influence the age reaction of collagen in skin. *Gerontologia (Basel)* 9:209–221.

Vetukhiv, M. (1957). Longevity of hybrids between geographic populations of *Drosophila pseudoobscura*. *Evolution* 11:348–360.

Victor, J., and Potter, J. S. (1935). Studies in mouse leukaemia: preleukaemic changes in lymphoid metabolism. *Br. J. exp. Pathol.* 16:243.

Vignal, L. (1919). Observations sur les *Rumina decollata. Bull. Soc. Zool. Fr.* 44:115.
—— (1923). De la durée de la vie chez l'*Helix spiriplana* Olivi. *J. Conchol.* 67:262.
Vischer, A. L. (1947). *Old Age, its Compensations and Rewards.* London: Allen and Unwin.
Visscher, M. B., King, J. T., and Lee, Y. C. P. (1952). Further studies of the influence of age and diet upon reproductive senescence in strain A female mice. *Am. J. Physiol.* 170:72–76.
Vogt, C., and Vogt, O. (1946). Age changes in neurones. *Nature* 158:304.
Vogt, W. (1949). *The Road to Survival.* London and New York:
Von Borstel, R. C., Prescott, D. M., and Bollum, F. J. (1966). Incorporation of nucleotides into nuclei of fixed cells by DNA polymerase. *J. Cell Biol.* 29:21–28.
von Hagen, W. (1938). Contribution to the biology of *Nasutitermes* s.s. *Proc. Zool. Soc. (Lond.)* 108, A:39.
Von Hahn, H. P. (1971). Failures of regulation mechanisms as causes of cellular aging. *Adv. Geront. Res.* 3:1–38.
Von Hahn, H. P., and Fritz, E. (1966). Age-related alterations in the structure of DNA. *Gerontologia* 12:237–249.
Von Hahn, H. P., and Verzár, F. (1963). Age-dependent thermal denaturation of DNA from bovine thymus. *Gerontologia* 7:105–108.
von Hansemann, D. (1914). Über Alterserscheinungen bei *Bacillus rossii. Sitzb. Nat. Fr. Berlin,* pp. 187–191.
von Hessling, T. (1859). *Die Perlmuscheln und ihre Perlen.* Leipzig.
von Reden, K. A. (1960). Sterblichkeitsmaxima bei *Daphnia magna* Straus. *Z. f. Wiss. Zool.* 164:119–126.
Vrbiescu, A., and Domilescu C. (1965) In *Intl. Conf. Gerontology Budapest Acad. Sci.* (Ed. Balázs, A.), pp. 737–762.
Waddington, C. H. (1957). *The Strategy of the Genes.* London: Allen and Unwin.
Wagner, E. (1971). Die physiologischen klinischen Laboratoriumswerte in Alter. *Actuelle Gerontol.* 9:531–538.
Walburg, H. E., and Hoel, D. E. (1972). Life-shortening and accelerated aging. *Radiat. Res.* 51:478.
Waldenstrom, J. (1970). Maladies of derepression: pathological, often monoclonal, derepression of protein-forming templates. *Schweiz. Med. Wschr.* 100:2197–2206.
Walford, R. L. (1962). Autoimmunity and aging. *J. Gerontol.* 17:281–285.
—— (1964). Further considerations towards an immunologic theory of aging. *Exp. Gerontol.* 1:67–76.
—— (1969). *The Immunologic Theory of Aging.* Copenhagen:Munksgaard.
Walford, R. L., and Liu, R. (1965). Husbandry, lifespan and growth rate of the annual fish Cynolebias adloffi E. Ahl. *Exp. Gerontol.* 1:161–172.
Walford, R. L., Liu, R. K., Gerbase-Delima, M., Mathies, M. and Smith, G. S. (1974). Longterm dietary restriction and immune function in mice. *Mech. Ageing Dev.* 2:447–454.
Walker, A. I., Stevenson, D. E., Robinson, J., Thorpe, E. and Roberts, M. (1969). Toxicology and pharmacology of dieldrin. *Tox. Appl. Pharmacol.* 15:345–360.
Walker, B. E., and Boothroyd, E. R. (1953). Chromosome numbers in somatic tissues of mouse and man. *Genetics* 39:210.
Walker, D. G., Asling, C. W., Simpson, M. E., Li, C. H., and Evans, H. M. (1952). Structural alterations in rats hypophysectomised at six days of age and their connection with growth hormone. *Anat. Rec.* 114:19.
Wallace, D. C. (1967). The inevitability of growing old. *J. Chron. Dis.* 20:476–486.
Wallach, Z., and Gershon, D. (1974). Altered ribosomal particles in senescent nematodes. *Mech. Ageing. Dev.* 3:225–234.
Walne, P. R. (1961). Observations on the mortality of *Ostraea edulis. J. Mar. Biol. Ass. (U.K.)* 41:113–122.

Waloff, N., Norris, M. J., and Broadhead, E. C. (1947). Fecundity and longevity of *Ephestia elutella* Hubner. *Proc. R. Soc. (Lond.)* 99:245.

Walsh, R. J. (1964). Variations in the melanin content of the skin of New Guinea natives at different ages. *J. Invest. Dermatol.* 42:261–265.

Walter, E. (1922). Über die Lebensdauer der freilebenden Süsswassercyclopiden und andere Fragen ihrer Biologie. *Zool. Jb.* (Syst. Abt.) 44:375.

Walters, H., and Walford, R. L. (1970). Latent period for outgrowth of human skin explants as a function of age. *J. Gerontol.* 25:381–383.

Walterstorff, W. (1928). *Triton (Cynops) pyrrhogaster* 25 Jahre. *Blatt. Aquar. Terrar. Kde.* 39:183.

Walton, C. L., and Hones, W. W. (1926). Further observations on the life history of *Limnaea truncatula*. *Parasitology* 18:144–147.

Wardle, R. A., and McLeod, J. A. (1952). *The Zoology of Tapeworms*. Minneapolis: Univ. Minn. Press.

Waring, M. J. (1968). Drugs which affect the structure and function of DNA. *Nature (Lond.)* 219:1320–1325.

Warren, S. (1956). Longevity and causes of death from irradiation in physicians. *J.A.M.A.* 162:

Warthin, A. S. (1929). *Old Age, the Major Involution; the Physiology and Pathology of the Ageing Process*. New York: Hoeber.

Watkin, E. E. (1941). The yearly life cycle of the amphipod *Corophium volutator*. *J. Anim. Ecol.* 10:77.

Watkins, B. E., Meites, J., and Riegle, G. D. (1975). Age-related changes in pituitary responsiveness to LHRH in the female rat. *Endocrinology* 97:543–548.

Webb, S., and Tribe, M. A. (1974). Are there major degenerative changes in the flight muscle of aging diptera? *Exp. Gerontol.* 9:43–49.

Weber, R. (1942). Höhes Alter verschiedenen Tiere in Düsseldörfer Zoologischen Garten. *Zool. Gart.* 14:208.

Weblicki, W. B., Luna, Z., and Nair, P. P. (1968). Sex and tissue specific differences in concentration of α-tocopherol in mature and senescent rats. *Nature* 221:185–186.

Weismann, A. (1882). *Über die Dauer des Lebens*. Jena.

——— (1891). The duration of life, in *Essays upon Heredity*. Oxford: Univ. Press.

Weiss, J.,and Lansing, A. I. (1953). Age changes in the fine structure of anterior pituitary of the mouse. *Proc. Soc. Exp. Biol. (N.Y.)* 82:460.

Weiss, P. (1950). Perspectives in the field of morphogenesis. *Q. Rev. Biol.* 25:177–198.

Welch, R. (1901). Longevity of land molluscs. *Irish Nat.* 10:145.

Wellensieck, U. (1953). Die Allometrie Verhältnisse und Konstruktionsänderung bei dem kleinsten Fisch im Vergleich mit etwas grösseren verwandten Formen. *Zool. Jb. (Anat.)* 73:187.

Wendt, A. (1934). Verjungung eines Marmormolches. *Blatt. Aquar. Terrar.* 45:281.

Werner, C. W. O. (1904). *Über Katarakt in Verbindung mit Sklerodermie*. Inaugural Dissertation, Kiel.

Westoll, T. S. (1950). Some aspects of growth studies in fossils. *Proc. R. Soc.* 137(B):490–509.

Wexler, B. C. (1976). In *Hypothalamus, Pituitary and Aging* (Eds. Everitt, A. and Burgess, J. A.). Springfield, Ill.: C. C. Thomas.

Weyer, F. (1931). Cytologische Untersuchungen am Gehirn alternden Bienen und die Frage nach dem Alterstod. *Z. Zellforsch.* 14:1–54.

Weymouth, F. W. (1923). The life history and growth of the Pismo clam. *Fish. Bull. No. 7, Calif. State Fish and Game Commission,* Sacramento.

——— (1931). The relative growth-rate and mortality of the Pacific razor clam (*Siliqua patula* Dixon) and their bearing on commercial fishery. *Bull. U.S. Bur. Fish.* 46:543.

Weymouth, F. W., and McMillin, H. C. (1931). The relative growth and mortality of the Pacific razor clam (*Siliqua patula* Dixon) and their bearing on the commercial fishery. *Bull. U.S. Bureau Fish.* 46:543–567.

Weymouth, F. W., and Thompson, S. H. (1930). The age and growth of the Pacific cockle. (*Cardium corbis* Martyn). *Bull. U.S. Fish. (Wash.)* 46:633–641.

Wheeler, J. F. G. (1934). On the stock of whales at South Georgia. *Discovery Rep.* 9:251.

Wheeler, K. T. and Lett, J. T. (1974). On the possibility that DNA repair is related to age in nondividing cells. *Proc. Nat.Acad. Sci.* 71:1862–1865.

Wheelwright, O. M. (1941). Life span of foxes. *Field (Lond.)* 197:438.

Whitney, J. E., Bennet, L. L., Li, C. H., and Evans, H. M. (1948). Effect of growth hormone on the N_2 excretion and body weight of adult female rats. *Endocrinology* 43:237.

Widdowson, E. M., and Kennedy, G. C. (1962). Rate of growth, mature-weight, and life-span. *Proc. R. Soc.* 156:96–108.

Wiedenreich, F. (1939). The duration of life of fossil man in China and the pathological lesions found in his skeleton. *China Med. J.* 55:34.

Wiesner, B. P. (1932). The experimental study of senescence. *Br. Med. J.* II:585.

Wiesner, B. P., and Sheard, N. M. (1934). The duration of life in an albino rat population. *Proc. R. Soc. Edinb.* 55:1.

Wiesner, B. P., and Yudkin, J. (1952). Inhibition of estrous by cultivated gromwell. *Nature* 170:474.

Wigglesworth, V. B. (1934). Physiology of ecdysis in *Rhodnius prolixus* (Hemiptera). II. Factors controlling moulting and metamorphosis. *Q. J. Microstruct. Sci.* 76:269.

—— (1953a). Hormone balance and the control of metamorphosis in *Rhodnius prolixus* (Hemiptera). *J. Exp. Biol.* 29:620.

—— (1953b). The thoracic gland in *Rhodnius prolixus* (Hemiptera) and its role in moulting. *J. Exp. Biol.* 29:561.

Wilkes, M. M., et al. (1975). *Proc. 10th Intl. Congr. Gerontol.* 2:39

Wilkins, G. L. (1948). Prolonged dormancy of *Planorbis corneus* L. and *Limnaea peregra* Muller. *J. Conchol.* 22:303.

Will, L. C., and McCay, C. M. (1943). Ageing, basal metabolism and retarded growth. *Arch. Biochem.* 2:481.

Williams, C., Moorhead, L. V., and Pulis, J. F. (1959). Juvenile hormone in thymus, human placenta and other mammalian organs. *Nature* 183:405.

Williams, L. W. (1910). *The Anatomy of the Common Squid* (*Loligo pealii* Leseur). Leiden: E. J. Brill.

Williamson, A. R., and Askonas, B. A. (1972). Senescence of an antibody-forming cell clone. *Nature* 238:337–338.

Wilson, D. P. (1949). Notes from the Plymouth aquarium. *J. Mar. Biol. Ass. (U.K.)* 28:345.

Wilson, M. A. (1950). Duration of life in *Rana temporaria* Linn. *Br. J. Herpetol.* 3:66.

Wilson, P. D., Hill, B. T., and Franks, L. M. (1975). The effect of age on mitochondrial enzymes and respiration. *Gerontologia* 21:95–101.

Wilson, R. H., and de Eds, F. (1959). Toxicity studies on the antioxidant 6-ethoxy-1, 2-dihydro-2, 2, 4-trimethylquinoline. *J. Agr. Food Chem.* 7:203–206.

Wimpenny, R. S. (1953). *The Plaice*. London: Arnold.

Winsor, C. P., and Winsor, A. A. (1935). The longevity and fertility of the pond-snail *Limnaea columella. J. Wash. Acad. Sci.* 25:302–307.

Witschi, E. Gonadotropins of the human hypophysis, particularly in old age. *J. Gerontol.* 7:307.

—— (1966). Endocrine aspects of aging in the guppy. I. The thyroid gland. *Exp. Gerontol.* 1:315–330.

—— (1967a). Effects of food restriction on thyroid activity in the guppy Lebistes reticulatus (Peters). *Exp. Gerontol.* 2:49–56.

—— (1967b). Endocrine aspects of aging in the guppy. II. The interrenal gland. *Exp. Gerontol.* 2:159–172.

Woodhead, A. D., and Ellett, S. (1969). Endocrine aspects of aging in the guppy. III. The testis. *Exp. Gerontol.* 4:17–26.

—— (1969). The ovary. *Exp. Gerontol.* 4:197–205.

Wolfe, J. M. (1941). Effects of testosterone propionate on the structure of the anterior pituitaries of old male rats. *Endocrinology* 29:969.

—— (1943). The effects of advancing age in the structure of the anterior hypophysis and ovaries of female rats. *Am. J. Anat.* 72:361.

Woodruffe, G. E. (1951). A life-history of the brown house moth, *Hofmanophila pseudospretella* Faint. *Bull. Ent. Res.* 41:529.

Woolley, G. (1946). In Hamilton, J. B. (1948). *Rec. Prog. Horm. Res.* 3:257.

Woolley, G. W., and Little, C. C. (1946). Prevention of adrenal cortical carcinoma by diethylstilbestrol. *Proc. Natl. Acad. Sci. (U.S.A.)* 32:239.

Wright, E. A., and Spink, J. M. (1959). A study of loss of nerve cells in the central nervous system in relation to age. *Gerontologia* 3:277–287.

Wright, M. N. (1936). The oldest jennet? *Field,* p. 1556.

Wright, S. (1926). Effect of age of parents upon characteristics of the guinea pig. *Am. Nat.* 60:552.

Wulff, V. J., Quastler, H., and Sherman, F. G. (1962). A hypothesis concerning RNA metabolism and aging. *Proc. Natl. Acad. Sci. (U.S.A.)* 48:1373–1375.

Wurmbach, H. (1951). Über Wachstum und Altern der Fische. *Z. Altersforsch.* 5:277.

Wust, C. J., and Rosen, L. (1972). Aminoacylation and methylation of t-RNA as a function of age in the rat. *Exp. Gerontol.* 7:331–344.

Wuttke, W., and Meites, J. (1973). Effects of electrochemical stimulation of medical preoptic area on prolactin and LH release in old female rats. *Pfluegers Arch.* 341:1–6.

Wyatt, H. V. (1961). The reproduction, growth and distribution of *Calyptraea chinensis* (L.). *J. Anim. Ecol.* 30:283–302.

Yablokov, A. V., and Andreyevna, T. V. (1965). Age determination in baleen whales. *Nature (Lond.)* 205:412–413.

Yacob, M., and Swaroop, S. (1945). Longevity and old age in the Punjab. *Br. Med. J.* 2:433.

Yagil, G. (1976). Are altered glucose-6-phosphate dehydrogenase molecules present in aged liver cells? *Exp. Geront.* 11:73–78.

Yiengst, M., Barrows, C., and Shock, N. (1959). Age changes in the chemical composition of muscle and liver in the rat. *J. Gerontol.* 14:400–404.

Yonge, C. M. (1962). On the biology of the mesogastropod *Trichotropis cancellata* Hinds, a benthic indicator species. *Biol. Bull.* 122:160–181.

Young, F. G. (1953). Growth hormone and diabetes. *Rec. Prog. Horm. Res.* VIII:471.

Young, L. J. T., Medina, D. D., De Ome, K. B., and Daniel, C. W. (1971). The influence of host and tissue age on the lifespan and growth rate of serially transplanted mouse mammary gland. *Exp. Gerontol.* 6:49–56.

Young, T. E. (1899). *On Centenarians and the Duration of the Human Race.* London: Layton.

Yuan, G. C., and Chang, R. S. (1969). Testing of compounds for capacity to prolong postmitotic lifespan of cultured human annion cells. *J. Gerontol.* 24:82–85.

Yuhas, J. M. (1971). Age and susceptibility to reduction in life expectancy: an analysis of proposed mechanisms. *Exp. Gerontol.* 6:335–343.

Zannas, E., and Auboyer, J. (1960). *Khajuráho.* The Hague: Mouton.

Zelinka, C. (1891). Studien über Rädertiere—III. *Z. Wiss. Zool.* 53:323.

Zeman, W. (1971). The neuronal ceroid-lipofuscinoses (Batten-Vogt syndrome)—a model for human aging? *Adv. Geront. Res.* 3:147–170.

Zondek, B., and Aschheim, S. (1927). Hypophysenvorderlappen und Ovarium. *Arch. Gynaek.* 130:1.

Zuckerman, S. (1951). The number of oocytes in the mature ovary. *Rec. Prog. Horm. Res.* 6:63.

Subject index

Index of generic names